The Protection of the Underwater Cultural Heritage

Publications on Ocean Development

A SERIES OF STUDIES ON THE INTERNATIONAL, LEGAL, INSTITUTIONAL AND POLICY ASPECTS OF OCEAN DEVELOPMENT

General Editors

VOLUME 104

The titles published in this series are listed at *brill.com/pood*

The Protection of the Underwater Cultural Heritage

National Approaches and Perspectives, Third Edition

Edited by

Jason Lowther
Joanne Sellick
Mike Williams

BRILL | NIJHOFF

LEIDEN | BOSTON

The Library of Congress Cataloging-in-Publication Data is available online at https://catalog.loc.gov
LC record available at https://lccn.loc.gov/2025933462

Typeface for the Latin, Greek, and Cyrillic scripts: "Brill". See and download: brill.com/brill-typeface.

ISSN 0924-1922
ISBN 978-90-04-51087-6 (hardback)
ISBN 978-90-04-51088-3 (e-book)
DOI 10.1163/9789004510883

This book is printed on acid-free paper and produced in a sustainable manner.

Printed by Printforce, the Netherlands

Contents

Preface

A considerable time has passed since the publication of the last edition of this title, and we are delighted, as well as perhaps *slightly* daunted, that Professor Dromgoole was amenable to our becoming the custodians – albeit in somewhat unexpected circumstances – of this third edition in the series. We hope to have stayed true to her vision in assembling an inclusive and comparative reference resource for global underwater cultural heritage legal scholarship. A great deal happened in between the first and second editions of the book, most notably the adoption of the UNESCO Convention on the Protection of the Underwater Cultural Heritage 2001. In those subsequent years, more nations have become State Parties to, and/or ratified, the 2001 Convention. In the eighteen years since the last edition there have been significant subsea discoveries, accelerating intrusive seabed development, across the globe: in some cases, this has prompted litigation, and in others, State cooperation to ensure that underwater cultural heritage (UCH) receives, at the very least, the legal, if not always physical, protection it merits so as to preserve its cultural integrity, rather than solely to reflect its monetary value to salvors.

More recently, the UN's Ocean Decade Programme's Cultural Heritage Framework Programme, which engages with cultural heritage within the UN Decade for Ocean Science, offers another means by which the cause and basis of UCH protection is actively promoted. Wider appreciations of the concept of UCH as a finite resource have prompted enhanced consideration of notions of cultural sustainability in the management of such assets, which can only add value to ontological discourses pertaining to its conservation as heritage assets of significance to both current and future generations.

As with the previous editions, the aim of this volume is to provide a contemporary account of national law and policy, and how that ultimately shapes practice within the jurisdictions considered. Applying a level of criticality to the considerations hopefully permits some deeper thinking around the core issues and may contribute to the further development of comprehensive and effective responses to safeguard UCH in a sustainable manner. The breadth of coverage has increased with a number of first-time assessments of country-specific measures, whether or not the State concerned is party to the 2001 Convention. We have taken tentative steps to add to the global picture, including Latin American and East Asian chapters to complement the previous focus and move in a small way towards realising Sarah's ambitions as stated in the preface to the last edition. It paints a picture which is both less Euro-centric and less dominated by common law jurisdictions, as noted in the

Editors' Introduction, reflecting the heterogeneity of cultural values and the responses undertaken to celebrate and conserve them.

Our sincere thanks must go to the contributors who have brought their expertise and wisdom to offer comprehensive analyses of their respective jurisdictions. We especially acknowledge their patience and good humour when the inevitable hiccups, some less foreseeable than others, have created challenges which we have worked collaboratively to overcome. As editors, we have relied upon our contributors to enable us to curate significant scholarship in a consistent and, hopefully, page-turning manner. We also must acknowledge the support and counsel of the whole team at De Gruyter Brill, including, but not limited, to Beth Derr, Marie Sheldon, and Jade Mambre, who went above and beyond on many occasions. Finally, the editorial team would like to acknowledge the contribution of Josh Martin, who initiated the proposal to develop a third edition. As a result of unforeseen circumstances, Josh had to step away from the project in its very early stages and was thus unable to see the germ of the idea through to fruition.

Developments in UCH protection have continued apace and appear to be gaining momentum. We sincerely hope that you will agree that by virtue of the extended breadth to the coverage and the scholarship of the contributors, we have managed to do justice to Sarah's original vision.

*Jason Lowther, Jo Sellick, and Mike William*s
Plymouth
March 2025

Notes on Contributors

Thomas Adlercreutz

born in 1944, holds a law degree (jur. kand) from Uppsala University (1971). He has served as a judge at district courts in Sweden, at the Svea Court of Appeals and at the Stockholm Court of Administrative Appeals. He has been a legal adviser at several Swedish ministries and legal counsel for the National Heritage Board, the Swedish government's cultural heritage agency. Thomas had leave from 1994 to 1996 to draft legislation for the government's Cultural Heritage Enquiry (publications SOU 1995:128 and SOU 1996:128). He is the author of Kulturegendomrätt – med en kommentar till kulturminneslagen (2001, Cultural Property Law – with a Commentary to the Cultural Monuments Act), which he updates in the Swedish internet publication JUNO. His publications in English include 'The Protection of the Cultural Heritage' in Swedish National Reports to the XIII th International Congress of Comparative Law (1990); Legal Protection of the Cultural Heritage in the USA (1991); Four Issues of Cultural Heritage Law in Six European Countries (France, Germany, Hungary, Italy, Sweden and United Kingdom) (1993); 'Civil Liability for Costs for Archaeological Investigation Necessitated by Criminal Negligence – A Swedish Supreme Court Case' in International Journal of Cultural Property (1997), and "The Swedish Royal Placat of 1666. The First Antiquities Legislation in the World?" in Art Antiquity and Law 2021. He wrote for Sweden in the previous editions of 'Legal Protection of the Underwater Cultural Heritage; (1999, 2006), and in 'Handbook on the Law of Cultural Heritage and International Trade' (2014). He is a member of the ICOMOS International Scientific Committee on Legal, Financial and Administrative Issues and a member of the International Law Association's Committee on Safeguarding Cultural Heritage in Armed Conflict. Having served as legal counsel for the National Fortifications Agency of Sweden until 2012, he is now retired.

Mariano J. Aznar

is Professor of Public International Law at the University Jaume I of Castellón, Spain, since 2008, previously professor at the University of Valencia and Visiting professor in several European and American universities. Mariano was a founder member of the European Society of International Law (ESIL) and member of its Board (2004–2012) and was Editor-in-Chief of the Spanish Yearbook of International Law (2013–2021). He is a life Member of Clare Hall College (Cambridge) and Consultant Scholar to the Penn Museum. Member of the International Committee on the Underwater Cultural Heritage (ICUCH/

ICOMOS). Patron of the National Museum of Underwater Archaeology (ARQVA). Member of the Spanish Royal Academy of the Sea. Co-author of the Green Book for the Protection of the Spanish Underwater Cultural Heritage (2010), Dr. Aznar is a legal expert on the protection of the underwater cultural heritage, acting both for the Spanish Government and for UNESCO. Advocate and counsel of the Kingdom of Spain before the International Tribunal for the Law of the Sea. Representative of Spain before the Meeting of States Parties of the UNESCO Convention on the Protection of the Underwater Cultural Heritage, he has participated in the drafting of the Operational Guidelines of this Convention and the new Spanish Law on Maritime Navigation, as well as legally advice on the drafting of cultural and maritime domestic legislation of several States. He has recently published for Brill a monograph titled Maritime Claims and Underwater Archaeology. When History Meets Politics (2021).

Karl Brady
is senior manager in the Licensing and Planning Unit (heading up the marine and inland waterways brief) and senior manager of the Wreck Inventory of Ireland Unit. Karl has directed many surveys and excavations of multi-period underwater sites, including the ongoing extensive work in Lough Corrib on multi-period logboats and associated artefacts. Karl has a broad publication record, in peer reviewed journal and chapters in books. These include his work on sites and topics ranging from early maps, medieval ship graffiti, logboats, the Spanish Armada, World War I and World War II wrecks, early medieval ecclesiastical remains, management of maritime cultural heritage and shipwrecks. Karl has published and co-edited two books: The Shipwreck Inventory of Ireland: Louth, Meath, Dublin & Wicklow (2008) and Warships, U-boats & Liners: A Guide to Shipwrecks Mapped in Irish Waters (co-authored with C. McKeon, J. Lyttleton & I. Lawler; 2012). He is also co-author of the book, RMS Lusitania: the Story of a Wreck (with F. Moore, C. Kelleher, C. McKeon & I. Lawler; 2019).

Yasin Çakır
is a partner at Gurulkan Çakır Günay Attorney Partnership, a boutique law firm in Istanbul specialized in corporate, commercial, financial and maritime law. He received his LL.B. degree from Bilkent University. Yasin has achieved 15 years in legal practice, advising domestic and international clients particularly in the fields of corporate and commercial, international trade, banking and finance law related transactions. His practice incorporates advisory and transactional work for clients doing business in a diversity of industries including shipping, banking and insurance. Throughout his career, Yasin dealt with

many international business transactions involving corporate and commercial laws of multiple jurisdictions which gives him a comparative perspective as well as solid cross-border work experience. He has been continuously advising foreign businesses in their transactions involving Turkish law. Yasin is an active member of the Istanbul Bar Association and International Bar Association.

Laura R. Carrillo Márquez
received a bachelor's degree in Archaeology from the National School of Anthropology and History; a degree in Underwater Archaeology from the National School of Anthropology and History; a degree in Introduction to Management strategies for Heritage sites from the National School of Conservation, Restoration and Museography; a degree in Underwater Archaeology from the UNESCO-ARQUA, Cartagena, Spain; and became an International tutor in Coastal and Maritime Archaeology, a title awarded by the Nautical Archaeology Society, in the United Kingdom. She is a researcher at the Underwater Archaeology Vice-directorate of the National Institute of Anthropology and History where she has taken part in the following projects: the New Spain fleet project from 1630–31 (1996–1999); the Regularization of land tenure in the National Palenque Park Project, (1999–2000). She was the planning process director at heritage sites at the Directorate of Site Operation, (2000–2001). She was the project manager of projects developed by the Underwater Archaeology Vice-directorate, such as: Underwater Archaeological Prospection in Bahia de Vergara, Veracruz (2008–2021); Inventory and Diagnosis of the Underwater Archaeological and Historical Heritage at the Biosphere Preserve Banco Chinchorro, Quintana Roo (2008–to date); Underwater Archaeological Rescue in Marina Veramar, Veracruz (2010–2013) and Documentation of the Underwater Archaeological Heritage in Surrounding Areas of Bahia Vergara, Veracruz (2015–to date). She has given lectures in Mexico and other countries and has published scientific and dissemination papers. Her main interest is to promote legal instruments for the protection of Mexican underwater cultural heritage.

Barbara Davidde Petriaggi
is Director of the Underwater Archaeology Unit at the Central Institute for Restoration in Rome (Italy). She had already directed the Unit between 2011 and 2023. From 2019 she has been a Member of the Scientific and Technical Advisory Body for the 2001 Convention and was President between 2021 and 2022. Between December 2022 and January 2024, she was Director of the National Superintendency for Underwater Cultural Heritage Between February 2021 and November 2022, she also acted as the interim Director of the Soprintendenza per i beni archeologici artisti e storici per le province di Brindisi e

Lecce (MiC – Italy). From 2018 to present, she is the Scientific Coordinator and Director, charged by the Italian Archaeological School of Athens (SAIA), for the Research Projects "Underwater Archaeology Research in the Island of Lemnos", and "Underwater Archaeological Mission in Epidaurus-Palaia Epidavros" – Two Collaborative programs between SAIA, the ICR, the National Superintendency for Underwater Cultural Heritage (since 2021) and the Greek Authorities. Her research focus since 2001 has been on the in-situ preservation and restoration of UCH as part of the research team within the Restoring Underwater Project. Since July 2011 she both designed and directed several national and international projects for the development of technologies for underwater archaeological research and for the conservation and enhancement of UCH heritage. Since 2009 she is visiting professor at the Roma Tre University, where she teaches "Underwater archaeology", a role she also performs at the Politecnico di Bari-Scuola di Specializzazione in Beni Architettonici e del Paesaggio. The author of over 100 publications (books, chapters and scientific papers), Barbara has also held the role of professor of Methodology of Archaeological research at the ICR MA School for Cultural Heritage Conservation and Restoration (SAF), Matera. Italy and as professor of Classical Archaeology at the ISCR MA School for Cultural Heritage Conservation and Restoration (SAF), Rome. Italy.

Piers Davies

is a retired maritime lawyer living in Auckland. He has had a particular interest in salvage, wreck and underwater cultural heritage for 50 years. He was one of the Law of the Sea specialists consulted in the 2019 UNESCO Review of the 2001 Convention on the Protection of the Underwater Cultural Heritage. He has been the co-author of the Shipping section of the Encyclopaedia of New Zealand Forms and Precedents (LexisNexis). He is a member of the Participation in Global Cultural Heritage Governance Committee of the International Law Association and convenor of the Auckland sub-branch of the International Law Association. He is a member of the Maritime Law Association of Australia and New Zealand and of the New Zealand Archaeological Association.

Edwin Egede

is a Professor of International Law and International Relations at Cardiff University's School of Law and Politics. He also serves as an Adjunct Professor at Nelson Mandela University's Department of Public Law in South Africa. Furthermore, he is a Fellow of the Learned Society of Wales (FLSW), Wales' National Academy for Arts and Sciences. He has also worked as a consultant for international organisations such as the United Nations, the International Seabed Authority and the African Union, and is currently a member of the Legal and Technical Commission of the International Seabed Authority. Additionally, he is a member of the Advisory Board of the Brazilian Yearbook of Law of the Sea and one of the editors of a six-volume book project on The Law of the Sea – Contemporary Norms and Practice in Africa (BYLOS). He undertakes interdisciplinary teaching and research in the fields of Law of the Sea, Public International Law, Human Rights in Africa, and International Organizations, particularly the United Nations and the African Union. In these fields, he has published widely and given academic and professional presentations at a number of international conferences.

María Luz Endere
is a lawyer and an archaeologist. She has a MA in museum and heritage studies and a PhD in archaeology (Institute of Archaeology, University College London). Dr Endere is currently a senior researcher of the National Council of Science and Technological Research (CONICET) at the Institute INCUAPA and professor of law and heritage studies at the Department of Archaeology, Faculty of Social Sciences, University of the Centre of Buenos Aires Province (UNICEN), Argentina. She is the head of the Heritage Studies Interdisciplinary Research Group named PATRIMONIA and director of the PhD in Archaeology Programme at the same university. Her research interests include legal protection of cultural heritage, Indigenous people rights and public archaeology issues. She was a Facility Advisory Group member on the Restoring Dignity project (2018–2020), funded by the Australian Research Council.

Craig Forrest
is a Professor of Law and Director of the Marine and Shipping Law Unit at the University of Queensland. Craig was a member of the South African delegation to UNESCO to negotiate the 2001 UCH Convention and has undertaken a number of activities and consultancies for UNESCO, including: acting as an independent advisor to UNESCO regional cultural meetings in Solomon Islands, Cambodia, St.Kitts and Nevis, Indonesia and Antigua and Barbuda; with the UNESCO secretariate drafting a Model Law for the implementation of the UNESCO UCH convention for the Caribbean States; completing a UNESCO consultancy with Dr Bill Jeffery (University of Guam) on the protection of underwater cultural heritage in the States of Micronesia and, together with Major Projects Foundation, undertaken a national Interest Analysis and Gap study on the protection of underwater cultural heritage in Solomon Islands (2012), Marshall Islands (2022) and Fiji (2023). Professor Forrest is an

Australian representative on the International Law Association's Committee on Safeguarding Cultural Heritage in Armed Conflict and a member of the International Council of Monuments and Sites (ICOMOS) International Committee on Underwater Cultural Heritage. Craig is also a Federal Attorney-General appointed Australian correspondent to the International Institute for the Unification of Private Law (Rome). Craig is the general editor of the Australian and New Zealand Maritime Law Journal, and on the editorial boards of the World Maritime University Journal of Maritime Affairs, Journal of Ocean Law and Governance in Africa and the International Maritime and Commercial Law Yearbook.

Ulrike Guerin
holds a PhD in Comparative Law and an LLM. After having worked as a lawyer at Freshfields in Munich, she came in 2005 to UNESCO. Since then, she has worked for several Conventions on cultural heritage, among others the 1970 and the 2001 Conventions. With the latter, the 2001 Convention on the Protection of the Underwater Cultural Heritage,she was involved throughout the process of its entry into force, as well as building the statutory framework and the various partner networks. She advises States in the ratification and implementation of the Convention and helps them to harmonise their national heritage laws.

M. Barış Günay
is a partner at Gurulkan Çakır Günay Attorney Partnership, a boutique law firm in Istanbul specialized in corporate, commercial, financial and maritime law. He pursued his undergraduate degree at Ankara University (2000) and received his LL.M. degree from the University of Nottingham (2002). Dr. Günay obtained his Ph.D. degree from the University of Exeter with his thesis on maritime liens (2007). His field of research includes maritime law, insurance law and transport law. He worked and lectured in various law schools in Türkiye as an associate professor. His principal teaching interest is maritime and insurance law but his interests extend to commercial law. He has extensive experience in dealing with corporate and commercial transactions. Dr. Günay has also taken part in numerous litigations at commercial and admiralty courts. He has written books and articles on maritime liens, cargo claims, salvage, limitation of liability, marine pollution, arrest of ships and underwater cultural heritage. He is one of the authors of Transport Law in Turkey (Wolters Kluwer, Second Ed. 2016). Fourth edition of his book on insurance law was published in 2022. He is an active member of the Istanbul Bar Association and International Bar Association.

Haluk Gurulkan

is a partner at Gurulkan Çakır Günay Attorney Partnership, a boutique law firm in Istanbul specialized in corporate, commercial, financial and maritime law. He studied law at Ankara University and holds LL.M. degrees from Goethe University Frankfurt (financial law) and the LSE (corporate and commercial law). He is currently pursuing another LL.M. degree at Erasmus University Rotterdam (maritime and transport law). Haluk has more than 20 years of experience in corporate, commercial, maritime, banking and financial law related matters. He has been providing a wide range of legal services to clients from all around the world in a broad array of industries and sectors from banking to shipping. He has solid expertise and experience in relation to maritime matters. Within this context, he has extensively worked on drafting, negotiation, execution and management of all kinds of shipping related contracts including but not limited to MOA s, facility agreements, ship management agreements, service agreements, charterparties, contracts of affreightment and bunkering, as well as other related matters such as registration and deregistration of vessels and mortgages in various jurisdictions and handling demurrage claims. Haluk is an active member of the Istanbul Bar Association, International Bar Association and Dutch Transport Law Association.

Georgia Holly

is an interdisciplinary ocean and social scientist at the University of Edinburgh with a background in marine biology and archaeology. Her research contributes to understanding, documenting, and equitably including cultural heritage within marine conservation management. Georgia has contributed to and led multiple research missions focused on the protection of marine cultural heritage in the UK and abroad. Her work now emphasizes translating these efforts into policy and practice, particularly through the UN Ocean Decade Programme's Cultural Heritage Framework Programme, which engages with cultural heritage within the UN Decade for Ocean Science. Her PhD research specifically examined the benefits marine heritage offers to society and the ocean by integrating shared values of nature, heritage, and the blue economy into policies for sustainable ocean and coastal community development both in Scotland and globally. Georgia is also the Editor-in-Chief and Founder of SeaVoice, an online platform dedicated to sharing diverse ocean stories from scientists, community members, advocates, and artists.

Akifumi Iwabuchi

is Professor of Maritime Anthropology and Nautical Archaeology at Tokyo University of Marine Science and Technology, which is a member institution of the UNESCO UNITWIN Network for Underwater Archaeology, and a Lecturer at the School of Law, Waseda University. He received his DPhil from the University of Oxford in 1990. He is the ICOMOS-ICUCH National Representative for Japan, a Vice-President of the Japan Society for Nautical Research, a director of the Asian Research Institute of Underwater Archaeology, and a director of the Japan Maritime Promotion Forum. He has published numerous books and articles on tangible and intangible cultural heritage in English, Japanese, or Bahasa Indonesia, including The People of the Alas Valley: A Study of an Ethnic Group of Northern Sumatra (Oxford, 1994) or Cultural Heritage under the Sea: An Introduction to Underwater Archaeology (Kyoto, 2012). The latter is the first introductory book to the UNESCO Convention 2001 in his mother tongue. An action project of the UN Decade of Ocean Science for Sustainable Development (2021–2030) titled 'Indigenous People, Traditional Ecological Knowledge, and Climate Change: The Iconic Underwater Cultural Heritage of Stone Tidal Weirs', which is led by him and his university, has been endorsed by the IOC-UNESCO.

Roberto Junco Sánchez
studied his bachelor's degree at the American University of Paris. He is an archaeologist, graduate of the Escuela Nacional de Antropología e Historia (ENAH) where he studied a master's degree and PhD in Archaeology. He received a diploma in Historical Archaeology from the University of Leicester, United Kingdom. He is currently an Affiliated Scholar of the Institute of Nautical Archaeology, member of the Society for Historical Archaeology and a Board Member of ACUA. He has been at the head of the Subdirección de Arqueología Subacuática SAS of the Instituto Nacional de Antropología e Historia INAH since 2017, where he has worked since 2004, succeeding Pilar Luna. He spearheaded projects such as: Underwater Archaeology in the Volcano Nevado de Toluca; Manila Galleon, Baja California; Maritime Archaeology of the Port of Acapulco and Underwater Archaeology in Villa Rica. His academic interests include the study of Chinese porcelain, the archaeology of Manila Galleons and navigation in colonial times. He has published several books on these topics, as well as organised different strategies to share UCH with the general public, such as: exhibits, public talks, documentaries, publications, theatre plays, among many others.

Connie Kelleher
is senior manager of the NMS' Underwater Archaeology Unit (UAU) and senior archaeological advisor for the World Heritage Site of Sceilg Mhichíl. Connie is a graduate of University College Cork (UCC) with an MA in maritime

archaeology and a PhD in history and archaeology from Trinity College Dublin. She is a commercially trained underwater archaeologist. She has directed many underwater projects on a variety of archaeological sites in both the marine and freshwater environments. She is visiting lecturer in underwater archaeology in University College Cork, and past visiting lecturer at Bristol University. She has lectured both nationally and internationally and published widely on her work on shipwrecks and underwater archaeological projects and on the history and archaeology of piracy in southwest Ireland. Along with publishing peer-reviewed papers in journals and chapters in books, she has published two books: The Alliance of Pirates: Ireland and Atlantic Piracy in the early seventeenth century (2020) and RMS Lusitania: The Story of a Wreck (co-authored with F. Moore, K. Brady, C. McKeon & I. Lawler, 2019). Connie is past council member of the Royal Society of Antiquaries of Ireland (RSAI), former chair of the Irish Post-Medieval Archaeology Group (IPMAG); she sits on the board of the International Advisory Council on Underwater Archaeology (ACUA) and is secretary of the International Committee on the Underwater Cultural Heritage (ICOMOS-ICUCH).

Seán Kirwan

has had, on a longstanding basis, a close involvement in the development of policy and legislation on the protection of the archaeological heritage. This is in particular relation to national policy on archaeological heritage and development, including the Framework and Principles for the Protection of the Archaeological Heritage, issued in 1999 and the newly enacted Historic and Archaeological Heritage and Miscellaneous Provisions Act 2023. He was a member of the Irish delegation to the Meetings of Governmental Experts that drafted the 2001 UNESCO Convention on the Protection of the Underwater Cultural Heritage, and was elected in two successive years as chair of the Working Group, which finalised the text of the Rules of the Annex for inclusion in the Convention. As well as holding an MA in archaeology from University College Dublin (1989), he was called to the Bar of Ireland in 2005 and holds an LLM in Environmental and Natural Resources Law from University College Cork (2021). In addition to a wide range of other responsibilities within NMS, he is currently serving as chair of the National Advisory Committee that advises on the implementation by Ireland of the 1954 Convention on the Protection of Cultural Property in the Event of Armed Conflict and its Second Protocol of 1999.

Andrea Klomp

is a senior policy advisor on underwater cultural heritage at the Netherlands Cultural Heritage Agency (RCE). She has a background in Roman archaeology of Northwestern Europe. In 2002 she joined the maritime team at RCE, which carries responsibility for the management of maritime heritage within both Dutch waters and the Dutch maritime heritage abroad. Since 2016 she has been part of the working group responsible for the ratification and implementation of the UNESCO 2001 Convention within the Kingdom of the Netherlands.

Norma Elizabeth Levrand
is a lawyer and specialist in labour law. She has a Doctorate in Law (Universidad Nacional del Litoral) with the thesis "Legal Regulation of World Cultural Heritage in Argentina". Dr Levrand is currently an assistant researcher of the National Council of Science and Technological Research (CONICET) at the Institute of Social Studies (CONICET-UNER). She is a Professor at the National University of Litoral and at the Autonomous University of Entre Ríos (Argentina). She currently directs and participates in research projects on the legal problems of the management of cultural and natural heritage with special emphasis on the mechanisms of citizen participation and the links between different jurisdictions.

Jason Lowther
is an Associate Professor in Law at the University of Plymouth. In addition to the law relating to UCH, his interests and expertise are in relation to environmental law and enforcement, and he is widely published in these areas. Jason led a project for Historic England on Enhancing Protection of Underwater Heritage Assets and contributed a chapter, concerning offshore environmental assessment, to Historic England's Marine Archaeology Legislation Project. More recently, he has worked on developing a Common Enforcement Manual for UK agencies with a capability offshore, to interrupt, investigate and enforce crimes against UCH; and a project reflecting on 50 years of the UK's Protection of Wrecks Act. In conjunction with the charity MAST, he was involved in the production of guidance for the Foreign and Commonwealth Office's Antarctic Headline strategy for the conservation and protection of underwater cultural heritage in the British Antarctic Territory. Jason is a member of the Joint Nautical Archaeology Policy Committee, the Association of Inshore Fisheries and Conservation Authorities' law subgroup, the Chartered Institute for Archaeology's enforcement subgroup, and the United Kingdom Environmental Law Association's conservation and marine subgroups. He sits on the Editorial Boards of the Environmental Law Review, the Journal of Environmental Law and Management, and the (online) Plymouth Law Review.

Martijn Manders
is a maritime and underwater archaeologist for the Netherlands' Government since 1990. After years of focusing on inventories, assessments and field

excavations he moved to the heritage policy department in 2003 and from 2011 he has been leading the maritime programme for the Cultural Heritage Agency of the Netherlands (RCE). After merging into the archaeology department, he shifted his focus on international maritime heritage management and Dutch shipwrecks overseas. He and his team are responsible for the management of almost 1600 Dutch shipwrecks all over the world. Martijn is also Professor by Special Appointment in underwater archaeology and maritime cultural heritage management at Leiden University, vice-president of the International Scientific Committee for Underwater Cultural Heritage (ICUCH) of ICOMOS and coordinator/trainer for the UNESCO Foundation Courses in Underwater Cultural Heritage Management.

Maija Matikka
is a Senior Advisor at the Cultural Environment Services Department, Finnish Heritage Agency (FHA) where her work concerns maritime and underwater cultural heritage. She holds a Master's degree in ethnology and history of art from Helsinki University 1992. Since 1990s she has been involved in administration and protection of underwater cultural heritage, including assessing the impact of construction and land use projects on the UCH and writing statements on these projects. Her responsibilities also include the development and maintenance of the Ancient Relics Register, co-operation with wreck divers, expert opinions and guidance on legislative matters and best underwater archaeological practices. Due to her work, she has been heard as an expert in her field in all national trials related to underwater cultural heritage in Finland since 1990s. Currently she is working for the maritime heritage expert team of the FHA, which among other things draws up the water related heritage action plans in consultation with regional museums and other partners.

Fionnbarr Moore
heads up the Research and Publications Unit in the National Monuments Service. He has a BA and MA in Archaeology and Early Irish History from University College Dublin. In his previous role as head of the Underwater Archaeology Unit (UAU) he project-managed and directed investigations at several significant underwater sites, including that of the wrecks of the 1588 Spanish Armada in Streedagh Bay, Co. Sligo. He has contributed papers and chapters to peer-reviewed journals and books on underwater archaeology and maritime history and has co-authored RMS Lusitania: The Story of a Wreck (with C. Kelleher, K. Brady, C. McKeon & I. Lawler, 2019). He is a former council member of the Royal Society of Antiquaries of Ireland, The Discovery Programme (for archaeological research) and former Chair of the EAC Underwater Cultural Heritage Working Group. As well as the above he has a particular interest in

the Early Medieval and Medieval periods and has published numerous papers on ogham inscriptions which was the subject of his MA and Ardfert Cathedral (2007) detailing results of his major excavation at Ardfert Cathedral, Co. Kerry, which he directed on behalf of the National Monuments Service. He was also responsible for overseeing the archaeological aspects of the conservation of National Monuments in the northwest of Ireland from 2000–2015 and was joint editor of the recently published monograph Boyle Abbey, Co. Roscommon: Conservation, Architecture and Archaeological Excavations 1982–2018 (with Dr Geraldine Stout, 2022).

Paul Myburgh
is a Professor at Auckland University of Technology Law School, New Zealand, and a Visiting Professor at the Centre for Maritime Law (CML) at the National University of Singapore. He previously held faculty positions in Singapore, New Zealand and South Africa. He has also held visiting teaching positions and research fellowships at the University of Queensland, the University of Oslo, and at City University of Hong Kong. Paul is the editor of The Arrest Conventions: International Enforcement of Maritime Claims (Hart, 2019), the author of New Zealand Transport Law (2nd ed, Kluwer, loose-leaf), and has published widely on admiralty and shipping law, maritime conflict of laws, and underwater cultural heritage issues. He is the New Zealand correspondent for Lloyd's Maritime and Commercial Law Quarterly and sits on the editorial boards of the Journal for International Maritime Law and the Maritime Business Review. He is also the general editor of the CML CMI database of judicial decisions on international maritime Conventions.

Nessa O'Connor
is an archaeologist and senior Assistant Keeper in the Irish Antiquities Division of the National Museum of Ireland (NMI). She holds BA and MA degrees in archaeology from University College, Dublin. She holds a Doctorate in Governance from the Law School of Queen's University Belfast. As part of her brief with NMI, Nessa carried out underwater archaeological inspections and surveys, several directly relating to specific sites including the Streedagh Armada wrecks in Sligo and in the inland waterways. She is the author of the 'Ireland' chapters in the previous two volumes of papers addressing national and international perspectives on the legal protection of the underwater archaeological heritage (Dromgoole, S. 1999 and 2006). She has also contributed to specific publications on wrecks, including that of RMS Lusitania: The Story of a Wreck (F. Moore, C. Kelleher, K. Brady, C. McKeon & I. Lawler, 2019).

Bobby C. Orillaneda
is currently a Senior Museum Researcher and Officer-In-Charge of the Maritime and Underwater Cultural Heritage Division (MUCHD) at the National Museum of the Philippines. He is completing his doctorate studies at the Oxford Centre for Maritime Archaeology (OCMA). He serves as the President of the Kapisanan ng mga Arkeologist sa Pilipinas, Inc. (KAPI), the Professional Guild of Archaeologists in the Philippines, and is an Expert Member of the ICOMOS International Committee on the Underwater Cultural Heritage (ICUCH).

Ville Peltokorpi
is a Finnish lawyer who also studied maritime history and archaeology at the University of Helsinki, where he holds a master's degree in law. His main areas of interest concern the protection of sunken warships and underwater cultural heritage in the Baltic region. He currently sits in the board of the Finnish Scientific Diving Steering Association (FSDSA) and is a member of the non-profit Badewanne dive team that documents shipwrecks in the Baltic Sea. He is also a trained scientific and technical diver having participated in many diving expeditions in the Baltic Sea, as well as archaeological inventory surveys and underwater excavations, including the Finnish Sveaborg fortress and the Swedish Viking Age harbour of Birka.

Carlo Emilio Piazzini Suárez
is an anthropologist from the University of Antioquia, Ms. in history from the National University of Colombia and Ph.D. in history from the Universidad de los Andes. He has experience in archaeological, historical, and anthropological research, and has participated in academic postgraduate training initiatives in the field of space and society studies. He has served as scientific deputy director of the Colombian Institute of Anthropology and History-ICANH, consultant for environmental studies, advisor on land use planning and cultural policies, and university professor for undergraduate, master's and doctorate degrees. He is currently professor at the Institute of Regional Studies-INER, of the University of Antioquia.

Marnix Jacques Pieters
has master's degrees in history (1984, Ghent University, Belgium), and soil science (1986, Ghent University, Belgium) and secured a PhD in History (2002, Free University of Brussels (VUB, Belgium)) with a dissertation on the material living world of fishing societies in the southern part of the North Sea in late medieval and early modern times. After having participated as a soil scientist

to the archaeological excavations at the site of the Louvre Museum (Paris, France, 1989–1991), he directed from 1992 to 2005 a large-scale archaeological excavation project at Walraversijde (Ostend, Belgium), a lost late medieval fishing settlement along the Flemish coast. From 2003 onwards his research focused increasingly on underwater cultural heritage (UCH) and as a result he could contribute to the ratification by Belgium of the UNESCO Convention for the protection of the cultural heritage underwater in 2013 and to the realization of the federal implementation laws of 2014 and 2021. From 2013 he teaches a course on 'Archaeology of Coast and Sea' as guest professor at the Free University of Brussels (VUB). He is a member of ICUCH (the ICOMOS's International Committee on Underwater Cultural Heritage) since 2006 and in 2021 joined the Scientific and Technical Advisory Board (STAB) of the UNESCO Convention for the Protection of the Underwater Cultural Heritage. Marnix has been employed by the Flanders Heritage Agency since 1992, first as a scientific collaborator, then as research director archaeology, and most recently Senior Archaeologist.

Gonzalo Rodríguez Prado
is a lawyer who graduated from Universidad de la República, Uruguay, where he teaches Public International Law. He is a United Nations– Nippon Foundation Fellowship Programme Alumni, specialising in the legal protection and management of underwater cultural heritage. He is a member of the Pool of Experts of the Regular Process for Global Reporting and Assessment of the State of the Marine Environment, including socio-economic aspects, contributing to the second and third cycles. He has also provided legal advice to national institutions for a better understanding of the 2001 Convention and the United Nations Convention on the Law of the Sea. Since 2019 he has been working as a consultant and legal advisor to the National Directorate of Aquatic Resources of the Ministry of Livestock, Agriculture and Fisheries of Uruguay, developing proposals for the strengthening of the national legal framework on fisheries in accordance with international instruments. He is President of the NGO Oceanids, a multidisciplinary team created with the aim of articulating initiatives for training, preservation and dissemination of maritime heritage.

Maili Roio
is a maritime archaeologist, and she has a master's degree from the University of Tartu on the topic of the protection of underwater cultural heritage. She has worked at the Estonian National Heritage Board since 2004. Her assignment is to organise the management of underwater cultural heritage, which includes documenting and monitoring underwater monuments, evaluating

the preservation status and conducting surveillance. She has delivered courses in underwater/ maritime archaeology and heritage management at the University of Tartu and Tallinn University. She is a member of the Baltic Sea Region Underwater Cultural Heritage Working Group.

Massimiliano Secci
graduated in Archaeology at the University of Florence, Italy in 2007, and later obtained a masters in Maritime Archaeology at Flinders University, Australia. Between 2010 and 2016 he worked at the University of Sassari (Italy), where secured a scholarship to develop a strategic plan for the public interpretation of the Sardinian maritime cultural heritage. A second scholarship followed in 2013 to research underwater remote sensing technologies for the location of underwater archaeological sites off the west coast of Sardinia. In 2016 was awarded his PhD which focused on a theoretical and methodological analysis of the photogrammetric techniques employed in underwater archaeology. In 2016–2017, he worked as Post-Doctoral Researcher at the Iuav University of Venice (Italy), where he was part of a team developing a virtual reality (VR) application on the Italo-French brigantine Mercure, excavated nearby Venice by the Univeristà Ca' Foscari of Venice. Between September 2017 and February 2018, Massimiliano was an iMareCulture Fellow at the M.A.RE.Lab, Department of History and Archaeology (University of Cypruswithin the European funded project IMARECULTURE. In May 2018, he was also an iMareCulture Fellow at the Department of Informatics at Mazaryk University in Brno (Czech Republic). Between 2018 and 2020 he held a Post-Doctoral Research position at the Department of History and Archaeology (University of Cyprus), and between 2021 and 2023 he was Principal Investigator of the Mare Cyprium Project, funded by the Honor Frost Foundation and hosted by the University of Cyprus. Massimiliano is a specialist in underwater photogrammetry and has been participating in various projects around the Mediterranean. He has collaborated with several Italian and International Institutions, including in Greece, the USA, the UK, and Cyprus. He has published close to twenty journal articles and book chapters on his major research interests.

Joanne (Jo) Sellick
is an Associate Professor in Law at the University of Plymouth and a former Associate Dean of Teaching and Learning. Her teaching experience includes European Union (EU) Law and UK Constitutional Law, in which she has written several texts, along with Public International Law. Jo's research rests primarily in environmental law, in which she has published articles and case commentaries with an EU focus, including for example on water policy and

legislative developments, animal testing, and EU enforcement, whilst also having several publications devoted to the embedding of sustainability in the legal curriculum. Jo is the EU law editor on the editorial boards of the Journal of Environmental Law and Management, and the Journal of Water Law.

Trpimir M. Šošić
is Assistant Professor of Public International Law at the University of Zagreb, Faculty of Law (Croatia). Apart from teaching Public International Law at the University of Zagreb, he has taken on other teaching assignments at the graduate and postgraduate level, including specialised courses on International Law of the Sea and International Cultural Heritage Law. Since 2020 he has been the legal expert for Croatia in the Coordination Committee for the Protection of the Underwater Cultural Heritage on the Skerki Bank and the Sicilian Channel, the first of its kind to be established under the consultation scheme of the 2001 UNESCO Convention. He currently also serves as member of the Croatian Commission for the Implementation of the Convention for the Protection of Cultural Property in the Event of Armed Conflict, including the First and Second Protocols to the Convention (since 2017). In the past he served as expert to the Croatian delegation in the Council of the European Union's Working Party on the Law of the Sea (COMAR) (2019–2023) and was part of the Croatian legal team in the matter of the arbitration under the Arbitration Agreement between the Government of the Republic of Croatia and the Government of the Republic of Slovenia (2011–2015). After completing his doctoral dissertation on The Protection of the Underwater Cultural Heritage in International Law (in Croatian), he continued researching and publishing on the subject, both in Croatian and English. He is a member of the Association Internationale du Droit de la Mer (AssIDMer) and an associate member of the University of Macerata's (Italy) Interdepartmental Research Center on the Adriatic and the Mediterranean (Centro interdipartimentale di Ricerca sull'Adriatico e il Mediterraneo–CiRAM).

Kathleen Felise Constance Dela Cuesta Tantuico
is a lawyer from the Philippines with a Master of Arts in Archaeology and Juris Doctor Degrees from the University of the Philippines and Bachelor of Arts in Social Sciences, specialising in Cultural Heritage and Minor in History from the Ateneo de Manila University. She has participated in numerous archaeological excavations, the most recent excavation being in Callao Cave, Penablanca, Cagayan Valley, the site where human remains of the newly identified Homo luzonensis species were uncovered. She worked as a litigation and dispute resolution associate lawyer in one of the Philippines' top law firms before

working as a public interest lawyer for two non-governmental organisations. Her law-related interests include legal ethics in the practice of archaeology, cultural rights, and the repatriation of colonial cultural materials. At the time of writing, she is currently completing a Master of Law in International Law, minor in Law and Society, at the University of Kent at Canterbury, Kent, UK.

Ole Varmer

is a Senior Fellow at The Ocean Foundation (TOF) with over 30 years of experience providing advice to the National Oceanic and Atmospheric Administration, intergovernmental agencies, NGOs and others regarding ocean law, jurisdiction, science and heritage. Ole represented NOAA on the United States (US) delegation that negotiated the International Agreement on Titanic and the UNESCO meetings that resulted in the 2001 Convention. He continues to provide advice on world heritage (natural and cultural), ocean governance, integrated ocean management, marine spatial planning, large marine ecosystems, and marine protected areas. Ole was the law of the sea and UCH law expert for the team of authors that produced the UNESCO Report on the Evaluation of the 2001 Convention on the Protection of UCH (2019). More recently Ole contributed to the Major Projects Foundation UCH Law Gap Analyses for UNESCO, the Solomon Islands and The Republic of the Marshall Islands. Ole has dozens of publications including The Duty to Protect UCH and to Cooperate for that Purpose in The Legal Regime of Underwater Cultural Heritage and Marine Scientific Research(Ankara U., 2020), K. Gjerde & O. Varmer, Chapter on the Sargasso Sea: An Innovative Approach to Governance in Areas beyond National Jurisdiction, in Frontiers in International Environmental Law Oceans and Climate Challenges (Brill-Nihoff 2021) and his chapters on US UCH law in the first and second editions of Legal Protection of the Underwater Cultural Heritage: National and International Perspectives (Kluwer Law International, 1999 and Brill, 2006). His UCH Law Study (2014) provided the foundation for this United States chapter.

Andrew (Andy) Viduka

is a maritime archaeologist and archaeological objects conservator employed by the Australian Government as the Assistant Director of Underwater Cultural Heritage. Andy co-drafted the Australian Government's Underwater Cultural Heritage Act 2018 which he administers, leads the Australian Underwater Cultural Heritage Program, and Australia's consideration of ratification of the UNESCO 2001 Convention on the Protection of the Underwater Cultural Heritage. Andy is actively involved in maritime archaeological projects with the not-for-profit research group Wreck Check Inc. continuing his research interest in linking community outcomes with the discovery and protection of underwater cultural heritage. In 2022, he co-authored a book based on Wreck Check research in 2015–2016 titled, 'Misadventures in Nature's Paradise: Australia's Cocos (Keeling) Islands and Christmas Island during the Dutch era'. Andy's PhD was on 'A public good conservation approach for underwater cultural management through citizen science' and in 2018 he founded the citizen science project Gathering Information via Recreational and Technical (GIRT) Scientific Divers. He is the Director of GIRT Scientific Divers Pty Ltd, an Honorary Associate of the University of New England (Armidale, Australia), a Fellow of the Society of Antiquaries, and an ICOMOS– ICUCH Bureau Member. Andy is also a member of ICOMOS– ICAHM, the Australian Citizen Science Association and a Board Member of the Ocean Decade Heritage Network.

Michael V. (Mike) Williams
is a Visiting Professor in Law at Plymouth University, and a former Honorary Professor at the Institute of Archaeology, UCL. He has published extensively on the law relating to the foreshore and seabed and underwater cultural heritage. He has advised government departments and agencies, both in the UK and abroad and was retained as an advisor to the Crown Estate (Marine Division) on foreshore and seabed law. Mike sits on the UK's Joint Nautical Archaeological Policy Committee, is a member of the Ministry of Defence's Expert Panel on HMS Victory 1744, is Chair of the Devon & Severn Inshore Fishery and Conservation Authority, Vice Chair of the Association of IFCAs, is the Honorary Secretary of the Nautical Archaeology Society (a UK registered charity), a Director of Mast Heritage, a Harbour Commissioner, an accredited UNESCO NGO Expert and a member of Devon & Cornwall Police's Peninsula Heritage Crime Partnership. Mike is a qualified commercial and recreational diver, and as a member of the Southwest Maritime Archaeology Group conducted archaeological operations on several protected wreck sites.

EDITORS' INTRODUCTION

The Protection of Underwater Cultural Heritage: Past, Present and Future

Jason Lowther, Joanne Sellick and Michael V. Williams

1 Introduction

The history of protecting underwater cultural heritage (UCH) has a significantly different provenance from, albeit one related to, terrestrial conservation measures to create rules of protection for sites and artefacts. Traceable to Greek and Roman rules to preserve buildings, graves, and other works of humanity, subsequent historical periods have continued the evolution of legal principles in a non-linear manner. The Hague Convention on the Protection of Cultural Property during Armed Conflict 1954 was the first international agreement focused on protecting cultural heritage – its preamble stating that 'any damage to cultural property, irrespective of the people it belongs to, is a damage to the cultural heritage of all humanity'.[1] This was followed by two UNESCO international agreements in the 1970s: the Convention on the Means of Prohibiting and Preventing the Illicit Import, Export and Transfer of Ownership of Cultural Property 1970,[2] and the Convention concerning the Protection of the World Cultural and Natural Heritage 1972.[3] The focus of the latter was for many years on terrestrial heritage but evolved to protect heritage under the sea.

In 1982, unprecedented international agreement resulted in the UN Convention of the Law of the Sea (LOSC)[4] which has become the primary legal framework for all activities at sea. However, only two of its provisions, Articles 149 and 303, expressly relate to objects of an archaeological or historical nature. Article 149 relates principally to such objects found in the Area, and that they 'shall be preserved or disposed of for the benefit of mankind as a whole' with particular emphasis placed upon preferential rights of the State of cultural, historical and archaeological origin. Article 303(1) provides that 'States have the duty to protect objects of an archaeological and historical nature found at sea

1 249 UNTS 215.
2 823 UNTS 231.
3 1037 UNTS 151.
4 1833 UNTS 3.

 | DOI:10.1163/9789004510883_002

and shall cooperate for this purpose'. However, whilst both Articles establish a duty to protect such objects, they unfortunately contain little to no guidance on how to implement such an obligation. It was not until 2001 and the UNESCO Convention on the Protection of the Underwater Cultural Heritage (2001 Convention), adopted at the 31st Session of the UNESCO General Conference that there emerged a clear definition of UCH.[5] The 2001 Convention offers a detailed legal framework for the protection of UCH, including its definition; a requirement that 'activities directed at [UCH]' must be authorised in a manner consistent with it; and, under Article 4, an express ban on the application of the laws of salvage and finds, unless consistent with the Rules contained in the Annex to the Convention, which codified the international standards and practice for research and recovery of UCH.

The first and second editions of this text, both edited by Professor Sarah Dromgoole, were published in 1999 and 2006 respectively. The first was thus published whilst UNESCO was drafting the 2001 Convention. It provided explanation and analysis on the national laws and policies related to UCH across thirteen States and an additional chapter considering this in the context of the seabed beyond national jurisdiction, namely the Area. A consistent theme in the first edition was that the primary threat to be addressed was the challenge posed by the plunder of UCH by treasure hunters, particularly given increased opportunities for retrieval brought about by technological innovation – innovation that continues apace and remains a consistent theme as a result. The edition explored a difference in approach between civil law traditions, such as that in France, Greece, Italy, Poland and Spain, and common law traditions in countries such as the United Kingdom (UK), United States of America (USA) and Australia.

The second edition, published in 2006, post-dated agreement of the text of the 2001 Convention, and reflected on both its generation and related corresponding developments. An issue of overarching significance identified in the second edition was the failure of efforts to reach agreement on the 2001 Convention's regulatory framework. The resulting final text could be described as one reflecting constructive ambiguity as a means of facilitating the agreement of as many delegations as possible. This resulted in eighty-seven nations doing so, with four voting against[6] and fifteen abstaining.[7] The second edition noted the significance of the fact that those nations that opposed or abstained included major maritime powers, whose participation was understandably

5 2562 UNTS 1.

6 Russia, Norway, Turkey, and Venezuela.

7 Brazil, the Czech Republic, Columbia, France, Germany, Greece, Ireland, Israel, Guinea-Bissau, the Netherlands, Paraguay, Sweden, Switzerland, the United Kingdom, and Uruguay.

important, particularly given they comprised those nations with the technological capability to explore and exploit deep water resources, including UCH. The USA, UK, and France, for example, did not sign in 2001 because of the ambiguity of the legal regime for cooperation on the control and regulation of UCH on the Continental Shelf (CS) and Exclusive Economic Zone (EEZ) and concerns that it would in practice be an extension of coastal State jurisdiction, i.e., 'creeping jurisdiction' as elaborated by the chapter contributors for those States. There were additional concerns that a coastal State 'should', rather than 'must', seek the consent of the foreign flag State before authorising activities directed at foreign sunken State vessels within its Territorial Sea (TS) and internal waters, which would not be in harmony with the requirement that they 'shall' seek the consent in the other maritime zones, including the CS/EEZ. In short, the apparent discretion of 'should' did not sit well with the imperative of 'shall' and was seen as a dilution of the principle of sovereign immunity of sunken State vessels used for non-commercial purposes at the time of their sinking.[8]

At the point of the publication of the second edition of this text, only six States had ratified the 2001 Convention.[9] With its requirement under Article 27 for entry into force following ratification, acceptance, approval or accession by 20 State Parties, the second edition's Editorial Introduction predicted this was likely, but that it would take some time, analogous to entry into force of the LOSC.[10] Indeed, following acceptance by Barbados in October 2008, the 2001 Convention entered into force on 2 January 2009. A lag in entry into force of maritime international agreements is not unusual, often related to issues of jurisdiction, as seen in not only LOSC and the 2001 Convention, but other instruments such as the International Convention on Salvage 1989, which entered into force in 1996.[11] It is also likely to be the case with the recently adopted Agreement under LOSC on the Conservation and Sustainable Use of Marine Biological Diversity of Areas beyond National Jurisdiction 2023 (BBNJ Agreement).[12]

This third edition reflects the fact that since the second the 2001 Convention has entered into force and, at the time of writing, the UNESCO depository

---

8 P. O'Keefe, A. Gonalez, M.V. Williams, 'The UNESCO Convention on the Protection of the Underwater Cultural Heritage: A Future for our Past?', International Journal of Conservation & Management of Archaeological Sites Vol. 11(1), 2009, pp. 54–69.

9 Panama, Bulgaria, Croatia, Spain, Libya, and Nigeria.

10 S. Dromgoole (ed), *The Protection of the Underwater Cultural Heritage, National Perspectives in Light of the UNESCO Convention 2001*, (2006) (Brill) at XXVIII.

11 1953 UNTS.

12 For updates on status see the UN Treaty Collection at <https://treaties.un.org/pages/ViewDetails.aspx?src=TREATY&mtdsg_no=XXI-10&chapter=21&clang=_en>.

records 78 State Parties.[13] It builds upon the foundational themes identified within the previous editions and has expanded the number and global spread of national jurisdictions considered. This edition offers analysis of both enduring and emerging challenges with respect to the management and preservation of UCH. In general terms, it would appear there is a positive direction of travel. A notable example of this is that of the fifteen nations that abstained in 2001, France, Guinea-Bissau, Paraguay, and Switzerland have subsequently become State Parties and at the time of writing other nations are in the process of developing legislation to implement the 2001 Convention apparently with a view towards becoming Parties. Such progress can be observed in, for example, the chapters related to Australia, Ireland, and the Netherlands, by Craig Forrest and Andrew Viduka, Connie Kelleher *et al.*, and Andrea Klomp and Martijn Manders respectively.

As the 2001 Convention approaches its 25th anniversary, the progress to date in recognising more than the monetary value of UCH would appear unquestionable, arguably representing a clear endorsement of its original purposes. From the international legal void reflected in the first edition, this third edition documents an increasingly sophisticated legal and policy environment. This is evident in both active participation of States via ratification and implementation of the 2001 Convention, but also in non-State Party practice, for example as seen in the UK's adoption of the Rules of the Annex as marine archaeological policy, which subsequently informs marine licensing decisions as discussed in this edition's chapter by Jason Lowther *et al.* The reasons for this are numerous, nuanced and discussed at length by the contributors to this edition. For example, there would appear to be little evidence of the 'creeping jurisdiction' that originally concerned the major maritime powers, as discussed in the chapter on the Netherlands by Andrea Klomp and Martijn Manders. In addition, whilst unresolved satisfactorily for some nations, potential inconsistency between the LOSC and the treatment of sunken warships, including the

13 Albania, Algeria, Antigua & Barbuda, Argentina, Bahrain, Barbados, Belgium, Benin, Bolivia (the Plurinational State of), Bosnia & Herzegovina, Bulgaria, Cabo Verde, Cambodia, Costa Rica, Croatia, Cuba, the Democratic Republic of the Congo, Dominican Republic, Ecuador, Egypt, Estonia, France, Gabon, Gambia, Ghana, Grenada, Guatemala, Guinea-Bissau, Guinea, Guyana, Haiti, Honduras, Hungary, Iran (the Islamic Republic of), Iraq, Italy, Jamaica, Jordan, Kuwait, Lebanon, Libya, Lithuania, Madagascar, Malawi, Mali, Malta, Mauritania, Mexico, Micronesia (Federated States of), Montenegro, Morocco, Namibia, Nigeria, Niue, Oman, Panama, Paraguay, Poland, Portugal, Qatar, Romania, Saint Kitts & Nevis, Saint Lucia, Saint Vincent & the Grenadines, Sao Tome and Principe, Saudi Arabia, Senegal, Slovakia, Slovenia, South Africa, Spain, State of Palestine, Switzerland, Togo, Trinidad & Tobago, Tunisia, Ukraine, and Yemen.

vexed question of sovereign immunity, does not appear to have manifested to the extent originally feared. Indeed, as noted in some contributing chapters to this edition there have been encouraging examples of practice demonstrating respect for the ownership and sovereign immunity of sunken State vessels (including aircraft) that lie within coastal State jurisdiction of Parties to the 2001 Convention.

However, whilst, as noted above, subsequent years have witnessed a growing willingness by States to ratify the 2001 Convention, there remain challenges in protecting UCH. The chapter contributors attest to both the successes and the obstacles, including the theoretical and practical means to overcome them. Such challenges include apprehension of 'creeping jurisdiction', *in situ* preservation, and the '100-year rule', as well as the need for greater inter-State collaboration, education, and outreach in the requirement to preserve and protect UCH. These key themes, as well as others specific to a region or State perspective, are outlined below and examined more fully and critically in the national context within individual chapters, the high-level content of which is elaborated in section 3 below.

2 Key Themes

As the effective management and conservation of UCH becomes a more prominent policy imperative, the ontologies of, *inter alia*, jurisdiction, *in situ* preservation, commercial salvage and treasure hunting, and sovereign immunity, become susceptible to refinement or reinterpretation. While the dial has shifted, positively in most cases, towards the enhanced protection for UCH, regarding key themes identified in previous editions, certain issues persist and the solutions to some extent remain elusive. These are identified below, and, whilst in no order of significance, evidently appear to impact on ratification of the 2001 Convention and its practical implementation.

2.1 *Creeping Jurisdiction*

In the second edition, the theme of 'creeping jurisdiction' was in the vanguard of reasons offered for reticence, particularly by major maritime States, to sign the 2001 Convention, let alone ratify it. The 78 current State Parties indicate that perhaps this issue was not quite the obstacle originally perceived. This may be due to the constellation of subsequent oceans-governance related measures, as well as the observable practice of States, and this appears to be so whether the State is a Party to the 2001 Convention or not. For example, Türkiye, the USA, the UK and others have aligned their domestic law and practice in a manner reflecting the spirit and objectives of the 2001 Convention and its Annex.

As Ulrike Guerin, Secretary to the 2001 Convention since 2005, notes in her chapter reflecting on a range of pertinent issues, "the 2001 Convention does not regulate any issue in contradiction to LOSC ... [and] ... does not contain regulations constituting a 'creeping jurisdiction'". This dimension to the 2001 Convention is presented more fully in jurisdictional terms in section 3 below.

2.2 *The 100-Year Rule*

The 100-year rule of mandatory protection of sites, is a *minimum* requirement established under Article 1(1)(a) of the 2001 Convention, as noted by Ulrike Guerin. The second edition of this work presented a significant range of perspectives on this theme and identified examples of where a shorter period has been applied, such as Chuuk Lagoon in the Federated States of Micronesia and the wrecks in Scapa Flow, Scotland. This edition includes further examples such as the scheduling of Second World War (WWII) amphibious tanks in England, discussed by Jason Lowther *et al.* as representing a significant change in English UCH policy, and Marnix Pieters offers the example of HMS *Wakeful* as a protected site in Belgian waters less than 100-years old. Maili Roio recognises that within Estonian waters UCH less than 100-years old may hold cultural value and is therefore able to be protected. In federal jurisdictions such as the USA, Ole Varmer reflects a non-uniform approach between States, Washington for example setting a limit as low as 30 years, with submerged vessels including aircraft becoming the property of the State.

2.3 *In Situ Preservation*

A further theme is the oft vexed question of *in situ* preservation. Article 2(5) of the 2001 Convention states that 'preservation in situ of [UCH] shall be considered as the first option for allowing or engaging in any activities directed at this heritage'. Again, in framing this issue from the perspective of the 2001 Convention's Secretariat, Ulrike Guerin is very clear that the *in situ* preference should be approached as a precautionary management tool and not a legal mandate, which is reflected by the majority of contributors to this edition. That said, there is at least a possibility that some regulators may hide behind the requirement as a means to avoid potentially costly interventions. The 2001 Convention, however, is clear in that it anticipates artefacts may require recovery. Article 2(6) for example, provides that 'recovered UCH shall be deposited, conserved and managed in a manner that ensures its long-term preservation'. The more emotive issue of human remains for which provisions are made in Article 2(9) of the 2001 Convention is considered at 2.5 below.

2.4 *Commercial Salvage and Treasure Hunting*

Article 2(7) of the 2001 Convention plainly states that UCH 'shall not be commercially exploited'. As noted above, the technology available to commercial salvors and treasure hunters appears to have increased in its scope and effectiveness in an analogous way to IT over the decades. Such advances continue to pose existential threats to UCH. While discoveries, such as *Endurance* under the Antarctic ice sheet and the USS *Samuel B Roberts* at a depth of nearly 7 kilometres, the deepest wreck of a warship found to date, are without doubt awe inspiring, they should prompt a note of caution within the subsea archaeological community.

Such technology, for example, permitted the surreptitious recovery of a cargo claimed to be protected under sovereign immunity which ultimately became the subject of a recent UK Supreme Court decision. The case centred on an *in rem* claim to a cargo of South African owned silver bullion recovered from a liner, SS *Tilawa*, sunk in the Indian Ocean by Axis forces during WWII with the loss of 280 lives.[14] While the case was not premised on an interference with UCH, the judgment offers clarity in terms of what constitutes a non-commercial purpose. Here the bullion was to be minted into State currency, and the Supreme Court held that this was non-commercial, at least insofar as UK salvage law is concerned. Whilst, the *Tilawa* litigation was concluded under principles of English law, the judgment is likely to be of interest to both treasure hunters and the authorities in other States, given the value of the cargo and the costs of recovery.

Those seeking to commercially exploit UCH have also had recourse to advances in other areas, such as Human Rights law. Ville Peltokorpi and Maija Matikka reflect on the position in Finland with respect to proprietary title in litigation concerning the salvage of the *Vrouw Maria* wreck. Uncertainties in Finnish law created potential lacunae and the protracted proceedings eventually became a claim before the European Court of Human Rights, which on a procedural point did not accept the case. The many complexities involved demonstrate the need for clear national legislation on title and State intervention.

Treasure hunting *per se* is discussed by, for example, Kathleen Tantuico and Bobby Orillaneda, who reflect on the loss of cultural artefacts taken from wrecks in the Philippines by highlighting potential discrepancies and misunderstanding in respect of treasure hunting permits, which were previously

---

14 *Argentum Exploration Ltd* v *Republic of South Africa* [2024] UKSC 16. The case post-dated the writing of the UK Chapter and for reference the full judgment is available at <https://www.supremecourt.uk/cases/uksc-2022-0162.html>.

permitted in that jurisdiction, although there has been no repeal of the law that enables their issuance. Treasure hunting under the guise of legitimate archaeological investigation and recovery has tested the legislative response, an example of which is provided by Roberto Junco Sánchez and Laura Carrillo Márquez reflecting on the Mexican experience and specifically the *Matancero* wreck.

It has also resulted in examples of litigation specifically related to the commercial exploitation of UCH. This includes Mariano Aznar's detailed explanation in the chapter on Spain of the unauthorised salvage by an American company of the wreck site of *Nuestra Señora de las Mercedes* and the subsequent, successful, litigation to recover the valuable cargo from the salvor. An American perspective on the *Mercedes* litigation is presented by Ole Varmer. A further example, resulting in litigation involving the same company, is the case of HMS *Victory 1744*, as discussed by Jason Lowther *et al.* Other examples of successful recovery of illicitly removed UCH include those offered by Maria Luz Endere and Norma Levrand in the chapter on Argentina, including cannon offered for sale on the internet and subsequently confiscated, although without further sanction being imposed.

2.5 *Sovereign Immunity*

Continuing the above theme there have been examples of military and/or State vessels to which sovereign immunity would be expected to apply that have been subject to plunder in recent years. Anecdotally, this has been a consequence of global scrap metal values, and specifically the value of pre-nuclear steel.[15] The Netherlands, Australia and the UK have all experienced losses, as noted by the authors in the respective jurisdictional chapters of this edition. For example, significant wrecks including, *inter alia*, HNLMS *De Ruyter*, HMAS *Perth* and HMS *Exeter* have been entirely removed from the seabed in the Java Sea, unlawfully, by foreign salvors. Craig Forrest and Andrew Viduka, offer a detailed analysis from the Australian perspective of the threats to out of jurisdiction wrecks in this context, whilst Andrea Klomp and Martijn Manders, note the prompt to greater international cooperation that these incidents have secured. Additional examples include those identified by Jason Lowther *et al.*, and Mariano Aznar, concerning recoveries from HMS *Victory 1744* and the *Mercedes,* as referred to above. This contentious issue remains without adequate

15 See for example, Oliver Holmes, Monica Ulmanu and Simon Roberts, 'The world's biggest grave robbery: Asia's disappearing WWII shipwrecks', (The Guardian, 3 November 2017). Interactive resource at, https://www.theguardian.com/world/ng-interactive/2017/nov/03/worlds-biggest-grave-robbery-asias-disappearing-ww2-shipwrecks>.

resolution, more so where there has been significant loss of life and that those human remains may have been disturbed or removed.

Article 2(9) of the 2001 Convention states that Parties 'shall ensure that proper respect is given to all human remains located in maritime water'. The human remains issue is one which receives significant consideration in Akifumi Iwabuchi's chapter on Japan. As a professor of anthropology and an ICOMOS-ICUCH expert on maritime archaeology, he highlights Japan's interest in the recovery of human remains from warships under the Promoting the Recovery of the Remains of Japanese War Dead Act 2016. While he expresses concern that this conflicts with the *in situ* provisions in the 2001 Convention, UNESCO's 2019 report on the 2001 Convention clarifies that the *in situ* provision is a policy preference, not a legal requirement, and the 2001 Convention

> ... aims to ensure the protection of these human remains but the decision on whether to remove them or not ultimately lies with each country ... [and] that the application of the provisions of the Convention needs to be carried out in respect of the diversity of religious and or cultural sensitivities.[16]

Reflecting the opinion of the UNESCO Secretariat, it is the view of Ole Varmer that Japan has discretionary authority to remove human remains that may be in its public interest as reflected in the above Act.

2.6 *Slow and Inconsistent Progress*

It is undeniable that the narrative with respect to enhanced protection for UCH is significantly more positive than it was even in the years immediately following the conclusion of the 2001 Convention. That said, to draw a comparison with protection of the natural environment, there are very observable phases of progress and common purpose evident, by both sovereign States and the international community. Conversely, there have been significant periods of stasis, or even backsliding. This is mirrored in the sometimes stop-start characterisations of jurisdictional political support for the cultural environment in general, and measures to protect UCH more specifically. States have signed and ratified in greater numbers, although as observed in the last edition, not always the traditionally conceived 'maritime powers'. Indeed, many of these nations continue to sit outside the 2001 Convention's scheme of regulation. It is worth

16 Meeting of States Parties to the Convention on the Protection of the Underwater Cultural Heritage, 7th, Paris, 2019, UNESCO UCH/19/7.MSP/INF.9 at p. 7.

noting perhaps that rather than considering this a setback in UCH protection, it may instead reflect a siloed, as opposed to a signalling, mindset. Evidence of this view exists in the contributions of authors who chart measures adopted within their jurisdictions, which even if not replicating the 2001 Convention or its Annex, come close to doing so and thus represent significant protective measures. As is also observable, not all jurisdictions have developed laws relating specifically to UCH, for example the Philippines, as explored by Kathleen Tantuico and Bobby Orillaneda, but have other measures in place that are able to extend protection into the offshore realm. Conversely, this edition contains chapters on States, for example Türikye and the USA, as discussed by as Barış Günay *et al.* and Ole Varmer respectively, which whilst not Party States to the 2001 Convention, or indeed LOSC, have effective UCH specific legislation.

Political will to undertake measures is often but not always linked to capacity in several States. Capacity building is identified as significant by a number of contributors as a resourcing issue. When there is perceived, tangible as well as intangible, value in UCH protection, resources may be more forthcoming. Perhaps linked is the temptation for politicians favouring a neo-liberalist approach and/or private sector involvement to prefer commercial exploitation over the preservation of cultural integrity. In addition, economic inequalities between States will remain key determinants in their abilities to ensure compliance with the 2001 Convention and will undoubtedly continue to shape their attitudes towards it. Sarah Dromgoole noted in the second edition the pressures in respect of less wealthy nations, with the example of the Federated States of Micronesia as reflected by Bill Jeffries' contribution, "to commercially exploit the bullion laden ships of former colonial powers that lie in their waters".[17] Those pressures have not lessened and have recently been brought into sharp focus following Colombia's stated intention to undertake survey work related to the wreck of the Spanish galleon *San José*, sunk by the British in 1708 in the Caribbean Sea. At present the Colombian approach, as analysed by Carlo Emilio Piazzini Suárez, has been to declare the site a protected area, although ownership of the ship and its cargo, valued in the billions of dollars, has been separately claimed by both a private American company, and Spain, and highlights difficult issues of arbitration.[18]

In the Philippines' chapter, Kathleen Tantuico and Bobby Orillaneda offer a further dimension capable of shaping political thinking via the presence of the

17 Sarah Dromgoole Ed etc, Editor's introduction page XXXII.

18 The most recent evaluation of the situation is available from a blog post by Paul Stevenson, 'Are We Yet at the Heart of the San José? Interested Parties Continue to Trade Blows', The Institute of Art & Law <https://ial.uk.com/heart-of-the-san-jose/>.

Gordian Knot of competing claims to jurisdiction. Specifically, they present this in the context of the situation in the South China Sea, relating to China's territorial claims under its 'Nine-Lines' policy, despite the decision of the International Tribunal on the Law of the Sea on the matter.[19]

Domestic factors, such as the lack of either political will or scope within legislative priorities, may also be responsible for lack of implementation and/or domestic inertia. Both constraints have been identified by authors to this edition. Examples include the situations in Italy, Nigeria, and the Philippines where a history of aspirational intent has not to date always been matched with the creation of equivalent practical measures. This is not uniform and indeed is very much contained within a spectrum of action/inaction and is often dependent upon political cycles and the ideological stances of particular governments. It would appear this is irrespective of membership of the 2001 Convention, such as in the cases of Nigeria and Italy, or non-membership, such as in the case of the Philippines and to an observable degree the UK. In the case of the latter, in the second edition, Sarah Dromgoole reported that the UK was undertaking a review of two of its key legislative provisions: the Protection of Wrecks Act 1973 and the Protection of Military Remains Act 1986. However, neither has subsequently been amended.

2.7 *International Cooperation*

The precarity of UCH offers itself to broader and deeper international cooperation, which may assist to alleviate the impact of political cycles and enhance capacity building. The 2001 Convention's Preamble, Article 19, and Rule 8 of its Annex all encourage and recognise the value of cooperation between States. This edition contains a number of more recent examples of such cooperation, while reflecting that there is certainly scope to improve the operational effectiveness of this dimension. There has, for example, been novel international cooperation under the auspices of the Antarctic Treaty,[20] where for the first time UCH was protected after agreement via Annex V to the Environmental Protocol 1991. The protection of the *Endurance*, and subsequently the *San Telmo*, were, at the time, of interest on the basis that the location of both was unknown, and in the case of the latter remains so. Jason Lowther *et al.* consider this development, while Mariano Aznar in the Spain chapter notes the search

19 *The South China Sea Arbitration* (*The Republic of Philippines v. The People's Republic of China*), Permanent Court of Arbitration, 2013–19. Available at <https://pca-cpa.org/ar/cases/7/>.

20 402 UNTS 71.

for the *San Telmo* as evidence of a more proactive approach in the evolution of Spain's attitudes and responses to its extensive and global UCH.

Other examples where international cooperation is evidenced, include those noted by Craig Forrest and Andrew Viduka in the chapter on Australia, reinforced by Andrea Klomp *et al.*, in the Netherlands chapter – recent cooperation relating to the threats posed to the respective States' military wrecks in the Java Sea. Additionally, the UK and the Netherlands have co-operated in relation to the VOC wreck of the *Rooswijk*, which is designated as protected in UK waters. Similarly, the nations have co-operated in respect of the *Klein Hollandia*, which was made subject to legal protection in 2019.[21] In the chapters on Estonia and Sweden, Maili Roio and Thomas Adlercreutz elaborate on inter-State agreements reached in respect of the MV *Estonia*, which have evolved since the previous edition of this work. Mariano Aznar charts Spain's extensive efforts at international cooperation, and otherwise States have entered into bi-lateral agreements, such as with the RMS *Titanic*, brought into a modern context by Ole Varmer.

Increasingly, shared heritage initiatives have become a useful vehicle to promote greater interest, appreciation, and thereby protection, of UCH. For example, the UK and Canada have entered into agreements in respect of HMS *Terror* and *Erebus*, with the unusual outcome of the UK ceding sovereignty to Canada over the vessels.[22] A more recent example, as analysed in some detail in Gonzalo Rodriguez Prado's chapter on Uruguay, is HMS *Agamemnon*. Significant work between Uruguayan and UK specialists have recovered, restored, and curated a series of artefacts that would otherwise have been lost to the impacts of shipworm. Shared heritage initiatives perhaps offer a means by which States outside of the 2001 Convention, and in the case of the majority of Latin American nations unlikely to join, may secure mutually beneficial outcomes. María Luz Endere and Norma Levrand's chapter on Argentina offers a slightly different perspective in its analysis of HMS *Swift*, and its importance in developing UCH-related measures in Argentina.

2.8 *Education, Access and Specialist Units*

In the context of the protection of UCH, education works in two principal ways. First, it enables the recognition of more than the monetary value of UCH

21 Mark Beattie-Edwards, Unknown Wreck off Eastbourne: Conservation Statement and Management Plan, (2024), Nautical Archaeology Society, Historic England Project Number 8572.

22 Ministry of Defence, 'UK gifts historic shipwrecks to Canada', 26 April 2018. MoD London, available at <https://www.gov.uk/government/news/uk-gifts-historic-shipwrecks-to-canada>.

amongst policy and law makers, which in turn engages the public and stimulates interest in cultural property and attendant values. Examples here include Trpimir Šošić's coverage on the position in Croatia, which refers to the Museum of the Apoxyomenos, amongst others. Second, upskilling and capacity building within and between nations facilitates cooperation and understanding, while innovating best practices in terms of investigation, recovery (if necessary), preservation and curation. The Croatia chapter reflects on multi-State cooperation on the Skerki Bank project, which is also discussed in the context of Italy by Massimiliano Secci and Barbara Davidde Petriaggi and Ulrika Guerin in the opening chapter.

The emergent 'Blue Growth Agenda' provides an opportunity to place greater focus upon the educational value of UCH alongside its economic potential. The protection of UCH could be maximised by the realisation that its educational value is a necessary and complementary corollary of any attributable economic value. The chapter on Uruguay by Gonzalo Rodriguez Prado contextualises this admirably, offering insight into the practicalities of achieving this.

As with education, the question of access is multi-faceted. First, as noted above, constant technological innovation grants access to UCH in unprecedented ways. The routine use of ROVs/UAVs undoubtedly creates both opportunities for study of, and existential threats to the integrity of, UCH in those deep sea environments where direct human access is impossible. However, where undertaken sensitively and within at least the scope of the Rules of the Annex to the 2001 Convention, unique opportunities for access without causing harm is possible. Issues related to this include disparities in capacity, as noted above, although perhaps of equal import is the vexed question relating to the governance of the Area.

Overall, greater public accessibility to UCH promotes positive engagement with history and culture. A number of contributors to this edition have indicated national approaches that recognise this value, and encourage responsible, sometimes curated, access to UCH. This may be evidenced, for example, by a 'look but do not touch' approach to a specific wreck or asset. It may also involve the creation of diver trails and, where necessary, land-based exhibition, in some cases involving international exchanges and cooperation, as in the case of Türkiye discussed by Barış Günay and his co-authors. Determining which UCH assets are able to be made generally accessible, however, is not necessarily a straightforward decision. Sensitivities, particularly in cases of human loss, may be difficult to overcome, as noted above. The freedoms of the past are now conditional upon assessments of cultural and/or educational value, perhaps analogous to the paradigm shift in governance brought about by the LOSC: *Mare Liberum* now giving way to *Mare Nostrum*. Sometimes, however, it remains necessary to maintain the integrity of UCH by denying access.

The means by which States have approached this conundrum with respect to UCH is appreciable, albeit inconsistent, in terms of the development, growth and value of specialist units with investigatory, archaeological and enforcement missions, such as the issuance of conditional diving/ remote access permits. In part, disparities between States' abilities to achieve this, as reflected in the content of this third edition, are a consequence of the capacity and political themes previously identified. There are numerous examples of what may be termed best practice in this edition. However, technological innovation is often market-driven, and the resources available to commercial interests are significantly greater than the majority of States would be willing or able to commit to their regulators, necessitating adaptive responses.

2.9 *Enforcement, Regulation and Sanctions*

A factor that has come to the fore more recently is enforcement: the offshore environment being so difficult to police effectively, all the more at the margins of the territorial/offshore capabilities of State Parties and/or where UCH that they may lay claim to appears in the Area or within the territorial jurisdiction of other States. Shared heritage or international cooperation may offer partial solutions in some cases – however, this is not a panacea. Dissuasive and proportionate enforcement cannot solely occur in the courts. Whilst many of the contributions to this edition identify cases where the shared cultural value of UCH has been recognised or upheld by the judiciary, the reality is that irreversible harm has been caused to the asset, which was the subject of the litigation, as discussed in 2.5 above. There are numerous examples within this edition that are suggestive of inconsistent State practice in relation to the 2001 Convention's Article 17 requirements that sanctions 'shall be adequate in severity to be effective in securing compliance … discourage violations … and deprive offenders of the benefit deriving from their illegal activities'.

The preference to protect UCH more consistently, and in accordance with the 2001 Convention, should be on prevention, with enforcement and regulation operating as a deterrent in order to do so. Yet, the characterisation of current practice across those nations examined within this edition is undoubtedly one of 'after the event'. In addition, even where there are sophisticated pre-intervention controls, penalties for unlawful disturbance and/or recovery remain wanting in many cases given the unique harms being perpetrated to what, in most jurisdictions, is considered to be a State or shared non-renewable resource.

The challenges and significant costs of gathering evidence and attempting enforcement interventions at sea, combined with the fact that the expense increases exponentially the further offshore the incident is, present very real choices and challenges for enforcement authorities even in well-resourced States. Ville Peltokorpi and Maija Matikka give an illustrative account of such difficulties in the example of the Porvoo looting case. Generally, according to the contributions in this edition, those States with the capacity to do so have opted for targeted interventions, often intelligence based, where is evidence or likelihood that UCH may be the subject of plunder or unlawful salvage and have built or considered mechanisms for doing so, good examples being Spain, Finland, and to a lesser extent the UK. Otherwise, enforcement is charted as occurring via the disruption and investigation of sales platforms, examples include Maria Luz Endere and Norma Levrand's explanation in the chapter on Argentina.

2.10 *Greater Ocean Governance, Marine Spatial Planning and Environmental Impact Assessment*

The very well-rehearsed concerns around 'creeping jurisdiction' appear to be perhaps now shown to be somewhat of a canard, in that there is arguably greater emphasis on the systematic management of both territorial and extra-territorial ocean spaces. Although beyond the scope of this text, there have been a series of progressive interventions, from more effective fisheries management to the creation of Marine Protected Areas predicated on the protection of species, which demonstrate the ability of States to agree on jurisdictional impacts where necessary. Additionally, greater emphasis, particularly within, although not limited to, European Union Member States, has been placed on spatial planning of the marine environment. 'Environment' taken at its broadest interpretation includes the cultural environment, thereby encompassing UCH. The result should be that UCH, known or otherwise, is factored into development decisions in the EEZ/CS of coastal States. The extent to which this occurs is currently not well understood given that marine spatial planning is a relatively contemporary practice. Some chapters in this edition, including for example that on the UK, have reflected on this development, although the area is under-researched.

Whilst formal marine planning requirements are a relatively recent phenomenon, in comparison the use of environmental impact assessments (EIA) to determine how negative environmental effects of offshore interventions may be avoided or mitigated has an established pedigree, including for UCH, in several jurisdictions. Chapters discussing the process for pre-development EIA include Belgium, the Netherlands and the UK – the utility of this means of regulation would be a useful expansion of the obligations contained in the Annex to the 2001 Convention.

In addition to the above key themes prevalent throughout the three editions of this text, are the emerging issues and threats to UCH that are identified in the conclusion to this Editorial Introduction, and which in the future are likely to require greater national and international focus.

3 The National Perspective

This third edition contains explanation and analysis of the protection of UCH from the perspective of 21 nations. These are arranged alphabetically but in this Editorial Introduction are considered, first, in the context of those that have ratified the 2001 Convention, followed by those that are yet to do so. The themes identified above are discussed within them to varying degrees, a reflection of national drivers in policy and law, and thus also both opportunities and challenges in securing the effective protection of UCH in its multiplicity of forms.

The chapters analysing national jurisdictions are preceded by one authored by Ulrike Guerin, providing a non-academic commentary reflecting a view on the UNESCO Secretariat's position on the 2001 Convention. This chapter considers in some detail the operational workings of the 2001 Convention, and challenges head-on various critiques, including perceptions of 'creeping jurisdiction', noting that the 2001 Convention has brought positive changes in respect of the recognition, value and protection of UCH. The chapter provides an expert, practical legal interpretation of the terms of art contained within the 2001 Convention and comprises an effective contextual baseline to set the scene for the jurisdictional commentaries that follow.

3.1 *States Party to the 2001 Convention*

There are eight chapters on the domestic UCH laws and policies of nations that are Parties to the 2001 Convention: Argentina, Belgium, Croatia, Estonia, Italy, Mexico, Nigeria, and Spain. Apparent from them, is a lack of evidence to support notions of 'creeping jurisdiction' or inconsistency with the LOSC. There is, additionally, some evidence of practice that respects the limits of coastal State jurisdiction in the CS and EEZ. There are also examples of cooperation with foreign flag States that demonstrates respect for ownership and sovereign immunity.

Argentina ratified the 2001 Convention in 2010. As noted by the authors, María Luz Endere and Norma E. Levrand, "[t]his country played a prominent role during the Convention discussion process ... especially by the young diplomat Ariel W. González ...", a consistent voice for the need for coastal States to have a leading role for the cooperative protection of UCH in their respective EEZs that resonated with many in the G77. As the authors note, Argentina's interest in UCH research, law and policy is traced to the discovery of HMS *Swift*, an 18th century British sloop that sank in Argentinian territorial waters, providing a springboard for Argentina's UCH management in a manner consistent with the LOSC and the 2001 Convention.

Belgium ratified in 2013 and, as Marnix Pieters explains, the 2001 Convention has been a key driver in its legal evolution regarding the protection of UCH. The Belgian Government has asserted title over reported finds and offers an example of respect for the ownership and sovereign immunity of foreign flagged State vessels, the author notes that:

> … this was of course not applicable to ships or craft that belonged to a State at the moment of sinking or crashing since such sites in general benefit from sovereign immunity, especially if they were used for non-commercial purposes.

In 2004, Croatia was the third country to ratify the 2001 Convention. Trpimir Šošić notes that while Croatia has not enacted specific legislation on UCH protection, it relies on a comprehensive law regulating the protection of all cultural heritage that is applicable to UCH and on its Maritime Code, which is consistent with the LOSC in regard to maritime zones, including the EEZ, and implements the International Convention on Salvage 1989,[23] which respects the ownership and sovereign immunity of sunken State vessels used for non-commercial purposes. While Croatia would arguably benefit from more clarity on control of activities beyond its Territorial Sea, the lack of assertion of coastal State jurisdiction over wrecked foreign flagged vessels and respect for the ownership of UCH is further evidence of its implementation of the 2001 Convention in a manner consistent with the LOSC.

Estonia, as noted by Maili Roio, is a relatively young country that was inspired by the 2001 Convention to develop UCH legislation as part of its process to become a Party in 2020. Like other nations, Estonia protects some of its more significant UCH through designation of monuments. From the author's perspective, there has been no assertion of 'creeping jurisdiction' or failure to respect foreign flag State sovereign immunity or ownership. Indeed, the chapter notes examples of coordination between nations to determine ownership and final disposition, including reliance on treaty and diplomatic

23 1953 UNTS.

correspondence with foreign flagged States, including non-State Parties such as Germany and the UK.

As explained by Massimiliano Secci and Barbara Davidde Petriaggi, the Italian delegation played a leadership role in the development of the 2001 Convention, becoming a State Party in 2010. They track early interest in protecting UCH and how Italy "started off on the right foot" but that a "lightening start" has unfortunately not been followed by the political will to design a complex infrastructure, both legislative and institutional, capable of managing this heritage. Italian waters are host to extensive UCH, as is the case with many Mediterranean nations, and its involvement in co-operative agreements, such as the Skerki Bank project mentioned above, evidences its commitment to the protection of UCH despite an absence of national legislation to further the objectives of the 2001 Convention.

Roberto Junco Sánchez and Laura Carrillo Márquez provide an overview of the development of the law in Mexico, starting with the establishment of measures relating to monuments and moving on to Pilar Luna's robust leadership in using these laws to protect UCH against pillaging by treasure hunters. Mexico became a Party to the 2001 Convention in 2006, relying on existing law to protect terrestrial heritage, which was subsequently consolidated in 2014. In doing so clarity was provided that it extended to UCH, demonstrating respect for the sovereign immunity of foreign flagged State vessels and the balance of interests under the LOSC. Again, the authors note no assertion of 'creeping jurisdiction' and offer examples of demonstrable cooperation, such as with Spain.

In 2005, Nigeria was the sixth, and the first African nation, to ratify the 2001 Convention, as highlighted by Edwin Egede. However, as the author summarises, Nigeria still has a long way to go as regards domestic implementation. As with several jurisdictions included in this edition there remains the need to create awareness amongst relevant local stakeholders of the importance and value of UCH, and to build the required capacity to engage with UCH, aligning with the key themes outlined above. Whilst Nigeria's domestic legislation on cultural heritage generally could be interpreted as applying also to UCH, and includes protection of antiquity and monuments, both natural and cultural 'made or fashioned before the year 1918', the author notes that express authority to protect and manage UCH is needed.

Spain has played a leading role in developing law and policy to protect UCH. It was the fourth country to ratify the 2001 Convention and continues to play a significant role in fulfilling the duty to cooperate to protect UCH, including through agreements with non-Party States. Mariano Aznar notes when negotiations on the 2001 Convention started, Spain, as a 'maritime power', was among the so-called 'like-minded' group of States (e.g., USA, UK, Germany, and France) concerned about 'creeping jurisdiction' and the treatment of sunken State craft. However, as a former colonial power Spain's UCH is located around the globe, and thus as negotiations proceeded, Spain's position evolved to support the 'constructive ambiguity' that afforded coastal States a primary coordinating role within the EEZ/CS. The chapter also demonstrates Spain's leadership by intervening in US Admiralty court cases which resulted in landmark rulings that respect the ownership and sovereign immunity of its sunken State wrecks, including the *Juno*, the *La Galga* and the *Mercedes*, as the author engagingly depicts.

3.2 *The Practice of Nations Not Party to the 2001 Convention*

There are 13 chapters in his book on the domestic UCH laws and policies of nations that are not Parties to the 2001 Convention: Australia, Colombia, Finland, Ireland, Japan, the Netherlands, New Zealand, the Philippines, Sweden, Türkiye, the UK, Uruguay, and the USA.

Australia, whilst not yet a Party, appears inexorably to be moving in that direction, as explored by Craig Forrest and Andrew Viduka. The authors examine development of contemporary domestic law that appears to have Australia better poised to implement the 2001 Convention than many existing Parties, since it may represent a model on implementing the 2001 Convention in a manner consistent with LOSC. This is one to watch with the hope this aim is soon realised. The authors' analysis offers no evidence of 'creeping jurisdiction' or lack of respect for foreign flag State ownership and sovereign immunity. Australia also demonstrates leadership in fulfilling the duty to protect UCH and international cooperation for that purpose.

Carlo Emilio Piazzini Suárez summarises Colombia's treatment of historic resources from 'treasure' to 'heritage', highlighting how commercial interests remain in potential conflict with the evolving legal and academic structure for preserving its heritage. He notes the Colombian delegation actively promoted protecting UCH during negotiations on the 2001 Convention that resonated with Latin American and Caribbean States. However, it did not become a signatory, noting concern on the principle of *in situ* conservation as being extremely protectionist, a position it appears influenced by the potential recovery of the remains of the Spanish galleon *San José*. As this involves a foreign sunken State craft on Colombia's CS, the international community is no doubt watching developments and delicate negotiations between the two States on the final disposition of shared heritage, which the author hopes will be consistent with the 2001 Convention and the LOSC. As the author notes, Colombia is at a crossroads in the protection of UCH.

Ville Peltokorpi and Maija Matikka summarise development of historic preservation law in Finland. Cooperation between government authorities and diving groups, as stakeholders, is active and important, as access is not prohibited. The authors note that while resources are limited and there has been no nationwide strategy focusing solely on UCH, the basic elements necessary for its protection exist in territorial and inland waters and are in the authors' opinion considered consistent with the spirit of the 2001 Convention. The authors report that preparations for reform of national legislation are underway but that there are no apparent plans for starting the process for becoming a Party.

The protection of Ireland's heritage can be traced to an ancient monuments law pre-dating independence in 1922, following which the Irish National Monuments Act 1930 was enacted and subsequently amended in 1987 to protect UCH. As noted by the authors, Connie Kelleher *et al.,* Ireland relies on its maritime law to protect UCH from commercial exploitation. As the authors note, the rulings of the Irish High and Supreme Courts have established important principles supporting the protection of UCH, including restrictions on the application of commercial salvage law and finds of objects with no known owner that are considered part of the heritage of Ireland. It appears that Ireland has taken care to regulate its UCH in a manner consistent with the LOSC and the 2001 Convention and its law has been revised since the second edition placing it in a position to ratify the 2001 Convention, which would now appear likely.

The Japanese perspective is provided by Akifumi Iwabuchi. An important aspect of the chapter relates to WWII losses, reparations and title to vessels. The author contends that title to Japanese warships was transferred to the Allies in the Treaty ending WWII. While this could be a position the Japanese Government may raise, the USA Government disagrees, and a review of the Treaty makes no explicit reference to wrecks or shipwrecks whereas it does reference fleets, arms, munitions etc. At a Project Tangaroa Workshop in 2024, Professor Tatsuya Nakada from Kobe University stated that the transfer of the ships in the Treaty did not include shipwrecks.[24] Despite potential dispute over title and ownership, the Japanese Government is voluntarily assisting in preservation efforts including removal of pollutants from sunken

24 Project Tangaroa is running workshops to address the issues flagged in its book: "Threats to Our Ocean Heritage: Potentially Polluting Wrecks", to create a framework for proactive management of PPWs. It plans to provide a tool kit or draft international standards for consideration by nations and international organizations that work on these PPWs issues. It' isa partnership initiated by The Lloyd's Register Foundation, with The Ocean Foundation, the Waves Group, the IUCN, ICOMOS-ICUCH and others. See <https://www.project-tangaroa.org/>.

warships in, for example, Chuuk Lagoon. However, as noted by the author, the perception of *in situ* preservation acting as an obstacle to recovery, along with the issues of title and sovereign immunity, appear to be significant hurdles to Japan acceding to the 2001 Convention.

Andrea Klomp and Martijn Manders (with a special mention of the late Thijs Maarleveld) provide an overview of the law in the Netherlands, which has historically been at the forefront of the development of the Law of the Sea. When concerns were raised about whether the 2001 Convention was consistent with the LOSC, it did not sign as a State Party. Regardless, the 2001 Convention and particularly the Annex influenced the development of the management of its UCH. Since the second edition the Netherlands has revisited its views and concerns and requested advice from the Advisory Committee on Public International Law on the relationship between the 2001 Convention and the LOSC, particularly on 'creeping jurisdiction'. The Committee subsequently concluded that the 2001 Convention was not in contradiction with the LOSC, which may potentially pave the way for the Netherlands to reassess its position and to accede to the 2001 Convention.

Like many other nations, the history of New Zealand/Aotearoa's cultural preservation law starts around the turn of the 20th century and extends to indigenous, colonial and post-colonial era UCH. The authors, Piers Davies and Paul Myburgh, note that New Zealand/Aotearoa's existing domestic legislative framework for heritage management addresses many issues covered in the 2001 Convention but also that gaps or shortcomings can be identified, not least in enforcement provisions and the lack of legal protection for UCH situated within the EEZ/CS.

Kathleen Tantuico and Bobby Orillaneda provide an overview of the cultural heritage legislation of the Philippines that has been applied to protect UCH. With colonial links to both Spain and the USA, the legal architecture appears to reflect aspects of both traditions. While there are provisions consistent with the 2001 Convention regarding policy to conserve categorised heritage, a treasure hunting permit system remains a major obstacle to becoming a Party to the 2001 Convention. The Philippines and its UCH would clearly benefit from becoming so, particularly in applying blanket protection from commercial treasure salvage. However, there appears to be no political will for change at this time, which the authors speculate may be at least in part a reflection of maritime territorial conflict between the Philippines and China.

Thomas Adlercreutz charts the evolution of Sweden's heritage system, from an early provenance to the Ancient Monuments Act 1942. Amendment in 2014 protected 'craft' underwater for at least 100 years, but further amendment applied a date of 1850. Since this would exclude all aircraft, the author notes that 'special reasons' may be promulgated to ensure protection of UCH arising post that cut-off point. Whilst Sweden has legislative provisions that may be considered as implementing LOSC Articles for UCH protection in the Area and within the CZ, the author's analysis of issues Sweden has with the 2001 Convention's compatibility with the LOSC indicates that it has little or no interest in becoming a Party at the current time.

Türkiye remains a non-signatory, of both the 2001 Convention and the LOSC. Nevertheless, as Barış Günay and his co-authors note, there is a rich history in terms of scientific investigation and the curation of recovered UCH. The chapter offers a detailed discussion of the key definitions of movable and immovable cultural heritage, the compulsory notification obligation, and reward mechanisms provided in the Law on Protection of Cultural and Natural Heritage 1983. In addition to this overarching measure, and the permitting system it creates, enforced though the criminal law, the chapter considers other related regulatory interventions. It concludes with a reflection on the fact that despite not being a signatory, Türkiye has developed a relatively sophisticated legal ecosystem targeted towards the protection of UCH.

As explained by Jason Lowther *et al.*, the UK is yet to become a Party to the 2001 Convention. As with the USA, there remain reservations about upsetting the delicate balance of flag and coastal State jurisdiction in the EEZ/CS. While many hope the UK revisits its position, it has taken positive steps since the 2006 edition, which the authors reflect critically upon. For example, the Marine Policy Statement 2011 explicitly recognises UCH, and it is clearly integrated into EIAS. 'Environment' is not limited to natural resources and includes 'cultural heritage', and thus UCH. In addition, since the second edition the UK has claimed an EEZ and placed a robust contemporary focus on enforcement. However, as highlighted in the chapter, the devolved nature of administration in the UK has resulted in differences of approach, specifically in Scotland.

Ole Varmer provides a summary of the patchwork of laws regulating activities directed at UCH in the USA and focuses on significant developments since the second edition, including salvage law cases involving RMS *Titanic* and the *Mercedes*. It offers a gap-analysis and recommendations for their rectification using the 2001 Convention as the benchmark. It also documents State practice in adhering to the duty to protect UCH and to cooperate for that purpose, making some progress over the last 16 years in developing laws and policies to implement its duties of protection and cooperation respecting UCH. However, the author reflects that there is still much to do, including building upon on an integrated approach to conserving the ocean heritage and using the best available science as a beacon.

Gonzalo Rodríguez Prado's chapter analyses Uruguay's treatment of commercial exploitation, ownership, sovereign immunity, and conservation of UCH before sharing lessons learned and best practices for its protection and management. Consistent with the 2001 Convention, he confirms the incompatibility of private for-profit projects to sell UCH and sees it "giving rise to a new sustainable blue economy context". Uruguay actively participated in the 2001 Convention negotiations but ultimately abstained – the principal objections being in relation to sovereign immunity of foreign flagged vessels and existing State contracts with private companies for the extraction of shipwreck remains. Case studies support the author's conclusion that Uruguay's experience subjecting UCH to commercial exploitation was negative. In 2006, granting new permits was suspended, and now only scientific projects approved by the National Heritage Commission are authorised. While the cultural authorities have expressed interest in becoming a Party to the 2001 Convention, the author notes that the Foreign Ministry view is unknown.

4 The Future for the Global Protection of UCH

Alongside the identified common themes, the contributors' presentations and analyses of the situations pertaining in their respective jurisdictions paints a picture of innovation and creativity as responses to the obligations generated by the 2001 Convention. This is witnessed not just for those States that have ratified the 2001 Convention but also non-signatories, where the conservation and sustainable use of UCH assets appears to have a degree of recognition and, in some cases, real traction. The expansion of national contributors in this edition garners broader insight into legal systems that have not always received considerable attention in this respect, so presenting them here, it is hoped, will lead to further, and perhaps more regionalised, examinations within academic literature. It is unquestionable that there is scope to learn and develop further best practices in the regulation and management of UCH assets and to appreciate how these might arise in a particular geographical and/or geopolitical context.

Looking ahead to the possible future, a more coherent integration of both cultural and natural assets has the potential to offer a catalysing effect on the more effective protection and management of both sectors. Presently, there is a definite sense of silos, with environmental interest in UCH often negatively focused upon impacts of spilled cargo, bunker oil, or other toxics, as opposed to the potential for positive outcomes. Contemporary discussion of concepts should recognise that marine 'natural' capital includes, and may be co-located with, the cultural, so that protected UCH may provide an additional refuge for biodiversity.[25] Many coastal States are now looking to exploit the offshore environment as a means for renewable energy generation, carbon capture and storage and the like, meaning more threats for the loss of, or damage to, previously undiscovered UCH resources, but also opportunities to discover lost cultural gems for future generations to investigate and enjoy. There remains the spectre of seabed mining in the Area, and while most concerns relate to the loss of biodiversity, it is highly likely that undiscovered UCH may be lost without effective means of regulation and/or obligations placed on developers.

The BBNJ Agreement adopted in June 2023, while not yet in force and currently a long way short of the 60 ratifications necessary for it to do so (15 at the time of writing), offers a vision of what could be. While the Agreement is wholly focused on biodiversity as currently constituted, reflecting a narrow interpretation of the environment, it contemplates global consensus on High Seas/ Area management tools, including Marine Protected Areas (MPAS) and effective EIAS. Neither MPAS nor EIAS are novel, for example the OSPAR[26] and Barcelona Conventions[27] (relating to the North-East Atlantic and the Mediterranean respectively) contemplate their use even in areas beyond national jurisdiction. Indeed, the Barcelona Convention includes a specific mechanism to afford protected area status to heritage assets, although to date this has been underutilised. As we are now well progressed into the UN Decade of Ocean Science 2021–2030, it would be timely to better reflect UCH overtly in a more holistic consideration of the marine environment.[28]

The significant 'elephant in the room' is climate change. The threat manifests in various ways including, but not limited to, reshaping the territorial limits of coastal States because of sea level rise. Further effects include the impact of altered chemical composition of the oceans as carbon is absorbed more rapidly, alongside increased frequency and power of extreme weather events reshaping the benthos. Finally, the ability of certain damaging organisms, such as shipworm, to proliferate in locations previously hostile to their survival poses a real threat to UCH. Its intrusion into those places where it is currently not present, such as the polar seas (as seen in the stunning state of

---

25 See, for example, Jenny Hickman, Joe Richards, Adam Rees, and Emma V. Sheehan, 'Shipwrecks act as de facto Marine Protected Areas in areas of heavy fishing pressure', (2024), Marine Ecology, Vol. 45(1) e12782.

26 2354 UNTS 67.

27 1102 UNTS 27.

28 UN Decade of Ocean Science for Sustainable Development 2021–2030, UNESCO, see <https://www.unesco.org/en/decades/ocean-decade>.

preservation of Shackleton's *Endurance*), must be a concern for future UCH management.

The contributions to this edition provide insight into the significant progress made in extending protection to UCH since the earlier editions of this text. The sincere hope of the editors it that the next will reflect even greater progress.

All websites last accessed March 2025.

Acknowledgements

The editorial team acknowledge with thanks the contribution of Ole Varmer (Senior Advisor on Ocean Heritage, The Ocean Foundation) to this introduction.

CHAPTER 1

UNESCO 2001 Convention on the Protection of the Underwater Cultural Heritage: Progress and Prospects

*Ulrike Guerin**

1 Introduction

The 2001 UNESCO Convention on the Protection of the Underwater Cultural Heritage (2001 Convention)[1] was adopted in 2001 in order to combat the extensive pillage, commercial exploitation, and illicit traffic of underwater cultural heritage (UCH) and came into force on 2 January 2009. It is a comprehensive treaty, which fully addresses these issues regarding all waters – oceans, lakes, and rivers. It increases the legal protection of sites *in situ* and prohibits the illicit and/or unethical recovery and traffic of artefacts. The 2001 Convention is thus very relevant at a time when the pillage and commercial exploitation of UCH, as well as the industrialisation of the seabed, constitute major issues that have not yet found an appropriate solution in most regions of the world.

The 2001 Convention, however, goes further than that. It also responds to the need for scientific guidance and the facilitation of States' cooperation. Underwater archaeology is still a developing discipline. Around 71 per cent of the Earth is covered by oceans and the majority of the global seabed has not yet been researched for heritage. Research capacities are still lacking and awareness of the immense patrimony lying on the seabed, as well as internal waters, is very low. Only through exchange of knowledge and training can this situation be improved, bringing the importance of UCH to the attention of the public.

Last, but certainly not least, the 2001 Convention addresses the needs to mitigate the impact of industrial seabed activities, such as trawling, dredging, mineral extraction and so on, with the protection of submerged archaeological sites. These impacts are considerable, but with wise planning and

* Secretary of the Convention of the Protection of the Underwater Cultural Heritage, UNESCO. All views given in this article are those of the author only, do not commit UNESCO and are not binding in the interpretation of the Convention, which belongs to States Parties alone.

1 2563 UNTS 1.

 | DOI:10.1163/9789004510883_003

collaboration, not only excellent results for heritage protection and the development of underwater archaeology can be achieved, but also the enterprises concerned can benefit in terms of corporate responsibility and public image.

The 2001 Convention was drafted exclusively as a heritage protection treaty. It provides a blanket protection to all traces of human existence of a cultural, historical, or archaeological character, which have been partially or totally under water, periodically or continuously, for at least 100 years. It does not address the ownership of heritage, nor does it change maritime zones or jurisdiction.

As of, February 2025 the Convention has 78 States Parties,[2] and can rely on an extensive cooperation system and is supported by a functioning Scientific and Technical Advisory Body (STAB) that has already executed numerous missions to help States Parties in cases of emergency and need.[3] Despite not all States ratifying the 2001 Convention, others, for example the United Kingdom, have adopted the Annex to the Convention (the Rules), which sets out 'best practice' for UCH protection and management, in to their domestic policies.

This chapter offers an explanation of some of the principal regulatory mechanisms of the 2001 Convention and considers progress, prospects, and challenges.

2 The Definition of UCH

A first important aspect of the 2001 Convention is its approach to heritage. According to Article 1(a), for the purposes of the Convention, and as adopted by many heritage laws worldwide, 'underwater cultural heritage', as stated above, means:

> all traces of human existence having a cultural, historical or archaeological character, which have been partially or totally underwater, periodically or continuously, for at least 100 years.

The definition covers all traces of human existence, ranging from wrecks to prehistoric materials to sunken cities. It does not, however, cover fossils or

2 See generally <https://www.unesco.org/en/underwater-heritage>.

3 At the time of writing, there have been 8 STAB missions, detail on these can be found at <https://www.unesco.org/en/node/85043?hub=412>.

natural marine formations. The criterion that there has to be a 'cultural, historical or archaeological character' is only a reiteration, as essentially any trace of human life or activity has a cultural or historical character. Article 1(a) further elaborates on what may fall within the definition of UCH, such as:

(i), Sites, structures, buildings, artefacts and human remains together with this archaeological and natural context;
(ii), Vessels, aircraft, other vehicles or any part thereof, their cargo or other contents, together with their archaeological and natural context; and
(iii), Objects of prehistoric character.

As this is not an exclusive list, it is of no significance that the addition of the words 'together with their archaeological and natural context' has been left out of Article 1(a)(iii), despite their mention in paragraphs (i) and (ii), and it can be concluded that this equally applies to prehistoric sites. There was much debate during the drafting of the 2001 Convention, on whether to include objects of paleontological character, but it was decided not to. Under Article 1(b), '[p]ipelines and cables placed on the seabed and still in use' are not considered UCH, nor are 'installations' on the seabed and still in use (Article 1(c)).

2.1 *No Requirement of a Degree of Significance*

The UNESCO 2001 Convention's definition of UCH does not contain any 'significance' benchmark for the inclusion of an item or site. Firstly, because significance is difficult to measure; it can be different at the local, national, or international levels and depend, for instance, on the strength of historic relations or religious associations. Second, it could also operate as a delaying exercise to evaluate significance, before affording protection. An authority would be forced to evaluate a site before pursuing a pillager who may be destroying it. The States in drafting the text of the 2001 Convention took this into account in guaranteeing a blanket protection. This was a deliberate decision, following discussion during negotiations on the final text. Thus, from the outset the Convention has sought to offer protection to all sites against pillage and destruction. There is also no requirement for a site or artefact to be 'listed', or otherwise designated, for the Convention to apply.

The lack of a significance benchmark in the definition does not mean that States Parties have to excavate all submerged heritage. The 2001 Convention states in Article 2(5) that the preservation *in situ* of UCH shall be the first option, before allowing or engaging in any activities directed at this heritage. Rule 1 of the Annex adds that such activities may be authorised for the purpose of making a significant contribution to protection or knowledge or enhancement of

UCH. Therefore, there is no significance benchmark for protection, but there is a significance benchmark for the activity, which justifies excavation or the recovery of artefacts.

2.2 *Protection of Repetitive Items*

Moreover, the 2001 Convention's definition does not contain a benchmark for representation or singularity. The fact that an item is found, while a similar item has already been discovered, does not change its character as UCH within the contemplation of the 2001 Convention. This is important and gives a strong statement for protection, for instance in the case of coin finds on historic wrecks. The reasoning behind this is that repetitiveness can provide valuable scientific information, for instance on the size of trade, vehicles, armament, or the exhortations put on a population in order to obtain the materials in question. Furthermore, one item is never identical to another, and the differences observed can be of scientific interest.

3.3 *Protection of Cargoes*

Article 1(a)(ii) of the 2001 Convention cites explicit examples of UCH as:

> ... vessels, aircraft, other vehicles or any part thereof, their cargo or other contents, together with their archaeological and natural context ....

Thus, the 2001 Convention stresses the heritage character of the cargoes of vessels, without making any differentiation of their value, purpose, or initial destination. Any *per se* exclusion of commercial loads consisting of materials of value or materials still in their raw state, movable items, which had exchange or tax value such as coins and bullion, and industrial loads from the identification as UCH is not in line with the 2001 Convention's definition. Despite some argument to the contrary,[4] there is no reason why an item, which served as merchandise in ancient times, could not be considered as cultural heritage today.

2.4 *Protection of Recent Shipwrecks*

Many relatively recent sites bear witness to important historic events, such as the large battlefield sites in the Asia-Pacific region and in Europe. The nuclear test site of Bikini Atoll, in the Marshall Islands archipelago, and sunken vessels

---

4 Ancient Coin Collectors Guild spokesman, Wayne G. Sayles, commented in the October 2010 issue of The Celator magazine: "[coins are] utilitarian objects that were created in the millions and are not in any way of significant cultural value to any state."

associated with it have been listed as a UNESCO World Heritage Site.[5] The question put often forward is whether these more recent sites can be protected under the 2001 Convention.

In general, States Parties to the 2001 Convention must respect the benchmark of 100 years as the *minimum* requirement, set out in by Article 1(1)(a) and mandatorily protect sites older than 100 years. They cannot make an exception for any ancient site from the protection conferred to it by their ratification of the 2001 Convention, other than by a reservation concerning the geographical area it is located in.[6] However, States can act more protectively than the Convention's minimum standard. This means they can extend protection to more contemporary sites, such as those from World War II, as for instance those of Chuuk Lagoon in the Federated States of Micronesia or in Scapa Flow, Scotland, UK. Thus, for example, when a national law foresees protection of sites that are only 50-years old, that law does not need to be changed when a State becomes party to the 2001 Convention, since it is already in compliance with the Convention on this point.

Supporting this, the STAB has recommended protection of World War II sites on several occasions, see for example Recommendation 4 of the Fifth Meeting of the STAB for instance, where it:

> Recommends to the Meeting of States Parties, to encourage the States Parties to also consider to ensure proper protection is given to UCH sites from World War II and to educate the public in this regard.[7]

In addition, the Meeting of the States Parties has also considered more recent sites – for instance Resolution 4/MSP 5:

> … encourages States, even if they have not yet ratified the Convention, to apply the Rules of the Annex of the Convention as best practice for any activities directed at submerged parts of World Heritage properties and to strengthen their protection.[8]

---

5 See <https://whc.unesco.org/en/list/1339/#:~:text=Criterion%20(iv)%3A%20Bikini%20Atoll,develop%20increasingly%20powerful%20nuclear%20weapons>.

6 However, a mitigation of industrial activity impact on a site can include a balancing of protective interests in comparison to economic interests (see Article 5).

7 STAB 5, UCH/14/5.STAB/6, 15 June 2014, available at <https://unesdoc.unesco.org/ark:/48223/pf0000231863>.

8 MSP Fifth Meeting, UCH/15/5.MSP/11, 5 May 2015, available at <https://unesdoc.unesco.org/ark:/48223/pf0000233623?1=null&queryId=de8bfeda-52ea-4914-b319-04b97d377ac2.>.

This evidence thus supports inclusion of World War II sites and the importance of the application of the Rules of the Annex to more recent sites, such as Bikini Atoll.

3 Objectives

Article 2(1) of the 2001 Convention sets out its overall goal, which is to '*ensure and strengthen the protection*' of UCH. This underlines that the Convention will not deal with the rights of owners, in any other issue than in respect of the need to protect cultural values of interest to humanity. The 2001 Convention is not about attribution. It functions in a similar way to a protection plan of a historic city centre, focusing solely on cultural values.

3.1 *Obligation and Right to Cooperation*

Article 2(2) sets out a mandatory obligation for all States that ratify the 2001 Convention to cooperate. Cooperation remains the *Leitmotiv* in all further Articles. This right to, and obligation of, cooperation is not an option, but a dictate. The term used is 'shall': presumably, the details of how to achieve this are left the States themselves to consider on a case-by-case basis.

3.2 *Obligation to Take Measures*

Article 2(3) and (4) obliges States to take measures to protect their submerged heritage. Again, the term used is 'shall'. It remains the case that UCH is most often afforded less protection than land-based heritage and that less action is taken to safeguard it. Many domestic legislative efforts concentrate only on heritage located within the land territory of a State. This is due to higher visibility and, until recently, easier accessibility to land-based heritage. While archaeology on land has some 200 years of history, underwater archaeology, and with it the scientific appreciation of UCH, has only become possible since the 1940s. The 2001 Convention thus seeks to harmonise protection standards by protecting underwater sites as well as ensuring the rightful place of UCH in the body of the world's heritage. Article 2(3) hence underlines that protection is to be provided 'for the benefit of humanity', recalling the universal importance of heritage as well as the overall responsibility of States Parties to protect it. Article 2(4) provides that States have to take measures, individually or jointly, as appropriate, using 'the best practicable means at their disposal and in accordance with their capabilities'. This provision takes into account that many States do not yet possess competent underwater archaeologists and technical equipment. Also, financial restrictions can be a serious issue, when considering which measures can and should be taken in order to ensure protection.

4 Consideration of *in Situ* Preservation

According to Article 2(5) of the Convention:

> The preservation *in situ* [i.e., in its original location] of UCH shall be considered as the first option before allowing or engaging in any activities directed at this heritage.

Rule 1 of the Annex then adds and clarifies:

> Accordingly, activities directed at underwater cultural heritage shall be authorized in a manner consistent with the protection of that heritage, and subject to that requirement may be authorized for the purpose of making a significant contribution to protection or knowledge or enhancement of underwater cultural heritage.

No provision in the 2001 Convention has been as much misunderstood as the recommendation to give due consideration to *in situ* protection. It has sometimes even been perceived as a discouragement for scientific excavation. This is not the case: the Convention does not envisage empty museums. The Convention continues to allow scientific excavations and recovery, when advisable.

In fact, the recommendation to give consideration to *in situ* preservation is based on the recognition of two important challenges: first, the challenge to ensure proper conservation and storage of artefacts recovered from the water, especially from salt water; and, second, recognition of the importance of the interplay between the site and its context, reflecting lessons learned from the large-scale displacements of heritage to European museums in the nineteenth century, which are now perceived as destroying the original site and its spirit (*genius loci*).

Past recoveries of large-scale UCH, such as the *Mary Rose* and *Vasa*, demonstrated that the conservation and storage of large vessel hulls necessitates a significant human and financial investment. It requires specific knowledge and capacity to enable the conservation of water-logged materials. While building such museums is essential to share heritage with the public, it would be difficult to replicate such recoveries. Many shipwrecks' hulls have been recovered nevertheless, only to suffer for lack of conservation. Hence, the Annex to the

2001 Convention sets very strict rules for what has to be considered, before artefacts are recovered.

First, there must be a good reason to recover an artefact. As commercial exploitation is forbidden selling the heritage is not a good reason, whereas according to Rule 1 of the Annex 'making a significant contribution to protection or knowledge or enhancement of UCH' would be. While it is relatively clear what protection and knowledge means, it is arguable as to what constitutes 'enhances' UCH. It can be supposed that exhibition in a museum is such an enhancement.

Second, the Rules also require assurance that proper conservation treatment and storage takes place, as well as for a capable team to be involved. Every national authority, considering a Project Document submitted in order to obtain authorisation for an activity directed at a UCH site, has an obligation to verify and ensure that these conditions are fulfilled. This principle is also clearly enshrined in the overarching principles of the Convention text itself in Article 2(6), which states that 'recovered UCH shall be deposited, conserved and managed in a manner that ensures its long-term preservation'. Even if a State has not declared its intention to apply the Annex to its inland waters, it is recommended to take them into account in such cases. *In situ* preservation is the reasonable option, particularly when there is no danger threatening the site, and/or there is insufficient museum or technical space to exhibit or house the discovery.

5 Public Access

According to Article 2(10) of the 2001 Convention:

> Responsible non-intrusive access to observe or document *in situ* underwater cultural heritage shall be encouraged to create public awareness, appreciation, and protection of the heritage, except where such access is incompatible with its protection and management.

The 2001 Convention expresses a clear view of the importance of public access and engagement for heritage managers and underwater archaeologists. Access to and engagement with the authentic remains of a historic event by the public are important. The more that is known about an artefact, the more meaning is ascribed to the physical remains that constitute it. Granting an archaeological site a historical and cultural meaning may be appreciated differently by diverse parts of society. Even though such valorisation can differ geographically, culturally, or temporally, it always reinforces the existing links between societies and their cultural heritage, and it helps preserve the sites in question.

Article 2(10) of the 2001 Convention calls for the development of 'responsible non-intrusive access' to UCH, and makes, according to Article 20, the States Parties managers of the adoption of 'practicable measures to raise public awareness regarding the value and significance of underwater cultural heritage and the importance of protecting it'.

UCH is a legacy for humanity, and the public has a right to access and develop an appreciation for it. However, the 2001 Convention is very clear in its message: no public access should be allowed if it is incompatible with the protection and management of the UCH concerned. Therefore, in order to avoid negatively impacting the UCH by making it accessible to the public, control mechanisms should be established and respected. This guarantees the protection and preservation of the heritage that is on display, either in museums or *in situ*. While the 2001 Convention refers to *in situ* access, the focus does not discourage establishment of museums, but rather to emphasise the encouragement to also open underwater sites to the public, which is still often avoided or neglected by competent authorities. Attention is drawn to UNESCOs initiative to designate Best Practices in access to UCH. Already 12 projects or sites have been designated and offer an insight into how access to UCH can be best achieved.[9]

6 No Regulation of Ownership

Also, the question of who owns and has the right to possess often valuable[10] cargo of ancient shipwrecks is frequently raised by concerned parties and States. The 2001 Convention does not regulate the ownership of wrecks and cargoes. This is reiterated expressly in its Operational Guidelines.[11] This issue was considered too delicate and complicated to be resolved by a heritage protection treaty. This is also not the 2001 Convention's objective, as its sole goal is to protect heritage for the benefit of humanity. To determine ownership, many

9 Some of these were evaluated by the Seventh Meeting of the States Parties, UCH/19/7.MSP/7 10 January 2019. For information generally on 'Best Practices' see <https://www.unesco.org/en/underwater-heritage/best-practices?hub=412.>.

10 In this context 'value' is most generally conceived of in financial terms, although this is not to say that such cargoes would not have an equally significant cultural value.

11 Operational Guidelines, CLT/HER/CHP/OG1/REV, August 2015, available at <https://unesdoc.unesco.org/ark:/48223/pf0000234177?posInSet=1&queryId=60227917-d258-4890-bb60-cfa5d467f12f>.

practical, moral, and legal issues need to be considered, including legal questions, such as which country's law is to be applied.

It is often very difficult to identify a shipwreck, especially if ancient. Even when the wreck can be identified, controversies arise, such as who was its last owner and who is the successor. In case of State ships this question is at least somewhat easier to answer, the Netherlands for instance now own, at least according to Dutch law, the ancient VOC shipwrecks.[12] However, not all States' laws align, for example, where all heritage older than a certain number of years becomes State owned. The issue is even more difficult in the case of merchant shipwrecks, where relevant enterprises may no longer exist, have become property of an insurance company, or may have been split in an inheritance. In some cases, even State vessels have been disposed of to private enterprises for scrapping.[13]

Even if the hull of the wreck has an identifiable owner, the question of who owned the cargo it contained at the time of its sinking often remains a further unclear question, and ownership might be difficult to prove if no written records remain, or if there were many owners. Even if the original owners are identified, they have, in cases of physical persons most probably died, or in cases of legal persons, might no longer exist. Again, the search for owners or heirs would be necessary.

Even if all these riddles can be resolved there may remain questions of applicable law. France for instance, has a law regulating that all ancient shipwrecks in its waters, where ownership is unclear, belong to France.[14] Sometimes the boundaries of maritime zones are still under discussion, the Mediterranean being one example – in cases of similar laws, as with the cited French one, it becomes crucial to determine to whom a certain maritime area belongs. Last but not least, many moral considerations must be examined as to the rights to certain artefacts seized during occupation, colonisation or war from certain regions or countries. For instance, Peru claimed a portion of the coins which were included in the cargo of the Spanish warship *Nuestra Señora de las*

---

12 See the Chapter in this book on the Netherlands.

13 See the cases of the British World War I warships HMS *Cressi*, HMS *Aboukir*, and HMS *Hogue* wrecks, torpedoed and sunk 22 September 1914. In 1954, the British Government sold the salvage rights to all three ships to a German company, and they were subsequently sold again to a Dutch company, which began salvaging the wrecks' metal in 2011; Ambrogi, Stefano (12 October 2011), 'Scrap metal hunt is wrecking UK warship graves-veterans' <https://news.yahoo.com/news/scrap-metal-hunt-wrecking-uk-warship-graves-veterans-163450791.html?fr=sycsrp_catchall>.

14 Loi n°89-874 du 1er décembre 1989 relative aux biens culturels maritimes et modifiant la loi du 27 septembre 1941 portant réglementation de fouilles archéologiques.

Mercedes. The cargo had been recovered without permission by a US firm, and Peru argued that the coins had been minted in Peru during colonial times.[15]

As the only aim of the 2001 Convention is to preserve UCH and to safeguard it for humanity, it was hence decided not to take part in these complicated and delicate debates and the Convention does not regulate ownership.

7 Consistency of the UNESCO 2001 Convention with the UN Convention on the Law of the Sea (LOSC)

The 2001 Convention was the result of a long and laborious effort made by the international community to adopt a comprehensive and effective framework of rules that can achieve the preservation of UCH. While the Convention has been welcomed by the scientific community and ratified and implemented by a large number of States the Convention is not adhered to by some. This is because they perceive a lack of integration with an existing and significant treaty, namely the United Nations Convention on the Law of the Sea 1982 (LOSC).[16]

Consequently, and in order to facilitate adherence of these States to the 2001 Convention, it is important to fully explain and illustrate the consistency of the 2001 Convention with LOSC. The following will show that:
- There is a complementary relationship between the 2001 Convention and LOSC;
- The 2001 Convention does not regulate any issue in contradiction to LOSC;
- The 2001 Convention and LOSC are fully compatible and there is an express obligation in Article 3 of the 2001 Convention to always interpret its provisions in a positive manner, i.e., consistent with LOSC; and
- The 2001 Convention does not contain regulations constituting a creeping jurisdiction.

7.1 *The Complementary Relationship between the 2001 Convention and LOSC*

The first question to be addressed, even if it has been openly repeated over the last decades, is whether there can be a Convention on issues beyond LOSC concerning the oceans, and whether one takes precedence over the other.

15 Peru had argued the gold and silver on the ship would have been mined, refined, and minted in its territory, which at the time was part of the Spanish empire. See NBC News 2/27/2012, <http://www.nbcnews.com/id/46544785/ns/technology_and_science-science/t/spain-fends-claims-shipwrecks-treasure/#.V8BhBBvymUk>. See for further discussion the Chapter in this book on Spain.

16 1833 UNTS 397.

As the subject of the 2001 Convention is UCH, which is largely located in the oceans, the Convention necessarily intersects with the law of the sea. It applies in an area in which the question of who has legal authority over a territory or a vessel is defined by this law of the sea. Primarily, this law is codified by LOSC.

Some legal advisors of States doubting the 2001 Convention seemed, especially in its early days, to proceed from the implicit premise that the provisions of LOSC are of a quasi-'constitutional' nature and that they enjoy a superior status to other treaties or agreements, including the 2001 Convention. The 2001 Convention would hence have a subordinate status and could not regulate anything regulated by LOSC or even come close to its content.

The general rules of treaty interpretation are worthy of note here, such as the rule of *lex specialis* and *lex posterior*. These provisions provide that a more specific treaty or a later treaty, between the same Parties, has priority over a more general or earlier treaty on the same subject. From the legally doubtful viewpoint of opponents of the 2001 Convention, such treaty interpretation rules would not come into operation when it comes to the relationship between LOSC and the 2001 Convention. According to these opponents, all other international agreements, or treaties on the protection of the UCH should operate within the framework of rules circumscribed by LOSC. Therefore, what they can do is limited to the clarification or supplementation of LOSC. In this scenario, subsequent agreements or treaties should and could not attempt to amend or abrogate LOSC's provisions. LOSC is 'the constitution of the ocean' not only figuratively but also normatively.

First, as Keun-Gwan Lee remarked in 2001, no treaty or convention should be immune from change when facing ever-changing real life and facts.[17] Thus, 'permanent treaties' do not exist. Secondly, LOSC itself contains a series of provisions relating to its amendment (Articles 312–316). Thirdly, Article 303(4) provides expressly for the role of other (future) international agreements and rules of law regarding the protection of objects of an archaeological nature. Therefore, the opposition to the 2001 Convention, which proceeds from the, often unstated, premise of LOSC being a closed system, is untenable.[18]

The next question is whether LOSC is at a normatively superior level compared to other 'ordinary' treaties or agreements, including the 2001 Convention. Article 311(2) LOSC addresses this question when it provides that:

17 Prof. Keun-Gwan Lee,' An Inquiry into the Compatibility of the UNESCO Convention on the Protection of the UCH 2001 with LOSC 1982', published in L. Prott (ed.), Finishing the Interrupted Voyage, papers of the Hong Kong 2003 UNESCO meeting on the 2001 Convention.

18 *Ibid.*

> This Convention shall not alter the rights and obligations of States Parties which arise from other agreements compatible with this Convention and which do not affect the enjoyment by other States Parties of their rights or the performance of their obligations under this Convention.

Notwithstanding this provision, there were still substantial uncertainties over this question, especially in the first years of the 2001 Convention. If superiority was only a very limited role or function (i.e., that of clarification or supplementation) it would be accorded to treaties or agreements subsequent to LOSC. In this scenario, the normative legitimacy or tenability of the 2001 Convention would be addressed only from the narrow angle of its compatibility or complementarity to LOSC, in particular, to Article 303.[19]

It is generally agreed that the controversial category of 'peremptory norms' allowing no derogations has little relevance to the law of the sea and LOSC. The concerns regarding this issue started in 2001, the year of the adoption of the 2001 Convention, mainly from lawyers that had been actively involved in the process of the elaboration and adoption of LOSC and who may have been influenced by their past experiences.

The refusal of the idea of any exclusivity of LOSC in matters of UCH does not mean that there could be no difference in terms of relative importance among the provisions of LOSC. For instance, the articles providing the fundamental legal structure of the oceans, e.g., those providing for the Territorial Sea (TS) up to 12nm or the 200nm Exclusive Economic Zone (EEZ), are the result of long and arduous negotiations, or "the Herculean labours of the many distinguished lawyers and statesmen".[20] As such, it could be argued that within the framework of LOSC these provisions of a 'fundamentally norm-creating character' enjoy a higher level in the hierarchy of rules than other provisions, suggesting, arguably, that there exists some element of normative hierarchy within LOSC. This, however, certainly does not apply to UCH, which was included in LOSC as a last-minute compromise between seven States, represented respectively by Greece and the United States.

From this fact alone, one can argue that the provisions of LOSC concerning UCH are not entitled to the same normative authority as is enjoyed by other LOSC provisions of more general and fundamental importance. Secondly, as pointed out by some leading commentators, some parts of Article 303 are "clumsy" in terms of logic or systematic coherence or "counterproductive" in

19 *Ibid.*

20 Churchill, R.R. and Lowe, A.V. *The Law of the Sea*, (Manchester University Press, Manchester, 3rd ed. 1999) 22.

their practical effect on the protection of UCH.[21] This also negatively affects the normative status of the provisions.

Thirdly, and more importantly, paragraph 4 of Article 303 stipulates that '[t]his article is without prejudice to other international agreements'. This provision does not proceed from the normative superiority of the given article to the provisions of other (future) international agreements. Rather, it is based on the normatively equal status of Article 303 and the relevant provisions of other international agreements.[22]

The main implication is that the substantive part of Article 303 (in particular, paragraphs 2 and 3) is susceptible to the rules of treaty interpretation, in particular the *lex specialis* and *lex posterior* rule. It is hence fully possible to also legally regulate the issues governed by them through another, later, international convention, such as the 2001 Convention.

7.2 *Compatibility of the 2001 Convention and* LOSC

After having illustrated that the 2001 Convention can fully and rightfully regulate issues in the realm of the law of the sea and in particular UCH, it shall also be shown, that all items regulated by the 2001 Convention are in full harmony with LOSC, without contradiction.

LOSC says little about the protection of the UCH.[23] It contains only two provisions referring to UCH, Articles 149 and 303. As noted, both were last minute introductions into its text and remained general in their formulations. When LOSC was created, underwater archaeology was in its infancy and the importance of UCH was underestimated. Article 149 LOSC provides for, without giving details, the protection of underwater heritage in the 'Area', i.e., 'the seabed and ocean floor and subsoil thereof, beyond the limits of national jurisdiction'. Article 303 LOSC sets a general obligation for States to protect their UCH. However, it gives them only effective protective powers up to the limits

---

21 See Camarda and Scovazzi, (eds), The Protection of the UCH, Legal Aspects, Milano, 2002.

22 Compare Article 303(4) with Article 103 of the UN Charter ('In the event of a conflict between the obligations of the Members of the United Nations under the present Charter and their obligations under any other international agreement, their obligations under the present Charter shall prevail'.) and Article 20 of the League of Nations Covenant ('The Members of the League of Nations severally agree that this Covenant is accepted as abrogating all obligations or understanding inter se which are inconsistent with the terms thereof, and solemnly undertake that they will not hereafter enter into any engagements inconsistent with the terms thereof').

23 "For some of its aspects ... it can even be considered not only insufficient, but also counterproductive and corresponding to an invitation to the looting of the heritage in question": Tullio Scovazzi in Wolfrum (Ed.) *The Max Planck Encyclopedia of Public International Law* (2008).

of the Contiguous Zone (CZ), i.e., up to 24 nautical miles from the coast and not beyond.[24]

Therefore, in the large space between the Area and the CZ, i.e., the remaining EEZ and on the Continental Shelf (CS), UCH remains mostly unprotected by LOSC. To compound this, Article 303(3) stipulates that '[n]othing in this article affects ... the law of salvage or other rules of admiralty ...'. While in many States with a civil law tradition salvage is only related to the efforts of saving a ship in danger and not to wrecks, particularly if these have been underwater for over 100 years, some common law countries have developed a concept of salvage law that extends to commercial exploitation of submerged archaeological sites. The LOSC regime as currently formulated, therefore leaves room for the commercial exploitation of UCH and, in consequence, has been criticised as containing a 'legal vacuum' and as representing an 'invitation to looting'.[25] While LOSC does reflect such a legal vacuum – stating that its regulations are 'without prejudice' to salvage law – this does not mean it *permits* commercial exploitation. It only contains a negation to regulate the issue, leaving room for another convention to regulate it.

The wording of Article 303(2) of LOSC also leaves a need for further regulation. The coastal State is empowered to prevent and sanction the 'removal from the sea-bed' of objects of an archaeological and historical nature. However, the Article is silent on when such objects, instead of being removed, are simply destroyed in the place where they are located (for instance, if they are destroyed by a company holding a licence for oil exploitation).

This legal vacuum is rectified by the 2001 Convention, for which LOSC leaves express room in Art. 303(4).[26] The 2001 Convention explicitly prohibits the intrusion into and destruction of UCH sites for commercial exploitation and without respect for the need to protect and preserve such sites. Furthermore, the 2001 Convention covers all waters and maritime zones, greatly extending the legal protection of submerged sites against all kinds of damaging actions. It also contains strong anti-pillaging measures and gives the States the right

24 See Art. 303(2).

25 See n.2.

26 Tullio Scovazzi, Wolfrum (Ed.), *The Max Planck Encyclopedia of Public International Law* (2008): "Some prospects to find some remedy to the unsatisfactory regime of the UNCLOS could be drawn from Art. 303 para. 4. It provides that Art. 303 does not prejudice "other international agreements and rules of international law regarding the protection of objects of an archaeological and historical nature". The UNCLOS itself seems to allow the drafting of more specific treaty regimes which can ensure a better protection of the underwater cultural heritage. The UNCLOS itself seems to encourage filling in the gaps and eliminating the contradictions that it has generated."

to close ports to pillagers, to seize materials and to apply sanctions for the destruction of heritage.

The 2001 Convention, however, does not alter LOSC, but complements it, and is thus in full harmony with it.[27] Article 3 precisely states:

> Nothing in this Convention shall prejudice the rights, jurisdiction and duties of States under international law, including the United Nations Convention on the Law of the Sea. This Convention shall be interpreted and applied in the context of and in a manner consistent with international law, including the United Nations Convention on the Law of the Sea.

This means that the 2001 Convention regulates issues that LOSC leaves open, but it does not contradict it in any way. Any other interpretation is against the very text of the 2001 Convention.

7.3 *No 'Creeping Jurisdiction'*

Some legal experts have questioned the issue of potentially extended jurisdictional rights by the State cooperation system provided for in the 2001 Convention. Admittedly, its regulations on the protection of UCH outside of the TS are complex. The reason being that the 2001 Convention's regulations in this regard have been forced into the complicated framework of LOSC. Every single detail of LOSC was taken into account in a lengthy drafting process, partly conducted in the presence of the LOSC Secretariat.

The underlying idea of the State cooperation mechanism of the 2001 Convention is that each State collects from its vessels and nationals information on activities concerning UCH in the EEZ or in the Area. The State then distributes the information to the other States Parties, which can then declare if the issue is of interest to them and if they wish to be consulted, and to be included in a group of coordinating States discussing protection measures. A coordinating State then leads the discussions on the measures to be taken and is charged with implementing them. When the site concerned is in the EEZ, the State closest to the site is usually chosen, if it is in the Area a State is chosen freely.

The view that the function of a coordinating State would extend jurisdictional rights of States arises from an erroneous understanding of this system and does not sufficiently take into account the clear regulation of Article 2(11) of the 2001 Convention. This provides that:

---

27 See Article 3 of the 2001 Convention.

> No act or activity undertaken on the basis of this Convention shall constitute grounds for claiming, contending or disputing any claim to national sovereignty or jurisdiction.

The coordinating State does not receive more jurisdictional rights. It only coordinates actions and implements what all States have decided together. That means that it does not receive any special powers from the 2001 Convention, but from the other States Parties in a form of jurisdictional help. The jurisdiction always remains with the State Party that initially held it.

The 2001 Convention is clear, Article 10(6) stating that:

> In coordinating consultations, taking measures, conducting preliminary research and/or issuing authorizations pursuant to this Article, the Coordinating State shall act on behalf of the States Parties as a whole and not in its own interest. Any such action shall not in itself constitute a basis for the assertion of any preferential or jurisdictional rights not provided for in international law, including the United Nations Convention on the Law of the Sea.

It could not be clearer. If, for instance, a coordinating State relies on the 2001 Convention to prevent a pillager from another State Party accessing a site, the powers to intervene in this immediate danger are a pre-agreed legal help from the other States Parties to prevent the pillaging or destruction of a site. They are not a lasting transferral of jurisdictional rights.

Even if a State Party that holds jurisdictional powers over a vessel of pillagers does not declare its interest in being consulted and is not member of the consulting group of States, by ratifying the 2001 Convention it has undertaken an obligation to cooperate with the other States Parties: it promises to help in the protection of UCH and to give assistance through its jurisdictional powers. Hence, this legal help enables the pursuit of the pillager, but does not constitute *per se* a newly existing jurisdictional power. Finally, to conclude, since the adoption of the 2001 Convention, no legal disputes resulting from its application have arisen. States have demonstrated the will to cooperate in the protection of their UCH. There has not been a single instance of an accusation or suspicion of an abuse of any of the provisions of the 2001 Convention.

The great importance of UCH and concern about the threats faced to it have been the principal interests of all the States ratifying the 2001 Convention. The rising number of States Parties indicates that the legal concerns about its interrelationship with the LOSC have been overcome and that the main issue looked at by States today is care for the due implementation of the 2001 Convention in the interest of the safeguarding of humanity's common underwater legacy. A special first implementation case of this cooperation system protecting UCH in international waters is now underway through the initiative to protect the UCH of Skerki Banks in the Mediterranean, with eight States collaborating in a common protection effort.[28]

8 The Interrelationship of the 2001 Convention with LOSC

A separate question is whether a State that is not party to LOSC and does not wish to be bound to it in the future, can join the 2001 Convention without becoming bound to LOSC. Arguably, this is the case for only a few States, but there are several that are very active in underwater archaeology and are concerned by this question, even if for many of them LOSC will apply as customary international law, e.g., the United States of America.

8.1 *The Use of Terms*

The first issue concerns the definition of the various maritime zones used in both LOSC and the 2001 Convention. In its provisions, the 2001 Convention adopts the same terminology as LOSC. However, it does not link their definition to LOSC (or any other treaty, for that matter). Only one of the terms used is defined by the 2001 Convention. The 2001 Convention defines in Article 1(5) the term Area ('seabed and ocean floor and subsoil thereof, beyond the limits of national jurisdiction'), but uses, without definition the terms 'Territorial Waters', 'Continental Shelf' and 'Exclusive Economic Zone'. Therefore, it remains unstated how these terms should be defined, i.e., according to LOSC or elsewhere, the 2001 Convention only providing in Article 3(2) on the relationship between the 2001 Convention and other treaties, which, as noted above, includes the LOSC. The use of 'including' means that it includes LOSC, but at the same time does not exclude any other international law applied by States not Party to LOSC and objecting to the latter.

The flexibility of the definition of terms used to describe the various maritime zones reflects a relationship of independence between the 2001 Convention and LOSC. The various maritime zones (excepting the Area) have to be interpreted by each State concerned according to the law of the sea applicable to it.

---

28 See generally <https://www.unesco.org/en/skerki-bank-mission>.

8.2 *Pillage, Exploitation, and Salvage*

While UCH is increasingly attracting the attention of the public and archaeologists, it has also become prey to commercial enterprises intending to exploit submerged archaeological sites, with the aim of selling retrieved artefacts for profit. These enterprises benefit from weak legal protection and site monitoring, as well as from a lack of awareness of the cultural value of the concerned sites. Several hundred major shipwrecks, each containing many thousands of artefacts, have been destroyed in this manner over the years, and thousands of other sites have been severely damaged. Just three examples include: the 'Belitung shipwreck' (60,000 artefacts); the 'Cirebon shipwreck' (500,000 artefacts); and the wreck of the *Nuestra Señora de las Mercedes* (500,000 artefacts).

The 2001 Convention stipulates in Article 2(7) as an overarching principle that UCH should not be commercially exploited. This regulation is in conformity with the moral principles that already sometimes apply to cultural heritage on land. It is not to be understood as preventing archaeological research, either by governmental institutions or by private undertakings holding a permit from a competent authority, or from paid tourist access.

It may be surprising, then, that this provision created significant objections during the drafting of the 2001 Convention. However, considering the ongoing commercial exploitation of UCH, which every year concerns hundreds of thousands of artefacts, and given the presence of treasure hunting operators at the discussions held at the General Conference of UNESCO, only illustrate that there remains a strong misconception regarding UCH. Commercial salvage is chosen over scientific excavation due to the perception of shipwrecks as lost treasures and due to pressure from the antiques market, which faces a decreasing availability of terrestrial artefacts. Additionally, some national authorities, which would otherwise not be able to finance projects, use commercial salvage to obtain artefacts from previously inaccessible sites through fund-sharing agreements, while allowing the sale of repetitive artefacts.

One background reason is the relative invisibility to the public of submerged sites. UCH is still too often reduced to the image of a recovered artefact instead of that of a full-scale archaeological site. The objection to the idea of 'seeking the treasure', which is very strong in national authorities when it comes to land-based heritage, is, in some regions, not yet as strong regarding UCH. This concerns either, regions with a long tradition of recovery of wreck materials for profit (mainly common law countries), or regions with a low number of professional underwater archaeologists, capable of giving scientific advice. The commercial exploitation of UCH is thus accepted by certain countries in several regions of the world.

The 2001 Convention is clear, setting UCH as equal to land heritage: no commercial exploitation of UCH from archaeological sites is permitted and the 'harvesting' of heritage for profit is considered profoundly unethical. Rule 2 of the Annex states '[t]he commercial exploitation of underwater cultural heritage for trade or speculation, or its irretrievable dispersal is also considered fundamentally incompatible' with its protection and thus, UCH 'shall not be traded, sold, bought or bartered as commercial goods'.

'Commercial exploitation', as used by the text of the 2001 Convention, could be understood as including all permitted or legal activities directed at UCH with the goal of the later commercial sale of all or of a part of the recovered artefacts, or of an introduction of at least a part of the artefacts into a private collection not accessible to the public or researchers. 'Permitted' in this context could mean that the activity is authorised by a valid activity permit from a competent national authority. A commercial excavation, however, can in some instances not be permitted, but remain legal, when the activity in question does not need any permission, for instance when domestic laws do not contain protective provisions. In comparison, 'looting' and 'pillaging' could be understood as the destructive and illegal recovery of artefacts from a heritage site against the provisions of the applicable national law. These definitions are offered as a suggestion, and the binding interpretation of the 2001 Convention is of course left to the States Parties.

8.3 *The Law of Salvage and the Law of Finds*

Article 4 of the 2001 Convention, another product of intense discussions in the intergovernmental meetings preceding its adoption, regulates the application of the Convention to the law of salvage and the law of finds. According to Article 4, an activity shall not be subject to the law of salvage or the law of finds, unless it is authorised by the competent authorities, and is in full conformity with the 2001 Convention, and ensures that any recovery of the UCH achieves its maximum protection. These are cumulative conditions.

This formulation has been called a "formal possibility, but practical impossibility of salvage".[29] Indeed, there is no known case of any treasure hunter having fully respected all scientific regulations of the Annex of the 2001 Convention when intervening on a site, despite contrary statements. A 2015 evaluation of a shipwreck recovery by a foreign enterprise in Mozambique, completed by the Mozambican Edouard Mondlane University, indicates in an exemplary fashion the discrepancy between the lip-service paid by the salvagers and the actual

29 Prof. Mariano Aznar in a regional meeting in Bahrain in 2013.

work carried out.[30] The same is true for the work done by treasure hunters on the Panamanian *San José* shipwreck, evaluated by the STAB.[31]

The word 'salvage' requires some explanation to better understand it. In general, the notion of salvage applies to attempts to save a ship or cargo from imminent marine peril on behalf of its owners. It is not intended to apply to submerged archaeological sites or to ancient sunken ships which, far from being in peril, have been definitively lost for hundreds or even thousands of years. This has also been reflected in the International Convention on Salvage of 1989.[32]

However, in a minority of common law countries the concept of salvage law has been enlarged by some national court decisions to cover activities which have in the opinion of this author very little to do with the proper sphere of salvage.[33] In such countries this leads to the situation that under the law of finds:

> ... a person who discovers a shipwreck in navigable waters that has been long lost and abandoned and who reduces the property to actual or constructive possession, becomes the property's owner.[34]

The application of this national law of salvage, which seems, according to these judgments, to go further than the law of finds, gives the salvor a *lien* (or right *in rem*) over the object.

In reality the application of this widened concept of 'the law of salvage and other rules of admiralty' (as mentioned also in Article 303 LOSC) means the application of a 'first-come-first-served' or 'freedom-of-fishing' approach, which serves the interests of private commercial gain. This 'law of salvage and other rules of admiralty' is today typical only of a few common law systems, especially the US, as regards ancient wrecks, but remains a stranger to the

30 2015 – Universidade Eduardo Mondlane, Departamento de Arqueologia e Antropologia, Resultados da avaliação do projecto PI/AWW, respeitante ao patrimônio arqueológico subaquático, na Ilha de Moçambique de 22 a 25 de Julho de 2014.

31 See Report of the mission to Panama (6–14 July and 21–29 October 2015) to evaluate the Project related to the wreck of the *San José*, <http://www.unesco.org/new/fileadmin/MULTIMEDIA/HQ/CLT/pdf/STAB-Panama-Report-EN-public.pdf>.

32 1953 UNTS 165.

33 For example, the US Court of Appeals for the Fourth Circuit in RMS *Titanic, Inc. v. Haver* 171 F.3d 943 (4th Cir. 1999) stated that the law of salvage and finds is a 'venerable law of the sea'. It was said to have arisen from the custom among 'seafaring men' and to have "been preserved from ancient Rhodes (900 B.C.E.), Rome (Justinian's Corpus Juris Civilis) (533 C.E.), City of Trani (Italy) (1063), England (the Law of Oleron) (1189), the Hansa Towns or Hanseatic League (1597), and France (1681), all articulating similar principles".

34 *Ibid.*

legislation of other countries. Due to the lack of corresponding concepts, the very words 'salvage' and 'admiralty' can thus not even be properly translated into languages different from English. In the French and Spanish official texts of LOSC they are hence rendered with expressions ('droit de récupérer des épaves et ... autres règles du droit maritime'; 'las normas sobre salvamento u otras normas del derecho marítimo') which have a broader and very different meaning.[35]

8.4 *No Pre-Planned De-Accessioning*

Given the prohibitive view taken by the 2001 Convention on the law of salvage, some treasure hunters proposed to utilise the concept of 'de-accessioning'.[36] This is the formal process of the removal of an object from a collection, register, catalogue, or database. One of the reasons why materials can be de-accessioned and disposed of by a museum, for example, is that they are duplicates. Usually a de-accession, which signifies the fact that the museum does not need the artefact, is not planned by the museum before the object has even been found or recovered. Commercial treasure hunters proposed however, to recover all cargo, and to foresee before the outset, the later de-accessioning of repetitive materials, such as coins.

The STAB has taken a formal view on this. It its Recommendation 5/STAB 3, endorsed by the States Parties by Resolution 4/MSP 4, on the financing of excavations by de-accession of the artefacts it:

> recommends to the Meeting of States Parties to consider that the financing of excavations by the process of the de-accessioning of the artefacts from the concerned site is not consistent with the Rules annexed to the 2001 Convention.

Indeed, it is understood as seeking to circumvent the prohibition of commercial exploitation by the 2001 Convention, by pretending to excavate for scientific purposes and then to de-accession the sellable artefacts.

There are some cases of recovery which lay between easily recognisable commercial recovery and ethical recovery. The boundaries between them may

35 Tullio Scovazzi, The entry into force of the 2001 UNESCO Convention on the Protection of the UCH, Aegean Institute of the Law of the Sea and Maritime Law 2009.

36 In Cultural Artefacts and Trade Goods: The Odyssey Model, Ellen C. Gerth writes on the commercial exploitation of an American salvor firm: "In light of the growing economic challenges confronting museums today, understanding the current conditions driving museums, including deaccessioning efforts and refined collecting policies, provides a logical backdrop for proposing Odyssey's Cultural Artefacts and Trade Goods model".

become blurred in some exceptional cases. One example is the RMS *Titanic* artefact salvage. In 1987, Titanic Ventures Inc. and the French Institute for Ocean Science began to salvage artefacts from the field around the two large hull portions of the wreck. These were not sold but presented in an exhibition. After legal exchanges, covenants were drafted, providing for the protection of the artefacts, which now cannot be sold separately. It has not been determined yet whether the *Titanic* artefact recovery was a commercial salvage or not. The sale of some of the artefacts is however now intended.[37]

Other commercial gain from shipwrecks such as dive tour offers, exhibitions or films do not fall under the commercial exploitation term of the 2001 Convention. They are similar to heritage access offers on land. They are not directed at UCH in the sense that they do not intrude on it and do not alter it (see Rule 2 of the Annex).

8.5 *Activities Incidentally Affecting* UCH

The oceans and the seabed are increasingly exploited in order to extract aggregates, sand, or gravel,[38] to catch fish, and to recover oil and lay pipelines. There is also increased construction of coastal installations, artificial islands, ocean-located wind turbines and energy-producing structures. Many of these activities impact on the environment and can also affect UCH sites, such as sunken cities or ancient shipwrecks. Indeed, a large number of ancient shipwrecks carry scars from trawling, and many wrecks are covered by nets lost from fishing boats, causing damage and making research impossible. This raises questions of mitigation of these extensive industrial-scale, non-desired and non-intended impacts.

In the above-described situation, Article 5 of the 2001 Convention is an ally for national authorities and its importance should not be underestimated. It offers a recognised international standard and backs up an authority's stance in negotiations with a commercial enterprise. In cases of industrial works

---

37 The salvor RMS Titanic Inc (RMST) filed for bankruptcy in 2016 and requested permission to sell artefacts it salvaged from *Titanic* in 1987 with IFREMER. A French Tribunal awarded RMST title to those artefacts subject to certain conditions that they not be sold for commercial purposes but be maintained for public benefit. The US intervened in the bankruptcy proceeding as amicus noting that it had an interest in keeping the collection together and that the sale of the 'French Collection' would be inconsistent with the conditions of the award by the French Tribunal. The bankruptcy court agreed with the US and dismissed the request for emergency sale of artefacts from the 'French Collection' but did so in a manner that RMST could sue France over those conditions, which it did.

38 See <https://www.unep.org/news-and-stories/press-release/our-use-sand-brings-us-against-wall-says-unep-report>.

potentially impacting UCH sites, it is highly desirable to adhere to recognised international standards for heritage protection and mitigation. Article 5 of the 2001 Convention provides:

> Each State Party shall use the best practicable means at its disposal to prevent or mitigate any adverse effects that might arise from activities under its jurisdiction incidentally affecting [UCH].

It is important to underline that this is an obligation, not a choice. A protective effort has to be made. The 2001 Convention thus clearly encourages States to enact national legislation obliging enterprises to take into account UCH, to assess its presence and significance and to mitigate any potential impacts. Adopting such a policy is usually very beneficial for a State, allowing it not only to protect its heritage, but also to enlarge its underwater archaeology capacity and research. The requirement to either pay archaeological taxes according to the territory impacted, as employed in France, or requiring proof of the assessment of archaeological potential in an area before approval of a project, can be an important funding source for underwater archaeological work.

Paragraphs 48 and 49 of the Operational Guidelines to the 2001 Convention add that States should endeavour to establish national rules for the authorisation of interventions on UCH sites.[39] These rules should also cover activities which only incidentally affect UCH sites, as well as areas where the sites' existence is not certain but where their presence is a possibility. States are encouraged to require the approval of their national competent authorities, as described in Article 22(1) of the Convention, for any such intervention. Where appropriate, local communities directly linked to UCH sites should be engaged in any activity directed towards them.

From the moment of the site's discovery and onwards, an authority should monitor the compliance with the Rules annexed to the 2001 Convention, especially regarding preventive excavations or intrusive research in the context of an industrial activity. These Rules apply to activities directed at heritage, not to incidental impacts. However, once an assessment has been made and sites have been identified as being present in the area, any activity relating directly to them becomes an activity 'directed at' the heritage. Rule 13 provides:

> in cases of urgency or chance discoveries, activities directed at the underwater cultural heritage, including conservation measures or activities for

39 *Supra* n.11.

a period of short duration, in particular site stabilization, may be authorized in the absence of a project design in order to protect the underwater cultural heritage.

Thus, the authorities may allow activities in the absence of a Project Design. An authority can better understand and monitor if, and how, heritage will be impacted though a Project Design provided to it by the enterprise, enabling consideration of measures to be taken to minimise any damage, balancing economic benefit and heritage significance. Every competent authority should exercise caution when considering permitting interventions not based on a Project Design.

Finally, the 2001 Convention also facilitates cooperation among different international stakeholders. Often, oil or seabed work companies come from a foreign country that has ratified the 2001 Convention. According to Article 16, vessels flying the flags of those countries and their nationals are obliged by their own State's national law to operate in compliance with the 2001 Convention principles in all activities that may affect UCH, wherever it is found.[40] Additionally, cultural heritage aspects are included in the work to achieve Sustainable Development Goal 14 (SDG14)[41] and in the currently ongoing Ocean Decade, which is supported by a dedicated Ocean Decade Heritage Network, cooperating closely with UNESCO and the Secretariat of the 2001 Convention.[42]

9 Ratification, Meeting of States Parties and the STAB

The deposit of an instrument of ratification, acceptance, approval, or accession with the Director-General of UNESCO expresses the consent of the concerned State to be bound by the 2001 Convention and is necessary in order to join.[43] This is due to the fact that according to the 2001 Convention, UNESCO is the depositary for such declarations (meaning all have to be sent to UNESCO instead of all other States that have adopted the convention or to any other organisation). A simple signature or an exchange of instruments constituting the Treaty among the concerned States is, in the case of the 2001 Convention,

40 Article 16 – Measures relating to nationals and vessels. States Parties shall take all practicable measures to ensure that their nationals and vessels flying their flag do not engage in any activity directed at UCH in a manner not in conformity with this Convention.

41 See generally <https://sdgs.un.org/goals>.

42 See generally <https://www.oceandecacdeheritage.org>.

43 See generally <http://www.unesco.org/en/undewater-heritage/ratification>.

not sufficient to become party to it. This means that UNESCO is the competent authority to accept declarations of ratification of the Convention and only those instruments handed over to UNESCO have legal effect.

Ratification of the 2001 Convention does not bind a State to any obligatory financial contribution. The harmonisation of national laws with the Convention might however be needed and Article 22 encourages States to establish competent authorities, or reinforce existing ones, where appropriate. States may also face certain costs for implementation in terms of heritage protection, awareness raising and education. Nevertheless, the 2001 Convention is explicit that States Parties need to take these measures using for this purpose the best practicable means at their disposal and in accordance with their capabilities. Indeed, in cooperating with other States and in obtaining technical assistance from UNESCO through the 2001 Convention, most States may reduce the costs incurred for underwater archaeological work.

9.1 *Meeting of States Parties and the STAB*

In terms of the day-to-day functioning of the Convention, its Meeting of States Parties is the main organ. It gathers the representatives of the States Parties, observers from other UNESCO Member States delegates from accredited NGOs and invited experts. The Meeting is convened in ordinary session by the Director-General of UNESCO at least once every two years. At the request of a majority of States Parties, the Director-General can convene an extraordinary session.

The first Meeting of States Parties to the Convention established the STAB. This is a subsidiary organ to the Meeting of States Parties and assists it in questions of a scientific or technical nature. Its tasks and responsibilities are regulated by its Statutes or through the Secretariat. It is for instance sent on technical emergency missions only after a decision of the Bureau or the Meeting of States Parties or of the Meeting itself. Currently, the Advisory Body comprises 14 expert members, although it may be increased to a total of 24. The members are selected with due regard to the principle of equitable geographical distribution and the desirability of a gender balance as well as a balance of expertise. They reflect the elite underwater archaeologists of the States having ratified the Convention.

Members are nominated by their State and elected in the Meeting of States Parties. They represent their State in the STAB[44] and do not function as fully

---

44 Rule 21 of the Rules of Procedure of the Meeting of States Parties: 'If the Meeting decides, in conformity with Article 23.4 of the Convention, to establish a Scientific and Technical Advisory Body, a State Party may nominate an expert for elections to represent it in the Advisory Body'.

independent experts, even if their impartiality is desired.[45] This makes the STAB a hybrid between an expert council and an Intergovernmental Committee and is why the States Parties attach great attention to the equal geographical distribution of the expert members. After its recent emergency missions to several States Parties, i.e., Haiti, Madagascar, Panama, Bulgaria, and Guatemala (a further mission to Paraguay being underway), the importance and recognition of the Advisory Body has greatly increased.[46] It offers assistance to those States that need it in a fast and hands-on way, making a true difference to the States requesting the help.

9.2 *Secretariat for the Convention*

The Secretariat for the 2001 Convention is provided by UNESCO. It organises the sessions of the Meeting of States Parties and its STAB and assists States Parties in the implementation of the decisions taken. According to the Rule 26 Rules of Procedure of the Meeting of States Parties, the Director-General of UNESCO or their representative participate in the work of the Meeting, without the right to vote. They may, at any time, make either oral or written statements to the Meeting on any question under discussion. The Director-General of UNESCO appoints also an official of the Secretariat of UNESCO to act as Secretary to the Meeting, and other officials who together constitute the Secretariat of the Meeting.

10 Conclusion

The above discussion has sought to show that the 2001 Convention has, after over 20 years of existence, become a centre point of the dialogue of experts with governments and the United Nations. It has brought a very positive change to the protection and visibility of UCH in considerably changing legal texts and the approach to the management of sites. It is to be expected that this positive impact will increase over the coming years as a result of UNESCO's and its partners' efforts to obtain a stronger insertion of cultural aspects into the efforts to protect the ocean, via the UN Ocean Decade[47] and the work to achieve SDG14.

All websites last accessed February 2025.

---

45 Article 2.b: 'The members of the Advisory Body shall work impartially and in compliance with the principles of the Convention'.

46 See generally <https://www.unesco.org/en/node/85043?hub=412>.

47 See <https://oceandecade.org/>.

CHAPTER 2

Argentina

María Luz Endere and Norma E. Levrand

1 Introduction

The intergovernmental negotiation to reach the agreements that allowed the adoption of the UNESCO Convention on the Protection of the Underwater Cultural Heritage (2001 Convention) began more than a decade earlier, with the genealogy even older.[1] Dromgoole indicates that the origin of the Convention dates back to 1988.[2] However, the United Nations Convention on the Law of the Sea 1982 (LOSC) already contained provision on the protection of underwater heritage.[3]

The difficulties in reaching agreements regarding this subject resulted on one hand from the fact that there are different legislative models incorporating various legal mechanisms established to protect underwater cultural heritage (UCH).[4] On the other hand, it has been stated that:

> The [UNESCO] Convention not only attempted to regulate a novel aspect of the international protection of cultural and natural heritage, but touched on a diversity of fiercely competitive interests, mainly cultural, historical, archaeological, economic/commercial, military, and humanitarian.[5]

Argentina took part in the negotiations of the Convention instrument, maintaining a broad concept of the protection of underwater heritage.[6] This was

---

1 2562 UNTS 1.

2 S. Dromgoole, 'Convention on the Protection of the Underwater Cultural Heritage (2001)', in C. Smith (ed.) *Encyclopaedia of Global Archaeology* (Springer, 2018).

3 1833 UNTS 397, Arts. 149 and 303.

4 T. Scovazzi 'Underwater Cultural Heritage: International Law Regime', in C. Smith (ed.) *Encyclopaedia of Global Archaeology* (Springer, 2018).

5 A. González, P. O'Keefe and M. Williams, 'The UNESCO Convention on the Protection of the Underwater Cultural Heritage: a Future for our Past?' 11(1) (2009) *Conservation and Management of Archaeological Sites*, 55.

6 This country played a prominent role during the Convention discussion process as part of the task carried out by the Permanent Delegation of Argentina at UNESCO Headquarters, especially by the young diplomat Ariel W. González (who died in 2011). It was also remarkable the advice given by national experts, especially those of the National Institute of Anthropology and Latin American Thought (INAPL).

 | DOI:10.1163/9789004510883_004

based on three aspects: the importance of the Convention as an international cooperation mechanism; the relevance of scientific-technical cooperation; and the need to have a specific normative instrument for this category of cultural property.[7] Despite the fact that Argentina was significantly involved in these negotiations, ratification of the Convention was only carried out in August 2010 by National Law 26,556.[8] This delay was produced, among other reasons, by an internal process of updating legislation protecting cultural heritage.[9] Based on recognition of the right to cultural heritage as a fundamental right in the National Constitution in 1994, and with the incorporation of various Human Rights Treaties with constitutional hierarchy, reforms were promoted of cultural heritage in various protective norms. Among them, national regulation regarding archaeological heritage was completely modified in 2003 by Law 25,743.[10]

Argentina is a federal republic divided into 23 provinces, one autonomous city, and is administered by the national government in Buenos Aires. According to the National Constitution, natural and cultural resources – including cultural heritage and territorial waters – are part of the provincial domain, and the National Congress can only enact minimal budgetary laws on such matters. This means that heritage should be governed by national legislation and controlled by national authorities in coordination with provincial governments. This complexity in the administrative and legislative sphere is combined with the existence of relevant groups of experts, from scientific organisations and national universities, that have carried out important projects to secure UCH since the end of the 1980s.

Archaeological heritage in Argentina is protected by law at various levels. National Law 25,743 defines it as cultural elements which are in an archaeological context on land or underwater for at least 100 years (Law 25,743 and Decree

7 A. González, 'La Argentina y la Convención sobre la Protección del Patrimonio Subacuático: hacia una relación simbiótica' (2010) *Revista Jurídica* 5 (5): 39–68.

8 Law N° 26.556 The National Legislature (November 18, 2009) Convention on the protection of the underwater cultural heritage. Ratification. B.O. 31.802 (16-12-2009).

9 M. Endere, *Arqueología y legislación en Argentina. Cómo proteger el patrimonio argentino* (UNICEN, 2000); M. Endere, *Management of Archaeological Sites and the Public in Argentina* (Oxford, 2007), M. Endere and J. Prado, 'Criterios de selección, valoración y zonificación de yacimientos arqueológicos y paleontológicos' in M. Endere (ed.) *Patrimonio, ciencia y comunidad. Un abordaje preliminar en los partidos de Azul, Olavarría y Tandil* (UNICEN, 2009); N. Levrand, 'Política legislativa vs. diversidad cultural: el desafío de proteger nuestro patrimonio cultural' in G. Sozzo (ed.) *La protección del patrimonio cultural. Estudios socio jurídicos para su construcción* (UNL, 2009).

10 Law N° 25.743 The National Legislature (June 4, 2003) Protection of archaeology and palaeontology cultural heritage. B.O. 30.179 (26-06-2003).

1022 /04).[11] The Province of Tierra del Fuego has a similar legal framework (Provincial Law 370) with an additional Decree which protects all historic shipwrecks lying within its jurisdictional waters (Decree 858/98).[12] Finally, in 2010 Argentina became a State Party to the 2001 Convention, which as noted above, was ratified by National Law 26,556.

Regarding the richness and diversity of Argentine underwater heritage, Elkin has pointed out that:

> Only in La Plata River, for example, more than 1,200 shipwrecks were registered from the sixteenth century to the first decades of the twentieth century. Other regions dangerous for navigation, such as the southern tip of America, were also the scene of hundreds of maritime tragedies.[13]

The objective of this chapter is to describe the current legislation regarding the protection of UCH in Argentina and to analyse the impact of the incorporation of the 2001 Convention in the protection of these properties. In order to achieve this aim, the following section presents the main research background. Then the main legal provisions related to the protection of underwater cultural assets at the national and provincial levels are outlined, characterising several draft proposals of laws presented in the National Congress. Afterwards, the main cases of successful wreck conservation as well as the recovery of stolen underwater heritage objects are discussed. Based on the development of the Argentine legal and administrative framework, certain reforms are proposed that, prospectively, may be relevant to strengthen the protection of underwater heritage in this country.

2 The Research Background on Underwater Cultural Heritage in Argentina

In the international sphere, the possibilities of finding and studying wrecks increased in the second half of the twentieth century: in Argentina, the 1982 discovery of a sunken wreck in the Deseado River estuary gave rise to underwater

---

11 See note 10 and Decree 1022 /04. The National Executive Power (August 10, 2004) Reglamentation of Law N° 25.743. B.O. 30.462 (12-08-2004).

12 Decree 858/98 The Executive Power of Tierra del Fuego (May 5, 1998). Reglamentation of Provincial Law N° 370. B. O. 935.

13 D. Elkin, 'Arqueología Subacuática' (2014) 23–138 *Ciencia Hoy* <https://cienciahoy.org.ar/arqueologia-subacuatica/>.

archaeological research. The actions carried out by professionals, as well as by local inhabitants, aimed to conserve and protect what they understood was a cultural heritage asset. Shortly after the discovery of the wreck of the Corvette HMS *Swift*, the Mario Brozoski Provincial Museum was founded as a Regional Museum. The primary purpose of this institution was to protect the cultural heritage of the Santa Cruz Province, particularly that originating from the discovery of this shipwreck. Currently the institution is under the sphere of the Municipality of Puerto Deseado. Since its establishment, it has recruited conservation and restoration experts in order to preserve the objects recovered from the sea.[14]

In 1987, the Underwater Heritage Working Group (GTPS) was created within the framework of the Argentine Committee of the International Council for Monuments and Sites (ICOMOS, Argentina). This Group collaborated with the Mario Brozoski Museum by carrying out a diagnosis of the state of the wreck, the conditions of the site and an estimate of the resources necessary to carry out the retrieval and conservation of the objects found. This Group also carried out research in the fluvial areas of the Province of Santa Fe and Misiones. According to Ciarlo,[15] during the 1990s the group was dissolved, and the activities continued through an NGO: the Albenga Foundation for the Preservation of Underwater Cultural Heritage.

Despite the lack of legal protection and regulation, the interest in underwater archaeological heritage and research in Argentina has been boosted by major developments in recent decades. In 1995, the National Ministry of Culture formally created the Research and Conservation of the Argentinean Underwater Cultural Heritage Program, which is currently being developed within the framework of the National Institute of Anthropology and Latin American Thought (INAPL). This institution, created in 1943, brings together experts from the areas of social anthropology, folklore and archaeology. Its purpose is mainly scientific and academic. Its specialists carry out projects dedicated to the recovery, documentation and management of cultural heritage, and provide training, postgraduate seminars and dissemination courses. The first study carried out by this program was devoted to the HMS *Swift* wreck. According to Elkin, "… thanks to this discovery, not only the local Mario

14 H. Santos and D. Elkin, 'El surgimiento de la arqueología naval en el marco del Museo Territorial' in M. Vázquez, D. Elkin and J. Oría (eds.) *Patrimonio a orillas del mar: Arqueología del litoral atlántico de Tierra del Fuego* (Tierra del Fuego, 2017).

15 N. Ciarlo, 'La arqueología subacuática en Argentina. Reseña histórica de los antecedentes, desarrollo de la especialidad y estado actual de las investigaciones' (2008) 26 *Revista de Arqueología Americana* 41–70.

Brozoski Museum ... was born, but also the specialty in underwater archaeology in our country".[16]

In this way, the emergence of underwater archaeology in Argentina is contemporary with that of neighbouring countries such as Brazil, Chile and Uruguay and has developed primarily in the context of historical or post-Hispanic navigation.[17] Later called the Underwater Archaeology Program (PROAS), it has concentrated its research on post-Hispanic navigation. In fact:

> ... most of the sites studied (...) are related to some of the shipwrecks that occurred on the Patagonian coast, particularly in the provinces of Chubut and Santa Cruz.[18]

In 1996, the Underwater Archaeology Research Group was created at the National University of Rosario, dedicated to complementing terrestrial archaeological investigations. Among its most remarkable works are its research of the submerged area of the Santa Fe La Vieja (founded in 1573) as well as the submerged remains of the Franciscan settlement of San Bartolomé de los Chaná,[19] both located in Santa Fe Province. The Albenga Foundation team frequently works with the Department of Anthropology, University of Rosario, Santa Fe Province.[20] Their studies have mainly focused on submerged sectors adjacent to archaeological sites, predominately located in inland rivers and lakes that have zero visibility and high currents.

In addition to the research carried out by these groups, many underwater cultural objects have been found by private parties, removed from their underwater environment, and are currently in museums or private collections. The activities of amateur divers has caused concern, in relation to both site

16 D. Elkin, 'Un naufragio, un diario y un hombre' (2011) 69 *Novedades de Antropología* 12.

17 Ciarlo, *supra* note 15.

18 Ciarlo, *supra* note 15, at. 27.

19 San Bartolome de los Chaná was a founded by Hernando Arias de Saavedra in 1616 as part of his regional policy and as a means to dominate the indigenous populations of semi-nomadic life in the tributaries of the Parana, between Asuncion and Buenos Aires. Source: <https://rephip.unr.edu.ar/handle/2133/14922#:~:text=San%20Bartolom%C3%A9%20de%20los%20Chan%C3%A1%20fue%20una%20reducci%C3%B3n%20de%20indios,entre%20Asunci%C3%B3n%20y%20Buenos%20Aires>.

20 G. Bonel, 'El aporte del sector privado a la arqueología subacuática. El caso de la Fundación Albenga.' (1998) 21 *Noticias de Antropología y Arqueología. – Revista electrónica de difusión científica;* J. García Cano and M. Valentini, 'Arqueología subacuática en una fundación española del siglo XVI. Ruinas de Santa Fe La Vieja, un enfoque metodológico' (1997) 3 *Anuario de la Universidad Internacional SEK* 25–48. This foundation was founded in the 1990s and it was managed by the architect Javier García Cano.

damage, and the treatment of discovered objects, which can be exposed to rapid degradation processes that may destroy them and thus impact their cultural significance. To protect against this, underwater archaeologists stress the need to stabilise, conserve and preserve the artefacts extracted from the seabed with the use of specialised techniques.[21]

The main aim of PROAS is to coordinate cooperation for the protection of underwater cultural heritage among the different jurisdictions. From the meetings held in 2020, two lines of work were defined: inventory and dissemination.[22] As a result, it is preparing a database based on written and oral sources of the location of wrecks alongside references obtained using GIS tools.[23] PROAS has also held meetings with officials responsible for the archaeological heritage of those provinces on the Argentine maritime coast (including Buenos Aires, Río Negro, Chubut, Santa Cruz and Tierra del Fuego and the Autonomous Government of Buenos Aires city). This working group also comprises representatives of the National Park Administration and those of the National and La Plata River Coastguards.

In Argentina there is no specific regulation of UCH, as outlined in section 3 below. Thus, the acts of protection, research and conservation of these assets adopt the international norms of soft law as a legal framework. That is to say, documents that are not legally binding upon the State, although they have, at the same time, a certain legal relevance.[24] In this field, the ICOMOS International Charter on the Protection and Management of Underwater Cultural Heritage,[25] the documents of the Council of Europe on Underwater Cultural Heritage[26] and the Buenos Aires Draft Convention on the Protection of

21 I. Srong, 'Current status of the draft UNESCO/DAOLOS Convention for the Protection of the Underwater Cultural Heritage', (1999) 3 *Conservation and Management of Archaeological Sites* 157; UNESCO, 'Preliminary study on the advisability of preparing an international instrument for the protection of the underwater cultural heritage' (1995) *General Conference*, twenty-eighth session, 6.

22 Cristian Murray, pers. comm., 02/17/2021.

23 D. Elkin, 'Argentina: Maritime Archaeology' in C. Smith (ed.) *Encyclopedia of Global Archaeology* (Springer, 2018).

24 E. Mereminskaya and A. Mascareño, 'Desnacionalización del derecho y la formación de regímenes globales de gobierno' in M. Martinic (Ed.) *Sesquicentenario del Código Civil de Andrés Bello: Pasado, presente y futuro.* (Lexis-Nexis, 2005); S. Ratner, 'International Law: the trials of global norms' (1998) 110 *Foreign Policy* 65–80.

25 ICOMOS Charter on the Protection and Management of Underwater Cultural Heritage [1996] Ratified by the 11th ICOMOS General Assembly in Sofia, Bulgaria.

26 See Parliamentary Assembly of the Council of Europe '*Recommendation 848 on the Underwater cultural heritage*' (Strasbourg, 1978), published in Council of Europe, Texts *Adopted by Assembly,* Session 30–32 (1978–81) (30th Ord. Sess.); and Draft European Convention on the Protection of the Underwater Cultural Heritage (1985).

the Underwater Cultural Heritage[27] have become relevant. The mechanism by which these non-binding legal norms are applied to UCH is through their observance by administrative bodies, particularly those made up of experts. Thus, Galbraith and Zaring affirm that, as a common factor, the implementation of international standards formalised through soft law rests with administrative agencies.[28] In this sense, the role of the specialists working at the INAPL as well as at the Fundación Albenga-UNR group makes it possible to analyse the interaction between this expert knowledge and the administration of UCH. In turn, this may prompt the observation that in a UCH context expert interpretation of the data of scientific agents may appear to be politicised, in the sense that it may lack scientific objectivity.[29]

3 Legislation Applicable to Underwater Heritage in Argentina

National legislation applied to archaeological resources is limited and inefficient even though the first federal law,[30] which provided protection for archaeological and palaeontological resources, was passed in 1913. Although this law, which placed archaeological resources under federal jurisdiction, was never applied, it has been heralded as a cornerstone of the national legal system for archaeological heritage protection.[31] In 2014, the Argentinean National Civil and Commercial Code established that archaeological heritage of scientific value belongs within the public domain and should be administered by the State[32] regardless of whether the find lies on public or private land. In other words, the State assumes legal authority for national heritage, as well as responsibility for its protection.

A 1994 amendment to the National Constitution resolved any conflict between federal and provincial laws with respect to ownership and jurisdiction

---

27 The International Law Association, *Buenos Aires Draft Convention on the Protection of the Underwater Cultural Heritage*, Report of the Sixty-Sixth Conference, held at Buenos Aires, Argentina, 14 to 20 August 1994, Buenos Aires, 1994, at 15–21, with comments at 432–47.

28 J. Galbraith and D. Zaring, 'Soft law as Foreign Relations Law' (2014) 99 *Cornell Law Review*, 748.

29 D. Kennedy, 'Challenging Expert Rule: The Politics of Global Governance' (2004) 27 *Sydney Law Review* pp. 1–24.

30 Law N° 9080 The National Legislature (February 26, 1913) Ruins and archaeological sites. LE-9080-1913-PLN.

31 E. Berberián, *La protección jurídica del patrimonio arqueológico en la República Argentina* (Comechingonia, 1992).

32 Law N° 26.994 The National Legislature (October 1, 2014) Civil and Commercial Code of the Argentine Republic (Article 235 clause h). B.O. 39.285 (08/10/2014).

over archaeological resources. The amended National Constitution recognised provincial ownership over archaeological heritage and established that the State was duty-bound to collaborate with provincial governments in order to develop heritage management and protection policies.[33] It was therefore necessary to adopt a new federal law to enable this constitutional position and to resolve legal loopholes, such as those relating to the protection of UCH. As indicated, this law was not approved until 2003.

The federal law for the protection of the archaeological and paleontological heritage (National Law 25,743)[34] passed in June 2003, presents a characterisation of the assets that are within its orbit based on a conceptualisation of such heritage. Thus, Article 2 states that archaeological heritage consists of:

> … movable and immovable things or vestiges of any nature that are on the surface, subsoil or submerged in jurisdictional waters, which can provide information on the sociocultural groups that inhabited the country from pre-Columbian times to recent historical eras.

Regulatory Decree 1022/2004 defines 'recent historical eras' indicating that it covers the last 100 years from the happening of the events and grants the power to national enforcement agencies to define terminology such as: archaeological object, fossil, lot, collection, site, and geological past, in order to develop a uniform administrative organisation.

National Law 25,743 recognises the duty of the State to preserve and safeguard this heritage and exercise the law aimed at it. Likewise, it establishes the guardianship of these assets in order to promote research into and dissemination about them. Furthermore, the State must defend and exercise custody over archaeological heritage by preventing and/or sanctioning its illegal trafficking, as well as managing the return of assets to the country of origin. For this, the law establishes administrative and criminal sanctions.

One of the strengths of this law is the explicit designation of enforcement agencies at national level, and the exhortation to provinces to identify their own competent authorities. At national level, the body that enforces the provisions on archaeological heritage is INAPL, which has a responsibility for research and protection of UCH, as indicated above. Another virtue of this law is the creation and organisation of registers for both archaeological and palaeontological heritage. Three registers were created, one of sites, another of

---

33 National Constitution of Republic of Argentina (1994), Article 41, Id SAIJ: LNS0002665.

34 Law N° 25.743 The National Legislature (June 4, 2003) Protection of the archaeological and paleontological heritage. B.O. 30.179 (26/06/2003).

objects and collections, and the third concerning law breakers. They are established, in the first instance, by the enforcement agencies of each province, and INAPL subsequently collates this information to compile its own second-degree registers.

Although National Law 25,743 includes underwater assets as part of archaeological heritage, and even adopts the temporality established in the 2001 Convention, it has notable shortcomings. The main one refers to the social and cultural de-contextualisation of the protected assets. The lack of an integrated vision of archaeological heritage, which allows consideration of its various scales (object, site, landscape), makes it difficult to guard the context of the location of underwater heritage assets.

Rivers, lakes, navigable lagoons, including their beds, belong to the public domain of the provinces.[35] However, the overlap of various administrative bodies with functions in these spaces can make conservation difficult. Thus, for example, the control of river navigation is charged to a national body (Prefectura Naval Argentina), while the authorisation of economic undertakings, such as mineral extraction or public works that may affect riverbeds, rivers, lakes, and lagoons, is the responsibility of the provinces. They are also in charge of the designation of the competent body for the application of the archaeological and palaeontological heritage law. Unfortunately, coordination and cooperation between these agencies is seldom achieved in practice. Therefore, the creation of the working group on underwater heritage convened by PROAS in 2020, previously mentioned, is indeed relevant.

Another difficulty in applying the law refers to the terminological confusion that it presents between the 'holder', the 'possessor in good faith' and the 'owner' of archaeological assets. Article 9 of National Law 25,743 establishes that archaeological assets are in the public domain of the State. However, when establishing a register of archaeological collections or objects, the law recognises that they may be in the possession of individuals. The rights enjoyed by individuals owning collections or archaeological objects have been the subject of debate in legal doctrine and, as explained below, they have tried to obtain recognition of their rights in courts of law.[36]

---

35 National Constitution of Republic of Argentina (1994), Article 124, Id SAIJ: LNS0002665 and Law N° 26.994 The National Legislature (October 1, 2014) Civil and Commercial Code of the Argentine Republic, Article 235, subsection a, b and c.

36 E. Berberian, *La protección del patrimonio cultural argentino: arqueológico y paleontológico* (Brujas, 2009); A. Calabrese 'Propiedad, posesión y tenencia en la ley 25.743 de protección del patrimonio arqueológico y paleontológico nacional' (2004) 14 *Novedades de Antropología* 48; A. Calabrese *La protección del patrimonio cultural argentino. Arqueológico y paleontológico* (Lumière, 2012).

It is relevant to highlight the insufficient consideration of the cultural ascription of archaeological assets in the regulation. Given that underwater cultural heritage items may belong to indigenous cultures, the lack of provisions guaranteeing the participation of those communities in the management of these cultural resources has been contested.[37] In this sense, National Law 25,517[38] requires the consent of indigenous communities in any scientific research related to their historical and cultural heritage, thus complying with the principles established by the International Labour Organization's Indigenous and Tribal Peoples Convention 1989.[39]

Beyond these provisions, other rules complement State guardianship over UCH assets. In 1999, the National Cultural Heritage Register was created under Federal Law 25,197 which creates an obligation to carry out an inventory of cultural property, including "the materials recovered through land and underwater archaeological and palaeontological surveys and excavations".[40] Although this law provides insufficient protection to archaeological resources due to its limited aims, it had a significant impact on underwater heritage protection policies because, for the first time, its existence and value was recognised by a national heritage law. It is important to note that many objects of UCH recovered through archaeological investigations, as well as by amateur divers, are found in national or provincial museums.[41] However, the necessary reglementary decree to implement this registry was not enacted until August 2020. For this reason, the survey, and the attributes of the cultural assets of the Nation are not yet publicly available.

In order to preserve and direct activities related to conservation of historical and artistic heritage, the National Commission of Monuments, Places and Historic Assets (NCMPHA) was created in 1940 by National Law 12,665 which was modified in 2015 by Law 27,103.[42] Through this modification new heritage categories were incorporated, including 'asset of national archaeological

37 M. Endere, M. Mariano, M. Conforti and C. Mariano, 'La protección legal del patrimonio en las provincias de Buenos Aires, La Pampa y Río Negro. Viejos problemas y nuevas perspectivas' (2015) 16 *Intersecciones en antropología* 207–219.

38 Law N° 25.517 The National Legislature (November 21, 2001) Dead remains of indigenous communities. B.O. 29.800 (20-12-2001).

39 ILO Convention 169.

40 Law N° 25.197 The National Legislature (November 10, 1999) Cultural Heritage Registration Regime, Article 2, B.O. 29.293 (15/12/1999).

41 Ciarlo, supra note 15.

42 Law N° 12.665 The National Legislature (September 30, 1940) National Commission of Museums, and Monuments, and Historical Sites, B.O. 13.851 (15/10/1940). Law N° 27.103 The National Legislature (December 17, 2014) Monuments and Historical Sites, B.O. 33.056 (23/01/2015).

interest', 'national historical tomb' and 'national cultural landscape', among others in Article 4 of National Law 12,665. Previously, categories included in international regulations had not been accepted as such in national heritage regulations.[43] However, despite the novelty of the legal recognition of these categories, some had already been recognised by NCMPHA. For example, in 2001, the area of the South Atlantic Ocean where the wreck of the cruiser ARA *General Belgrano* is located, with the remains of 323 crew members, was declared a national historic site and war grave by National Law 25,546.[44] In the same category were listed the site of the land and naval Battle of Vuelta de Obligado by Decree 120,411/1942,[45] and the naval Battle of Los Pozos by Decree 120,412/1942.[46] However, despite the relevance of this recognition for the protection of UCH sites, the functions of the Commission only focus on supervision of research activities, interventions carried out on these assets, and the review of the evaluation criteria of the assets themselves.

The legal status of UCH in Argentina is particularly critical not only because of the cultural heritage legislation issues already discussed, but also because of loopholes in maritime legislation. For example, Federal Law 20,094/73 concerning maritime navigation, permits the salvage of shipwrecks and their cargo by private investors, and does not consider wrecks to be of cultural value.[47]

To avoid wreck looting by amateur divers, a statement approved by National Decree 2,750/77 laid down three criteria that have to be met before gaining access to shipwrecks of historic value: firstly, the authorisation of the Argentinean Coastguard (Prefectura Naval Argentina); secondly, the supervision of the divers by the Coastguard; and, thirdly, the surrender of any finds to the Coastguard. This rule does not mention any requirement related to professional skills, archaeological methodologies or conservation strategies. However, by preventing recovered materials from falling into private hands, the

43 N. Levrand and M. Endere, 'Nuevas categorías patrimoniales. La incidencia del soft law en la reciente reforma a la ley de patrimonio histórico y artístico de Argentina' (2020) 16 *Direito GV* 2.

44 This warship of the Argentine Navy was sunk in 1982 during war between the United Kingdom and Argentina. Law N° 25.546 The National Legislature (November 27, 2001) National historic sites. Remains of the Cruiser ARA *General Belgrano*. B.O. 29.812 (09/01/2002).

45 This battle took place at a bend in the Paraná River between Buenos Aires and an English-French squadron in 1845. Decree 120.411 The National Executive Power. (May 29, 1942) Historical Sites. BO. 14325 (29/05/1942).

46 This battle took place in the Río de la Plata, in 1826, between the fleet of the Empire of Brazil and Argentina. Decree 120.412 The National Executive Power. (May 29, 1942) National Historic Monuments. B.O. 14.325 (29/05/1942).

47 Law N° 20.094 The National Legislature (January 15, 1973) Navigation. Articles 389 and 402. B.O. 22.619 (02/03/1973).

requirements do go some way towards deterring looters. Moreover, National Decree 166/2001, punishes those who violate extant legislation by the cancellation of diving licences.[48]

3.1 *Draft Proposals of Law on UCH*

Since 1988, seven draft proposals for laws related to UCH have been presented to the National Congress, although none has been passed, and a new proposal is awaiting consideration at the Senate. The only one specifically aimed at creating a regime for underwater cultural heritage was presented by Senator Leopoldo Moreau in 2000 but was rejected in 2002.[49] There were two draft proposals for a cultural heritage law that established the legal category of UCH by reference to the provisions of the 2001 Convention, but neither was approved. A summary of each proposal is outlined below.

3.1.1 1988 Draft Legislative Proposal

This brief proposal aimed to declare of national interest the archaeological heritage formed by sunken ships and their remains existing in Puerto Deseado, Santa Cruz Province and others located in the South Atlantic Ocean, which could be added in the future on scientific grounds.[50] It arose as a response to the discovery of the English corvette HMS *Swift* in Puerto Deseado, a case examined more fully below. The purpose of protecting and studying this find is evidenced in the designation, as enforcement authorities, of two scientific bodies, INAPL and the National Council for Scientific and Technical Research (CONICET), while fostering exchange with universities and specialised institutions abroad. This proposal was not approved.

3.1.2 1991 Draft Legislative Proposal 'on the Defense, Preservation, Conservation and Enhancement of the Underwater Cultural Heritage'

This was presented for the first time in 1991.[51] None of the proposals were approved, however, their provisions are significant for understanding the course of underwater heritage legislation in Argentina. These proposals established a broad definition of UCH, including, in Article 1, all objects found within

---

48 Decree 166 The National Executive Power (February 9, 2001) Regulation of sport diving activities. B.O. 29.587 (13/02/2001).

49 M. Endere, *Arqueología y legislación en Argentina: Cómo proteger el patrimonio arqueológico* (UNICEN, 2000).

50 TP Nº 216, date 04/13/88: 2997.

51 T.P. year 1991: 1457), re-admitted in 1994 (1,000 1-D.-94), in 1996 (801-D.-96) and in 1998 (462-D.96: 585).

national territory, including any water basin. They considered both marine, river, lake and even dried basins. They indicated that:

> … all those objects that are in a state of 'hydric or water saturation' were part of the underwater heritage, even if they did not have a geographical proximity relationship with any current water basin (Article 3).

The property in these objects was to belong to the Nation or Provincial State, according to the place of discovery. In this case, the competent authority was the NCMPHA in coordination with provincial agencies. As indicated above, the strength of this agency is not found in the investigation and protection of assets, but in the control of compliance with current legal regulations. However, the proposal envisaged the creation of a Fund for the Sustaining of the Underwater Cultural Heritage that would be administered by the Commission. Under the axiom 'protect rather than excavate' it was established that "assets considered underwater cultural heritage were inseparable from their environment" and could not be displaced or removed, "unless it resulted from force majeure or social interest".[52]

3.1.3 1992 Draft Legislative Proposal for the 'Protection and Preservation of the Underwater Cultural Heritage'

This draft law was promulgated to protect "the underwater cultural assets existing in the jurisdictional limits of the Argentine Republic, including the exclusive economic zone", and "declared these assets of national interest".[53] Article 2 adopted a broad definition including all movable or immovable property; which was the product of the activity of man or of the combined action of man and nature; that have historical, archaeological, anthropological, scientific, artistic, religious, documentary or any other interest for cultural heritage; and is located in the bed or subsoil of any 'aquatic space'. This included the sea, rivers, lakes, including coastline and riverbanks. A 50-year age requirement was imposed, although an *ad hoc* commission formed by specialists had discretion to decide about any asset that had the characteristics referred to in Article 2.

Establishing 'protection zones' of adequate breadth was considered necessary to ensure the protection of the property discovered. In addition, limits to domain were possible and the commission would authorise the carrying out of public or private works that could affect these assets. The inclusion of the Exclusive Economic Zone (EEZ) within the scope of this proposal was

52 Endere, *supra* note 49, at p. 106.

53 TP N°136/92: 6371.

undoubtedly its most innovative provision, inspired by the concept of a 'cultural protection zone', used in the recommendation on Underwater Cultural Heritage adopted by the Council of Europe in 1978.[54]

3.1.4 1997 Draft Proposal for the Protection of UCH

Presented in 1997, Article 1 of 1.900-D.97: 1960 declared of national and cultural interest all the existing underwater cultural assets within the jurisdictional limits of the Argentine Republic, including the EEZ. It adopted a broad concept of underwater heritage, similar to the 1992 proposal, although it did not extend protection to the context of the assets.

Both the age of the assets included, reduced to at least 25 years, and the omission of consideration of the degree to which the asset is submerged, especially those found on the coasts and beaches, offered a wide scope of application, albeit one that was questioned.[55] On the other hand, some ambiguities in the determination of the enforcement authority would have been difficult to overcome had the law been approved.

3.1.5 1999 and 2000 Draft Proposals for UCH Protection

The 1999 proposal reproduced many of the provisions of those previous.[56] For example, it continued the broad definition of heritage including:

> … all movable and immovable property produced by the activity of man or the combined action of man and nature, which has historical, archaeological, anthropological, scientific, artistic, religious, documentary value, and/or any other interest for cultural heritage, and it is located in the bed or subsoil of any aquatic space.

Additionally, both interior and exterior waters were 'aquatic spaces', and it imposed a 50-year requirement to determine if an asset may be classed as underwater heritage. It provided for protection areas and the need to obtain prior authorisation for works that could affect underwater heritage and established penalties for those damaging, altering, removing, hiding, or stealing these assets.

---

54 Parliamentary Assembly of the Council of Europe '*Recommendation 848 on the Underwater cultural heritage*' (Strasbourg, 1978), published in Council of Europe, Texts *Adopted by Assembly,* Session 30–32 (1978–81) (30th Ord. Sess.).

55 Endere, *supra* note 49.

56 See 1552-B.-99: 1904.

In 2000, a similar proposal was not approved, before expiring in 2003.[57] Many of the observations made regarding the other proposals are applicable to it, including applicable jurisdiction, extension of the protected heritage, professional responsibilities to act as underwater archaeologists, as well as the need to establish mechanisms for the protection of heritage in danger.

3.1.6 Other Draft Legislative Proposals

Additional to those dedicated exclusively to the protection and regulation of activities related to UCH, since 2000 a series of proposals have been presented at the National Congress aiming to establish a general regime for cultural heritage. At least three of them included UCH. For example, proposal 1223/00 contained a section devoted to underwater heritage, which included provisions similar to the 1999 and 2000 draft proposals. However, this proposal was shelved a few months after it was presented.

Furthermore, proposals presented in 2010 and 2012[58] had the objective of establishing a general legal framework on Argentine cultural heritage, within which UCH was recognised as a special category. However, they referred to the 2001 Convention, without incorporating specific norms regulating the application of these provisions in Argentine territory. Both incorporated the possibility of citizen participation in proposing objects or sites to be declared as part of the Argentine cultural heritage.

To conclude this brief exposition, interest in regulating underwater heritage in Argentina predates the adoption of the 2001 Convention. Several legislative initiatives were presented but failed to become law. In general, the draft proposals considered the assets of underwater heritage as belonging to the public domain of the State, in accordance with the provisions of the Civil and Commercial Code; and they established the duty of the State to protect and preserve them. There is important consensus regarding the definition of these assets, as well as the inclusion of items found both in marine and inland waters. Distinctions refer to antiquity requirements (25, 50 or 100 years); the enforcement authority; the regulation of a protection zone adjacent to the assets; and the penalties provided. The failure of these draft legislative proposals was due more to a lack of interest than to true political opposition, with most of them losing parliamentary status without even being dealt with in the chambers.

57 Endere, *supra* note 49.

58 Senate of the Argentine Nation, Draft Legislative Proposal 4449-D-2010 and Senate of the Argentine Nation, Draft Legislative Proposal 1731-D-2012, Cultural Heritage of Argentine.

At present, there remains no specific regime for UCH, which is framed in the general standards set for archaeological heritage. This resulted, in 2019, in a request for reports from the Executive on the application of the 2001 Convention.[59]

3.2 *Provincial Legislation*

The provinces of Argentina predate the Nation and are recognised as fully autonomous. Thus, they can establish their own Constitutions that, in general, guarantee the right to cultural heritage, and which in some cases includes archaeological heritage. This right is principally a State obligation, although in Tierra del Fuego, Córdoba, and Chubut Provinces it is considered a duty of all people. All provinces have laws that protect cultural heritage. In some cases, the preservation of archaeological heritage is regulated independently. However, even though the category of archaeological heritage is always recognised, there are no specific provisions concerning UCH. Many of the provincial regulations adhere to the concept of archaeological heritage stated in National Law 25,743, although some do not define it.

There are several provincial laws worthy of mention. For example, the Provinces of San Luis, Santa Cruz, Río Negro, Mendoza and San Juan[60] recognise as archaeological zones or sites, places with remains of human settlements or related assets 'susceptible to be studied with archaeological methodology'. This definition includes both recovered materials and those kept *in situ*, whether they are on the surface, in the subsoil or underwater.

It is worth highlighting the Province of Tierra del Fuego, where Provincial Law 370/1997 on cultural and paleontological heritage contemplates, in Article 13, archaeological heritage that is found 'on the surface of the land, in the subsoil or under territorial waters'. The heritage condition of other types of cultural property, such as historical and architectural assets, must be recognised individually through a declaration. In 1998, National Decree Nº 858 was promulgated, which establishes that all shipwrecks are part of the provincial historical heritage. In this way, the conflict raised by the request for the rescue of the *Purísima Concepción* shipwreck made by a treasure hunter, discussed below, was resolved and, at the same time, general legal protection was provided to other historical wrecks found in the provinces.[61]

---

59 Senate of the Argentine Nation. *Request for a report to the executive branch on various points related to the Law 26.556 – approval of the Convention on the Protection of the Underwater Cultural Heritage.* File 3238/19.

60 Respectively: Law 11-0526-2006, Law 3137/2010, Law F 3656/2007, Law 6034/1993 and Law 6801/1997.

61 Santos and Elkin, *supra* note 14.

4 Relevant Case Studies Relating to Argentinian UCH

4.1 *Successful Case Studies*

4.1.1 The HMS *Swift* Case

HMS *Swift* was part of the naval fleet located in the British settlement in Malvinas/Falkland Islands at the end of the eighteenth century. In 1982, a group of local amateur divers found this shipwreck off the coast of Puerto Deseado city, Santa Cruz Province, within the Argentinean Territorial Sea. Therefore, it belongs to the provincial cultural heritage although it is also under the federal jurisdiction of the Prefectura Naval Argentina which controls maritime navigation. In 1977, a natural reserve was created to protect the area and in 1983 the site of HMS *Swift* was declared "a provincial site of historic interest and part of the protected regional heritage" by Provincial Decree 1430.[62]

In 1984, one of the amateur divers who found the wreck in 1982 began an administrative procedure to exercise the 'right of first refusal' granted by Article 390 of the Navigation Law 20,094. The administrative procedure requires prior notification to the owner of the wreck and, if the vessel is of a foreign flag, to the respective consul, so they may file opposition. Although the vessel was a British Crown warship, the administrative authority understood that the notification should be made to the Province of Santa Cruz, which according to the aforementioned Provincial Decree claimed its ownership. In this instance, the province expressed its opposition to the recovery, and, on that basis, the Maritime Authority denied it. The claimant filed a judicial appeal, but the administrative decision was ratified. Central to the decision of the Supreme Court of Justice of the Nation, was that the administrative authority had acted in accordance with the law since the Court had no jurisdiction to determine questions about the legitimacy of the province as 'owner'. According to the Supreme Court, had the plaintiff wanted to question the legitimacy of the Provincial Decree that declared the ownership of the province over the wreck, he should have filed an action based on the unconstitutionality of it. However, two judges dissented on this point, representing a minority view.

In 1986, the local Municipality contacted the ICOMOS-Argentina Underwater Heritage Working Group (GTPS) asking for assistance to recover and preserve the remains. In 1994, the Albenga private foundation carried out fieldwork activities and, from 1997 onwards, research was carried out by the newly created Underwater Archaeology team of INAPL in coordination with local

62 V. Dellino and M.L. Endere, 'The HMS *Swift* wreck and the development of underwater heritage protection in Argentina', (2001) 4 *International Journal of Conservation and Management of Archaeological Sites* 219–231.

and provincial authorities.[63] It is also notable that the first underwater archaeology programme arose as a result of this discovery and that until then, there were no qualified personnel to undertake the recovery, research and preservation of such remains. The role of museum experts and INAPL researchers was significant in enabling the management of these assets. Additionally, the HMS *Swift* project has also provided opportunities for international collaboration and training expertise between England and Argentina.[64] For all these reasons, it has become a paradigmatic case in the development of underwater archaeology and heritage in Argentina.

4.1.2 The *Purísima Concepción* Wreck

The Spanish frigate *Purísima Concepción*, en route from Cádiz, Spain to the port of El Callao, Peru, was shipwrecked off the Atlantic coast of Tierra del Fuego in 1765. At the end of the 1990s, Javier Curra Donati, head of the Pecios firm, requested authorisation from the national and provincial governments to remove materials from the *Purísima Concepción* despite its exact location being unknown at the time. It was a purely commercial undertaking, focused on:

> … the rescue of the treasure that, in his opinion, was transported by the *Purísima Concepción* at the time of the shipwreck, in exchange for keeping much of it as remuneration.[65]

According to his estimates, the "shipment of silver and gold could reach a value of three billion dollars".[66] Governmental agencies requested information from organisations linked to UCH, specifically the GTPS of ICOMOS-Argentina, PROAS-INAPL and the Albenga Foundation, which agreed that the recovery was incompatible with the research and protection of the wreck. However, the legal regulations in force at that time were not enough to stop Donati's claim:

---

63 D. Elkin, C. Murray, R. Bastida, M. Grosso, A. Argüeso, D. Vainstub, C. Underwood and N. Ciarlo, *El Naufragio de la HMS Swift (1770) – Arqueología Marítima en la Patagonia* (Vázquez Mazzini Editores, 2011).

64 González, *supra* note 5, at p. 59; H. Roberts 'The British ratification of the underwater heritage convention: problems and prospects', (2017) 67 *International & Comparative Law Quarterly* 833–865; D. Elkin 'HMS *Swift*: Scientific Research and Management of Underwater Cultural Heritage in Argentina' in R. Grenier, D. Nutley and I. Cochran (eds) *Underwater Cultural Heritage at risk: Managing Natural and Human Impacts* (UNESCO 2006).

65 Santos and Elkin, *supra* note 14, at p. 126.

66 See notice in *Diario Clarín* (newspaper), 29 September 1997, cited by Santos and Elkin, *supra* note 14.

National Law 25,743 was not yet in force, and the old Law 9080 on archaeological and paleontological heritage of 1913 did not contemplate historical or underwater assets. For its part, although Tierra del Fuego's Provincial Law 370 included submerged assets within its scope, it was limited to remains linked to indigenous peoples. Given the situation, the Director of Museums, Monuments and Historical Sites of Tierra del Fuego decided to promote an executive decree to protect historic shipwrecks, such as the *Purísima Concepción*, and began a campaign to raise public awareness.[67] Finally, as noted above, in 1998 National Decree No 858 was passed, establishing that all shipwrecks are part of the provincial historical heritage and, in this way, the *Purísima Concepción* could be protected.

Ultimately, as Santos and Elkin point out, Donati could never prove that he had located the wreck, and the supposed silver coin that he had recovered from it was confiscated by the Rio Grande Naval Prefecture by court order. An expert in numismatics was able to verify that the coin was not contemporary to the *Purísima Concepción* since it post-dated the wreck.

The Museum of the End of the World in Ushuaia (Tierra del Fuego) has had a noteworthy role, not only in the promotion of naval archaeology in the region, but also in coordinating preservation activities with other research institutions such as CADIC (Austral Scientific Research Centre – CONICET) and the Argentine Navy. In 1981, an expedition organised by this museum found an iron cannon supposedly from this shipwreck on the Atlantic coast, a few kilometres from Caleta Falsa. In 2014, the site of the *Purísima Concepción* shipwreck was found in the same area and since 2017, systematic research has been developed there by a team of PROAS.[68]

4.2 *Recoveries of Stolen Underwater Cultural Property*

The 2001 Convention contributed to reinforcing and completing the system of protection against illicit trafficking of cultural property by extending the scope of existing Conventions[69] to the underwater environment. Indeed, Article 2(7)

---

67 Santos and Elkin, *supra* note 14, at p. 126.

68 D. Elkin, 'Arqueología marítima histórica en Argentina: investigaciones de naufragios acaecidos entre los siglos XVII y XX' (2019) 6 *Magallánica – Revista de historia moderna* 237–275.

69 i.e. UN Educational, Scientific and Cultural Organisation (UNESCO), The First Protocol to the Convention for the Protection of Cultural Property in the Event of Armed Conflict, 14 May 1954; UN Educational, Scientific and Cultural Organisation (UNESCO), Convention on the Means of Prohibiting and Preventing the Illicit Import, Export and Transfer of Ownership of Cultural Property, 14 November 1970 and International Institute for the

establishes a general principle that 'underwater cultural heritage shall not be commercially exploited'.

Article 17 establishes that 'each State Party shall impose sanctions for violations of measures it has taken to implement this Convention'. Specifically, it states:

> Sanctions applicable in respect of violations shall be adequate in severity to be effective in securing compliance with this Convention and to discourage violations wherever they occur and shall deprive offenders of the benefit deriving from their illegal activities.

It also establishes according to Article 18(1) that:

> Each State Party shall take measures providing for the seizure of underwater cultural heritage in its territory that has been recovered in a manner not in conformity with this Convention.

It must also, under Article 18(4):

> … ensure that its disposition be for the public benefit, taking into account the need for conservation and research; the need for reassembly of a dispersed collection; the need for public access, exhibition and education; and the interests of any State with a verifiable link, especially a cultural, historical or archaeological link, in respect of the underwater cultural heritage concerned.

These provisions complement those contained in National Law 25,743 on archaeological heritage. To demonstrate the application of these regulations, some relevant case examples in which stolen underwater heritage assets were recovered are outlined below.

4.2.1 Anchor from the Battle of La Vuelta de Obligado

In 2012, INAPL filed a complaint with the National Centre for the Protection of Cultural Heritage because an anchor was being offered for sale on Mercado Libre, a popular online shopping platform. It was an admiralty anchor from the nineteenth century, measuring approximately 1.20 cm and weighing 200 kg, illegally removed from the site of the Battle of La Vuelta de Obligado, in the

Unification of Private Law (UNIDROIT), Convention on Stolen or Illegally Exported Cultural Objects, adopted 24 June 1995.

town of San Pedro, Province of Buenos Aires. It had been declared a National Historic Site in 1942 as the location of a land and river battle in 1845 and where some vestiges remained, including the anchor.[70] Therefore, it is an underwater cultural asset protected by National Archaeological Heritage Law 25,743 and National Law 26,556 that ratifies the 2001 Convention. In 2013, a search warrant was issued, and the piece was recovered in the city of Quilmes, Buenos Aires Province and taken to the INAPL repository. The purported seller received no sanction.

4.2.2 Armstrong Cannon Belonging to the Argentine Navy

In 2021, an English naval Armstrong cannon was recovered. It is a steel breech-loading barrel, approximately 4m in total length. It has an inscription with the legends 'SIR W.G. ARMSTRONG & Co', which corresponds to the manufacturer,[71] and the number '3639', which corresponds to the part number.

This artillery cannon has great cultural value since it would have belonged to the Argentine Navy, dated between 1850 and 1860. It was offered for sale on the internet with a monetary value of €12,000. An investigation was initiated following a complaint made in Spain, and with the intervention of the Civil Guard. After verifying that the piece would be in Argentine territory, the Department for the Protection of Cultural Heritage of the Argentine Federal Police sought to determine its location, and in 2019 it was discovered in the city of Mar del Plata. The local Federal Justice finally ordered the confiscation. A specialist from INAPL, part of PROAS, intervened in the case to identify the piece. In the report it was affirmed that it was the piece sought, protected by the scope of both Law 25,743 and Law 26,556.

4.2.3 Spanish Cannon Used in the Battle of Puente de Márquez

In 2019, a search warrant was issued by a court in the city of San Isidro. As a result, a muzzle-loading cannon, of Spanish origin from the eighteenth century, belonging to the Argentine Navy, was confiscated. It weighs 363 kg, has an inscription '7024' that indicates its serial number and would have been used in the Battle of Puente de Márquez in 1821.[72]

70 See note 45.

71 The manufacturer was W. G. Armstrong, of Newcastle, England, established in 1864.

72 The Battle took place in Buenos Aires Province, on 26 April 1829, as part of the civil war between Unitarians and Federals in Argentina. On that occasion, the forces led by the governor of the Province of Santa Fe, Estanislao López, defeated those led by the unitary General, Juan Lavalle.

This cannon was offered for a starting bid of €12,000 on an international online buying and selling platform and was detected by the periodic monitoring of this type of activity carried out by the Department for the Protection of Cultural Heritage of the Argentine Federal Police. INAPL specialists were able to verify its authenticity and identity and so, protected by current regulations, it was left in judicial deposit. Again, the purported seller did not receive any sanction.

4.2.4 Wooden Baskets with Historic Pottery Found at Playa Donata

In 2016, a group of ATV riders found several wooden baskets containing a large amount of historic pottery. These baskets were deposited at the coast of Playa Donata, an inhospitable area with difficult access located on Península Mitre, Tierra del Fuego Province. The finders collected some material, disturbing the archaeological context. Some of them commented on the event through Facebook and added photographs. A local archaeologist realised the objects had archaeological value and contacted the provincial authorities. Noting the circumstances of the discovery, the Secretary of Culture of Tierra del Fuego contacted the persons in possession of the pottery and requested return of them as part of provincial cultural heritage.[73] Subsequently, the PROAS team conducted rescue archaeological fieldwork on the site with the support of the provincial authorities and the Museo del Fin del Mundo in Ushuaia. It was identified that the eleven baskets were part of the cargo of a vessel heading to the Pacific Ocean along the Cape Horn route. They contained nineteenth century British pottery and glassware. However, it was not possible to determine their provenance as no wreck site had been identified in the area.[74]

5 Final Comments and the Future Agenda

It is clear that Argentina acknowledges the importance of UCH, is aware of the need to protect this heritage in its inland waters and Territorial Sea and agrees with the principles promoted by the 2001 Convention. However, if Argentine

---

73 Martín Vázquez, pers. Comm., 03/01/21.

74 D. Elkin, 'Arqueología histórica del litoral atlántico fueguino: El cargamento de vajilla de Playa Donata' in J. Gómez Otero, A. Svoboda y A. Banegas (Ed.) *Arqueología de la Patagonia: el pasado en las arenas* (Instituto de Diversidad y Evolución Austral, 2019); Elkin, D. 'Not just divers and fishermen: increasing the public involvement in the safeguarding of underwater cultural heritage in Tierra del Fuego, Argentina' in A. Hafner, H. Oniz, L. Semaan L. and C.J. Underwood *Cultural Heritage Under Water at Risk: Threats, Challenges and Solutions* (ICOMOS, 2020).

authorities would like to fully apply the Convention in its jurisdiction, a priority is to enact a federal UCH law designed according to its principles, objectives and aims. This law must declare that national navigation law is no longer applicable to the exploitation of underwater cultural heritage. In this way, the 2001 Convention's standards would contribute to the exercise of effective jurisdiction over Argentine maritime space, generating a "natural integration of international regulations".[75]

Changes in provincial heritage laws would also be necessary to make them correspond with the desired new national legislation and thus the 2001 Convention. Although some provinces have adopted specific UCH measures, the provisions referring to exploration, research and safeguarding of this heritage are still limited, as are sanctions and the mechanisms for their application – essentially judicial procedure and competent courts.

It is worth noting that at provincial level the most remarkable legislation was not the result of a planned policy on UCH, but instead the result of archaeology's sporadic appearance on the agendas of legislators, usually prompted by the effort and influence of archaeologists, or by a spectacular discovery. For example, the finding and research of the HMS *Swift* wreck not only prompted the enactment of a new provincial heritage law (2472/97) – which includes the protection of submerged sites – but also resulted in the drafting of a federal law for the protection of underwater national heritage. In the same sense, the claims for the rescue of the *Purísima Concepción* wreck prompted the approval of Provincial Decree 858/98 in Tierra del Fuego.

If there is to be new law, it would be reasonable that the INAPL be the competent authority at national level, designated to carry out effective safeguarding of underwater cultural heritage, create a specific official inventory, as well as continue other activities, including research and education, in accordance with Article 22 of the 2001 Convention. It should act in coordination with provincial cultural authorities and the Coastguard (Prefectura Naval Argentina). In this event, it would be convenient to also reimagine the underwater archaeology programme (PROAS), positioning it as an area within INAPL dedicated to the management of this heritage and to technical coordination with the provinces.[76] More generally, the availability of technological and financial resources is also required, as well as international assistance and support, in order to help the authorities accomplish basic measures for the protection of UCH.

75 González, *supra* note 7, at p. 66.

76 See González, *supra* note 7, at p. 63.

Another key issue is the need to maintain and update an inventory of UCH. Although a non-official inventory began some years ago, financing is required given the magnitude of the task, considering the extent of Argentine territory and the significant number of shipwrecks that can be found on the route to Cape Horn. Within this framework, it would be opportune to establish priorities for the preservation of UCH, applying criteria such as importance and vulnerability. This would allow action in urgent cases without compromising the idea of comprehensive protection that should govern both, internationally and nationally.[77]

Argentina's archaeological heritage management system has, in short, been rendered less effective by the inadequacy of current legislation. However, any sanction applied by an archaeological heritage law does not imply, by itself, the effective safeguarding of this heritage. The specificity of this type of cultural asset requires consistent legal provisions, which provide for integration with navigation legislation, the preservation of protected natural areas and the recognition of protection zones adjacent to the underwater cultural assets found. In addition, the fragmentation of responsibility and accountability between provincial and national authorities makes it difficult to implement protection policies and impose sanctions on offenders.

Despite these shortcomings, some underwater heritage assets have been successfully safeguarded. In this sense, the political work of PROAS and academic institutions such as the UNR allowed local managers to be made aware of the relevance of these assets. Likewise, the Department for the Protection of Cultural Heritage of the Argentine Federal Police carries out persistent work to detect and report situations of illegal commercialisation and export of underwater heritage objects. However, the absence of a specific norm that establishes significant sanctions limits the administration of justice in this area.

Argentina has the strength of having qualified human resources with experience in underwater exploration and research, being one of the pioneer countries in these developments in Latin America. There is already abundant scientific production and consolidated research teams, despite the fact that an underwater archaeology career path does not yet exist in the country.[78] In this context, international technical and financial cooperation is crucial in

---

77 See González, *supra* note 7, at p. 60; and also see Endere and Prado, *supra* note 8.

78 Such an express provision would allow Argentina (according to A. González 'La Argentina y la Convención sobre la Protección del Patrimonio Subacuático: hacia una relación simbiótica' (2010) *Revista Jurídica* 5 (5): 39–68) to aspire to become a sub-regional or regional centre under the auspices of UNESCO for training and awareness-raising in the field of UCH.

encouraging positive actions for the protection and management of underwater cultural heritage in this country. Alternative funding sources and sponsorship – such as through private investors – should be explored as much as the promotion of institutional arrangements among different interest groups. Last but not least, public support is crucial to safeguard underwater cultural heritage, as their engagement in the conservation philosophy is essential to guarantee its long-term preservation.

All websites last accessed February 2025.

Acknowledgements

We are grateful to those people who generously provided information, especially to Comisario Mayor Marcelo Daniel El Haibe (Policía Federal Argentina), Dr. Dolores Elkin and Arch. Cristian Murray. This chapter was carried out within the framework of research carried out by PATRIMONIA (Interdisciplinary Program for Heritage Studies) of the INCUAPA Institute (Executive Unit of CONICET – UNICEN) and was financed through the projects PIP 736/21 CONICET, directed by Maria Luz Endere.

Selected Bibliography

N. Ciarlo 'La arqueología subacuática en Argentina. Reseña histórica de los antecedentes, desarrollo de la especialidad y estado actual de las investigaciones' (2008) 26 *Revista de Arqueología Americana* 41–70.

V. Dellino and M.L. Endere 'The HMS *Swift* wreck and the development of underwater heritage protection in Argentina' (2001) 4 *International Journal of Conservation and Management of Archaeological Sites* 219–231.

D. Elkin 'Argentina: Maritime Archaeology' in C. Smith (ed.) *Encyclopedia of Global Archaeology* (Springer, 2018).

M. Endere 'Arqueología y legislación en Argentina: Cómo proteger el patrimonio arqueológico' (UNICEN, 2000).

A. González 'La Argentina y la Convención sobre la Protección del Patrimonio Subacuático: hacia una relación simbiótica' (2010) *Revista Jurídica* 5 (5): 39–68.

N. Levrand and M. Endere 'Nuevas categorías patrimoniales. La incidencia del soft law en la reciente reforma a la ley de patrimonio histórico y artístico de Argentina' (2020). *Revista Direito GV* 16 (2). Doi:10.1590/2317-6172201960.

CHAPTER 3

Australia

Craig Forrest and Andrew Viduka***

1 Introduction

Australia is a large island nation with an extended Continental Shelf (CS) and the third largest Exclusive Economic Zone (EEZ) in the world, such that its maritime jurisdiction exceeds that of its land territory. Given its size, Australia has a relatively small population of approximately 27 million people, most of whom live on the coastal fringe.

Australia is made up of six States, two territories[1] and a number of external territories.[2] In 1901, the separate British colonies of Queensland, New South Wales, Victoria, Tasmania, South Australia and Western Australia united to form the Commonwealth of Australia. The federal nature of this Commonwealth is such that the Constitution vested specific powers in the Commonwealth while each State retained the residual powers that existed pre-federation. The exact division of powers has not always been clear and has shifted over time with evolving constitutional interpretations. This has been particularly marked when addressing issues of maritime jurisdiction, with a corresponding impact on the protection and management of underwater cultural heritage (UCH).

2 Australia's Underwater Cultural Heritage

Australia's indigenous population is believed to have first arrived from South-east Asia between 50,000 and 65,000 years ago. Given sea level rises since then, there exists the possibility of some underwater remains that date back to these times down to approximately 125 metres below present sea level; though little investigation has so far been undertaken, the current boom in near and

* Professor and Director. Marine And Shipping Law Unit, TC Beirne School of Law, University of Queensland.

** Assistant Director Underwater Cultural Heritage, Cultural Heritage Section, Department of Climate Change, Energy, the Environment, and Water, Australian Government.

1 The Australian Capital Territory and the Northern Territory.

2 Norfolk Island, Heard and McDonald Islands, Cocos (Keeling) Islands, Christmas Island, Ashmore and Cartier islands, Coral Sea Islands and the Australian Antarctic Territory.

 | DOI:10.1163/9789004510883_005

offshore energy is driving increased assessment.[3] The first Europeans to arrive on Australian shores were Dutch explorers in 1606 and shipwrecked sailors during the early age of exploration, with the oldest known shipwreck in Australian waters being the British East Indiaman *Trial* that sank in 1622. Since then, approximately 7,500 known shipwrecks have been recorded as sunk around the coastline, from early Dutch wrecks, numerous colonial-era wrecks to more recent wrecks of the First and Second World Wars. Since colonisation in 1788, the remains of jetties, piers and other maritime property, submerged aircraft, as well as the remains of 65,000 years of indigenous habitation, have also revealed much about early Australia, making up a rich body of UCH.[4]

3 The Evolving Legislative Regime

In the 1950s, the relatively affluent Australian coastal community eagerly embraced the use of Self-Contained Underwater Breathing Apparatus (SCUBA). This quickly led to the discovery of shipwrecks. There was no specific protection for these important archaeological and historical shipwrecks, which were subject to the salvage regime as embodied in the Navigation Act 1912 (Cth) (NA 1912).[5] This required finders of wrecks to report such finds to the Receiver of Wreck and to deliver up any recovered artefacts to the Receiver so that they could be returned to the original owner in exchange for a salvage reward. Importantly, recovered artefacts that were not claimed by their original owner within a year, were vested in the Commonwealth.[6]

By the early 1960s, Australian sports divers were discovering important shipwrecks, particularly four Dutch shipwrecks; *Vergulde Draak* (*Draeck*) (1656), *Batavia* (1629), *Zuiddorp* (*Zuytdorp*) (1712) and *Zeewijk* (1727).[7] Some of these, and other finds, were not always reported to the Receiver of Wreck and were often retained by those that had recovered them. While there was some enforcement of the NA 1912, this appears to have been unusual given the difficulty of enforcing these provisions when recoveries were made

3 B. Jeffrey, 'Australia' in S. Dromgoole (ed) *Legal Protection of the Underwater Cultural Heritage: National and International Perspectives* (Kluwer Law 1999) 2.

4 M. Nash (ed) *Shipwreck Archaeology in Australia* (University of Western Australia Press, 2007).

5 The Commonwealth's Navigation Act 1912 was repealed and replaced with the Navigation Act 2012 (Cth).

6 NA 1912 (Cth) ss 302 & 308.

7 G. Henderson, *Maritime Archaeology in Australia* (University of Western Australia Press, 1986) 94–96.

underwater and then simply retained.[8] Concerns over the recovery of artefacts and especially those from the Dutch wrecks, which included silver coins, led to the first legislative attempt to regulate access to and interaction with shipwrecks: in 1964, the Western Australian Museum Act 1959 was amended to protect historic wrecks and their associated artefacts found off the coast of Western Australia.[9]

The vexed question of ownership of the Dutch wrecks was addressed in 1972 with the conclusion of an Agreement between the Netherlands and Australia concerning Old Dutch Shipwrecks (ANCODS Agreement), which transferred the rights, title and interest to wrecked vessels of the Dutch East India Company lying off the coast of Western Australia to the Commonwealth of Australia, which accepted that right, title and interest.[10] Following this, specific shipwreck legislation, in the shape of the Maritime Archaeology Act 1973, was adopted by Western Australia.

Coincidently, the Commonwealth was dealing with the difficult question of maritime jurisdiction as between it and the States and Territories. To regulate activities such as oil and gas exploration off Australia, the Commonwealth adopted the Seas and Submerged Lands Act 1973 (Cth) (SSLA) which asserted Commonwealth jurisdiction over the Territorial Sea (TS).[11] The effect of this was that the individual States were only able to legislate to regulate matters off their coast extra-territorially when doing so was for the peace, order or good government of their State. The regulation of historic shipwrecks by the State would therefore have to accord with those limitations to be valid. In 1977, this led to a successful constitutional challenge to the validity of the Maritime Archaeology Act 1973 by one of the finders of the *Vergulde Draack (Draeck)*.[12]

The extent of the Commonwealth's jurisdiction over the TS meant that the Commonwealth and not the State or territories was responsible for regulating all activities, including those relating to historic shipwrecks, in the TS. This led

8 K. Hosty, 'Historic shipwreck legislation and the Australian diver. Past, present and future' (1986) 11(1) *Bulletin of the Australian Institute of Maritime Archaeology* 21.

9 G.A. Kennedy, 'Discovery, Legislation and Litigation' in J. Green, M. Stanbury and F. Gaastra (eds.), *The ANCODS Colloquium. Australian National Centre of Excellence for Maritime Archaeology, Special Publication No.3* (1998) 33.

10 Agreement between Australia and the Netherlands concerning Old Dutch Shipwrecks, done at the Hague on 6 November 1972 ATS 18; HSA Schedule 1, 34.

11 *New South Wales v Commonwealth* (1975) 135 CLR 337. See also now Seas and Submerged Lands (Historic Bays) Proclamation 2016.

12 *Robinson v Western Australian Museum* (1977) 138 CLR 283. P. Ryan, 'Legislation on Historic Wreck', Papers from the First Southern Hemisphere Conference on Maritime Archaeology, Perth, Western Australia, Australian Sports Publications, 1977) 23–27.

to the Commonwealth adopting the Historic Shipwrecks Act (HSA) in 1976.[13] The States and Territories remained responsible for regulating historic shipwrecks within internal waters and continue to do so, by way of State legislation.[14] The Commonwealth was reluctant to legislate and manage all activities within the TS and, in 1979, entered into an agreement, the Offshore Constitutional Settlement,[15] with the States and Territories that would allow for State and Territory regulation of some activities in the first 3nm of the TS; termed 'State coastal waters'.[16] The Offshore Constitutional Settlement provided that the Commonwealth would be responsible for the protection and management of shipwrecks in the TS including State coastal waters in accordance with the HSA. Other UCH in State coastal waters would be protected by the relevant jurisdiction.

4 The Historic Shipwrecks Act 1976 and National Management Framework

The HSA provided that historic shipwrecks and their associated relics (all objects/artefacts that are cargo, part of the ship, personal possessions, or human remains) were of value to all Australians and incorporated the principles from the ANCODS agreement of 'being available to the public and the scholar'.[17] Initially the HSA only applied to specifically declared shipwrecks. It was soon realised that the inefficiencies of a front-loaded significance assessment system facilitated opportunities for individuals to damage significant but as yet undeclared wrecks. In 1985 the HSA was amended to provide for blanket protection of all shipwrecks 75 years or older, though this actually only took effect from 1 April 1993.[18]

---

13 For an account of events leading to the adoption of the HSA see Henderson, *supra* note 7, at pp. 67–78; Jeffrey *supra* note 3, at pp. 5–6.

14 Queensland Heritage Act 1992 (Qld), Heritage Act 1977 (NSW), Heritage Act 2017 (Vic), Historic Shipwrecks Act 1981 (SA), Historic Cultural Heritage Act 1995 (Tas), Maritime Archaeology Act 1973 (WA); and Heritage Act 2011 (NT). As to the extent of the States' maritime jurisdiction, particularly with respect of historic bays in South Australia, see Jeffrey *supra* note 3, at p 2.

15 AGD 2021, Attorney-General's Department Offshore Constitutional Settlement <https://www.ag.gov.au/international-relations/international-law/offshore-constitutional-settlement>.

16 Coastal Waters (State Powers) Act 1980 (Cth).

17 P. Ryan, 'Legislation on Historic Wreck', Papers From the First Southern Hemisphere Conference on Maritime Archaeology, 1977 Perth, Western Australia, Australian Sports Publications, 23–27.

18 W. Cassidy, 'Historic shipwrecks and blanket declaration' (1991) 15(2) *Bulletin of the Australian Institute for Maritime Archaeology* 4–6. On the HSA see further Jeffrey *supra* note 3, at p 1.

Approximately 7,500 shipwrecks were protected by the HSA in Australian waters, which includes the TS with the incorporated State coastal waters, and out to the edge of the CS and EEZ. Importantly, the HSA also protected relics recovered from historic shipwrecks, including those recovered prior to the Act coming into force. Since many relics had been recovered and not reported to the Receiver of Wreck they were not held legally, and those in possession did not have legal title as the relics vested either in the original owner or the Commonwealth, in accordance with the NA 1912 or by way of treaty.[19] As such, the HSA could govern the possession of these relics even though they had been acquired prior to the Act coming into force. That said, concerns did exist as to whether salvage rights granted in the NA 1912, or some other residual proprietary right, might vest with those who had recovered relics. The HSA therefore included a provision giving effect to the Commonwealth Constitution[20] providing for compensation on just terms for the acquisition of proprietary rights.[21] In any event, regardless of title, the associated relics of a protected wreck site were subject to the HSA and its regulatory requirements.

That said, relics recovered from historic shipwrecks since the 1950s were in private possession and being traded despite questions of title, and often on the erroneous assumption that title was indeed being passed by way of sale. The HSA addressed this by requiring possessors to report their possession of relics and to obtain a permit to transfer possession to another.[22] Many of those in possession of relics recovered prior to the HSA coming into force were nevertheless reluctant to report their possession, fearing prosecution or the loss of the relic. In 1993, to coincide with the 75-year blanket protection regime coming into force, an amnesty was granted allowing the reporting of possession without enforcement of the Act – approximately 20,000 previously unrecorded relics were declared.[23]

The day-to-day management of historic shipwrecks in accordance with the HSA was by way of a cooperative arrangement between the Commonwealth

19 This including not only the 1972 ANCODS Agreement but others regarding specific wrecks such as that between United Kingdom and Australia with respect to sovereign vessels such as HMS *Sirius* (1790) and HMS *Pandora* (1791). A. Viduka and G. Luckman, 'The management of protected underwater cultural heritage artefacts in public and private custody in Australia' in S. Thomas, B. Pitblado, B, Schroeder and M. Rowe, *Advances in Archaeological Practice* special (2022, in review).

20 Commonwealth of Australia Constitution, clause 51 (XXXI).

21 HSA S.21.

22 HSA ss. 9 and 13.

23 J. Rodrigues, 'An Amnesty Assessed. Human Impact on Shipwreck Sites; the Australian Case' (2009) 38 *International Journal of Nautical Archaeology* 153–162.

and the States and Territories; a feature of all maritime activities in Australia as reflected in agreements such as the Offshore Constitutional Settlement. This permitted Commonwealth delegation of powers to individual States and the Northern Territory. The resulting 'Historic Shipwreck Program' facilitated a national collaborative approach to the management of Australia's shipwrecks and associated artefacts, coordinated and led by the Commonwealth.

In 2009, the HSA was reviewed, in part to address concerns and gaps in the legislative regime and the Historic Shipwreck Program and to consider the possible ratification and implementation of the 2001 UNESCO Convention for the Protection of the Underwater Cultural Heritage (2001 Convention).[24] The review led both to a decision to consider ratification of the 2001 Convention and the legislative changes that would be needed to implement it, and also in 2010 to a new collaborative regime between the Commonwealth and the States and the Northern Territory for the implementation of the HSA, namely the Australian Underwater Cultural Heritage Intergovernmental Agreement.[25] This Agreement codified the practices and processes for administering Australia's UCH that had been in use for over 20 years and committed all States and the Territories to amend their legislation to meet the requirements of the 2001 Convention.

In light of the 2009 review, the Underwater Cultural Heritage Act 2018 (Cth)[26] (UCH Act) was adopted, repealing the HSA and enabling Australia to actively consider ratification of the 2001 Convention.[27]

---

24 2562 UNTS 1. The HSA had previously been reviewed in 1990 and 2001, leading to amendments including the 1993 75-year blanket protection regime. See F.J. Kendall, *An assessment of the effectiveness of existing legislative arrangements for protecting and preserving Australia's Underwater Cultural Heritage*. Unpublished report. Department for Environment and Heritage. Canberra, 1990; B. Jeffery and V. Moran, 'The foundering of the National Historic Shipwrecks Program' (2001) 25 *Bulletin of the Australasian Institute for Maritime Archaeology* 121–127.

25 AUCH IGA, 2010, Australian Underwater Cultural Heritage Intergovernmental Agreement, <https://www.environment.gov.au/heritage/publications/agreements/underwater-cultural.html>.

26 Act no. 85, 2018 in force on 1 July 2019.

27 The Underwater Cultural Heritage (Consequential and Transitional Provisions) Act 2018 ensured that declarations, permits, databases and other regulatory features of the HSA would continue as if these had been regulated by the UCH Act. For an overview of the UCH Act see A. Alpin, 'The Underwater Cultural Heritage Protection Act: charting a New Course for Cultural Heritage Management in Australia? (2019) 21 *Journal of Art Crime* 37 and G. J. Dwyer, 'Ship shape or all at sea? A preliminary assessment of Australia's recent legislative reforms concerning underwater cultural heritage' (2019) 32 *Australian and New Zealand Maritime Law Journal* 71.

5 The Underwater Cultural Heritage Act 2018

The UCH Act has three objectives. The first is 'to provide for the identification, protection and conservation of Australia's underwater cultural heritage'.[28] The improved regime includes key features such as: prohibiting impacts on UCH without a permit; providing for the declaration of protected zones around UCH to regulate activities undertaken in the zone; enabling the gathering of information on the location of UCH including recovered artefacts and giving directions in relation to their possession and care; establishing a register of UCH; regulating the trade, possession, import and export of protected UCH; and protecting Australia's UCH in waters outside Australia from actions by Australians.

The second objective is 'to enable the cooperative implementation of national and international maritime heritage responsibilities'.[29] This addresses the need for a cooperative regime in the Australian federal system that allocates jurisdiction and responsibilities between the different States, Territories and the Commonwealth itself, as set out in the 2010 Intergovernmental Agreement. Indeed, the UCH Act was drafted to be consistent with the 2010 Intergovernmental Agreement and to broadly align with the 2001 Convention facilitating Australia's potential ratification.

The third objective is 'to promote public awareness, understanding, appreciation and appropriate use of Australia's underwater cultural heritage'.[30] This reflects a key element of Australia's UCH management; to balance appropriate public engagement and site access with site management and protection outcomes.

5.1 *Defining Underwater Cultural Heritage*

The definition of UCH in the Act is almost identical to that set out in the 2001 Convention, but it functions differently.[31] The Act defines UCH in general terms, and later goes on to specify what aspects of that UCH are protected. As such, the most important difference in the definitions is that the Act makes no reference to a limiting period of 100 years. Instead, the Act addresses a subset of that UCH which is automatically protected[32] and that which may be declared to be protected.[33] Before turning to these subsets of UCH, the other difference

28 UCH Act s.3(a).
29 UCH Act s.3(b).
30 UCH Act s.3(c).
31 UCH Act s.15(1).
32 UCH Act s.16.
33 UCH Act s.17.

in the definitions is that the Act includes 'animal remains' but makes no reference to 'objects of prehistoric character'. Nothing much turns on this as the inclusion of the latter in the 2001 Convention appears to 'simply make it absolutely clear that an object dating from prehistoric times can qualify as a 'trace of human existence''.[34]

Section 16 of the UCH Act automatically protects all remains of vessels and aircraft that have been underwater for 75 years.[35] It thus provides a more stringent protective regime than the 2001 Convention and, importantly, it covers all UCH from World War II.[36] It also covers 'every article that is associated with' a vessel[37] or aircraft or the remains of a vessel or aircraft.[38] The UCH Act addresses the inclusion of articles in some detail, taking pains to ensure that no gap is left in the application of its protective regime. So, for example, the UCH Act specifies that an article is 'associated with' a vessel, aircraft, or other vehicle if it:

a. appears to have formed part of the vessel, aircraft or other vehicle; or
b. appears to have been installed or carried on the vessel, aircraft or other vehicle; or
c. is remains of humans or animals that appear to have been on board the vessel, aircraft or other vehicle; or
d. appears to have been constructed or used by a person associated with a vessel.[39]

Importantly, this covers cargo carried on a vessel or in an aircraft, which is addressed in the definition of UCH in the 2001 Convention, but not explicitly in the general definition of UCH as set out in the UCH Act. This ensures that

---

34 S. Dromgoole, *Underwater Cultural Heritage and International Law* (Cambridge University Press, 2013) 88.

35 The Act uses the term 'in waters' which includes the UCH (a) being in, or forming part of, the seabed or the subsoil of the seabed, beneath those waters; or (b) being on, or forming part of, a reef in those waters. UCH Act s.9(1).

36 This is particularly important with respect to the protection of HMAS *Sydney*, as well as the other important World War II wrecks in Australian waters such as the AHS *Centaur*, USS *Lexington*, USS *Neosho*, USS *Simms*, HSK *Kormoran*, SS *Macumba* and SS *Florence*, the submarines *I-124* and *M-24* as well as a number of aircraft: Catalina A24-24, and A24-25.

37 A vessel means any kind of vessel used in navigation by water, however propelled or moved, including the following: (a) a barge, lighter or other floating craft; (b) an aircushion vehicle, or other similar craft, used wholly or primarily in navigation by water: UCH Act s. 9(1).

38 UCH Act s.16(1)(b) and (d). A reference in the UCH Act to (a) the remains of a vessel; or (b) the remains of an aircraft; or (c) an article; includes a reference to part of the remains or article: UCH Act s. 9(2).

39 UCH Act s.10(1).

in substance, the effect is the same as that in the 2001 Convention. This definition also includes an article that appears to have been constructed or used by a person associated with a vessel and allows for the protection of secondary heritage sites such as shipwreck survivor or salvage camps that are associated with the primary protected UCH site.[40]

In case this is not sufficiently comprehensive, the UCH Act then provides, in a somewhat convoluted way, that a:

> ... thing is not to be taken to not be an article for the purposes of this Act only because it is attached to: (a) the remains of a vessel; or (b) the remains of an aircraft; or (c) a reef; or (d) the seabed: or (e) the subsoil of the seabed.[41]

In part, this caution is a response to gaps that were evident in the HSA and because the UCH Act addresses in some detail recovered UCH, some of which may be in private ownership, but still within the remit of the Act.[42] As such, an article is associated with a vessel, aircraft or other vehicle even if the article has been wholly or substantially incorporated into another object or thing.[43] Finally, and importantly, vessels, aircraft and associated artefacts underwater for more than 75 years are protected 'whether or not the existence or location of the article is known'.[44]

Vessels, aircraft, and associated artefacts are thus a subset of UCH as defined in the Act, but which is included in the category of 'protected underwater cultural heritage'. Section 17 then addresses other UCH that may be declared to be protected. There are really two categories covered here: vessels, aircraft or associated artefacts that have not been underwater for more than 75 years: and all other UCH covered in the general definition. For these to be 'protected UCH', the Minister must be satisfied that each has heritage significance.[45] The criteria to be used to assess the heritage significance of this UCH are set out in the

---

40 These are particularly noticeable in the Old Dutch Shipwrecks where the survivors' sites were usually found before the wreck site itself. See Henderson *supra* note 7, at pp. 80–99.

41 UCH Act s.9(3).

42 UCH Act s.16(3) This covers, for example, coins that might have been combined with contemporary materials to make jewellery, or ships fittings incorporated into furniture. See further section 5.7.

43 UCH Act s.10(2).

44 UCH Act s.16(2). Note that here the term 'article' includes a vessel or aircraft itself as well as articles associated with the vessel or aircraft.

45 UCH Act s.17(1).

Underwater Cultural Heritage Rules 2018.[46] Having these rules in subordinate legislation allows for flexibility in amending them to reflect contemporary values. That said, the criteria are in themselves flexible given their very general scope. Section 5 of the UCH Rules merely requires the Minister to consider the significance of the particular UCH in question, taking into matters such as its place in Australian history or its association with a community in contemporary Australia.

5.2 *Jurisdiction*

The protection of UCH in Australia is complicated by the federal nature of the Australian Constitution. Reflecting this division of powers, the UCH Act defines 'coastal waters' as the waters, seabed and subsoil of a State or Territory that are within 3nm of the baseline of the TS and landward of the TS baseline.[47] 'Commonwealth waters' is the TS beyond the 3nm coastal waters as well as the waters above the CS (including the EEZ and Contiguous Zone (CZ)), as well as the relevant seabed and subsoil.[48] Finally, 'Australian waters' are those over which the Commonwealth has the widest jurisdictional mandate, extending from the TS baseline out to sea to include the TS and the sea above the CS (including the EEZ and CZ), as well as the seabed and subsoil.[49]

These jurisdictional arrangements in the UCH Act stem from the 1979 Offshore Constitutional Settlement (discussed above in section 3) and reconfirmed in the 2010 Intergovernmental Agreement. A consequence of this and the existing constitutional structure is that the UCH Act has a split jurisdictional arrangement, with shipwrecks protected from the TS baseline, designated at the Lowest Astronomical Tide, out to the end of the CS, while other UCH, including aircraft, are only regulated by the UCH Act beyond the 3nm limit of coastal waters out to the end of the CS.[50] State and Northern Territory legislation provides protection for those waters not covered by the UCH Act.

5.3 *Protected UCH*

In summary, as we have seen, protected UCH includes vessels that have been underwater in Australian waters for at least 75 years and those that have been

---

46 By reference UCH Act s.22.

47 UCH Act s.12.

48 UCH Act s.13.

49 UCH Act s.11(1).

50 The UCH Act makes provisions for agreement between the Commonwealth and the relevant State or Territory when the UCH lies partly in one jurisdictional zone and another, or which has been recovered from one jurisdictional zone but left in another: UCH Act ss.11(2)–(3) and 13(2)–(4).

underwater for less than 75 years but determined to have heritage significance;[51] aircraft that have been underwater in Commonwealth waters for at least 75 years and those that have been underwater for less than 75 years but determined to have heritage significance;[52] and any other UCH having heritage significance in Commonwealth waters.[53] In addition, articles associated with a vessel or aircraft are also protected UCH if the article has been underwater for at least 75 years or been individually declared.[54] This also applies to articles that might have been lost from a vessel or aircraft that did not sink.[55] Section 19 of the UCH Act provides for provisional declaration of protected UCH for up to five years in circumstances where it may have heritage significance but further investigation is necessary,[56] which will continue even if the UCH is actually recovered.[57]

The UCH Act also allows the Minister to declare UCH that lies outside of Australian waters (beyond the CS) to be protected UCH, even if it is subsequently moved.[58] While this might apply to UCH that lies in the Area, it may also apply to UCH that lies on some other State's CS or within another State's CZ or even TS. This raises significant jurisdictional sensitivities, as does Australia's jurisdiction with respect to UCH in the CZ, CS and EEZ, which domestically is a continuation of jurisdiction under the HSA. The Explanatory Memorandum declares that such a declaration 'would only be made after consultation with the Government of the nearest coastal state'.[59] Similar provisions in the Environment Protection and Biodiversity Conservation Act 1999 (Cth) have recognised the declaration of Anzac Cove in Turkey/Türkiye and the Kokoda Track in Papua New Guinea as overseas places of historic significance to Australia.[60] Such designations do not, however, allow Australia to regulate these sites in any way and the relevant provisions only apply to Australian citizens, Australian corporate entities and Australian registered vessels. While it is not likely that this provision will be often used, possible candidates for such a

---

51 UCH Act ss. 16(1)(a) and 17. See section 5.1.

52 UCH Act ss. 16 and 17.

53 UCH Act s.17.

54 UCH s16(1)(b) & (d) and 3. See further section 5.7.

55 For example, anchors or cannon thrown overboard to lighten a ship, such as the anchor from *Endeavour* abandoned by Captain Janes Cook after the ship had stranded on the Great Barrier Reef in 1770. See National Museum of Australia <https://www.nma.gov.au/learn/kspace/endeavour-river-1770/teacher-resources/primary-source-study>.

56 UCH Act s.19.

57 UCH Act s.19(2).

58 UCH Act s.18(1).

59 Explanatory Memorandum, Underwater Cultural Heritage Bill 2018 (Cth) and Underwater Cultural Heritage (Consequential and Transitional Provisions) Bill 2018 (Cth), 6.

60 Environment Protection and Biodiversity Conservation Act 1999 (Cth), Ch 5A, Prt 15A.

declaration include HMAS *Perth* (1942) in Indonesian waters, HMAS *AE1* (1914) in the waters of Papua New Guinea and HMAS *AE2* (1915) in Turkish waters.

5.4 *Extent of Australian Jurisdiction*

While the UCH Act extends to 'acts, omission, matters and things outside Australia',[61] the extent of that jurisdiction differs in the different maritime zones. In relation to the regulation of activities involving UCH in the TS, the UCH Act applies to all persons and vessels, including those that are foreign.[62] A lesser jurisdiction applies in the CZ in that foreign persons or foreign vessels are not subject to all provisions; while these foreign persons and vessels are subject to the prohibition of conduct having an adverse impact on protected UCH without a permit in the CZ,[63] they are not subject to other prohibited activities, such as the possession of UCH without a permit in that zone.[64] This reflects the generally understood jurisdictional limits of States as reflected in the United Nations Convention on the Law of the Sea 1982 (LOSC).[65] As such, beyond the CZ the UCH Act only regulates activities of Australian citizens, corporate entities, and registered ships.[66]

Importantly, this jurisdictional arrangement is subject to international law and international agreements that Australia has entered into.[67] This might include the 2001 Convention and any agreement entered into by Australia in accordance with the 2001 Convention by which Australia is a coordinating State for the protection of UCH on the CS of Australia or in the Area (or possibly some other State's CS where Australia has an interest in the relevant UCH and the coastal State has requested that Australia act as coordinating State, and Australia has agreed to that request).

5.5 *Discovery of UCH*

Always a problematic provision to administer, the notification of discovery of UCH (whether the site of a vessel, aircraft, or artefact) is vitally important to the effective administration of the UCH Act. Section 40 of the UCH Act requires a person who finds an article of UCH in Australian waters that appears to be

61 UCH Act s.7(1).
62 UCH Act s.7(3).
63 UCH Act s.7(4).
64 UCH Act s.31.
65 1833 UNTS 397.
66 UCH Act s. 7(6).
67 UCH Act s.7(5).

of archaeological character to provide the Minister with written notice of the discovery within 21 days of the find. It is an offence to fail to do so.[68]

5.6 *Protection in Situ and Permits*

The primary focus of the UCH Act is to protect UCH *in situ*. The largest threat to such heritage occurs along the coastal margin, where development and human activity is at its greatest. The UCH Act thus operates a permit application system for specified conduct in relation to UCH. Part 3 of the UCH Act deals with the regulation of protected UCH and covers: issuing permits, permits subject to conditions, varying permits, suspending, or revoking permits and transferring permits.[69] All permit holders contravene the UCH Act if they act inconsistently with permit conditions and are required to produce their permit at the request of an Inspector.[70]

At the heart of the protection regime then is the prohibition, without a permit, of any conduct that 'has, will have or is likely to have an adverse impact' on protected UCH.[71] Conduct having an 'adverse impact' on protected UCH is defined as conduct that:

a. directly or indirectly physically disturbs or otherwise damages the protected underwater cultural heritage; or
b. causes the removal of the protected underwater cultural heritage from waters or from its archaeological context.[72]

Importantly, this conduct is not simply that 'directed at' UCH,[73] but also conduct that might 'incidentally affect' UCH, such as dredging or resource extraction.[74] This regime also ensures that while protected UCH *in situ* may be visited and dived on, it cannot physically be disturbed.

The UCH Act also provides the Minister with the power to declare an area containing protected UCH to be a protected zone within which certain activities are prohibited without a permit.[75] A protected zone may be established, for instance, when the UCH in question is of particular national or international significance, is rare or is subject to an international treaty or agreement; where

68 UCH Act s.40(5)–(6).
69 UCH Act ss 23–27.
70 UCH Act ss. 28 and 37.
71 UCH Act s.30(1).
72 UCH Act s.30(2).
73 2001 Convention Art. 1(6).
74 Explanatory Memorandum, Underwater Cultural Heritage Bill 2018 (Cth) and Underwater Cultural Heritage (Consequential and Transitional Provisions) Bill 2018 (Cth), 28.
75 UCH Act ss. 20(1) and 29. The Minister also has the power, by legislative instrument, to vary or revoke a protected zone declaration: UCH Act s.21.

the UCH is environmentally, socially or archaeologically sensitive; or where the UCH is under threat of interference, damage, destruction or removal. It might also be that the UCH poses a danger to the public; where there is a need to ensure effective monitoring of the UCH in remote locations or where there is a need to improve management of the UCH and its surrounding environment, which may be subject to impacts from visitation or development activity.[76] The protected zone may vary in size and in terms of the prohibited activities, allowing it to be tailored to each specific site.[77] A larger area might be declared where a site lies in deep-water and has an extensive debris field on the sea floor, or where it is far offshore and there is a need for a large-scale surveillance capability. Examples of activities that might be prohibited or regulated in the protected zone are stated in the UCH Act and include the entry or movement of persons or vessels; trawling or fishing; conducting underwater activity; the anchoring or mooring of vessels; and the release or deposit of objects or materials in the zone.[78] It is an offence then to engage in such conduct unless a permit to do so has been obtained.[79]

To contextualise this, protected zones have been established around only 28 of the approximately 7,500 known shipwrecks.[80] Different conditions apply in each protected zone depending on the reasons for its declaration, as does the size of each. By way of example, a protected zone of 800 metre radius has been established around the wreck of the Australian Hospital Ship *Centaur* (sunk in 1943) as it is of particular significance to Australia and environmentally, socially and archaeologically sensitive. Within this zone, stationary vessels, underwater activities within 200 metres of the seabed and the release or deposit of objects or materials are all prohibited without a permit.

5.7 *Recovered UCH*

Protected UCH is not only that *in situ*, but also that which has been recovered. Indeed, an important objective of the UCH Act is to regulate the way recovered artefacts are dealt with, including those recovered before any legislative protective regime was established.[81] The new legislation thus protects the property rights of individuals, better regulates the trade of legally notified UCH, and

---

76 UCH Act s.20(3).

77 A Guide to the Protected Zones Declared Under the Underwater Cultural Heritage Act <https://www.environment.gov.au/heritage/underwater-heritage/protected-zones>.

78 UCH Act s.20(7).

79 UCH Act s.29(1)–(2).

80 Underwater Cultural Heritage Act 2018 (Protected Zones) Declaration Instrument 2019.

81 For a full account of the development of the management regime for artefacts, see Viduka and Luckman, *supra* note 19.

prohibits any trade of protected UCH that is not legally notified or recovered after the UCH came into force.

The UCH Act continues in a modified form the existing regime that applied to recovered UCH – referred to as 'relics' in the HSA but as 'articles' in the new Act. There are approximately 500,000 recovered UCH artefacts in Australia, of which about one-tenth are in private possession, custody, and control by permit. As discussed earlier, few of the private individuals in possession of recovered UCH acquired ownership at the time of the recovery given the terms of the NA 1912. There may, however, be exceptions and indeed, the UCH Rules recognise and require that the ownership of protected UCH, if known, must be specified in any permit authorising possession, custody, or control, and for other permit purposes such as import and export.[82] While some might have acquired ownership from the original owners, or in lieu of a salvage award, most will have dubious bases for ownership. Nevertheless, the UCH Act applies irrespective of ownership and at times treats those in possession as if they had acquired ownership. The intent is to regulate possession rather than to take possession or to address the issue of ownership. Thus, the permit system established in the HSA has been transposed and updated in the UCH Act.[83]

The UCH Act prohibits a person from having possession, custody, or control of protected UCH without a permit.[84] Since a permit would have been required to recover protected UCH,[85] a permit to possess recovered UCH would have been acquired at the same time for recoveries after the Act came into force. The permit requirement though is relevant not only to protected UCH that had been recovered after the Act came into force, but to all protected UCH, including that recovered prior to both the UCH Act and the HSA coming into force, as well as any earlier legislative regime. This arises because protected UCH is defined to include 'every article that is associated with a vessel (or aircraft) or the remains of such, that has been in Australian waters for at least 75 years'.[86]

The permit to possess protected UCH must identify the UCH in possession[87] and have a description that is sufficient to allow it to be so identified.[88] It must also identify the possessor, whether persons generally, a class of persons or an

82 UCH Rules s.7(2)(c).
83 Underwater Cultural Heritage (Consequential and Transitional Provisions) Act 2018 (Cth) s.6.
84 UCH Act s.31.
85 UCH Act s.30.
86 UCH Act s.16(1).
87 UCH Act s.23(5)(a).
88 UCH Rules s.7(2)(b).

individual,[89] the period the permit is to be in force and any specific conditions imposed.[90] Importantly, the permit must have a unique registration number in the Australasian Underwater Cultural Heritage Database.[91]

The UCH Act recognises not only that private individuals may possess protected UCH, but that there is a market for these articles. Rather than address the complex issue of ownership, the UCH Act seeks to authorise and record all such transactions, thus giving at least an appearance of recognising some form of proprietary interest in the protected UCH by those in possession. The UCH Act thus allows, by permit, the supply by way of sale, exchange, gift, lease, hire or hire-purchase of protected UCH, or for dealers to offer to supply such protected UCH.[92] Where a permit allows the sale of the relevant UCH, the permit number must be included in any advertisement for the sale.[93] When sold, if the permit is transferable it should be transferred to the purchaser; in all cases the seller is required to inform the Department of the transfer within 14 days.[94] It is an offence to fail to produce a permit when required to do so by an Inspector.[95] The UCH Act does enable the Minister to direct a person who has UCH in their possession, custody or control to deliver it into the custody of another specified person.[96]

The regulation of possession of protected UCH also extends to its import and export.[97] The trade in cultural heritage is subject to the Protection of Movable Cultural Heritage Act 1986 (Cth) (PMCHA) which was adopted to give effect to Australia's obligations as a party to the 1970 UNESCO Convention.[98] Included in the list of archaeological objects subject to the PMCHA are 'objects relating to seagoing exploration, transportation, supply and commerce, including ordnance, coins, ship's gear, anchors, cargo and personal items from shipwrecks, sunken ships and landfalls, ships' logbooks and other documentation'.[99] The permit required for import or export under the UCH Act requires the Minister to take into account the 'relevant government guidelines relating to the

89 UCH Act s.23(5)(b).

90 UCH Act ss.23(5)(e) and 24. Permit conditions may be varied when appropriate: UCH Act s.25 and UCH Rules s.8.

91 UCH Act s.23(5)(f) and UCH Rules s.7(2)(a).

92 UCH Act s.32(1)–(2).

93 UCH Act s.33(1)–(2).

94 UCH Act ss.24(2)(a) and 27. Some permits, such as a site permit, are not transferrable.

95 UCH Act s.37.

96 UCH Act s.39.

97 UCH Act ss. 34(1)–(2) and 35(1)–(2).

98 1970 UNESCO Convention on the Means of Prohibiting and Preventing the Illicit Import, Export and Transfer of Ownership of Cultural Property, adopted on 14 November 1970, entered into force 24 April 1972, 823 UNTS 231.

99 Protection of Moveable Cultural Heritage Regulations 2018 (Cth) Sch 1, Pt 2.2(a).

importation or exportation of protected underwater cultural heritage, as in force from time to time',[100] as well as 'obligations under any relevant international conventions, agreements or treaties, as in force from time to time'.[101] While these are considerations the Minister must have regard to, the PMCHA is not made inapplicable to UCH and needs to be complied with separately.

The UCH Act recognises the need for the Department to be able to identify who might have possession of UCH, including that which may have been recovered some time ago. It thus grants the Minister power to communicate with those thought to have, or have had, possession, custody or control of protected UCH to ascertain its provenance in terms of possession.[102] Furthermore, the Minister is also empowered to give directions to the person in possession or custody of the protected UCH, such as taking steps to preserve the UCH; placing the UCH with a collection of articles that has been, or is to be, established; or exhibiting, or providing access to, the UCH.[103] This enables the Department to ensure that artefacts from one site that have been dispersed can be brought back together for study or exhibition. In this way, protected UCH is allowed to circulate whilst maintaining a record of all transactions and its actual physical location.

Given Australia's experience with the *Tek Sing* (1822) cargo,[104] the UCH Act also includes a provision that makes it an offence to import into the country any foreign UCH without a permit.[105] 'Foreign underwater cultural heritage' is defined as:

> … an article that has been removed from waters and, at the time the article was removed from waters, the article: (a) had been in waters for at least 100 years; and (b) was underwater cultural heritage of a foreign country.[106]

100 UCH Rules s.6(b).
101 UCH Rules s.6(d)(iii).
102 UCH Act s.38.
103 UCH Act s.39.
104 The *Tek Sing* was an early nineteenth century Chinese trading vessel wrecked in Indonesian waters, and whose cargo of ceramics was salvaged without Indonesian permits. Between 1999 and 2000, 47 containers of the salvaged ceramics were shipped through Adelaide, Australia. By the time the PMCHA could be activated, all but one had left Australia. The remaining container was seized and returned to Indonesia.
105 UCH Act s.36.
106 UCH Act s.9(1).

The reference to the 100-year period is clearly in anticipation of the 2001 Convention being widely ratified and governing the international threshold for the recognition of UCH. This requirement for an import permit is in addition to the obligations contained in the PMCHA that require any import of a protected object from a foreign State not to be illegal in terms of that foreign State's laws.[107]

The Underwater Cultural Heritage Rules 2018 (Cth) set out in some detail the matters the Minister must have regard to when considering applications.[108] This includes whether the person applying for a permit is fit and proper to engage in the conduct proposed to be authorised,[109] with specific consideration given to whether they have been convicted of a previous offence related to cultural heritage.[110] If the permit is for conduct that will have or is likely to have an adverse impact on protected UCH (such as excavation and/or recovery of UCH), the import or export of protected UCH, or the possession of such UCH, the Minister is required to consider whether that conduct is consistent with the objectives of the Act; relevant government guidelines relating to the protection or management of Australia's UCH; and the Annex to the 2001 Convention.[111] Consideration is also to be given to whether appropriate consultation has been undertaken with relevant stakeholders relating to shared heritage interests; issues of ownership or sovereignty; and obligations under any relevant international conventions, agreements or treaties, as in force.[112]

The enforcement of the provision relating to possession and trade of protected UCH is by way of both criminal and civil penalty provisions.[113] Importantly, the UCH associated with the commission of any offence or resulting in a civil penalty order may, by court order, be forfeited[114] and either sold or otherwise dealt with as the Minister thinks fit.[115] This means that protected UCH not yet notified to the Department is liable for forfeiture. Current Departmental policy is to seek forfeiture of relevant UCH when prosecutions for breaches of

107 PMCHA s.14.

108 UCH Act s.23(4) provides for the rules to regulate applications.

109 UCH Rules s.6(2).

110 UCH Rules s.6(3). These convictions include those for breaches of the UCH Act, the HSA, the PMCHA or the Customs Act 1901, similar cultural heritage laws of a State or Territory or a law of a foreign State that relates to UCH.

111 UCH Rules s.6(4)(a)–(c).

112 UCH Rules s.6(4)(d).

113 See further below.

114 UCH Act s.47.

115 UCH Act 47(3).

the UCH Act are successful. However, un-registered protected UCH continues to come to light, especially when it comes into the hands of descendants of original possessors who may not have been aware of its original recovery. In these circumstances, Departmental policy is to proceed on a case-by-case basis taking mitigating circumstances into account. Such a case, for example, may merely lead to the registration of the protected UCH rather than any enforcement for a strict liability offence.[116] However, it may be that on ratification of the 2001 Convention and its coming into force for Australia, all unregistered protected UCH will thereafter be forfeited.

5.8 *Ownership and Sovereignty*

While the UCH Act focuses on management, there are three provisions that specifically deal with issues of ownership and sovereignty. The first touches on the issue of Dutch shipwrecks and associated articles and essentially confirms the existing arrangements made in the ANCODS Agreement.[117] Specifically, it confirms the agreement with respect to the transfer of all rights, titles and interests relating to the *Batavia, Vergulde Draack* (*Draeck*), *Zuiddorp* (*Zuytdorp*) and *Zeewyjk* to Australia.[118]

The second addresses other UCH. The Commonwealth is entitled to all unclaimed wreck in the Territorial Sea or internal waters[119] and may conclude an agreement with a foreign State (other than the Netherlands) with respect to the ownership of a shipwreck, aircraft, or some other UCH. It may also be that to give effect to the UCH Act, ownership of UCH needs to be vested in some governmental entity, either State, Territory or Commonwealth. In all these circumstances, the Minister may, by legislative instrument, declare ownership to be vested in the relevant entity.[120] While ownership might also be vested in any specified person, this will only arise when it is necessary to give effect to the UCH Act. This could arise in cases where, for example, a charity, private museum or some other community group may be vested with ownership in order to protect and manage the relevant UCH. The UCH Act also contains a safeguard should a declaration by the Minister that vests ownership of UCH

116 The UCH Act s.31(5) provides for an offence of strict liability with a penalty of 60 penalty units (Aus$13,320). The value of a penalty unit is prescribed by the Crimes Act 1914 and is currently Aus$222 for offences committed on or after 1 July 2020.

117 UCH Act s.50.

118 UCH Act s.14.

119 NA 2012 s. 228. On the constitutional framework that underpins this, see D.J. Cremean, 'Ownership of unclaimed wreck' (2018) 92 *Australian Law Journal* 667.

120 UCH Act s.51.

in an entity be subsequently found to have impacted an existing ownership right in that UCH. Section 53 provides that compensation be payable when this amounts to an acquisition of property other than on just terms, the amount of which may be determined by the Federal Court of Australia or the Supreme Court of a State or Territory.

The third provision that touches on ownership addresses the sensitive issue of sovereign vessels; and does so out of an abundance of caution. Whilst it is arguable that customary international law recognises the continued ownership and sovereign immunity of sovereign non-commercial vessels, especially warships,[121] the unauthorised salvage of HMAS *Perth*, and the discovery of HMAS *AE1*, have prompted an express assertion of Australia's ownership and sovereign immunity in such vessels when they lie in waters outside the outer limits of Australian waters.[122] The UCH Act also codifies the customary international law exceptions to this continued ownership and sovereign immunity, being either an express relinquishment of rights or the capture and surrender to a foreign State before the vessel sank.[123]

5.9 *The Australasian Underwater Cultural Heritage Database*

The Commonwealth Department of Climate Change, Energy, the Environment, and Water is currently responsible for administering the UCH Act, which protects approximately 8,000 known historic shipwrecks and submerged aircraft in Australian waters and approximately 500,000 associated artefacts. The UCH Act requires the Minister to establish and maintain a register for the purposes of the Act.[124] The pre-existing Australian National Shipwreck Database (ANSDB) had evolved over the decades from a number of different States' paper-based regimes into a limited database with 53 fields of information. Largely maintained by the Western Australian Museum from 1983 to the late 1990s, it was transferred to the Commonwealth where it was modernised and modified by

121 See C. Forrest, *Maritime Legacies and the Law* (Edward Elgar, 2019) 237–271; N. Ronzitti, 'The Legal regime of Wrecks of Warships and Other State-Owned Ships in International Law' (2015) 76 *Yearbook of the Institute of International Law* 267; M. Williams, 'War graves and Salvage: Murky Waters?' (2000) 5 *International Journal of Maritime Law* 151. S. Dromgoole, 'Military Remains on and around the Coast of the United Kingdom' (1996) 2 *International Journal of Marine and Coastal Law* 23.

122 UCH Act s.52(1).

123 UCH Act s.52(2).

124 UCH Act 4.48(1).

2009 with significantly expanded capabilities that links sites, artefacts, notifications, permits, and client records.[125] The ANSDB is not merely a repository of information, but a portal through which many statutory obligations occur, such as permit applications, notifications and reporting obligations. In 2018, in line with the introduction of the UCH Act, the database's name changed to the Australasian Underwater Cultural Heritage Database (AUCHD).[126]

5.10 *Compliance and Enforcement Provisions*

The UCH Act aligns compliance and enforcement with the general Commonwealth framework adopted in the Regulatory Powers (Standard Provisions) Act 2014 as well as the Maritime Powers Act 2013. With reference to, and incorporating the terms of these Acts, the UCH Act addresses monitoring, investigation powers, general criminal offences, strict liability offences, civil penalties provisions; infringement notices, enforceable undertakings and injunctions.[127] Taken together, this enables the Commonwealth to act in a range of ways in response to activities regulated by the Act.

An important enforcement provision is the power of courts to order the forfeiture of any vessel, equipment or articles used or otherwise involved in the commission of an offence governed by the UCH Act.[128] This includes any protected UCH actually recovered. The forfeiture of valuable property, especially a vessel, acts as a significant deterrent to those who may be tempted to interfere with protected UCH.

The UCH Act provides for three different levels of penalties for breaches of specific provisions. The first and lowest level provides for the breach to constitute a criminal offence of strict liability.[129] This obviates the need to prove that the accused either intended, or was aware of, the fact that their conduct was prohibited. As such:

> ... strict liability is used in circumstances where there is public interest in ensuring that regulatory schemes are observed, and it can reasonably be expected that the person was aware of their duties and obligations.[130]

125 G. Luckman and A. Viduka, 'The Australian National Shipwreck Database' (2013) 37 *Bulletin of the Australasian Institute for Maritime Archaeology* 76–86.

126 AUCH Database 2021, Australian Government Australasian Underwater Cultural Heritage Database <https://www.dcceew.gov.au/parks-heritage/heritage/underwater-heritage/auchd >.

127 UCH Act s.46.

128 UCH Act ss.41–47.

129 Strict liability offences apply for breaches of UCH Act ss.27–39.

130 Explanatory Memorandum, Underwater Cultural Heritage Bill 2018 (Cth) and Underwater Cultural Heritage (Consequential and Transitional Provisions) Bill 2018 (Cth), 8.

The second level provides for a civil penalty, which imposes a financial penalty without raising the conduct to a criminal level.[131] It requires the lower civil burden of proof of finding the prohibited conduct to have occurred only be on the balance of probabilities, rather than beyond reasonable doubt.[132] The third and highest level is a criminal offence in which the accused's *actus reus* and *mens rea* must be proved beyond reasonable doubt, for which a custodial sentence may be imposed.[133] The most serious offences are for breaches of the provisions relating to conduct in a prohibited zone, conduct having an adverse impact on protected UCH, possession, custody or control of protected UCH or export of protected UCH, for which a term of imprisonment for five years or fine ranging from 330 penalty units (Aus$99,000) to the maximum of 800 penalty units (Aus$264,000) may be imposed.[134]

5.11 *Delegation of Power*

The UCH Act continues the collaborative administration of the legislation between the Commonwealth and the States and the Northern Territory that had been initiated in 1983 as the Historic Shipwrecks Program (noting the Delegation for Norfolk Island Territory was revoked subsequent to administrative changes from 1 July 2017). Now called the Australian Underwater Cultural Heritage Program (AUCHP) it is underpinned by the delegation of powers by the Minister to the senior heritage official responsible for similar legislation in each State and the Northern Territory.[135] Funding for the AUCHP comes from within Departmental resources and is allocated directly to the States and the Northern Territory through a multi-year funding arrangement to partially cover costs associated with their undertaking delegated activities. With the support of the Minister's delegates, other funding from the AUCHP is provided to the Norfolk Island Museum and the Australasian Institute for Maritime Archaeology to educate and engage with the public in line with the objectives of the UCH Act.

5.12 *Appointment of Authorised Officers*

To facilitate compliance activities, the Department can train and authorise Commonwealth, State and Northern Territory officers as Inspectors under the

131 Civil liability offences apply for breaches of UCH Act ss.27–40.

132 see Dwyer *supra* note 27, at p. 109.

133 Custodial sentences may be imposed for breaches of the UCH Act ss.27–36.

134 For a breakdown of the penalties see Explanatory Memorandum, Underwater Cultural Heritage Bill 2018 (Cth) and Underwater Cultural Heritage (Consequential and Transitional Provisions) Bill 2018 (Cth), 8.

135 UCH Act s.56.

UCH Act.[136] Inspectors are appointed from persons who operationally work on the water regularly in government roles, or who are experienced compliance officers. As such, most Inspectors are appointed from Fisheries and Marine Park State-based officers, distributed around the country. These officers become the eyes and ears of the national compliance programme, with a primary remit to communicate the requirements of the UCH Act and to enforce compliance.

In line with the Australian Government's legislative drafting policy guidelines, when drafting the UCH Act the Department was required to map all compliance and enforcement provisions to the Regulatory Powers (Standard Provisions) Act 2014 and or Maritime Powers Act 2013. Ironically, even though a major reason in modernising the HSA was to update and strengthen the compliance regime, this legislative drafting policy requirement resulted in two changes between the HSA and the UCH Act, which significantly diminished on-water compliance capacity. The first change was that Commonwealth, States and Northern Territory Police officers were no longer appointed *ex officio* as Inspectors. Previously, the Department had received significant support from the Police force because of this provision. The second and most negative change was that the power to board, search and seize artefacts, diving gear and or boats without warrant was not able to be replicated from the HSA.[137]

5.13 *Public Engagement*

While the UCH Act introduced several important legislative changes that will assist in the preservation of UCH *in situ* in Australian waters and *ex situ*, arguably the most significant amendment was to provide a legislative basis for the rights and role of the public into the objects of the UCH Act, which can be found in section 3: 'to promote public awareness, understanding, appreciation and appropriate use of Australia's underwater cultural heritage'.

A key element of Australia's UCH management is to balance appropriate public engagement and site access with site management/protection outcomes. In saying that, without the public's participation in heritage there is little that can be effectively done to prevent its destruction and loss.[138] Only

136 UCH Act s.60.

137 These changes resulted from a broader Commonwealth review of policing and police powers.

138 A. Viduka, 'Going for the win-win: including the public in underwater cultural heritage management through citizen science' (2020) 49 *International Journal of Nautical Archaeology* 87; A. Viduka, 'Public Engagement, Community Archaeology and Underwater Cultural Heritage Management – An Australian Case Study' in A. Hafner, H. Oniz, L. Semaan and C. Underwood, (Eds) *Heritage at Risk* (ICOMOS 2020)152; A. Viduka, 'A maritime archaeological conservation focussed citizen science program for individual benefit and

through an informed and engaged public can Australia hope to discover, document, monitor and protect its UCH sites. This *realpolitik* of UCH site management was recognised early in Australia and underpinned the effort of every jurisdiction to create avocational maritime archaeology groups.[139] Today, a small number of heritage agency-initiated public archaeology groups remain, however, other community-based groups have appeared and continue to discover, monitor and protect Australia's UCH.[140] The most recent is the Gathering Information via Recreational and Technical (GIRT) Scientific Diver citizen science program (GIRT Scientific Divers 2021) which is now an endorsed action of the UN Decade of Ocean Science for Sustainable Development 2021-2030.[141]

6 Ratification of the 2001 Convention

Should Australia decide to ratify the Convention, a number of minor provisions need to be drafted to enable its ratification in line with the obligations Australia would take on as a State Party. For example, minor amendments to the UCH Rules may require drafting to ensure that activities directed at UCH align with the requirements of the Annex Rules.

Potentially, there may also be a need to draft additional amendments to the UCH Act in line with the enabling provisions. For example, while shipwrecks and submerged aircraft in Australia are currently covered by a 75-year rolling date protection provision, other UCH is subject to individual declaration following a significance assessment. This structure was adopted because the Commonwealth only protects other UCH from 3nm–200nm and in this zone, and more importantly at this depth, no Aboriginal or Torres Strait Islander UCH has ever been discovered. In enabling the 2001 Convention, an issue of equity and optics would occur if the Australia Government only protected

public good outcomes: the GIRT Scientific Diver programme' (2020) *Journal of Community Archaeology and Heritage* <https://www.tandfonline.com/doi/full/10.1080/20518196.2020.1858544?scroll=top&needAccess=true>.

139 G. Henderson, (ed) Guidelines for the Management of Australia's Shipwrecks, Australian Institute for Maritime Archaeology and the Australian Cultural Development Office, 1994; 1996, Historic Shipwrecks Public Access Guidelines, Commonwealth of Australia.

140 Such as MAAV 2021, Maritime Archaeological Association of Victoria, <https://home.vicnet.net.au/~maav/>, MAAWA 2021, Maritime Archaeological Association of Western Australia, <http://www.maawa.net> ; NSW Wreckspotters 2021, New South Wales government web pages for Wreckspotters program, see Viduka, 'Public Engagement' *supra* note 139, at p. 152.

141 A. Viduka, B. Sutton, A. Hutchison, T. Dempsey and C. Low, 'A Report on the GIRT Scientific Diver Survey of the Rainbow Warrior, Cavalli Islands, New Zealand' (2020) 16 *Journal of Maritime Archaeology* 3; GIRT Scientific Divers 2021, <https://www.girtsd.org/>.

Aboriginal or Torres Strait UCH in line with the Convention's 100-year blanket protection rolling date rather than adopting the 75-year date as for shipwrecks and submerged aircraft. An additional issue is the need to specifically recognise Aboriginal and Torres Strait Islander UCH as its own class, rather than leaving it as a subset of 'other UCH'.

In a major development, on 8 February 2022, at the request of the Minister for the Environment, the Australian Government Minister for Foreign Affairs tabled the 2001 Convention and an associated National Interest Analysis document in Parliament for consideration by the Joint Standing Committee on Treaties (JSCOT).[142] This was a significant step in Australia's ratification process and signified that consultation between the Commonwealth, States and the Northern Territory and within the Australian Government was concluded and in-principle supportive. Prior to a mid-year general election, JSCOT, whose consideration process takes 20 joint sitting-days (when both the House of Representatives and the Senate sit on the same day), had already concluded a call for public submissions, which concluded on 11 April 2022.

Following the general election, and at the request of the new Minister for the Environment, in October 2022, the Convention was re-tabled for further JSCOT consideration by the new Minister for Foreign Affairs. On 10 February 2023, JSCOT held a public hearing into the 2001 Convention and on 7 March 2023 produced a final report with the following recommendation: "3.128 The Committee supports the Convention on the Protection of the Underwater Cultural Heritage and recommends that binding treaty action be taken".[143]

Australia's possible ratification of the 2001 Convention is now subject to the introduction of enabling legislation, approval by the Federal Executive Council of Australia and normal treaty making processes.

7 Conclusion

Since coming into force, the regulatory regime to administer the UCH Act is being established and the protection of UCH has been extended to include other types of UCH in Commonwealth waters. The protection of the proximal environment of sites is a significant and positive shift, recognising the importance of the environment in itself, and in its potential preservation of UCH *in*

142 <https://www.aph.gov.au/Parliamentary_Business/Committees/Joint/Treaties/UnderwaterHeritage-UN/Treaty_being_considered>.

143 Parliament of Australia, Report 207, *Australia-Iceland Double Taxation; Underwater Cultural Heritage* (JSCOT) March 2023, viii and 55.

situ. The inclusion of a public outcome in the objects of the UCH Act is one of its most important provisions and will help continue to focus the day-to-day administration on management and protection activities.[144] With JSCOT's support for ratification of the 2001 Convention, the next questions are: how long it will take for enabling legislation to be drafted and introduced; and what other potential amendments will be included, all of which will warrant analysis in the future.

All websites last accessed February 2025.

Select Bibliography

Guidelines for working in the near and offshore environment to protect Underwater Cultural Heritage, Australian Government, Department of Climate Change, Energy, the Environment and Water, Canberra, July CC BY 4.0.

S. Dromgoole, *Underwater Cultural Heritage and International Law* (Cambridge University Press, 2013).

G. J. Dwyer, 'Ship shape or all at sea? A preliminary assessment of Australia's recent legislative reforms concerning underwater cultural heritage' (2019) 32 *Australian and New Zealand Maritime Law Journal* 71.

G. Henderson, *Maritime Archaeology in Australia* (University of Western Australia Press, 1986).

G. Henderson and A.Viduka, (eds) *Towards Ratification: Papers from the 2013 AIMA Conference Workshop* (Australasian Institute for Maritime Archaeology Special Publication no.17, 2014).

M. Nash, (ed) *Shipwreck Archaeology in Australia* (University of Western Australia Press, 2007).

A. Viduka and G. Luckman, 2022, The Australian Management of Protected Underwater Cultural Heritage Artifacts in Public and Private Custody. *Advances in Archaeological Practice,* 1–14. doi:10.1017/aap.2022.16.

A. Viduka 2012, '1976 and beyond – managing Australia's underwater cultural heritage' *Bulletin of the Australasian Institute for Maritime Archaeology*, Ed. Jeremy Green and Myra Stanbury, No. 36: pp 1–9.

144 UCH Act s.3(1)(c).

CHAPTER 4

Belgium

*Marnix J. Pieters**

1 Introduction

In Belgium, underwater cultural heritage (UCH) slowly emerged in terms of its recognition, both legally and scientifically, during the first two decades of the twenty-first century.[1] Three successive legal frameworks at federal level, respectively adopted in 2007, 2014 and finally in 2021, progressively extended enhanced protection to UCH. At the start of this legal odyssey, in 2007, only shipwrecks and parts thereof were in scope. Following the adoption of the 2021 Belgian legal framework, all the various types of UCH, as defined by the UNESCO Convention on the Protection of the Underwater Cultural Heritage (2001 Convention), are encompassed.[2] In addition, fossil, animal and plant remains with a scientific character and invertebrate, vertebrate and plant fossils together with their paleontological context are within scope of the latest legal framework.

The ratification of the 2001 Convention by Belgium in August 2013 was a key moment for the recognition of this, until then, largely undervalued heritage, consequently providing a catalyst for further legal development. The ratification continues to act as a driver to improve current practice within the Belgian system, as will be explored in more detail in section 3. The latest legal framework even refers to the 2001 Convention in its title.

In June 2014, less than a year after the 2001 Convention's ratification, a completely new law on UCH, replacing the preceding 2007 legislation, came into force.[3] The territorial application of the 2014 Act on the Protection of UCH

* Senior Archaeologist, Flanders Heritage Agency.

1 Pieters M., et al., 'Belgium – Finds from Trawl Fishing, Dredging and Beach Walking' in Anders Fisher and Lisbeth Pedersen (eds), *Oceans of Archaeology* (Jutland Archaeological Society and Aarhus University Press 2018). Pieters M. and Delaere C., 'UCH in Belgium: Recent Developments 2012–2019' in Albert Hafner and others (eds), *Heritage under Water at Risk. Threats-Challenges-Solutions* (The International Council on Monuments and Sites (ICOMOS) and International Scientific Committee on UCH (ICUCH 2022).

2 2562 UNTS 1.

3 4 April 2014 – Wet betreffende bescherming van het cultureel erfgoed onder water (1) Belgisch Staatsblad 2014-04-18 (Ed. 3) (2014 Act on the Protection of UCH (2014 APUCH)). <http://www.ejustice.just.fgov.be/eli/wet/2014/04/04/2014014248/staatsblad>; 25 April 2014 – Koninklijk besluit betreffende de bescherming van het cultureel erfgoed onder water,

 | DOI:10.1163/9789004510883_006

(2014 APUCH) extended to the Belgian sector of the North Sea, to include all of the Territorial Sea (TS), the Exclusive Economic Zone (EEZ) and the Continental Shelf (CS). The Act thus allowing, for the first time in the Belgian part of the North Sea, underwater archaeological sites to be protected *in situ*. By the end of 2018, 11 archaeological sites were protected/ recognised as UCH via ministerial decrees (although in these cases not as *in situ* UCH, which had to be undertaken via Royal Decrees according to the 2014 APUCH) including a German World War I (WWI) submarine (U-boat) identified in 2017. The 2014 APUCH and its corresponding Royal Decree also installed a procedure for reporting UCH found incidentally in the North Sea.[4] In 2018, two UCH sites attracted international attention: one was the identification of a previously unknown German WWI U-boat and the other was the discovery of a crash site of a B-17 Flying Fortress.[5] The newly identified German U-boat was subsequently the focus of a 'UCH Forum' organised collaboratively by Flanders and Germany in the context of the 'European Year of Cultural Heritage' in Berlin on 4 December 2018. The Forum discussed legal aspects related to the implementation of the 2001 Convention and gave an anthology of different approaches to and opportunities in respect of WWI UCH present in European waters,[6] and contributions are available via the website of the German National Committee for Monument Protection (DNK).[7]

The year of the 2001 Convention's ratification also saw the start of a multiannual (2013–2016) research project focused on UCH in Belgium, known as SeArch.[8] This was funded by Flanders Innovation and Entrepreneurship

Belgisch Staatsblad 2014-05-14 (Ed. 2) (2014 Royal Decree on the Protection of UCH). <http://www.ejustice.just.fgov.be/eli/besluit/2014/04/25/2014014267/staatsblad>.

4 Art. 5 2014 APUCH and art. 2 of the corresponding Royal Decree.

5 A B-17 Flying Fortress is a four-engined heavy bomber developed by Boeing. This type of airplane was intensively employed during World War II by the United States Army Air Corps, see for example 'Boeing B-17 Flying Fortress' <https: //en.wikipedia.org/wiki/Boeing_B-17_Flying Fortress>.

6 Tell C., and Pieters M., (eds), *Forum für Unterwasserarchäologie 2018/UCH Forum 2018. Dokumentation der Tagung des Deutschen Nationalkomitees für Denkmalschutz (DNK), des auswärtiges Amtes der Bundesrepublik Deutschland und der Flämischen Agentur für Kulturerbe am 04. Dezember 2018 in Berlin/Documentation of the conference of the German National Committee for Monument Protection (DNK), the Foreign Office of the Federal Republic of Germany and the Flanders Heritage Agency on 04 December 2018 in Berlin* (Schriftenreihe des Deutsches Nationalkomitees für Denkmalschutz band 95 2022).

7 See <https://www.dnk.de/mediathek/#publikationen>.

8 Missiaen T., et al., 'The SeArch Project: Towards an Assessment Methodology and Sustainable Management Policy for the Archaeological Heritage of the North Sea in Belgium' in Bailey G., Harff J., and Sakellariou D., (eds) *Under the Sea: Archaeology and Palaeolandscapes of the Continental shelf* (Springer 2017).

(VLAIO), the Flemish point of contact for all entrepreneurs in Flanders and with a mission to stimulate and support innovation and entrepreneurship, for example via accessing different types of subsidies.[9] The SeArch project[10] developed an assessment methodology and a sustainable management policy for archaeological heritage located in the Belgian part of the North Sea and offered the actors at sea, such as recreational divers, fisherpersons and crews of ships involved in works at sea (such as dredging, sand extraction, building activity, cable laying, and dealing with unexploded ordnance), a set of clear instructions on how to deal with incidentally found UCH by introducing bespoke protocols for each type of activity zone. Three separate protocols were prepared: one for finds at sea (TS, as well as CS),[11] a second for finds on the beach and in the intertidal zone,[12] and lastly a third for finds on terrestrially-located facilities for dealing with marine aggregates resulting from various activities at sea.[13] The main results of the project were synthesised into a best practice brochure.[14] The final chapters of this are devoted to advice for the industries active at sea and in the intertidal zone and advice for the authorities. The latter is primarily in the context of such authorities exercising legislative powers to deal with identified flaws in the 2014 APUCH. In parallel with the SeArch project, two PhD-research projects were initiated at Ghent University: one on legal aspects related to UCH and a second, geological one on drowned landscapes on the Belgian CS.[15]

The first experiences with the practical application of the 2014 APUCH in the period 2014–2018, the results of SeArch and the PhD research, established that some improvements to the law were highly desirable, as explained below. In 2018, the federal government took the initiative to start preparations for

9 See <https://www.vlaio.be/en/about-us/let-us-introduce-ourselves> and <https://www.vlaio.be/en/subsidies>.

10 The results and outcomes of the SeArch Project such as the protocols mentioned in the text are available via <https://www.vliz.be/projects/sea-arch/nl/resultaten-1.htm>.

11 Sven Van Haelst, Marnix Pieters and Ine Demerre, 'Protocol voor het melden van archeologische vondsten gedaan tijdens werkzaamheden op zee' (SeArch Project 2016).

12 Sven Van Haelst, Marnix Pieters and Ine Demerre, 'Protocol voor het melden van archeologische vondsten op het strand of in de getijdenzone (SeArch Project 2016).

13 Sven Van Haelst, Marnix Pieters and Ine Demerre, 'Protocol voor het melden van archeologische vondsten op werven voor zeegranulaten (SeArch Project).

14 Missiaen T., et al., 'Erfgoed in zee : wat moet ik ermee ? Richtlijnen voor de gebruikers van de Noordzee met betrekking tot het cultureel erfgoed onder water' (SeArch Project 2016).

15 Thary Derudder, Our Past Beneath the Waves. The Legal Protection of UCH from an International, North Sea and Belgian Perspective (DPhil thesis Ghent University 2018–2019). Maikel De Clercq, Drowned Landscapes of the Belgian Continental Shelf. Implications for northwest European Landscape Evolution and Preservation Potential for Submerged Heritage (DPhil thesis Ghent University 2017–2018).

amending, or even replacing, the 2014 APUCH by a new law, mainly in order to realise these improvements, but at the same time to optimise the implementation of the commitments agreed to by ratification of the 2001 Convention. The third UCH law finally entered into force in 2021.[16]

Before commencing an overview and discussion of the legal evolution in the period 2007–2021 linked to the growing appreciation for underwater archaeological heritage, or even broader UCH in Belgium, it is useful first to outline Belgian State structures and the possible impact of them upon the management of UCH.

2 Responsibility for UCH in Belgium

Between 1970 and 2014, Belgium went through a series of six constitutional reforms, evolving during that period from a unity constitutional model, with one government and one parliament, to a federation consisting of Regions and Communities. Since the fourth constitutional reform in 1993, Belgium is a fully developed federal State consisting of three Regions (Flanders, Wallonia and Brussels Capital Region) and three language-based Communities (Flemish, French and German-speaking Communities).[17] The Regions have the responsibility for what are termed territorial matters or matters within their defined areas, including agriculture, public works, spatial planning, nature preservation, housing and immovable heritage. As the Communities are based on the language spoken, they have responsibility for what are termed personal matters or matters linked to the person, such as culture, health care and education. The areas of the Regions are different from those of the Communities: the Flemish Community consists of the region of Flanders plus a part of Brussels Capital Region; the French Community consists of the region of Wallonia plus the other part of Brussels Capital Region and minus the relatively small

16 23 April 2021 – Wet tot implementatie van het UNESCO-verdrag van 2 November 2001 ter bescherming van het cultureel erfgoed onder water en de bescherming van waardevolle wrakken, Belgisch Staatsblad, 2021-05-25 (Ed.1) (2021 Act to Implement the 2001 Convention and to Protect Valuable Wrecks (2021 AICPVW), available from <http://www.ejustice.just.fgov.be/eli/wet/2021/04/23/2021041529/staatsblad>. 30 July 2021 – Koninklijk besluit tot uitvoering van de wet van 23 April 2021 tot implementatie van het UNESCO verdrag van 2 November 2001 ter bescherming van het cultureel erfgoed onder water en de bescherming van waardevolle wrakken, Belgisch Staatsblad 2021-09-06 (Ed. 2) (Royal Decree for the 2021 AICPVW) <http://www.ejustice.just.fgov.be/eli/besluit/2021/07/30/2021042757/staatsblad>.

17 See <https://www.vlaamsparlement.be/nl/over-ons/de-geschiedenis-van-het-vlaams-parlement>.

German-speaking Community consisting of nine municipalities in the eastern part of the province of Liège.[18]

Archaeology is predominantly a territorial matter and thus the Regions have the responsibility for archaeology within their area. Consequently, each Region has its own legislation dealing with archaeology (for example, inventorying, scheduling, granting permits etc.). This responsibility exists only until any archaeological objects, and the corresponding documentation of an archaeological excavation for instance, are transferred to a museum, an archive, or a repository. Following such a transfer, the Communities become responsible for archaeology, as it is deemed then to have become a personal matter based on museums, archives and repositories being considered as culture. A good example are the finds assembled from the archaeological excavation of a Merovingian cemetery at Broechem[19] (which is managed subject to the regional legislation of Flanders). These finds are considered as having exceptional value and, as such, are protected based on the appropriate Flemish Community legislation.[20] These are known as 'the finds assemblage of the Merovingian cemetery of Broechem' on the list of exceptional value that currently includes 891 objects.[21]

Flanders is the only Region with a coastline bordering the North Sea. In addition, as the intertidal area of the North Sea forms part of the Region, Flanders also has responsibility for the UCH in this physical transition zone between the North Sea and the mainland. The Federal State has territorial authority over the Belgian TS and CS, but has no responsibility for archaeology, which has been devolved to the Regions and Communities as explained above. Thus, there is no specific archaeological legislation at the federal level. However, in the North Sea the Federal State has a so-called residual competence on archaeology or UCH. This is because the Belgian sector of the North Sea, including the TS, EEZ and CS, as a territory belongs neither to the Regions nor the Communities. This situation, 'between two chairs' as we say in Flanders, is the main reason why it took some time to put in place the necessary tools to deal with UCH for the Belgian part of the North Sea in a way that aligned with the evolution of international law.

---

18 See <https://www.belgium.be/nl/over_belgie/overheid/gemeenschappen>.

19 Rica Annaert, 'Het vroegmiddeleeuwse grafveld van Broechem. Analyses/The Early Medieval Cemetery of Broechem. Analyses (Flanders Heritage Agency 2018), available at <https://oar.onroerenderfgoed.be/publicaties/RELM/17/RELM017-001.pdf>.

20 See <https://codex.vlaanderen.be/Zoeken/Document.aspx?DID=1010774&param=inhoud>.

21 See <https://topstukken.vlaanderen.be/topstukken/>.

The complicated Belgian State structure also has consequences for the ratification process of international conventions dealing with competences belonging to the different constituent parts of the country. Ratification has to be at the federal level but cannot be done without the prior consent of the Regions and the Communities. Thus, each parliament of the Regions and the Communities has to give its consent to allow the Federal State to ratify on its behalf. The Belgian ratification of the 2001 Convention in August 2013 was a commitment to not only abide with that Convention but also to subsequently implement all the requirements in the domestic laws of the constituent parts of the federation as necessary. Some countries work in a different way and may first adapt the relevant and necessary domestic legislation ahead of ratification. Both approaches have their benefits and limitations but given the Belgian situation, with a complex constitutional infrastructure, the 'commitment-approach' is doubtless the most workable.

3 The 2004 Cooperation Agreement and UCH Related Acts: 2007, 2014 and 2021

The positive evolution in respect of UCH in Belgium started with a cooperation agreement[22] for the protection of maritime heritage, concluded between Flanders (the Region) and the Federal State. This was signed in Raversijde (Ostend) on 5 October 2004 by Minister Johan Vande Lanotte (on behalf of the Belgian Federal Government) and by Minister Dirk van Mechelen (on behalf of the Flemish Government).[23] The wording of the agreement speaks about 'maritime heritage' in order to also comprise maritime heritage on land, such as harbour infrastructure, fishing settlements and landing places and has, as a consequence, a very wide scope, extending much wider than the concepts of maritime archaeology or even UCH. Under the terms of the agreement, Flanders agreed to establish within 18 months a first database of maritime archaeological heritage present in the Belgian part of the North Sea and to put this database at the disposal of the Federal Government for planning and management purposes. The Federal Government correspondingly agreed to select

22 Concluding cooperation agreements between the Federal State and the Regions and Communities is made possible by one of the Constitutional Reform Acts (Derudder, *supra* n 15, 335).

23 Samenwerkingsakkoord tussen het Vlaams Gewest en de federale overheid houdende het maritiem erfgoed (2004 Cooperation agreement between Flanders and the federal authorities dealing with maritme heritage).

some sites from the database to be protected on environmental or biodiversity grounds and to ensure that archaeological heritage was taken into consideration before permits for infrastructural or other works at sea were undertaken. The 2004 cooperation agreement can be considered as a letter of intent, marking in fact the start of a long legal journey, since whilst the database was realised within the promised 18 months (and since 2006 can be freely consulted online),[24] no sites were selected by the Federal Government for protection.

Despite its limited success, and lack of legal force, the 2004 cooperation agreement certainly raised awareness at the political level and probably also inspired and stimulated the realisation of the first federal legislative initiative[25] for the protection of shipwrecks and parts thereof with an archaeological and historical value. This new Act on the Discovery and Protection of Wrecks (ADPW) was drafted in 2006 and adopted in 2007.[26] Unfortunately, this piece of legislation was drafted without consulting archaeologists, UCH experts, or experts in archaeological conservation in its early stages. As a result, the important and complex issues of long term (one year and more) conservation and adequate storing of archaeological finds raised from an underwater environment containing soluble salts was completely overlooked in the drafting of the Act. This was especially evident in Article 11 of the ADPW, which merely stipulated that finds had to be kept by the finder or the authorities for one year so as to give the original owner the possibility to recover their property. Keeping finds retrieved from a submerged context in good condition, thereby preventing their decay, requires knowledge and infrastructure that cannot automatically be expected to be available. Once this shortcoming was identified, close collaboration started between the Federal State and the Flemish Government to draft the Royal Decree necessary for this Act (Acts require the approval of Parliament; Royal Decrees (or Royal Orders) are federal government decrees exercising legislation, or powers the legislature has delegated), taking the conservation issue into consideration, together with a proposal for a cooperation agreement including financial engagements between both partners. Due to a lack of time, the Royal Decree needed to allow the ADPW to enter into effective operational force, as well as to introduce some additional measures, was never published and thus the Act did not come into force. After the federal elections

24 The database, launched in 2006, is still operational and can be accessed at <www.maritieme-archeologie.be>.

25 9 April 2007 – Wet betreffende de vondst en de bescherming van wrakken (1), Belgisch Staatsblad 2007-06-21 (Ed. 1) (Act on the Discovery and Protection of Wrecks (2007 ADPW), see <http://www.ejustice.just.fgov.be/eli/wet/2007/04/09/2007014194/staatsblad>.

26 Derudder, *supra* n 15, 336–37.

of 10 July 2007[27] and a consequent change in political priorities, the ambition to finish the work related to the Royal Decree needed for the ADPW to enter into force disappeared and the project was put on hold for several years.

The ADPW focused on the discovery and the protection of shipwrecks and parts thereof found in the Belgian TS. Although, as explained, it never came into force, it had an impact in laying down the basis for further legal work on UCH. This impact included the introduction into Belgian legal thinking on maritime and underwater heritage of the idea and concept of the 'Receiver of Wreck', a similar but not completely identical function as in the United Kingdom and in some other countries. This the Act attempted to achieve via regulating the finding, reporting and ownership of wrecks, with the Receiver acting as a key figure, discussed below.

Most significantly, for the first time in Belgian law, the ADPW envisaged the protection of shipwrecks solely based on their archaeological and historical value, and independently of any nature conservation or ecological motive. Naturally, shipwreck sites may meet both criteria, that of offering habitat type and of being of cultural value. For example, a research project carried out between 2003 and 2006 of shipwreck sites in the Belgian part of the North Sea, an area with a rather monotonous sandy seabed, discovered they acted as hotspots for marine biodiversity.[28] The project demonstrated that the shipwrecks acted as additional hard substrates and as such enhanced marine biodiversity by allowing hard substrate species to spread more easily via using the network of shipwrecks as 'stepping stones'.

In addition, Article 22 of the ADPW (the only provision of the Act to come into immediate effect) abolished the 'Edict of Charles Quint of 10 December 1547'.[29] This Edict, still in application in an actualised version in 2007, speaks of an ' Ontfanghere van den extraordina(i)ris van Vlaendren'[30] (extraordinary receiver), effectively a 'civil servant' to which goods found at sea and on the beach had to be reported. Given its date, naturally this Edict had no archaeological ambition or purpose, but instead looked for additional income for the State Treasury, with the role also operating in relation to finds at sea and on the beach in fifteenth century Burgundian Flanders, and in the Flanders bailiffs

27 See <https://verkiezingen2007.belgium.be/nl/index.html>.

28 Mallefet J., et al., 'Belgian Shipwreck: Hotspots for marine biodiversity (BEWREMABI) (Belgian Science Policy 2008).

29 2007 ADPW Section VIII, Article 22.

30 Alexander Korthals Altes, 'Prijs der zee. Raakvlak van redding, strandrecht en wrakwetgeving' (Tjeenk Willink 1973).

of the fourteenth century.[31] However, whilst the Edict was abolished, as noted above the ADPW alternatively referred to the Receiver of Wreck. In the most recent Belgian legislation in 2021 (see below) echoes of the Edict can still be traced in the use of a title of 'Receiver of cultural heritage underwater', which could be interpreted as a successor to the extraordinary receiver from the sixteenth century.[32] Besides the similarity in title, both 'civil servants' basically share a similar task, being official persons to whom 'finds' at sea have to be reported. However, beyond the mere reporting of finds, the processes and goals are very different. The result of the abolition of the Edict of Charles Quint combined with the failure to adopt a Royal Decree for the ADPW was significant, since it left shipwreck sites and parts thereof totally unprotected by any form of legislation for seven years.

On 25 April 2014, the Royal Decree needed for the entrance into force of a revised law on the protection of UCH, the Act on the Protection of UCH (APUCH), was adopted.[33] This expanded the geographical scope of UCH protection to the Belgian part of the North Sea, including its TS, EEZ and CS. Its focus was also expanded, so that it was no longer restricted to shipwrecks and parts thereof, but applied to all types of cultural heritage underwater, as defined in the 2001 Convention.[34] It is noteworthy that the time-criterion, or the cut-off date, of 100 years, as provided in the 2001 Convention, was not taken into consideration regarding UCH present in the TS.[35] Thus, UCH sites known to be less than 100-years underwater in the TS could via the APUCH also be protected, in contrast to such sites present in the EEZ and CS, where the age requirement of the 2001 Convention was applied. This was an important aspect of the new law for two reasons: first, as a lot (or even most) of the known UCH

31 Louis Sicking and Jan De Klerk, 'The Law of Wreck in Flanders, Holland and Zeeland in the Late Middle Ages' in Claire Weeda, Robert Stein and Louis Sicking (eds) *Communities, Environment and Regulation in the Premodern World* (Brepols Publishers 2022). Marleen De Groote, 'De baljuwrekening : venster op de praktijk van het middeleeuws strandrecht in Vlaanderen' (1999) 13 Madoc : Tijdschrift over de Middeleeuwen. Themanummer Middeleeuwen aan Zee 258.

32 2021 AICPVW Article 1, 8°: ontvanger: de door de Koning aangewezen ontvanger van het cultureel erfgoed onder water.

33 4 April 2014 – Wet betreffende bescherming van het cultureel erfgoed onder water (1) Belgisch Staatsblad 2014-04-18 (Ed. 3) (2014 Act on the Protection of UCH (2014 APUCH)), see <http://www.ejustice.just.fgov.be/eli/wet/2014/04/04/2014014248/staatsblad> 25 April 2014 – Koninklijk besluit betreffende de bescherming van het cultureel erfgoed onder water, Belgisch Staatsblad 2014-05-14 (Ed. 2) (2014 Royal Decree on the Protection of UCH), see <http://www.ejustice.just.fgov.be/eli/besluit/2014/04/25/2014014267/staatsblad>.

34 2014 APUCH Article 2, 1°.

35 2014 APUCH Article 3, 1° and 2°.

is located in the TS and, second, much valuable UCH dates from both World Wars and that linked particularly to WWII would have to wait far too long to obtain protection if applying the Convention's age requirement. In addition, as above, the APUCH introduced the role of 'Receiver of cultural heritage underwater' (Receiver) analogous to the Receiver of Wreck in the ADPW and made a distinction between 'finds', those 'finds recognised as UCH' (via ministerial decision) and those '*in situ* protected UCH' (via Royal Decree). The UNESCO definition of UCH is given to 'finds' in the APUCH[36] and these can only acquire the status of UCH via a ministerial decision based on a research report made by the Receiver.[37] There is thus no automatic assignation of heritage status, or so-called blanket protection, to 'all traces of human existence having a cultural, historical or archaeological character which have been partially or totally under water periodically or continuously for at least 100 years'. Once a find has been recognised as UCH, it can also additionally be protected *in situ*.

The Receiver is a key player with a considerable range of tasks and responsibilities under the APUCH. These include requirements to create and maintain a publicly accessible electronic register[38] that contains all reported finds;[39] to draft research reports on reported finds with advice for the minister as to whether or not to recognise the find as UCH;[40] to communicate via a website[41] which finds have been reported, have been recognised as UCH, or are protected *in situ*; to notify the Director-General of UNESCO;[42] to consult other States that have made a declaration;[43] to deliver grants for activities directed at UCH; and to grant authorisations to bring a find to the surface.[44] The governor of the province of West-Flanders, the only Belgian province with a coastline bordering the North Sea, is appointed by Royal Decree as the Receiver.[45] To support them with tasks related to the APUCH, two protocols of collaboration were signed, one with the Flanders Heritage Agency,[46] and the other with the Flanders Marine Institute.[47] These agreements were intended to provide

36 2014 APUCH Article 2, 1°.
37 2014 APUCH Article 8 § 1.
38 See <http://www.vondsteninzee.be/overzicht-registraties>.
39 2014 APUCH Article 7.
40 2014 APUCH Article 8 § 1.
41 See <http://www.vondsteninzee.be/>.
42 2014 APUCH Article 9.
43 2014 APUCH Article 5 § 2.
44 2014 APUCH Article 6 § 1.
45 Article 1 of the Royal Decree for the 2014 APUCH.
46 See <https://www.onroerenderfgoed.be/>.
47 See <https://www.vliz.be/>.

the Receiver with adequate storage capacities, provided by Flanders Marine Institute at their land based facilities, and with the necessary archaeological advice, provided by the Flanders Heritage Agency.

In order to be able to comply with its obligations under the 2001 Convention, the Belgian Federal Government thought it necessary that title over reported finds was immediately awarded to the Belgian State. This was naturally not applicable to ships or craft that belonged to a State at the moment of sinking or crashing,[48] since such sites in general benefit from sovereign immunity, especially if they were used for non-commercial purposes.[49] If a find recognised as UCH is by Royal Decree protected *in situ*, ownership remains with the State. In all other situations, ownership may be transferred to the person that claims, and can prove, they were the original owner of the UCH and after having paid any costs incurred for the conservation of the UCH by the Receiver and/or the finder. A public administration, an institution of public interest, or a museum can also show their interest to the Receiver to become owner of the find, even when ownership is claimed by the original owner, which to become effective requires payment of a mutually accepted fee based on the value of the find. In the event of a conflict over the value of the fee between the original owner and a public administration, an institution of public interest or a museum, the find remains property of the original owner.[50] If no one claims ownership, it can be awarded to the finder

Under the APUCH, by the end of 2018, 11 archaeological wreck sites were recognised as UCH for their archaeological and historical values.[51] These 11 shipwreck sites constitute significant material sources of important aspects, events or periods of the maritime history of Belgium, such as, for example, the organisation of safety at sea, the WWI U-boat war, the Saint George's Day raids on Ostend and Zeebrugge, the evacuation of Dunkerque (Operation Dynamo) and the role played by the harbour town of Ostend. Five of these shipwreck sites can additionally be qualified as 'war graves'. Via their status as UCH, they benefit from protective measures. Although they have never strictly speaking been officially recognised by the King of Belgium as *in situ* protected UCH via an individual Royal Decree, a Royal Decree from 2016 installed some regulatory

48 2014 APUCH Article 5 § 2.

49 Garnett R., 'Foreign State Immunity and Marine Wrecks' [2021] *Australian and New Zealand Maritime Law Journal* (The University of Queensland) 1, available at <https://papers.ssrn.com/sol3/papers.cfm?abstract_id=3973287 >.

50 2014 APUCH Article 12.

51 Sven Van Haelst and Marnix Pieters, 'Vissen naar wrakken en beenderen. Archeologisch onderzoek op het strand en in de Noordzee' (2018) 37(2) *Monumenten, Landschappen en Archeologie*. Tweemaandelijks Tijdschrift 39.

measures for the protection *in situ* of such UCH. The same Royal Decree also stipulated that, contrary to the text of the APUCH,[52] from 2016 onwards individual protective measures for sites should be adopted through ministerial decree and not through Royal Decree, which is to be reserved for regulatory measures.[53] Before the King can decide to protect UCH *in situ,* according to the APUCH the advice of those stakeholders active at sea (such as windfarms, aggregate extraction, fishing industry etc.) is needed.[54] Their support for the protection of UCH at sea is crucial to guaranteeing the sustainability of protection and the above mentioned 11 shipwreck sites all benefitted from such support.

Although the 2014 legislation was a major and significant step forward, even if the 2007 ADPW had entered into force, there remained scope for work to be done to fully secure the level of protection required under the 2001 Convention. The main issues detected by Derudder in her PhD thesis related to the distinction between finds, finds recognised as UCH, and *in situ* protected UCH, and to the lack of provisions to implement Article 5 of the 2001 Convention, namely, to effectively deal with activities incidentally affecting UCH, including unknown finds.[55]

The issues raised by Derudder, together with the advice given by the SeArch project and experiences with the APUCH in the period 2014–2018, led to the decision by the Federal Secretary of State to start preparatory work to explore potential amendment or replacement of the 2014 APUCH. The outcome was new law, adopted in 2021, coincidentally seven years after the 2014 APUCH, which itself came seven years after the 2007 ADPW.[56]

The 'law implementing the UNESCO Convention of 2 November 2001 on the protection of the underwater cultural heritage and on the protection of valuable wrecks' (AICPVW) was adopted on 23 April 2021 and the corresponding Royal Decree dates from 30 July 2021.[57] First of all, this law abolished the 2014 APUCH distinction between 'finds' and 'finds recognised as UCH' and by doing so contributed to administrative and legislative simplification. In terms of definitions, that for UCH is entirely in line with the 2001 Convention's definition

---

52 2014 APUCH Article 8 § 3.

53 21 september 2016. Koninklijk besluit betreffende de reglementaire maatregelen ter bescherming van het cultureel erfgoed onder water, Article 7 – Royal Decree related to regulatory measures for the protection of UCH, Article 7 <http://www.ejustice.just.fgov.be/eli/besluit/2016/09/21/2016014315/staatsblad>.

54 2014 APUCH, Article 8 § 3.

55 Derudder, *supra* n 15, 386.

56 Missiaen T., et al., *supra* n 14.

57 2021 AICPVW and corresponding Royal Decree, *supra* n 16.

but moreover expands the Convention's definition in order to also cover paleontological remains. It achieves this by adding to the definition of UCH from the 2001 Convention 'and fossil animal and plant remains with a scientific character' and expands the wording of 'objects of prehistoric character' with 'and all fossils from vertebrate and invertebrate animals and plants together with their paleontological context'.[58] Aside from administrative simplification, this definition has an additional advantage in that it clarifies the situation in relation to the obligation to report finds. For example, there is no more need to discuss whether a fossil elephant tusk found by fishers should be reported or not since it is clear that it should. Another important concept related to definitions is that of 'wrecks' as opposed to 'underwater cultural heritage': 'wrecks' are defined as:

> ... ships, aeroplanes and other means of transportation or parts thereof with their cargo or other content that are less than 100 years situated under water.[59]

The law thus distinguishes 'wrecks' from 'underwater cultural heritage' and from '*in situ* protected underwater cultural heritage'. 'Wrecks' and 'underwater cultural heritage' are dealt with by the Receiver (as noted above),[60] whereas '*in situ* protected underwater cultural heritage' is dealt with by the relevant minister.[61] The minister can decide to equate 'wrecks' to 'underwater cultural heritage' and once the case may subsequently also decide to protect them *in situ*.[62] However, once a wreck is submerged underwater for 100 years it acquires the status of UCH automatically, regardless of whether or not it has previously been designated as UCH.[63]

58 2021 AICPVW, Article 2, 1° and 1° c: 1° cultureel Erfgoed onder water: alle sporen van menselijke aanwezigheid evenals gefossiliseerde dierlijke of plantaardige overblijfselen met een wetenschappelijk karakter met een cultureel, historisch of archeologisch karakter die zich deels of volledig, tijdelijk of permanent sinds ten minste 100 jaar onder water bevinden, in het bijzonder:

c. prehistorische voorwerpen en alle fossielen van gewervelden, ongewervelden en planten evenals hun paleontologische context.

59 2021 AICPVW, Article 2, 2°: wrakken: schepen, luchtvaartuigen, andere vervoermiddelen of delen daarvan met hun vracht of andere inhoud die zich minder dan honderd jaar onder water bevinden.

60 2021 AICPVW, Article 6.

61 2021 AICPVW, Article 8.

62 2021 AICPVW, Article 11.

63 2021 AICPVW, Article 11, §1.

Ownership of 'wrecks' and 'underwater cultural heritage' remains with the owner at the moment of sinking or crashing and, if the owner at that moment cannot be identified, reverts to the finder.[64] The minister can also decide that a 'wreck' or 'UCH' is a part of the 'Belgian national heritage'.[65] This decision has the benefit of making it significantly easier for a public administration, an institute of public interest, or a scientific institute to become an owner since it has only to reimburse the finder for any proven costs. When the minister decides that a wreck or UCH does not belong to the 'Belgian national heritage', the public administration, institute of public interest, or scientific institute can if it wishes, become the owner by simply making an offer to the finder. If no agreement can be reached with the finder, the public administration, institute of public interest, or scientific institute can bring legal proceedings for a decision on the price to pay to the owner.[66]

With 'underwater cultural heritage' status in the AICPVW being automatically assigned to heritage (including fossils) that has lain underwater for at least 100 years in the Belgian part of the North Sea, as at August 2022, 56 shipwreck sites have gained such status: 55 of these are known to have been underwater for at least 100 years.[67] The remaining one, the HMS *Wakeful* shipwreck site,[68] situated in the Belgian TS, is the only shipwreck site less than 100 years old to receive UCH status. This offers the site some measure of protection, such as the need for prior consent by the Receiver to bring objects to the surface or to engage in archaeological or other activities affecting UCH.[69] For 18 of these 56 sites, additional individual protective measures have been published in 18 individual ministerial decrees (as at 10 March 2022) all providing for[70] identical protective measures. Under these measures, anchoring, line fishing, trawling and dredging is forbidden in a circular zone with a radius of 150 metres around the central coordinate.

64 2021 AICPVW, Article 14.

65 Royal Decree for the 2021 AICPVW (16), Article 7 § 2.

66 Royal Decree for the 2021 AICPVW (16), Article 7 § 3.

67 Ine Demerre, Sven Van Haelst and Matthias Sandra, 'Inventaris 100-jarige scheepswrakken in het Belgische deel van de Noordzee' (FOD Volksgezondheid, Veiligheid van de Voedselketen en Leefmilieu 2020).

68 Dirk Termote and Tomas Termote, 'Schatten en Scheepswrakken. Boeiende onderwaterarcheologie in de Noordzee' (Davidsfonds 2009).

69 2021 AICPVW, Article 6.

70 As an example the reference to one of these 18 ministerial decrees: 10 March 2022 – Ministerieel besluit betreffende de bescherming van de VORPOSTENBOOT STHAMER als cultureel erfgoed onder water <http://www.ejustice.just.fgov.be/eli/besluit/2022/03/10/2022020591/staatsblad> (ministerial decree on the protection of the VORPOSTENBOOT STHAMER as UCH).

As of 10 March 2022, a total of 29 shipwreck sites are now protected *in situ*: 11 were extended protection under the 2014 APUCH and 18 under the 2021 AICPVW. Under the Royal Decree for the AICPVW, diving on UCH that is *in situ* protected is not prohibited, but any person intending to should, at least four hours prior to diving, give notice to the responsible federal administration via a digital form.[71] A total of 13 of the 29 *in situ* protected sites are currently subject to this additional requirement.[72] This is because although the Royal Decree stipulates in Article 10 that diving should be reported on every *in situ* protected wreck site, only those sites with important parts protruding from the seafloor into the water column have been made subject to this additional measure. In practice, the others are not interesting for divers and thus this additional restriction is considered unnecessary.

To facilitate the implementation of the AICPVW and to ensure the new legislation achieves its goals, a protocol of collaboration has been concluded between five partners: the governor of West-Flanders as Receiver of UCH, Flanders Marine Institute, Flanders Heritage Agency, the Royal Belgian Institute of Natural Sciences[73] and the Directorate-General for Shipping.[74]

The AICPVW deals very well with protection of known UCH and with regulating activities directed at it. The aspect of activities 'incidentally' affecting 'unknown' UCH, as noted in Article 5 of the 2001 Convention, is not really addressed within its framework, but it is debatable whether this would in any case be the right place to deal with it. This aspect of activities would probably be best dealt with in the specific, mainly federal, legislation devoted to works at sea (including, *inter alia*, installing windfarms, dredging, aggregate extraction) where the ambition should be to meet the requirements of the Valletta Convention, which is ratified by Belgium and implemented in the three Belgian Regions.[75]

Legally protecting UCH is a significantly important first step, but physical inspections and monitoring actions are a very much-needed next step.[76] It is very positive that since 2019 the federal authorities are devoting financial means to improve the physical situations of the *in situ* protected shipwreck sites. In addition, the potential for conditions of the protected UCH in the Belgian part of the North Sea to be improved has been facilitated as a result of action taken by Federal Public Service (FPS) Health, Food Chain Safety and

71 Royal Decree for the 2021 AICPVW, Article 10.

72 See <https://mobilit.belgium.be/nl/scheepvaart/pleziervaart/onderwatererfgoed>.

73 See <https://www.naturalsciences.be/nl/museum/home>.

74 See <https://mobilit.belgium.be/nl/over-de-fod/activiteiten/dg-scheepvaart>.

75 European Convention on the Protection of the Archaeological Heritage (Revised) Valletta 16.1.1992. European Treaty Series n° 143 <https://rm.coe.int/168007bd25>.

76 Martijn Manders, Rob Oosting and Wil Brouwers, 'MACHU Managing Cultural Heritage Underwater. Final Report (Machu 2009).

Environment, DG Environment Marine Environment Service. In tandem with Belgium's development of a Marine Spatial Plan, the FPS published a Marine Litter Action Plan, on the basis that the issue of marine litter "affects our marine ecosystem in the long-term" and requires a "specific approach".[77] Section 4.3 of the Plan contains actions related to 'cleaning' operations, and 4.3.4 is of significance in improving the quality of UCH sites. It recognises the significance of wrecks as artificial reefs supporting biodiversity, but that their fixed structure attracts the accumulation of litter. In recognition of this, the Plan committed to a "systematic clean-up", financed by the Environmental Compensation Fund of offshore wind farms, of one of the first protected wreck sites, the *West-Hinder*, a former lightship that sank in 1912, with an almost intact hull lying upright on the sea floor.[78] The following 2019 clean-up operation gathered about 4.5 tonnes of marine litter from the wreck site, which today forms an artificial reef of about 33 metres length, and is considered a hotspot for biodiversity.[79] The accumulated litter recovered included about 2000 kg of iron (mainly chains and other parts from fishing nets), 1000 kg of lead (mainly fishing leads from line fishing) and 1500 kg of fishing nets and other kinds of plastics.[80] After the successful cleaning operation of the *West-Hinder* it was decided to undertake a similar operation with the British cargo vessel SS *Kilmore*, which sank in 1906 following a collision, and which rests on the sea floor close to the *West-Hinder*.[81] This cleaning operation started in 2021. Together with regular inspections, these cleaning operations improve the general quality of *in situ* protected wreck sites, including for divers, whilst at the same time helping to eliminate important poisonous substances, such as significant amounts of fishing leads, from the sea bottom.

4 Conclusions

The legal and archaeological research situation related to UCH in the Belgian part of the North Sea including the intertidal zone is clearly evolving in the right

77 Philippe de Backer, State Secretary for the North Sea, Foreword, Marine Litter Action Plan, page 3. For full access to the Marine Litter Action Plan see <https://www.health.belgium.be/nl/actieplan-marien-zwerfvuil>.

78 For more detail on the wreck site see <https://www.wrecksite.eu/wreck.aspx?1193> and from a divers perspective <https://www.divers-guide.com/en/lichtschip-west-hinder>.

79 See <https://www.health.belgium.be/nl/news/45-ton-afval-bovengehaald-bij-schoonmaak-wrak>.

80 Ibid.

81 For more information on the SS *Kilmore* see <https://www.health.belgium.be/nl/news/45-ton-afval-bovengehaald-bij-schoonmaak-wrak>.

direction as seen from the heritage perspective over the past two decades, with the drafting of three various successive Acts (2007, 2014 and 2021) that have progressively offered more and better protection. Today, under the 2021 legislation, not only shipwreck sites and parts thereof are in scope, but also paleo landscapes and even paleontological remains, not only in the TS but also in the vergulde and CS of the Belgian part of the North Sea. Moreover, since 10 March 2022, 56 shipwreck sites have acquired some form of protection as UCH, with 29 of these extended *in situ* protection. For 18 of these, uniform protective measures such as a ban on line fishing, trawling, dredging and anchoring in a circular zone with a diameter of 300 metres around the central part of the wreck site also apply.

These developments are an important improvement compared to the protection offered by the 2014 APUCH with strongly diverging protection measures for each individual *in situ* protected site. The protective measures were tailormade for each site, but this led to some confusion. The uniformity of the 2021 AICPVW is more straightforward and easier for raising awareness amongst stakeholders. The numbers of now protected UCH sites were completely unexpected when the legislative work started about 20 years ago. It gives clear proof of the successful appreciation of UCH by the public and by stakeholders at sea. The challenge is now to complement the mainly legal protective measures with physical measures where needed. The cleaning of the protected wreck sites from marine litter and lost fishing tackle such as fishing nets, iron hooks and lead weights is a good start. It cleans the environment and improves the integrity and quality of the sites and when linked to periodical inspection allows the monitoring of their evolution. As a result, legal protection gets translated into physical terms with real impact.

A second area where improvement can be realised is in relation to Article 5 of the 2001 Convention and confrontation of the continuing challenge posed by dealing with activities incidentally affecting unknown UCH. This was already noted as one of the shortcomings of the 2014 legal framework, although it is noteworthy that most of the other shortcomings of the 2014 APUCH have been tackled successfully with the 2021 AICPVW.

A third challenge is actually to achieve the same positive evolution in relation to inland waters, mainly rivers, in the three Belgian Regions (Flanders, Brussels and Wallonia). Significant UCH-threatening activities occur in rivers, such as construction works, for example tunnelling and dredging activities. In the context of inland waters, it sometimes seems more difficult to apply the protective measures prescribed by the 2001 Convention. This observation is not necessarily reflective of a lack of awareness but of practical matters, such as challenging visibility, strong currents, little chance to avoid UCH and very high traffic densities.

Reflecting upon two decades of legal work for the benefit of the protection of UCH in the Belgian part of the North Sea leads to some observations. First, Belgian law-making in relation to UCH is a gradual work in progress, with each new law using elements of the preceding one as a start point and baseline, indeed even the 2021 AICPVW echoes regulation from many centuries previously. Such a developmental approach does not bring about revolutionary changes, but each new UCH law does systematically allow mapping with increasing detail of the work still to be done and as such serves to stimulate progress in this particular field.

The fact that each new law improves the level of protection of UCH seems to be linked with increased general awareness, not only at the political level but also at the level of the scientific community and the public at large. A positive indication can be found in the fact that in the protocol for collaboration linked to the implementation of the 2021 AICPVW, the Royal Belgian Institute of Natural Sciences (RBINS) – a leading federal institute – is involved for its scientific advice. In contrast, under the preceding 2014 APUCH, only scientific advice at the level of the Flemish Region was looked for by the federal authorities. The joining of the RBINS seems to indicate that from 2021 onwards UCH belongs to its fields of research.

The fact that 56 UCH sites are given some form of legal protection was completely unexpected at the start of the described legal journey. That the advice of stakeholders working at sea has to be asked before a UCH site can be *in situ* protected, is a key element in making these protective measures sustainable. The support of these stakeholders is certainly needed to allow the protection to be more than a written legal text. This is without doubt an unexpected strong element in the legal frameworks of 2014 and 2021 and shows that the heritage sector and the industry working at sea can indeed join forces, work together for the benefit of UCH, and are not doomed to be adversaries.

All websites last accessed February 2025.

Selected Bibliography

Demerre I., Van Haelst S. & Sandra M. 2020: Inventaris 100-jarige scheepswrakken, Oostende.

Derudder T. 2018: Our Past Beneath the Waves. The Legal Protection of UCH from an International, North Sea and Belgian Perspective, PhD thesis, Ghent University, Belgium.

Korthals Altes A. 1973: *Prijs der zee. Raakvlak van redding, strandrecht en wrakwetgeving*, W.E.J. Tjeenk Willing, Zwolle.

Missiaen T., Derudder T., Rabaut M., Van Haelst S., Pieters M., Lettany R., Pirlet H., Maes F; 2016: *Erfgoed in zee: wat moet ik ermee? Richtlijnen voor de gebruikers van de Noordzee met betrekking tot het cultureel erfgoed onder water.* SeArch brochure, Gent.

Missiaen T., Pieters M., Maes F., Kruiver P., De Maeyer P. & Seys J. 2017: The SeArch Project: Towards an assessment methodology and sustainable management policy for the archaeological heritage of the North Sea in Belgium. In: Bailey G. N., Harff J. & Sakellariou D (eds.) *Under the sea: archaeology and palaeolandscapes of the continental shelf.* Springer, Cham, 415–424.

Pieters M., De Clercq M., Demerre I., Missiaen T. & Van Haelst S. 2018: Belgium – finds from trawl fishing, dredging and beach walking. In Fischer A. & Pedersen L. (eds) *Oceans of archaeology.* Jutland Archaeological Society and Aarhus University Press, Aarhus, 88–93.

Pieters M. & Delaere C. 2020: UCH in Belgium: recent developments 2012–2019, in: Hafner A., Öniz H., Semaan L. & Underwood C.J. (eds.): *Heritage under water at risk. Threats-Challenges-Solutions*, ICOMOS Paris, 46–49.

Tell C. & Pieters M. (eds.) 2022: *Forum für Unterwasserarchäologie 2018/UCH Forum 2018. Dokumentation der Tagung des Deutschen Nationalkomitees für Denkmalschutz (DNK), des auswärtiges Amtes der Bundesrepublik Deutschland und der Flämischen Agentur für Kulturerbe am 04. Dezember 2018 in Berlin/Documentation of the conference of the German National Committee for Monument Protection (DNK), the Foreign Office of the Federal Republic of Germany and the Flanders Heritage Agency on 04 December 2018 in Berlin*, 1. Auflage 2022, Schriftenreihe des Deutsches Nationalkomitees für Denkmalschutz, band 95, Berlin.

CHAPTER 5

Colombia

*Carlo Emilio Piazzini Suárez**

1 Introduction

Colombian waters in the Caribbean Sea have a high potential for obtaining evidence of ancient shipwrecks, as established by historical analyses and archaeological studies of the sinking of ships returning to Spain with cargoes of what had been extracted by Europeans in America. In recent decades, as with other countries in the region, this potential wealth has drawn the attention of numerous foreign private companies interested in the recovery, financial speculation, and sale of these cargoes of shipwrecks from the colonial period. In Colombia, these commercial interests have come into conflict with a legal and academic structure built throughout the twentieth century that considers the remains of these shipwrecks as part of the national archaeological heritage, and in that sense not subject to commercial exploitation.

This tension has become particularly apparent in the alleged discovery of the remains of the galleon *San José*, as discussed below, a ship of the Spanish 'Flota de Tierra Firme' (Mainland Fleet) that, having set sail from Portobello in Panama en route to Cartagena, was sunk in 1708 near the Islas del Rosario by the English Admiral, Charles Wager, who intended to capture its precious cargo.

Since the end of the 1970s, entrepreneurs dedicated to the business of underwater treasure hunting, under the name, first, of the Glocca Morra Company, subsequently renamed Sea Search Armada, took steps against different Colombian Governments, seeking to modify local legislation so that it could permit exploration and extraction contracts for the most valuable commercial contents of the *San José* and other shipwrecks.[1] At that time, a combination of factors prevented the project going from the exploration to the recovery phase. These included changes in the terms of distribution of what could be

* Full Professor, Instituto de Estudios Regionales de la Universidad de Antioquia.

1 This is the case of the galleon *San Roque*, one of the ships that made up the Tierra Firme fleet of Luis Fernández de Córdoba, sunk around 1605, and which, according to some interested parties in its extraction, is located near the Serranilla Keys in the Colombian Sea. Padilla, N. F., (2011). 'Proponen al Gobierno rescate del galeón San Roque', El Espectador, 19 de febrero de 2011. <https://www.elespectador.com/investigacion/proponen-al-gobierno-rescate-del-galeon-san-roque-article-251973/>.

 | DOI:10.1163/9789004510883_007

found, the interests of other companies seeking to enter the market for shipwrecked antiques, and the relatively strong opposition of some legislators and politicians. In response, Sea Search Armada sued the Colombian State in national and international courts, culminating in a legal process of more than two decades.

Without these issues being completely resolved, a more robust and well-structured strategy has been implemented to allow the establishment of exploitation contracts that have greater economic and commercial value. Under the leadership of former President Juan Manuel Santos (2010–2018), a series of legal and political actions were considered to fundamentally modify the existing legislation on underwater cultural heritage (UCH), permitting the signing of an exploration contract between the Colombian State and the firm Maritime Archaeology Consultants. In 2015, this led to the discovery of artefacts that apparently corresponded to the wreck of the galleon *San José*. Immediately afterwards, the State wanted to enter into another contract with the same company, for the recovery phase, to establish a scheme of distribution for the goods found. The scheme would have permitted, in addition to covering the costs of the operation, the securing of economic gains for the contractor and the State, with the remainder of the finds granted to a public museum in Cartagena.[2]

In 2022, the transaction was cancelled because of strong opposition voiced by some academic sectors in the country and abroad, as well as legislators and regulatory institutions, which considered such contracts a risk both to cultural heritage and to the country. However, there remain inconsistencies related to commercial involvement in the Colombian legal framework on UCH, leaving the door open for the commercial interests of private actors and their political allies to flourish once again. In the international context, the essentially commercial treatment that was proposed for the recoveries from the shipwreck in question alarmed multilateral entities such as UNESCO, as well as governments which, like the Spanish in terms of the galleon *San José*, consider such wrecks their sovereign property and thus entitled to sovereign immunity from salvage. Some of the events in this case have been widely reported in the media, mostly episodically and with a sensationalist tone. The result of this coverage has

2 The case of the galleon *San José* has been the subject of numerous writings that, from different perspectives, have narrated both the characteristics of the ship, the historical reconstruction of the shipwreck, as well as the details of the initiatives aimed at its extraction. For a historical view, see: C. Rahn, *The treasure of the San José: death at sea in the War of the Spanish Succession.* (Johns Hopkins University Press, 2007). For a synthesis of the legal problems, see M. Żenkiewicz and T. Wasilewski ''The Galleon *San Jose*. Almost 4 Decades of Legal Struggles on the National and International Plane' (2019) 25 *Comparative Law Review* 319.

meant that their connections to wider processes, as well as the scale of their impact on the country's cultural policies, have tended to be overlooked.

The case of the galleon *San José* is the most visible example, but not the most well-understood, of a larger issue in Colombia relating to the divergence between different value regimes for archaeological artefacts: on the one hand, as treasures with economic value, the exploitation of which must be defined commercially; and on the other, as property that is part of the Nation's archaeological heritage, which is of a public nature and thus excluded from the market.[3] This chapter presents a comprehensive review of the current situation and prospects for the management of UCH in Colombia based on a historical analysis of how these two value regimes were formed. It concludes by offering potential solutions. First, a subject-specific public policy is needed to fully restore the value of underwater archaeological material as scientific and cultural property, thus removing the commercial dimension. Second, the promotion and strengthening of the application of local capacities to ensure its conservation and better understanding. Finally, the promotion of a heritage concept favourable to the creation of a greater link between archaeological evidence and an understanding of the history of the various social groups that form the Colombian Nation today.

2 From Treasure to Heritage

The historiography of archaeology in Colombia contains a large body of research and evidence that allows for in-depth examination of the transformations and tensions that have marked the subject's emergence and development as a distinct field of study.[4] Archaeology, cultural heritage, and legal studies, on the other hand, contribute significantly to our understanding of the legal measures that the State has enacted to regulate the treatment of archaeological artefacts.[5] Based on these disciplinary perspectives, the main features

3 I take the concept of regimes of value, in the sense proposed by Appadurai in his theory on the social life of merchandise: A. Appadurai 'Introduction: commodities and the politics of value' in A. Appadurai (ed.) *The social life of things. Commodities in cultural perspective*, (Cambridge University Press, 1986).

4 For an analysis of the relevant literature see: E. Piazzini, 'Historiografía de la Arqueología en Colombia. Una Aproximación Geográfica' (2015) 51 *Revista Colombiana de Antropología* 15.

5 G. Castellanos, *Régimen jurídico del patrimonio arqueológico en Colombia* (Instituto Colombiano de Antropología e Historia. 2011). L. Duque *Colombia. Monumentos históricos y arqueológicos. Libro Primero. Monumentos y Objetos Arqueológicos* (Instituto Panamericano de Geografía e Historia, 1955). L. Duque, 'Prehistoria: etnohistoria y arqueología' in Academia

of the transformation process, from the colonial regime of value based on the category of treasure, to the most recent regime of archaeological evidence as archaeological heritage, are examined below.

An analysis of the pertinent content of the so-called 'Leyes de Indias' (Laws of the Indies) between 1519 and 1596, reveals two statutes under which indigenous materials were evaluated in the Spanish overseas colonies since the sixteenth century. First, treasures ('tesoros'), which included scarce objects with economic value, such as pieces made of gold, silver or alloys, and pearls or precious and semi-precious stones, which were obtained through 'discovery' in burials, houses, temples, and other indigenous places, and which ended up being smelted or put to commercial use. Second, shrine goods ('bienes de adoratorios'), objects that had to be destroyed because they were associated with places and practices considered by the Christian church as idolatrous, although high economic value items were excluded from destruction and considered as treasures. By default, all those artefacts and ruins that were insignificant from the point of view of the economic or religious enterprises of the Crown and its subjects remained unclassified but latent.[6]

This classification system appears to have prevailed until the mid-eighteenth century and even into the middle of the next, when the category of 'antigüedades' (antiquities) began to be used with some frequency in enlightened discourses. People from the literate elites of the new Republic of Colombia (also known as Nueva Granada, Confederación Granadina and Estados Unidos de Colombia, during the nineteenth century), amassed collections of indigenous objects and, on occasion, wrote texts about their physical characteristics, origins, and function. Travellers, dilettantes, European and North American scholars also became involved, some of whom added material to their personal collections or sent pieces to imperial collections such as the British Museum, the Ethnological Museum of Berlin, the National Museum of the United States,

---

Colombiana de Historia (ed.) *Historia Extensa de Colombia*, Vol. 1, Tomo 1. (Editorial Lerner, 1965). L. Duque, 'Defensa del Patrimonio Histórico y Artístico de Colombia, Legislación' (1966) 11 *Boletín de Arqueología* 43. C. García 'Caminos Recorridos, Fronteras por Superar. Arqueología Subacuática en Colombia' in C. del Cairo and C García (comp.) *Historias sumergidas. Hacia la protección del patrimonio cultural subacuático en América Latina* (Universidad Externado, 2006). G. Jaramillo and E. Piazzini, (comp.) *Bienes arqueológicos: una lectura transversal sobre legislación y políticas culturales – Argentina, Colombia, China, Francia, Gran Bretaña e Italia* (Universidad de Los Andes, 2013). J. Martín, F. Pérez and W. Gómez, 'Underwater Archaeology in Colombia: Between Commercial Salvage and Science' (2021) *International Journal of Historical Archaeology* <https://doi.org/10.1007/s10761-021-00610-x>.

6 *Recopilación de Leyes de los Reynos de las Indias. Mandadas imprimir y publicar por la magestad católica del Rey Don Carlos II. Nuestro Señor* (Andrés Ortega, 1774).

and the Field Museum of Chicago, among others.[7] Introduction of the denomination 'antigüedades indígenas' (indigenous antiquities) and its correlate term 'antiquarios' (antiquarians) related to a transformation of both the symbolic and economic values of archaeological artefacts. On the one hand, they began to be considered as 'testimony' or 'proof' of temporalities and remote societies, while on the other, an economic value, derived from the pieces' status as ancient and exotic artefacts, rather than the mere value of the gross weight of the raw materials, was afforded to them. This then allowed pieces elaborated with materials that previously had no commercial value, such as stone, bone, textiles, and ceramics, to gain the status of exotic goods. When these two valuations were combined, indigenous antiques became prestigious goods that served to strengthen the academic, social, economic, and political esteem of their owners and of those who studied them. All this occurred while an active international market for antiquities was being established, in which pieces circulated from archaeological sites, where they were obtained by 'guaqueros' (people who dug for treasures), transferred thereafter to antiquarians, sometimes through intermediaries, until they reached collections in Colombia and abroad.[8]

There are suggestions that, throughout the nineteenth century, perceptions were shaped in a similar manner to those that now surround the category of archaeological heritage, such as admiration and respect for the material remains of the past and their belonging to a national community. During the struggles for independence, some Colombians were interested in antiquities as a rhetorical and symbolic resource for the foundation of new regional and national identities that sought to locate themselves in the American indigenous past.[9] At that time, a renowned antiquarian, Ezequiel Uricoechea, came to refer to the existence of an 'arqueología patria' (homeland archaeology).[10] In 1882, as a result of the sale and export from the country of one of the most valuable archaeological collections held in Bogotá, that of Gonzalo Ramos Ruiz,

---

7 C. Botero, *El redescubrimiento del pasado prehispánico de Colombia: viajeros, arqueólogos y coleccionistas 1820–1945* (Instituto Colombiano de Antropología e Historia; Universidad de los Andes, 2008).

8 E. Piazzini, 'Guaqueros, anticuarios y letrados: la circulación de artefactos arqueológicos en Antioquia (1850–1950)' in C. Langebaek and C. Botero, (comp.) *Arqueología y Etnología en Colombia. La creación de una tradición científica* (Universidad de Los Andes-Banco de la República, 2009).

9 C. Langebaek, *Los herederos del pasado. Indígenas y pensamiento criollo en Colombia y Venezuela* (Universidad de los Andes, 2009).

10 E. Uricoechea, *Memorias sobre las antigüedades Neo-granadinas* (Librería de F. Schneider y Cia., 1854).

the government was criticised in some newspaper columns for not purchasing it for preservation in the Museo Nacional (National Museum).[11] Critics also questioned President Carlos Holguin's gift of the famous Quimbaya Treasure to the Queen Regent of Spain in 1892, an issue that is still debated today, not only in the press, but also in the courts, with claims for its repatriation.[12] Finally, and in contrast, another antiquarian, Leocadio María Arango, was reluctant on several occasions to sell pieces from his valuable collection. Thus, his ceramic, stone, and metal artefacts remained in Colombia, ultimately serving as the basis for the creation of two of the most important archaeological museums in the country: the Museo del Oro del Banco de la República (Gold Museum of the Bank of the Republic) and the Museo de la Universidad de Antioquia (Museum of the University of Antioquia).[13]

Despite the occurrence of these cultural changes during the nineteenth century, issues related to the legal management of indigenous antiquities were fundamentally a matter of private law applied to transactions between landowners, guaqueros, and antiquarians. The State's role was reduced to regulating the business through mining codes and regulations on treasure finds. In legal terminology, the colonial category of 'tesoro' (treasure) was still the best label to refer to indigenous antiquities.[14]

Arguably, it was not until the first decades of the twentieth century that official provisions or regulations were issued under the assumption that antiquities had 'monumental', 'historical', and 'patriotic' value. In 1902, the Academia Nacional de Historia y Antigüedades (National Academy of History and Antiquities) was created. Its imperatives focused upon the importance of safeguarding archaeological objects in museums, as well as the study of indigenous antiquities.[15] Almost at the same time, a law was passed recommending the organisation of museums and the publication of catalogues of their collections.[16] However, it was not until 1918 that what is possibly the first legislation expressly aimed at regulating the issue of archaeological artefacts

11 P. Gamboa, *El tesoro de los Quimbayas: historia, identidad y patrimonio* (Planeta, 2002), 51.

12 P. Gamboa, *El tesoro de los Quimbayas: historia, identidad y patrimonio* (Planeta, 2002).

13 E. Piazzini, 'La Colección de Antigüedades de Leocadio María Arango Uribe'in S. Robledo (ed.) *Colecciones y coleccionistas en Colombia*, (Revista Credencial Historia, 2021). See: <https://www.banrepcultural.org/bogota/museo-del-oro>; and <https://www.udea.edu.co/wps/portal/udea/web/inicio/cultura/museo-universitario>.

14 See: Ley de 13 Junio de 1833, and Ley 38 del 15 Marzo de 1887, In: F. Vélez *Datos para la Historia del Derecho Nacional* (Imprenta del Departamento,1891).

15 H. García, '¿Qué Hay en un Nombre? La Academia Colombiana de Historia y el Estudio de los Objetos Arqueológicos' (2009) 13 *Memoria y Sociedad* 41.

16 Ley 39 de 1903.

was enacted. The law was concerned with prohibiting the destruction of 'pre-Columbian monuments' considered to be 'material of the homeland history', without government authorisation.[17] Two years later, another law made it illegal to take any object of historical importance to the Nation out of the country without prior authorisation.[18] To some extent, these two laws were a response to public concern over the recovery and export of artefacts by foreign archaeologists, such as Konrad Preuss of the Ethnological Museum of Berlin and Alden J. Mason of the Field Museum of Chicago. However, when viewed in context, these laws clearly articulated the emergence of a new regime of value, in which archaeological remains are incorporated into the concept of a State's sovereignty.

In the following decades, it was considered to be the duty of the State to protect archaeological sites and study them scientifically. Thus, in 1931, Ley 103 de 1931 declared that the "monuments and archaeological objects of the regions of San Agustín, Pitalito, Alto Magdalena, and those of any other place in the Nation" were to be for 'public purposes', or the benefit of the public. Fines were to be imposed upon any "person or entity that destroys, in whole or in part, said monuments"; the sale and export of artefacts was prohibited; and there would be financing of archaeological research, the setting up of a museum in San Agustín, and the purchase of land for the creation of a National Park.[19] The promulgation of these first laws on archaeological monuments may have been linked to the participation of Colombian delegates in the Pan-American Conferences. Following the Second Conference (1901–1902), it was recommended that the member countries create an 'International Commission of Archaeology', and in the framework of the Fifth Conference (1923), they were invited to adopt measures for the protection of 'documentos arqueológicos' (archaeological documents), including their investigation and even expropriation if applicable.[20]

However, it was during the so-called Liberal Republic (1930–1946), characterised by the elaboration of public policies in education, culture, and science premised upon the concept of State modernisation, that international recommendations were accepted by the signing of treaties and the establishment of legal entities responsible for their realisation. In 1935, Colombia formalised, through two legislative measures, the Treaty on the Protection of Artistic and

17 Ley 48 de 1918.

18 Ley 47 de 1920.

19 Ley 103 de 1931, Articles 1º and 3º. This law was amended by the Decreto 904 de 1941.

20 Carnegie Endowment for International Peace *Conferencias Internacionales Americanas 1889–1936*. (Carnegie Endowment for International Peace, 1938).

Scientific Institutions and Historic Monuments, better known as the 'Roerich Pact'.[21] Consequently, in 1938, the Servicio Arqueológico Nacional (National Archaeological Service) was created as an agency attached to the Ministry of Education, overseeing the conduct of archaeological research. In the following year, the Sociedad Colombiana de Estudios Arqueológicos y Etnográficos (Colombian Society of Archaeological and Ethnographic Studies) was founded, the Museo Nacional was transformed into the Museo Arqueológico y Etnográfico de Colombia (Archaeological and Ethnographic Museum of Colombia), and the Museo del Oro was created.[22] A decisive step was taken in 1941, with the founding of the Instituto Etnológico Nacional (National Ethnological Institute), where the first Colombian anthropologists would be trained.[23] The Institute promoted the creation of satellite entities, attached to public universities, which operated as regional nodes in charge of developing research and disseminating information in archaeology and other anthropological sub-disciplines.[24]

Thus, by the mid-twentieth century, legal and institutional structures had been established to remove the issue of monuments and archaeological objects from the domain of the private and free market, with the State taking control of these on behalf of the Nation. It reflects a nascent political philosophy of archaeological heritage that became more visible when, in 1959, the first law entirely focused on the specific management of cultural heritage in Colombia was enacted.[25] The definition of immovable and movable monuments already established at the Seventh Pan-American Conference in Montevideo[26] was accepted, and the concept of 'patrimonio' (heritage) was introduced and qualified as "national historical and artistic heritage" to refer, among other expressions, to:

---

21 Ley 14 and Ley 36 de 1936.

22 M. Echeverri, 'El Museo Arqueológico y Etnográfico de Colombia (1939–1948): La Puesta en Escena de la Nacionalidad a Través de la Construcción del Pasado Indígena' (1999) 3 *Revista de Estudios Sociales* 104. J. Perry, *Caminos de la antropología en Colombia: Gregorio Hernández de Alba* (Universidad de los Andes, 2006).

23 M. Jimeno, 'Consolidación del Estado y antropología en Colombia' in J. Arocha and N. de Friedeman (ed.) *Un siglo de investigación social* (Editorial Etno, 1984). E. Restrepo, 'Antropología Hecha en Colombia' (2014) 1 *Revista Antropologías del Sur* 83–104.

24 R. Pineda, 'Cronistas Contemporáneos. Historia de los Institutos Etnológicos de Colombia (1930–1952)' in C. Langebaek and C. Botero (ed.) *Arqueología y Etnología en Colombia. La creación de una tradición científica* (Universidad de Los Andes-Banco de la República, 2009).

25 Ley 163 de 1959. This law was regulated by Decrees 264 de 1963 and 1397 de 1989.

26 Carnegie Endowment for International Peace *Conferencias Internacionales Americanas 1889–1936*. (Carnegie Endowment for International Peace, 1938).

> … monuments, pre-Hispanic tombs, and other objects, whether they are the work of nature, or human activity, that are of special interest for the study of past civilizations and cultures, history or art, or for paleontological research, and that have been preserved on the surface or in the national subsoil.[27]

Specifically, regarding 'monumentos arqueológicos', the rights of the Nation to material discovered during the course of works and earthworks was protected. Findings were required to be reported to the Ministry of National Education immediately, and the obligation to have excavation and archaeological exploration licenses was established, taking into account "the scientific solvency of the interested parties and the strictly cultural motives of such explorations".[28] A registry of artefacts already in the possession of private individuals was also implemented, and although purchase of archaeological artefacts remained possible, it was understood that there was a mechanism for the State to reacquire them in order to conserve, study and exhibit them. In addition, they were expressly removed from classification as 'tesoros', as provided for in the Civil Code,[29] marking a fundamental transformation in the regime of value of archaeological artefacts in the country.

In the decades that followed, a geopolitics of heritage began to emerge, which has since gravitated, with few exceptions, around the concepts, sophisticated terminology, and management models recommended by UNESCO.[30] Thus, Colombia adopted both the 1972 Convention Concerning the Protection of the World Cultural and Natural Heritage[31] and the 1970 Convention on the Means of Prohibiting and Preventing the Illicit Import, Export, and Transfer of Ownership of Cultural Property.[32]

To align with these international tools, while also consolidating a political philosophy of cultural heritage, the new Political Constitution of Colombia

---

27 Ley 163 de 1959, art. 1.

28 Ley 163 de 1959, art. 11.

29 CódigoCivil, Article 700.

30 E. Piazzini, 'Cronotopos, memorias y lugares: una mirada desde los patrimonios' in E. Piazzini and V. Montoya (ed.) *Geopolíticas: espacios de poder y poder de los espacios* (Editorial La Carreta-Instituto de Estudios Regionales, 2008).

31 UN Educational, Scientific and Cultural Organisation (UNESCO), *Convention Concerning the Protection of the World Cultural and Natural Heritage,* 16 November 1972. 1037 UNTS 151. Made effective in Colombia by Ley 45 de 1983.

32 UN Educational, Scientific and Cultural Organisation (UNESCO), *Convention on the Means of Prohibiting and Preventing the Illicit Import, Export, and Transfer of Ownership of Cultural Property*, 14 November 1970. 823 UNTS 231. Made effective in Colombia by Ley 63 de 1986.

(1991) established a higher status for both heritage and archaeological property, in particular by incorporating them as foundational concepts of nationality, within the framework of the rule of law, and among the cultural rights of citizens. Among its fundamental principles, the Constitution specified the joint responsibility of the State and the people in the protection of the "cultural riches of the Nation."[33] It also established the State duty to promote and foster the access of all Colombians to culture, the development of research, and the dissemination of the cultural values of the Nation. It stated unequivocally that the cultural heritage of the Nation "is under the protection of the State", and that "the archaeological heritage and other cultural property that comprise the national identity belong to the Nation, it is inalienable, non-attachable, and imprescriptible".[34] Since then, these constitutional principles and developments have been affirmed and regulated through a series of general norms on cultural heritage, and particularly archaeological heritage.[35] This, when combined with a series of judgments issued by the high courts,[36] forms a relatively extensive body of jurisprudence that, with notable exceptions referring to UCH, currently governs the issue of archaeological heritage in the country.

Similarly, and in keeping with the geopolitics of alignment with UNESCO, in the last decades, Colombia approved the 1954 Hague Convention for the Protection of Cultural Property in the Event of Armed Conflict,[37] and the Second Protocol of the Convention signed in 1999.[38] Other international agreements added to the constitutional block include the 1995 UNIDROIT Convention on Stolen or Illegally Exported Cultural Objects[39] and Decision 861 of 2020 on the Protección y Recuperación de Bienes del Patrimonio Cultural de los Países Miembros de la Comunidad Andina (Protection and Recovery of Cultural

33 Constitución Política de Colombia, Article 8°.

34 Constitución Política de Colombia, Articles 63°, 70°, and 72°.

35 Ley 397 de 1997, modified and expanded by Ley 1185 de 2008, and regulated by the Decrees 833 de 2002 and 763 de 2009.

36 Among others, rulings C-474 of 2003, C-668 of 2005, and C-264, C-553, and C-572 of 2014, issued by the Constitutional Court.

37 UN Educational, Scientific and Cultural Organisation (UNESCO), *Convention for the Protection of Cultural Property in the Event of Armed Conflict,* 14 May 1954. 249 UNTS 215. Made effective in Colombia by Ley 340 de 1996.

38 UN Educational, Scientific and Cultural Organisation (UNESCO), *Second Protocol to the Hague Convention of 1954 for the Protection of Cultural Property in the Event of Armed Conflict The Hague,* 26 March 1999. 2253 UNTS 172. Made effective in Colombia by Ley 1130 de 2007.

39 International Institute for the Unification of Private Law (UNIDROIT), *Convention on Stolen or Illegally Exported Cultural Objects,* 24 June 1995. 2421 UNTS 457. Made effective in Colombia by Ley 1304 de 2009.

Heritage Property of the Member Countries of the Andean Community), which takes into account archaeological heritage property.[40] However, it is important to highlight Colombia's refusal to sign the 2001 UNESCO Convention on the Protection of the Underwater Cultural Heritage (2001 Convention), which highlights a legal anomaly described below.[41]

3 From Heritage to Treasure

In Colombia, since at least the 1960s, a series of regulations, under the term 'especies náufragas' (shipwrecked objects), reintroduced a concept of value typical of the old colonial term of 'tesoros' into the legislation. As a result of advances in technology for the exploration of deep underwater environments, the 'especies náufragas', which maintain high economic value in the art and antiquities markets, became the focus of foreign private companies. Their representatives and financial backers lobbied and exerted pressure on the governments and legislators of the day to create a more favourable legislative environment. As a result, decrees granted the national government and/or certain State agencies the authority to sign agreements or contracts with private individuals who reported the discovery of shipwrecks, granting those individuals commercial rights over some of the property contained therein, whether in kind or in money.[42] However, until the 1990s, it had not been possible for these companies to achieve their ultimate goals. This was due to various factors such as competition between companies, changes in alliances with members of the Colombian Government, or those close to it, and the refusal of some legislators and officials to allow this type of business with property already considered part of the Nation's archaeological heritage.

However, the partial progress of some of these initiatives had already created risks for the UCH located in Colombian waters, as well as creating an anomaly in the legislation on archaeological heritage. This anomaly was highlighted very clearly in the General Law of Culture of 1997,[43] which, while being entirely consistent with the constitutional status of archaeological goods as

---

40 Consejo Andino de Ministros de Relaciones Exteriores, *Decisión 861 Protección y recuperación de bienes del patrimonio cultural de los Países Miembros de la Comunidad Andina*, 8 de julio de 2020.

41 2562 UNTS 1.

42 Decreto 655 de 1968, Decreto-ley 2349 de 1971, Decreto-ley 12 de 1984, Decreto-ley 2324 de1984, and Ley 26 de 1986.

43 Ley 397 de 1997.

national heritage, introduced the term 'especies náufragas' in a contradictory manner. It states:

> With regard to the underwater cultural heritage, they belong to the cultural or archaeological heritage of the Nation due to their historical or archaeological value, which must be determined by the Ministry of Culture, the cities or cemeteries of disappeared human groups, human remains, the shipwrecked species constituted by the ships and their content, and other movable property lying within them, or scattered on the seabed, that is found on the marine floor or subsoil of internal waters, the territorial sea, the continental shelf, or exclusive economic zone, whatever their nature or state, and the cause or time of the sinking or shipwreck. The remains or parts of boats, contents or goods that are in similar circumstances, also have the character of shipwrecked species.[44]

Further, procedures were established to deal with complaints about discoveries of shipwrecked objects, which appear to contemplate apportioning of the monetary value of the find:

> If, as a result of the complaint, the rescue occurs in the geographical coordinates indicated by the complainant, the latter will be entitled to a percentage of the gross value of the shipwrecked objects that will be regulated by the National Government, after hearing the opinion of the National Council of Culture.[45]

The ambiguity produced by the tension between the differing regimes applied to the value of underwater archaeological artefacts as either heritage, or treasure, was also revealed when the Colombian State decided not to sign the 2001 Convention. Although the Colombian delegation, which had participated in the preparatory meetings for the Convention and actively promoted a position supportive of Latin American and Caribbean States adopting the common position of protecting UCH, when the time came to actually support it, there were debates in the Congress of the Republic that influenced the official decision not to sign. In coming to this decision, arguments were presented about the principle of *in situ* conservation as being extremely protectionist. In addition, parts of the 2001 Convention concerned with marine jurisdiction were considered an inconvenience as they related to the sovereign management of

44 Ley 397 de 1997, Article 9º.

45 Ley 397 de 1997, Article 9º, parágrafo 1º.

the shipwrecked objects present in Colombia's aquatic environment. These positions, ironically dressed up in nationalist rhetoric by some politicians, turned out, however, to favour foreign commercial interests over the UCH existing in Colombian waters.[46]

However, until 2010, the legislation on 'especies náufragas' was not sufficient to allow the legal commercial exploitation of UCH property in Colombia. Faced with this situation, under the administrations of former President Juan Manuel Santos (2010–2018), a combined political-legislative strategy was launched to favour commercial involvement. It was expressly aimed at making possible the signing of contracts with private companies for the identification, recovery, and commercial exploitation of those more economically valuable goods in colonial shipwrecks. Initially, a ruling was issued that established mechanisms expressly aimed at ensuring that some goods could be released from the constitutional status of inalienable objects of the archaeological heritage, to allow their management as merchandise. This was in apparent contrast to the official media version of events, which extolled the cultural and patriotic value of cultural heritage. Indeed, while in some newspapers the defence and protection of UCH was promulgated,[47] the law was specifically targeted towards the most valuable objects on the international antiquities market: gold bars, gold and silver coins, pearls, and precious, and semi-precious stones, as well as those repeated objects of any material and characteristics.[48]

At the time, the Corte Constitucional (Constitutional Court) reviewed this law and declared some its provisions would violate the constitutional framework for the valuation of archaeological heritage.[49] However, despite this, not

46 For a defence of the Colombian opposition to the 2001 Convention, see: A. Rengifo, 'Las Objeciones de Colombia a la Convención Internacional de la Unesco sobre Protección del Patrimonio Cultural Subacuático'. (2009) 25 *Pensamiento Jurídico* 117. For a reading of the debate in the Colombian Congress, see: 'Acta de Comisión 10 del 23 de octubre de 2001 Senado' (2002) 164 *Gaceta del Congreso*. <http://svrpubindc.imprenta.gov.co/senado/index2.xhtml?ent=Senado&fec=17-5-2002&num=164&consec=4505>.

47 See for example: <https://www.semana.com/aprueban-ley-protegera-patrimonio-cultural-sumergido/348279-3/>.

48 According to Article 3° of the Ley 1675 de 2013, known as the Law of Underwater Cultural Heritage, the repetition criterion refers to the «Quality of a good or set of movable goods by which they are similar, given their characteristics, their serial condition and for having exchange or fiscal value, such as coins, gold and silver ingots or rough precious stones». This law was regulated by decrees 1698 de 2014, 1530 de 2016, 1389 de 2017, and 204 de 2022.

49 Sentencia C-264 de 2014, declared numerals 1 and 2 of Article 3° of the Ley 1675 unenforceable. These numerals were intended to exclude the following goods from the condition of archaeological heritage: "Commercial cargo consisting of materials in their raw

all the negative impacts upon UCH and the previous regulations that protected it were overruled. Once the legislative door was opened for the deregulation of the special regime for the protection of archaeological heritage, the Maritime Archaeology Consultants company was hired, which resulted in the discovery of the remains of what was presumed to be the galleon *San José*, in November 2015. This identification phase was carried out secretly, citing reasons of national security. Subsequently, a tender was structured for a public-private partnership contract that would allow the recovery and commercial exploitation of the identified shipwreck, with Maritime Archaeology Consultants as the company favoured to carry it out. The contract was expected to be signed before the end of the second government of Santos (July 2018), but a few days before his term of office ended, and as a result of a series of complaints and demands, the bidding process entered into a dynamic of suspensions, extensions, and modifications.[50]

The criticisms made by different sectors of the national and international academy, as well as by multilateral organisations dating back to early 2011, had a powerful impact on the failure of this political-legislative strategy.[51] Included

state, whatever their origin, such as pearls, corals, precious and semi-precious stones, sand and wood" and "movable property identified with serial numbers that would have had an exchange or fiscal value such as coins and ingots." Regarding the criterion of repetition, one of the most contentious aspects of the Law, the Court declared it enforceable but conditioned its application in three ways: first, to the extent that it cannot be applied in isolation when determining whether or not a property is part of the UCH, but rather it must be done in conjunction with the other criteria, that is, in an integral way; secondly, insofar as in each find the criterion of cultural unity must be respected, which would be lost if one or more of the goods that make it up is detached from the group because of its character as a repeated object. Finally, the Court reasoned that even in the case of those serialised objects with an exchange value, such as precious materials in their raw state, ingots, bars or coins, that the National Council of Cultural Heritage could consider as not belonging to the UCH due to the repetition criterion, a representative sample of them must be reserved, in order for them to fulfil a cultural function.

50 Presidencia de la República de Colombia, 'Declaración del presidente Juan Manuel Santos sobre el Galeón San José, 23 de julio de 2018', see <https://www.youtube.com/watch?v=_V1SN9tBTcA>.

51 When the drafting of the Bill began in 2011, the ICANH issued a technical concept that drew early attention to aspects that ran the risk of being unconstitutional and could hinder the fight against illicit trafficking of cultural property. Likewise, the Attorney General's Office warned on several occasions about the risks of the violation of constitutional rights on account of the law and the bidding of the public-private alliance. Between 2011 and 2022, criticism of the law and the contracting process has been publicly expressed by the former directors of ICANH, the Colombian Society of Archaeology-SCAR, the Colombian Association of Archaeology-ACOARQ and the University Network of Underwater Cultural Heritage (RUPCS). The presidents of the World Congress of Archaeology, the

amongst the latter are UNESCO petitions to the Colombian Government to amend the Law on UCH, passed in 2013, and to suspend the tender for the recovery of the remains of the galleon *San José*.[52]

In what at first glance would seem to correspond to a change in strategy, during the administration of President Iván Duque (2018–2022), the entire wreck was declared 'bien cultural del ámbito nacional' (national cultural property),[53] a category that, in accordance with Colombian legislation, shields the remains of the galleon *San José* from otherwise probable commercial exploitation. More recently, the Ministry of Culture publicly announced the cancellation of the tender for contracting the recovery of said property.[54] However, although these decisions are, in principle, related to the regime of value for UCH as part of the national archaeological heritage, the ultimate purpose of the principles and mechanisms that will be adopted to deal with this and other underwater archaeological contexts remains unclear. In any case, the decisions made do not eliminate the current and future risks of commercial exploitation of archaeological heritage, nor do they overcome the legal anomaly created by the reintroduction of the category of 'tesoro' in Colombian regulations on the subject.

4 The Need for Public Policy

There are several structural factors that have deprived Colombia of consistent legislation on the protection of UCH and consequently, on several occasions the government has agreed to contract shipwreck recovery projects, mainly by commercially oriented interests. First, in addition to the pressure and lobbying that companies interested in the business of 'especies náufragas' have deployed over the last five decades, certain political sectors have maintained

---

American Society of Archaeology and the European Association of Archaeology also spoke critically.

52 In 2011, the Sub-directorate General for Culture of UNESCO called the Colombian Government's attention to the fact that the Bill went against the rules established by that body for the protection of UCH, and also promoted the treasure hunting business. Correspondence UNESCO CLT/CEH/CHP/11/179 swl 16th November 2011. This warning was reiterated in 2018 by the UNESCO Scientific and Technical Advisory Council on Underwater Cultural Heritage, when the terms of the contract for the recovery of goods from the *San José* were made public. Underwater Cultural Heritage/18/9.STAB/10, 24 April 2018. Resolution 4/STAB 9. See <https://unesdoc.unesco.org/ark:/48223/pf0000261338>.

53 Resolución 0085 del 23 de enero de 2020, of the Ministry of Culture.

54 Resolución 0113 del 4 de marzo de 2022, of the Ministry of Culture.

a discourse of poverty, which takes for granted that the country does not have sufficient financial, scientific, and technological capacities to effectively manage the protection and research of UCH in its maritime waters. A second key factor has been the lack of State policy on the subject, without which the treatment of legislation and related actions is dependent on changing decisions based on the interests of incumbent governments.

By way of example regarding the first factor, in 2001, in the Congressional debate relating to the defeated proposal to adhere to the 2001 Convention, a senator said emphatically: "everyone knows that there is no money for priority things in the country, much less for exploration that can give many surprises." He then added, referring to the principle of *in situ* conservation promoted by the 2001 Convention, that:

> ... there are about 1,100 shipwrecks with historical importance, deteriorating underwater, being lost with all their cargo under the seas of Colombia, with an invaluable cultural and historical wealth, with goods of incalculable value, while here the press periodically publishes that the culture is bankrupt, that museums, hospitals, and schools are closing.[55]

The same argument of an economically poor country accompanied the Congressional debates in 2013 prior to approval of the Law on UCH.[56] However, it is not only about understating economic capacity, but also the scientific and technological abilities of the country. This is evident in the contempt shown by politicians and officers aligned with the Santos Government's political-legislative strategy toward technical and scientific arguments that opposed them or did not serve their interests. At the same time, the official news of the discovery of the galleon and the subsequent bidding process for its recovery was imprinted with a scientific rhetoric that placed the capacities abroad, and in the sphere of private business.[57]

---

55 Acta de Comisión 10 del 23 octubre de 2001 Senado (2002) 164 *Gaceta del Congreso*: <http://svrpubindc.imprenta.gov.co/senado/index2.xhtml?ent=Senado&fec=17-5-2002&num=164&consec=4505>.

56 See the interventions of the senators Carlos Roberto Ferro Solanilla (Party of the U) and Jorge Hernando Pedraza Gutiérrez (Conservative Party), in the minutes 1.03:00 and 2:36:00 of the public hearing in the Colombian Congress in 2013: <https://www.youtube.com/watch?v=B48ZEjTUrlA&ab_channel=CarlosFerro>.

57 Santos claimed that for the discovery and rescue of the remains of the *San José*, a "dream team had been formed, bringing together the most important experts in the world at each step, with the most advanced technology in the world". República de Colombia. Relatoría de la primera sesión de la Comisión Nacional de Moralización, 9 de abril de 2018..

However, there are enough indications to believe that Colombia has the capacity to implement collaborative schemes for underwater archaeological heritage training, research, and assessment, without jeopardising the principle of self-determination in the management of its heritage property. Between 2010 and 2011, the Instituto Colombiano de Antropología e Historia (Colombian Institute of Anthropology and History, ICANH) organised an exercise to analyse the country's capabilities in underwater archaeology and related fields, with the participation of national and international experts.[58] The general balance showed that State entities and public or private universities had a long history of local research experience, training, international cooperation schemes in archaeology and related areas, as well as technological resources in the nautical field, which could be used for the protection, conservation, better knowledge, and appreciation of the UCH located in the country's continental, island, fluvial, and maritime territories.

These conditions have been strengthened in the last decade, hand-in-hand with the improvement of postgraduate programmes in anthropology, archaeology, history, restoration, and conservation offered by Colombian universities. This is coupled with the improvement of the investigative capacity of their professors and students, including pertinent postgraduate training abroad, as well as the establishment or strengthening of networks of academic exchange and international cooperation. However, it is worth noting that, in the absence of a clear policy position on the valuation of archaeological heritage as common

58 Among the national participants were members of the Armada Nacional, the Dirección General Marítima, Colciencias, the Comisión Colombiana del Océano, as well as teachers and researchers from higher education entities such as the Universidad Nacional de Colombia, the Universidad de Antioquia, the Universidad de los Andes, the Universidad del Magdalena, the Universidad del Cauca, the Universidad de Caldas, the Universidad Externado de Colombia, the Universidad Jorge Tadeo Lozano, and the Fundación Terra Firme. From the international sphere, professionals included those attached to UNESCO, State entities such as the Instituto Nacional de Antropología e Historia de México and the Instituto Nacional de Antropología y Pensamiento Latinoamericano de Argentina, as well as universities and research centres with scientific expertise in training and research projects in underwater archaeology such as the University of Southern Denmark, Texas A&M University, Australia Flinders University, the United Kingdom's Nautical Archaeological Society (NAS), and the Spanish Museo Nacional de Arqueología Subacuática (ARQUA), Instituto Colombiano de Antropología e Historia-ICANH. 2010–2011. Arqueología subacuática en Colombia: hacia la generación de capacidades locales para la investigación y la gestión del patrimonio cultural subacuático. Unpublished reports of the meetings called by ICANH and held in Bogotá on November 19, 2010 and between September 7 and 9, 2011. Bogotá: Instituto Colombiano de Antropología e Historia.

good and public heritage, as well as the ethical implications of the professional practice of underwater archaeology and related knowledge, these capacities run the risk of serving the regime of value of such heritage as 'tesoro'.

Regarding the second structural factor, the lack of a State policy on UCH, many rulers, legislators, and officials have ignored the long journey, and the efforts that have been made in the country to build a regime for the valuation of this heritage as common good and outside of the world of commerce. Strategically there is an urgent need to formulate a public policy on the subject, composed of legal, scientific, technological, and social guidelines in order to remedy this situation.[59]

Along with guidelines, the UCH law and its regulations (Ley 1675 de 2013) must be substantively revised in order to eliminate those provisions that allow the questionable management of a portion of the materials that comprise the UCH as if they were merchandise. More broadly, progress must be made in a legislative development that is in tune with the conceptualisation of archaeological heritage as part of collective rights and interests, as has been highlighted in recent Colombian jurisprudence.[60]

It is also necessary to transform the perception of alleged economic precariousness and the lack of scientific and technological capacities on the part of State institutions and the local academic community. This can be accomplished through the design and implementation of public policies in terms of scientific and technological investment, and responsible treatment of UCH as a common good. Based on this, local expertise should be used and strengthened, establishing alliances and international cooperation schemes, clearly guided by criteria of Colombian leadership and ethical positioning.

In terms of what would be a critical geopolitics of heritage, it is necessary to adopt a criterion of self-determination that seeks to protect the interests and collective rights of the Nation and the citizenry over the UCH in the spaces of sovereignty of the country. This should be achieved without the favouring of foreign interests in the contracting frameworks for the exploitation of shipwrecks, nor adopting nationalist postures that, paradoxically, have served such

59 The need for such a public policy and the proposal of possible lines for its development have been expressed in recent years by the University Network of Underwater Cultural Heritage. See: Red Universitaria de Patrimonio Cultural Sumergido-RUPCS. 2018. Sobre la necesidad de una Política de Estado en materia de Patrimonio Cultural Sumergido. Comunicación abierta desde las universidades colombianas al Nuevo Gobierno. 23 de julio de 2018: <https://www.academia.edu/37143076>.

60 Sentencia SU-649 del 19 de octubre de 2017, available at <https://www.corteconstitucional.gov.co/relatoria/2017/SU649-17.htm>. Fallo 02704 de 2018 Consejo de Estado, available at <https://www.alcaldiabogota.gov.co/sisjur/normas/Norma1.jsp?i=85245>.

interests. For better or worse, the Colombian State bears primary responsibility for the protection, conservation, research, and social valuation of the archaeological heritage found in its continental, island, and maritime territories.

5 Conclusions

Colombian legislation on UCH currently exhibits ambiguities resulting from the tension between two opposing regimes of value of archaeological material, either as inalienable property of archaeological heritage, or as treasure. There have been advances for decades in the transformation of the value regime of past materials, granting them the former status of inalienable property of the archaeological heritage, public in nature, and placed outside the world of commercial exploitation. However, since the end of the twentieth century, and with remarkable intensity in the last decade, there have been legislative and administrative actions that have sought to restore their value as exotic goods with defined economic value in the realm of private business.

From a historical perspective, the recent regulations on UCH, added to the series of provisions on 'especies náufragas' that were issued during the second half of the twentieth century, constitute a legal anomaly. They generate significant inconsistencies with the broader legislative hierarchy that, in line with international treaties on cultural heritage, the country has been building since the 1930s. Furthermore, recent legal provisions that treat a portion of the national archaeological heritage as if it were treasure, constitute a regression insofar as, rather than gradually expanding citizens' rights to culture and, in particular cultural heritage, they restrict them, putting at risk the very integrity of the property that comprise said heritage, both on land and in water.

It should be noted that the ways in which the regimes of value that have categorised underwater archaeological materials as treasures or heritage have gradually been taking shape and do not correspond to teleological, linear, or finished processes. For this reason, it is in the hands of legislators, governments, and academics to finish opening or closing the door to the current processes of deregulation of the norms on archaeological heritage as public property, and to the reduction of the duties of the State and of citizens in relation to its protection and valuation. To close the door, as is proposed here, is not easy. The necessary legislative adjustments, design, and implementation of a public policy on UCH in Colombia must consider an updated discussion of national experiences in professional training, research, conservation, and restoration as a framework for establishing strategies aimed at decisively strengthening capacities in this field.

In this perspective, it is necessary to specify a clear geopolitical position of the Colombian State in relation to the international and local dynamics that affect the future of UCH today. On the one hand, and without putting the principle of self-determination in doubt, international cooperation and alliances should be fostered, based on symmetrical, not deferential or dependent relationships, and clearly guided by fundamentally scientific and cultural interests. On the other hand, it is necessary to better understand, and take into account, the diverse and changing forms of relationship that local communities establish with the archaeological material that rests in the Nation's aquatic spaces. Without a doubt, a full understanding of archaeological heritage as a common good demands a creative transformation of the State's traditional mechanisms of hegemonic and centralised treatment for its valuation, protection, intervention, and enjoyment. Overall, these transformations should not overlook the progressive legislative legacies mentioned here, valuing them in their respective historical context.

All websites last accessed February 2025.

Acknowledgements

The author wishes to express his gratitude to Professor Gustavo Zapata Giraldo, for his valuable support with the translation of the original text in Spanish.

Selected Bibliography

Botero, Clara. 2008. *El redescubrimiento del pasado prehispánico de Colombia: viajeros, arqueólogos y coleccionistas 1820–1945*. Bogotá: Instituto Colombiano de Antropología e Historia; Universidad de los Andes.

García, Catalina. 2006. Caminos recorridos, fronteras por superar. Arqueología subacuática en Colombia. En *Historias sumergidas. Hacia la protección del patrimonio cultural subacuático en América Latina*, compiled by Carlos del Cairo and Catalina García, pp. 177–192. Bogotá: Universidad Externado.

Jaramillo, Luis Gonzalo y Carlo Emilio Piazzini (comps.). 2013. *Bienes arqueológicos: una lectura transversal sobre legislación y políticas culturales – Argentina, Colombia, China, Francia, Gran Bretaña e Italia*. Bogotá: Universidad de Los Andes.

Langebaek, Carl. 2009. *Los herederos del pasado. Indígenas y pensamiento criollo en Colombia y Venezuela*. 2 Tomos. Bogotá: Universidad de los Andes.

Martín, Juan, Felipe Pérez y William Gómez. 2021. Underwater Archaeology in Colombia: Between Commercial Salvage and Science. *International Journal of Historical Archaeology*. 10.1007/s10761-021-00610-x.

Piazzini, Emilio. 2008. Cronotopos, memorias y lugares: una mirada desde los patrimonios. In: *Geopolíticas: espacios de poder y poder de los espacios*, editado por Emilio Piazzini y Vladimir Montoya, pp. 171–183. Medellín: Editorial La Carreta-Instituto de Estudios Regionales.

Piazzini, Emilio. 2015. Historiografía de la arqueología en Colombia. Una aproximación geográfica. *Revista Colombiana de Antropología* 51 (2): 15–48.

Żenkiewicz, Maciej y Tadeusz Wasilewski. 2019. The Galleon San Jose. Almost 4 Decades of Legal Struggles on the National and International Plane. *Comparative Law Review*, 25: 319–342.

CHAPTER 6

Croatia

*Trpimir M. Šošić**

1 Introduction

As elsewhere in the Mediterranean, the sea off the Croatian Adriatic coast contains numerous Underwater Cultural Heritage (UCH) sites from various periods of history, be they wrecks of ships lost on their voyages to and from the ports of the Adriatic, or settlements and harbour works submerged due to sea level rise.[1] Thus, it is not surprising that in Croatia underwater archaeology as a discipline is, comparatively, rather well developed. With some sporadic campaigns undertaken in the first half of the twentieth century, since the 1960s activities in relation to maritime archaeological research have become more intense and systematic.[2] Instances of important discoveries stemming from this activity include the finds of two well-preserved boats dated to the medieval Kingdom of Croatia, and a Renaissance shipwreck off the islet of Gnalić,[3] on which research continues.[4] Probably the most famous find is that of a rare, Hellenic, bronze statue, known as the Croatian Apoxyomenos, towards the end of the 1990s, now in independent Croatia. It was the story of this statue that brought UCH protection into the purview of the wider public.[5]

That Croatia affords a fair degree of importance to UCH protection may be deduced from the fact that it was the third country to ratify the UNESCO Convention on the Protection of the Underwater Cultural Heritage (2001 Convention), back in 2004.[6] After its entry into force, a Croatian expert in underwater

* Assistant Professor of Public International Law, University of Zagreb, Faculty of Law.

1 In an informative text on underwater archaeology on the website of the International Centre for Underwater Archaeology, some 400 known sites are mentioned, although a smaller number have effectively been protected (see note 23); see <https://www.icua.hr/en/underwater-archaeology>.

2 I. Radić Rossi, 'Underwater Cultural Heritage and Maritime Archaeology in Croatia: An Overview' (2012) 15 *European Journal of Archaeology* 285, at pp. 287–98.

3 *Ibid.*, at pp. 288–89.

4 I. Radić Rossi, M. Nicolardi, K. Batur, 'The Gnalić Shipwreck: Microcosm of the Late Renaissance World' in D. Davison *et al.* (eds.), *Croatia at the Crossroads* (Archaeopress Archaeology, 2016) 223.

5 See 3.5.3., notes 135–136.

6 (2009) 2562 UNTS 51.

 | DOI:10.1163/9789004510883_008

archaeology was elected to the first Scientific and Technical Advisory Body (STAB).[7] Another testimony to the efforts of Croatian experts in the field of UCH protection came with conferral of the status of a UNESCO regional centre for underwater archaeology upon the International Centre for Underwater Archaeology in Zadar (ICUA), which to date remains the only such institution.[8]

Thus, given that the outlook of Croatia on the 2001 Convention appears to be evidently positive, the focus of the discussion in this chapter will be on how its rules have shaped Croatian municipal law. First, an overview of the institutional framework of UCH protection in Croatia will be given. Croatia does not have a separate law on UCH protection, instead it adopts the model of one, comprehensive, law that regulates the protection of all cultural heritage, including UCH. At the time this chapter was finalised, this still was the Act on the Protection and Preservation of Cultural Objects (COA), adopted in 1999,[9] two years prior to the completion of the 2001 Convention, and repeatedly amended.[10] In November 2023, the Croatian Ministry of Culture and Media publicised a legislative proposal with the draft text of an entirely new Act on the Protection and Preservation of Cultural Objects (2023 Draft Act),[11] which in the following discussion could only be considered to a limited extent.

7 The expert was Jasen Mesić. See Resolution 7/MSP2, Convention on the Protection of the Underwater Cultural Heritage, Meeting of States Parties, 2nd session, Paris, 1–2 December 2009.

8 See 2., notes 34–37.

9 Narodne novine [Official Gazette of the Republic of Croatia; NN] no. 69/1999. An English translation of the initial text can be retrieved from the UNESCO Database of National Cultural Heritage Laws, <https://www.unesco.org/en/cultnatlaws>. The original Croatian term for what has, in lack of a more apt formulation, been translated into English as 'cultural object' is *kulturno dobro*. Much like the French expression *bien culturel*, the term connotes not only material but also immaterial values and aspects, and may, thus, be used in connection with intangible cultural heritage, as well. *Cf.* T. M. Šošić, 'Pojam kulturne baštine – međunarodnopravni pogled' ['The Concept of Cultural Heritage – an International Law Perspective'] (2014) 51 *Zbornik radova Pravnog fakulteta u Splitu* [*Collected Papers of the Law Faculty of the University of Split*] 833, at pp. 837–38.

10 Subsequent amendments and/or corrections in NN nos. 151/2003, 157/2003, 100/2004, 87/2009, 88/2010, 61/2011, 25/2012, 136/2012, 157/2013, 152/2014, 98/2015, 44/2017, 90/2018, 32/2020, 62/2020, 117/2021. In addition, the legislation has been amended converting fines into Euros in line with Croatia's joining of the Eurozone in 2023, see NN no. 114/2022.

11 It may be observed that according to the proposal the law's title will not be altered. The proposal is expected to enter parliamentary procedure during the first trimester of 2024. During the public consultation process the text of the 2023 Draft Act has been available online (in Croatian only): <https://esavjetovanja.gov.hr/ECon/MainScreen?entityId=25710>.

2 The Institutional Framework of UCH Protection under the COA

In Croatia, distinct State-run institutions for UCH exist at the level of archaeological and conservation work and expertise (namely the Croatian Conservation Institute's Department for Underwater Archaeology and the International Centre for Underwater Archaeology, discussed below), but administrative decisions in relation to UCH, such as those on permits for archaeological research or on protection measures, are taken and relevant procedures conducted by State authorities responsible for the protection of cultural heritage generally. This accords with Croatia's approach of one law encompassing all cultural heritage.

Administratively, management of cultural heritage is organised and coordinated by the ministry competent for cultural affairs, originally called the Ministry of Culture, but since 2020, due to enlargement of its competence, renamed the Ministry of Culture and Media (the Ministry), which:

> ... performs administrative and expert work on the protection and preservation of cultural objects ... and inspections in the area of protection and preservation of cultural objects.[12]

Within the organisational structure of the Ministry, this task is realised by the Directorate for the Protection of Cultural Heritage. However, under the COA most object and site specific administrative decisions, including fieldwork permits and the prescription of protection measures, are taken by 19 regionally competent conservation departments, operating under the umbrella of the Ministry's Directorate for the Protection of Cultural Heritage.[13] As a rule, they are set up in the prinicipal city of a county and territorially cover the area of that county. Among the conservation departments, nine cover coastal areas on the Adriatic Sea, including the appurtenant maritime spaces, i.e. Internal Waters and Territorial Sea (TS).[14] In practice, it will be one of these

---

12 COA, Article 77.

13 The Zagreb City Institute for Cultural and Natural Heritage Conservation, which fulfils the functions of a conservation department for the area of Croatia's capital, has a somewhat different legal status. In the 2023 Draft Act the possibility of organising the Ministry's work through the establishment of regional conservation services, offices and departments is retained (Art. 96(3)). A novelty in the 2023 Draft Act is that it spells out a set of 11 general protective measures (Art. 26(1)). Amongst these general measures figures the requirement of digitisation of cultural objects which is further elaborated in a separate article (Art. 27).

14 Namely the Conservation Departments in Pula, Rijeka, Gospić, Zadar, Šibenik, Trogir, Split, Imotski and Dubrovnik.

conservation departments that, according to territorial remit, issues administrative orders and decisions in respect of a specific maritime UCH site. The lack of a specialised, central administrative body for the coordination of activities in respect of UCH has been perceived by Croatian archaeologists as a hindrance to attaining an effectively systematic approach to UCH protection.[15]

Under the COA, an important tool of cultural heritage management in Croatia is the Register of Cultural Objects. It comprises three lists, covering 'Protected Cultural Objects', 'Cultural Objects of National Importance' and 'Objects under Preventive Protection'. Before being permanently protected by entry in the 'List of Protected Cultural Objects', prospective cultural objects are, as a rule, placed under preventive protection.[16] Preventive protection is the first step in the process of determining the value of a cultural object and is, thus, necessarily temporary. It may last for up to four years, with an exception regarding archaeological sites, both on land and underwater, in which case the period of preventive protection may be extended up to six years.[17] The entire set of rules and regulations on cultural heritage protection is applicable to objects placed under preventive protection.[18] For entry in the 'List of Cultural Objects of National Importance', a special evaluation process is laid down.[19] A mere 42 cultural objects had made it onto the List,[20] none of them UCH sites or artefacts of underwater provenance, not even the Croatian Apoxyomenos statue. Although it had been suggested that inclusion on the 'List of Cultural Objects of National Importance' might be deemed an indispensable step in the process of an immovable cultural object's bid for the World Heritage List,[21] not even those already on that List, let alone those on

15 In the early 1970s, when Croatia had been a federal unit of socialist Yugoslavia, such a body had been established, but its functioning as such was gradually discontinued. See Radić Rossi, *supra* note 2, at pp. 289–93. According to the 2023 Draft Act the situation will remain unchanged, since there are no provisions on an administrative body specialised for UCH.

16 COA, Articles 10–11.

17 COA, Article 10(3).

18 COA, Article 11(1). The 2023 Draft Act, in essence, retains the concept of preventive protection, although a different term – temporary protection – has been introduced (Art. 17). The general period of temporary protection has been shortened to two years, but the maximum temporary protection period for land and underwater archaeological sites remains at six years (Art. 17(5)).

19 COA, Article 13.

20 The List of Cultural Objects of National Importance is not available online. However, it was furnished by the Ministry upon request from the author.

21 See J. Antolović, *Zaštita i očuvanje kulturnih dobara* [*The Protection and Preservation of Cultural Objects*] (HADRIAN, 2009), at p. 263.

Croatia's tentative list, had been added to Croatia's 'List of Cultural Objects of National Importance'. Thus, one might conclude that the use of this List as such has never really materialised in practice as an effective cultural heritage management tool.[22]

UCH sites are classified in the Register either as underwater or mixed land/underwater archaeological zones/sites, and are treated as immovable property.[23] Individual artefacts recovered from the sea, as a rule permanently preserved in a museum or other cultural institution, are also entered into the 'Register of Cultural Objects', but as movable property and taking into account that such items may form part of a collection.[24]

Another body established by the COA is the Croatian Council for Cultural Objects (the Council), consisting primarily of distinguished experts in the field of cultural heritage protection.[25] Its main purpose is "to monitor and improve the condition of cultural objects."[26] The Council has advisory functions,[27] but, given the authority and expertise of its members, it may still exert a great deal of influence, and in certain cases its prior opinion is mandatory, such as before a cultural object may be delisted from the 'Register of Cultural Objects',[28] and it is on the Council's recommendation that the Minister of Culture will designate a cultural object as being in danger.[29]

Activities concerning the protection of cultural heritage on the level of archaeological, conservation and other specific expertise are performed by museums, galleries, conservation institutions, archives and libraries.[30] These are primarily public or publicly funded institutions. However, the COA takes into account that the necessary expertise for specific tasks, and in respect of

22 This proposition is corroborated by the 2023 Draft Act, which has no provisions on 'cultural objects of national importance' as a distinct statutory category.

23 There are currently 160 underwater archaeological sites, which are registered as protected cultural objects, while a further 19 are registered as being under preventive protection. In addition, nine mixed land/underwater archaeological sites figure in the Register as protected cultural objects, and another three have been accorded preventive protection. The data concerning immovable cultural objects entered in the Register of Cultural Objects is available online (in Croatian only), see <https://registar.kulturnadobra.hr/#/>.

24 See 3.5.3., note 134.

25 COA, Article 104.

26 COA, Article 102.

27 COA, Article 103.

28 COA, Article 15(2).

29 COA, Article 71. According to the 2023 Draft Act the competences of the Council remain largely the same.

30 COA, Article 77(2).

specific cultural objects, may also be provided by specialised private entities, both legal persons, e.g., corporations or associations, and individual experts.[31]

When it comes to public institutions with specialised expertise and activities in the field of UCH protection, one should first mention the Croatian Conservation Institute (CCI).[32] The CCI is the foremost Croatian public institution for research, including archaeological research, conservation, restoration and presentation of movable and immovable cultural objects, and as such also figures in the COA.[33] It was established in 1996, but has a longer pedigree, with its two predecessor institutions having been founded in 1966. The Institute's Division for Archaeological Heritage hosts a specialised Department for Underwater Archaeology, whose staff have both led and participated in numerous underwater archaeological research missions.

As previously noted, the ICUA also plays a pivotal, contemporary role in specialised UCH protection.[34] It was established in 2007, initially as an organisational unit within the framework of the CCI, but soon became an independent, public institution. Based on a bilateral treaty concluded between Croatia and UNESCO, in 2008[35] the ICUA was the first body accorded the status of a regional centre for underwater archaeology under the auspices of UNESCO. The ICUA undertakes a wide range of activities in respect of UCH protection, with an emphasis on international collaboration. These activities encompass all aspects of archaeological research, but also conservation and restoration of recovered artefacts. A core task of the Centre lies in the field of education and training, with numerous international workshops and educational programmes.[36] An evaluation conducted by UNESCO assessing the ICUA's performance, published in 2022 and utilised in the process of determining renewal

31 COA, Article 77(3).

32 Croatian Conservation Institute (Croatian: *Hrvatski restauratorski zavod*), <https://www.hrz.hr/en/index.php>.

33 COA, Article 95. In the 2023 Draft Act the position of the CCI has been solidified even further, with an entire and rather extensive article (Art. 114) being devoted to its functions and role.

34 ICUA, <https://www.icua.hr/en>.

35 Agreement between UNESCO and the Government of the Republic of Croatia regarding the Establishment of the Regional Centre for Underwater Archaeology in Zadar, Croatia, as a Category 2 Centre under the Auspices of UNESCO, Narodne novine – Međunarodni ugovori [Official Gazette of the Republic of Croatia – Treaties; NNMU] no. 1/2009.

36 ICUA's activities include the publication of a bilingual (English/Croatian) yearbook on UCH entitled *Submerged Heritage*. The volumes published thus far are available on ICUA's website: <https://www.icua.hr/en/icua-publications>.

of its status, identified the Centre as having made significant progress, with public exposure supported by the media.[37]

3 The 2001 Convention and Croatian Municipal Law

This part will analyse how the 2001 Convention has been implemented in Croatian municipal law and assess the extent to which the solutions contained in domestic legislation correspond with it. In that respect, the primary source of national legislation to be scrutinised is the COA. However, other laws enacted by the Croatian Parliament (Sabor), such as the Maritime Code[38] and the Act on the Coast Guard of the Republic of Croatia (CGA),[39] as well as ministerial acts and orders issued on the basis of statutory authorisations, are also relevant. Before considering the provisions of these laws, it is pertinent to explain the position given to treaties as a source of international law within the Croatian constitutional order, which must be considered when applying the 2001 Convention.

3.1 *The Position of Treaties in the Croatian Constitutional Order*

According to Article 134 of the Croatian Constitution:[40]

> International treaties which have been concluded and ratified in accordance with the Constitution, which have been published and which have entered into force shall be a component of the domestic legal order of the Republic of Croatia and shall have primacy over domestic law.

Since the constitutional provision does not refer to sources of international law other than treaties, i.e., particular rules of international law expressly accepted as binding by Croatia, which are required to fulfil the prescribed conditions, the constitutional approach towards the relationship between international

37 Renewal Evaluation of the International Centre for Underwater Archaeology in Zadar, Republic of Croatia, Final Report, January 2022, available at: <https://en.unesco.org/sites/default/files/evaluation_report_icua_final_2022_0.pdf>.

38 NN nos. 181/2004, 76/2007, 146/2008, 61/2011, 56/2013, 26/2015, 17/2019.

39 NN no. 125/2019.

40 Constitution of the Republic of Croatia, NN nos. 56/1990, 135/1997, 113/2000, 28/2001, 76/2010, 5/2014. An English translation prepared by the Croatian Constitutional Court is available at: <https://www.usud.hr/en/the-constitution>.

and municipal law may be regarded as partially monistic.[41] If the requirements are met, however, such treaties will, in the hierarchy of legal sources, feature above laws enacted by the Sabor. This is certainly true for the 2001 Convention. Consequently, an interested party might invoke the direct application of the 2001 Convention's provisions, even if not formally transposed into national legislation, provided that these are detailed enough to be applicable in practice without prior implementing legislation. Arguably, the Rules in the Annex to the 2001 Convention have these characteristics. Nevertheless, in the COA there is no express reference to the 2001 Convention, or to any other UNESCO convention, while, in comparison, the pertinent EU legislation has been listed in the COA since Croatia's accession.[42]

3.2 *Definition of UCH*

The COA does not define the term 'cultural object' in the strict sense,[43] let alone provide a definition of UCH.[44] Article 2 of the COA stipulates that cultural objects are of interest to the Republic of Croatia and as such enjoy its special protection,[45] and, furthermore, that they represent national treasures.[46] Thereafter, a broad determination is given of what the term 'cultural object' includes. This comprises: movable and immovable objects of artistic, historical, palaeontological, archaeological, anthropological and scientific significance; archaeological sites and cultural landscapes with artistic, historical and anthropological value; intangible cultural heritage; and buildings for the

---

41 *Cf.* J. Andrassy, B. Bakotić, M. Seršić, B. Vukas, *Međunarodno pravo: 1. dio* [*International Law: Part 1*] (Školska knjiga, 2010), at p. 7.

42 COA, Article 1a.

43 Šošić, *supra* note 9, at pp. 852–53.

44 Interestingly and rather oddly, instead of a law on cultural heritage protection enacted by the Sabor, the 2001 Convention's definition of UCH had been contained in regulations issued by the Minister of Defence in implementation of the first Coast Guard Act (NN no. 109/2007), namely in the 'Regulations on the cooperation of the Coast Guard with the bodies competent for the protection of cultural objects in the sea, on the seabed and in its subsoil' (NN no. 56/2009). Different from the Convention, the temporal cut-off was set at 50 years, in line with the practice of the Croatian cultural heritage protection services. See T. M. Šošić, 'Konvencija UNESCO-a o zaštiti podvodne kulturne baštine i jurisdikcija država u Jadranskome moru' ['The UNESCO Convention on the Protection of the Underwater Cultural Heritage and State Jurisdiction in the Adriatic Sea'] (2010) 49 *Poredbeno pomorsko pravo* [*Comparative Maritime Law*] 101, at pp. 129–30. However, in 2019 the Sabor adopted a new Coast Guard Act, and the mentioned Regulations were abrogated. Anyway, from what could be gathered, it seems that they were never effectively applied in practice. On the role of the Coast Guard in UCH protection, see 3.4.3., notes 100–106.

45 COA, Article 2(1).

46 COA, Article 2(2). This paragraph was added in implementation of EU law.

keeping and presentation of cultural heritage.[47] Thus, the concept of 'cultural object' under the COA encompasses a significance criterion, as opposed to the ambiguous compromise formula of the 2001 Convention's definition of UCH, which speaks of "all traces of human existence having a cultural, historical or archaeological *character*".[48]

It may be discerned already from the scope of the term 'cultural object' in Article 2 that the COA distinguishes between three basic categories of cultural heritage, i.e., movable and immovable cultural objects, as well as intangible cultural heritage, which should allow for enough flexibility and adaptability as to the dynamics of cultural heritage protection.[49] Subsequent provisions enumerate examples for all three categories of cultural heritage. UCH will necessarily be classified either as an immovable cultural object in the case of underwater sites, or as a movable cultural object in the case of artefacts recovered from the seabed. However, it is only in the list of immovable cultural objects provided in Article 7 that UCH is specifically referred to, namely within the listed example of "archaeological sites and archaeological zones, including underwater sites and zones." However, the lists are non-exhaustive, providing typical examples for each of the three categories of cultural heritage.[50]

The COA does not contain a specific age-limit for cultural objects akin to the 2001 Convention's definition of UCH.[51] Instead, the assessment has been left

---

47 COA, Article 2(3).

48 2001 Convention, Article 1(1)(a); emphasis added. For the view that the Convention's wording does not amount to a significance criterion, see e.g., S. Dromgoole, '2001 UNESCO Convention on the Protection of the Underwater Cultural Heritage' (2003) 18 *International Journal of Marine and Coastal Law* 59, at p. 64. For a different view, see C. J. S. Forrest, 'Defining "Underwater Cultural Heritage"' (2002) 31 *International Journal of Nautical Archaeology* 3, at p. 9.

49 Cf. Antolović, supra note 21, at p. 242.

50 The 2023 Draft Act, in substance, follows the COA's approach in defining cultural objects. In respect of immovable cultural objects other than individual immovable objects, the 2023 Draft Act envisages the possibility of establishing a 'contact zone' around a heritage site in which specific measures might be applied with a view to securing its value as a cultural object (Art. 18). Such contact zones will be mandatory for sites on the World Heritage List (Art. 18(3)).

51 A novelty in the 2023 Draft Act is a list of four categories of cultural objects which, regardless of the otherwise required evaluation process, are *ipso iure* taken to have that status (Art. 14(1)). Time criteria are used in determining these categories, and one of the categories, i.e., archaeological material older than 100 years, might be particularly relevant in the context of UCH protection. However, for any other objects not listed in that Article the status of cultural object is to be determined in an evaluation process. The criteria to be pondered in that process have been elucidated with more precision (Art. 15) than has been the case under the COA, but none of them expressly factors in time.

to the Croatian cultural heritage protection services. In practice, the Croatian authorities have applied a more flexible time-criterion than the 100-years cut-off adopted in the 2001 Convention. Thus, many underwater sites have been placed under protection as registered cultural objects before coming within the remit of the 2001 Convention's definition, including from the Second World War. One famous example being the intact and well-preserved wreck of a US bomber, Boeing B-17G Flying Fortress, which sank off the island of Vis in 1944 after an emergency landing into the sea.[52] This was true also for sites from the period of the First World War, before they had come within the remit of the 2001 Convention's definition.[53]

3.3 *Salvage Law, Law of Finds and Ownership of UCH*

The 2001 Convention eventually did not expressly exclude the application of salvage law and the law of finds to UCH. Nonetheless, for State Parties opting to retain salvage law and the law of finds in respect of UCH, Article 4 prescribes strict requirements, which ultimately aim to guarantee the application of the Convention's protection regime, including the Rules contained in the Annex.[54]

As a country of continental Europe, Croatia follows the approach of other civil law systems, whereby the legal concept of salvage does not extend to objects deemed as cultural heritage. The rules on salvage[55] and the removal of wrecks and other objects from the sea[56] are contained in the Maritime Code. According to the Maritime Code, any activities undertaken towards the removal of a wreck or recovery of a submerged object, which may be presumed to be a cultural object, requires the prior consent of the Ministry.[57] If

52 It was entered in the List of Protected Cultural Objects (see note 16) under no. Z-17; see entry with description in Croatian at: <https://registar.kulturnadobra.hr/#/details/Z-17>. See also D. Frka, J. Mesić, *Treasures of the Adriatic* (Adamić, 2013), at pp. 280–85.

53 T. M. Šošić, 'The 2001 UNESCO Convention and the Protection of the Underwater Cultural Heritage in the Adriatic and Ionian Seas' in A. Caligiuri (ed.), *Governance of the Adriatic and Ionian Marine Space* (Editoriale Scientifica, 2016) 119, at pp. 122–23.

54 See e.g., G. Carducci, 'The Crucial Compromise on Salvage Law and the Law of Finds' in R. Garabello, T. Scovazzi (eds.), *The Protection of the Underwater Cultural Heritage: Before and After the 2001 UNESCO Convention* (Martinus Nijhoff Publishers, 2003) 193; C. J. S. Forrest, 'Historic Wreck Salvage: An International Perspective' (2009) 33 *Tulane Maritime Law Journal* 347.

55 Maritime Code, Articles 760–788.

56 Maritime Code, Articles 840a-840z. In implementation of the 2007 Nairobi International Convention on the Removal of Wrecks ((2007) 46 *International Legal Materials* 697), the removal of wrecks and other objects from the sea was regulated more precisely, and the pertinent provisions were structurally encompassed in a separate chapter of the Maritime Code.

57 Maritime Code, Articles 840ć(6), 840j(4).

the status of the object as a cultural one has been established only after its removal from the sea, the legal consequences that would otherwise ensue are expressly excluded.[58] The COA itself contains a further safeguard provision in connection with the recovery of submerged objects. Accordingly, before the locally competent harbour master's office may issue a recovery permit, it must seek the opinion of the competent conservation department of the Ministry to ensure that the objects at hand "are not or are not presumed to have the capacity of a cultural object".[59] Considering this approach to salvage and the removal of objects from the sea, it should come as no surprise that Croatia, when acceding to the 1989 International Convention on Salvage,[60] entered a reservation so as to exclude its application to "maritime cultural property of prehistoric, archaeological or historic interest".[61]

In Croatia, the legal rules on finds[62] are in principle applicable to cultural heritage, including UCH,[63] although the status and protection of cultural objects under the COA remain unaffected by their operation. The rules on finds will primarily be relevant for the collection of a reward on the part of the finder.[64] Objects presumed to be cultural objects, found in the earth, in the sea or otherwise underwater, become the property of the Republic of Croatia.[65] This provision obviously includes UCH within its scope. A person claiming to be the owner of a cultural object thus found, may institute proceedings before a court to establish the legitimacy of such a claim.[66] Even so, the presumption of ownership will operate in favour of the Republic of Croatia.

According to the COA, ownership over cultural objects must be ascertained. In case a cultural object does not have an owner, or the owner is unknown

---

58 Maritime Code, Articles 840f(1)(b), 840i, 840u(1).

59 COA, Article 50.

60 (1996) 1953 UNTS 194.

61 International Convention on Salvage, Article 30(1)(d). See *Status of IMO Treaties*, 5 January 2024 (available on the web site of the IMO, <https://www.imo.org/>), at p. 497; Act on the Confirmation of the 1989 International Convention on Salvage, NNMU no. 9/1998, Article 2(2).

62 Finds are regulated in the Act on Ownership and Other Property Rights (OPORA), consolidated text in NN nos. 81/2015, 94/2017. The OPORA distinguishes finds of objects that were recently lost or stolen, where the owner is usually known or at least more easily determinable (Art. 134), from objects, primarily valuables, lost or misplaced for such a long time that their owner is no longer known, and which are referred to as treasures (Croatian: *blago*) (Art. 140). Finds of objects that may be deemed as cultural heritage will, as a rule, fall under the latter category.

63 COA, Article 19(3).

64 OPORA, Articles 137, 140(5).

65 COA, Article 19(1).

66 COA, Article 19(2).

or cannot be determined, ownership will again fall to the Republic of Croatia.[67] It is important to note that cultural objects, even if privately owned, fully remain within the purview of the COA. Thus, any owner will have the obligation, amongst others, to respect and fulfil the protection measures prescribed by the competent authorities in accordance with the law.[68]

3.4 *Jurisdiction Concerning UCH in Maritime Zones*

3.4.1 Internal Waters and Territorial Sea

Since the United Nations Convention on the Law of the Sea (LOSC)[69] places Internal Waters and the Territorial Sea (TS) under the sovereignty of the coastal State ,[70] here the Republic of Croatia, thus forming part of its sovereign territory, the provisions of the COA extend fully to UCH found there. In fact, all the UCH sites that have so far been listed in the Croatian Register of Cultural Objects, either as protected cultural objects or as objects under preventive protection,[71] are located within the 12-nautical mile TS limit.

According to an express provision, all of the COA's rules on archaeological excavations and research are equally applicable to underwater archaeological research.[72] As already discussed, it will be the regionally competent conservation department of the Ministry that ordinarily issues administrative orders and decisions, including permits for fieldwork and protection measures, in respect of UCH sites in both Internal Waters and the TS.[73] In that respect, the Minister of Culture, in line with the relevant provisions of the Maritime Code, is authorised to issue more detailed regulations on requirements and procedure for archaeological research. That authorisation extends to regulations on requirements and procedure for permissions in respect of other underwater activities at UCH sites, primarily concerning public access by sports divers.[74]

---

67 COA, Article 18.

68 COA, Article 20. According to the 2023 Draft Act the provisions concerning the ownership of cultural objects will essentially remain the same.

69 (1994) 1833 UNTS 397.

70 LOSC, Article 2.

71 See note 23.

72 COA, Article 49(1).

73 COA, Articles 47, 55.

74 COA, Article 49(2). This has been done through two sets of regulations: the 'Regulations on archaeological research', NN nos. 102/2010, 2/2020, which cover both land and underwater archaeology; and the 'Regulations on the procedure and modalities for the issuance of permissions regarding underwater activities in the Internal Maritime Waters and the Territorial Sea of the Republic of Croatia in areas where cultural objects are located', NN nos. 49/2019, 55/2019, 79/2020. See 3.5. According to the 2023 Draft Act both sets of regulations will remain applicable until the issuance of regulations under the new law (Art. 135(3)).

The COA also contains a provision requiring the competent authorities to exercise control over underwater archaeological research and other activities at UCH sites.[75] In the Internal Waters and the TS, apart from the Ministry and the harbour master's office, it will primarily be the police fulfilling this function, while the Coast Guard covers the Continental Shelf (CS) and the Exclusive Economic Zone (EEZ).[76]

The provisions of the COA concerning competence as regards UCH sites are supplemented by the Maritime Code with a view to taking account of the safety of navigation. Part II of the Code comprises the basic rules regarding the maritime zones of the Republic of Croatia, which largely reflect the international law of the sea as codified in the LOSC.[77] However, in connection with permissions for surveys, research, documentation and hydrographic activities in the Internal Waters and the TS, there are distinct provisions regarding UCH. The regulation is identical for both Internal Waters[78] and the TS.[79] Accordingly, domestic and foreign, legal and natural, persons may conduct archaeological research, photographing and/or other forms of documentation in respect of UCH sites in Croatian Internal Waters and its TS only with permission granted by the Ministry: essentially, this refers to the competent conservation department under the COA. Thus far, the provisions of the Maritime Code are congruent with the COA. However, the Maritime Code additionally requires the prior consent of the Ministry of Defence and the locally competent harbour master's office be obtained to ascertain that the intended activities will not compromise the safety of navigation. Such consent must be given within 30 days of a request.

3.4.2 Contiguous Zone

Croatia has not proclaimed a Contiguous Zone (CZ). The Maritime Code does not mention this legal concept and, hence, does not provide the legal basis for a possible proclamation in the future, as it had done for the EEZ. The reasons why this potentially important legal tool for the governance of maritime spaces has largely been disregarded by Croatian policymakers remain elusive.[80]

---

75 COA, Article 49(3).

76 See 3.4.3., notes 100–106.

77 Maritime Code, Articles 6–46.

78 Maritime Code, Article 13(8)–(9).

79 Maritime Code, Article 31(8)–(9).

80 *Cf.* B. Vukas, 'Pomorski zakonik Republike Hrvatske i međunarodno pravo mora' ['The Maritime Code of the Republic of Croatia and the International Law of the Sea'] (2008) 58 *Zbornik Pravnog fakulteta u Zagrebu* [*Collected Papers of the Zagreb Faculty of Law*] 181, at pp. 185–86.

However, as has been argued,[81] the use of the jurisdictional powers regarding UCH on the seabed beyond the TS up to the 24-nautical mile limit by the coastal State is not necessarily dependent on the prior proclamation of a CZ. This was true already based on Article 303(2) LOSC,[82] but all the more so for Parties to the 2001 Convention with its clearer regulation in Article 8.[83] In light of the duty to protect UCH and to cooperate with other States in that respect, as enshrined before the 2001 Convention in Article 303(1) LOSC, it might even be contended that an obligation exists for coastal States when it comes to protecting UCH on the seabed in the maritime area up to the 24-nautical mile limit. In any case, the coastal State certainly cannot remain entirely passive, if conscious of reports that UCH in this area is in danger.[84] Yet, neither the COA nor other Croatian laws or regulations had endorsed provisions based on either Article 303(2) LOSC or Article 8 of the 2001 Convention and considering the proposals for a new law contained in the 2023 Draft Act such a legal situation will, regrettably, persist in the foreseeable future.

3.4.3 Continental Shelf and EEZ

Part II of the Maritime Code contains rules on the maritime zones of Croatia including both the CS[85] and the EEZ.[86] The Code's provisions are to a great degree reflective of the LOSC, and do not specifically refer to UCH.[87]

---

81 T. M. Šošić, 'The 24-Mile Archaeological Zone: Abandoned or Confirmed?' in R. Wolfrum, M. Seršić, T. M. Šošić (eds.), *Contemporary Developments in International Law – Essays in Honour of Budislav Vukas* (Brill-Nijhoff, 2016) 305. *Cf.* M. J. Aznar, 'The Contiguous Zone as an Archaeological Maritime Zone' (2014) 29 *International Journal of Marine and Coastal Law* 1; M. J. Aznar, *Maritime Claims and Underwater Archaeology: When History Meets Politics* (Brill, 2021), at pp. 30–38.

82 Šošić, *supra* note 81, at pp. 318–19, 326–27.

83 *Ibid.*, at p. 322.

84 *Ibid.*, at pp. 319, 324.

85 Maritime Code, Articles 42–45.

86 Maritime Code, Articles 32–41.

87 Interestingly, the 1987 Yugoslav Act on the Coastal Sea and the Continental Shelf of the Socialist Federal Republic of Yugoslavia had extended the sovereign rights of Yugoslavia on the CS to the exploration and exploitation of "archaeological and other submerged objects". See M. Škrk, 'The 1987 Law of Yugoslavia on the Coastal Sea and the Continental Shelf' (1989) 20 *Ocean Development & International Law* 501, at p. 508; B. Vukas, 'Uz Zakon o obalnom moru i epikontinentalnom pojasu SFR Jugoslavije od godine 1987.' ['As to the 1987 Act on the Coastal Sea and the Continental Shelf of the SFR Yugoslavia'] (1987) 34 *Jugoslovenska revija za međunarodno pravo* [*Yugoslav Review of International Law*] 199, at pp. 206–07. It would appear, however, that this provision did not have any noteworthy practical effects. Anyway, after the dissolution of Yugoslavia, it was not retained in the 1994 Croatian Maritime Code (see next note).

When the first Maritime Code was adopted by the Sabor back in 1994, it had included provisions on the CS, as well as the EEZ. However, although providing legal basis for an EEZ, no proclamation was effected at the time, owing principally to political considerations, and was left for the future.[88] Ultimately, rather than claiming a fully-fledged EEZ, the Sabor, in its 2003 Decision on the Extension of the Jurisdiction of the Republic of Croatia in the Adriatic Sea,[89] opted for a *sui generis* zone, labelled the 'ecological and fisheries protection zone' (EFPZ). The reasons for this were again primarily of a political nature.[90] It should be noted that the 2003 EFPZ Decision did not make mention of possible jurisdictional powers in respect of UCH.

With the enactment of the currently applicable Maritime Code in 2004, the Sabor expressly reserved Croatia's right to upgrade its EFPZ to a fully-fledged EEZ in accordance with the LOSC.[91] This finally happened in 2021, based on the Decision of the Proclamation of the Exclusive Economic Zone of the Republic of Croatia in the Adriatic Sea,[92] which is quite concise and as concerns substantive provisions, in essence simply points to Part V of LOSC and the pertinent chapter of the Maritime Code. Given this, predictably there is no reference to jurisdiction regarding UCH.

In the course of the 2020 amendment of the COA,[93] the Minister of Culture's authorisation to issue more detailed regulations on the procedure and requirements for underwater archaeological research and for permissions in respect of other underwater activities at UCH sites was extended to the EFPZ and the CS.[94] Although the EFPZ has, in the meantime, been turned into an EEZ proper, this should not affect the Minister's statutory authorisation. In any case, more than two years have elapsed since the amendment and such specific regulations for the CS and the EEZ have still not been enacted. Although the introduction of a reference to UCH beyond the TS in the COA should be viewed positively as a step in the right direction, and mindful of the fact that the pertinent regulations are yet to be elaborated, the approach taken appears more like the application of a 'sticking-plaster' than a systematic outlook towards full implementation of the 2001 Convention.

---

88 1994 Maritime Code, NN nos. 17/1994, 74/1994, 43/1996, Article 1042.

89 NN nos. 157/2003, 77/2004, 138/2006, 31/2008.

90 Vukas, *supra* note 80, at pp. 193–99; D. Vidas, 'The UN Convention on the Law of the Sea, the European Union and the Rule of Law: What Is Going on in the Adriatic Sea?' (2009) 24 *International Journal of Marine and Coastal Law* 1, at pp. 9–14.

91 Maritime Code, Article 1018(2).

92 NN no. 10/2021.

93 NN no. 62/2020.

94 COA, Article 49(2). See note 74.

Indeed, it should first be noticed that neither on ratification of the 2001 Convention, nor any time later, did Croatia make a choice under Article 9(2) as to its preferred reporting procedure concerning finds of UCH on the CS and in the EEZ.[95] The COA already had included a provision stipulating that all citizens had the duty to report the existence of an object presumed to be a cultural object to the competent authority, i.e., the regionally competent conservation department of the Ministry.[96] However, it is unclear to what extent this provision, without expressly stating so, is applicable beyond the TS, i.e., beyond Croatia's territory.[97] Regardless, without specific rules it is not immediately clear which particular State administrative body is competent to administer not only the reporting procedure under Article 9 of the 2001 Convention but also the Article 10 consultation and cooperation mechanism. This is especially the case should Croatia take on the role of the 'coordinating State' in respect of UCH located on its CS and in its EEZ. In this situation it could not be one of the Ministry's regional conservation departments since their spatial area of competence does not extend beyond the TS. Given the institutional framework of cultural heritage management in Croatia, the logical solution might be that administrative decisions and procedures regarding UCH on the CS and in the EEZ be handled at the level of the Ministry's Directorate for the Protection of Cultural Heritage. However, in the absence of unequivocal regulation, this remains an assumption based on systemic considerations. Verifying, in this context, the list of national competent authorities according to Article 22 of the 2001 Convention on UNESCO's website,[98] it is noteworthy that Croatia still has not made the required notification as to its competent authority for UCH protection.[99]

In Croatia, the Coast Guard is set up as an organisational unit of the Croatian Navy,[100] with the general purpose of monitoring and protecting the rights and interests of the Republic of Croatia on the sea.[101] Since the CGA currently in force was adopted in 2019, predating the proclamation of the EEZ, the primary function of the Coast Guard is stated as the:

---

95 See the declarations of States Parties to the 2001 Convention on UNESCO's website: <https://www.unesco.org/en/legal-affairs/convention-protection-underwater-cultural-heritage?hub=412>.

96 COA, Article 4(3).

97 Šošić, *supra* note 44, at p. 127.

98 See UNESCO website at: <https://www.unesco.org/en/underwater-heritage/national-competent?hub=412>.

99 Šošić, *supra* note 44, at p. 125, note 97.

100 CGA, Articles 2(1)(1), 7(1).

101 CGA, Article 1(1).

control over and protection of the ecological and fisheries protection zone and the continental shelf, in respect of which the Republic of Croatia exercises sovereign rights and jurisdiction.[102]

Indeed, pending amendment, this reference to the EFPZ should now be read as signifying the EEZ. Unlike the first Coast Guard Act in 2007,[103] the current CGA no longer expressly mentions the monitoring and protection of UCH on the CS and in the EEZ as a specific task. However, this should not be construed as the Coast Guard's competence having been limited in that respect. In fact, the CGA contains a safeguard provision envisaging that the Coast Guard may perform other tasks in accordance with special laws.[104] As indicated,[105] the 2020 amendment of the COA, obviously taking account of the new CGA's contents, provided a role for the Coast Guard in connection with the control over underwater archaeological research and other activities at UCH sites.[106] However, since the Minister of Culture's specific regulations on underwater archaeological research and other activities at UCH sites on the CS and in the EEZ are yet to be drawn up, this provision awaits further elucidation.

To conclude this section, it must be noted that to date no systematic survey of Croatia's CS, or even parts thereof, has been undertaken with a view to determining the locations of potential UCH sites. Considering the importance of the Adriatic Sea as a route for maritime trade and navigation, sites of shipwrecks from various periods of history must undoubtedly be present and may yield important data that will further our historical knowledge. On the other hand, Croatia did not hesitate to express its interest in being part of the consultation and cooperation mechanism for the UCH on the Skerki Banks, which was triggered by Italy under Article 10 of the 2001 Convention and resulted, as a pioneering endeavour, in the formation of the Coordination Committee for the Protection of the UCH on the Skerki Bank and in the Sicilian Channel.[107]

---

102 CGA, Article 5(1)(1). As concerns the Internal Waters and the TS, the Coast Guard principally acts in support of other competent State authorities (CGA, Art. 5(2)). See 3.4.1.

103 2007 Coast Guard Act, NN no. 109/2007, Article 36(1). See Šošić, *supra* note 44, at p. 129; Šošić, *supra* note 53, at p. 132.

104 CGA, Article 5(1)(12).

105 See 3.4.1., notes 75–76.

106 COA, Article 49(3).

107 See UNESCO's website: <https://www.unesco.org/en/skerki-bank-mission?hub=412>. See also T. M. Šošić, 'The Protection of Underwater Cultural Heritage beyond the Exclusive Jurisdictional Reach of Coastal States' in A. Caligiuri, G. Cataldi, N. Ros (eds.), *L'évolution du droit de la mer: Réflexions à l'occasion du 20ème anniversaire de l'AssIDMer (2001–2021)/ The Evolution of the Law of the Sea: Reflections for the 20th AssIDMer Anniversary (2001–2021)* (Editoriale Scientifica, 2023) 175, at pp. 183–85.

It is to be hoped that the experience of Croatia's participation on the Coordination Committee and its involvement in putting into effect the Article 10 State cooperation mechanism, will bring the potentially important UCH lying on Croatia's CS more into the focus of the Croatian cultural heritage services, although the piecemeal implementation of the pertinent rules of the 2001 Convention does not facilitate progress towards that end. One may be further disillusioned by the fact that the 2023 Draft Act does not contain any new provisions concerning UCH on the CS and in the EEZ; the situation remains much the same as it has been under the COA.

3.5 Rules of the Annex

Neither the COA, nor the regulations enacted by the Minister of Culture based on statutory authorisations, contain a reference to the archaeological and technical standards in the Annex to the 2001 Convention (the Rules). It is true that the COA was enacted two years before the adoption of the Convention, but numerous amendments to the COA have been made since and the drafters of both the initial legislative text and the subsequent amendments were certainly mindful of current archaeological principles and standards.[108] The same may be said of the 'Regulations on archaeological research' (ARR), which in their current version were enacted by the Minister of Culture in 2010.[109] The ARR set the requirements and modalities for archaeological research in general, but also explicitly pertain to underwater archaeological research.[110] In that sense, the ARR do not closely follow the structure of the Rules, but the contents of the latter are, essentially, reflected in the provisions of the former, especially regarding project design, documentation, conservation, reporting and dissemination. It should also be noted that the ARR, as they concern maritime zones, are applicable only to archaeological research in the Internal Waters and the TS, not the CS or the EEZ (i.e., EFPZ). In contrast, it is explicitly stated that the ARR do extend to UCH in rivers and lakes, even though Croatia did not clarify its position on this point by making an express declaration on the application of the Rules to inland waters not of a maritime character, in accordance with Article 28 of the 2001 Convention.

108 *Cf.* J. Mesić, 'Protezione del patrimonio culturale subacqueo in Croazia' in F. Maniscalco (ed.), *Tutela, conservazione e valorizzazione del patrimonio culturale subacqueo* (Massa Editore, 2004) 243, at p. 244.

109 See note 74.

110 ARR, 2(2).

3.5.1 The Preservation of UCH 'in situ'

The principle that, in line with modern archaeological standards and practice, the preservation *in situ* of UCH shall be considered as the first option is enshrined in Article 2(5) of the 2001 Convention, among the objectives and principles of the Convention's UCH protection regime, and prominently reiterated and further elaborated in Rule 1 of the Annex.[111] Preservation *in situ* as such is not spelled out in Croatian legislation, in either the COA or the ARR. However, the drafters of the COA did bear in mind the contemporary approach to *in situ* preservation, pertaining to both underwater and terrestrial archaeology. This consideration is discernible in the stated objectives of cultural heritage protection under the COA, which features the objective "to protect and preserve cultural objects in their *unaltered* and *original* condition and pass cultural objects to future generations".[112]

This is reflective of the fact that from the early 1970s Croatian underwater archaeologists had advocated *in situ* preservation of UCH as the preferred method.[113] Croatia, amongst others, also devised the use of protective cages in the early 1990s, which was a rather novel approach at the time to preservation *in situ*.[114] Shipwreck sites from the Roman period especially, often with considerable cargoes of amphorae, are protected by this method, implemented for the first time in respect of two such sites discovered off the island of Lastovo at the end of the 1980s.[115] Although this method of protecting sites by iron cages has proven functional, in that the site is preserved for future research whilst simultaneously ensuring accessibility to divers as a tourist attraction,[116] criticism has been advanced that financial, ecological, aesthetic, maintenance and safety aspects have not been fully assessed, and that there have been no long-term management plans as concerns the flow of visitors to such sites.[117]

---

111 See e.g., M. J. Aznar, 'In Situ Preservation of Underwater Cultural Heritage as an International Legal Principle' (2018) 13 *Journal of Maritime Archaeology* 67.

112 COA, Article 5; emphasis added.

113 Radić Rossi, *supra* note 2, at p. 290.

114 M. Pešić, '*In Situ* Protection of Underwater Cultural Heritage' in L. Bekić (ed.), *Conservation of Underwater Archaeological Finds: Manual* (2nd edn., International Centre for Underwater Archaeology, 2014) 97, at p. 103; available on ICUA's website: <https://www.icua.hr/en/icua-publications>.

115 Radić Rossi, *supra* note 2, at p. 300.

116 See 3.5.3.

117 Radić Rossi, *supra* note 2, at p. 301. In 2021, the ICUA launched a multiannual programme with the long-term aim of establishing an effective system for the inspection and monitoring of UCH sites in Croatia. During the programme's first year three sites were inspected, including a shipwreck from antiquity near Cavtat protected by a cage and the wreck of

2.5.2 The Prohibition of Commercial Exploitation of UCH

The COA does not explicitly formulate a prohibition upon commercial exploitation akin to that in the 2001 Convention, based on Article 2(7) and Rule 2 of the Annex. However, that cultural objects must not be treated as ordinary goods in commerce is obvious, considering the whole range of legal consequences that the cultural heritage protection regime, as established by the COA, contemplates. In that sense, the objectives of COA's protection regime are to "prevent illicit conduct in respect of and the illicit traffic in cultural objects, and to control the export, removal and import of cultural objects". A further aim is to "create conditions that will allow for cultural objects to serve the needs of individuals and the *common interest*, in conformity with their purpose and significance".[118]

In addition, it should be remembered that the application of the COA extends to all cultural heritage, including real property. It would be counterproductive to generally prohibit commercial activities in all historic buildings that have been registered as immovable cultural objects. Thus, with certain exceptions,[119] for commercial activities in immovable cultural objects, such as hotels, restaurants, cafés or shops, the COA has established a two-fold system that envisages concessions, on the one hand,[120] and so-called monument annuities, on the other,[121] the latter being applicable as the general rule in default of the former. The collected revenues, notably those from monument annuities, are used for the financing of cultural heritage protection activities.[122] Naturally, the commercial activities taking place in cultural objects will have to conform to all protection measures prescribed by the cultural heritage services under the COA.

Although there is no express provision to that end, in practice the COA's rules on concessions and monument annuities will not be applicable to UCH sites due to their specific nature. On the other hand, because of Croatia's status as a tourist destination, UCH sites represent a valuable resource in that they are

the *Baron Gautsch* (see 3.5.3., note 133). See R. Surić, 'Inspecting and Monitoring Croatia's Protected Underwater Sites' (2021) 11 *Submerged Heritage* 20 (see note 36).

118 COA, Article 5, emphasis added.

119 Manufacturing and production activities are exempt from the payment of monument annuities (COA, Art. 114(9)).

120 COA, Articles 43a–43k. As opposed to the payment of monument annuities which is established practice, the provisions on concessions have been used only sporadically.

121 COA, Articles 114–114c.

122 COA, Article 114b. The model of concessions and monument annuities has been retained in the 2023 Draft Act.

attractive destinations for divers.[123] That said, diving activities at UCH sites are handled by a set of special regulations, enacted by the Minister of Culture, and are discussed next in the context of public access to UCH.

3.5.3 Public Access to UCH

Rule 7 of the Annex to the 2001 Convention, on the promotion of public access to UCH *in situ*, should be read in conjunction with the objective in Article 2(10), emphasising non-intrusiveness and the creation of public awareness, and Article 20 regarding efforts of the State Parties to raise public awareness as to the importance of UCH protection. As follows from these provisions, public access should only be allowed if compatible with the proper management and protection of the UCH site at hand.[124]

In Croatia, public access to UCH *in situ* is governed by the 'Regulations on the procedure and modalities for the issuance of permissions regarding underwater activities in the Internal Maritime Waters and the Territorial Sea of the Republic of Croatia in areas where cultural objects are located' (UAR), enacted by the Minister of Culture based on statutory authorisation.[125] As is clear from the lengthy title of the Regulations, their spatial application extends only to the Internal Waters (of maritime character) and the TS,[126] and does not encompass the CS or EEZ.[127] In Croatia, at protected UCH sites, only organised diving conducted in accordance with the UAR is allowed, while individual diving is explicitly prohibited.[128] Permissions for organised diving are issued on the basis of a five-year programme of activities adopted by the Minister of Culture, which lists all the sites, some grouped into areas. The programme indicates the number of permissions available for each of the sites/areas and fixes the annual fees to be paid.[129] Those eligible for obtaining permissions, as a rule licensed diving centres, must go through a selection process following a call for applications publicised by the Ministry.[130]

For the diving centres that have obtained the required permissions, the organisation of such diving expeditions is primarily appealing as an offer to

123 I. Radić Rossi, 'Podvodna arheološka baština i turizam'/ 'Underwater Archaeological Heritage and Tourism' in S. Mihelić (ed.), *Arheologija i turizam u Hrvatskoj/ Archaeology and Tourism in Croatia* (Arheološki muzej u Zagrebu, 2009) 456.

124 2001 Convention, Article 2(10); Annex, Rule 7.

125 COA, Article 49(2). See note 74.

126 UAR, Article 1.

127 See 3.4.3.

128 UAR, Article 2(1).

129 UAR, Article 3.

130 UAR, Articles 4–6.

tourists who are sports divers with the necessary skills. Thus, it is important to note that the holder of the permission must ensure compliance with all protective measures prescribed by the cultural heritage services for the UCH site at hand.[131] The most interesting sites for tourist diving expeditions are the many twentieth century shipwrecks in the Adriatic, and those sunk up to the end of World War II have more often than not been placed under protection as registered cultural objects in accordance with the COA.[132] An example is the wreck of the *Baron Gautsch*, a passenger steamship which was the pride of the Austrian Lloyd shipping company.[133]

If, following underwater archaeological research, it is decided to recover artefacts from a UCH site, these will usually be displayed in a museum and that way public access will be assured. In Croatia, the approach is to keep artefacts from a particular site together as a unit. A further principle is that they should be curated and displayed in a local or regional museum close to the site of the find unless there are sound reasons for a different course of action. An example of these principles in operation is the collection of artefacts recovered from a sixteenth century shipwreck near Gnalić, which is curated by the Heritage Museum in Biograd na Moru.[134] The most prominent artefact found on the seabed of the Croatian maritime space is probably the bronze statue of a Greek athlete belonging to the rare *Apoxyomenos* sculptural type. It was discovered in 1996 off the islet of Vele Orjule near the island of Lošinj and raised from the sea in 1999. After a long-lasting process of meticulous conservation and restoration works, involving also foreign experts and institutions, the Croatian Apoxyomenos was finally presented to the public in 2006. The statue is a good example of how UCH forms part of the cultural heritage of humanity, and thus surpasses not only local, but national sentiments and affiliations.[135] In view of this, opinions were voiced that the Croatian Apoxyomenos should be permanently displayed in a museum of national significance in

131 UAR, Article 10.

132 See 3.2., notes 51–53. For descriptions of the most attractive wreck sites in the Eastern Adriatic, see Frka, Mesić, *supra* note 52.

133 The *Baron Gautsch* tragically foundered off the coast of Istria at the very beginning of World War I while transporting mostly civilians from Kotor to Trieste in the service of the Austro-Hungarian Navy. Due to an evident mistake of the captain, the ship sailed into a minefield laid to secure the naval port of Pula. More than 150 lives were lost. *Ibid.*, at pp. 26–31. For an example of a licensed diving centre, see the website of *Rovinj Sub*: <https://rovinj-sub.hr/index.php>.

134 See Radić Rossi, Nicolardi, Batur, *supra* note 4, at pp. 227, 228, 231, 232–243.

135 T. M. Šošić, 'The Common Heritage of Mankind and the Protection of the Underwater Cultural Heritage' in B. Vukas, T. M. Šošić (eds.), *International Law: New Actors, New Concepts – Continuing Dilemmas. Liber Amicorum Božidar Bakotić* (Martinus Nijhoff Pub-

Zagreb, the capital city of Croatia. Nonetheless, in line with the established approach, the decision was taken to reconstruct the historic Kvarner Palace on the waterfront of Mali Lošinj, the island of Lošinj's main town, into a museum that would house the statue as its sole artefact. The result is the remarkable Museum of the Apoxyomenos, which opened its doors to the public in 2016.[136]

3.5.4 Project Design and Management of Archaeological Research

Regarding project design and the management of archaeological research, the ARR, as mentioned, do not follow the Rules in the Annex to the 2001 Convention literally, not least because they regulate archaeological research in general. Nevertheless, the standards contained in the Annex Rules have essentially been built into the ARR. In connection therewith, some of the more important aspects should be highlighted.

First, archaeological research, including underwater research, may only be conducted under a permit issued by the competent conservation department of the Ministry. As concerns the contents of the request for a permit, including the submission of corroborating documentation, the ARR, amongst others, stipulate that a project leader must be designated and all the participants in the project must be listed. For divers, their diving qualification and category must be indicated, including the diving equipment and instruments that will be used.[137] Project leaders are limited to persons holding either Croatian citizenship, or citizenship of a Member State of either the EU or the European Economic Area. They must have a university master's degree or a specialist professional qualification in the field of archaeology, experience in organising archaeological research and a record of at least 24 months practical fieldwork experience. In addition, the project leader of an underwater campaign must have an appropriate diving certification, at least CMAS 3* or an equivalent category.[138] Foreigners and foreign institutions may participate in the research on the basis of reciprocity.[139]

The project leader is responsible for ensuring that the research is conducted in accordance with professional standards and that the project is realised

---

lishers, 2010) 319, at pp. 319–20, 349–50. *Cf.* Aznar, *supra* note 81 (*Maritime Claims…*), at pp. 97–101.

136 See the website of the Museum of the Apoxyomenos: <https://www.muzejapoksiomena.hr/en/>.

137 ARR, Article 5.

138 ARR, Article 7.

139 ARR, Article 9.

within the limits of the secured financial resources.[140] According to specific provision, samples that need to be analysed and movable finds, essentially recovered artefacts, may be sent abroad only with the express permission of the competent conservation department,[141] although this would also follow from the pertinent rules of the COA. In case of underwater research, the project leader must see to it that the area of underwater activities is properly marked, e.g., with buoys, in line with the pertinent rules concerning the safety of navigation.[142] The competent harbour master's office must be informed of the commencement, suspension, resumption and ultimate termination of the underwater activities in connection with archaeological research.[143]

The ARR contain no detailed provisions on funding. However, the request for a permit must be accompanied by a financial plan covering research, conservation and restoration of the site and the finds, and by proof that the financial resources have been secured.[144]

An expert report, the contents of which are further prescribed depending on the type of research conducted,[145] has to be furnished to the competent conservation department by the project leader within three months of completion of the research campaign, while a summary report is submitted to the Ministry for publication.[146] With the intensification of archaeological fieldwork during the 2000s, the Ministry launched a special periodical, the Croatian Archaeological Yearbook, in which all summary reports created since 2004 have been published.[147]

The project leader and their associates have the exclusive right to first publish the documentation and the finds, which as a rule should occur no later than two years after the completion of the research. It seems that to fulfil the requirements of this provision a descriptive communication will suffice. This first publication must be in Croatia.[148] The project leader, or a person duly authorised by them, moreover, has the exclusive right to first publish the

140 ARR, Article 8.
141 ARR, Article 20.
142 ARR, Article 13.
143 ARR, Article 14.
144 ARR, Article 5(3).
145 ARR, Articles 17–19.
146 ARR, Article 16.
147 Antolović, *supra* note 21, at p. 290; Radić Rossi, *supra* note 2, at p. 299. The volumes of the Croatian Archaeological Yearbook (as a rule, for each report an abbreviated English summary is included) are successively made available on the website of the Ministry: <https://min-kulture.gov.hr/izdvojeno/kulturna-bastina/izdavacka-djelatnost/hrvatski-arheoloski-godisnjak/8334>.
148 ARR, Article 21.

results of the research and the expert evaluation of the finds. What the drafters of the ARR had in mind here are probably more analytical papers published in periodicals of a scientific nature. This should be done within five years after the research has been completed.[149] However, from what could be gathered, the two provisions on dissemination are applied rather flexibly, with the one requirement strictly adhered to being that the first results be published in Croatia.

4 Conclusion

Croatian underwater archaeologists, working with the competent State authorities for cultural heritage protection, have achieved noteworthy, indeed laudable, results in respect of UCH protection. As has been observed, however, these efforts have so far not been extended to the UCH located beyond the outer limits of Croatia's TS. Aside from the undoubted difficulties in securing sufficient financial resources, another contributing factor in such a state of affairs might be the partial and unsystematic approach towards the implementation of the 2001 Convention into Croatian municipal law.[150] In light of Article 134 of the Croatian Constitution, one could indeed argue in favour of the direct application of the 2001 Convention, but this alone cannot resolve more intricate procedural aspects, such as those related to the competence of administrative bodies for UCH protection on the CS and in the EEZ.

Thus, considering that UCH protection on the CS and in the EEZ could well be the next major challenge for underwater archaeology in Croatia, it is submitted that such endeavours should be supported by an adequate legislative framework. The expectation that the project of an entirely new and revised law might be used to achieve this objective has, regrettably, not been met. Since the publication of the 2023 Draft Act, which is unlikely to be amended significantly during the parliamentary legislative procedure, it is clear that the opportunity has been missed. Judging from the Ministry's proposal not even

149 ARR, Article 22.

150 Another issue not addressed by the COA and not specifically discussed in this chapter, is the status of wrecks of State vessels and aircraft, especially warships and military aircraft. Regarding the wreck of the Italian ironclad *Re d'Italia*, sunk in battle in 1866 and discovered in 2005 on the seabed of the Croatian TS, Degan has argued that Italy lost its entitlements to the wreck based on the rules of war in force at the time of sinking. See V.-Đ. Degan, 'The Legal Situation of the Wreck of the Ironclad *Re d'Italia* Sunk in the 1866 Battle of Vis (Lissa)' (2012) 51 *Poredbeno pomorsko pravo* [*Comparative Maritime Law*] 1. See also Frka, Mesić, *supra* note 52, at pp. 304–13.

the title of the law will be changed, which should also have been a consideration in view of a shared terminology reflecting the modern idea and concept of cultural heritage.

All websites last accessed in January 2024.

Selected Bibliography

V.-Đ. Degan, 'The Legal Situation of the Wreck of the Ironclad *Re d'Italia* Sunk in the 1866 Battle of Vis (Lissa)' (2012) 51 *Poredbeno pomorsko pravo* [*Comparative Maritime Law*] 1.

D. Frka, J. Mesić, *Treasures of the Adriatic* (Adamić, 2013).

I. Radić Rossi, 'Underwater Cultural Heritage and Maritime Archaeology in Croatia: An Overview' (2012) 15 *European Journal of Archaeology* 285.

T. M. Šošić, 'The Common Heritage of Mankind and the Protection of the Underwater Cultural Heritage' in B. Vukas, T. M. Šošić (eds.), *International Law: New Actors, New Concepts – Continuing Dilemmas. Liber Amicorum Božidar Bakotić* (Martinus Nijhoff Publishers, 2010) 319.

T. M. Šošić, 'The 24-Mile Archaeological Zone: Abandoned or Confirmed?' in R. Wolfrum, M. Seršić, T. M. Šošić (eds.), *Contemporary Developments in International Law – Essays in Honour of Budislav Vukas* (Brill-Nijhoff, 2016) 305.

T. M. Šošić, 'The Protection of Underwater Cultural Heritage beyond the Exclusive Jurisdictional Reach of Coastal States' in A. Caligiuri, G. Cataldi, N. Ros (eds.), *L'évolution du droit de la mer: Réflexions à l'occasion du 20ème anniversaire de l'AssIDMer (2001–2021)/The Evolution of the Law of the Sea: Reflections for the 20th AssIDMer Anniversary (2001–2021)* (Editoriale Scientifica, 2023) 175.

CHAPTER 7

Estonia

*Maili Roio**

1 Introduction

The Republic of Estonia is located in the north-eastern part of the Baltic Sea in northern Europe. It borders Finland across the Gulf of Finland in the north, Sweden across the Baltic Sea in the west, Latvia in the south and Russia in the east, and shares a maritime border with all these neighbouring countries. Estonia's maritime space is divided into three parts: the inland sea, the Territorial Sea (TS), and the Exclusive Economic Zone (EEZ). The total area of the maritime waters under the jurisdiction of the Republic of Estonia is approximately 36,500 km^2, of which the EEZ accounts for almost one third, i.e., nearly 11,300 km^2. The length of the coastline of mainland Estonia is 1,242 km, including islands this increases to a total length of 3,793 km.

Depending on their history, the Baltic Sea countries have adopted different approaches to underwater cultural heritage (UCH).[1] In recognised maritime nations, the foundations of maritime governance are based on centuries of seafaring history, resulting experience and international authority. In Estonia, previous experience of the national organisation of both maritime affairs and heritage protection is limited to just over two decades in the first half of the last century (1918–1940). At the beginning of the Second World War, the Soviet Union occupied Estonia on 17 June 1940, staged a coup d'état on 21 June 1940 and annexed the Republic of Estonia on 6 August 1940. On 22 June 1941, Germany started a war against the Soviet Union, and the territory of Estonia was occupied by Germany from September 1941 to October 1944. For many countries, the consequences of the Second World War remained unresolved, and the Baltic States remained annexed by the Soviet Union until 1991.[2]

The Second World War and the occupations had a devastating effect on Estonia's existing heritage protection arrangements, and many monuments

---

* Estonian National Heritage Board.

1 RUTILUS Strategies for a Sustainable Development of the Underwater Cultural Heritage in the Baltic Sea Region, Swedish National Maritime Museums report dnr 1267/03-51, 2006 (NCM). <https://cbss.org/baltic-heritage/working-groups/underwater-heritage/>.

2 A. Pajur & T. Tannberg, *Eesti ajalugu VI. Vabadussõjast taasiseseisvumiseni.* (Tartu, 2005).

DOI:10.1163/9789004510883_009

were destroyed or damaged. First and foremost, the Republic of Estonia with its established laws and institutions had ceased to exist. Since the new regime replaced the existing laws with those in force in the Soviet Union, a legal vacuum was created in the field of heritage protection, as there was no such legal protection in the Soviet Union. The existing Estonian Soviet Socialist Republic Act on the Conservation of Cultural Monuments was enforced only in 1961.[3] It was the first law of its type in the entire Soviet Union.[4] After the restoration of the Republic of Estonia in 1991, the Heritage Conservation Act was enacted in 1994.[5] The protection of UCH was regulated under this Act only in 2011,[6] as part of the process of accession to the UNESCO Convention on the Protection of the Underwater Cultural Heritage (2001 Convention).[7] In October 2020, the Government of the Republic of Estonia approved its accession to the 2001 Convention, which was adopted in November 2020 and entered into force on 2 February 2021. A new Heritage Conservation Act[8] (hereinafter referred to by the Estonian acronym MuKS) was passed in 2019, under which regulation for the protection of UCH remained largely the same.

Prior to 2011, the protection of underwater sites was addressed in a similar way to the protection of monuments on land. An attempt was made to bridge the gaps in maritime legislation and to regulate the investigation and protection of sunken ships, as well as the import of diving equipment, via a regulatory measure concerning "[o]rganisation of the investigation, raising and protection of sunken ships and their remains", which was in force until August 2006.[9] On the basis of the Merchant Shipping Code[10] (hereinafter referred to by the Estonian acronym KMSK) in force at the time and the Heritage

3 Eesti Nõukogude Sotsialistliku Vabariigi seadus Eesti Nõukogude Sotsialistliku Vabariigi kultuurimälestiste kaitse kohta. – Eesti Nõukogude Sotsialistliku Vabariigi Ülemnõukogu ja Valitsuse Teataja, 23 (76), 15.06.1961, see <https://www.digar.ee/arhiiv/et/perioodika/60637>.

4 A. Tvauri, 'The Conservation of Archaeological Heritage in Estonia'in V. Lang & M. Laneman (eds.) *Archaeological Research in Estonia, 1865–2005. Estonian Archaeology 1.* (Tartu University Press, 2006).

5 Heritage Conservation Act of 1994 no 289 (RT I 1994, 24, 391), see <https://www.riigiteataja.ee/akt/28649>.

6 Heritage Conservation Act of 2002 (RT I, 21.03.2011, 8), see <https://www.riigiteataja.ee/en/eli/521042014009/consolide>.

7 2562 UNTS 1.

8 Heritage Conservation Act of 2019 (RT I, 19.03.2019, 13), see <https://www.riigiteataja.ee/en/eli/513122020003/consolide>.

9 Government of the Republic Regulation No 271 of 26 July 1994.

10 Merchant Shipping Code of 1991 (RT 1991, 46, 577), see <https://www.riigiteataja.ee/akt/30363>.

Conservation Act,[11] ownerless wrecks were designated as belonging to the State and the procedure for issuing wreck diving permits was set out. The legality of the regulation was questioned by divers, its provisions were controversial, and it was not respected. Initially, the Border Guard Board also approved control procedures over the activities of wreck divers at sea, but without a legal basis this too remained ineffective.[12] The regulation, a concise document of about a page, proved difficult to implement because of its generality. Unfortunately, repeal of the regulation did not entail a substantive analysis of the loopholes in the law and the introduction of the necessary additions to the sectoral rules to close them.

There are gaps in every legal order since positive law, as a product of human creation, can never be a finished system. In the case of the Estonian legal order, this is compounded by a characteristic factor, its youth. Undoubtedly, there are far fewer gaps apparent in countries with continental legal systems whose national legal systems date back more than 100 years, than there are in the Estonian legal order. However, the overabundance of legislation is cited as a shortcoming in the law of many modern countries.[13] The Estonian legal system is certainly more characterised by the existence of gaps than by any such overabundance.

2 Estonian Legislation

The Ministry of Culture is responsible for organising the protection of UCH, while the National Heritage Board is responsible for the management and national supervision of heritage conservation activities. In Estonia, the study and protection of cultural heritage is governed by a number of legislative Acts. Cultural heritage, including UCH, is protected by being classified variously as 'cultural monuments', 'archaeological finds', or 'archaeological sites'. The regulation of investigations for the conservation of UCH that is not recognised as a monument or archaeological site comes under the MuKS. The conservation of

11 Heritage Conservation Act of 1994 no 289 (RT I 1994, 24, 391), see <https://www.riigiteataja.ee/akt/28649>.

12 A. Kraut, 'Protection of Underwater Cultural Heritage in Estonia – current situation' in J. Litwin (ed.) *Baltic Sea Identity. Common Sea – Common Culture? 1st Cultural Heritage Forum. Gdansk 3rd-6th April 2003 at the Polish Maritime Museum in Gdansk.* (Gdansk, 2003).

13 See E. Catta, 'Kodifitseerimise ja süstematiseerimise tähtsus õige seaduse leidmise lihtsustamisel' (2002) 588 *Juridica* 9.

UCH is also supported by several other laws[14] under which planned activities in the sea and in inland waters are regulated.

2.1 *Underwater Monuments*

The definition of 'underwater monument' is given in the MuKS as a monument located in inland waters, Territorial Sea (TS), transboundary water bodies or the EEZ, together with the archaeological and natural surroundings.[15] The definition of the term and the regulation of activities are based on the 2001 Convention. An underwater monument is not a separate type of monument (archaeological, historical, and architectural monuments can all be found underwater), but the need for separate regulation of an underwater monument is important because of the special nature of its location.

An archaeological monument is the remains, thing or set of things of human activity and other traces which indicate the multiple layers of time on a cultural landscape, and which provide scientific information on the history of mankind and human relations with the natural environment. An archaeological layer is an important part of an archaeological monument.[16] An archaeological layer means a deposit accumulated as a result of direct human activity or human impact, which may include the remains of construction, wrecks, human and animal bones, archaeological finds, including tools and utility articles, remains or production and similar.[17] The term 'wreck' has been separately defined, as the approach in the MuKS differs from the traditional definition of a wreck, which is mainly the hull of an end-of-life vehicle (e.g., a ship, an aircraft or other vehicle). The definition of a wreck is given under the section on archaeological layers. A wreck means the remains of a water, air or other craft, or a part or parts thereof, together with the area underneath it and the cargo or other objects associated with the wreck.[18] Shipwrecks are considered archaeological monuments. The archaeological layer of a wreck consists of the hull and the detached parts of the ship and other objects associated with the wreck. In many cases, people have died with the ship, and the sea has become their final resting place.

The MuKS does not set an age-limit for declaring an item a monument. This is compatible with the 2001 Convention since it does not prohibit a State Party

---

14 These laws include the Water Act (RT I, 29.06.2022, 12), Building Code (RT I, 29.06.2022, 5), Exclusive Economic Zone Act (RT I, 19.03.2019, 101).

15 MuKS 'para. 12(1).

16 MuKS 'para. 11(3).

17 MuKS 'para. 6(1).

18 MuKS 'para. 6(2).

from treating remains less than 100-years old as UCH. This does not, however, mean that, all shipwrecks that are less than 100-years old have historical or other value and therefore can be wholly protected by the legislation. The temporal dimension to cultural objects has been dealt with solely by regulating their export, as under the Intra-Community Transport, Export and Import of Cultural Objects Act[19] (hereinafter referred to by the Estonian acronym KultVS). This applies to cultural monuments, temporarily protected objects, as well as to watercrafts built in Estonia and their parts, freight and other content originating from pre-1945, and watercrafts found from the territories under the jurisdiction of the Republic of Estonia and their parts, freight and other content originating from pre-1945.[20]

Under the MuKS, the prerequisite for being included under State protection is that the thing or area of cultural value represents a valuable part of the tangible cultural heritage of Estonia, which has scientific, historical, artistic or other cultural value, or attracts a duty of preservation arising from an international agreement.[21] The 2001 Convention imposes an obligation to protect UCH that has been partially or totally underwater, temporarily or permanently, for at least 100 years. Nevertheless, during the procedure for designation as a monument under the MuKS, the National Heritage Board must also assess the condition of the object, its integrity, its source value, i.e., the scientific value and uniqueness of the information, its preservation in its original location etc. As a criterion for the presumption of national protection, the partially or wholly underwater location of the object is specifically mentioned, emphasising the conditions of preservation created by the underwater environment and the special experience it offers (remains of sunken water, air, and other craft, together with freight, furnishings, and commodities; underwater ancient settlements and burial sites, etc.).

However, the process of getting a monument listed is lengthy and bureaucratic, which must be preceded by a relatively thorough survey to assess the condition and extent of the object. This is why, currently, only just over 100 underwater monuments are protected. Since the number of known underwater monuments of cultural value today is close to 700, this is a very modest result. Looking to the future, recent advances in underwater archaeology (in terms of techniques, methods and software) have made it possible, for the first

19 Intra-Community Transport, Export and Import of Cultural Objects Act of 2007 (RT I 2008, 3, 24). See <https://www.riigiteataja.ee/en/eli/514032019003/consolide>.

20 KultVS 'para. 2(1) cl 16.

21 MuKS 'para. 10(1).

time in history, to study and record wrecks after a short time in the field and to document them in their entirety.[22] These developments should offer the scope to certainly speed up the process of placing objects under protection.

2.2 *Archaeological Finds and Sites*

Items of UCH are protected not only through their recognition as cultural monuments, but also through the regulation of archaeological finds and sites. The MuKS allows for the protection of UCH as archaeological finds if it meets the definition of being an object or set of objects created by human activity and sedimented or hidden in the ground or on the surface of the ground, inside a structure, water body or the sediments thereof, which has an archaeological, including historical, artistic, scientific or other cultural value and which has no owner or the owner of which cannot be ascertained,[23] or, if the discovered finds refer to a cultural layer, also as an archaeological site.[24]

Designation as an archaeological site does not impose the same restrictions on the landowner that apply to an archaeological monument. Activities that may have an impact at an underwater site, which must be preceded by an investigation, are separately specified. These include trawling, dredging and solids dumping.[25] The purpose of imposing the investigation obligation prior to these activities is necessary to protect UCH and to ensure that important information is not lost. However, this obligation does not entail any restriction or prohibition of these activities. The investigation obligation is also a preventive measure. If there is sufficient evidence of the possibility of finding archaeological remains, an investigation before the work is carried out will also be less burdensome for the landowner or developer than stopping the works already started, because of the discovery of an archaeological find.[26]

The National Heritage Board may determine a reward payable to the finder of an archaeological find. The reward to the finder is an incentive to hand over the find to the State in accordance with the procedure laid down by law.[27]

---

22 One of the outputs is 3D modelling of the objects, which give a complete picture of their condition and preservation. See for example <https://sketchfab.com/muinsuskaitseamet>.

23 MuKS 'para. 24(1).

24 MuKS 'para. 25.

25 MuKS 'para. 26(1). Applies to all ships operating in Estonian waters. Trawling has caused major damage to historic shipwrecks in Estonian waters, and whilst this has been in force since 2011, no disputes have arisen.

26 MuKS 'para. 31. Not all activities are subject to an environmental impact assessment. If one is required, the study must be carried out within this framework.

27 MuKS 'para. 28(2).

However, circumstances where the finder will not be granted an award are also stipulated. This will be the case if it is determined that the find is a wreck of a water, air or another craft, a part thereof, or a cargo associated with the wreck or other objects.[28] One of the reasons for this is that the locations of vehicles (wrecks, tanks etc.) are often known from archival material or other information and are deliberately sought. When they are found, it is not a typical stray find, but rather a question of pinpointing the exact location. The second reason is that the same wreck may be found repeatedly, making it virtually impossible to identify the original finder. For example, the locations of many wrecks may have already been identified by fishing vessels trawling during the Soviet period; the captain of each vessel would mark these places on a map, but the information may not have been recorded beyond the captain's bridge. Coastal communities are often also aware of the locations of sunken ships. The third important factor is that there may be no way to determine the owner of an archaeological find, which is of particular relevance in the case of historic shipwrecks.

The MuKS provision on archaeological finds and sites sets out the obligation of notification. If an archaeological find is found within the EEZ, Continental Shelf (CS) or seabed of another State, an Estonian citizen or a captain of a ship sailing under the Estonian flag shall be required to immediately notify the National Heritage Board of the find.[29] Inclusion of such an obligation ensures compliance with Article 9 of the 2001 Convention.

In the decade leading up to the introduction of the new MuKS in 2019, there were two occasions when diplomatic notes were exchanged with neighbouring countries to clarify the fate of a find. In 2011, Estonian fishermen hoisted a nineteenth century figurehead aboard a fishing trawler flying the Finnish flag and headed for a port in Estonia, where locals reported the find. The National Heritage Board handed the figurehead over to the Estonian Maritime Museum for temporary storage and initial conservation work until the establishment of the circumstances of the find. As the finder of the figurehead had transmitted the coordinates of the site, which was located in the Finnish EEZ, an exchange of diplomatic notes between Estonia and Finland started, with the aim of clarifying the fate of the figurehead and whether there was a wreck with fresh damage at the site. On 21 September 2011, the Finnish Ministry of Foreign Affairs officially stated that Finland made no ownership claims in respect of the figurehead: since the figurehead was found in its EEZ, Finland did not consider that handing it over was necessary and agreed to leave it in Estonia

28 MuKS 'para. 28(4) cl 1.

29 MuKS 'para. 27(4).

as common UCH, which Estonia undertook to conserve and exhibit properly. It was also confirmed that the wreck had been found at the coordinates provided. The figurehead was conserved in Sweden and then brought back to the Estonian Maritime Museum, where it is part of a permanent exhibition in the Fat Margaret Tower.[30]

The second case was similar, in both the circumstances of the discovery and the solution. In 2018, a wooden box, which had the imprints of two nineteenth century coins inside, got caught in the trawl of a fishing vessel flying the flag of Finland. A crew member contacted the Estonian Maritime Museum to hand over the box. According to the finders, the box came from the Gulf of Bothnia in the Swedish EEZ. The official position of Sweden was also that it had no ownership claim on the box but would like the opportunity to exhibit it in the Swedish National Maritime and Transport Museums in the future. However, the box is currently in the collection of the Estonian Maritime Museum.

While reporting a find is a universal obligation, in practice fishers do not always do so – in the first example above, the figurehead was not reported by fishers but instead by local people. This identified mismatch between obligation and practice highlights the need for systemtic data collection.

2.3 *Ownership*

Issues related to the ownership of the UCH are regulated through the concepts of 'underwater monument' and 'archaeological finds'. The MuKS stipulates that an underwater monument which does not have an owner, or the owner of which cannot be ascertained, belongs to the State.[31] The administrative body responsible for underwater monuments belonging to the State is the National Heritage Board.[32] An archaeological find belongs to the State regardless on whose immovable property it was found or in whose possession it is. An archaeological find cannot be acquired in good faith.[33] A prerequisite for State ownership is that the underwater monument or archaeological find does not have an owner, or the owner cannot be ascertained.

The national legislation in Estonia that regulates sunken goods is the Merchant Shipping Code (KMSK). This includes the raising and removal from the water of property (vessels, their remains, equipment and freight, including

30 See R. Alatalu & M. Roio, 'International cooperation. Case study: Figurehead from a merchant ship in Finnish Exclusive Economic Zone' in L. Witt, D. Shaft (eds.) *The UNESCO Convention on the Protection of Underwater Cultural Heritage: how do we make it work* (Amersfoort: Cultural Heritage Agency of the Netherlands, 2017).

31 MuKS 'para. 12(2).

32 MuKS 'para. 12(3).

33 MuKS 'para. 24(4).

vessels and their remains, equipment and freight cast ashore and on shoals), which has sunk in the Estonian TS, inland sea, EEZ or in navigable inland waters.[34] Sunken property of cultural value is an exception to this, as the protection, research and raising of such property must be carried out in accordance with the procedure laid down in the MuKS.[35] According to the KMSK,[36] the owner loses the right to the sunken property if they fail to raise it within one year of sinking. This means that the owner must show interest within a certain period of time, and failure to do so can result in the wreck being considered abandoned. This includes when the owner of the wreck is unidentifiable.

Due to the political situation, the issue of determining the ownership of Russian warships in the listing process rose to the top of the agenda in 2014. In previous years, the question of wreck ownership had not been addressed so sharply and clearly in this process, with expert opinions on listing mainly stating that it was not possible to ascertain the wreck's owner. As of 2014, the wrecks of Imperial Russia[37] in Estonian waters were declared the property of the Republic of Estonia under the Treaty of Tartu.[38] Article XI of the Tartu Peace Treaty, signed between the Republic of Estonia and Soviet Russia in 1920, stipulates that:

> Russia gives up all movable and immovable national property of the Russian State from its transfer to it or the payment of its value, whatever property this may be, including military and other buildings, fortifications, ports, all types of ships, including warships, ship freight, etc., as well as any rights of the Russian State to the movable and immovable property of individuals that does not belong to it, insofar that all of these listed properties are in the territory of Estonia, within the borders determined

---

34 KMSK 'para. 110.

35 KMSK 'para. 118^1.

36 The respective regulation of the Merchant Shipping Code has essentially been in force during the Republic of Estonia 1918–1940, as well as during the Soviet period.

37 The expert assessment of the wreck of the submarine *Akula*, which belonged to Imperial Russia, defined the question of ownership in relation to the Tartu Peace Treaty for the first time.

38 The peace treaty between the Republic of Estonia and Soviet Russia was signed in Tartu on 2 February 1920. The Treaty marked the end of the Estonian War of Independence, which had lasted for about a year and a half and was the first major achievement in the foreign relations of the young Estonian State. The eastern border of Estonia was determined in the Treaty and Soviet Russia recognised the independence of the Republic of Estonia for all time. It also opened the road to international recognition for Estonia as an independent State. The ratification instruments of the Treaty were exchanged in Moscow on 30 March 1920, and it entered into force on that date.

> in this treaty or in waters adjacent to the territory of Estonia or were there by the time of the German occupation, i.e. by the twenty-fourth day of February one thousand nine hundred and eighteen, also any rights to ships, including warships, that came there during the German occupation or, ultimately, have been captured in the subsequent war between Estonia and Russia by the Estonian military forces or by others, and have been transferred to Estonia. All of the above properties are declared to be in the sole ownership of Estonia, free of any commitments, as of the fifteenth of November one thousand nine hundred and seventeen, or if Russia has acquired them later, as of the time of their acquisition.

The Treaty of Tartu defines Estonia as the sole owner of the ships in the territory of Estonia as well as in the waters adjacent to its territory, including any warships and the property onboard. As the property of the Russian State could potentially also include German ships, including warships, the Treaty of Tartu also expands to German vessels in this regard.

The ownership of other wrecks, mainly from World War II and the Soviet period, is defined by the Government of the Republic Act.[39] With this legislation, in the context of its withdrawal from Estonian territory, the Government of the Republic decided to transfer buildings, facilities and other property used by the armed forces of the USSR to the ownership of the Estonian State Chancellery. It can be concluded from this that all the equipment and property left behind by the Soviet armed services, including ships and their wrecks, was transferred to the Republic of Estonia. Russia has subsequently made no claims to sovereign immunity.

The conservation and protection of wrecks, both on its territory and in the EEZ, can only be ensured by a coastal State. In Estonia, different regulations apply primarily through designation as a monument. This process usually involves communication with countries of origin or Flag States, as necessary, through diplomatic channels. In this respect, diplomatic notes have been exchanged with Germany. However, since Germany has expressed no interest and made no formal submissions, it can be implied that it has relinquished its ownership of the World War II shipwrecks located in Estonian waters. There is a constrasting situation with the United Kingdom (UK) since its position in communication with the Republic of Estonia is historically different. While Russia and Germany attacked the territory of Estonia and lost their warships in

39 'Otsus Eesti Vabariigi territooriumil endise NSV Liidu relvajõudude halduses olevate hoonete, rajatiste, relvastuse, lahingutehnika, varustuse ja muu vara Eesti Vabariigi omandiks tunnistamise kohta', 23.01.1992. – ERA.R-3.3.16671.

the process, the wrecks belonging to the UK (and which are listed) are located in Estonian waters for different reasons.[40] The UK expressed a clear position in the exchange of diplomatic notes on the recognition of the wreck of submarine HMS *E18* as a monument.[41] Furthermore, to ensure the sanctity of such sites, the UK has protected warship wrecks from unauthorised disturbance under the Protection of Military Remains Act 1986. Section 1(6), extends such protection to international waters, defined under section 9(1) as any part of the sea outside the seaward limits of the territorial waters adjacent to any country or territory. Thus, the UK designates wrecks of warships located in the Estonian EEZ, but not its TS or inland waters. However, in international waters, such as the Estonian EEZ, the Act only applies to British nationals or British-flagged vessels.[42] In terms of diving on such wrecks, the UK does not consider it necessary to restrict such activity, as long as sanctity is guaranteed.[43]

Where possible, Estonia has also considered the interests of the countries of origin, where this is justified and not contrary to law. The wreck of the Latvian minesweeper *Virsaitis*,[44] which sank in the Estonian EEZ, was discovered by Finnish divers in 2005, who recovered the ship's bell during a dive for identification purposes in 2008. The National Heritage Board learned of the find in 2012, and contacted the divers, who provided the footage and agreed to hand over the bell. As a ship of historical importance for Latvia, the position of the National Heritage Board was that since the ship's bell had already been

40 During World War I, the British Government decided to send a flotilla of submarines to the Baltic Sea to prevent the exportation of iron ore from Sweden to Germany and to participate in patrols and reconnaissance missions, sinking German warships whenever possible. After World War I, it was correctly assumed that Soviet Russia was going to try to conquer the newly independent Baltic States. To prevent the spread of Communism, the British Government decided to provide armed support to the Republic of Estonia on 20 November 1918. At the same time, it refused to send military units to the Baltic States, as the Entente Powers were not officially at war with Soviet Russia. Therefore, a limited form of intervention policy was pursued. For this purpose, a squadron of warships was formed, one of the aims of which was to demonstrate Britain's political support for Estonia with its presence in Baltic ports.

41 „Kultuurimälestiseks tunnistamine". Directive of the Minister of Culture, 29.08.2014 No 220. <https://www.riigiteataja.ee/akt/302092014004>.

42 The Protection of Military Remains Act 1986, section 1((6).

43 Securing the sanctity of a wreck is ensured through the regulation of diving on the monument, see above.

44 In 1919, the *Virsaitis* was incorporated into the fleet of the Republic of Latvia. The *Virsaitis* was the flagship of pre-war Latvia. At the start of the Soviet occupation in 1940, the vessel was incorporated into the Baltic Fleet. In late autumn 1941, the *Virsaitis* participated in the evacuation of the Hanko military base to Kronstadt, hit a mine in the Gulf of Finland, and sank on 3 December 1941.

brought up, it should be transferred to the appropriate Latvian State authority or national museum, where its preservation and display would be ensured. Handover to the Latvian War Museum took place in Estonia in 2013, with the cooperation of the Ministry of Defence.[45]

2.4 *Public Access to Underwater Monuments*

Diving is regulated in order to ensure responsible access to an underwater site *in situ* in a way that does not harm cultural heritage. Thus, public access to an underwater monument can be described as permitted on a 'look, but don't touch' basis. Any physical intervention by people, such as cleaning the various surfaces and objects of the wreck of the layers that have built up over time, is tantamount to deterioration of the monument. In the case of monuments that are more sensitive to human impacts, where diving has been identified as having an adverse impact on their preservation, or where diving poses a risk to people (e.g., risk arising from an explosive device on board a wreck), the National Heritage Board may restrict or prohibit access.[46]

Diving to underwater monuments and their buffer zones is allowed under the instruction of a competent person or a business operator that offers diving services within the scope of its economic activities or under a diving permit. A diving permit can only be used by the holder of the permit and is issued for an unspecified term.[47] In order to avoid endangering heritage unknowingly when diving, and to ensure understanding of the rights and obligations when diving on a site, it is necessary to undergo training before applying for a permit.[48]

The competent person, including of any company providing the diving service, must hold a certificate of competence issued by the National Heritage Board.[49] Holding a diving permit and an internationally recognised diving instructor's licence is a precondition to getting this.[50] The competent person may take an unlimited number of people on the dive.

---

45 Republic of Estonia Ministry of Defence, 'Latvian and Estonian defence ministers commemoirate sunken flagship' 4 September 2013 available at <https://www.kaitseministeerium.ee/en/news/latvian-and-estonian-defence-ministers-commemorate-sunken-flagship> and „Kultuurimälestiseks tunnistamine". Directive of the Minister of Culture, 28.02.2014 No 79. <https://www.riigiteataja.ee/akt/305032014003>.

46 MuKS 'para. 82(3).

47 MuKS 'para. 42.

48 MuKS 'para. 42(2).

49 MuKS 'para. 68.

50 MuKS 'para. 71(4).

A notification must be sent to the National Heritage Board both before and after the dive. The number of divers, as well as information on any possible changes in the status of the monument, must be given in the report submitted after the dive. This notification system has two important outcomes. Above all, it ensures an operational and continuous exchange of information on underwater sites between the Board and the divers. It also ensures the Board has knowledge of the sites frequented by divers and how often they are visited, which in turn is the basis for choosing where to install mooring, used to help divers descend to the wreck, which supports wreck protection and safe diving.

2.5 *Conducting an Investigation*

The quality of the execution and the final result of the archaeological investigation is very important. Achieving this relies first and foremost on a responsible specialist with good skills and knowledge. The competence of a company or other legal entity to carry out an underwater archaeological investigation is assessed through the evaluation of its personnel. A company is competent if its competent person is qualified, which is attested by a certificate issued under the MuKS. Similarly, the competence of individual persons is assessed by the National Heritage Board by issuing a certificate for a limited period.[51] The purpose of setting the term is to ensure that the qualifications of the person supervising the work are maintained and monitored since without frequent practice, skills can be forgotten. Applicants for a certificate of competence in archaeological investigation must have a master's degree and they must have been continuously engaged in the activity in question for at least the last four years. In principle, the formal Higher Education requirement and the professional experience that a person can provide should ensure that an underwater archaeological investigation is properly carried out.[52]

A certificate of competence can be requested for underwater archaeological research, during which diving may or may not take place.[53] If the case, the prerequisite for conducting the research is diving skill, and for where diving is not conducted, competence in techniques such as sonar investigations, and/or research with underwater robots or underwater drones. Considerably more research is being conducted using such remote technical means, which is more effective and safer. Often, for example, when filming a single wreck with an

51 MuKS 'para. 71.

52 MuKS 'para. 48(3).

53 The requirements for conducting research (research plan, research notification and certificate of competence) are in line with the relevant rules of the 2001 UNESCO Convention.

underwater robot, the result is better because all the work can be done at the same time and the quality of material collected in similar environmental conditions is more consistent. In comparison, a dive requires the cooperation of one or more photographers and filmmakers, and multiple dives are required to cover an entire wreck.[54]

The MuKS also addresses the conservation of UCH that has not yet been discovered or explored, which means it has been impossible to take measures to conserve it. Research must be conducted in inland waters, the TS, transboundary water bodies or an EEZ before any construction, including the installation of plant and equipment, or any other activity likely to compromise the conservation of UCH.[55] The purpose is to identify the impact of the proposed activity on UCH and, if necessary, to take measures to ensure its protection, either by designating it as a monument or a site. The need for and the scope of the study will be determined by the Board on the basis of the nature and extent of the proposed works, for example before granting consent to another administrative body or in the permit to carry out the works. This applies to various developments (e.g., offshore wind farms, cable lines, fish farms, etc.), for which the National Heritage Board sets conditions through various authorisation procedures. According to estimates, less than 20 per cent of marine areas and even less of inland waters have been explored in depth, so the first priority is to conduct underwater archaeological research. As a rule, changing the locations of wind turbines or route corridors in later stages has proven to be practically impossible, so the research should be conducted within the scope of the environmental assessment. The scope and extent of the research, as determined by the Board, must be properly implemented. This requirement is rigid in the context of projects of high public interest, where the risks to the public interest must be identified to the extent possible, whereas, in contrast, in the case of research of a different nature (e.g., in the context of scientific research), the public interest may not be as demanding for the full scope of the research. In the first case, the researcher does not have the right to set or change the scope

54 For comparison, see the 3D model of the wreck of the schooner *Gullkrona*, filmed with an underwater robot, available at <https://skfb.ly/opDQS> and a 3D model of the wreck of mine trawler number 1 filmed during several dives, available at <https://skfb.ly/6Ysru>. The change in water conditions is noticeable on the model.

55 MuKS 'para. 32. This section is the basis for the determination of underwater archaeological research at the different stages of the authorisation procedures and is based on principles of EIA regulated by the Environmental Impact Assessment and Environmental Management System Act (hereinafter referred to as the Estonian acronym KeHJS). See <https://www.riigiteataja.ee/akt/103012022010?leiaKehtiv>.

of the research. This must be met to the full extent of the public interest served by the research.

According to Article 2(5) of the 2001 Convention, the conservation of UCH *in situ* is considered the first option before any activity impacting it is authorised or commenced. The MuKS follows the same principle. First, the MuKS emphasises that the principle of minimal intervention is followed when planning or conducting research. Also, the law provides that "[t]ypes of research, procedure for reimbursement of research costs and related costs, and the formal requirements and notification procedure for the research report", and stipulates that in the case of underwater archaeological research preference is given to the preservation of objects and details in the original location of discovery.[56] Underwater archaeological research methods, especially for shipwrecks, have become increasingly more technical and less destructive of heritage than archaeological research on land. Often, the information obtained on the object proves to be fully sufficient and accurate to determine its origin and condition. For this reason, the excavation and raising of one of the most abundant types of UCH, shipwrecks, is usually not justified. The only requirement that alters the condition of the wrecks in the research designated by the Board is the taking of wood samples for dendrochronological analysis.

If raising UCH during underwater archaeological excavation is unavoidable, then the long-term preservation of that raised heritage must be ensured. Due to the change in the environment, salvaged materials require immediate conservation and storage in a location that meets the temperature and humidity requirements. In Estonia, archaeological finds are stored in scientific collections and in major museums to ensure they are properly preserved. However, the conservation and storage of excavated large shipwrecks is problematic. This need may arise in or around historic harbour sites, where active development and construction are ongoing and where the public interest in urban development is greater, or more important, than preserving UCH in its original location. In Estonia, a typical area like this is Tallinn Old Harbour and its immediate surroundings, where the first reports of wreck finds date back to the eighteenth century.[57] While only scant and incomplete descriptions of earlier finds are available, the most recent finds include shipwrecks. In addition, the

56 Minister of Culture Regulation No 25 of 15 May 2019. See <https://www.riigiteataja.ee/akt/116052019003>.

57 M. Roio, 'Tallinn Harbour from the Middle Ages: Studies of the Former and Current Seabed' in J. A. Rodrigers and A. Traviglia (eds.) IKUWA6 Shared Heritage: Proceedings of the Sixth International Congress for Underwater Archaeology. (Archaeopress Publishing Ltd, 2020).

research documentation and the individual finds are preserved for the long-term. In each case, the situation and storage options in the original location will be assessed and a considered decision will be taken. The current practice of decision-making is different from the past and is set out below.

2.5.1 Preservation In Situ

The preferable option is to preserve the wreck *in situ*, assuming that this environment is maintained and restored after the development, so that the wreck is in a stable environment. Several wrecks in Kadriorg, for example, have been preserved in their original location (between new buildings, in one case under the road and promenade).[58] Wrecks are not left under the foundations/floors of new buildings, because the pressure of the building could cause damage and because the possibilities to both study the wreck and if necessary transfer it (e.g., should something happen to the general water level in the area) would be lost.

2.5.2 Transfer of UCH

Pursuant to the MuKS, in the public interest, monuments may be transferred to another suitable location if preservation of the monument in the present location is endangered, and its preservation cannot be ensured in any other manner. Such transfer of an underwater monument occurred from the third quay of Tallinn Old Harbour.[59] This quay is in everyday use, as it hosts daily ferries on the Tallinn-Stockholm line. An inspection in autumn 2017 revealed that the wreck in question was completely clear of sediment and its preservation was under threat due to intense ferry traffic. The wreck had also moved significantly away from the edge of the quay when compared to 2008. At a meeting of the National Heritage Board and Port of Tallinn representatives, a joint conclusion was reached that it was impossible to protect the wreck at its current location as both its preservation and the safety of ferry traffic were impacted. The Port of Tallinn undertook the transfer of the wreck in accordance with the project and special conditions drawn up by the National Heritage Board.

If permission is given to examine and transfer a wreck, the long-term preservation of it and the possibility of future research must be secured. The alternatives are the current practices of transfer to a museum or more often to the

---

58 See A. Läänelaid, A. Daly, M. Roio, R. Bernotas, 'Dendrochronological dating of an 18th century shipwreck from the Tallinn harbour'(2020) 235 *Archaeological Fieldwork in Estonia 2019*.

59 Cultural monument No 30190, see more information in the National Registry of Cultural Monuments. See <https://register.muinas.ee>.

UCH storage area near Naissaar Island (e.g., a wreck from Kalaranna).[60] Wreck excavation is based on the principle that the wreck site must be investigated in its entirety, even if it extends partially outside the construction area.

In 2015, two medieval shipwrecks were found in the course of construction work for apartment buildings near Tallinn Old Harbour in the area between Kadriorg and the sea.[61] It was reclaimed land filled in less than 100-years ago that was historically used as an anchorage. At the start of excavations, because the wrecks would be located under planned apartment buildings, it was decided that the wrecks should be excavated in their entirety and preserved for the long term. The excavation pits had to be drained of water every day in order to make it possible to excavate the wrecks using archaeological methods meant for dry land. Sinking the wrecks in the Tallinn Bay was seen as a solution. This had previously been done in 2006 in the case of a wreck that emerged during construction work at the Old Harbour of Tallinn but unfortunately only a few fragments reached the seabed.

One of the discoveries found in 2015 turned out to be the remains of a wreck from the early fourteenth century, the so-called *Peeter* cog, where a relatively large number of various finds were preserved. Part of the wreck (less than a third) was outside the construction area. The developer's proposal was to saw the wreck in half, both vertically and horizontally (i.e., not to go deeper with excavations than the plan required). The National Heritage Board did not accept this proposal, as it would have completely destroyed the wreck and the changed environmental conditions would not have ensured its preservation for further research, as it would have remained largely under the building. Thus, the *Peeter* cog was excavated, conserved and is on display in the permanent exhibition of the Estonian Maritime Museum in the Fat Margaret Tower. The second wreck found, the so-called *Viljo* wreck, was sunk in the designated place in Tallinn Bay.[62]

---

60 The Kalaranna wreck represents probably a two-masted ketch, a typical fishing vessel used in the North Sea region. The results of the dendrochronological investigation show that it was made of oak felled around 1841–1852. See more A. Läänelaid, A. Daly, R. Bernotas, and V. Mäss, 'Dendrochronological dating of the Kalaranna wreck from Tallinn' (2021) 243 *Archaeological fieldwork in Estonia 2020*.

61 See M. Roio, L. Lõugas, A. Läänelaid, L. Maldre, E. Russow, and Ü. Sillasoo, 'Medieval ship finds from Kadriorg, Tallinn' (2016) 139 *Archaeological fieldwork in Estonia 2015*.

62 The National Heritage Board expressed a clear demand that that in the course of extending the harbour the wreck would be studied *in situ*, then should be lifted up compact and re-sunk. The lifting process destroyed all compact details of the wreck, hence the National Heritage Board decided to preserve only the remains of the keel and some parts of the frames. After archaeological work was concluded at the wreck, the responsible archaeologist failed to turn over the finds, which caused the loss of copper plates from the

3 UCH Underwater Storage Areas in the Sea

The spatial planning of maritime areas is a tool for long-term planning use of the sea. The purpose of maritime spatial planning is to agree on long-term principles for the use of Estonia's maritime area in order to contribute to achieving and maintaining good environmental status of the marine environment and to promote the maritime economy.[63] At the national level, a plan acts to guide such spatial development, and in the case of Estonia, the Planning Act, passed in 2015, provides guidelines for preparing these. This sets out the long-term vision, defines the principles of spatial development and provides general guidelines and conditions for the use of the Estonian maritime area. Shipwrecks, for which the Baltic Sea offers unique preservation conditions, are the most abundant part of the heritage resting on its seabed, where the environmental conditions (low salinity, relatively cool water temperature, absence of shipworm) are favourable for the long-term preservation of wooden wrecks and offer alternative options for wreck preservation.

UCH underwater storage areas in the sea are included within the maritime spatial plans. The purpose of designating storage areas is to ensure the preservation of the UCH that has been discovered in situations where it cannot be preserved in its original location or conserved, stored or exhibited in museum collections. In the public interest, an underwater monument and archaeological find may be transferred from its location to the preservation area specified in the plan if preservation of the monument/find in the present location is endangered and cannot be ensured in any other manner. The conditions for the transfer of underwater monuments and archaeological finds are determined by the National Heritage Board.[64] The Water Act stipulates the registration of activities involving risk to the aquatic environment when sinking an underwater object of cultural value in an area defined in a spatial plan.[65] The

bottom and some other parts of the wreck. See K. Ilves, 'Archaeological monitoring during reconstruction works in Tallinn Old City Harbour' (2008) 205 *Archaeological fieldwork in Estonia 2007*. F. Lüth, 'Review of the article, 'Archaeological monitoring during reconstruction works in Tallinn Old City Harbour', by Kristin Ilves' (2008) 216 *Archaeological fieldwork in Estonia 2007*. V. Mäss 'Review of the article, 'Archaeological monitoring during reconstruction works in Tallinn Old City Harbour', by Kristin Ilves' (2008) 217 *Archaeological fieldwork in Estonia 2007*. M. Roio, 'Some remarks on the archaeological rescue work at the Tallinn Old Harbour' (2008) 219 *Archaeological fieldwork in Estonia 2007*.

63 The Planning Act 2015, see Chapter 3. <https://www.riigiteataja.ee/en/eli/515072022012/consolide>.

64 MuKS 'para. 40(3).

65 Water Act 2019 'para. 196(2) cl 11. See <https://www.riigiteataja.ee/en/eli/530062022002/consolide>.

respective regulation was effective from 2019 and has greatly accelerated the whole process. For example, in 2015 a permit for a special use of water had to be requested for the transfer of the *Viljo* wreck to Tallinn Bay. At the time of the request for the permit, the issuer had to decide whether or not to initiate an environmental impact assessment, making the process of obtaining the permit relatively long and stressful, in a situation where the shipwreck would need to be sunk immediately after excavation to minimise the damage caused by the wreck drying out. The UCH storage area in Tallinn Bay is still in use today, and four shipwrecks have been transferred there.

4 Topical Issues

4.1 *Environmentally Hazardous Shipwrecks*

Twentieth century heritage in Estonian waters is known to amount to approximately 500 vessels.[66] The use of fuel oils increased early in the twentieth century, bringing the risk of pollution from sunken ships. In addition to pollution caused by fuel oils, sunken ships may also pose a threat to the environment in two other respects – ghost fishing and explosives. Coastal States face the challenge of identifying and addressing these environmental risks. Whilst the rights and practices of Flag States and the sovereignty of warships are subject to international law, there is no equivalent and widespread practice in the case of the environmental threat that may arise from such a wreck. However, a start point is that both rights and obligations should stem from ownership.

Dealing with the issue of environmentally hazardous wrecks is likely to be one of the biggest challenges in coming years, as corrosion of metal-hulled ships has reached a stage that could lead to petroleum products seeping into the marine environment, including the Baltic Sea. Identification of the environmental hazards of historic wrecks has so far been carried out in cooperation between the Ministry of the Environment, the National Heritage Board and the Police and Border Guard Board. In 2019, the project 'Mapping, documentation and risk assessment of environmentally hazardous wrecks', coordinated by the National Heritage Board, was completed, resulting in a list of twentieth century shipwrecks and an analysis of their environmental hazards.[67]

---

66 See the Wreck Register, available at <https://register.muinas.ee/public.php?menuID=en_wreckregistry>.

67 <https://www.muinsuskaitseamet.ee/et/ameti-tegevus/keskkonnaohtlike-vrakkide-kaardistamine-dokumenteerimine-ja-riskide-hindamine>.

The results, based on historical sources of the maximum amount of fuel that could be contained in the tanks of a particular vessel, identified around 400 vessels as posing a low or no risk to the environment; 72 vessels that could pose a medium risk; and one that could pose a high risk. Where possible, wreck conditions (e.g., whether cut down to scrap or whether an explosion had occurred at the location of the fuel tanks, etc.) were also considered. To date, of those wrecks identified as posing a risk, 44 have been recovered; the locations of the remaining 28 are unconfirmed, although approximate ones have been identified.[68]

4.2 *Violations and Enforcement*

One of the biggest shortcomings in the Estonian system for the protection of UCH is the detection and handling of violations. Regulating activities and imposing restrictions do not serve their purpose if compliance is not monitored and there are no proportionate consequences for non-compliance. In misdemeanour proceedings, the principle of mandatory initiation of violation proceedings applies according to the Code of Misdemeanour Procedure (hereinafter referred to by the Estonian acronym VTMS).[69] The principle of expediency of State supervision is laid down in the Law Enforcement Act (hereinafter referred to as the Estonian acronym KorS), according to which the law enforcement authority shall act expediently and effectively when exercising State supervision and shall apply State supervision measures flexibly within the limits of legitimate considerations.[70]

When the elements of a misdemeanour are revealed, proceedings must be conducted unless there are circumstances that preclude this. The commencement of misdemeanour proceedings is not required in the case of a minor misdemeanour. However, an act that causes damage (such that if a monument is damaged) cannot be considered minor. One exception is that where damage has been caused, proceedings may be dismissed if the person who has committed the offence has voluntarily compensated or remedied the damage. In such circumstances, the prosecutor can elect not to initiate proceedings and to give the offender a verbal warning. They also have the right to decide not to open proceedings if it is unlikely that the person who committed the misdemeanour

68 See I. Treffner, '20. sajandil uppunud vrakkide keskkonnaohtlikuse analüüs. '(2019). <https://www.muinsuskaitseamet.ee/sites/default/files/content-editors/Veealune/vrakkide_keskkonnaohtlikkuse_analuus.pdf>.

69 VTMS 'para. 31. See <https://www.riigiteataja.ee/en/eli/515072022014/consolide>.

70 KorS 'para. 8(1). See <https://www.riigiteataja.ee/en/eli/526082022003/consolide>.

can be identified, or if the conduct of proceedings would be unreasonably costly in view of the circumstances of the misdemeanour.[71]

The majority of violations qualify as criminal cases,[72] which can only be processed by the Police and Border Guard Board. For various reasons, the majority of violations that have qualified as criminal cases have not reached a satisfactory outcome as regards cultural heritage.[73] In order to be able to deal with violations, the National Heritage Board must assess and quantify the extent of the damage and there is a growing need to detect, assess and deal with violations. This is particularly the case since today violations are no longer linked solely to the taking of souvenirs from wrecks: expanding organised crime has become an increasingly serious phenomenon,[74] which to be effectively tackled also requires international cooperation.

5 Conclusion

The legal protection of UCH in Estonia is regulated at several levels and is in line with the 2001 Convention. The new MuKS was adopted in 2019 and, based on practice so far, it can be said to work in terms of the conservation of UCH, with no major additions or amendments to the law being necessary. Minor additions and clarifications have been made, and others possibly need to be made, primarily to other legal measures introduced under the MuKS, which were not previously stipulated with sufficient clarity, or where clarification is essential for the sake of legal certainty. So far, there are also no court rulings related to the regulations on UCH in the new MuKS that highlight major loopholes in the legislation. In terms of the low representation in supervisory procedures, this does not necessarily indicate law-abiding behaviour, but rather could be a result of deficiencies of a more general nature in the response to violations and the conduct of procedures.

Legal clarity on ownership at the international level (including the concept of abandonment), Flag State and owners' rights and obligations, is also necessary. The expectation of cooperation from countries of origin are equally

71 VTMS 'para. 31(3).

72 Under MuKS 'para. 34.

73 For example, during the excavations of the wreck described above in Tallinn Old Harbour in 2006, some wreck parts were lost. The Estonian National Heritage Board made a statement to the police in order to start an investigation. Criminal proceedings were not commenced within the limitation period.

74 For example, systematic looting of historic shipwrecks and selling of archaeological artefacts.

justified because the history of one ship, from the time it is built until wrecked, is commonly linked to many different countries and the ship's crew is often international.

The relevant provisions of the MuKS apply to the protection and conservation of the underwater heritage in its original location when it is granted the status of a monument. However, considering that only 106 sites have been declared such cultural monuments in nearly 30 years, the Board's performance in terms of designation is arguably too low and does not meet expectations. Therefore, the protection of identified sites should be one of the top priorities for the coming years.

All websites last accessed February 2025.

Selected Bibliography

V. Lang & M. Laneman, (eds.) *Archaeological Research in Estonia, 1865 – 2005. Estonian Archaeology 1.* (Tartu University Press, 2006).

A. Kraut, 'Protection of Underwater Cultural Heritage in Estonia – current situation' in J. Litwin (ed.) *Baltic Sea Identity. Common Sea – Common Culture? 1st Cultural Heritage Forum. Gdansk 3rd-6th April 2003 at the Polish Maritime Museum in Gdansk.* (Gdansk, 2003).

M. Roio, L. Lõugas, A. Läänelaid, L. Maldre, E. Russow, and Ü. Sillasoo, 'Medieval ship finds from Kadriorg, Tallinn' (2016) 139 *Archaeological fieldwork in Estonia 2015.*

K. Ilves 'Archaeological monitoring during reconstruction works in Tallinn Old City Harbour' (2008) 205 *Archaeological fieldwork in Estonia.*

M. Roio, 'Tallinn Harbour from the Middle Ages: Studies of the Former and Current Seabed' in J. A. Rodrigers and A. Traviglia (eds.) IKUWA6 Shared Heritage: Proceedings of the Sixth International Congress for Underwater Archaeology. (Archaeopress Publishing Ltd, 2020).

CHAPTER 8

Finland

*Ville Peltokorpi and Maija Matikka**

1 Introduction

Finland is located in the northern part of the Baltic region, surrounded in the west by the Gulf of Bothnia and in the south by the Gulf of Finland, with Sweden and Norway to the west and Russia to the east. Finland's coastline is diverse and long, comprising of 46,000 km of shoreline and approximately 97,000 islands. There are some 190,000 lakes, covering approximately a tenth of the country's total land area. The northern part of the Baltic Sea is especially favourable for the preservation of underwater cultural heritage (UCH) since due to the low salinity of the water, molluscs that destroy organic materials, such as the shipworm *Teredo navalis*, are not present. Therefore, wooden wrecks in particular survive well in the northern Baltic Sea, and bones, textiles, leather, and other organic remains can be found.

While the legislation described below also applies to inland waters and to all kinds of cultural heritage, the focus of this chapter is on maritime UCH. It excludes the legislation of the Åland Islands, an almost entirely autonomous, politically neutral and completely demilitarised region of Finland, consisting of an archipelago at the entrance to the Gulf of Bothnia.[1]

According to an old saying, Finland is an island. From prehistoric times to the present day, the Baltic Sea has been an important transport network for people and goods in Finland and its neighbours. Today about 80 per cent of Finnish foreign trade takes place by sea. Finland was part of Sweden until 1809 and then an autonomous Grand Duchy within the Russian Empire before becoming independent in 1917. As a result, Finland's waters contain numerous

* University of Helsinki and senior advisor for the Finnish Heritage Agency, respectively.

1 According to the Act on the Autonomy of Åland, the Åland Islands have legislative powers over prehistoric relics and the protection of buildings and artefacts with cultural and historical value. As defined by the regional law, UCH includes all underwater cultural material and shipwrecks that have been underwater for over 100 years. In certain cases, the regional government has to ask for an expert opinion from the FHA. Regarding the Åland *Champagne Schooner*, see V. Peltokorpi 'Impacts and Issues of the Commercial Exploitation of the Åland 'Champagne Schooner'' (2020) in *IKUWA6. Shared Heritage* (*Proceedings of the Sixth International Congress for Underwater Archaeology: 28 November–2 December 2016, Western Australian Maritime Museum Fremantle, Western Australia*) (Archaeopress Publishing, 2020).

 | DOI:10.1163/9789004510883_010

old Swedish and Russian sunken warships, while the incomplete mapping of Finland's waters during the age of sail, and more than 60,000 naval mines laid during World War II, all contribute to its UCH.[2]

Centuries of Baltic Sea trade, along with naval wars, has defined what UCH is found in Finnish waters. Following the founding of St. Petersburg at the beginning of the eighteenth century, the Gulf of Finland became an important trade route between Russia and Western Europe. There are many known wrecks of merchant ships in Finnish waters, including Dutch vessels assumed to have been *en route* to or from St. Petersburg, such as the *Vrouw Maria*, which sank in 1771.[3]

Well into the twentieth century, the concept of preserving historic wrecks as cultural heritage and sources of historical information was unthought of in Finland. Shipwrecks were mainly seen as sites from which financially valuable or interesting artefacts could be obtained without archaeological research. The beginning of the documentation of underwater sites was strongly related to the development of SCUBA diving equipment and the beginning of recreational diving in the 1950s. Information about UCH has been collected in official registers and archives since the 1960s. At present, the Finnish Heritage Agency (FHA) keeps a register of archaeological sites jointly with regional museums. In 1968, an office of maritime archaeology was established within the FHA, responsible for preserving cultural heritage. From the outset, the problem regarding the preservation of shipwrecks has been unauthorised appropriations from them. However, there seems to be less, if any, large-scale professional treasure hunting and commercial exploitation of historical wrecks around Finland.

2 Relevant Domestic Legislation, Policies, Practice and International Conventions for the Protection of UCH in Finland

In Scandinavia, it is customary that the State is responsible for the protection and preservation of ancient sites and all forms of cultural heritage. The Finnish Constitution is also central to the protection of cultural heritage, section 20 of which places the responsibility for maintaining cultural heritage on everyone.

2 Regarding World War I, see J. Flinkman & J. Polkko The Fog of War – *The First World War in the Gulf of Finland* (John Nurminen Foundation, 2024) and the 'Fog of War' online museum available at <https://digimuseo.fi/en/exhibitions/sodan-sumua/>.

3 For further information, see R. Alvik, 'The merchant vessels *St. Michel* and *Vrouw Maria* and their cargo' in E. Ehanti, J. Aartomaa, I. Lounatvuori & E. Tirkkonen, (eds) *Lost at Sea, Rediscovered* (Otavan Kirjapaino Oy, 2012).

The FHA monitors the protection of ancient relics, their study, and issues research permits to applicants in accordance with the Antiquities Act 295/1963. Collections consisting of ancient relics are largely centralised at the FHA. Previously, it made agreements with regional museums for performing certain tasks relating to provincial archaeological cultural heritage. It was not until the amended Museums Act 314/2019, in force early 2020, that some cultural heritage related responsibilities were permanently devolved to regional museums. However, of the 20 of these, only one has an employee who can dive and use a side-scan sonar. Thus, regional museums currently only have responsibility for UCH sites within 'wading depth'.

2.1 *Finnish Heritage Agency Act 282/2004 and the Government Decree on the Finnish Heritage Agency 407/2004*

The FHA's duties include taking care of the collection, maintenance and exhibition of culturo-historical national heritage, acting as a specialist authority responsible for the protection of cultural heritage and the cultural environment. It oversees the preservation and supervision of ancient relics and, if not within the remit of another authority, the management and supervision of the cultural environment, as well as researching and ensuring information on cultural heritage is recorded, preserved, and made accessible. The FHA's tasks are also regulated in more detail by a government decree on the FHA (407/2004).

2.2 *Antiquities Act 295/1963*

The most important instrument for protecting archaeological cultural heritage in Finland is the Antiquities Act 295/1963. The overriding principle is that archaeological remains are collective national and cultural heritage that must be preserved for future generations. Therefore, all immovable ancient relic sites are protected memorials of Finland's past settlements and history. Consequently, everyone has a right to free information on them and access to view and study recovered ancient relics. This is made possible by the fact that the responsibility for archaeological heritage has been given to legally appointed public authorities in charge of keeping the Ancient Relics Register and managing the archive, artefact collection and customer service. The register contains basic information of the ancient relics in mainland Finland, and other archaeological sites on land and at sea. The information is freely accessible through the Cultural Environment Service portal.[4] Presently, there are approximately 2,300 UCH sites, 800 of which are protected ancient relics, in contrast to approximately 60,000 archaeological sites on land, 35,000 being protected ancient relics.

---

4 Available in Finnish, see <https://www.kyppi.fi/>.

Ancient relics are automatically protected by law, and thus their protection does not require separate administrative decision. The relic also encompasses an area necessary for the preservation of the remains in question. It is forbidden to excavate, cover, alter, damage, or remove ancient relics, or to disturb them without lawful authorisation.

Finland is in the process of preparing a comprehensive amendment of the Antiquities Act, which started in 2020 under the Ministry of Education and Culture. The government proposal and draft for the new Law on the Archaeological Cultural Heritage was completed on June 30, 2023. The final content of the law and possible changes to the government proposal are not yet known, but at least the principle of automatic protection will evidently be preserved. However, ancient relics subject to automatic protection will be redefined, in which case a certain age or time limit is likely to be chosen as the basis for protection. The current Act only applies a rolling limit of 100 years to ship finds and movable antiquities. At the moment there is no more detailed information about the entry into force of the final law.

2.2.1 Immovable Ancient Relic Sites, Movable Antiquities and Ship Finds

The Antiquities Act covers ancient relics on land and in water within Finland's inland and maritime areas. The Act regulates immovable ancient relic sites, movable antiquities and ship finds. The regulations contain a nine-item list of site types and finds considered to be immovable ancient relics. Underwater ancient relics include, for example, remnants of military history, past settlements, historical traffic and economic sites.

According to provisions concerning movable antiquities, anyone who finds money, a weapon, tool, dish or any other item on the ground or underwater whose owner is unknown, and which can be presumed to be at least 100-years old must immediately deliver the object to the FHA with information about the location and the conditions in which it was found. The FHA may redeem the artefact or transfer the right of redemption to another museum or institution. If the FHA does not want to redeem the artefact, the finder may keep it. If a movable antiquity is redeemed, reasonable compensation determined by the FHA shall be paid. By way of derogation from the above general rule, artefacts that are found in, or are apparently derived from a protected wreck, belong to the State without redemption, and shall otherwise be subject, *mutatis mutandis*, to the provisions on movable antiquities.

Shipwrecks are not considered to be immovable ancient relic sites, nor movable antiquities, which have their own provisions in the law. However, regulations on immovable ancient relic sites apply *mutatis mutandis* to shipwrecks, so a wreck is legally comparable to an ancient relic, in or near which antiquities have been found.

2.2.2 Essential Provisions Relating to Wrecks

Under s.20 of the Antiquities Act, wrecks and parts of wrecks found in the sea or water bodies, and which can be assumed to have sunk more than 100-years ago are protected. Accordingly, unauthorised excavation, covering, alteration, damage, removal and disturbance of the wreck or part thereof are prohibited.

If, on the basis of external circumstances (determined on a case-by-case basis), it is obvious that the owner has abandoned the wreck, which is considered to be an antiquity, it belongs to the State. Artefacts in shipwrecks that have sunk over 100-years ago, or that appear to be from such a wreck, also belong to the State. A wreck that sank more than 100-years ago may also have a known owner. In this case, the State does not own the wreck, but it is still subject to the protection provisions of the Antiquities Act. Therefore, a permit from the FHA is required for any changes to the wreck, such as salvage. A person who finds a wreck or an artefact referred to in s.20 must immediately notify the FHA.

Diving is considered an everyman's right, so all protected wrecks not within a special protective area established under the Antiquities Act or the Territorial Surveillance Act 755/2000 can, in principle, be dived on without permission. Any activity that alters or damages a wreck or involves removing artefacts requires permission from the FHA, so diving must be non-intrusive. A protective area may be established around an ancient relic in accordance with the Antiquities Act, and, if necessary, special regulations may be issued to safeguard the relic. At present, there are six wrecks in Finland considered of exceptional significance from a historical and research point of view and diving on these requires a permit. An exception is diving on warships owned by the Finnish Defence Forces, which requires a permit from the Military Museum. The permit application must state e.g., the time and purpose of dives and information about the divers. In addition, all dives must be reported using a separate report form. Permit control is carried out in cooperation with the FHA, the Finnish Navy, and the Finnish Border Guard.[5]

Wrecks can be searched for and located without permission. However, under the Territorial Surveillance Act, any systematic sea surveying and examinations of the composition of the seabed are subject to authorisation, with the Defence Command as the licensing authority. If a search results in the

5 In 2015, the FHA, the Finnish Border Guard and the Finnish Defence Forces drew up internal guidelines on cooperation and information sharing between authorities, particularly for the protection of sunken warships and the artefacts derived from them.

discovery of a wreck that is presumed to be more than 100-years old, the find must be immediately reported to the FHA.

2.2.3 Taking Ancient Relics into Account in Construction Projects

When planning a general construction project or zoning, it must be ascertained in good time whether the work will affect an immovable ancient relic site. If this is the case, the FHA must be notified and consulted. If a previously unknown immovable ancient relic site is found during construction, the work must be suspended, and the FHA notified so necessary measures can be taken. If the general construction project requires examination of any relic or measures for its preservation, the developer must compensate or contribute to research costs. Underwater relics are subject to similar regulations.[6]

The Land Use and Building Act,[7] Decree 895/1999, the Water Act[8] and Decree on Water Management[9] and the Act and Decree on the Environmental Impact Assessment Procedure are also related to the protection of UCH in water use projects.[10] Under these laws, examinations of UCH are required, if necessary, to obtain sufficient information about the UCH well before the execution of the project. Ancient relics are marked on zoning maps, with the provisions obliging them to be protected.

2.2.4 Offences Pertaining to Ancient Relics

Offences against ancient relics may be punishable under the Antiquities Act or general criminal law. Depending on the activity, it can either be an antiquity offence; an offence against the protection of buildings under criminal law; or a property crime, i.e., theft, aggravated theft or petty theft under criminal law. Penalties vary from fines to four years' imprisonment, depending on the legislation in question, but the maximum sentence of four years can only be imposed for aggravated theft.[11]

---

6 Antiquities Act 295/1963, Section 13–15 §.

7 Land Use and Building Act (132/1999) was in force until 31 December 2024. New Building Act (751/2023) mostly replacing the Land Use and Building Act entered in force 1 January 2025 but the relevant provisions on cultural heritage have basically remained unchanged.

8 Water Act (587/2011).

9 Decree on Water Management (1560/2011).

10 Act (252/2017) and Decree (277/2017) on the Environmental Impact Assessment Procedure, respectively.

11 One view on how UCH can be protected and looting of historic shipwrecks prevented by imposing penal sanctions has been presented by E. Pirjantaniemi, 'Shipwreck Heritage Management – A Criminal Law Perspective' in H. Rak & P. Wetterstein (eds) *Shipwrecks in International and National Law: Focus on Wreck Removal and Pollution Prevention – Papers from a Seminar 13–17 June 2007, Kasnäs, Finland* (Uniprint, 2008).

What little case law there is, shows that the current provisions are not fully appropriate given the nature of cultural heritage protection. The difficulty of obtaining evidence can lead to the expiration of the right to prosecute before the offence has even been established, as the limitation period is calculated from the date of the offence.

Violations of antiquities are regulated under s.25 of the Antiquities Act. A person who intentionally, negligently, or without permission disturbs protected relics or violates the notification obligation can be fined. In addition, a person who fails to deliver to the relevant authority any found movable antiquities, or fails to submit a prescribed notice of it, or otherwise conceals, bequeaths, acquires or exports such an object, which should have been delivered to the FHA, or damages or alters it shall also be convicted of an antiquity offence, as well as losing any rights based on the discovery.

Offences relating to the protection of buildings are regulated under the Criminal Code 39/1889, Chapter 48, s.6. A person who intentionally or through gross negligence dismantles, destroys, or damages an immovable ancient relic site within the terms of the Antiquities Act, or the wreck of a ship or a part thereof without a permit required by law, or in violation of the conditions of the permit, will be convicted of an offence against the protection of buildings. The authors hold the view that unauthorised removal of artefacts from a wreck could fulfil the characteristics of an offence relating to the protection of buildings, since the destruction of contextual information caused by undocumented removals of artefacts can also lead to the destruction of an immovable antiquity. In such cases, the offence should not always be seen as mere artefact theft but, on a case-by-case basis, as the destruction of an ancient relic through looting.

Theft offences are divided into petty thefts, thefts, and aggravated thefts, based on the seriousness of the action, the value of the stolen property, and other circumstances. Because the characteristics of theft and other crimes involve intention on the perpetrator's part, it may also be considered on a case-by-case basis whether the perpetrator knew they stole from a shipwreck that sunk more than 100-years ago and was protected under the Antiquities Act.

With property crimes related to wrecks, it can be particularly difficult to determine the value of the property in question and how the nature of the crime creates other adverse effects, such as damage to the site and loss of context and research data. Damage like this cannot be measured monetarily because the lost data is site-specific and therefore irreplaceable and invaluable. In this respect, it has been stated in the preparatory works of the Criminal Code in Finland that the application of the theft provision does not require that the action has caused financial damage to someone. Therefore, the object of the crime does not necessarily have to be of economic value.[12] Nevertheless, assessing the value of the stolen property other than in terms of its alleged economic value has been difficult in practice. This leads to a situation where the damage is only measured financially when assessing the harmfulness of a crime, for example based on antique markets or auctions. This completely disregards the fact that the property in question would not have been put up for sale by its owner, i.e., the State, under any circumstances. In addition, the removal of even worthless property from the wreck always destroys, either in part or in full, the context of the item discovery, because the wreck and its artefacts always form a coherent research entity. In this case, the greatest damage and negative change in the value of cultural property is the loss of information and the general harmfulness of the crime to scientific research.

2.3 *International Treaties and Conventions*

As regards the internal implementation of international agreements, Finland applies a dualist system under which they must be transposed into national law before they can be applied, for example, by public authorities and courts. The FHA oversees the implementation of cultural heritage conventions.

2.3.1 International Treaties and Conventions Ratified by Finland

In 1995, Finland ratified the revised European Convention for the Protection of the Archaeological Heritage 1992.[13] At the time, this did not necessitate amendment to the Antiquities Act.

In 1996, Finland ratified the United Nations Convention on the Law of the Sea (LOSC).[14] Construction projects in the Exclusive Economic Zone (EEZ) require a permit from the government in accordance with the Act on the Exclusive Economic Zone of Finland and a permit from the environmental authorities, in accordance with the Water Act.[15] In the authorisation process under the Water Act, the FHA has been able to present its position referring, *inter alia,* to Article 303 LOSC on large construction projects in the EEZ, such as the Nord Stream gas pipeline projects. The mapping of UCH and the protection of identified sites have been preconditions for permit issue and also been approved and made a condition for the project permit itself.

---

12 Government proposition 66/1988 to Parliament, at 36. Given that cultural heritage is shared by all and that the responsibility for cultural heritage lies with everyone, it is inarguable that the value of cultural heritage is, in itself, indisputable and widely recognised.

13 ETS 142.

14 1833 UNTS 397.

15 Exclusive Economic Zone of Finland (1058/2004) and Water Act (587/2011) respectively.

In 1990, Finland signed the International Convention on Salvage 1989,[16] with reservations, but this was not ratified until January 2007. This led, in part, to the initiation of a dispute over the salvage of the *Vrouw Maria*, because the Salvage Convention for the Unification of Certain Rules of Law respecting Assistance and Salvage at Sea 1910[17] was still applicable in Finland at the time the wreck was found. Part of the problem was that the 1910 Salvage Convention did not make clear how it was to be applied to an ownerless, eighteenth century shipwreck of mainly historical significance. For its part, the protection of UCH is facilitated by the fact that Finland has included a reservation in accordance with Article 30.1(d) of the 1989 Convention. Consequently, the provisions of the Maritime Act concerning salvage at sea do not apply to the ships and property referred to in the Antiquities Act, unless otherwise agreed.[18]

In 2018, Finland ratified the Council of Europe Convention on the Value of Cultural Heritage for Society, which emphasises cultural heritage as a common resource and the right of individuals and communities to benefit from cultural heritage and to participate in the enrichment of it.[19] Additionally, Finland is also a Party to a number of treaties drafted under the auspices of UNESCO.[20]

2.3.2 UNESCO Convention on the Protection of UCH 2001

In 2001, Finland voted to approve the text of the 2001 Convention, agreeing with its main objectives, its substantive approach and the regulatory regime it established for the protection of UCH, although with scope for clarification and criticism of the Convention's provisions. At present, preparations for the ratification of the 2001 Convention have not begun, but nor has Finland decided that it will not be ratified. At the FHA, ratification of the 2001 Convention has been considered important.

At a general level, the 2001 Convention contains many of the same key principles as the Antiquities Act already in force and adopted practices relating

16 1953 UNTS 194.

17 212 CTS 187.

18 For a recent account on the Finnish legislation on the salvage of wrecks, see J. Aminoff, 'Salvage of Wrecks in the Baltic Sea – A Finnish Perspective' in H. Ringbom (ed.) *Regulatory Gaps in Baltic Sea Governance: Selected Issues* (Springer, 2018).

19 CETS 199.

20 These comprise, Convention for the Protection of Cultural Property in the Event of Armed Conflict, in force 7 August 1956, 249 UNTS 240; Convention for the protection of the world cultural and natural heritage, in force 17 December 1975, 1037 UNTS 151; Convention on the Means of Prohibiting and Preventing the Illicit Import, Export and Transfer of Ownership of Cultural Property, in force 24 April 1972, 823 UNTS 231; and Convention for the Safeguarding of the Intangible Cultural Heritage, in force 20 April 2006, 2368 UNTS 3. For further information, see <https://museovirasto.fi/en/about-us/international-activities/>.

to UCH in Finland. The management and protection of cultural heritage has been assigned to a public authority and that authority maintains a register of cultural heritage sites. Disturbances of sites are only to be carried out with the permission of the authorities, which provide information about the sites and their research. *In situ* preservation is a common and recommended practice. Activities that are not primarily targeted at antiquities but may nevertheless affect them, are monitored and potential damage minimised. Finds discovered during excavation are conserved, catalogued, and preserved in public collections for research. Excavations are undertaken purely for information, not for financial gain. Access to cultural heritage sites is encouraged, and cooperation between the authorities and enthusiasts is active. Furthermore, in 2007 the FHA reviewed the rules for maritime archaeological field surveys in the Annex to the 2001 Convention, concluding the procedures listed were already being applied in Finland, so committing to them would not be problematic.

However, the working group preparing amendment of the Antiquities Act has stated that ratification and implementation of the 2001 Convention would require its own preparatory project to assess the effects more widely than only in relation to archaeological cultural heritage. Since this is not possible during preparations for the current reform, ratification of the Convention is unlikely to take place for a few years.

2.4 *Other Relevant Regulations and Procedures*

The Territorial Surveillance Act is the most important law on the surveillance and safeguarding of Finland's territorial integrity, which also affects UCH since some wrecks are located within protected areas under the Act.[21] SCUBA diving and underwater activities normally not associated with navigation may not be practised without a permit in areas protected by the Act. Licensing for SCUBA diving is handled and determined by the Navy General Staff.

The 2007 EU INSPIRE Directive contributed to improving the availability of data on underwater sites.[22] In November 2010, data on wrecks and other underwater sites were merged into one register of archaeological sites and made publicly available. Previously, information on the means for protecting underwater sites, especially wrecks, was limited. However, implementation of the Directive did not lead to an expedient outcome in all respects concerning

21 Territorial Surveillance Act (755/2000).

22 Directive 2007/2/EC of the European Parliament and of the Council of 14 March 2007 establishing an Infrastructure for Spatial Information in the European Community (INSPIRE), in force 15 May 2007. Official Journal of the European Union, L 108, 25 April 2007, at 1.

UCH, as can be seen in the court case described below at 3.3: the disclosure of extensive new spatial data immediately led to looting at a number of previously unknown wreck sites.

Finnish Guidelines for the Quality of Archaeological Fieldwork were introduced for the first time in 2013.[23] Their purpose is to harmonise archaeological fieldwork practices, to ensure the quality of reports and to provide the basis for protection and future work. Underwater fieldwork is not addressed separately in the guidelines, but the instructions are intended to be applied to it. Because underwater surveying for purposes other than locating archaeological sites has often been proposed for underwater inventories and the equipment may not have been suitable for archaeological purposes, it was necessary to provide guidance on surveying to detect UCH. The guidelines prepared by the FHA for underwater surveying were completed in 2020.

3 Notable Cases and Recent Developments

3.1 *The Vrouw Maria*

The *Vrouw Maria* was a twin-masted Dutch merchant vessel shipwrecked in the Finnish Archipelago Sea in 1771.[24] One of the largest research projects has been '*Vrouw Maria* Underwater', which aimed to present the wreck and analyse her cargo,[25] which revealed coffee beans, tobacco, and indigo, among other things.[26]

The fate of the *Vrouw Maria* has been known since the 1970s when Dr. Christian Ahlström found documents about the shipwreck in archives.[27] The Pro *Vrouw Maria* Association, expressly established to support locating

23 For further information, see <https://www.museovirasto.fi/en/cultural-environment/archaeological-cultural-heritage/studying-archaeological-cultural-heritage/quality-instructions-on-archaeological-fieldwork>.

24 O. Gelderblom, ʹCoping with the Perils of the Sea: The Last voyage of Vrouw Maria in 1771ʹ (2003) *International Journal of maritime history, Vol. 15*(2).

25 For further information, see *The Vrouw Maria Underwater Project 2009–2012 final report*, National Board of Antiquities' Reports 2 (2014), available online at < https://www.museovirasto.fi/en/services-and-guidelines/publications/electronic-publications >.

26 These findings are analysed in the doctoral thesis by MA Riikka Alvik, currently in preparation at the University of Helsinki. For further information, see also R. Alvik 'Vrouw Maria' in A. Arnberg, O. Johansen, P. Widén, (eds) *Under the Surface. Stories from Vrak – Museum of Wrecks* (Elanders Sverige AB, 2021).

27 See (in Swedish) C. Ahlström *Sjunkna skepp* (Lund, 1979) and C. Ahlström *Looking for Leads: Shipwrecks of the Past Revealed by Contemporary Documents and the Archaeological Record* (Finnish Academy of Science and Letters, 1997).

and investigating the wreck and comprised of many members with experience of working with the FHA, succeeded in locating it in 1999, led by the Finnish professional diver, Rauno Koivusaari. Following its discovery, planning for joint research began but proved challenging and the basis of dispute. In the end, Koivusaari, the company owned by him, and another member of the Pro *Vrouw Maria* Association sued the Finnish State.[28]

In summary, through the proceedings the plaintiffs sought confirmation that, first, they had carried out the salvage referred to in the Maritime Act by raising three clay pipes, a clay bottle, a seal and a zinc ingot and that they were entitled to a salvage reward for raising these objects. Second, they had the right to salvage, based on either the contract or the right of the first salvor, as regards all other objects in or near the wreck and the right to a salvage reward for all objects raised from or in the vicinity of the wreck. Finally, they contended that they had ownership of the wreck and thus the right to salvage it and all items in and near it, as well as a right to determine who would undertake these salvage operations. In the alternative, the plaintiffs claimed that if the court ruled ownership of the wreck was vested in the State, they had the right to salvage it on the basis of either the contract or the right of first salvor, as well as a right to a salvage reward under the Maritime Act.

3.1.1 The Relationship between the Antiquities Act and the Maritime Act

The State had submitted, and the District Court accepted, that the Antiquities Act would override the application of the Maritime Act primarily because the former is *lex specialis* and hierarchically superior to the Maritime Act, under which a person who "salvages a shipwrecked vessel or ship in danger, or goods on board or something belonging to such a ship or its cargo" is entitled to a salvage reward.[29] Subsequently, the Court of Appeal concluded that the concept of 'salvage' could not always be interpreted as meaning the rescue from some danger, nor was there a provision in the Antiquities Act prohibiting the application of the salvage regulations specified in the Maritime Act to shipwrecks referred to in the Antiquities Act. Thus, the *Vrouw Maria* was considered a shipwrecked vessel, in which case the salvage provisions also applied to it. Consequently, in contrast to the decision of the District Court, the Court of

28 *Koivusaari, Martikainen & Top Shark Oy v. State.* Turku Court of Appeal, judgment 787, 23 March 2005 (S 04/2163) and *Koivusaari, Martikainen & Top Shark Oy v. State.* Turku District Court (sitting in admiralty), judgment 04/4302, 16 June 2004 (H 99/8603).

29 In this respect, it should be noted that the term 'shipwrecked' was added to the Maritime Act, although there is no mention of a shipwrecked vessel in the 1910 Salvage Convention, on which the Act's provisions on salvage were based.

Appeal concluded that the Antiquities Act did not override the Maritime Act, so that both laws had to be applied.

3.1.2 The Plaintiffs' Right to the Wreck of the Vrouw Maria

The plaintiffs argued that they had become the owners of the wreck at the time of its discovery, or, in any event, at the latest by the declaration of lost property. During the proceedings, in 2002, s.20 of the Antiquities Act (relating to the discovery of ships) was amended so that the ownership of a wreck of a ship or other vessel found in the sea or another body of water and which can be presumed to be at least 100-years old, would always belong to the State if apparent that it has been abandoned by the owner. In accordance with the provisions for its entry into force, the Act was also applied to protected wrecks before the amendment came into force.

The plaintiffs argued that the amendment should only have been applied retroactively if the wreck had no owner. The plaintiffs considered that the wreck was owned when the amendment came into force because they had legally claimed control of it at the time of discovery. In addition to this presumption of ownership, the plaintiffs sought to obtain ownership of the wreck by making a declaration in accordance with the Lost Property Act and asserted ownership after the expiration of the time limit specified in it.[30]

The District Court held that under the provisions of the Antiquities Act in force before and after the entry into force of the above amendment, the wreck had been protected directly, and disturbance of it without the permission of the FHA was prohibited. Thus, the FHA had, and retained, the right to take possession of the wreck and, if necessary, move it to another location. Although the plaintiffs had found the wreck and swum above it, they were not allowed to touch or otherwise manage it due to the provisions of the Antiquities Act. Therefore, the plaintiffs were not able to take possession of the wreck in such a way that they could claim ownership of it.

The Court of Appeal held that a claim may establish ownership of an abandoned object, such as the discovered wreck. However, this was conditional on the claimant acquiring control of the object in question, which means a *de facto* relationship of power over it. Since the wreck was protected directly under the Antiquities Act, any disturbance of it without the permission of the FHA was prohibited. Thus, the Court of Appeal, like the District Court, ruled that the protection provisions of the Antiquities Act prevented the finders

30 In the Act on Lost Property (778/1988), lost property refers to an object that has fallen out of the possession of its owner or holder. However, the law does not apply to an object that has apparently been abandoned by its owner.

from gaining *de facto* power over the wreck, thereby denying the plaintiffs' right of ownership.

3.1.3 Entering into a Salvage Agreement

The plaintiffs submitted that a salvage agreement had been concluded between the parties for the salvage of the wreck and its cargo, at least regarding the artefacts raised from it. They submitted, *inter alia*, that a few days after the wreck was found, a representative of the FHA was on the site when Koivusaari had offered to raise artefacts. The removals had been negotiated between the parties and as a result the artefacts listed above were raised. The plaintiffs argued that the salvage operation was initiated by the FHA and that, in practice, it had accepted the assistance provided by them, thus meeting the conditions for the conclusion of a salvage agreement.

In the FHA's view, the plaintiffs had not carried out salvage at sea in accordance with the Maritime Act, nor had such a salvage been agreed upon. Representatives of the FHA had not perceived the chain of events as salvage, and there was no discussion on a salvage agreement or other compensation between the parties. Rather, it was normal cooperation between the FHA and volunteer divers. The raising of artefacts carried out by decision of the FHA was solely research activity referred to in the Antiquities Act, based on the consent of the Agency for determining the date and origin of the wreck, with no salvage agreement concluded. In addition, all the measures relied on by the plaintiffs as the basis for the salvage agreement were, in the view of the FHA, simply routine research as referred to in the Antiquities Act, which the FHA had already carried out for several years in cooperation with the plaintiffs and other members of the same diving crew. The FHA also argued that the plaintiffs were aware that raising the wreck would require a special decision by the authorities and funds to be set aside in the State budget. Moreover, the cost of this would be so high that the project would have to be put out to tender, as required by public procurement processes. Considering the evidence presented, both the District Court and the Court of Appeal concluded there had been no salvage agreement.

3.1.4 Right of the First Salvor and the State's Right to Prohibit Salvage

Under the Maritime Act, anyone who has participated in salvage contrary to the master's express and legitimate prohibition, is not entitled to a salvage reward. The right of prohibition also applies to the so-called first salvor, who is not placed in any special position under the Maritime Act.

In this respect, it was undisputed that the State already owned the wreck's cargo directly under the Antiquities Act, in addition it had also been declared the owner of the wreck in the Court of Appeal. The question was therefore whether the State had been entitled to prohibit the plaintiffs from salvaging the wreck and its cargo. The plaintiffs had appealed, arguing that the wreck could be robbed or that anchoring over or close to the wreck could damage it, placing it in danger within the meaning specified in the Maritime Act.

The District Court addressed, more widely than the Court of Appeal, how the term 'shipwrecked' was to be interpreted and how the concept of danger should be assessed. In this regard, the District Court made the following observations:

> In this case, the salvage and raising of the wreck and the objects inside it must be seen as a whole, which includes not only the raising and moving of the wreck and objects but ensuring the conservation and preservation of the wreck and objects, which also requires the construction of a storage room for the wreck and objects (cf. the Swedish ship Vasa). […] The salvage has not been completed until the preservation of the wreck and its objects has been secured by conservation and other necessary measures, all of which are not even known at this stage. […] When a wreck is found, the state would be faced with the fact and responsibility for paying the salvage reward, even if no salvage agreement has been concluded, no danger would exist, and there was no intention of raising the wreck and the objects in it. It is therefore not a genuine salvage situation within the meaning of the Maritime Act, which would entitle the first salvor to take salvage action and to receive a salvage reward. […] The need to raise the wreck and the objects found therein may be mainly archaeological and historical, as regulated by the provisions of the Antiquities Act, which give the FHA exclusive discretion and control over what is done with the wreck and the objects within. As stated above, the wreck is already protected directly under the provisions of the Antiquities Act.[31]

The District Court concluded that the Antiquities Act precluded the possibility of the provisions of the Maritime Act concerning salvage and salvage rewards applying in cases regarding such wrecks and related goods. The Court of Appeal stated that the first salvor may carry out salvage against the will of the owner of the property where there is a concrete danger necessitating a salvaging operation. In the case at hand, it was of the opinion no such danger existed, because the wreck and its cargo had been lying at the bottom of the

31 Turku District Court, judgment 04/4302, 16.6.2004 (H 99/8603), at 33–37.

sea for over 230 years. In addition, the wreck and at least some of its cargo were in good condition at the time it was found, and it was to be expected that they would remain so for several decades. The wreck did not pose any danger to shipping since it was at a depth of 42 metres, and in a difficult location as regards navigation. As to possible property thefts, the Court of Appeal held that long stays at the shipwreck site without the intervention of the authorities would be unlikely because it was under surveillance by them. On these grounds, among others, the Court of Appeal held that the State was entitled to prohibit the salvage.

3.1.5 Appeal to the Supreme Court

Both the plaintiffs and the State sought leave to appeal to the Supreme Court, which was ultimately refused. Due to amendments to the Antiquities and Maritime Acts, it is very unlikely that a similar dispute will arise again. In their application for leave, the plaintiffs waived their claims regarding the ownership of the wreck, reiterating all their other original claims. For its part, the State maintained its position that the Antiquities Act would completely override the application of the Maritime Act. The plaintiffs' decision to waive the claim of ownership subsequently became one of the key issues when the proceedings continued before the European Court of Human Rights.

3.2 *Vrouw Maria in the European Court of Human Rights*

3.2.1 The Application to the European Court of Human Rights

In 2006, the plaintiffs appealed to the European Court of Human Rights (ECtHR), which unanimously decided not to accept the case.[32] The appeal mainly concerned the appellants' dissatisfaction with the national courts' decision to reject their claims regarding the ownership of the wreck and that they were not entitled to any kind of salvage reward.

The appellants attempted to rely on Article 1 of Protocol No. 1 (A1FP) to the European Convention on Human Rights 1951 (ECHR),[33] on the protection of property, and in connection with this, the lack of effective legal remedies in accordance with Article 13 of the ECHR. In addition, the appellants considered that their right to a fair trial had been violated, contrary to Article 6, and that they had been discriminated against in violation of Article 14 and/or Article 1 of Protocol No. 12.[34]

---

32 See further, *Rauno Koivusaari and others v. Finland (dec.)*. European Court of Human Rights, Application no. 20690/06, 23 February 2010 (inadmissible).

33 ETS 5.

34 ETS 177. Regarding the complaints, see *Rauno Koivusaari and others v. Finland,* at 9–10.

3.2.2 Amendment of the Provisions on Shipwreck Discoveries

At the time of the discovery of the *Vrouw Maria* wreck, the Antiquities Act did not contain an express provision as to who owned the wreck itself, or part thereof, in the event of unknown ownership, nor did the law explicitly provide that a wreck considered to be an antiquity belonged to the State. There was no case law in this context, and it had not yet been addressed in academic literature.[35]

In response, an amendment to s.20 of the Antiquities Act concerning ship discoveries was proposed in 2002, so that the wreck of a ship or other vessel, or part of such a wreck found in the sea or a waterway and presumed to be at least 100-years old would always be owned by the State if external circumstances indicated that the owner had abandoned the ship. The purpose of the amendment was to clarify determination of ownership pertaining to a ship protected as an antiquity or the ownership of other vessels or parts thereof. As a result, s.20(1) of the Antiquities Act was amended to its current form, so that the timing specified in the provision was tied to the ship's or vessel's moment of sinking, adding greater precision than the previous wording.[36] Simultaneously, a new subsection 2 was added, according to which, if external circumstances clearly indicate that the owner had abandoned the wreck or part thereof as referred to in s.20(1), it would always belong to the State.

The amended law was also applied to the wreck of a ship or other vessel (etc.) that had been protected as an antiquity before the amendment entered into force, again if external circumstances clearly indicated that it had been abandoned by its owner. This retrospective application was particularly criticised by the finders of the *Vrouw Maria* and led to the proceedings before the ECtHR.

It was concluded in the drafting of the law that although not explicitly stated, the original intent was that historic shipwrecks belong to the State. The preparatory work addressed this deficiency as well as setting out a number of other guiding policy objectives.[37]

The Constitutional Law Committee did not consider the amendment to be problematic, stating in its opinion, *inter alia*, that:

> According to the Bill, the wreck or part thereof referred to in the Bill belongs to the state if external circumstances make it obvious that it

---

35 See further, the Government Bill for the amendment of Section 20 of the Antiquities Act (HE 80/2002 vp).

36 The earlier, less precise wording was: 'a wreck that can be assumed to be at least 100 years old, or part of such a wreck'.

37 The Government Bill for the amendment of section 20 of the Antiquities Act, HE 80/2002, at 7–8.

> has been abandoned by the owner. The subject of the regulation is thus the so-called orphan object, the owner of which has relinquished their right of ownership without transferring it to another, i.e., abandoning the object in an orphaned state. Such an object has no owner, and therefore making the object the property of the state does not infringe on anyone's property rights protected by the Constitution (*cf.* Government Bill PeVL 10/1961 to Parliament, Government Bill PeVL 8/1966 to Parliament). The purpose of the Bill is to implement the provision of section 20(1) of the Constitution on the responsibility of everyone for cultural heritage. [...] Shipwrecks and their parts that are at least one hundred years old are protected under the current Antiquities Act. Thus, under the current law, it has not been possible to validly acquire ownership of them, for example on the basis of discovery and claim. However, in some foreseeably unlikely cases, the shipwreck may have a new legal owner. In such cases, the ownership of the wreck will not be transferred to the state under the proposed regulation.[38]

Because the actual control of the wrecks protected under the Antiquities Act already belonged to the State, and as the number of wrecks protected under the law was found to be significant, the provision was concluded to apply to all underwater wrecks of ships or other vessels or parts thereof already protected or to be protected under the law.

3.2.3 Complaint Concerning the Ownership of the Wreck (A1FP)

First, the applicants complained about the deprivation of property or an interference with the peaceful enjoyment of possessions, specifically by the retroactive enactment of the 2002 legislation. Furthermore, they complained about the misuse of the State's legislative powers to refuse salvage in order to safeguard archaeological heritage so as to deprive the applicants completely of their rights, and about the refusal to pay any compensation for the deprivation and/or interference.[39]

The State considered the appellants to have expressly waived their claims related to the ownership of the wreck with the application for leave to appeal to the Supreme Court. Therefore, the appellants had neglected their obligation under the ECHR to exhaust all national legal remedies, a condition precedent to the admissibility of the case. The appellants considered that the remaining

38 The statement of the Constitutional Law Committee PeVL 29/2002 vp – HE 80/2002 vp, p. 2.

39 *Rauno Koivusaari and others v. Finland*, at 11.

national legal remedies were no longer effective due to the retroactive amendment of s.20 of the Antiquities Act, since under this ownership undeniably belonged to the State, its ownership could no longer be questioned in the same way as when the national trial began, taking into account the fact that the Constitutional Law Committee had deemed the amended law in accordance with the Finnish Constitution. In addition, the case had also lost its precedential value in the Supreme Court, because it was highly unlikely that a similar situation would arise again due to the 2002 amendment.

On this point, the ECtHR concurred with the State. It went on to observe that:

> ... the examination of the application does not disclose the existence of any special circumstance which might have absolved the applicants, according to the generally recognised rules of international law, from exhausting the remedy available to them. The fact that the Antiquities Act had been amended recently does not render the examination of the applicants' claim before the Supreme Court ineffective. Even though the Supreme Court cannot challenge the validity of legislation, it can, in accordance with Article 106 of the Constitution, give primacy to the constitutional provisions, including the right to property, if an Act were found to be in obvious conflict with it.[40]

The ECtHR concluded that the applicants had failed to exhaust domestic remedies insofar as the complaint concerned ownership of the wreck application.

3.2.4 Complaint Concerning the Right to Salvage Remuneration (A1FP)

The State maintained that the entire application was also inadmissible because the applicants had neither been in enjoyment of any possession (protection of property), nor any civil right (right to a fair trial) as regards the amendment of the Antiquities Act.[41] Furthermore, the State submitted that the application was in any case totally incompatible *ratione materiae* with the provisions of the ECHR.

The State pointed out that A1FP did not guarantee a right to acquire any property. Thus, the question was whether the applicants had had a legitimate expectation of receiving an object (i.e., the wreck) or a benefit having a net asset value (i.e., a salvage reward). The appellants had submitted to the ECtHR two expert opinions on the value of the wreck and its cargo, as well as the amount

40 Ibid., at 12–13.

41 Pursuant to Article 6 ECHR.

of the salvage reward. According to these, the appellants allegedly suffered financial damages of around €7 million by not receiving the salvage reward; and the value of the wreck with its commercial rights was conservatively estimated to be at least €40–50 million. However, the State submitted that the possibility of receiving salvage remuneration was based on the Finnish Maritime Code, which was open to various interpretations, meaning the right to salvage remuneration was not absolute, and presupposed, among other things, that the vessel had been in danger, which both domestic courts had held was not the case. The Court of Appeal found that the first salvor could have conducted salvage notwithstanding the will of the property owner if a concrete danger had been at hand. Moreover, the domestic proceedings had involved adjudication of difficult questions of the relationship between the Maritime Code and the Antiquities Act, and the significance of international treaties in a dispute in which the domestic courts had come to a certain conclusion.[42]

The applicants claimed that the right of the first salvor had been a definite legal right, recognised by both courts, and that this right had had an actual value as the State would either have had to allow the applicants to lift the wreck and to pay them for that, or to compensate them if it had preferred to perform the operation itself or had it done by a third party. The applicants had thus a legitimate expectation of a benefit having a net asset value. They also stated that the reason why their claim was ultimately not successful, was the retrospective legislative amendment that had given the State, as an owner, the possibility to prohibit salvage.[43]

The ECtHR noted that the protection of property applied only to a person's existing possessions. Thus, future income could not be considered to constitute possessions unless it had already been earned or was definitely payable. In the present case, the applicants had no existing possession within the meaning of the ECtHR's jurisprudence, but a proprietary interest in the form of a claim. Thus, it concluded the applicants had no concrete proprietary interest and no legitimate expectation. The ECtHR further observed that both domestic courts had held that the wreck was not in danger when it was discovered by the applicants. The ECtHR did not consider the treatment of the applicant's claim by the national courts as arbitrary, while noting that it had only limited power to deal with alleged errors of fact or law committed by them in their interpretation and application of domestic law.[44]

---

42 *Rauno Koivusaari and others v. Finland*, at 13–14.

43 Ibid.

44 Ibid., at 15–17.

The ECtHR concluded that the claim for salvage remuneration did not qualify as an asset attracting protection, and thus the applicants did not have possession, so the complaint was rejected as being incompatible *ratione materiae* with the provisions of the ECHR.[45]

3.2.5 Alleged Violation of the Article 6 of the Convention (Right to a Fair Trial)

The applicants also complained the amendment of the Antiquities Act had been designed to deprive them, with retroactive effect, of rights that they had enjoyed at the time of the find, reasoning that vesting of ownership to the State retrospectively made it possible for the State to object to salvage. According to the applicants there had been a significant possibility that the State would have lost the first salvor claim without this retrospective amendment. Since there had been no similar cases before domestic courts, the only case that was affected by the retrospective amendment was that of the *Vrouw Maria*.

The State observed that the amendment took effect 18 months before the Maritime Court passed its judgment. In domestic proceedings both parties had an opportunity to state their positions vis-à-vis the amendment, which they had done: the significance of which, including the decisions of the higher courts, was part of the consideration in assessing leave to appeal. The State also referred to the reasoning of the Government Bill noted above, arguing that even though the amendment contained a reference to the *Vrouw Maria*, its purpose and intent had been pursuit of the public interest by filling a legislative gap regarding ownership of old and abandoned shipwrecks by clarifying the wording of the Antiquities Act, and not to intervene in the present case.[46]

Ultimately, the question the ECtHR faced was whether the amendment had in fact any effect, even indirectly, on the applicants' rights as well as on the proceedings pending at the time of the entry into force of the amendment, because the only effect that the modified provision of the Antiquities Act had on the applicants' right to salvage remuneration as first salvors had been that the owner of the wreck, i.e. the State, could prohibit salvage in the case of no danger and thereby also the right to salvage remuneration. In the present case the missing element rendering the applicants' claim unsuccessful was the lack of danger, noted above. The ECtHR concluded that it was irrelevant whether the State could have prohibited the salvage or not, as the element of danger was missing. Thus, according to the national law, as interpreted by the Court of Appeal, the entry into force of the amendment did not change the applicants' situation in respect of their right to receive salvage remuneration and thus the

45 Ibid., at 17.

46 Ibid., at 20.

amendment could not have influenced the outcome of the present case. For this reason, the intention of the authorities was also irrelevant regarding the retrospective effect that ownership of wrecks was to be vested in the State. Further, there was no indication that had the amendment not entered into force, the applicants would have been successful in their claims.

On this reasoning the Court concluded that the applicants could not sustain a complaint that they were denied the right to a fair hearing in the determination of their property interests, leading to a rejection of the complaint as being manifestly ill-founded.[47]

3.2.6 The Remainder of the Application

Additionally, the applicants complained that the proceedings before the FHA and/or the Maritime Museum had failed to meet the requirements of a fair and unbiased hearing and treatment of the applicants' claims and representations, and that the outcome had been arbitrary and unsupported by reasons. The applicants also complained that the Finnish legislature and/or other Finnish authorities had discriminated against the applicants by favouring the interests of the Maritime Museum. These remaining complaints were found either incompatible *ratione materiae* with the provisions of the Convention and/or manifestly ill-founded under the Convention since no civil right was being determined before the FHA and the Maritime Museum.[48]

3.3 *Porvoo Looting Case*

After the data on underwater sites known to the FHA was published in late 2010, there has been an apparent increase in observed and reported vandalism and artefact losses at protected shipwreck sites. A documentary filmmaker and diver decided to make a documentary on the subject. While gathering material and interviewing divers, he became aware of a possible suspect in connection with artefacts taken from the unidentified wreck of a merchant ship. The creator of the documentary delivered the material he had collected to the police for investigation in 2013.[49] During the preliminary investigation, the suspect admitted to taking numerous artefacts from the wreck, in addition to which he named three other divers involved. The prosecutor decided to prosecute all four for theft. The Court of Appeal fined the main suspect for theft, in addition to which he was sentenced to forfeit the financial benefit gained to the State.[50]

---

47 Ibid., at 20–22.

48 Ibid., at 22–23.

49 Maija, Matikka, pers comm. 2016. The documentary is available online in Finnish (Finnish and Swedish subtitles are available): see <https://areena.yle.fi/1-2483225>.

50 *District prosecutor v. A. J. H.* Helsinki Court of Appeal, judgment 16/121044, 20 May 2016 (R 15/1905) and *District prosecutor v. A. J. H. and others*, Itä-Uusimaa District Court, judgment

3.3.1 Legal Issues

Even though this was an isolated case, the main problems relating to it are very general. The first central issue and problem was determining what items had been taken from the site and by whom. One of the characteristics of underwater sites is the challenge to monitor activities undertaken at them. Again, the biggest problems were related to the evaluation of the evidence. Based on the case, it appears that proving guilt would often require the perpetrators to be caught red-handed, or by eliciting a confession.

The second issue concerned the age of the wreck and whether the parties were aware, or whether it was probable that they should have considered that the ship had sunk more than 100-years ago and was therefore directly protected by law. In reality, it would be considered very unlikely that the perpetrators would not normally be aware of the presumed age and historical significance of the site, particularly as the wreck was entered in the Ancient Relics Register at the time of the interference.

The third issue was determining the charges, considering the Antiquities Act and the criminal offences. What seemed to be particularly difficult was determining whether the theft of individual artefacts could also fulfil the characteristics of an offence against the protection of buildings on the grounds that the wreck had been damaged in terms of its context. Since crimes against cultural heritage are still officially quite rare in Finland, the fact that courts do not recognise the special nature of cultural heritage may be problematic.

The fourth issue related to the appropriate punishment and assessment of damage incurred. For example, how should the removal of artefacts relevant for the possible identification of the site and the destruction of contextual information be assessed, and on the other hand, could the value of the artefacts also somehow be measured in monetary terms? The penalty of forfeiture also stipulates that the economic benefit obtained through the crime – the value of the stolen property – be determined. In this respect, the situation was very incongruous because UCH is common cultural heritage and should not be economically exploitable by private parties. Nevertheless, the economic value of artefacts must be determined in criminal proceedings, which means commercialising cultural heritage, at least indirectly. Based on the findings of the case and the research data provided by the site, its cultural value should be more clearly recognised in legislation, preferably directly, in the wording of the law.

15/124953, 5 June 2015 (R 14/936).

3.3.2 Reflections on the Case

Prior to the trial the main suspect confessed to the police to having removed items from the wreck. In the District Court, however, he withdrew his confession. The three other defendants denied their involvement from the beginning. Because the witnesses did not have concurrent recollections that would have supported the prosecution, the District Court ended up dismissing the charges against all four individuals.

The prosecutor requested that the main suspect be punished for theft. With regard to the criminal characteristics, the District Court considered that his actions could at most satisfy the characteristics of a petty theft, because:

> ... the FHA's assessment of the value of the artefacts is not sufficiently specified and, for want of a better assessment, the value of the artefacts was considered to be very low.[51]

In this regard, the District Court erroneously overlooked the fact found in the preliminary works of the criminal law that the object of the crime does not necessarily have to have economic value.

As regards the FHA's alternative charge against the defendant for the offence against the protection of buildings, the District Court first referred to the government's motion concerning offences against the protection of buildings, stating that:

> ... [h]owever, in the legal provision, as well as in the Antiquities Act, the wrecks of ships or other vessels and the parts thereof are comparable to immovable ancient relic sites whereas the artefacts that are found in them and derived from them are movable antiques. A criminal provision for violating the regulations on movable antiquities would still be included in the Antiquities Act (Section 25).[52]

The District Court held that:

> ... if the criminal protection of the movable artefacts in question were extended as suggested by the FHA, it would lead to such a broad interpretation of criminal law provisions which is prohibited.[53]

---

51 *District prosecutor v. A. J. H. and others*, Itä-Uusimaa District Court, judgement 15/124953, 5 June 2015 (R 14/936), at 10.

52 Government proposal 94/1994 to Parliament, at 199.

53 *District prosecutor v. A. J. H. and others*, Itä-Uusimaa District Court, judgement 15/124953, 5 June 2015 (R 14/936), at 12.

In this respect, the District Court's interpretation can be considered erroneous. It is not a question of a broad interpretation of Criminal Code provisions, but of the fact that the removal of artefacts from a shipwreck almost invariably also leads to the deterioration of the site. Thus, the removal of artefacts should not be assessed only as a crime against those objects, but by looking holistically at the site as an archaeological entity that is damaged by artefact theft. As the matter can be considered open to interpretation, it would be advisable to reform the legislation and the characteristics of the crimes in such a way that any damage to research values is more clearly considered when assessing the adverse cultural impact of the offences.

Following the prosecution's appeal, the Court of Appeal fined the main suspect only, for theft. In addition, he was sentenced to forfeit the economic benefit obtained by the crime to the State. In its ruling, the Court of Appeal held that the main suspect had stolen culturally and historically valuable artefacts belonging to a shipwreck owned by the Finnish State, thus committing theft.[54] The Court of Appeal held that the severity of the fine should reflect the quantity and quality of the stolen property and the manner in which the offence was committed. With regard to the forfeiture, the FHA stated that the value of the artefacts was solely informative since the Agency would not have sold the items. As a result, the artefacts were appraised only on the basis of an online antique shop, considering the information available on the quality and quantity of the stolen property. The Court of Appeal settled the FHA's evaluation.

In conclusion, the difficulty of obtaining evidence is highlighted, especially in crimes against UCH. Usually, artefact theft from a protected wreck is not discovered until later, when a conservation-minded diver, who knows the shipwreck and has previously dived on it, re-visits it. When the crime was committed is usually a matter of speculation and the time range can be as long as several years. In effect, this may prevent investigation, because the right to prosecute becomes statute barred.

4 Concluding Remarks

For about 60 years, Finland has had the Antiquities Act in force, which encompasses UCH. The law was progressive when it came into force in 1963, because it

54 The Court of Appeal found that the main suspect had taken a part of a mug, two teacups, bottles and a plate on the first dive; bottles, berry bowls, teacups and glassware on the second dive; berry bowls on the third dive and a clay dish and an earthenware jar on the fourth dive.

required ancient relics to be taken into account in connection with construction and zoning. After diving and interest in historic wrecks began to become more common in the 1960s, a Maritime Archaeological Office was established at the FHA, responsible for archaeological heritage, to collect information on wrecks and other sites and to manage their protection. However, resources for UCH underwater conservation tasks were very limited, and this remains the case.

Tasks are largely centralised in the FHA, where the maritime cultural heritage team draws up periodic action plans for all matters pertaining to maritime cultural heritage. To date, there has been no nationwide strategy focusing solely on UCH. However, the basic elements necessary for its protection exist. The law protects UCH in territorial and inland waters, which is tasked to relevant authorities, for example, in addition to its main duties, the Finnish Border Guard monitors protected wrecks. An assistant professorship of maritime archaeology has been established at the University of Helsinki, in addition to which the Finnish Scientific Diving Academy (FSDA) has been founded.[55] Cooperation between the authorities and divers groups, as stakeholders, is active. Information on UCH is produced jointly, and it is openly shared in the Ancient Relics Register maintained by the authorities and in the services maintained by the wreck enthusiasts themselves.

The legislation in force in Finland and the procedures applied can be considered in line with the spirit of the 2001 Convention. Archaeological heritage is preserved for the common good, and the main method of preservation is *in situ*. The sites are considered valuable because of the information they contain, and the activities undertaken on them must follow the best principles of archaeological fieldwork. If wreck sites or related artefacts are raised while doing research, their long-term preservation is ensured through conservation and by the inclusion of the artefacts in professionally managed public collections. A report of the fieldwork is always made and is publicly available. The sites are not considered as instruments for salvage and economic benefit, nor are they otherwise valued financially. Cooperation and information sharing between different stakeholders is important and respectful access to UCH sites is encouraged. The general compatibility of the Finnish national legislation and currently applied archaeological principles can thus be considered in line with the spirit, as well as the object and purpose, of the 2001 Convention.

As noted above preparations for the reform of the Antiquities Act are currently underway in Finland. However, the ratification and implementation of the

---

55 FSDA was established in autumn 2021 to revitalise the training of scientific divers in Finland. For further details, see <https://www2.helsinki.fi/en/research-stations/tvarminne-zoological-station/courses/finnish-scientific-diving-academy>.

2001 Convention into Finnish law would require a separate drafting and impact assessment process, which has not yet begun. We hope that this preparatory process will be attained in the 2020s. In particular, new tools are needed to improve the possibilities for protecting UCH in the EEZ, the large-scale implementation of which would require wider acceptance of the 2001 Convention.

All websites last accessed February 2025.

Acknowledgements

The authors would like to thank former Development Manager Juha Flinkman (Finnish Environment Institute, Marine Research Centre, now retired). The views and opinions expressed in this chapter are those of the authors.

Selected Bibliography

R. Alvik, 'The merchant vessels St. Michel and Vrouw Maria and their cargo' in E. Ehanti, J. Aartomaa, I. Lounatvuori & E. Tirkkonen (eds) *Lost at Sea, Rediscovered* (Otavan Kirjapaino Oy, 2012).

J. Aminoff, 'Salvage of Wrecks in the Baltic Sea – A Finnish Perspective' in H. Ringbom (ed.) *Regulatory Gaps in Baltic Sea Governance: Selected Issues* (Springer, 2018).

N. Eriksson, J. Flinkman, M. Koivikko, M. Lempiäinen-Avci, M. Manders, L. Näsänen, J. Polkko, J. Reinders, E. Stockdale & I. Treffner 'Witte Swaen from 1636. The Discovery and Archaeological Survey of an Intact Fluit in the Gulf of Finland, Baltic Sea' in (2024) *International Journal of Nautical Archaeology.*

J. Flinkman & J. Polkko, *The Fog of War – The First World War in the Gulf of Finland* (John Nurminen Foundation, 2024).

O. Gelderblom, ′Coping with the Perils of the Sea: The Last voyage of Vrouw Maria in 1771′ (2003) *International Journal of Maritime History,* Vol. 15(2).

V. Peltokorpi, 'Impacts and Issues of the Commercial Exploitation of the Åland 'Champagne Schooner" (2020) in *IKUWA6. Shared Heritage (Proceedings of the Sixth International Congress for Underwater Archaeology: 28 November–2 December 2016, Western Australian Maritime Museum Fremantle, Western Australia)* (Archaeopress Publishing, 2020).

E. Pirjantaniemi in 'Shipwreck Heritage Management – A Criminal Law Perspective' in H. Rak & P. Wetterstein (eds) *Shipwrecks in International and National Law: Focus on Wreck Removal and Pollution Prevention – Papers from a Seminar 13–17 June 2007, Kasnäs, Finland* (Uniprint, 2008).

CHAPTER 9

Ireland

*C. Kelleher**, *S. Kirwan***, *N. O'Connor****, *F. Moore*****, *and K. Brady******

1 Introduction

In Ireland there have been several developments relating to the nature and rate of discovery of Underwater Cultural Heritage (UCH), as well as the manner in which underwater archaeology is addressed in terms of protection, policy and planning. This has unfolded against the background of a legal framework that has sustained and largely served underwater archaeology in Ireland well. Important case law has been among several factors that have influenced positively the exploration and protection of Ireland's underwater heritage. While many challenges continue or may emerge for Ireland's UCH, current work to strengthen legislation relating to UCH (and archaeological heritage generally) will support ongoing efforts to meet such challenges.

There are advantages of scale in Ireland: though there is an extensive coastline, marine area and very substantial inland waterways, it is a relatively small country. The strong legal framework noted above is supported by cross-departmental collaboration in government and a network of local community contacts interested in, and concerned for, the preservation of their local heritage. In summary, the protection of UCH is rooted firmly in statute, government policy and community awareness.

2 Roles of the National Monuments Service and National Museum of Ireland

The authors of this paper are employed, in Ireland, at the National Monuments Service (NMS) (Heritage Division) of the Department of Housing, Local

* Senior archaeologist, National Monuments Service (NMS) in the Department of Housing, Local Government and Heritage.

** Senior Archaeologist Grade I, National Monuments Service (NMS) of the Department of Housing, Local Government and Heritage.

*** Assistant Keeper, Irish Antiquities Division, National Museum of Ireland.

**** Senior archaeologist, National Monuments Service, Department of Housing, Local Government and Heritage.

***** Senior Archaeologist, National Monuments Service, Department of Housing, Local Government and Heritage.

 | DOI:10.1163/9789004510883_011

Government and Heritage and, in the case of one, at the National Museum of Ireland (NMI). There has been continuing fruitful cooperation between the NMS and the NMI as the main State organisations responsible for all archaeological heritage, including underwater archaeology, in terms of the protection of monumental and portable heritage respectively. This dual-stranded responsibility is reflected in the structure and provisions of the National Monuments Acts 1930 to 2014. For more than four decades, there has been a shared approach between the two organisations in relation to long-running issues pertaining to important underwater heritage sites.[1] Perhaps most notably in the public eye has been the case of the Spanish Armada wreck sites of 1588 at Streedagh Bay, County Sligo and that of the wreck of the RMS *Lusitania* which sank off the coast of County Cork in 1915.[2]

Within the NMS, the Underwater Archaeology Unit (UAU) has archaeological diving capacity unique within the State service. It has led marine, lacustrine and riverine investigations over the past number of decades, including at the sites of the Armada wrecks. Through its work, the NMS has aimed to secure the appropriate management and protection of both well-known wrecks, such as the RMS *Lusitania,* along with many other sites. These include those revealed through natural forces, marine and other developments, diver activities and through chance discoveries by the fishing community or members of the public. The NMS, on behalf of the Minister for Housing, Local Government and Heritage, is also the statutory authority for the key statutory permits relevant to protection of UCH under the National Monuments Acts.[3] The work of the State-employed archaeologists concerned comprises active field investigation, recording, conservation, research, provision of access through digital

1 N. O'Connor, 'The Irish Experience', in S. Dromgoole (ed.), *The Protection of the Underwater Cultural Heritage: National Perspective in the Light of the UNESCO Convention 2001*, (Leiden, 2006), 127. 11; S. Kirwan, 'Ireland and the UNESCO Convention on the Protection of the Underwater Cultural Heritage', 5(2) *Journal of Maritime Archaeology*, 2010, 115.

2 See below and O'Connor 2006, *op. cit.*; F. Moore, C. Kelleher, K. Brady, C. McKeon & I. Lawler 'Managing and Protecting the Wreck Site' in RMS Lusitania: The Story of a Wreck (Government Stationery Office Publications, Dublin 2019), 121; N. O'Connor, 'The Lusitania and the National Museum of Ireland' in F. Moore, C. Kelleher, K. Brady, C. McKeon & I. Lawler (eds.) RMS Lusitania: The Story of a Wreck (Government Stationery Office Publications, Dublin 2019), 124.

3 Licences for archaeological excavation under section 26, National Monuments Act 1930; consents for use of detection devices under section 2, National Monuments (Amendment) Act 1987; licences for damage to, removal from, diving on or survey of historic wrecks and underwater archaeological objects under section 3, National Monuments (Amendment) Act 1987.

resources, regulation through the licensing system and provision of advice in the context of the statutory planning process.[4]

The NMI claims, on behalf of the State, all unowned archaeological objects found in Ireland.[5] There are challenges in providing the necessary professional conservation facilities where just one exceptional underwater site may absorb a very high percentage of the NMI's professional conservation staffing and laboratory capacity, though of course these provide new and important archaeological knowledge and are a cultural and scientific resource for the future. The Director of the NMI also has a statutory relationship with the office of Receiver of Wreck under the terms of merchant shipping law as noted in 3.2 below.

3 Legislation and Policy

Ireland has robust heritage legislation that has protected its terrestrial archaeological resources since 1930, but it is only since 1987 that there has been statutory provision specifically for the protection of UCH.[6] The new Historic and Archaeological Heritage and Miscellaneous Provisions Act 2023, when fully operational, will further strengthen this protection. With over 18,000 wrecks recorded around the coast, Ireland's shipwreck heritage is rich and diverse. Not all of the recorded wrecks have known locations with only around 4,000 having identified positions or confirmed wreck remains. Other site types have also attracted attention in recent years, including crannogs,[7] fording points and ancient bridge crossings. With the increased availability of metal detectors and advances in underwater mapping technology these significant sites became a target for treasure hunters, with a virtual explosion of this activity in the 1980s. It was clear at that point that there was a real need to protect Ireland's underwater archaeological heritage, and this is the

4 K. Brady, C. Kelleher & F. Moore 'Ireland's Underwater Cultural Heritage: The Role of the Underwater Archaeology Unit in Documenting, Managing and Investigating the Maritime Archaeological Resource', in J. Higgins, A. Conneely & M. Gibbons (eds.), *Irish Maritime Heritage: Proceedings of the 3rd Galway International Heritage Conference 2013* (Crow's Rock Press, Galway, 2014), 165.

5 Sections 2, 3, 6 and 9 National Monuments (Amendment) Act 1994, (as amended by section 68 National Cultural Institutions Act 1997).

6 See previous publication in this book series: O'Connor 2006, *supra* n.1.

7 A crannog is an island, partly or wholly artificial, built up by dumping timber, earth and stones onto a lake or river bed, often riveted with timber piles or a palisade. Derived from the Irish word 'crannóg'; the Irish word for tree is 'crann' and 'crannóg' principally means a young tree, piece of wood or a structure of wood. These site types generally date from the early medieval to the post-medieval periods.

background to the enactment of the National Monuments (Amendment) Act 1987 (NM(A)A 1987; see 3.1 below).[8]

National policy on the protection of the archaeological heritage in the course of development also covers underwater archaeological heritage. This is set out administratively in the 1999 Framework and Principles for the Protection of the Archaeological Heritage, published following ratification by Ireland in 1997 of the 1992 Council of Europe European Convention on the Protection of the Archaeological Heritage (Revised).[9] The case law of the High and Supreme Courts of Ireland has also established important principles supporting the protection of UCH, in particular in terms of restriction of applicability of commercial salvage law and State ownership of heritage objects with no known owner.[10]

Ireland participated actively in the negotiations leading to the adoption of the 2001 UNESCO Convention on the Protection of the Underwater Cultural Heritage (2001 Convention) and strongly supported its adoption.[11] The new Historic and Archaeological Heritage and Miscellaneous Provisions Act 2023, detailed in 3.3, as well as strengthening heritage protection generally, now enables Ireland to ratify this Convention and this is now in progress. Other measures in the new Act include integrating historic wreck protection with protection for monuments, while also continuing the strong automatic protection afforded to all wrecks 100 or more year's old and archaeological objects. In addition, the new Act establishes on a statutory basis the inventory of historic wrecks currently maintained by the NMS on an administrative basis.

---

8 C. Kelleher 'Ireland's Treasure Hunting Past – the Case for Underwater Archaeology', in F. Castro & L. Thomas, (eds.) *Crossing Boundaries: ACUA Underwater Archaeology Proceedings 2011* (Advisory Council on Underwater Archaeology, Society for Historical Archaeology publications, 2011), 74.

9 Framework & Principles for the Protection of the Archaeological Heritage, Government of Ireland 1999; *European Convention on the Protection of the Archaeological Heritage (Revised)* (adopted 16th January 1992, entered into force 25th May 1995) Council of Europe Treaty Series No. 143.

10 N. O'Connor, 'Ireland', in Sarah Dromgoole (ed.), *Legal Protection of the Underwater Cultural Heritage: National and International Perspectives*, (Kluwer Law International Publications, The Hague, 1999), 87. O'Connor, 2006, *supra* n.1, 12, 14; *In re "La Lavia", "Juliana" and "Santa Maria de la Vision" King and Chapman v. The owners and all other persons etc.* [1999] 3 I.R. 413; see also: S. Kirwan & F. Moore, 'Update on Ireland and the UNESCO Convention on the Protection of the Underwater Cultural Heritage' in Robert A. Yorke (ed.) *Protection of Underwater Cultural Heritage In International Waters Adjacent to the UK: Proceedings of the JNAPC (21st Anniversary Seminar 2010,* published 2011), 51.

11 2562 UNTS 1; Kirwan 2010, *supra* n.10.

3.1 *National Monuments (Amendment) Act 1987*

The NM(A)A 1987 provided the first specific protection for UCH in Ireland. The core of this is provision under which any damage, removal, survey or salvage of a wreck more than 100 years old or an underwater archaeological object[12] is a criminal offence unless done under licence issued by the relevant Minister.[13] Provision was also made for the designation, by way of an underwater heritage order, of 'restricted areas' within which similar protection is applicable, key distinctions being that such orders can be made in respect of wrecks of any date and that such orders designate an area additional to specific wrecks and archaeological objects.[14] The definition of 'monument' (which underpins the scheme of protection of monuments under the National Monuments Acts) was amended so as to make clear that it could apply to underwater assets as well as those on land, and provision was made to ensure that the licensing requirement for archaeological excavation applies underwater as well as on land.[15] Combined with the introduction of a scheme regulating the use or possession of detection devices on a range of sites protected under the National Monuments Acts or their use anywhere to search for archaeological objects,[16] the NM(A)A 1987 put in place a strong and comprehensive regime of protection for historic wrecks (at least where over 100 years old) and underwater archaeological objects. The provision of clarity that monument protection and regulation of archaeological excavation were applicable underwater was also important, though in the former case monuments which do not come within the definition of 'wreck' or 'archaeological object' require (in most cases) an administrative decision to designate them under the Acts.[17] In that regard, the

12 The term 'archaeological object' is defined for the purposes of the National Monuments Acts 1930 to 2014 as meaning: 'any chattel whether in a manufactured or partly manufactured or an unmanufactured state which by reason of the archaeological interest attaching thereto or of its association with any Irish historical event or person has a value substantially greater than its intrinsic (including artistic) value, and the said expression includes ancient human, animal or plant remains'; see section 2, National Monuments Act 1930, as amended by section 14, National Monuments (Amendment) Act 1994.

13 Section 3(4) National Monuments (Amendment) Act 1987; the relevant Minister is, at the time of writing, the Minister for Housing, Local Government and Heritage.

14 Sections 3(1) and (3), National Monuments (Amendment) Act 1987.

15 Sections 3 and 11(a) and (c) National Monuments (Amendment) Act 1987, (latter amending section 2 National Monuments Act 1930 regarding the definition of 'monument' and making clear that references to 'land' in the Acts includes land covered by water).

16 Section 2, National Monuments (Amendment) Act 1987; the definition of 'detection device' covers devices designed or adapted for searching for metals or minerals including devices such as magnetometers.

17 Section 8, National Monuments Act 1930 (as amended by section 3, National Monuments (Amendment) Act 1954); section 4, National Monuments (Amendment) Act 1954;

scheme of automatic protection for wrecks and underwater archaeological objects may be seen, in fact, as more comprehensive than that for monuments, whether on land or underwater.

3.2 *Subsequent Legal Developments: Case Law, Merchant Shipping (Salvage and Wreck) Act 1993 and Maritime Jurisdiction Act 2021*

A key development in Irish archaeological law in the late 1980s, coming out of litigation arising from a major terrestrial discovery of Early Medieval metalwork, was that the State was entitled to claim ownership of archaeological objects with no known owner at the time of finding, with this seen as arising by implication from the Constitution of Ireland rather than from prerogative rights which had not survived the foundation of the State.[18] This principle was incorporated into statute in 1994[19] in relation to finds of archaeological objects generally, but in the meantime (in litigation focused on how matters stood considering only the NM(A)A 1987 and which related to the Armada wrecks at Streedagh), the applicability of the same principle to 'maritime archaeological wrecks' was accepted.[20] While specifically set out in part of the High Court's decision, to which the Supreme Court took a different approach (in relation to the claimed unreasonableness of a refusal of a licence), the principle regarding ownership of such wrecks also formed part of the High Court's reasoning in respect to exclusion of salvage law from historic wrecks, and seems generally implicitly accepted in the Supreme Court decision.[21] Moreover, a crucial aspect of the High Court's decision was that the law of commercial salvage should not be applied to historic wrecks analogous to the Streedagh Armada wrecks in terms of archaeological nature, a finding that was not disputed in the Supreme Court.[22] In terms of statute, it may be noted that the current procedures for disposal of unclaimed wreck under the Merchant Shipping (Salvage and Wreck) Act 1993 (not considered in the case dealing with the Streedagh Armada wrecks) expressly exclude wrecks to which section 3 of the NM(A)A 1987 applies. It nevertheless does provide a role for the NMI regarding decisions

---

section 14, National Monuments Act 1930 (as amended by section 5, National Monuments (Amendment) Act 2004); section 5, National Monuments (Amendment) Act 1987; section 12, National Monuments (Amendment) Act 1994.

18 *Webb v. Ireland* [1988] I.R. 353; see O'Connor 2006, *supra* n.1.

19 Section 2, National Monuments (Amendment) Act *1994*.

20 *Re "La Lavia", "Juliana" and "Santa Maria de la Vision" King and Chapman v. The owners and all other persons etc.* [1999] 3 I.R. 413, at 467.

21 *Ibid*, at 467, 460 and 477–481.

22 *Ibid*, at 459–60 and 477–481.

by Receivers of Wreck on other unclaimed wreck of historical or archaeological importance.[23]

Two further developments in case law, both arising in the litigation relating to the RMS *Lusitania,* are worth noting. Firstly, the acceptance by the High Court that a historic wreck (as it is legally a chattel) can, even if of relatively modern date, come within the scope of the definition of 'archaeological object' under the National Monuments Acts, both on grounds of archaeological interest and on grounds of association with an Irish historical event (the second element of the definition of 'archaeological object').[24] This principle has not been elaborated on in case law so far, but raises the interesting possibility that the legislation on archaeological objects (which provides automatic protection for all such objects[25]) could apply to a range of historic wrecks of relatively recent date, though the importance of this in practical terms diminishes as such wrecks pass over the 100 year old mark. Secondly, in its decision in the same case, the Supreme Court (while not giving as detailed a view on the legal status of the wreck and its associated material as archaeological objects) found that removal of silt did come within the scope of regulation of archaeological excavation under section 26 of the National Monuments Act 1930, and that both licensing regimes (i.e., that for interference, etc. with historic wrecks under section 3 of the NM(A)A 1987 and that for archaeological excavation) applied simultaneously in relevant cases.[26]

The NM(A)A 1987 provided for the possibility of underwater heritage orders being made on areas of Ireland's claimed Continental Shelf (CS), though none such were ever made, and section 3 appears to have been applied generally to such areas under the 1994 amending Act.[27] However, under amendments made by the Maritime Jurisdiction Act 2021 the relevant references to the CS have been replaced by ones to the Contiguous Zone (CZ) of the State.[28] Accordingly, Ireland may now be said to have adopted a '24 mile zone' approach to the

23 Section 49, Merchant Shipping (Salvage and Wreck) Act 1993.

24 *Bemis v. Minister for Arts, Heritage, Gaeltacht and the Islands & Ors* [2005] IEHC 207 (17 June 2005); see section 2, National Monuments Act 1930 (as amended by section 14, National Monuments (Amendment) Act 1994) for definition of 'archaeological object').

25 Section 25, National Monuments Act 1930 (as amended by section 20, National Monuments (Amendment) Act 1994).

26 *Bemis v. Minister for Arts, Heritage, Gaeltacht and the Islands & anor* [2007] IESC 10 (27 March 2007), at paragraphs 39–46.

27 Section 3(1), National Monuments (Amendment) Act 1987); section 18, National Monuments (Amendment) Act 1994 (inserting subsection (13) into section 3, National Monuments (Amendment) Act 1987).

28 Sections 26 and 27, Maritime Jurisdiction Act 2021.

protection of UCH, although this does not extend to claiming State ownership over archaeological objects found beyond the outer limit of the Territorial Sea (TS).[29] It should, however, be noted that the separate entitlement of the State to unclaimed wreck, including such wreck found outside the State but brought within it, continues as provided for under the Merchant Shipping (Salvage and Wreck) Act 1993.[30]

3.3 *Historic and Archaeological Heritage and Miscellaneous Provisions Act 2023*

In October 2023, the Historic and Archaeological Heritage and Miscellaneous Provisions Act was enacted (HAHMP). The Act is being brought into legal effect on a phased basis, which will, when completed, result in the full repeal of the existing National Monuments Acts, replacing them with a single revised and modernised Act.[31] This will, in broad terms, continue and indeed strengthen the level of existing protection for UCH, with several innovations. The system of automatic protection for wrecks 100 or more years old will be integrated with a new system under which archaeological sites of classes set out in secondary legislation will have automatic protection, without needing administrative designation while maintaining the high level of protection currently afforded to such wrecks.[32] Conversely, wrecks will be capable of specific designation under the new Register of Monuments.[33] The NMS' inventory of historic wrecks has now also been given mandatory statutory status.[34] The principles of State ownership of historic wrecks with no known owner and exclusion of salvage law from historic wrecks are given express recognition in statute.[35] The necessary measures are incorporated into domestic Irish law to enable Ireland to comply with the terms of the 2001 Convention, including the assertion of Irish jurisdiction over Irish citizens and vessels when engaged in activities directed at UCH beyond the territorial jurisdiction of the State.[36] In relation to Ireland becoming a party to the

---

29 Sections 2(1) and 1(2), National Monuments (Amendment) Act 1994 (as amended and affected by section 27, Maritime Jurisdiction Act 2021).

30 Sections 48 and 49 (see also section 44).

31 <https://www.irishstatutebook.ie/eli/2023/act/26/enacted/en/html>.

32 Historic and Archaeological Heritage and Miscellaneous Provisions Act 2023 (HAHMP Act 2023), sections 12, 13, 30 and 126.

33 HAHMP Act 2023, sections 2 (definition of 'relevant thing') and 14 (and related provisions on the Register of Monuments).

34 HAHMP Act 2023, section 158(2).

35 HAHMP Act 2023, sections 133 and 134.

36 HAHMP Act 2023, section 138 and Chapter 2 of Part 5.

2001 Convention, the formal decision to ratify will have to be made by the government and a parliamentary motion approving that decision will also be needed, but the complex work of putting in place domestic implementing legislation has been completed, subject only to completion of the process of bringing the relevant aspects of the new legislation into operation.

4 Statutory Consultation within the Planning Process

In recent years the growth of the Irish economy has seen an upsurge in commercial developments. A large percentage of these are focused along the coast and inland waterways and have the potential to negatively impact on UCH. With the increase in maritime traffic, harbour authorities have had to undertake new port developments and increased maintenance and capital dredging works in order to remain economically viable. In recognition of the growing threat from climate change impact there is now a greater emphasis on alternative energy possibilities and a consequential increase in proposals for developments, such as offshore windfarms. Through the planning process and under specific legislative measures various government agencies are involved in the processing and assessment of development proposals. The main agencies in this regard include the Foreshore Section of the Department of Housing, Local Government and Heritage (DHLGH), the Department of Agriculture, Food and the Marine (DAFF), the Environmental Protection Agency (EPA), Petroleum Affairs Division (PAD) and Local Authorities (LA).

4.1 *Maritime Area Planning Acts 2021 and 2022 (Amended) and MARA*

In July 2023, a new regulatory body, the Maritime Area Regulatory Authority (MARA), was established. The primary brief of MARA is to regulate activity within the marine area of Ireland's TS – an area seven times the size of its landmass. The brief of MARA has been set out in the 2021 and 2022 Maritime Area Planning Acts.[37] A streamlined consenting system will be in place to cover Maritime Area Consents (MAC) in advance of granting developments under the planning system, granting marine licences for specific activities, a specific role in compliance, inspections and enforcement. The National Monuments Service has been engaging in discussions with MARA since 2022, to highlight the need for consultation within the permitting process, in order to ensure that UCH is considered, assessed and protected.

37 <https://www.irishstatutebook.ie/eli/2021/act/50/enacted/en/print.html>; <https://revisedacts.lawreform.ie/eli/2021/act/50/front/revised/en/html>.

4.2 *Planning and Development Act 2000, Foreshore Act 1933 and Dumping at Sea Act 1996*

The Minister for Housing, Local Government and Heritage is a statutory consultee under the Planning and Development Act 2000[38] and the National Monuments Service advises the planning authority (Local, County and City Councils) in each county area on individual planning cases, proposed development projects and in relation to their County Development Plans. The Minister can recommend that archaeological conditions be attached to grants of planning permission or recommend refusal of permission by the planning authority to ensure the protection of the cultural heritage. The NMS assesses planning cases referred to the Minister and advises on the potential for direct or indirect impact from proposed developments on underwater heritage. Such planning cases can pertain to all aquatic environments: inland waterways, coastal, foreshore/inshore and offshore. In its consultative role, the NMS is also referred applications under the terms of other development control legislation. This can include instances of inshore and offshore development licensed under the terms of the Foreshore Act 1933 and relating particularly to the construction of marine interconnectors and submarine fibre-optic cables. The Dumping at Sea Act 1996, as amended, has implications for the archaeological impacts of harbour dredging works, for example, and the NMS has a close working relationship with the EPA, the body which regulates such works. In this connection, the importance of the EU's Environmental Impact Assessment Directive (as transposed into Irish law across a range of legislative codes) in ensuring that large scale development is planned to take account of cultural heritage impacts should be noted.[39]

4.3 *Integrating Archaeological Considerations into the Planning and Development Process*

Over the recent past, significant national infrastructural projects have come on-stream in Ireland, in particular, main drainage schemes, offshore windfarm developments and flood relief schemes. Strategies for mitigation of known and potential impacts upon underwater archaeology are developed in a variety of

38 Statutory Instrument No. 600/2001, Planning and Development Regulations 2001 (see for example Article 28).

39 Directive 2011/92/EU of the European Parliament and of the Council of 13 December 2011 on the assessment of the effects of certain public and private projects on the environment OJ L 26, 28.1.2012, p. 1–21, as amended by Directive 2014/52/EU of the European Parliament and of the Council of 16 April 2014 amending Directive 2011/92/EU on the assessment of the effects of certain public and private projects on the environment OJ L 124, 25.4.2014, p. 1–18.

ways. Initially pre-development archaeological assessments may be requested by the NMS, which could involve desktop assessments, non-intrusive underwater surveys and remote sensing surveys. Following on from this, additional survey, archaeological testing, preservation *in situ*, excavation (preservation by record) and/or archaeological monitoring may be recommended. The considerable scale of some of these developments dictates the need for a fully effective assessment process that may require engagement across a large number of interested parties, including, for example, central and local government, port authorities, private sector and individual applicants. The experience of flood relief schemes and port dredging operations has led to the development of workable sets of procedures involving contract archaeological companies and approved methodologies within the planning process. As part of established practice, the relevant regulatory authorities for development require those proposing or undertaking development to engage the services of suitably qualified private-sector archaeologists to implement the archaeological recommendations as advised by the NMS. Applications for relevant permits under the National Monuments Acts (e.g., archaeological excavation licences) are then made to the NMS, with accompanying method statements setting out how archaeological mitigation will be achieved. Through this process many private-sector archaeologists have been responsible for the identification of a large number of UCH sites and archaeological objects, and significant discoveries have resulted.[40]

To assist with ensuring that the appropriate levels of commercial underwater archaeological expertise are available, and to help mitigate against the potential shortage of commercially trained archaeological divers, the NMS runs a scheme to provide grants to assist archaeologists to gain the required commercial dive qualifications to work in an underwater environment in line with health and safety regulations.[41]

5 Archival and Digital Approaches as Management and Protection Tools

5.1 *Wreck Inventory of Ireland Database*

With the introduction of legal protection for historic wrecks, it soon became clear that a comprehensive inventory of shipwrecks in Irish coastal waters was

40 Brady et al., 2014, *supra* n.4, 171.

41 Statutory Instrument No. 254/2018, Safety, Health and Welfare At Work (Diving) Regulations 2018 and Statutory Instrument No. 180/2019 Safety, Health and Welfare At Work (Diving)(Amendment) Regulations 2019.

essential for their protection and management. Accordingly, the NMS has been compiling a comprehensive dataset of wreck sites around the coast, which is used as a management tool for addressing planning and development impacts, licensing dives and activities on protected wreck sites and carrying out monument protection duties related to UCH.[42] The primary element of this dataset is the Wreck Inventory of Ireland Database (WIID), which contains a detailed catalogue of all recorded ship losses and other wreck sites in Irish territorial waters and in the designated area of the CS.[43]

The WIID contains the records of over 18,000 vessels lost in Irish coastal and inland waterways, of which only 15 per cent have precise locations. This figure, which is revised regularly, is considered to represent only a fraction of the real number of wrecks in Ireland's waters. It is estimated that the true number could be as high as 30,000. Prehistoric logboats are the earliest vessels recorded in the inventory but the majority of wrecks in the database date to the eighteenth and nineteenth centuries. Given the increase in shipping activity in Irish waters due to the intensification of the fishing industry in the late medieval period, increased global trade from the sixteenth century onwards, along with later industrial trade (all resulting in increased shipping in the ports and harbours of Ireland) the number of shipwrecks is not that surprising. The heaviest concentrations of recorded wrecks occur along the east and south coast rather than the west, despite the relentless pounding of the Atlantic Ocean on the western seaboard that might have led to a far greater level of anticipated loss. The preponderance of wrecking and loss along the southern and eastern coastal areas can be explained, however, by the high levels of marine traffic moving through the Irish Sea and St George's Channel, inevitably leading to higher numbers of wrecks. A significant number of ship losses, approximately 1,800 in total, recorded in both inshore and offshore waters additionally reflect the submarine warfare that was a feature of major conflicts during World Wars I and II.[44] A wide variety of other vessel types are recorded in the WIID including currachs,[45] galleys, galleons, fully-rigged merchant ships, iron clad battleships,

42 K. Brady, C. Kelleher & F. Moore, 'Underwater Cultural Heritage', in R. Devoy, V. Cummins, B. Brunt, D. Bartlett and S. Kandrot (eds.) *The Coastal Atlas of Ireland* (Cork University Press, 2021), 501.

43 See for e.g., <https://www.archaeology.ie/underwater-archaeology-wreck-viewer>.

44 K. Brady, 'Ireland and the First Battle of the Atlantic', in R. Devoy, et al. (eds.) *Supra* n.42, 515.

45 Currachs (sometimes spelled 'curraghs') are traditional wooden framed craft over which animal hides or canvas is stretched, which is then tarred; their design is unique to Ireland, and they are especially associated with the west of Ireland where regional variations in building design are found.

steamships, submarines, warships, ocean-going liners and a broad range of more recent historic wooden sailing ships.[46]

The data contained within the WIID draws on a broad selection of sources including the wreck data in the United Kingdom Hydrographic Office (UKHO); eighteenth and nineteenth century surveys and sea charts; Lloyd's List and Lloyd's Register of Shipping; old newspaper sources; Parliamentary Papers; local and international journals; fishers' marks and charts, and cartographic sources.[47] Targeted fieldwork carried out by the UAU has also led to important information being identified on wreck sites, along with first-hand accounts from divers and fishers reporting possible wreck sites; coastal walkers, archaeologists and other marine and inland waterways users have also contributed valuable information for inclusion in the WIID. New resources have become available, particularly in the area of digital technology, including for example the use of innovative 3D survey and recording techniques, along with the multibeam echosounder that is enabling advances in seabed mapping and recording of UCH. The UAU has forged strong links with the Irish National Seabed Survey (INSS) and its successor programme INFOMAR which, under the direction of the Geological Survey Ireland and the Marine Institute, has carried out extensive seabed mapping programmes and shipwreck surveys in recent years. One of the significant by-products of the multibeam echosounder surveys undertaken by the INSS/INFOMAR in deep waters has been the discovery of numerous shipwrecks, many of which represent vessels lost during the course of World Wars I and II. New imagery has also been captured of earlier wrecks, including the French Armada frigate *La Surveillante,* scuttled in Bantry Bay in County Cork in 1797. This latest geophysical data was presented, within a historical context, for 60 of the more significant wrecks discovered and recorded, in the 2012 joint publication between the Geological Survey Ireland and the NMS.[48]

5.2 *Wreck Viewer*

In 2018, the NMS's Wreck Viewer was published online as a digital viewer.[49] This service shows the known location of nearly 4,000 historic wrecks while

46 Brady, Kelleher, Moore 2014, *supra* n.4, 168.

47 For a full list see bibliography in Brady et al., 2014, *supra* n.4, 178, and K. Brady, *Shipwreck Inventory of Ireland, Volume 1: Louth, Meath, Dublin and Wicklow* (The Stationary Office, Government of Ireland, 2008), 557.

48 K. Brady, C. McKeon, J. Lyttleton & I. Lawler (eds.) *Warships, U-Boats and Liners: A Guide to Shipwrecks Mapped in Irish Waters* (The Stationary Office, Government of Ireland, 2012).

49 <https://dahg.maps.arcgis.com/apps/webappviewer/index.html?id=89e50518e5f4437abfa6284ff39fd640>.

also facilitating access to the WIID and thus many more entries on historic wrecks with both known and unknown locations. It is a resource that can be used by researchers, developers, local authority planners, fishers, divers, teachers and the general public. As new discoveries are made or new locations pin-pointed for recorded wreck sites, the information on the Wreck Viewer is updated and expanded accordingly.

5.3 *The NMI's Digital Archive*

The archaeological archive at the Irish Antiquities Division of the NMI includes records of archaeological objects found in Ireland from the eighteenth century to the present. The archive relates to the locations of finds in terrestrial, maritime and inland waterways. The archive is constantly updated and there is digital access available to researchers on site to some of the records. As part of the requirements for appropriate archaeological assessment under the planning process, these sources, the NMI's Archive and the NMS' WIID, are consulted to inform all archaeological impact assessments and desk-based studies.

6 Threats and Challenges

Ireland's underwater cultural resource may represent a chronological locker containing the details to past human endeavours, but it is also part of a dynamic submerged ecosystem, on the one hand acting as a capsule of cultural memory while on the other, a living landscape within our underwater environment. With this dichotomy of values come equally contrasting threats by way of both natural and cultural pressures. In this time of heightened awareness of climate change and its impacts, our underwater heritage is more at risk than ever before. There has been physical impact from extreme storm events in Ireland with, for example, the exposure of the 1588 Armada wreck, *La Juliana* in Streedagh, Co Sligo, following a series of intense storms from late 2014 (Storm Darwin) into the first quarter of 2015.[50] The pressure on UCH from development works, inevitably arising as part of social and economic growth, have

50 F. Moore, K. Brady & C. Kelleher,' Cannon, Saints and Sunken Ships – An Armada Wreck Revealed', Archaeology Ireland 29(4), 2015, 10; C. Kelleher, F. Moore and Brady, K. 'Encounter with the Irish Coast: The 1588 wrecks of the Spanish Armada', in R. Devoy, et al., *supra* n.42 510; F. Moore, K. Brady & C. Kelleher, 'La Juliana: A Spanish Armada Ship wrecked at Streedagh Bay, Co. Sligo, Ireland in 1588: Rediscovery and Investigation', in I. Pérez Tostado & D. M. Downey (eds.), Ireland and the Iberian Atlantic: Migration, Military and Material Culture, (Albatros Publications, Valencia, Spain, 2020), pp. 447–460.

already been noted. Other anthropogenic risks include an increase in commercial marine salvage operations in Ireland's coastal waters. The management approaches taken in relation to threats to Ireland's underwater archaeology require continuous appraisal in order to ensure effective planning for climate adaptation and resilience.[51]

6.1 *Natural Threats*

Climate change impacts can lead to erosion, abrasion, burial/reburial, exposure or indeed complete destruction of sites and archaeological objects underwater. The threat from climate change is real, clearly identified across the globe as a danger to vulnerable sites everywhere.[52] At the same time as the exposure of the Armada wreck at Streedagh in Sligo in 2014/2015, the complete hull of the wreck of the nineteenth century schooner, *Sunbeam,* on Rossbeigh Strand in County Kerry was lifted and shifted by Storm Darwin in 2014. Broken in two, the bow section became lodged in the dunes while the stern lay some 100 metres away. Then, further intense weather in February of that year negated all temporary protective measures put in place by the NMS around the two sections of this wreck. Recording of the structure was undertaken nonetheless, having been once again impacted, broken up and dispersed over a wide area along the strand. The remains of the wooden schooner, a local landmark on the beach, became a victim once again to weather conditions that had originally led to its stranding on the beach more than a century previously, in 1904. In certain cases, therefore, while fulfilling the State's obligations to manage and protect vulnerable sites, management of loss may need to be considered, where the natural elements present insurmountable challenges, leading to a management strategy relying on recording in advance of inevitable destruction. Other natural forces, such as marine micro-organisms, while less obvious, can also lead to deterioration of underwater archaeological sites, particularly iron shipwrecks. To what degree, if any, micro-bacterial activity is occurring on the remains of the 1915 wreck of RMS *Lusitania* is not known but such studies, similar for instance to that which has taken place on the wreck of the RMS *Titanic,*[53] may lead to a revised interpretation and appreciation of the wreck

---

51 *Climate Change Adaptation Sectoral Plan for Built and Archaeological Heritage* (Department of Culture, Heritage and the Gaeltacht, 2019).

52 E. Perez-Alvaro, 'Climate Change and Underwater Cultural Heritage: Impacts and Challenges' *Journal of Cultural Heritage*, 21, 2016, 842.

53 R. Cullimore & L. Johnston, 'Rusticles Thrive on the Titanic', *Ocean Explorer*, (National Oceanic and Atmospheric Administration, 2003); see also <https://oceanexplorer.noaa.gov/explorations/03titanic/rusticles/rusticles.html>.

site from both a natural and cultural conservation perspective and inform management strategies for the site.[54]

It is not just marine archaeological sites that are at risk from natural forces, and vessels like logboats in our freshwater environments are also susceptible to freshwater woodborers and other organisms. Recent archaeological survey work in Lough Corrib by the UAU has revealed a significant array of well-preserved prehistoric and medieval logboats and a spectacular range of artefacts and weapons contained within them. These include iron, bronze and wooden spears and axes.[55] However, during these archaeological investigations it has become clear that these vulnerable sites are being damaged by recent introductions of invasive species. Both zebra mussels (*Dreissena polymorpha*) and invasive aquatic plants such as Curly Waterweed (*Lagorosiphon major*) are now widespread in Lough Corrib, causing problems for fisheries, survival of native species, navigation and, as is now evident, protection of UCH.

6.2 *Anthropogenic Threats*

Section 3 of the NM(A)A 1987 does not preclude diving on historic wrecks and underwater archaeological objects, rather it regulates such activities through licensing. Implementing the legislation effectively, while maintaining a positive relationship with the majority of divers who respect the underwater environment from both a natural and cultural perspective, represents an ongoing challenge for the NMS. Unfortunately, a small core group of treasure hunters is still actively and illegally looting sites within the coastal waters of Ireland. Policing underwater sites is inevitably challenging, a challenge which becomes only more difficult as the increased availability of technical diving technology allows greater access to deeper sites.

The answer to this challenge must be a combination of continued positive engagement with the wider diving community coupled with robust responses to serious contraventions of the legislation. The outcome of the 2007 Dunworley Bay Wreck case is an example of the latter, and, while it related to a shallow water site, should send a clear message to all contemplating breach of the legislation. The survey and excavation of the wreck site by the UAU informed the formal investigation carried out by An Garda Síochána.[56] The case concluded in February 2007 with the successful conviction of three

54 Moore, et al., *supra* n. 2, 2019, 120.

55 K. Brady, 'Secrets of the Lake: The Lough Corrib Logboats', *Archaeology Ireland*, 28 (4), 2014, 34.

56 Ireland's National Police Force.

individuals for tampering with, and damage to, the protected wreck site, contrary to section 3 NM(A)A 1987. It was the first time that individuals were successfully prosecuted under this provision.[57] The case demonstrates that the legislation can be enforced and result in the imposition of sanctions in appropriate cases.

Marine salvage operations directed in particular at wrecks of World War I and II, and potentially other historic wrecks located in Ireland's coastal waters, have increased over the last number of years. This activity, as explained, is difficult to regulate under national heritage legislation as many of the wreck sites are located outside Ireland's TS or CZ. The Merchant Shipping (Salvage and Wreck) Act 1993 is applicable for marine salvage cases when the salvor lands wreck material or objects in ports and harbours within the State, even if the wrecked vessel was located beyond Ireland's jurisdiction. In that regard, an example of a case dealt with by the relevant Irish authorities, in particular the Receiver of Wreck and NMI, was that of artefacts recovered from the wreck of the Cunard liner RMS *Laconia*, torpedoed off the coast of Cork in February 1917, and brought into the Port of Cork in 2011. A second example would be silver ingots recovered from the World War II steamship SS *Gairsoppa*, and landed at Foynes Port, County Limerick in 2013.[58] Both wrecks lie in international waters, on Ireland's CS.

The application of the relevant procedures as set out under the 1993 Act[59] yielded contrasting results in each case. The NMI retained the material from the RMS *Laconia*, which included personal items such as a woman's shoe, an option provided for under section 49 of the 1993 Act in relation to unclaimed wreck of archaeological or historical interest. In contrast, the cargo of silver ingots was not retained from the *Gairsoppa* wreck. The government of the United Kingdom is the owner of the remains of the vessel and had awarded a permit for the salvage of the cargo of silver.

57 *DPP v P. O'S & Ors 2007*, Cork Circuit Criminal Court; C. Kelleher, 'The Dunworley Bay Shipwreck: Seventeenth-Century Evidence for Piracy and Slavery in Ireland?' In C. Horrell and M. Damour, (eds.) *Coastal Connections: Integrating Terrestrial and Underwater Archaeology: ACUA Underwater Archaeology Proceedings 2010*, (Advisory Council on Underwater Archaeology, Society for Historical Archaeology publications, 2010), 138.

58 Receiver of Wreck Manual (Irish Tax and Customs 2022); <https://www.revenue.ie/en/tax-professionals/tdm/customs/Aviation-and-Marine/Receiver-of-Wreck.pdf>.

59 Sections 44 to 49, Merchant Shipping (Salvage and Wreck) Act 1993; Receiver of Wreck Manual (Irish Tax and Customs 2022); <https://www.revenue.ie/en/tax-professionals/tdm/customs/Aviation-and-Marine/Receiver-of-Wreck.pdf>.

7 Collaborations and Engagement

Ireland is alert to both national and international responsibilities to wreck and UCH of major importance where the cultural heritage of other countries is relevant. Larger wreck sites, like the ocean liner *Justicia* and RMS *Amazon*, both lost in 1918, have been targeted in recent times and portholes, whistles and other parts removed by divers. While the *Justicia* lies in the CZ it was targeted prior to it being automatically protected by the 100-year rule as provided for under the NM(A)A 1987. On the other hand, the RMS *Amazon* lies beyond the CZ, where Ireland's capacity to protect such sites is restricted. The difficulty in countering illegal activity is further compounded by divers arriving on wreck sites but not necessarily using Irish ports and harbours as their base. Indeed, even within Ireland's TS it is often only through sources such as social media that the NMS or NMI become aware that unlicenced diving has taken place on protected wrecks, and that wreck constituting archaeological objects has been removed and illegally exported.[60] Efforts to address such cases demand close collaboration across heritage, policing and other relevant agencies, though as seen from earlier discussion regarding the Dunworley case, the prospects for successful outcome are real and achievable if the right resources are in place.

7.1 *The UC-42 and Local Engagement*

The site of the World War I German mine-laying submarine *UC-42*, which sank 5 km south-east of Roche's Point outside Cork Harbour in 1917, is another instance of effective engagement across government and non-government agencies. The *UC-42* is perhaps one of the most accessible submarine wrecks, not just in Ireland but in all of Northern Atlantic waters, as it lies in just 27 metres of water. Its discovery significantly increased its susceptibility to interference and damage but, due to an increased appreciation of UCH generally, local divers, other seafarers and local activists continue to ensure that the site is actively protected. The NMS annually issues licences to dive clubs, dive operators and individual divers for the *UC-42*, who in turn report on the wreck's condition. Local operators in Kinsale, the nearest port to the wreck site, report to the NMS on any unusual activities near the site. Whilst one of the most complete examples of a World War I submarine in Irish territorial waters, the site is also a war grave, possibly containing the remains of 27 submariners and accordingly should be treated with appropriate respect and sensitivity. It has a particular significance in this regard due to it being a relatively recent German

60 Export of archaeological objects from the State requires a licence under section 50, National Cultural Institutions Act 1997.

naval loss and with crew who are known by name, many of whom are likely to have close living relatives. The Embassy of Germany in Ireland has indicated a legitimate concern for the protection, preservation and non-disturbance of the wreck site and the human remains within it.

This close engagement with key stakeholders has evolved over time, particularly as a result of interference with the submarine site in 2011. The U-boat still has a number of mines in place in its mine chutes and torpedoes scattered on the seabed, which were determined to be 'live' by the Irish Naval Service and the Irish Coast Guard and therefore still had the potential to detonate. A no-dive exclusion zone was agreed, to preclude recreational diving taking place for a time so as to provide divers from the Irish Naval Service with the opportunity to make the mines safe by capping the mine chutes that still retain their ordnance, in the interest of both marine safety and for those diving the wreck into the future. In 2013, however, unidentified divers removed the capping plates, along with warning signs that had been placed on the wreck by the Navy divers. Collaborative discussions then took place between the Naval Service and the Coast Guard, the Marine Safety Division of the Department of Marine, the National Parks and Wildlife Service (of the Department of Housing, Local Government and Heritage), and the NMS. These focused on safety issues and future access by sports divers, while acknowledging the importance and sensitivity of the wreck site from a heritage perspective.

Following publication by the NMS in the Irish Underwater Council's (now Dive Ireland)[61] diver magazine, *Subsea,* clarifying that each individual diver would be responsible for their own safety when on the wreck site, the Irish Naval Service removed the defined no-activity exclusion zone.[62] Although less than 100-years old at the time, because of the historical and archaeological importance of the wreck, the fact that in the light of the *Lusitania* High Court ruling it can also be defined as an archaeological object (for which there is no cut off point in terms of dating) and as a repository for archaeological objects, together with its significance as a war grave, the diving community was advised to apply to the NMS for licences under section 3 NM(A)A 1987 to dive on the site. This approach sought to put in place a regulatory regime for the site and a framework seeking to ensure that only appropriate and authorised diving took place. The wreck site is now, in any event, over 100-years old and the NMS, through its licensing system, continues to monitor activity at the site.

61 <https://diving.ie/>.

62 C. Kelleher, 'Diving the Wreck of the German Submarine *UC-42* in Cork Harbour', *Subsea* Diver Magazine, Irish Underwater Council, 2016.

7.2 *Engagement with Divers and the Fishing Community*

It is essential that a working relationship exists with the diving community in Ireland. On the whole this engagement is positive, and the NMS liaises with individual divers and dive clubs on a regular basis, through both the statutory licensing process but also on the ground when coordinating with them on new discoveries of sites and objects from an underwater context. This is a two-way process, and the NMS regularly supplies divers with locations for wrecks, which have not yet been dived and, in turn, the divers report on the nature, extent and condition of such wrecks. In this way trust has built up and there is a sense of collective responsibility for Ireland's UCH. Indeed, there is a cohort of technical divers who reliably assist with updating the WIID by adding to the record with high quality video and photography captured when diving the deep-water shipwrecks that are beyond the depth range of the UAU archaeologists.

The fishing community too has a significant role to play in the protection of Ireland's UCH. As individuals who are innately connected to the sea, they have extensive knowledge of the possible location of sites or artefacts and net-snagging locations that may indicate wreck sites. Many fishers have reported the recovery of archaeological objects as a result of their fishing activity, such as cannonballs, medieval pottery, ship timbers and anchors and this has subsequently led to the discovery and protection of both known and new archaeological sites. In 2017, during the course of trawl fishing, the taps from a bath were recovered in the nets of a fishing trawler. The discovery was reported to the NMS and subsequent engagement with the finder confirmed that the location of the recovery was the World War I liner SS *Hesperian*, lost off the south-west coast in 1915. Although the wreck is not protected under the National Monuments Acts as it is outside the CZ, the discovery of the taps highlights the need to liaise with fishers and share information on wreck sites so that archaeological objects can be taken into care, but also so that such sites can be avoided, thus preventing potential damage to these wrecks from fishing activity.

7.3 *Working with the Owner of a Major Historic Wreck*

An interesting aspect of the Irish experience in managing UCH has been the need, over a long period, to build and manage the relationship with the private owner of a major historic wreck, such as that of the RMS *Lusitania*. A full account of this process, which was not always an easy one for any of the parties, involved litigation at one point, and is beyond the scope of this chapter.[63]

63 Moore et al., *Lusitania: The Story of a Wreck*, 2019, *supra* n. 4.

However, noteworthy are the steps taken to facilitate the granting in 2007 and 2013 of multi-annual licences to enable the owner to progress a programme of forensic examination of the wreck and the putting in place of a Memorandum of Understanding (MoU) between the NMS and the owner in 2013. The objective of the MoU was to set the agenda for future research on the wreck, identify areas where there might be room for collaboration on projects and to set out clearly the respective positions of stakeholders so that there would be full understanding of aims, objectives and legal obligations.

Following the passing of the owner, Mr. F. Gregg Bemis, in 2020, title to the RMS *Lusitania* wreck transferred to the Lusitania Museum Old Head Signal Tower Heritage CLG. Contacts between the NMS and the Old Head Lusitania Museum are being developed with a view to exploring possibilities for collaboration in the context of the new owners' efforts to achieve their vision of a museum dedicated to the story of the RMS *Lusitania* and the maritime heritage of the south coast. Support by NMS by way of funding a professional consultant underwater archaeologist to review their *Lusitania* Museum proposal and providing direct advice to them, as well as liaising with with them on potential future surveys on the wreck site, is progressing.

8 Future Directions

The future management of UCH in Ireland will continue to be founded on a range of management tools, some specific to it and some shared with other aspects of heritage management. All have been touched on already, but it is worth emphasising again the benefits that integration of archaeological heritage considerations into the planning and development process will bring to UCH. In that regard, it will be important to ensure that the specific needs of UCH protection are fully recognised in the overall guidance and policies being developed in this field, and that UCH is appropriately reflected in relevant documents. A recent example of this is the publication in 2021 by the Office of the Planning Regulator (OPR),[64] in cooperation with the NMS, of 'Archaeology in the Planning Process', an information leaflet setting out the issues that may arise with developments that might affect the archaeological

64 The OPR was established in 2019 to ensure that local authorities and An Bord Pleanála (Ireland's national independent planning body that decides on planning appeals by local authorities and direct applications) support and implement planning policy; <https://www.opr.ie>.

heritage, including UCH.[65] The point is not to minimise or detract from the specific requirements and importance of UCH and its management, but to emphasise that UCH will benefit greatly when also recognised as a central part of archaeological heritage management in general.

With a view to establishing a national policy for UCH, in the summer of 2023 the NMS, in partnership with the NMI, initiated a process of developing a Proposal for a National Strategy for Ireland's Underwater Cultural Heritage that will define the nature and scope of what that national policy will comprise. It sets out a vision for the future protection and management of Ireland's underwater archaeological resource and will identify key actions and make recommendations in that regard. The broad framework covers UCH, and actions set out in the national heritage plan, Heritage Ireland 2030. The proposal will also address challenges and threats to UCH stemming from climate change, taking on board the objectives of the Built & Archaeological Heritage Climate Change Sectoral Adaptation Plan, published by the Department of Culture, Heritage and the Gaeltacht in 2019.[66] The drafting of the proposal is now at an advanced stage with suitably qualified professional underwater archaeological consultants engaged by NMS to carry out the drafting, which included circulation of a survey to inform a series of workshops, which took place in February 2024. Already gaps have been identified within the existing professional field of UCH in Ireland, and discussions have commenced with academic institutions and training colleagues to engage in constructive dialogue with a view to addressing this hiatus in practical training and education in Ireland.

One area where there is potential for a particularly new approach in the Irish context, is in the consideration being given to the establishment of a more comprehensive network of Marine Protected Areas (MPAs). In September 2022, the Irish Government approved the General Scheme of a Marine Protected Areas Bill. When enacted, it will designate, at a minimum, 30 per cent of Ireland's marine area as MPAs by 2030.[67] The challenge here will be to see if cultural heritage can be recognised as an integral part of such a network, as it already

65 <https://www.opr.ie/wp-content/uploads/2021/01/Planning-Leaflet-13-Archaeology-in-the-Planning-Process.pdf>.

66 <https://www.google.com/search?q=Press+release+-+minister+noonan+built+and+archaeological+heritage+climate+change+sectoral+plan>.

67 Expanding Ireland's Marine Protected Areas, Department of Housing, Local Government and Heritage, 2021; <https://www.gov.ie/en/publication/135a8-expanding-irelands-marine-protected-area-network/>.

is in comparable systems of reserves in other jurisdictions.[68] Consideration of UCH within existing and future expanded MPAs would positively support existing statutory protection measures by raising the profile of sites protected within those areas, but there will clearly be challenges in terms of securing an appropriate legal basis for inclusion of UCH and the necessary co-operation with other areas of heritage management. While the primary focus of the MPA legislation will be to protect the natural environment, NMS is engaging in discussions with relevant personnel centred on integrating the protection of Ireland's UCH. This aligns with the International Union for the Conservation of Nature (IUCN), which in its definition of MPAs includes 'any area of intertidal or subtidal terrain, together with its overlying water and associated flora, fauna, historical and cultural features.'[69] Integrating the protection of UCH, which by its nature is fragile and finite, very much ties in with the objective of the proposed expanded MPAs, with UCH sites (such as shipwrecks) themselves becoming distinct marine habitats, playing host to an abundance of marine life, and acting as living ecosystems.

9 Conclusion

While the underwater environment may provide exceptional levels of preservation, yielding evidence of the past otherwise unavailable, as well as telling the story of human interaction with the sea, rivers and lakes, that environment also presents particular challenges when taking action to protect cultural heritage. Some of these challenges are long recognised, such as the threat from treasure hunting, salvage operations and trawling, the need to integrate heritage considerations into important and beneficial marine development and the need to maximise protection, making the best use of (and work within the limitations of) complex maritime jurisdictional regimes and diverse statutory codes. These can include those regulating marine and developmental activities as well as those specifically directed at heritage protection. Other challenges, in particular the need to adapt to a rapidly changing climate, are only beginning to be tackled.

---

68 The Marine Protection Atlas (Marine Conservation Institute): <https://mpatlas.org/>; international examples include Thunder Bay Marine Sanctuary and Underwater Preserve on Lake Huron in the US, where over 100 shipwrecks are protected see for example <https://thunderbay.noaa.gov/>.

69 Emphasis added, see <https://www.iucn.org/sites/default/files/import/downloads/iucn_categoriesmpa_eng.pdf>.

The protection and management of Ireland's UCH has historically involved a range of stakeholders and actors, not just the State bodies specifically tasked with its protection. These include the sports diving community, fishing sector, marine development sector, academic sector and a range of other Government Departments and State agencies. Whatever the future challenges may be, it is clear that any successful approach to underwater archaeological protection and management in Ireland must continue to engage, and indeed increase the level of engagement, with all these stakeholders and actors. Given the presence in Ireland's waters of many wrecks with international associations and the prospect of participation by Ireland in the international co-operation system under the 2001 Convention, the consideration of relevant stakeholders and actors must include those at national and international level. This will become even more apparent when the new Historic and Archaeological Heritage and Miscellaneous Provisions Act 2023 is commenced fully, allowing for the ratification by Ireland of the 2001 Convention, which in itself will enable more far-reaching protection measures for UCH within the waters around and off Ireland's shores.

All websites last accessed February 2025.

Select Bibliography

Brady, K. *Shipwreck Inventory of Ireland, Volume 1: Louth, Meath, Dublin and Wicklow* (The Stationary Office, Government of Ireland, 2008).

Brady, K., Kelleher, C. & Moore, F. 'Ireland's Underwater Cultural Heritage: The Role of the Underwater Archaeology Unit in Documenting, Managing and Investigating the Maritime Archaeological Resource', in J. Higgins, A. Conneely & M. Gibbons (eds.), *Irish Maritime Heritage: Proceedings of the 3rd Galway International Heritage Conference 2013* (Crow's Rock Press, Galway, 2014), 165–182.

Brady, K., McKeon, C., Lyttleton, J & Lawler, I. (eds.) *Warships, U-Boats and Liners: A Guide to Shipwrecks Mapped in Irish Waters* (The Stationary Office, Government of Ireland, 2012).

Kelleher, C. 'Ireland's Treasure Hunting Past – the Case for Underwater Archaeology', in F. Castro & L. Thomas, (eds.), *Crossing Boundaries: ACUA Underwater Archaeology Proceedings 2011*, Advisory Council on Underwater Archaeology, (Society for Historical Archaeology publications, 2011), 74–83.

Kirwan, S. & Moore, F. 'Update on Ireland and the UNESCO Convention on the Protection of the Underwater Cultural Heritage', in Robert A. Yorke, (ed.), *Protection of Underwater Cultural Heritage in International Waters Adjacent to the UK: Proceedings of the JNAPC 21st Anniversary Seminar 2010*, (Published in 2011), 51–60.

O'Connor N. 'Ireland', in S. Dromgoole (ed.), *Legal Protection of the Underwater Cultural Heritage: National and International Perspectives*, (Kluwer Law International Publications, The Hague, 1999), 87–99.

O'Connor, N. 'The Irish Experience', in S. Dromgoole (ed.), *The Protection of the Underwater Cultural Heritage: National Perspective in the Light of the* UNESCO *Convention 2001*, (Leiden, 2006), 127–144.

CHAPTER 10

Italy

Massimiliano Secci and Barbara Davidde Petriaggi***

1 Introduction

More than 70 years have passed since underwater archaeology became appreciated in Italy. In the 1950s, Nino Lamboglia was the first Italian scholar to recognise the importance of underwater cultural heritage (UCH). Although he never discussed legislation or management *per se*, many of his efforts were devoted to creating a framework for the sound technological-scientific development of the discipline and the protection of UCH.[1] Throughout his career he struggled to gather sufficient funding and political support to ensure a solid research framework and infrastructure for the nascent discipline, touching early upon themes that are key to full implementation in Italy of the UNESCO Convention on the Protection of Underwater Cultural Heritage 2001 (2001 Convention).[2]

From 1950 onwards, in his 27 years of activity in the field, Lamboglia experimented and developed new methodologies. A centre for underwater archaeology was established in 1957,[3] and the first ship devoted to underwater archaeological research, the *Daino* (1959–1963) was utilised, with (then) state-of-the-art diving and safety equipment. A second smaller ship, the *Cycnus*

* The Maritime Research Laboratory, Archaeological Research Unit, Department of History and Archaeology, University of Cyprus.

** Director of the Underwater Archaeology operation Unit-Central Institute for Restoration (Rome -Italy), former Superintendent of the National Superintendency for Underwater Cultural heritage (Taranto-Italy).

1 F. Pallares, 'Nino Lamboglia e l'archeologia subacquea' (1997–1998), Rivista di Studi Liguri 63 – 64.

2 2562 UNTS 1; N. Lamboglia, 'Archeologia sul mare. I. 1950' (2007) 4 *Archaeologia Maritima Mediterranea* pp. 23–26; N. Lamboglia, 'L'avventura del «Cycnus» nel Golfo del Leone e a Maiorca' (2007) 4 *Archaeologia Maritima Mediterranea* pp. 27–36; Pallares *op cit* n.1; F. Pallares, 'Premessa ai manoscritti inediti di Nino Lamboglia' (2007), 4 *Archaeologia Maritima Mediterranea* pp. 13–21; R. Petriaggi, 'Nino Lambaglia, l'archeologia subacquea e la burocrazia: luci ed ombre di un rapporto tormentato' (2007), 4 *Archaeologia Maritima Mediterranea* pp. 37–43.

3 Namely the Centro Sperimentale di Archeologia Sottomarina, established within the Istituto di Studi Liguri, located in Albenga nearby Genoa.

 | DOI:10.1163/9789004510883_012

(1969–1981) with the same state-of-the-art equipment followed.[4] Lamboglia also stressed the importance of methodology, while emphasising the necessary recognition of roles and professionalism. While promoting the involvement of avocationals, he also stressed the required expertise to undertake activities directed at UCH. His experiences proved that sound collaboration between trained archaeologists and avocationals, is not impossible and that they can work well together to promote the study and protection of UCH. Unfortunately, following his death in 1977 and some debatable choices by the Ministry of Cultural Heritage, his legacy and insight were sadly lost. Ironically, recent innovations in Italian UCH management are re-proposing some of the key aspects of Lamboglia's vision, although on a different basis, as discussed in section 4 below. The new millennium has seen a renewed interest in UCH and capacity-building which is unprecedented in Italy. This chapter offers a timely opportunity to discuss the Italian system of UCH protection and offers the reader a thorough and comprehensive overview.

2 A Brief History of the Evolution of Legislation for the Protection of Cultural Heritage and UCH

Italy was officially established in 1861 as a Kingdom, under the sovereignty of the Royal House of the Savoy, following the unification of the various States and Kingdoms that had characterised the Italian peninsula until then. After the Fascist dictatorship and the Second World War and powered by the publics' distaste of the Savoy House's laxity during the Fascist period, the Italian Republic was established by way of a referendum in 1946. Despite its youth, the Italian Kingdom and then the Republic could count on a long civil law tradition based on the *Corpus Iuris Civilis* (Code of Justinian) developed over the centuries by the pre-unitarian States and Kingdoms, with numerous examples of an early general sensibility towards cultural heritage.[5]

Compared to other countries, it was not until recently that Italy formally included the protection of UCH within national legislation. Although it has always been protected under generic heritage legislation, it was not until recently that an explicit reference to the protection of UCH was made within national legislation. UCH was included in the legislative lexicon for cultural

4 Pallares *op cit* n.1 and 2.

5 G. Volpe, *Manuale di diritto dei beni culturali: storia e attualità*, (CEDAM 2007); S. Settis, *Paesaggio Costituzione Cemento: La battaglia per l'ambiente contro il degrado civile* (Einaudi 2010).

heritage in 2004,[6] when a reference to "*le cose* [...] *ritrovate nel sottosuolo o sui fondali marini*" (the objects [...] found under or on the seabed) was made in Article 94.1 of the Codice dei Beni Culturali e del Paesaggio. Article 94.1 dictated that the archaeological and historical objects found within Italy's Contiguous Zone (CZ) were to be dealt with according to the Rules annexed to the 2001 Convention. This was surprising, because at that time Italy had yet to ratify the 2001 Convention.

The chronological development is charted below. Various legislative measures on cultural heritage were issued by the Italian Kingdom between the end of the nineteenth and the first decades of the twentieth century. This was "one of the most tormented legislative" periods in the development of cultural heritage laws in Italy.[7] It was characterised by a struggle between two opposing factions: one that supported the *utilitas publica*[8] of cultural heritage protection and management; and the other seeking to uphold the inviolability of private property rights.[9] Such antagonism is not entirely settled and still plays an important role in the legislative measures in force and, to a certain extent, in public opinion. Nonetheless, some interesting improvements were made during these troubled times. In 1881, the Direzione Generale per le Antichità e Belle Arti (General Directorate for Antiquities and Fine Arts) was established within the Ministry of Education.[10] In 1907, under the same Ministry's direction[11], local Superintendencies[12] were established, whose duty was "protection of the archaeological and artistic interests".[13]

6 Decreto Legislativo 22 gennaio 2004, n. 42, 'Codice dei Beni Culturali e del Paesaggio'. Available at: <https://www.normattiva.it/uri-res/N2Ls?urn:nir:stato:decreto.legislativo:2004-01-22;42>.

7 T. Alibrandi and P. Ferri, *I Beni Culturali e Ambientali* (Giuffrè 2001), p. 6. The period in question includes the last two decades of the nineteenth century and the first three decades of the twentieth.

8 Settis *op cit* n. 5, p. 93.

9 V. Baldacci, *Il Sistema dei Beni Culturali in Italia* (Giunti 2004), p. 36; Settis *op cit* n. 5, p. 113.

10 M. Musacchio, *L'archivio della Direzione generale delle antichità e belle arti (1860–1890): inventario* (Ministero per i beni culturali e ambientali, Ufficio centrale per i beni archivistici 1994).

11 Legge 27 giugno 1907 n. 386, so called 'Legge Rava'. Available at: <https://www.normattiva.it/uri-res/N2Ls?urn:nir:stato:legge:1907-06-27;386>.

12 Local Heritage Offices within the Ministry delegated to the protection of cultural heritage. These were distributed throughout the national territory and subdivided according to the sector of competence (e.g., archaeological, monuments, archives etc.). Currently the nomenclature is Soprintendenze Archeologia, Belle Arti e Paesaggio (Superintendencies Archaeology, Fine Arts and Landscape).

13 Law 386/1907. Among other duties, they had to: (i) carry out archaeological excavations, while issuing permits to and supervising the fieldwork research done by other institutions or private persons; (ii) monitor the territory of competence for illicit excavations, transfer, or trafficking of CH; (iii) undertake or supervise conservation and restoration activities.

During the Second World War, in line with the high value placed on cultural heritage by Fascist propaganda, a substantial law was drafted,[14] which remained the principal Italian legislation on the subject until the end of the twentieth century.[15] Law 1089/1939 placed under a blanket protection "*le cose, immobili e mobili, che presentano interesse artistico, storico, archeologico o etnografico*" (the objects, immobile or mobile, which present an artistic, historic, archaeological or ethnographic interest), which were 50 years or older.[16] No specific reference to UCH was provided for in this legislation. Henceforth, UCH sites and artefacts have been protected as objects of archaeological interest, with no specific reference to their location or status.

Two more pieces of legislation contributed (and still contribute) to the protection of UCH: the Codice Civile (CC)[17] and the Codice della Navigazione (CN).[18] Article 826 of the CC formally states that "*le cose d'interesse storico, archeologico, paletnologico, paleontologico e artistico, da chiunque e in qualunque modo ritrovate nel sottosuolo*" (objects of historical, archaeological, paleontological, and artistic interest, found underground by anyone and in any way) belong to the "inviolable assets" of the State and "are subject to special laws".[19] Furthermore, in Article 828 CC, it is stated that the objects belonging to the State's " inviolable assets cannot be diverted from their intended purpose/use". In the case of cultural heritage, they are explicitly intended for the enjoyment of the community of citizens.

In addition, Articles 510 and 511 of the CN regulate the accidental discovery of wrecks. Specifically, Article 510 provides that "anyone who accidentally finds wrecks at sea must report them within three days to the nearest maritime authority".[20] However, Article 511 provides that, if the owner is unknown, the

14 Legge 1 giugno 1939, n. 1089; Legge 29 Giugno 1939, n. 1497. The two laws, conceived as a whole, were respectively devoted to the protection of the historical and artistic heritage (Law 1089/1939) and to the protection of the natural beauty (Law 1497/1939). Law 1089/1939 is available at: <https://www.normattiva.it/uri-res/N2Ls?urn:nir:stato:legge:1939-06-01;1089!vig=>. Law 1497/1939 is available at: <https://www.normattiva.it/uri-res/N2Ls?urn:nir:stato:legge:1939-06-29;1497>.

15 Law 1089/1939 underwent several amendments and integrations.

16 Law 1089/1939, Art. 1.

17 Regio Decreto 16 marzo 1942, n. 262. Available at: <https://www.normattiva.it/uri-res/N2Ls?urn:nir:stato:regio.decreto:1942-03-16;262!vig=2020-12-04>.

18 Regio Decreto 30 marzo 1942, n. 327. Available at: <https://www.normattiva.it/uri-res/N2Ls?urn:nir:stato:regio.decreto:1942-03-30;327>.

19 In the specific case of cultural heritage, currently, the special law is the Code.

20 This provision is integrated by Art. 90 of the *Codice* which concerns 'fortuitous discoveries' and by Art. 91, which concerns the 'belonging and qualification of the discovered things'.

"objects of artistic, historical, archaeological or ethnographic interest" found at sea "are devolved to the State". In any case, the discoverer has the right to a reward.[21]

Two years after the establishment of the Italian Republic in 1946, the protection and promotion of cultural heritage was made one of the fundamental principles of the newborn Republic and included in Article 9 of its Constitution. In 2003, former President Carlo Azeglio Ciampi highlighted how the merit of Article 9 lies in having conceived protection "not in the sense of passive protection, but in an active sense, that is, as a function of the citizens' cultural growth" to make "this heritage accessible to all".[22] Little changed in the following two decades, although an attempt was made to rationalise the disorganised multitude of laws and regulations, when, in 1964, a Parliamentary Commission was established to investigate matters regarding cultural heritage.[23] Published in 1967, under the title *'Per la salvezza dei beni culturali in Italia'* (For the salvation of cultural heritage in Italy),[24] the Commission's report offered a series of declarations providing insights towards an adaptation of the cultural heritage management system to the new challenges presented mainly from the economic boom and the consequent urban development that threatened the physical integrity of both natural and cultural heritage. The work of the Commission made no reference to UCH and was not followed by any reform of the cultural heritage management system.

However, UCH is mentioned in the 1972 Carta Italiana del Restauro (the Charter), drafted in close collaboration with art historian Cesare Brandi.[25] The Charter defines the precise typologies of objects that are subject to the activities of protection and restoration. For the first time in the Italian management

---

21 Concerning cultural heritage, the value of the reward is set by Art. 92 of the *Codice*.

22 Ciampi in S. Settis, *Battaglie senza eroi: I beni culturali tra istituzioni e profitto* (Mondadori 2005), pp. 195–196 e 373; Settis *op cit* n. 5, pp. 179 ss; M. Secci, 'Protection vs. Public Access: two concepts compared within the Italian underwater cultural heritage management system' (2011) 6 *Journal of Maritime Archaeology* 2., p. 118.

23 Established by the Legge 26 aprile 1964, n. 310, it became known as the Franceschini Commission based on the name of the Chair, Member of Parliament Hon. Francesco Franceschini. See M. Pallottino, 'La stagione della commissione Franceschini' in F. Perego, A. Clementi (eds) Memorabilia: il futuro della memoria. Beni ambientali architettonici archeologici artistici e storici in Italia (Laterza 1988).

24 F. Franceschini, *Per la salvezza dei beni culturali in Italia: atti e documenti della Commissione d'indagine per la tutela e la valorizzazione del patrimonio storico, archeologico, artistico e del paesaggio* (Colombo 1967).

25 Italian Charter for Restoration. The Charter was published in the Ministry of Education's Circular n. 117, 6 April 1972. Available at: <https://soprintendenzapisalivorno.beniculturali.it/wp-content/uploads/2019/08/circ-117-del-1972-Carta-del-restauro.pdf>.

system, these also included ancient remains discovered in both land and underwater research.

Annex A to the Charter sets out the procedures for interventions related to UCH, clearly reflecting the experiences, approaches and methodologies that had been developed by Lamboglia. It states that:

> ... the protection of the underwater archaeological heritage [... is] aimed at preventing the indiscriminate and reckless tampering with wrecks of ancient ships and their cargo, submerged ruins, and sunken sculptures.

Anticipating many concepts and approaches that are established best practices today, the Annex identified as a prerequisite the need to proceed to undertake a "systematic exploration of the Italian coasts with specialised personnel" in order to create a catalogue (*Forma Maris*) of the remains, which could then inform protection and research. It also stressed how eventual plans for the recovery and lifting of shipwreck hull remains should not start before the required infrastructure had been organised, such as premises, equipment, and expertise.

In 1975, a special Ministry for Cultural and Natural Heritage was created, integrating into one Ministry the competences that until then were split between the Ministry of Education, the Ministry of the Interior, and the Presidency of the Council of Ministers. Through a framework of central structures (General Directorates, Central Institutes) and peripheral structures (Superintendencies, which were previously established by Law 364/1909), under the direction of the Minister, the intention of the new Ministry was to promote a more focused approach and more professionalism in the management of cultural heritage.

Following the establishment of the Ministry, a first attempt was made to legislate on UCH matters in the same year, when a draft law was submitted for Parliamentary consideration by the Minister.[26] The proposed measure would have extended the protection provided by Law 1089/1939 to sites and artefacts of archaeological and historical interest found underwater, in the Territorial Seas (TS) and inland waters.[27] For the first time, it advocated for the establishment of a National Superintendency for the Sea, while contemplating the appointment of a Commission which would have drawn up a catalogue of UCH (*Forma Maris Antiqui*), to be published by the Ministry. Unfortunately, due to lack of political support, nothing came of it. Compared to Lamboglia's vision, the Ministry, universities, and the political environment lacked a broad

26 Pallares *op cit* n. 1, p. 48.

27 *ibid.*

structural programme for the full development of the discipline. This fact also explains why Lamboglia's commitment is still held up as an example in the Italian disciplinary field.

In 1982, to counter the problems highlighted by the discovery of the Riace Bronzes, discussed below, the Ministry set up a Commission, which unfortunately was quickly disbanded due to controversies surrounding the background, role, and expertise of some of its members.[28] During the 1990s, two further draft laws were proposed to the Parliament: the first in 1992[29] and the second in 1996.[30] They were composed of only a few articles, lacking the complex drafting necessary to reflect the manifold heritage and disciplinary objectives. The 1992 draft law suggested the extension of the protective measures provided for by Law 1089/1939, to UCH;[31] while a collaboration between the Ministry of Cultural and Natural Heritage and the Ministry of Shipping would have ensured protection, by employing naval vessels and aircraft of the Coast Guard.[32] To have a countrywide system of protection, specialised units were to be established within the local port authorities.[33] Article 2 dictated the establishment of a specific training system for the personnel of the Ministry and other entities engaging in the research and protection of UCH via a system of permits. Finally, Article 3 dealt with the coverage of the costs related to the new measures.

The main difference in the 1996 draft law was reference in Article 1.2 to the United Nations Convention on the Law of the Sea 1982 (LOSC), which Italy had ratified in 1994.[34] Article 1.3 recognised the role to be played in the protection of UCH by the Comando Carabinieri per la Tutela del Patrimonio Culturale (Carabinieri Command for the Protection of Cultural Heritage), established in

28 L. Vlad Borrelli, 'Prospettive per l'archeologia subacquea' in *Bollettino d'Arte. Supplemento 4 – Archeologia Subacquea* (Istituto Poligrafico e Zecca dello Stato 1982), p. 11; P. A. Gianfrotta 'Introduzione' in G. Volpe, (ed.) *Archeologia subacquea. Come opera l'archeologo sott'acqua. Storia delle acque. VIII Ciclo di Lezioni sulla Ricerca Applicata all'Archeologia, Certosa di Pontignano* (All'Insegna del Giglio 1998), p. 16.

29 A first draft law was submitted to the Parliament by Minister Alberto Ronchey on 16 November 1992: Available at: <http://legislature.camera.it/_dati/leg11/lavori/stampati/pdf/50166.pdf>.

30 Mirroring the one proposed in 1992, a second draft law was submitted to the Parliament by Minister Walter Veltroni on 25 July 1996: Available at: <http://leg13.camera.it/_dati/leg13/lavori/stampati/pdf/1984.pdf>.

31 Art. 1.1.

32 Arts. 1.2 and 1.4, respectively.

33 Art. 1.3.

34 1833 UNTS 397; Legge 2 dicembre 1994, n. 689. Available at: <https://www.gazzettaufficiale.it/eli/id/1994/12/19/094G0717/sg>.

1969 and recently integrated within the structure of the Ministry of Cultural and Natural Heritage through a ministerial decree.[35] However, due to changes in the legislature, i.e., appointed government Ministers and Members of Parliament, both draft laws were abandoned and never reproposed.

In 1997, it was realised how heterogeneous and disconnected the legislation within the cultural heritage sector was. Both the protection of cultural heritage and its management was complicated by the substantial number of laws and provisions in existence. An obligation was placed on policymakers to organise a rationalisation of the legislation within two years. To fulfil this mandate, in 1999 a consolidated text of the existing legislation was drafted, commonly known as the *Testo Unico* (TU)[36] and published in the Official Gazette of the Italian Republic.[37] Although it was praised as an "undeniable step forward" to define the "work to be done" in the light of "what has been done",[38] the TU was also criticised because it leaned towards a definition of cultural heritage based on its materiality and specificity. It drew additional criticism because of its narrow approach to protection, avoiding regulation of key aspects, such as a comprehensive definition of cultural heritage; a precise definition of the duties of the peripheral offices of the Ministry; the promotion of and public access to cultural heritage; and the relationship between the public and private sectors.

The reorganisation of the previous legislation provided for by the TU enabled some order to be applied to what was otherwise a particularly heterogeneous and fragmented situation. The result was the drafting and issuing of the current legislation on cultural heritage in Italy, the *Codice dei Beni Culturali e del Paesaggio* (the *Codice*).[39] The *Codice* has subsequently been amended and consolidated on numerous occasions.[40]

As previously mentioned, the *Codice* was the first legislation in Italy to make an express reference to UCH. In its original version, Article 94.1 stated that "the

35 Decreto Ministeriale 5 marzo 1992. Available at: <https://www.gazzettaufficiale.it/eli/id/1992/03/17/092A1217/sg>.

36 Decreto legislativo, 29 ottobre 1999 n, 490. Available at: <https://www.parlamento.it/parlam/leggi/deleghe/99490dl.htm>.

37 Gazzetta Ufficiale, 27 dicembre 1999. Available at: <https://www.gazzettaufficiale.it/eli/gu/1999/12/27/302/sg/pdf>.

38 M. Cammelli, 'Il Testo Unico, il commento e ... ciò che resta da fare' (2000), Aedon 2, pp. 26–27.

39 Code of Cultural Heritage and Landscape; Available at: <https://www.normattiva.it/uri-res/N2Ls?urn:nir:stato:decreto.legislativo:2004-01-22;42>.

40 The amending and integrating laws can be found at the above link under the heading 'aggiornamenti all'atto'.

objects indicated in Article 10, however and by whomever found underground or on the seabed, belong to the state [...]".[41] The scope of Article 10 includes both territorial waters, CZ and Exclusive Economic Zone. Article 94.1, applied the Rules annexed to the 2001 Convention to the "archaeological and historical objects found on the seabed in the area extended twelve nautical miles from the external limit of the territorial waters", i.e., in the CZ, according to Article 33, LOSC.[42]

Since its drafting and adoption, the 2001 Convention has been welcomed by the international community of practitioners as a much needed and comprehensive set of measures to protect UCH, while promoting cooperation between all the stakeholders, both at a national and international level. As far as Italy is concerned, this legal instrument had already acquired a formalised leading role on the subject since 2004, and it has acquired even more value following its ratification which entered into force on 8 April 2010.[43]

3 Establishment of a Management Framework for UCH and Relevant Issues

UCH has always been protected through the mandates of generic legislation on cultural heritage and, more specifically since the ratification of the 2001 Convention. However, the situation regarding the recognition of the required expertise and professionalism for the activities directed at UCH has been problematic. Moreover, the consistent lack at a national level of a structure specifically devoted to this type of heritage should be highlighted, with the exception of the Sicilian region, where, thanks to a special autonomy in the field of cultural heritage, matters are arranged slightly differently. This lack of a national-level structure devoted to UCH is due to a lack of political vision which has characterised the action of the Republic in this field until recently. Over the decades, at least since the 1970s and in conjunction with collateral events, this lack of vision has created a series of counterproductive measures, the effects of which are still felt today.

In 1972, during a fishing trip off the coast of Riace (south-western Italy), a spearfisherman discovered in very shallow waters two original Greek bronze

41 The last amendment to Art. 94.1, following the Decreto Legislativo 26 marzo 2008, was a merely formal modification, only changing the title of the Article to include a direct reference to the 2001 Convention.

42 Available at: <https://www.un.org/depts/los/convention_agreements/texts/unclos/unclos_e.pdf>.

43 Available at: <https://www.normattiva.it/uri-res/N2Ls?urn:nir:stato:legge:2009;157>.

statues: the 'Bronzi di Riace' (the Riace Bronzes). The enthusiasm for the discovery and the inappropriate media coverage of the event and of the exhibitions that followed the restoration,[44] triggered a "fever" that was, to say the least, poorly managed by the institutions entrusted with the management of UCH and by the disciplinary field at large.[45] The, to a degree, understandable "fever" taking hold of the general public was sadly mirrored by a sensationalist approach by some experts in the field who succumbed to the lure of media-driven celebrity.

In this same period, a series of measures of dubious merit were taken. A special provision, included in Article 15 of the Legge 28 febbraio 1986, n. 42, which came to be known as '*giacimenti culturali* '(cultural deposits), is particularly representative of the confusion and disjointed approach that characterised the cultural heritage sector at the twilight of the twentieth century. Providing for the cataloguing of cultural heritage with an eye to potentially sponsoring youth employment, the system was deluged with a large amount of funding. A lack of structural planning and programming completed the picture. Combined with the sensationalist frenzy of these decades, a negative *praxis* developed, causing many sites to be abandoned after a couple of seasons, once a new and more promising one was discovered.[46]

Additionally, and more relevantly, the very title of the provision is somehow equivocal. The term '*giacimenti* '(deposits) in the Italian language usually refers to reserves of oil, gold, or other precious and economically valuable materials. It was in fact part of a growing perception of cultural heritage as 'Italy's Oil',[47] triggering a vicious circle around the creation of a mysterious/sensationalist aura surrounding it. As Salvatore Settis correctly suggests, "labels matter", and unfortunately labels such as 'deposits' or 'oil' have the defect of creating a public opinion where cultural heritage is wrongly equated to a purely economic asset.[48]

---

44 The restoration took place in the period 1975–1980 at the Opificio delle Pietre Dure in Florence. Once the first restoration was concluded, the statues were taken on a traveling exhibition in Florence (1980–1981), in Rome (1981) and in Reggio Calabria (1981 onwards). They were again studied and restored by the Istituto Centrale per il Restauro (Rome) with the restorers of the responsible Soprintendenza from 1992 to 1995, and finally in 2009. The collaborative relationship between the two Institutions for the conservation of these two statues is still active.

45 Gianfrotta *op cit* n. 28, p. 16.

46 Gianfrotta *op cit* n. 28, p. 17.

47 The first use of the term 'Italy's Oil' has been attributed to a Minister of the Republic. A. Paolucci 'Prefazione' in V. Baldacci *Il Sistema dei Beni Culturali in Italia* (Giunti 2004), p. 10; S. Settis *Italia S.p.A.: L'assalto al patrimonio culturale* (Einaudi 2007), p. 35; A. Borchi 'Oil, gold, stones: cultural value in Italian cultural policy' (2019) 9 *Arts and the Market* 1.

48 Settis *op cit* n. 5, p. 53.

In 1986, the Servizio Tecnico per l'Archeologica Subacquea[49] (the STAS) was created within the Ministry, along the lines of the Superintendency imagined in the draft law of 1975, taking over from the Centro per l'Archeologia Sottomarina of Albenga, established by Nino Lamboglia.[50] In 1992 and 1993, the archaeologists and technicians of the STAS were officially authorised to undertake underwater archaeological research by a Decree of the then Minister of Cultural Heritage.[51]

The intention was to provide technical support to the local Superintendencies on practical matters relating to UCH, while they were to maintain the direction of protection and management of UCH. In the absence of sufficient specialised personnel in the Superintendencies, protection and research activities in Italy were carried out intermittently and not always according to common best practices. The activities were often contracted out to external archaeologists and private underwater archaeological companies that operated under the control of the Superintendencies. Although included in the Directorate General for Archaeology, the STAS has not been able to influence the planning and national coordination for underwater archaeology within the Ministry. Also, for this reason the STAS was harshly criticised by some for its approach.[52] Since the mid-1990s the Ministry of Cultural Heritage has preferred to decentralise the activities in this field, establishing underwater archaeology units within each of the various Superintendencies located in Italian territory. In 1996, the Ministry organised two training courses for its personnel to create a group that could operate underwater. One theoretical and practical course in underwater archaeology was organised by the STAS. The course was directed at public sector employees, such as archaeologists, architects, technicians, and custodians;[53] the training in the water was held by the diving units of the Fire Fighters and Carabinieri. A second course, which again reflected both theoretical and practical components, was organised by the Istituto Centrale per il Restauro (the ICR),[54] addressed to archaeologists, technicians, and restorers.[55] As a result, about 100 officers and technicians of the Ministry obtained a diving

49 Technical Section for Underwater Archaeology.
50 Petriaggi *op cit* n. 2, p. 41.
51 R. Petriaggi and B. Davidde Petriaggi, *Archeologia sott'acqua. Teoria e pratica* (Fabrizio Serra Editore 2015), pp. 56–58.
52 Gianfrotta *op cit* n. 28.
53 This limitation has caused considerable controversy.
54 Central Institute for Restoration. The ICR is one of the four institutes of excellence in Italy, renown internationally for its expertise in proactive protection, preservation, and conservation of CH.
55 Gianfrotta *op cit* n. 28.

certification and, following a Decree of the General Director, were authorised to operate underwater activities directed at UCH.

Between 1996 and 1997, underwater archaeological units have been established within the local Superintendencies and the ICR, under the direction, when present, of an underwater archaeologist. STAS continues to exist within the General Directorate of the Ministry under the new name of Sezione di Archeologia Subacquea (the SAS).[56] Thanks to targeted funding, during 2004 and 2011 the SAS organised and realised the 'Archeomar Project', focused on surveying and creating an archaeological catalogue of UCH sites along the coasts of the Basilicata, Campania, Calabria and Publica regions. Some years later, the survey was extended to the regions of Lazio and Toscana.[57] After the retirement of its director in 2010, the activities of the SAS ceased. Ever since, activities have been continued at a peripheral level, by local and regional Superintendencies, and at a national and international level by the ICR.

Apart from being disjointed and lacking a strategic vision, the measures taken had a further negative outcome by creating a protean approach to UCH. Many Superintendencies, for instance, established units for underwater archaeology with well-trained personnel, while others either did not establish such units at all or, if they did, they were devoid of trained personnel. As a final consequence, the activity in this field has long been left to good intentions, individual passion, and scientific and technical capabilities, without any overall structured planning. Furthermore, the personnel hired during this reforming period are now retiring. Inevitably, their jobs are becoming vacant, although with no identifiable structural plan on the horizon to replace these lost competences within governmental structures.

In 2018, the Direzione Generale Archeologia Belle Arti e Paesaggio (the General Directorate for Archaeology, Fine Arts and Landscape) of the Ministry of Cultural Heritage and Activities, felt the need to create a central coordinating role once again. This role was assigned to the Istituto Centrale per l'Archeologia,[58] with its main duties being to deal with the cataloguing of national UCH and to manage the funds granted by the General Directorate to the projects proposed by the local Superintendencies.

---

56 Underwater Archaeology Section.

57 C. Mocchegiani Carpano *et al.*, 'Un futuro per l'archeologia subacquea italiana; Il progetto Archeomar; Nuove tecnologie per la tutela del patrimonio archeologica sommerso' (2004) *Notiziario: Ministero per i beni e le attività culturali*, 19, 74–76.

58 Central Institute for Archaeology.

On a day-by-day basis since the establishment of a specific Ministry in 1975, cultural heritage has been managed within a pyramid system. Several reforms[59] followed, until in 2021 the Ministry of Cultural Heritage and Activities was transformed into the Ministry of Culture. The change was made in order to enable more coherent and comprehensive institutional activities.[60] The pyramid structure of the Ministry places the Minister at the top, playing a generic political and managerial role, providing a common direction based on the laws of the State and his own decrees. At the base are the local Superintendencies, distributed across Italian territory, enforcing the laws and management measures under the political guidance of the Ministry, providing research permits, and overseeing the application of the requirements of the law. Between these two extremes are a series of intermediate offices (i.e., General Directorates) which provide directives in their specific fields of competence.[61] The monitoring of action against disturbance, pillaging and trafficking of UCH is mostly done by the naval and aerial units of the policing forces.

Within the Ministry, a separate group is represented by the Nucleo per gli Interventi di Archeologia Subacquea (the Underwater Archaeology Unit, NIAS), established in 1997 within the ICR, which in addition to collaborating with the Superintendencies on specific case studies, has carried out autonomous and innovative projects experimenting with methodologies, materials and techniques for the conservation and restoration of recovered and *in situ* UCH. Additionally, the NIAS also provides training activities for underwater conservators.[62]

A fundamental role in the fight against crimes against cultural heritage, including UCH, is played by the Comando Carabinieri Tutela Patrimonio Culturale (the Command).[63] This was established in 1969, thus preceding by one year the UNESCO Convention 1970 on the Means of Prohibiting and Preventing the Illicit Import, Export and Transfer of Ownership of Cultural Property,[64]

59 Since 1975, there have been several reforms, the last being in 2021. For further information, including the relevant legislation, see <https://www.beniculturali.it/ministero>.

60 Decreto Legge 1 marzo 2021, n. 22, Art. 6.1. Available at: <https://www.normattiva.it/uri-res/N2Ls?urn:nir:stato:decreto.legge:2021;22~art10>.

61 See the interactive organisation chart of the Ministry at: <https://media.beniculturali.it/mibac/files/boards/be78e33bc8ca0c99bff70aa174035096/PDF/2022/organigramma2021_navigabile.pdf>.

62 For more information on the NIAS and its innovative projects see: <http://www.icr.beniculturali.it/pagina.cfm?usz=2&uid=171&umn=74&smn=102>; Petriaggi and Davidde Petriaggi *op cit* n. 51 pp. 251–264.

63 Command for the Protection of Cultural Heritage within the Carabinieri armed force.

64 823 UNTS 231.

which, among other things, invited Member States to take appropriate measures to prevent the illicit trafficking of cultural heritage, encourage the recovery of stolen artefacts, as well as to establish a specific service for these purposes. The Command, functionally operating within the Ministry of Culture as an Office of direct collaboration with the Minister, carries out tasks relating to the safety and protection of the national cultural heritage through the prevention and repression of violations to the relevant legislation. Diving units of the Carabinieri operate within the Command, carrying out their activities for the protection of UCH and directly collaborating with the National Superintendency, the territorial Superintendencies and the NIAS during their respective activities.

This type of protection was initially entrusted to the Command by a ministerial decree in 1992 and the pre-eminent role of the Carabinieri was subsequently confirmed in 2006.[65] Ever since, the Command has functioned as a hub for other policing authorities concerning information gathering and analysis in the frame of cultural heritage protection. In terms of ordinances to protect UCH *in situ*, by preventing navigation, fishing, diving, and other hazardous activities, Port Authorities take the lead role if requested by the National Superintendency or territorial Superintendencies.

4 Recent Developments in the UCH Management Structure

Following a promising start in the 1950s–1960s, Italian underwater archaeology has suffered a series of setbacks since the 1970s. In Italy, with the many problems and lack of good decision-making at the political level, the development and implementation of underwater archaeological research, protection and the preservation of UCH have until now been carried out with ups and downs. Despite this, it has not prevented the realisation of high quality scientific archaeological research, both of conservation and enhancement *in situ*. Over the years personalities and projects have distinguished themselves, in turn inspiring the international scientific community.

However, despite the role played by the Italian delegation in the formulation of the 2001 Convention, the concepts and best practices developed therein have been slow to find proper fulfilment within the Italian system. In addition to the issues described in this chapter, several others have been

65 Decreto del Ministro dell'Interno, 28 aprile 2006. Available at: <https://www1.interno.gov.it/mininterno/site/it/sezioni/servizi/old_servizi/legislazione/polizia/legislazione_769.html>.

identified elsewhere that jeopardise the fulfilment of the 2001 Convention's vision. In particular, the "governmental decentralizing administrative actions, put forward by" the Constitutional Reform in 2001,[66] created tensions in the collaborative scheme between central and local government bodies. In addition, some directives issued by the General Directorate of the Ministry of Cultural Heritage, have created tensions regarding collaboration and cooperation between the Ministry and universities in underwater archaeological research.[67] Furthermore, although the professionalism required to produce "activities directed at underwater cultural heritage", contemplated by Rules 22 and 23 of the Annex to the 2001 Convention, has now been recognised,[68] the measures taken during the 1990s, and the inability to create specific university education programmes in this field, remain a concern.[69]

Notwithstanding the limitations discussed above, the new millennium has also brought with it some interesting advancements in the field. Since 2004, thanks to the special political-administrative autonomy it enjoys,[70] Sicily has been the only Italian Region to establish a Superintendency of the Sea (SopMare), operating solely on Sicilian territory, dealing with the protection and study of UCH and also that of biodiversity and the marine environment in general. It was conceived by taking inspiration from the Greek Ephorate for underwater archaeology and has been able to activate numerous projects and collaborations. Amongst its achievements are establishment of a catalogue of UCH sites in Sicilian waters; a consolidated system of underwater trails in several locations around mainland Sicily and its small islands; and the development and testing of new technologies for, and approaches to, activities directed at UCH. Additionally, several collaborations have allowed SopMare to undertake projects which otherwise, with the limited capacity and funds available, may have been impossible. However, the most relevant achievement has been to act as a precedent and inspiration for the Italian underwater

66 M. Secci, P.G. Spanu, 'Critique of Practical Archaeology: Underwater Cultural Heritage and Best Practices' (2015) 10 *Journal of Maritime Archaeology* 1, p. 38.

67 ibid p. 39.

68 Legge 22 luglio 2014, n. 110. The law amended the *Codice* to include definitions of CH professions, as well as to establish national lists of experts. To be included in the list, each CH expert must hold a set of titles and skills (according to their career stage, experience, and ability to direct fieldwork). Superintendencies, institutions, and the private sector can draw from these lists whenever the necessity arises.

69 Secci, Spanu op cit n. 66, p. 40.

70 Four other Italian Regions enjoy an autonomous status which allows them to undertake legislative and administrative actions in specific fields, which can be supplementary and complementary to the State legislation but never in conflict.

archaeology sector. The hope is that the vision that informs SopMare can be carried forward.

Probably inspired by the Sicilian experience, and following the first attempt in 1975, new efforts were made to establish a National Superintendency for Underwater Archaeology, along the lines of SopMare. Two draft laws were submitted to Parliament in 2009[71] and 2013.[72] The former proposed to establish a National Superintendency within the central Ministry in Rome, while two technical offices would have operated in Venice and Orbetello. The former would have had competence in the Northern and Adriatic regions, and the latter competence in the Tyrrhenian, Liguria, and Sardinia regions. The 2013 proposal aimed at establishing an Istituto Centrale per l'Archeologia Subacquea (Central Institute for Underwater Archaeology, ICAS) within the central Ministry in Rome, and four local offices (Venice, Genoa and Cagliari, Rome, and Isola di Capo Rizzuto). Both proposals envisioned the central and local offices having administrative and financial independence, trained personnel, and competences over a specific and defined territory. As often occurs in Italy, following changes in the political landscape, both draft laws were abandoned.

In 2019, a specific decree (the Decree)[73] established the Soprintendenza Nazionale per il patrimonio culturale subacqueo (the National Superintendency).[74] The creation of this institute has finally brought Italy in line with other countries of the Mediterranean basin, which have been equipped with this type of body for decades.[75] Article 37 of the Decree stresses the obligations of the newly established body towards the protection, management, and

71 Proposta di Legge, 18 marzo 2009, n. 2302. Available at: <http://documenti.camera.it/_dati/leg16/lavori/stampati/pdf/16PDL0023550.pdf>, and: <https://leg16.camera.it/126?tab=&leg=16&idDocumento=2302&sede=&tipo=>.

72 Proposta di Legge, 21 marzo 2013, n. 470. Available at: <http://documenti.camera.it/_dati/leg17/lavori/stampati/pdf/17PDL0002500.pdf> and: <https://www.camera.it/leg17/126?tab=2&leg=17&idDocumento=470&sede=&tipo=>.

73 169/2019 DPCM.

74 National Superintendency for the Underwater Cultural Heritage. Decreto del Presidente del Consigli dei Ministri (DPCM), 2 dicembre 2019, n. 169. Available at: <https://www.normattiva.it/uri-res/N2Ls?urn:nir:stato:decreto.del.presidente.del.consiglio.dei.ministri:2019-12-02;169!vig=>. For more information, please visit the institutional website of the Superintendency at: <https://cultura.gov.it/ente/soprintendenza-nazionale-per-il-patrimonio-culturale-subacqueo>.

75 The draft Law 2302/2009 already criticised the backwardness of the Italian system in this sector, compared to neighbouring countries such as France (Départment des recherches archaéologiques subaquatiques et sous-marines – DRASSM), Spain (Museo Nacional de Arqueología Subacuática – ARQVA), Portugal (Centro Nacional de Arqueologia Náutica e Subaquática – CNANS), Greece (Εφορεία Εναλίων Αρχαιοτήτων), and finally Croatia (M Međunarodni centar za podvodnu arheologiju u Zadru – ICUA).

promotion of UCH in accordance with what is stated in Article 94 of the *Codice* and in Law 157/2009, i.e., the 2001 Convention ratification law. To achieve these aims, Article 37.1 of the Decree provides that the National Superintendency would operate through a central office in Taranto, with operational offices in Naples and Venice, with additional offices that may be identified with subsequent regulatory measures, according to Article 37.3 (in May 2023 an operational Office was established in the city of Olbia-Sassari).

In determining the activities and functions of the new National Superintendency, Article 37 makes express reference to both Article 94 of the *Codice* and the 2001 Convention.[76] Hence, it appears that the new institution is primarily focused upon the protection, management, and promotion of UCH discovered in or on the seafloor between 12 and 24 nautical miles from the baseline of the territorial waters (ex-Article 94, *Codice*), that is the Archaeological CZ. Furthermore, the Decree expressly attributes the functions deriving from Law 157/2009, which were previously assigned to the Ministry of Culture (MiC), to the National Superintendency.

The 2001 Convention established the responsibilities of the Member States for the proactive and sound protection of UCH over the limits of national jurisdiction, i.e., territorial waters. However, the tenor of some of the norms contained within it go beyond strict jurisdictional aspects, as they can be seen as provisions for the development of best practice. This is the clear case, for instance, with the Rules Concerning Activities Directed at Underwater Cultural Heritage annexed to the 2001 Convention, which state the general principles informing any activity for the protection of UCH, including those within the 12 nautical mile limit and internal waters.

In that connection, the National Superintendency was established precisely in accordance with the objective of Article 22 of the 2001 Convention, where it is stated that:

> In order to ensure the proper implementation of this Convention, States Parties shall establish competent authorities or reinforce the existing ones where appropriate, with the aim of providing for the establishment, maintenance and updating of an inventory of underwater cultural heritage, the effective protection, conservation, presentation and management of underwater cultural heritage, as well as research and education.

It is clear that Article 37 of the Decree, by attributing the competences for the execution of the 2001 Convention to the National Superintendency, is intended

76 Specifically, to the ratification law, Law 157/2009.

to entrust it with the delicate task of standardising every activity in the UCH field according to the 2001 Convention's principles. This would include tasks focused on the inventory and protection of UCH, not only in the context of the so-called Archaeological CZ, but also within 12 nautical miles from the coast or in inland waters. It is no coincidence that the last part of Article 37.1 of the Decree, states that the activities of the National Superintendency must be developed in connection with "the [territorial] Superintendencies for Archaeology, Fine Arts and Landscape", the offices tasked with the protection of the UCH in territorial waters. Pending the adoption of the implementation decrees referred to in Article 33 of the Decree, and aiming to harmonise the methods and procedures employed in the UCH field, a General Direction issued by the MiC has instructed the National Superintendent to, *inter alia*, coordinate the following activities that will be carried out in collaboration with the central and peripheral offices of the MiC:[77] first, to complete a national survey, catalogue and georeferencing for UCH;[78] second, to produce a set of guidelines for the standardisation of procedures in the field of UCH protection; third, to ensure the updating of professional diving training for ministerial personnel; and, finally, according to the current legislation on safety at work, develop uniform implementation procedures for the underwater activities conducted by MiC officers and technicians.

Competence is reaffirmed by a Circular on permits for archaeological research and excavations. The National Superintendency gives its expert opinion on all underwater archaeological research and excavations conducted by personnel in all the Offices of the Ministry (Superintendencies, Archaeological Parks, Regional Museum Directorates). For archaeological research and excavation permits requested by universities and research institutes within the national territory, permits are assessed and granted by a joint decision of the National Superintendency and the other territorial bodies that have competency for the area where the activities will be undertaken.

Finally, in a communication to the Ministry of Foreign Affairs and International Cooperation and the Permanent Representation of Italy to UNESCO,[79] the Secretary General of the MiC identified the National Superintendency as the competent body of the Ministry for the management and coordination at

77 Circular 08 February 2021, No. 7.

78 UCH Data Cards are part of the MiC National Cataloguing Systems 'Vincoli in Rete', available at: <http://vincoliinrete.beniculturali.it/VincoliInRete/vir/utente/login> and the 'Carta del Rischio', available at: <http://www.cartadelrischio.beniculturali.it/>.

79 Circular 20 January 2022, No. 1490, registered by the National Superintendency offices on 21 January 2022, No. 511.

a national level of activities directed at the protection, management, and promotion of UCH.[80] The 2024 organisation of the Italian Ministry of Culture confirms the competences on UCH of the National Superintendency based in Taranto while the competences on terrestrial CH have been transferred to the newly established Superintendency of Archaeology, Fine Arts and Landscape for the provinces of Brindisi, Lecce and Taranto.[81]

The establishment of the National Superintendency has opened a new page in the history of underwater archaeology in Italy. During its first year of activity, it activated a series of initiatives as part of a strategic programme focusing on three macro-areas: national UCH; the cultural heritage of Taranto and its territory; and international projects. Within this three-pillar scheme, the initiatives have been designed in respect of specific areas, including: research; terrestrial and underwater site monitoring (including through the implementation of new technologies); protection and preservation; the management and maintenance of archaeological areas and parks; the promotion of site accessibility (both land and underwater); and finally, the development of public access programmes.

The operational scenarios of the National Superintendency are strictly connected with the numerous development activities related to the Piano Nazionale di Ripresa e Resilienza (National Recovery and Resilience Plan, PNRR).[82] They also connect to maritime spatial management plans,[83] the implications of the ever-increasing dynamism of offshore exploration and exploitation of marine resources, and the vulnerability of coastal landscapes due to climate change. Furthermore, on a practical level, they include the cataloguing of UCH sites lying in territorial waters; the fight against looting and the consequent

80 A UNESCO Office operates within the Service II of the Secretariat General of the MiC. It is the Italian Office responsible for coordinating European and International activities affecting UCH in the country. It also coordinates the relationship with UNESCO on matters relating to the implementation and representation mechanisms of the 2001 Convention.

81 Decreto del Presidente del Consiglio dei ministri 15 marzo 2024, n. 57, and the Decreto ministeriale 05 settembre 2024, n. 270

82 For further information, see: <https://italiadomani.gov.it/it/home.html>. The PNRR aligns with the pillars set out by the Next Generation EU recovery plan: <https://europa.eu/next-generation-eu/index_en>.

83 The cataloguing activities of national UCH are included in the inter-ministerial project 'Planning of the maritime space' established pursuant to Legislative Decree 17 October 2016, n.201 implementing Directive 2014/89/EU OJ L2014 257/135. The Superintendent of the National Superintendency was in fact a member of the Technical Committee of the inter-ministerial project 'Maritime Spatial Planning' established at the Ministry of Infrastructure and Transport. In addition to participating in planning meetings, the National Superintendency was responsible for coordinating the cataloguing activities of the UCH sites in connection with the territorial Superintendencies and the Regions and their inclusion in the GIS, which is under construction. To date, about 1200 UCH sites have been recorded.

illicit trafficking of archaeological artefacts found underwater; and, finally, cooperation through the exchange of information and multilateral agreements with other countries of the Mediterranean basin.

The exploitation of new technologies, such as the 'internet of underwater things',[84] for the monitoring and enhancement of UCH and the need for highly specialised personnel have become essential factors in the attempt to expand the current state of scientific knowledge. In this sense, by implementing high-profile collaborations, the National Superintendency will undertake experiments with new tools and technologies, placing a focus on the development of good (and best) practices to share with the global scientific community. In this connection there are already active framework agreements in place with the ISPRA,[85] the DRASSM,[86] the Centre Camille Julian,[87] and universities and local government in the Region of Puglia.

The development of adequate tools and a solid technical-operational expertise must connect to new forms of cultural growth based on effective communication and promotion. In response to the exhortations of the 2001 Convention, which strongly advocates *in situ* preservation and public access, the MiC must find sustainable ways to reach more of the general public. This orientation, perhaps more than others makes the 2001 Convention a far-sighted and innovative regulatory device, requires the organisation of tools, infrastructures, and procedures for evaluating archaeological risk. To this end, adequate predictive models must be developed and functionally connected. These include models to assess the degradation of underwater movable and immovable artefacts and the *in situ* conservation and restoration requirements according to methodologies that, in Italy, have been developed as part of the 'Restoring Underwater' project conceived by Roberto Petriaggi of the Central Institute for Restoration.[88] Hence there is a need to promote conservation, public education and awareness, and responsible use directly *in situ* by encouraging, as stated in the 2001 Convention, a responsible and non-intrusive access to UCH.[89]

---

84 M. C. Domingo, 'An overview of the internet of underwater things' (2012) 35 *Journal of Network and Computer Applications* 6; R. A. Khalil *et al.* 'Toward the internet of underwater things: Recent developments and future challenges' (2020) 10 *IEEE Consumer Electronics Magazine* 6; S. A. H. Mohsan *et al.* 'Towards the internet of underwater things: a comprehensive survey' (2022) *Earth Science Informatics*.

85 Istituto Superiore per la Protezione e la Ricerca Ambientale: <https://www.isprambiente.gov.it/it>.

86 Département des recherches archéologiques subaquatiques et sous-marines: <https://archeologie.culture.fr/fr/drassm>.

87 Centre Camille Jullian:< https://ccj.cnrs.fr/>.

88 Petriaggi and Davidde Petriaggi *op. cit.* n. 51 pp. 251–264.

89 See for example Article 2.10; Rule 7 of the Annex.

The 'BlueMed' and 'BlueMed PLUS' projects adopt this concept.[90] Their aim is to share good practice for the design and management of innovative underwater archaeological trails. These trails use both innovative methods for *in situ* protection and preservation and innovative technologies for virtual access, allowing the non-diving public to access otherwise remote and inaccessible UCH sites. The 'BlueMed' multidisciplinary model for the management and sustainable promotion of UCH has been tested in Italy, Greece, and Croatia. The follow-up 'BlueMed Plus' project is led by the University of Calabria, with the National Superintendency an associated partner, and will transfer knowledge to two more countries, Montenegro and Albania. The objective is to build the capacity of partner countries to manage their UCH through the creation of knowledge and awareness centres in their territories, thus promoting new destinations as resources for the sustainable development of coastal tourism. The National Superintendency is also a partner of the 'CREAMARE' project, which aims to create a transnational and cross-sectoral collaboration framework in which cultural organisations, scientific/research bodies, creative professionals, and technology experts co-produce Creative Commons applications and media content to communicate, disseminate and promote UCH.

The National Superintendency has also launched the 'Amphitrite' project, which follows on from innovative methodologies already developed by Barbara Davidde during the ICR MUSAS Project. This project established a virtual museum, two underwater diving trails within the Archaeological Park of Submerged Baiae,[91] with another at the Roman Harbour of Egnatia, all enhanced using acoustic sensors and tablets to enrich the visitor experience.[92] The 'Amphitrite' project includes the recording, cataloguing and georeferencing of underwater archaeological sites and recording of GIS data for the MiC; underwater archaeological excavations and *in situ* restoration of selected archaeological sites; and the creation of new underwater archaeological trails open to the public, which will connect submerged and semi-submerged sites with nearby terrestrial cultural locations, such as archaeological sites and museums. Additionally, digital content will be shared through a web portal and mobile applications guiding visitors through integrated tours. As a result of the 'internet of underwater things', the created tours will become real digital parks. This represents an extremely innovative model to make Italian

90 BlueMed PLUS – Capitalisation by transferring to new Mediterranean territories the BlueMed multidisciplinary model for sustainable and responsible coastal tourism development. Available at: <https://bluemed.interreg-med.eu/>.

91 The Pisoni's Villa and the Nympheum of Punta dell'Epitaffio.

92 For further info, see: <https://www.progettomusas.eu/>.

UCH accessible, placing Italy as a leader in this sector. The outcomes of the 'Amphitrite' project encourage sustainable underwater cultural tourism while allowing the assessment of the state of conservation and the vulnerability of UCH through its continuous monitoring. Digital Parks will be implemented for the Marine Protected Areas in Crotone (Calabria), Isole Tremiti (Puglia), Capo Testa –Punta Falcone (Sardegna) and Portofino (Liguria), creating a unique, curated and innovative underwater visitor system.

Actions representing strategic sectors of the National Superintendency's activity also include deep-sea research and exploration and the commitment to international cooperation. The boundless potential of underwater archaeology in furthering the understanding of the past is illustrated by a recent study conducted by the National Superintendency on Corinthian ceramic artefacts. This was on the cargo of an early-archaic shipwreck, discovered off the Strait of Otranto, dated within the early decades of the seventh century B.C and recovered from the considerable depth of 780 metres. The site was discovered during a well-conducted and thorough archaeological impact assessment prior to the works for the Trans Adriatic Pipeline (TAP), a gas pipeline that will bring natural gas from Azerbaijan to Europe.[93]

Although the site represents a challenge due to the depth, it is also of exceptional historical and archaeological significance because it could contribute to a greater understanding of sea trade at the dawn of Magna Graecia. The National Superintendency and TAP AG have signed a donation and funding agreement for the restoration, scientific study, analysis and promotion of the recovered artefacts through an exhibition and a publication.[94] The MiC has also granted funding for the recovery, study and restoration of the entire cargo.

The National Superintendency participates with its own funds and scientific personnel in a three-year cooperation project between the Scuola Archeologica Italiana di Atene,[95] the Εφορεία Εναλίων Αρχαιοτήτων[96] and the Εφορεία Αρχαιοτήτων Λέσβου[97] to produce underwater archeological research on the Greek island of Lemnos. The project aims to identify ancient maritime sites and shipwrecks, understand their topography and contexts, as well as the

93 See <https://archaeonewsnet.com/2021/10/corinthian-shipwreck-from-7th-century.html> and B. Davidde Petriaggi (ed.), *Recuperati dagli Abissi. Il relitto alto arcaico del Canale d'Otranto* (Roma, Gangemi Editore 2023).

94 The publication of the first assessment and finds recovery is currently in process. For a brief overview, see <https://www.patrimoniosubacqueo.it/il-relitto-alto-arcaico-del-canale-di-otranto/>.

95 Italian Archaeological School in Athens.

96 Greek Ephorate of Underwater Antiquities.

97 Ephorate of Antiquities of Lesbos.

construction techniques of the emerged and submerged structures, through the implementation of systematic visual and remote sensing surveys.

Finally, Italian commitment has been key to the establishment of the first multi-lateral cooperation process coordinated by Tunisia, under the auspices of UNESCO. The 'Multilateral Underwater Archaeological Mission Under the Framework of UNESCO in the Skerki Bank and the Sicilian Channel' sees the collaboration of eight Mediterranean countries towards the protection of UCH in international waters.[98]

5 Conclusions: a Vision for the Future

The beginning of the millennium has witnessed a renewed political interest in UCH, both at regional and national level. Several rearrangements of the Italian management system, and the inclusion of UCH within legislative and administrative structures have already improved and will continue to significantly improve the general approach in this field.[99] The Sicilian and international collaborations have paved the way. With the ratification of the 2001 Convention, the legislature has finally recognised the value of this heritage, while there has been a much-needed recognition of the professionalism required to carry out archaeological research.[100] The establishment of the National Superintendency is potentially bound to act as a promoter of a uniform approach towards this type of heritage. These developments appear to build the capacity of the management system, in line with what is proposed by the 2001 Convention, which, as has been suggested has played some role in such developments.[101]

The issues that formerly characterised Italian UCH management have only recently been dealt with through a series of legislative measures. For example, the ratification of the 2001 Convention introduces within the Italian legal system a coherent set of rules for the protection of UCH. In addition, a law which provides clear parameters for the definition of professional underwater archaeologist acts in a complementary fashion. Finally, the establishment of

98 For more information, see: <https://www.unesco.org/sites/default/files/medias/fichiers/2022/09/Skerki%20Bank%20Fact%20Sheet%20ENGLISH.pdf>.

99 R. F. MacKintosh, *The 2001 UNESCO convention on the protection of the underwater cultural heritage: implementation and effectiveness* (Unpublished Doctoral dissertation, University of Southampton 2018).

100 Law 110/2014.

101 MacKintosh *op cit* n. 98.

a central institution fully devoted to UCH, which can favour a coherent and organic development of the discipline at national level, completes the picture.

As suggested elsewhere,[102] central government, through the legislature and the National Superintendency, must play a major coordinative role to develop a coherent, proactive, and uniform approach to UCH. Similarly, the actors and stakeholders involved should be fully recognised by the central government and provided with the ability to contribute proactively to the research and promotion of this heritage. A system of constructive collaboration between these stakeholders, such as the Ministry, Universities, cultural Institutions, and other actors, must be clearly formalised to profit from all the positive forces that the national disciplinary framework yields.[103]

This chapter has underlined how Italy started off on the right footing in the field of protection, research, and enhancement of UCH. Unfortunately, this 'lightning start' was not followed by a political will that could design a complex infrastructure (both legislative and institutional) capable of managing this heritage. The path had been traced by Lamboglia, and his contributions in the field of UCH management speak for themselves. Particularly illuminating is his reference to the "system of our statal administration", offering a subtle critique in respect of the complicated Italian bureaucratic machine.[104] In 1959, in a letter to the then Director General of Antiquities and Fine Arts, he warned of the "predicted destiny" of the ship *Daino*, equipped shortly before and given to the CSAS to use, if managed by the extremely bureaucratic statal system.[105] This is the same bureaucratic system that has been slow and sometimes unwilling to recognise the national relevance of the UCH field. Evidence of this 'bureaucratic beast' is seen in the numerous attempts made over the years to reform both the legislation on the subject and the governance structure for this heritage: arguably these have fallen on deaf ears. Something has changed in the last two decades, however. It is difficult to sustain the argument that the 2001 Convention played no role in this long-awaited awakening. We believe that it has provided opportunities and substance for reflection, it has applied peer pressure, and has finally facilitated the elaboration and application of the changes that have occurred.

---

102 Secci, Spanu *op cit* n. 68; M. Secci, M. Stefanile '"Sailing heavy weather". Underwater Cultural Heritage Management in Italy' in *Proceedings of the 5th International Congress of Underwater Archaeology. A Heritage for Mankind* (Ministero de Educacion, Cultura y Deporte 2016).

103 Secci, Spanu *op cit* n. 68.

104 Pallares *op cit* n. 1, p. 29; Petriaggi *op cit* n. 2, p. 40.

105 Petriaggi Op cit n. 2, p. 40.

Of course, the Italian UCH management system is not perfect, far from it, but the infrastructures, both conceptual and physical, are now in place. It would be a desirable reform for universities to be allowed to introduce specific courses or programmes in maritime and underwater archaeology to create a new generation of scholars and experts. Furthermore, the new National Superintendency will take charge to create a whole series of guidelines, best practices and regulations that can change the approach to UCH. This will be done with the involvement and consultation of all stakeholders, including scholars, experts, public and private stakeholders, amongst others.

The episodic and inorganic regulatory action that characterised this sector in the last century cannot be the answer to the internationally recognised problems and hazards that UCH faces. Without proper actions, management structure, funding and trained personnel, the extent of Italian waters is such that UCH therein cannot be properly guarded, let alone researched and studied. Until now, the activities in the field of underwater archaeological research and UCH management have been too often left to personal commitment, when this was possible, while cooperation and collaboration, both on a national and international basis, has occasionally been established only when the sensibility and available network of individual contacts permitted. The result of this situation was a waste of potential that could have been harnessed more proactively and proficiently in a formalised framework.

The widespread presence of archaeological evidence submerged in inland waters and in the sea is to be considered, as the Preamble of the 2001 Convention clearly states, "an integral part of the cultural heritage of humanity and a particularly important element in the history of peoples, nations". For these reasons, the States adhering to the 2001 Convention have not just the faculty but the obligation to protect and preserve this heritage and to pass it on intact to future generations. UCH, by virtue of the strong symbolic and evocative charge it bears, may constitute a privileged tool assisting nations to weave relationships of brotherhood: reflective of the universal and participatory perspective of UNESCO. This heritage may be a formidable inclusive factor and an instrument of dialogue between communities living along both the shores of the Mediterranean, and other seas. Knowing, conserving, protecting, and passing on to future generations this immense heritage, which is a cultural heritage for the whole of humanity, is a moral duty. Underwater archaeology opens new research perspectives that we hope will generally develop for the country and can offer the new generations of Europe and the world stimulating opportunities for knowledge, research, and job opportunities.

All websites last accessed February 2025.

Selected Bibliography

F. Pallares ,'Premessa ai manoscritti inediti di Nino Lamboglia' (2007) 4 *Archaeologia Maritima Mediterranea.*

R. Petriaggi, 'Nino Lambaglia, l'archeologia subacquea e la burocrazia: luci ed ombre di un rapporto tormentato' (2007) 4 *Archaeologia Maritima Mediterranea.*

R. Petriaggi and B. Davidde Petriaggi, *Archeologia sott'acqua. Teoria e pratica* (Fabrizio Serra Editore 2015).

M. Secci, 'Protection vs. Public Access: two concepts compared within the Italian underwater cultural heritage management system' (2011) 6 *Journal of Maritime Archaeology* 2.

M. Secci and P.G. Spanu, 'Critique of Practical Archaeology: Underwater Cultural Heritage and Best Practices' (2015) 10 *Journal of Maritime Archaeology* 1.

S. Settis, *Paesaggio Costituzione Cemento: La battaglia per l'ambiente contro il degrado civile* (Einaudi 2010).

CHAPTER 11

Japan

*Akifumi Iwabuchi**

1 Introduction

The Japanese Government currently has no national plan to ratify the UNESCO Convention on the Protection of the Underwater Cultural Heritage 2001 (the 2001 Convention).[1] In fact, as of 2022, no East Asian nation has ratified it, demonstrating little to no regional commitment. The 2001 Convention contains problematic issues, which East Asian nations appear unwilling to accept. These include the problem of ambiguity regarding the ownership of UCH, human remains as UCH, and the fundamental rule of preservation *in situ* against poor visibility in general within Asian waters, to name a few. For instance, at a Mongolian shipwreck site from the thirteenth century, located in western Japan, the water visibility is only a few metres at a depth of about 20 metres. In terms of *in situ* conservation in the context of poor water visibility, some believe that if wrecks are not completely or partially recovered it may become more difficult for scholars to study in detail a vessel's structure and/or its cargo. In addition, shipworm thrives in the warm Asian waters, which consume temporarily excavated wooden hulls left *in situ*.[2]

However, the most important external factor for the apparent unpopularity of the 2001 Convention is the fact that the Cold War has not yet ceased in Asia. Thus, in Asian waters, there has been considerable disagreement since 1945 concerning maritime national borders between a variety of nations, leaving them without demarcation, a situation that does not reflect the norms created by the United Nations Law of the Sea Convention (LOSC),[3] with which the

* Professor of Maritime Anthropology and Nautical Archaeology, Tokyo University of Marine Science and Technology.

1 2562 UNTS 1.

2 A. Iwabuchi, 'Risk and Problems Relating to Protecting and Researching Underwater Cultural Heritage in East and Southeast Asia' in A. Hafner, H. Öniz, L. Semaan and C. J. Underwood (eds.) *Heritage under Water at Risk: Threats, Challenges, Solutions* (ICOMOS, 2020) 23.

3 1833 UNTS 397.

DOI:10.1163/9789004510883_013

2001 Convention aligns regarding maritime boundaries. Since some Territorial Seas (TS) and/or Exclusive Economic Zones (EEZs) have not been precisely defined, many countries have been unable to legislate on the protection of UCH within them. In East Asia, ironically, it is Taiwan, which remains unaccepted as a member of both the United Nations and UNESCO, that upholds policies closest to the 2001 Convention, with adoption of the Underwater Cultural Heritage Preservation Act 2015, which are highly reflective of its ideas and principles of.[4] Japan ratified the LOSC in 1996, and subsequently enacted the Basic Act on Ocean Policy 2007, although this Act does not contain the terms 'culture', 'cultural property', or 'heritage' in any form.[5]

2 Act on Protection of Cultural Properties 1950, Revised 2021 (1950 Act)

Prior to the Second World War, Japan's legislation on cultural heritage was included in the Historic Sites, Places of Scenic Beauty, Natural Monuments Preservation Act 1919 (1919 Act),[6] the Act for the Preservation of National Treasures 1929 (1929 Act),[7] and the Act for the Preservation of Important Fine Arts 1933 (1933 Act).[8] According to the 1919 Act, some maritime archaeological sites were designated as Historic Sites. In 1921, Hakoishi Beach Buried Property in Kyoto prefecture became one of the first such Historic Sites. This site faces the Sea of Japan and was an international trading harbour built at the mouth of a river, active from prehistoric times until the medieval period. The most important excavated items are two Huo Quan coins from the Xin dynasty from A.D. 9

4 Law and Regulations Database of the Republic of China (Taiwan) 'Underwater Cultural Heritage Preservation Act' (2015), see <https://law.moj.gov.tw/ENG/LawClass/LawAll.aspx?pcode=H0170102>.

5 Japanese Law Translation 'Basic Act on Ocean Policy' (2007), see <https://www.japaneselawtranslation.go.jp/en/laws/view/3755>.

6 Ministry of Education, Culture, Sports, Science and Technology of Japan 'Historic Sites, Places of Scenic Beauty, or Natural Monuments Preservation Act' (1919), see <https://www.mext.go.jp/b_menu/hakusho/html/others/detail/1318165.htm>.

7 Ministry of Education, Culture, Sports, Science and Technology of Japan 'Act for the Preservation of National Treasures' (1929), see <https://www.mext.go.jp/b_menu/hakusho/html/others/detail/1318166.htm>.

8 Ministry of Education, Culture, Sports, Science and Technology of Japan 'Act for the Preservation of Important Fine Arts' (1933), see. <https://www.mext.go.jp/b_menu/hakusho/html/others/detail/1318167.htm>.

to 23.[9] The 1919, 1929, and 1933 Acts were consolidated into the 1950 Act[10] but nowhere does it contain any of the terms 'submerged site', 'underwater cultural heritage', or 'maritime cultural heritage'.

The 1950 Act classifies cultural properties into six categories: 'tangible cultural properties', 'intangible cultural properties', 'folk cultural properties', 'monuments', 'cultural landscape', and 'groups of historic buildings'.[11] The Agency for Cultural Affairs (ACA), an external bureau of the Ministry of Education, Culture, Sports, Science and Technology, designates important tangible cultural properties into several classes. These include 'Important Cultural Properties and National Treasures', which are more highly valued cultural properties, while cultural properties requiring preservation and proper usage are labelled as 'Registered Cultural Properties'.[12] The ACA also designates 'Important Intangible Cultural Properties', while it selects some as 'Intangible Cultural Properties Requiring Special Measures Such As the Creation of Records'. Additionally, the ACA designates important 'folk cultural properties' by reference to whether they are tangible or intangible, while it registers those particularly requiring preservation and proper usage, with some selected as 'Intangible Folk Cultural Properties Requiring Special Measures Such As the Creation of Records'. The ACA designates important monuments as 'Historic Sites', 'Places of Scenic Beauty', or 'Natural Monuments'. More important monuments are designated as 'Special Historic Site's, 'Special Places of Scenic Beauty', or 'Special Natural Monuments'. Where special measures are required, such monuments are classified as 'Registered Monuments'. Outstanding cultural landscapes are selected by the ACA as 'Important Cultural Landscapes' based on local governmental recommendations.

In addition to these categories, under the 1950 Act cultural properties and buried cultural properties are to be safeguarded via preservation techniques. The ACA specifies preservation techniques for cultural properties particularly requiring preservation as Selected Preservation Techniques.[13] 'Buried Cultural Properties' are defined as archaeological sites under the ground, including the seabed, and archaeological remains excavated from such sites.[14] However, not all remains are automatically classified as cultural property as soon as they are

9 Tango Kodai-no-Sato Museum, *Hakoishi Beach Buried Property and its Discoverers* (Tango, 2006) 3–34.

10 e-Gov 'Act on Protection of Cultural Properties' (1950), see <https://elaws.e-gov.go.jp/document?lawid=325AC0100000214>.

11 Respectively Chapters 3, 4, 5, 7, 8 and 9 of the 1950 Act.

12 Respectively Articles 27 and 57 of the 1950 Act.

13 Chapter 10 of the 1950 Act.

14 Chapter 6 of the 1950 Act.

excavated. If archaeological remains are found or excavated, the finder must notify and surrender the remains to the local police station nearest to the discovery within one week of the day of discovery, according to the Lost Property Act 2006.[15] Only when the Board of Education of the municipality in which the artefact was found designates them as cultural properties do they become cultural properties in law. In accordance with the Organization and Operation of Local Educational Administration Act 1956,[16] administration of the protection of Buried Cultural Properties is basically under the control of Boards of Education belonging to their municipal governments, such as cities, towns, or villages. Each municipal Board of Education could designate remains as cultural properties, but it could also register archaeological sites as 'Well-Known Places Containing Buried Cultural Properties' (WPCBCP). As Japan has an extensive history, nearly 500,000 WPCBCP have been registered by municipal Boards of Education. Since the number of places containing Buried Cultural Properties in the Japanese archipelago is beyond any agency's ability to count, in 1988 the ACA notified a set of 'Principles for the Scope of Buried Cultural Properties' to all municipal Boards of Education: Buried Cultural Properties could be all buried artefacts before the medieval period (pre-1599); those buried in the early modern period (1600–1867), or buried artefacts from the modern period that are specially important (1868 – present).[17] The same time division is applied to 'Historic Sites', 'Places of Scenic Beauty', and' Natural Monuments'.

According to the 1950 Act, moreover, each prefecture, city, town, or village may promulgate its own ordinances and designation procedures for locally arising cultural property, with a range of specific labels attached.[18] Sometimes these precede 'Important Cultural Properties', 'Historic Sites', or 'Places of Scenic Beauty' within the edicts of the 1950 Act. For instance, the Sanya Shell Midden at Sodegaura City, Chiba prefecture, immediately in front of Tokyo Bay, was designated as a 'Sodegaura City Designated Monument' in 2000 by the Board of Education at Sodegaura City, as a 'Chiba Prefecture Designated Historic Site' in 2009 by the Board of Education of Chiba prefecture, and then as a 'Historic Site in 2017 by the ACA. This shell midden, estimated to be 2,300–4,000 years old, is horseshoe shaped, measuring 140 metres from east to west

15 e-Gov 'Lost Property Act' (2006), see <https://elaws.e-gov.go.jp/document?lawid=418AC0000000073>.
16 e-Gov 'Organization and Operation of Local Educational Administration Act' (1956), see <https://laws.e-gov.go.jp/law/331AC0000000162>.
17 ACA of Japan 'Principles for the Scope of Buried Cultural Properties' (1988), see <https://www.bunka.go.jp/seisaku/bunkazai/shokai/pdf/hokoku_03.pdf>.
18 Article 182 of the 1950 Act.

and 110 metres from south to north, from which numerous inshore and pelagic fish bones, as well as shells, stoneware, and earthenware, have been excavated.[19] On the other hand, there are cases of 'Historic Sites' being designated as such from the start. For example, the remains of the Mietsu Naval Dock at Saga City, Saga prefecture, was designated as a Historic Site in 2013 by the ACA and then in 2015 registered as a UNESCO World Cultural Heritage Site (a 'Site of Japan's Meiji Industrial Revolution'). The dock was opened in 1858, and consisted of three sections: a traditional dockyard, a modern dockyard including a dry dock, and a venue for naval drilling. In the dry dock, the oldest in existence in Japan, the country's first domestically built steamship was constructed and numerous materials for building ships, such as rivets, bolts, nuts, and ropes have been excavated from the site.[20]

Under the 1950 Act, the first Historic Site of UCH in Japan, Wagae-no-shima, was designated in 1968 by the ACA. This site is the ruin of a medieval port off Kamakura City, Kanagawa prefecture. In 1192, the Kamakura shogunate was established at the city, while Japanese emperors remained at the old capital city of Kyoto in western Japan. Although a large quantity of various goods started to be transported from western Japan and China to Kamakura by ship, the city itself had no adequate harbour; almost the entire coastline in front of Kamakura consists of sand beaches with shallow foreshore and shoreface areas. The Kamakura shogunate requested that a priest, who was an experienced civil engineer, construct Wagae-no-shima, which was completed in 1232. The port consisted of numerous large boulders spread over an offshore reef in front of the beaches. The priest had constructed a similar port in northern Kyushu, western Japan, although sadly its remains have been buried because of land filling, and the site is not classified. Miraculously the ruin of Wagae-no-shima still remains today, but there remain problems to be solved. On the beaches in front of it, a small number of signboards displaying information on this site are in place, but at low tide during the spring local beachcombers, as well as amateur archaeologists, collect finds, such as celadon ceramics from China and unglazed wares from western Japan, in violation of the 1950

19 Board of Education at Sodegaura City, *The Comprehensive Report of the Sanya Shell Midden: A Large Shell Midden during the End and the Last Jomon Periods Existed at the Southernmost Part of the Boso Peninsula* (Board of Education at Sodegaura City, 2016) 1–20.

20 M. Tabata, N. Yagi, J. Nishimoto and A. Ghaffar, 'Estimation of Places of Production of Porcelains of Unknown Origins Excavated at the Mietsu Naval Facility Site Based on Differences in the Solubility of Trace Metals during the Elutriation Process' (2021) 36 *Journal of Archaeological Science: Reports* 1.

Act.[21] This unfortunate situation has arisen because the Board of Education at Kamakura City has no management plan for this Historic Site. Since the Board of Education also has no underwater archaeologist, no survey has been done around Wagae-no-shima, where some Chinese and domestic shipwrecks may still exist.

The most famous UCH site, and the first underwater one to be discovered in Japan, is the Sone archaeological site in Nagano prefecture. In 1908, a local schoolteacher found two prehistoric flint arrowheads at the bottom of the shallow Lake Suwa. Archaeologists at the University of Tokyo started to survey the lake, but, as draining it was impossible at that time, they used iron rakes to drag out archaeological items. At first, the Sone site was believed to be the remains of a lake dwelling, much like Prehistoric Pile Dwellings around the Alps (which became the first freshwater UNESCO World Cultural Heritage sites). These days, however, it is thought that the Sone site was originally a terrestrial settlement that was submerged as a result of fluctuation in the level of Lake Suwa. In 1972, it was designated as a 'Suwa City Designated Historic Site' by the Board of Education at Suwa city. Between the 1960s and 70s, during Japan's high economic growth period, many domestic archaeological sites were lost and destroyed. At the end of the 1970s, feeling threatened by this, the ACA asked all prefectural Boards of Education to update site maps. Under the leadership of the Board of Education of Nagano prefecture, in 1978 the Sone archaeological site was registered as a WPCBCP by the Board of Education at Suwa City.[22]

The first underwater archaeological project surveying a shipwreck in Japan started in 1974 and was of the warship *Kaiyo-maru*.[23] This vessel, constructed in the Netherlands, came to Japan in 1867 as a battleship in the Tokugawa shogunate navy. In 1868, however, she ran aground in a storm and sank off the port of Esashi, Hokkaido prefecture. As the wreck lay on the seabed at a depth of about 10 metres, the research went smoothly and succeeded in recovering more than 30,000 artefacts including cannon, cannon balls, firearms, ship fittings, fixtures, and utensils. In 1974, the Board of Education at Esashi town

21 T. Hayashibara, 'National Designated Historic Place: Wakae Jima (Island), Kamakura-city, Kanagawa Pref. and its Present State' (2005) 19 *KOSUWA Newsletter* 5; Iwabuchi, *supra* n. 2 at pp. 23–4.

22 Academic Society of the Sone Site, *The Study of Sone Historical Site 100 Years On* (Nagano Nippo, 2009) 10–54.

23 Wikipedia 'Japanese frigate Kaiyō Maru' (2025), see <https://en.wikipedia.org/wiki/Japanese_frigate_Kaiy%C5%8D_Maru>.

registered the shipwreck as a WPCBCP,[24] and in 1991 designated its recovered artefacts as 'Esashi Town Designated Tangible Cultural Properties'.

Underwater archaeological research on a larger scale, discovering shipwrecks and anchors, took place in the 1980s, investigating the sinking in 1281 of the Mongol fleet by a typhoon at Imari Bay, northwestern Kyushu. The Board of Education at Matsuura City, Nagasaki prefecture, registered approximately 1,500,000 square metres of the site as a WPCBCP in 1981, and a part of the site of 384,000 square metres was designated as a Historic Site in 2012 by the ACA. Among the recovered artefacts, 'A Copper Statue of Seated Buddha' was designated as a 'Nagasaki Prefecture Designated Tangible Cultural Property' in 1987, and in 1989 'A Bronze Seal of Authority Belonging to a Mongolian Commander of a Thousand-Man Group' was granted the same designation.[25]

In 2021, the revised 1950 Act came into effect.[26] The main purposes of this relatively large-scale revision were as follows: to promote broader use of cultural properties as expectations for utilising them for economic growth have grown significantly, and to strengthen prefectural power and authority. In addition, provision was made to transfer cultural property operations from Boards of Education to heads of municipal governments and a requirement to pay more attention to post-seventeenth century cultural properties was included. As to the first point, the effective use of UCH for education, community-based management, and/or tourism is highly recommended worldwide. In Japan, public access to and/or awareness of UCH sites is a top priority in order to foster recognition of cultural and historical sites, but this obviously requires a budget. Neither municipal nor prefectural Boards of Education have these budgetary levels, but the size of a prefectural budget is always more than that of a municipal one; it is thus expected that each prefecture will contribute more towards UCH. The point on post-seventeenth century cultural properties is good news for underwater archaeology, as many shipwrecks around the Japanese archipelago only date back to early modern times and designating such sites as WPCBC is greatly anticipated. Nevertheless, none of the terms 'submerged site', 'underwater cultural heritage' or 'maritime cultural heritage' were included in the revised Act.

---

24 Board of Education at Esashi Town, *Kaiyo-maru: The First Survey Report* (Board of Education at Esashi Town, 1975) 8–23.

25 Board of Education at Matsuura City, *Takashima Submerged Site at Matsuura City: The Complete Summary* (Board of Education at Matsuura City, 2011) 8–9.

26 ACA of Japan 'Act for Partial Revision of the 1950 Act' (2021), see <https://www.bunka.go.jp/seisaku/bunkazai/pdf/93084801_03.pdf>.

To date, the ACA has selected 65 outstanding cultural landscapes as 'Important Cultural Landscapes'. Selection is based on eight criteria: typical and exceptional landscapes of agriculture, pastoralism, forestry, fishery, water utilisation, industry, transportation, and compound. Out of these, eight are those of fishery and 30 are those of water utilisation, yet there is some evidence of overlap. For instance, the 'Important Cultural Landscape of Kure Port and Fishing Townscape' in Kochi prefecture consists of fishing and trading ports and town districts behind them, which comprise landscapes of both fishery and water utilisation. From its neighbouring archaeological sites, mainly dating from around the thirteenth century, many domestic and foreign pottery remains have been excavated.[27] However, no outstanding seascapes in Japan have been selected as 'Important Cultural Landscapes'. One site that perhaps should be, is Tomonoura, an old harbour in Hiroshima prefecture. A Joseon mission to Japan in 1711 described its seascape in front of the Inland Sea as the most beautiful in Japan.[28] In 1983, after Fukuyama City, Hiroshima prefecture, planned to build a long bridge directly across its harbour area, as well as large car parks, the famous 'Tomonoura Landscape Litigation' began.[29] As members of the International Council on Monuments and Sites (ICOMOS) inspected it and mass media voiced opposition, the initial plan was withdrawn, but Tomonoura's seascape has still not been classified as an Important Cultural Landscape.

In 2018, the Act on Promoting the Utilisation of Sea Areas for the Development of Marine Renewable Energy Power Generation Facilities 2018[30] was enacted, implementation of which is assigned to the Ministry of International Trade and Industry and the Ministry of Land, Infrastructure and Transport. As a result, offshore wind farms are planned directly in front of UNESCO World Cultural Heritage Sites, Places of Scenic Beauty, and Natural Monuments. These may obliterate seascapes, all without surveying any potential UCH

27 H. Edani, 'How to Deal with Wide-Area Cultural Landscapes: The Case of Shimanto River Basin' (2012) 1 *Journal of Japan Society of Water Policy and Integrated River Basin Management* 14.

28 T. Sato, 'Poems Written by Joseon Missions during the Shotoku Era at Fukuzenji Temple, Tomonoura: Or an Example of the Effective Use of Local Classical Chinese Heritage' (2018) 14 *Ronso Kokugo Kyoikugaku* 51.

29 M. Usui, 'Tomo-no-Ura Landscape Preservation Case: Decision by the Hiroshima District Court on 1 October 2009' (2010) 23 *The Chuo-Gakuin University Review of Faculty of Law* 39–40.

30 Japanese Law Translation 'Act on Promoting the Utilization of Sea Areas for the Development of Marine Renewable Energy Power Generation Facilities' (2018), see <https://www.japaneselawtranslation.go.jp/en/laws/view/3580>.

remains since whilst there should be an Environmental Impact Assessment, no Cultural Assessment is required.

In the case of UCH at Tokyo Bay Fortress, there has been observable bureaucratic rivalry between the Ministry of Land, Infrastructure and Transport and the Japanese administration of cultural properties. At the end of the nineteenth century, the Japanese Government began building fortresses to defend Tokyo Bay and its capital against foreign navies. Their construction was partially based on the Kronstadt Fortress off Saint Petersburg, now a UNESCO World Cultural Heritage Site. Construction of No. 1 Kaiho commenced in 1881 and was finished in 1890. No. 2 Kaiho was built between 1889 and 1914. A further Artificial Island Battery, No. 3 Kaiho, was started in 1892 and finished in 1921. Both No. 1 Kaiho, which is owned by the Ministry of Finance, and No. 2 Kaiho, which for all intents and purposes is owned by the Ministry of Land, Infrastructure and Transport, have been registered as WPCBCP by the Board of Education at Futtsu City, Chiba prefecture. However, the Ministry of Land, Infrastructure and Transport is now doing revetment works around No. 2 Kaiho, in violation of the 1950 Act. Because No. 3 Kaiho was in the way of seaborne traffic in Tokyo Bay, it was removed during 2000 to 2009; its remaining submerged foundation has been registered as a WPCBCP by the Board of Education at Yokosuka City, Kanagawa prefecture and parts of its demolished land structures are exhibited at parks in Yokosuka City.[31]

3 Sea Casualties Rescue Act 1899 (SCRA 1899)

In addition to the 1950 Act, the SCRA 1899 is applicable to some shipwrecks. This prescribes procedures for the rescue and protection of vessels in distress and for the securing and disposal activities for drifting or sunken objects.[32] Pursuant to this Act, anyone who finds shipwrecks, or their cargoes, must notify and hand them in to the head of the city, town, or village nearest to the find, as opposed to the police, as soon as possible. Then, such municipal heads must publish notices of the wrecks or cargoes. If no owner appears, the finder may take ownership after six months for drifting objects or after one year for sunken objects, paying their storage and noticing costs to the municipalities.

---

31 T. Noguchi, K. Uramoto and T. Suzuki, 'Construction Techniques of Modern Civil Engineering Heritage Sea Fort No. 2 in Tokyo Bay' (2014) 70 *Japanese Journal of Japan Society of Civil Engineers* 21–2.

32 e-Gov 'Sea Casualties Rescue Act' (1899), see <https://elaws.e-gov.go.jp/document?lawid=132AC0000000095>.

If owners appear, the finder may only claim one third ownership of their monetary value.[33]

Various cases have raised issues around the juxtaposition in applicability of the 1950 Act or the SCRA 1899. In 1957, 103 small oval gold coins and 63 rectangular gold pieces around 400 years old were recovered by fishermen off Oshima Island in the Izu Island chain, but no shipwreck was found, prompting discussion as to the applicability of either the 1950 Act or the SCRA 1899 to these salvaged items. In this case, as no owner made any claim to the authorities and these coins seemed to be Buried Cultural Properties, the conclusion was that the case fell under the 1950 Act.[34]

In 1890, *Ertuğrul*,[35] an Ottoman frigate, sank in stormy weather off Kii Oshima, Wakayama prefecture, on the way back from Japan to Istanbul. The frigate was first stranded against the offshore rock of Funagoura, water broke through into the engine room, and the vessel finally sank. The survivors then swam to the beach of Kii Oshima island and climbed a cliff in order to seek help at the Kashinozaki Lighthouse. In 2008, Turkish and US underwater archaeologists started recovering more than 1,000 artefacts, including pottery and copper objects from the shipwreck. As Turkey claimed ownership, in conformity with the principle of sovereign immunity, this underwater activity was conducted under the SCRA 1899, rather than the 1950 Act. Recovered items were sent to Turkey undergo desalination treatment, with making their way back to Japan to be exhibited at the Kushimoto Turkish Museum on Kii Oshima Island, by courtesy of the Turkish Government.[36] In 2020, the ACA consulted with the Council for Cultural Affairs regarding the heritage related to the *Ertuğrul*, with the proposal it be designated as a Historic Site. The Council's answer was that the Kashinozaki Lighthouse, including its Official Residence, the Offshore Rock of Funagoura, the Landing Beach of the Shipwreck Victims, as well as their Cemetery, should be Historic Sites under the 1950 Act. In contrast, neither the recovered artefacts at the Kushimoto Turkish Museum or the shipwreck itself have been designated as Important Cultural Property or Historic Sites under the 1950 Act, as they are owned by Turkey, rather than Japan.

---

33 Respectively Article 24, 25, 28 and 27 of the SCRA 1899.

34 R. Ono, 'Izu Island Chain' in Asian Research Institute of Underwater Archaeology (ed.) *The Database of Underwater Cultural Heritage and Promotion of Underwater Archaeology*, Vol. 4: The Pacific (Asian Research Institute of Underwater Archaeology, 2012) 50–7.

35 Wikipedia 'Ottoman frigate *Ertuğrul*' (2025), see <https://en.wikipedia.org/wiki/Ottoman_frigate_Ertu%C4%9Frul>.

36 T. Turanli and B. Lledo, 'The Frigate *Ertuğrul*: The 2008 Underwater Excavation Season' (2008) 2008 *The INA Annual* 80–91.

The following case illustrates greater complexity, where rather than the SCRA 1899, the 1950 Act was applied to a foreign shipwreck. In 1874, the *Le Nil*, a steel, cargo-passenger sailing ship of Messageries Maritimes, sank off the Izu peninsula, Shizuoka prefecture. In 2005, after a Japanese archaeological team under the leadership of the Board of Education of Shizuoka prefecture found what appeared to be part of its remains, the surrounding area was registered as a WPCBCP and named 'The (Alleged) Wreck Site of *Le Nil*'. Inclusion of the word 'alleged' in brackets ensured application of the 1950 Act, since the wreck site of *Le Nil*, the SCRA 1899 could be applicable. Additional justification for application of the 1950 Act to this foreign vessel stems from the fact the *Le Nil* carried many Japanese cultural artefacts at the National Treasure level, which were exhibited at the 1873 Vienna World's Fair, such as 'A Lacquered Casket Decorated with Laminae of Chrysanthemum Designed Mother-of-Pearls on Sprinkled Gold Background' from the twelfth century.[37] As much of the cargo belonged to Japan, and the ship was not a State vessel as compared to the *Ertuğru*', it is arguable that the application of the 1950 Act was more appropriate.

However, perhaps surprisingly, most shipwrecks around the Japanese archipelago are subject to neither the 1950 Act nor the SCRA 1899 because they fall through the net of domestic law, even though some are relatively famous shipwrecks that the ACA recognises. The main reason for this situation is because very few Boards of Education have no archaeologists, let alone underwater ones. They thus may be unable to distinguish domestic shipwrecks (governed by the 1950 Act) from foreign shipwrecks (normally governed by the SCRA 1899), or they are unable to distinguish between medieval shipwrecks (where the 1950 Act is *unconditionally* applicable) from modern shipwrecks (where the 1950 Act is *sometimes* applicable).

In most cases, nearly all Boards of Education leave shipwrecks as they are, leading to preservation *in situ*. One illustrative example is a wooden shipwreck lost circa 1700 off Hatsushima Island, belonging to Atami City, Shizuoka prefecture. This domestic freighter carried roof tiles to Edo Castle, many of which are still scattered on the seabed.[38] If this extremely important archaeological site were on land it would be immediately registered as WPCBCP. However, the Board of Education at Atami City remains inactive in respect of making any designation, partly because this is not a medieval shipwreck and partly

---

37 Y. Kakuyama, 'On *Le Nil*, a French Ship Sank off the Izu Peninsula' (1998) 48 *The Economic Review of Kansai University* 189–90.

38 N. Nagai and H. Akamatsu, 'Underwater Excavation of an 18th Century Wooden Shipwreck off Hatsushima Island, Japan' (2021) 9 *ACUA Student* 5.

because the city's archaeologist has no knowledge concerning UCH. To make matters worse, the Hatsushima Fisheries Cooperative Association and Atami Fisheries Cooperative Association are not on good terms. In practice, the Hstsushima Fisheries Cooperative Association, which has its own diving centre, manages this shipwreck, with the Tokyo University of Marine Science and Technology[39] providing archaeological oversight.

Another example of lack of designation can be seen in the treatment of the *Haya-maru*, a screw steamer built in the UK, sold to the US and then to Japan, which sank at the mouth of Tokyo Bay in 1869. The shipwreck remains, but no Board of Education has registered it as a WPCBCP, primarily because the ship's ownership has been transferred numerous times by court order, as its cargo is believed to be of some worth. In theory, the SCRA 1899 should be applicable, but no Board of Education nor the Ministry of Land, Infrastructure and Transport has ever declared that the SCRA 1899 would be applicable to the wreck and as with the wooden shipwreck off Hatsushima, they have remained inactive on the issue.[40]

Other examples include the USS *Oneida*, a screw sloop-of-war, which in 1870 collided with the *Bombay*, a UK steamer, and sank inside Tokyo Bay. Because USS *Oneida* is believed to have carried a significant amount of coinage from the sale of ammunition and gunpowder to the Japanese Government, salvage operations have been ongoing by several private companies. The wreck of this State vessel has not been registered as a WPCBCP.[41] The vessel *Hermann*, a chartered US side-wheel ship, run on a steam engine, sank in 1869 off the Boso peninsula in the Pacific. This wreck, which was neither a State vessel, nor carrying valuable cargo, has been researched professionally for an extensive period of time by Japanese underwater archaeologists. However, the wreck site has likewise never been registered as a WPCBCP and appears to be managed by the local Fisheries Cooperative Association.[42]

The 'Principles for the Scope of Buried Cultural Properties', published in 1988 by the ACA,[43] might justify why no shipwrecks sunk around the period of the Meiji Restoration in 1868, have been registered as WPCBCP, with the

39 A member institution of the UNESCO UNITWN Network for Underwater Archaeology.

40 T. Nakada, '*Haya-maru* and the *Oneida* from the Viewpoint of Sites which Contain Buried Cultural Properties: The Treatment Historical and/or Cultural Shipwrecks at Tokyo Bay' (2021) 19 *Constitutional Law Review* 109–19.

41 ibid.

42 T. Inoue and T. Tamai, 'A Reinforcement for the Battle of Hakodate: Discovery of the *Hermann* and its Underwater Archaeological Survey' (2000) 456 *The Archaeological Journal* 43–6.

43 ACA of Japan, *supra* n. 15.

exception of the *Kaiyo-maru*. This is because if the 1950 Act does not automatically apply, given the wrecks are not medieval ones, it is possible to argue that they may be managed under the SCRA 1899.

4 Fisheries Cooperative Associations and the Fishery Act 1949

In Japan, all adjacent waters immediately off the coast, where most UCH sites are situated, are practically managed by each local Fisheries Cooperative Association (FCA). Adjacent waters are different from the Territorial Sea; the former has its roots deep in the medieval era, implying waters or fishing grounds within view from the beach. FCAs have no connection with municipality groupings; sometimes a single Fisheries Cooperative Association crosses boundaries with several towns, whilst in contrast a single city may have a number of FCAs. Each is independent from its municipality and understandably from the Board of Education at the municipality.

Nominally, according to the Fishery Act 1949 (FA 1949)[44] it is the prefectural governor that grants fishing rights to each FCA. However, the fishing right itself seems to be an extra-legal entity. Its origin can be traced back to prestigious groups of fishermen in coastal villages from the medieval to early modern period. Nobody has succeeded in infringing on this historically vested right. Thus, when academics wish to undertake underwater archaeological activities in an adjacent water zone, they must first obtain permission from its FCA. Submitting notifications to Japan's Coast Guard, an external bureau of the Ministry of Ministry of Land, Infrastructure and Transport, is of secondary importance, and reporting to the local municipal Board of Education is not always required.

Every FCA retains exclusive powers over all activities in adjacent waters. If they say no, neither scientific activity nor public enterprise is permitted. Thus, when the Ministry of International Trade and Industry and the Ministry of Land, Infrastructure and Transport plan to build offshore wind farms, they first ask relevant FCAs. Although FCAs inevitably proclaim they 'own the sea', exceptionally there are examples of where they are less predominant, such as in the Ryukyu archipelago or contemporary Okinawa prefecture. The former Ryukyu Kingdom, which was dissolved by Japan in 1879, historically had no prestigious group of fishermen in its coastal villages, unlike mainland Japan. Therefore, the Japanese Coast Guard under the Ministry of Land, Infrastructure

44 Japanese Law Translation 'Fishery Act' (1949), see <https://www.japaneselawtranslation.go.jp/en/laws/view/3846>.

and Transport has succeeded in becoming central to the management of UCH exclusively in Okinawa prefecture.[45]

Stone tidal weirs are a commonly regulated UCH feature under the FA 1949. They are a type of fishing trap or gear, made of numerous rocks, which exist along the shoreline on a colossal scale, with many observed in Kyushu and the Ryukyu archipelago. According to the 2001 Convention, this is a typical or iconic, UCH relic.[46] Pursuant to the FA 1949, and administrated by the Ministry of Agriculture, Forestry and Fisheries, as a rule each FCA manages all stone tidal weirs inside its fishing grounds. In 2005, the Ministry endorsed the selection of 100 fishing industry and village locations as 'Historical and Cultural Heritage Sites' for future preservation. One of these is a stone tidal weir at Isahaya City, Nagasaki prefecture, also selected in 2008 as one of the 'Landscapes of Agricultural, Mountain, and Fishing Villages to Be Preserved for the Future' by the same Ministry.[47] The same site was also designated as an 'Isahaya City Tangible Folk Cultural Property' in 1987, but not as such by the ACA. In terms of the general protection of such iconic UCH, no stone tidal weir in Japan is either a Historic Site or a Buried Cultural Property pursuant to the 1950 Act. In a few regions in Japan, Boards of Education have tried to register their local stone tidal weirs as WPCBCP, but none has been successful, as negotiations with local FCA s have been unsuccessful.

5 Other Related Legislation

In addition to the 1950 Act, SCRA 1899, and FA 1949, there are other domestic laws relating to UCH in Japan: when underwater archaeologists excavate the seabed, their activities may be regulated. Pursuant to the Act on the Protection of Fishery Resources 1951,[48] anybody seeking to damage or destroy shore reefs

45 T. Yamazaki, S. Wakamatsu and N. Baba, 'Trial Study to Add New Information of the Underwater Cultural Heritages [sic] and Properties of Okinawa into the Marine Cadastre Database' (2015) 52 *Report of Hydrographic and Oceanographic Researches* 132.

46 A. Iwabuchi, 'SDG 14, Case Study: Research on the Underwater Cultural Heritage of Stone Tidal Weirs on the Earth' in S. Labadi, F. Giliberto, I. Rosetti, L. Shetabi and E. Yildirim (eds.) *Heritage and the Sustainable Development Goals: Policy Guidance for Heritage and Development Actors* (ICOMOS, 2021) 96–7.

47 Ministry of Agriculture, Forestry and Fisheries of Japan, *Landscapes of Agricultural, Mountain and Fishing Villages to Be Preserved for the Future* (Ministry of Agriculture, Forestry and Fisheries of Japan, 2008) 64–5.

48 Japanese Law Translation 'Act on the Protection of Fishery Resources' (1951), see <https://www.japaneselawtranslation.go.jp/en/laws/view/4011>.

or collect earth, sand or rock on the seabed under fishing ground waters, which would impact the spawning and growing environment for aquatic plants and animals, must obtain the permission of the prefectural governors. When an application for permission is filed, written consent by FCAs is necessary; thus, the practical authority granting permission is the relevant Association. Under the Mining Act 1950,[49] anybody intending to extract samples of mud sediment with piston corers or to drill below the seabed extensively, must, when appropriate, obtain special permission, administrated by the Ministry of International Trade and Industry. At the same time, this Act bans any mineral explorations that may have adverse effects on cultural properties.

In Japan, archaeologists engaging in underwater survey or excavation works are highly recommended to have a Diver's Licence. This is not a diving certification, but a national licence under the Ordinance on Safety and Health of Work under High Pressure 1972,[50] which is secondary legislation under the Industrial Safety and Health Act 1972,[51] administrated by the Ministry of Health, Labour and Welfare. The Diver's Licence was originally instigated for professional commercial divers working under the water or in caissons.

In short, the numerous governmental stakeholders under the various legislative measures have generated a fragmented bureaucratic authority.

6 Japanese UCH from the Second World War

Many war-related shipwrecks in the Asia-Pacific region are Japanese vessels from the Second World War during which over 7,000 Japanese ships sank. The breakdown is as follows: 500 warships including submarines, 2,500 freighters, 4,000 small boats under 100 tons such as fishing boats, and 50 others.[52] Japan surrendered to the Allied Powers on 2 September 1945, and on 24 September 1945, Japan and the Supreme Commander for the Allied Powers signed what is commonly referred to as SCAPIN-53.[53]

---

49 Japanese Law Translation 'Mining Act' (1950), see <https://www.japaneselawtranslation.go.jp/en/laws/view/2441>.

50 e-Gov 'Ordinance on Safety and Health of Work under High Pressure' (1972), see <https://elaws.e-gov.go.jp/document?lawid=347M50002000040_20200828_502M60000100154>.

51 Japanese Law Translation 'Industrial Safety and Health Act' (1972), see <https://www.japaneselawtranslation.go.jp/en/laws/view/3440>.

52 A. Iwabuchi, 'Japanese Shipwrecks and Human Remains from WWII' in B. Fahy, S. Tripati, V. Walker, B. Jeffery and J. Kimura (eds.) *Proceedings of the 3rd Asia-Pacific Regional Conference on Underwater Cultural Heritage*, Vol. 2 (Hong Kong: APCONF, 2017) 1098–103.

53 Supreme Commander for the Allied Powers Directives to the Japanese Government-53: Materials, Supplies, and Equipment Received and to Be Received from the Japanese Armed Forces.

1. … it is desired that the Imperial Japanese Government take immediate steps to prepare to turn over on demand to the Commanding Generals, Sixth and Eighth United States Armies, XXIV Corps, and Commanders, Fifth and Seventh Fleets, all arms, ammunition, explosives, military equipment, stores, and supplies and other implements of war of all kinds and any equipment or other property belonging to, used by, or intended for use by the Japanese armed forces or any members thereof in connection with their operations. Japanese armed forces include all Japanese and Japanese-controlled land, sea, and air forces and military and para-military organizations, formations, or units and their auxiliaries including Civilian Volunteer Corps wherever they may be located.
2. United States Occupation Force Commanders have been directed to destroy all equipment which is essentially or exclusively for use in war or warlike exercises and which is not suitable for peacetime civilian uses. After operational requirements of Occupational Forces have been met, equipment and supplies of the Japanese armed forces which are not essentially for war or warlike exercises, including scrap from implements of war destroyed, are to be returned to the Japanese Government except that in Korea.
3. The Home Ministry of the Imperial Japanese Government is hereby designated as the official agency to receive and account for such supplies, materials and equipment of the Japanese armed forces as are being returned to your control.
4. In order to administer these transactions, it is desired that the Imperial Japanese Government take the following action:
   a. Responsible Japanese Army and Navy Commanders will prepare inventories by location (generally corresponding to points at which the material is being assembled for turn over to the United States Occupation Forces) of all supplies, materials, and equipment in their possession. These inventories will be made available upon call to United States Occupational Force Commanders.
   b. The Home Ministry of the Imperial Japanese Government will send representatives to the Commanding General, Sixth and Eighth United States Armies, and Commander, Fifth Fleet, for the purpose of receiving supplies, materials, and equipment being returned to the Japanese Government. Sufficient personnel will be provided to accept these items at the locations where turned over by the Japanese armed forces.
   c. The Home Ministry of the Imperial Japanese Government will maintain records of all property so received and account for this

property in such form that the disposition of all supplies, materials, and equipment may be traced to the ultimate consumer. These records will be made available on call to the Supreme Commander for the Allied Powers, the United States Occupational Force Commanders, or authorized representatives.

5. You are informed that the supplies, materials, and equipment returned to your Government are for the purpose of civilian relief, and for use towards restoration of Japanese civil economy to the extent that it can provide the essentials of food, clothing, and shelter for the Japanese civilian population. The use of these supplies, materials, and equipment for any purposes other than the above is expressly forbidden.[54]

In summary, SCAPIN-53 proclaimed *inter alia* that the ownership of all arms and other military properties of the Imperial Japanese Navy and Army was to be transferred to the Allied Powers. This was ratified by the Treaty of San Francisco (the Treaty of Peace with Japan) in 1951.[55] The arms and properties included, for example, IJN *Nagato*[56] which met her end at the nuclear testing in the Bikini Atoll in July 1946 and IJN *Yukikaze*,[57] which was ceded to China as war reparation. The Supreme Commander for the Allied Powers took a severe attitude, particularly towards Japanese submarines: all combat-capable submarines such as IJN *I-400*, *I-401*, and *I-402*,[58] the largest submarines during the Second World War, were scuttled. At the beginning of the twenty-first century, the wrecks of IJN *I-400* and *I-401* were discovered off the Hawaiian Islands, while the remains of IJN *I-402* were found off the Gotō Islands, off the western coast of Kyushu. According to the Japanese Government, the ownership of the wrecks of these submarines, as well as IJN *Nagato*, still belong to the Allied Powers.

As for sunken and half-sunken naval shipwrecks around the Japanese archipelago, the Supreme Commander for the Allied Powers issued a number of orders that the Japanese Government demolish and remove them so that

54 E. Takemae, *The Total Collection of GHQ Instructions: SCAPIN*, Vol. 2 (MT Publisher, 1993) 90–1; National Diet Library of Japan 'SCAPIN-53: Materials, Supplies, and Equipment Received and to Be Received from the Japanese Armed Forces 1945/09/24' (1945), see <https://dl.ndl.go.jp/info:ndljp/pid/9885115>.

55 Ministry of Foreign Affairs of Japan 'Treaty of Peace with Japan' (1951), see <https://www.mofa.go.jp/mofaj/gaiko/treaty/pdfs/B-S38-P2-795_1.pdf>.

56 Wikipedia 'Japanese battleship *Nagato*' (2025), see <https://en.wikipedia.org/wiki/Japanese_battleship_Nagato>.

57 Wikipedia 'Japanese destroyer *Yukikaze* (1939)' (2025), see <https://en.wikipedia.org/wiki/Japanese_destroyer_Yukikaze_(1939)>.

58 Wikipedia 'I-400-class submarine' (2025), see <https://en.wikipedia.org/wiki/I-400-class_submarine>.

Japanese ports and waterways might be safely used, and that as soon as they were dismantled into scrap metal that their ownership should be returned to the Japanese Government. The first order was issued in April 1946, the second in June 1946, and the last in August 1947. The National Treasury incurred the costs associated with demolition and removal, but in return gain from the sale of scrap metal was returned to it. In fact, the shipwrecks were sold to private Japanese shipbuilding and salvage companies. According to the Ministry of Finance, Japanese ownership extends only to the scrap metal from such wrecks, meaning that ownership of war-related Japanese sunken shipwrecks that are yet to be discovered, salvaged and/or demolished remains with the Allied Powers.

There are still many war-related Japanese vessels even inside its Territorial Seas. Some are too deep for viable salvage, and others have not yet been located. For instance, the famous wreck of IJN *Yamato*[59] lies within Japanese Territorial Seas off the southern tip of Kyushu. Around the Bonin Islands, many Japanese shipwrecks from the Second World War rest inside a port. Because the Islands were returned to Japanese control only in 1968 by the Allied Powers, the Japanese Government was unable to demolish or remove these after the Second World War and is unable to apply the 1950 Act to establish any national management plans for researching or safeguarding these wrecks since SCAPIN-53 and the Treaty of San Francisco fix ownership of them with the Allied Powers.

SCAPIN-53 also applies to Japanese shipwrecks from the Second World War in the High Seas or in other nations' Territorial Seas. In these areas, as a result of progressive corrosion, loads including chemical ordnance and tanks have begun to rupture, resulting in leaks of oil, aviation fuel, or and toxic substances. Chuuk (or Truk) Lagoon, located in the Federated States of Micronesia, was Japan's primary naval base in the South Pacific. In 1944, US-led 'Operation Hailstone' destroyed the base, sinking 12 warships, 32 merchant ships, and 275 aircraft.[60] Waste oil from these wrecks is being treated by a Japanese NGO working alongside the Micronesian States' Government.

In contrast, scrap metal from Japanese shipwrecks in the Territorial Seas of the Philippines, was given over to the Philippine Government in 1953 under the Interim Agreement on Reparations Concerning Salvage of Sunken Vessels between Japan and the Republic of the Philippines:

---

59 Wikipedia 'Japanese battleship *Yamato*' (2025), see <https://en.wikipedia.org/wiki/Japanese_battleship_Yamato>.

60 See generally <https://www.thevintagenews.com/2018/07/28/truk-lagoon/?chrome=1>.

Whereas the Government of Japan is ready to make available to the Government of the Philippines the services of the Japanese people in the salvaging of the sunken vessels located in the mine-cleared areas of the Philippine territorial waters, with a view to assisting to compensate the cost of repairing the damage done by Japan during the war;

Therefore, the Government of Japan and the Government of the Philippines, in order to define conditions for providing the said services, have agreed as follows:

Article 1. The Japanese Government shall, in accordance with the provisions of the present Agreement, provide the Philippine Government with the services of Japanese people including the necessary operating equipment and supplies for salvaging sunken vessels located in the Philippine territorial waters.

Article 2. The Philippine Government shall cooperate with the Japanese Government to the extent permitted by Philippine laws in providing such facilities as are readily available locally in performing salvage operations and in procuring ordinary minor operational supplies that may be acquired locally.

The Philippine Government shall take adequate measures for the protection of the life and property of the Japanese nationals engaged in the salvaging operation. However, these responsibilities shall not include risks arising from normal operational hazards.

Article 3. Details for the execution of the present Agreement shall be agreed upon through consultation between the two Governments.

Article 4. The present Agreement will be approved by each Government in accordance with its constitutional procedures, and the present Agreement shall enter into force upon an exchange of diplomatic notes indicating such approval.

The present Agreement shall become an integral part of final arrangements on reparations which will be concluded between the Japanese Government and the Philippine Government.[61]

This interim agreement was confirmed by Article 8 of the Reparations Agreement between the Republic of Philippines and Japan in 1956:

1. The services which have already been supplied or may hereafter be supplied in accordance with the exchange of notes effected at Manila

61 Ministry of Foreign Affairs of Japan, 'Interim Agreement on Reparations Concerning Salvage of Sunken Vessels between Japan and the Republic of the Philippines' (1953), see <https://www.mofa.go.jp/mofaj/gaiko/treaty/pdfs/A-S38(2)-179.pdf>.

on January 24, 1953, in connection with the survey of sunken vessels in Philippine territorial waters or in accordance with the Interim Agreement on Reparations Concerning Salvage of Sunken Vessels between the Republic of the Philippines and Japan signed at Manila on March 12, 1953, shall constitute part of the reparations under Article 1 of the present Agreement.

2. The supply of the above-mentioned services after the coming into force of the present Agreement shall be subject to the provisions of the Agreement.[62]

Japan concluded a similar interim agreement with Indonesia in 1953[63] and with South Vietnam in 1955.[64] However, the former did not take effect and the latter was unilaterally broken by the Government of South Vietnam. Nevertheless, the philosophy of these interim agreements has something in common: Japan offered the necessary infrastructure for salvage, free of charge to each country and the gain from sales of the scrap metal, not the shipwrecks, was given to each as war reparation. Apart from these agreements, Japan has entered into no bilateral or multilateral treaty upon sunken Japanese vessels from the Second World War with any country.

According to SCAPIN-53, all loaded cargo such as war or raw materials contained within wrecks, were also turned over to the Allied Powers. However, the human remains of Japanese soldiers and sailors inside wrecks are believed to be owned by Japan on the basis they are not war materials. Since the Japanese Government promised those in its armed forces repatriation in the event of death overseas, the feeling is that Japan must recover such remains to consign them to land-based graves in their home country.

The 2001 Convention recognises submerged human remains as a type of UCH, and requires Parties ensure that proper respect is given to those located in maritime waters.[65] Additionally, its Rules in the Annex state that activities directed at UCH shall avoid the unnecessary disturbance of human remains or

62 Reparations Commission, *Report of the Philippine Reparations Mission, Tokyo, to the Reparations Commission, Manila, for the Period from September 21, 1956, to December 31, 1958* (Reparations Commission, 1959) 100.

63 Ministry of Foreign Affairs of Japan, 'Interim Agreement on Reparations Concerning Salvage of Sunken Vessels between Japan and the Republic of Indonesia' (1953), see <https://www.mofa.go.jp/mofaj/gaiko/treaty/pdfs/A-S38(2)-106.pdf>.

64 S. Tomotsugu, 'Japan-Cambodia Agreement on Economic and Technological Cooperation as "Quasi-reparation": Political Process in the Japanese Government and International Relations in 1955–59' (2019) 57 *Japanese Journal of Southeast Asian Studies* 39.

65 Art. 2(9).

venerated sites,[66] but it does not recommend recovering all human remains given its fundamental rule of preservation *in situ*. This is because some parts of the heritage value of shipwrecks might in turn be damaged or destroyed. The discrepancy between the Japanese Government's position, most recently reflected in the Promoting the Recovery of the Remains of Japanese War Dead Act 2016, discussed below, and the 2001 Convention in terms of recovering submerged human remains from the Second World War is one of the main obstacles for Japan in accepting the 2001 Convention.

More recently, as a result of rapid developments in underwater technology, Japanese human remains in the deeper parts of the sea, to which neither skilled divers nor underwater vehicles were previously able to gain access, have relatively easily attracted the attention of divers and/or remotely operated vehicles. In some places, foreign divers have recovered Japanese human remains as souvenirs.[67] In 2016, the Japanese Government enacted the above Act,[68] and in 2020 it formally began to recover all Japanese submerged human remains from the Second World War, which number approximately 300,000, including from aircraft. The stakeholder Ministry in the administration of this Act is not the Ministry of Defence, but the Ministry of Health, Labour, and Welfare. Section 7 of the Act expressly provides that the process should incorporate 'consultations etc. with the government of the countries concerned and obtain their understanding and co-operation'.

7 Conclusion – Future Direction

Following its ratification of the LOSC in 1996, the Japanese Government enacted the Basic Act of Ocean Policy 2007. Under the Act, the Headquarters for Ocean Policy was established, inside the Cabinet Secretariat, with the role of formulating national marine policies and solutions, which may involve several Ministries. The Secretary-General is a high-ranking official from the Ministry of Land, Infrastructure and Transport. The Ministries of Education, Culture, Sports, Science and Technology, Agriculture, Forestry and Fisheries, and Health, Labour and Welfare also provide supporting officials. In 2018, the

---

66 Rule 5.

67 A. Iwabuchi, 'The Shipwreck of the *Takachiho*, Japanese Cruiser Sunk off China in 1914' in UNESCO (ed.) *Underwater Cultural Heritage from World War I* (UNESCO, 2014) 45–7; Iwabuchi, *supra* n. 2, at p. 23.

68 e-Gov, 'Promoting the Recovery of the Remains of Japanese War Dead Act' (2016). <https://elaws.e-gov.go.jp/document?lawid=428AC1000000012_20160401_000000000000000>.

Headquarters for Ocean Policy published the Third Basic Plan on Ocean Policy.[69] In principle, deciding on and producing a coordinated, national policy on UCH, formulating national programmes concerning the financing and regulation of underwater archaeological research, and investigating the pros and cons of ratification of the 2001 Convention, ought to have been discussed by the Headquarters for Ocean Policy. In actual practice, however, the Headquarters does not function this way, rather it seems to be an organisation that reconciles differences of opinion between Ministries, with no national budget of its own. In contrast, in 2018, the Taiwanese Government established the Ocean Affairs Council and enacted the Ocean Basic Act 2019.[70] On the basis of this Act and the Underwater Cultural Heritage Preservation Act 2015, the Council is working for UCH research and management, in close coordination with Taiwan's Bureau of Cultural Heritage.

Although ownership of Japanese shipwrecks from the Second World War was shifted from Japan to the Allied Powers by SCAPIN-53 in 1945, confirmed by the Treaty of San Francisco in 1951, not all the Allied Powers signed it: Russia has not yet done so. Under these circumstances, some international commentators and some Ministries in Japan, such as the Ministry of Foreign Affairs, have started to insist that, because of the legal doctrine of sovereign immunity, all Japanese shipwrecks, in particular sunken State vessels located in its Territorial Seas, the High Seas, or the Territorial Seas of foreign countries are still owned by Japan. Indeed, it is a common claim under international law that sunken warships or State vessels maintain an entitlement to sovereign immunity as such vessels remain State property.[71] For example, the former Soviet Union, used to claim ownership of a special service vessel of the Russian Baltic Fleet that sank inside Japanese Territorial Seas, despite Russia's surrender at the end of the Russo-Japanese War in 1905; and the IRN *Oryol*,[72] a battleship of the Russian Baltic Fleet, captured by Japan after the Battle of Tsushima 1905, reconstructed and renamed IJN, *Iwami* while the Japanese request that Russia should hand over its warships to Japan at a port of a neutral nation was rejected. However, the view that sovereign immunity does not apply after warships have sunk (on the basis they no longer meet the definition of seagoing watercraft), seems to be increasingly common, but not universally accepted;

69 Available in full at <https://www8.cao.go.jp/ocean/english/plan/pdf/plan03_e.pdf>.

70 Law and Regulations Database of the Republic of China (Taiwan) 'Ocean Basic Act' (2019), see <https://law.moj.gov.tw/ENG/LawClass/LawAll.aspx?pcode=D0090064>.

71 J. A. Roach, 'Sunken Warships and Military Aircraft' (1996) 20 *Marine Policy* 352.

72 Wikipedia 'Russian battleship *Oryol*' (2025), see <https://en.wikipedia.org/wiki/Russian_battleship_Oryol>.

under this interpretation, the recovery of warships or items therefrom on the High Seas is subject to the same rules as those governing other wrecks and may therefore be undertaken by anyone, subject to the application of the ordinary rules of salvage.[73] The Japanese Government, in particular the Ministry of Finance, focuses on the fact that Japan surrendered to the Allied Powers in 1945 and therefore takes the latter view i.e., that sovereign immunity does not apply in these circumstances. This is complicated by the fact that there remain some countries that did not sign peace treaties with Japan following the end of the Second World War; many Pacific small island developing States have become independent since 1962; before the 1950s the 3 nautical mile limit of the Territorial Sea was still legitimate; and the safeguarding of UCH has only recently become a legal and policy objective. Existing evidence would suggest that a new multilateral international agreement for the region is needed in terms of safeguarding Japanese shipwrecks from the Second World War as UCH, as well as for finding solutions to issues surrounding their potential impact upon the environment and Japanese activity in recovering submerged human remains from them.

All websites last accessed February 2025.

Selected Bibliography

Iwabuchi A., 'The Shipwreck of the *Takachiho*, Japanese Cruiser Sunk off China in 1914' in UNESCO (ed.) *Underwater Cultural Heritage from World War I* (Paris: UNESCO, 2014) 41–9.

Iwabuchi, A., 'Japanese Shipwrecks and Human Remains from WWII' in B. Fahy, S. Tripati, V. Walker, B. Jeffery and J. Kimura (eds.) *Proceedings of the 3rd Asia-Pacific Regional Conference on Underwater Cultural Heritage*, Vol. 2 (Hong Kong: APCONF, 2017) 1098–113.

Iwabuchi, A., 'Risk and Problems Relating to Protecting and Researching Underwater Cultural Heritage in East and Southeast Asia' in A. Hafner, H. Öniz, L. Semaan and C. J. Underwood (eds.) *Heritage under Water at Risk: Threats, Challenges, Solutions* (Paris: ICOMOS, 2020) 22–5.

73 S. Dromgoole and N. Gaskell, 'Draft UNESCO Convention on the Protection of the Underwater Cultural Heritage 1998' (1999) 14 *International Journal of Marine and Coastal Law* 18; K. Oyama, 'Legal Status of Sunken State Vessels and Sovereign Immunity' in B. Fahy, S. Tripati, V. Walker, B. Jeffery and J. Kimura (eds.) *Proceedings of the 3rd Asia-Pacific Regional Conference on Underwater Cultural Heritage*, Vol. 1 (APCONF, 2017) 486.

Nagai, N. and Akamatsu, H., 'Underwater Excavation of an 18th Century Wooden Shipwreck off Hatsushima Island, Japan' (2021) 9 *ACUA Student* 5–6.

Oyama, K., 'Legal Status of Sunken State Vessels and Sovereign Immunity' in B. Fahy, S. Tripati, V. Walker, B. Jeffery and J. Kimura (eds.) *Proceedings of the 3rd Asia-Pacific Regional Conference on Underwater Cultural Heritage*, Vol. 1 (Hong Kong: APCONF, 2017) 483–99.

Tabata, M., Yagi, N., Nishimoto, J. and Ghaffar, A., 'Estimation of Places of Production of Porcelains of Unknown Origins Excavated at the Mietsu Naval Facility Site Based on Differences in the Solubility of Trace Metals during the Elutriation Process' (2021) 36 *Journal of Archaeological Science: Reports* 1–9.

CHAPTER 12

Mexico

Roberto Junco Sánchez and Laura R. Carrillo Márquez***

1 Introduction

The legal framework for the protection of underwater cultural heritage (UCH) in Mexico was finally consolidated in 2014 when, on the basis of the UNESCO Convention on the Protection of the Underwater Cultural Heritage (2001 Convention),[1] an addendum via Article 28 TER to the Federal Law on Monuments and Archaeological, Artistic and Historical Areas (Monumentos y Zonas Arqueológicos Artísticos e Históricos) (1972 Act) was implemented. However, prior to this amendment, there were various instances in which Mexico was forced to curb treasure hunters' attempts to plunder the nation's UCH, using the available legal instruments and through the robust defence put forward by Pilar Luna Erreguerena, the then head of the underwater archaeology department of the National Institute of Anthropology and History (INAH), a position she held for over three decades.

We shall provide an overview of the actions that led to the consolidation of the Mexican legislation on cultural heritage, parallel to the building of the Mexican State. We also examine the laws that were used prior to the 1972 Act to defend Mexico's UCH. At the same time, we will review the history of the consolidation of the INAH's Division of Underwater Archaeology (Subdirección de Arqueología Subacuática) (DUA), with a focus on examples of attempts to plunder shipwrecks, some of which were enabled by government institutions, ultimately leading to the need to strengthen the country's existing legal protection.

2 Legislation on Cultural Heritage

2.1 *Consolidation of the National Legal Framework*

The interest in the study and the protection of archaeological monuments of national interest traces its origins back to the Mexican 'Viceregal Period'

* Deputy Director of the Division of Underwater Archaeology, National Institute of Anthropology and History.

** Researcher at the Division of Underwater Archaeology, National Institute of Anthropology and History.

1 2562 UNTS 1. Ratified by Mexico on 5 June 2006.

 | DOI:10.1163/9789004510883_014

(1521–1821). However, strictly speaking, the Mexican tradition regarding this category of national interest protection started to take shape by adapting existing European traditions, in particular the Spanish one. This resulted in the consolidation of Mexico's own body of law as an independent nation. In this context, the discovery of pre-Hispanic monuments, demolished in the early decades of Spanish colonisation, during the undertaking of public works in the late eighteenth century, rekindled a nationalistic sentiment by granting them identitarian values. This also ignited the interest in the study of ancient monuments as a source of knowledge to learn about the country's history.[2]

Both aspects allowed for the construction, during the nineteenth century, of a legal framework that regulates and protects any assets of archaeological, historical, or artistic interest, which is strengthened with the enactment of several laws throughout the twentieth century. Some background worth mentioning is the rules and regulations established for the National Museum[3] and other isolated provisions between 1827 and 1864 that aimed to avoid the plundering and smuggling of cultural property, and to preserve archaeological monuments and ancient buildings.[4] Furthermore, since the promulgation of the Constitution of 1857, the Federal Government has exerted acts of ownership over archaeological monuments, without an explicit constitutional basis for such powers. A notable example was the below-mentioned addition of section XXV to Article 73 of Mexico's Constitution of 1917,[5] which ultimately laid the foundations for the protection of these assets. This document contains many of the ideas that motivated the Mexican Revolution, with a strong social content aimed at strengthening the State. Nevertheless, throughout its 105 years of existence, and especially during the last 40 years, the State has undergone various policy adjustments, in line with the country's lived reality.

The concern for the conservation of monuments of national interest stemmed from the dynamics that occurred surrounding archaeological property (antiques) since the time of the Spanish conquest. This interest was reinforced throughout the nineteenth century as the Mexican State was taking

2 B. Cottom, *Nación Patrimonio Cultural y Legislación: Los Debates Parlamentarios y la Construcción del Marco Jurídico Federal sobre Monumentos en México* (Miguel Ángel Porrúa, 2008).

3 Founded in 1825, by a decree of President Guadalupe Victoria and consolidated circa 1831 with the issuance of the Decree for the *Formation of an Establishment Comprising Antiques, Industrial Products, Natural History and Botanical Garden* or *Formación de un Establecimiento que Comprenda Antigüedades, Productos de Industria, Historia Natural y Jardín Botánico* by Anastasio Bustamante.

4 Cottom *supra* n.2 at pp. 79–99.

5 Constitución Política de los Estados Unidos Mexicanos, (last amendment dated November 18, 2022), *Diario Oficial de la Federación*, 1917, Mexico.

shape. Some of these dynamics are: its destruction, plundering and commercial exploitation (including both legal trade and illegal trafficking); its exploration by a multitude of actors, especially foreigners whose main interest was commercial rather than cultural; the continuous discoveries of such monuments throughout the country; and the emergence of research surrounding these discoveries and their ownership. These issues, together with a growing recognition of the value and importance of pre-Hispanic cultures for the shaping of a national and historic identity, prompted the Mexican State to implement a legal framework that would govern its actions over these archaeological goods.[6]

One of the government's first actions in 1885 was to create the post of 'inspector and conservator of archaeological monuments of the Mexican Republic,' within the Ministry of Justice and Public Instruction (Ministerio de Justicia e Instrucción Pública), which no longer exists as an entity. The first person to take on this responsibility was Leopoldo Batres, an archaeologist close to the then President, Porfirio Díaz. Soon after, in 1896, a Law on Archaeological Explorations (Ley sobre Exploraciones Arqueológicas) was issued, which stipulated the necessary requirements for individuals to obtain concessions for the exploration of archaeological monuments. This Act established for the first time the State's ownership over any archaeological property recovered during these interventions, although it also stipulated that the concessionaire may keep an artifact for themselves, provided that they find another one similar to the first.[7]

That same year, a first draft of the Law on Archaeological Monuments (Ley sobre Monumentos Arqueológicos) (1897 Act) was presented, which had two main intended purposes: the first was to establish the cultural value of these monuments and the second was to ratify the importance of archaeology as a science. This law was passed in mid-1897, despite opposition from certain parties whose individual interests were at stake, especially when it came to

6 Actions that motivated the formalisation of the legal protection of cultural heritage included those of Desiré Charnay, who had an exploration and export of archaeological goods permit issued by the Mexican Government itself, and which led to a dispute in the House of Representatives, and those of Edward Thompson, United States Consul in Mérida, who plundered over 30,000 artifacts from the Sacred Cenote in Chichén Itzá.

7 Biblioteca Jurídica Virtual del Instituto de Investigaciones Jurídicas de la UNAM, L. López *El Caso Particular de la Legislación sobre los Monumentos Arqueológicos* 185, <https://revistas-colaboracion.juridicas.unam.mx/index.php/rev-facultad-derecho-mx/article/viewFile/28863/26094#:~:text=El%20Congreso%20de%20la%20Uni%C3%B3n,de%20la%20Inspecci%C3%B3n%20de%20Monumentos>.

assigning ownership over archaeological property (a symbol of power), which was brought under the jurisdiction of the Federal Government.[8]

With this framework in place, the legal *corpus* was then shaped during the twentieth century to protect all paleontological, archaeological, historical, and artistic monuments, through an extensive drafting of laws prompted by attention from within the social sciences and the artistic sectors. One of the first laws to be enacted was the 1914 Conservation of Historical and Artistic Monuments and Natural Beauties Act (Ley de Conservación de Monumentos Históricos y Artísticos y Bellezas Naturales) (1914 Act), issued by the then President, Victoriano Huerta, through a concession granted to the executive by the legislature. The 1914 Act introduced for the first time the European concept of 'cultural heritage', in which 'monuments' are considered as akin to 'documents' that are capable of providing information on the history of the nation, and not just mere pieces of architecture, in juxtaposition to the nineteenth century perspective.[9]

After some years of uncertainty due to political instability in Mexico and the international conflict brought about by the First World War, two additional laws were created in 1930 and 1934. The first was the Law on the Protection and Conservation of Monuments and Natural Beauties (Ley sobre Protección y Conservación de Monumentos y Bellezas Naturales) (1930 Act), promoted by the interim administration of President Emilio Portes Gil. Interestingly, the proposed law included a reference to the lacuna that existed in the 1897 Act, with no mention of the 1914 Act, in which the conservation subjects were listed, namely 'monuments' and 'natural beauties'.[10] The second provision was the Law on the Protection and Conservation of Archaeological and Historical Monuments, Typical Populations and Sites of Natural Beauty (Ley sobre Protección y Conservación de Monumentos Arqueológicos e Históricos, Poblaciones Típicas y Lugares de Belleza Natural) (1934 Act), sponsored by the Ministry of Public Education (Secretaría de Educación Pública) (MPE) to address gaps and issues stemming from the implementation of the 1930 Act, which it superseded.

---

8 1897 Act, Article 1; see Cottom, *supra* n. 2, at pp. 143–178.

9 Cottom, *supra* n. 2, at pp. 187–188. Cottom, who cites Julio César Olivé, cultural law expert, states that the 1914 Act cannot "be formally invoked as an antecedent" since the provisions issued by General Victoriano Huerta, whom he considers a usurper, were nullified following his resignation. Cottom, *supra* n. 2, at p. 193.

10 One of the most important aspects of the 1930 Act is that it expresses interest in resolving the issue of the ownership of movable archaeological property through the creation of the Register of Archaeological Property (Registro de la Propiedad Arqueológica). Cottom, *supra* n. 2, at p. 212.

Within this legal dynamic, the Mexican Government's growing interest in protecting and studying its cultural heritage was reflected in the creation of the National Institute of Anthropology and History (INAH) in 1939, based on its Organic Law.[11] This Law gives it powers to explore, protect, preserve, and restore archaeological, historical, and artistic monuments, as well as to develop scientific research. Alongside the creation of this Institute by President Lázaro Cárdenas within the MPE, the 1934 Act was amended and some provisions added in order to establish its powers.

Decades later, in 1965, section XXV, Article 73 of the Constitution of the United Mexican States was added, whereby, after years of discussing the lack of constitutional underpinnings, the Union Congress was granted the authority to legislate on any archaeological, historical, and artistic monument whose conservation is of national interest. A special provision regarding certain vestiges and fossil remains was added to said section soon after.

Finally, since the INAH did not have adequate legal basis to carry out its duties, especially regarding the issue of national ownership of archaeological property, its jurisdiction, and the illicit trade in such property, in 1968 the Institute presented the Federal Cultural Heritage of the Nation Bill (Ley Federal del Patrimonio Cultural de la Nación), based on the amendment to the above-mentioned Article 73. Adopted in 1970, the Act once more touched upon the concept of 'cultural heritage', although somewhat ambiguously as it was not clear which items would be considered as heritage and which would not.[12]

The adoption of this Law generated several problems derived, above all, from the prohibition of private collecting and the mechanisms that were established to avoid and sanction it. These aspects constituted the main political obstacles for its implementation, causing it to be repealed in 1972 by the Law on Archaeological, Artistic and Historic Monuments and Zones (Ley Federal sobre Monumentos y Zonas Arqueológicos, Artísticos e Históricos) (the 1972 Act) which remains in force with various amendments and addenda. Regulations under this Act were added in 1975, and two other laws were enacted to protect cultural heritage, the 1946 Organic Law of the Institute of Fine Arts and Literature (Ley Orgánica del Instituto de Bellas Artes y Literatura) and the 2003 Law of the National Commission for the Development of Indigenous Peoples (la Ley de la Comisión Nacional para el Desarrollo de los Pueblos Indígenas).

Nowadays, this body of law is complemented by various laws, Federal and State regulations, official regulations, as well as various treaties, charters,

11 INAH's Organic Law (Ley Orgánica de INAH), *Diario Oficial de la Federación*, 17 December.

12 Cottom, *supra* n. 2, at p. 244.

recommendations, international conventions, and agreements dealing with the protection of cultural heritage. These include, *inter alia*, the 1970 Convention on Measures to be Taken to Prohibit and Prevent the Import, Export and Transfer of Illicit Ownership of Cultural Property;[13] the 1972 Convention for the Protection of World, Cultural and Natural Heritage;[14] and the 1982 United Nations Convention on the Law of the Sea (LOSC).[15]

2.2 *National and International Legislation on Protection of UCH*

2.2.1 National Legislation

The legal framework referred to above aims to safeguard Mexico's vestiges and fossil remains of organic beings, and archaeological and historic monuments. Nevertheless, the protection of those monuments in aquatic environments, specifically the items that could be classified as historical according to the 1972 Act's guidelines, was only explicitly established in 2015. In this regard, the chapter continues with a review of the legal instruments that, to some extent, seek to ensure and maintain the safeguarding of Mexico's underwater heritage assets.

In the Mexican Political Constitution, as was seen earlier, protection of archaeological and historical property is not provided for. However, Article 27 stipulates that:

> Ownership of the lands and waters within the boundaries of the national territory is vested originally in the Nation, [...] The Nation exercises control over an exclusive economic zone situated outside the territorial seas and adjacent to them, consistent with the rights of sovereignty and the jurisdictions established by the laws of Congress.[16]

Whilst this provision clearly provides for State ownership of territory, including both land and water, it does not extend ownership to underwater cultural heritage. Further, as noted above, the aforementioned Article 73, grants the Congress of the Union power to legislate on archaeological, artistic, and historic monuments, without making any distinction in terms of the context in which they are found.[17] In addition, the 1986 Federal Act relating to the

13 823 UNTS 231.

14 1037 UNTS 151.

15 1833 UNTS 397.

16 Art. 27 of the 1917 Political Constitution of the United Mexican States (Constitución Política de los Estados Unidos Mexicanos) (in force in 2021).

17 Art. 73, section XXV of the 1917 Political Constitution of the United Mexican States (in force in 2021).

Sea (Ley Federal del Mar) establishes that for any matter related to marine scientific research, which includes all research on submerged cultural heritage and its natural context, the sovereignty of the nation extends to the seabed and subsoil of the Territorial Sea (TS), the Exclusive Economic Zone (EEZ), Contiguous Zone (CZ), Continental Shelf (CS) and inland marine waters.[18]

Although since 1944 the General Law on National Property (Ley General de Bienes Nacionales) has regarded 'archaeological and historical buildings and ruins' as property of common use, their legal status was enhanced by reforms in 1982. These reforms established that federally-owned historic, archaeological, or artistic monuments, both movable and immovable, all constitute national property subject to the public domain regime. In other words, they constitute State or public administration property, and are inalienable, imprescriptible, and unseizable, thus unable to be traded or distributed between individuals.[19]

The protection of heritage in the institutional framework, is stipulated in Article 2 of the INAH's Organic Law. Under this, INAH has competence in scientific research pertaining to Anthropology and History, and also the conservation, restoration, and recovery of Mexico's archaeological, historical, cultural, and paleontological patrimony. INAH also promotes and publishes on its subject-matters and activities.[20] In this same framework, the 1972 Act (as amended) specifies that the research, protection, conservation, restoration and recovery of archaeological, artistic, and historic monuments and monumental sites are of collective public interest. This Act establishes in Article 27 that, given the fact that they are national property, all movable and immovable 'archaeological monuments' are inalienable and imprescriptible, which are defined as follows:

> ... movable and immovable property, product of cultures prior to the establishment of the Hispanic in the national territory, as well as the human remains, flora and fauna, related to these cultures.[21]

In turn, 'historic monuments' are defined in Article 35 as:

> All property linked with the nation's history from the time of the establishment of Hispanic culture in the country shall be considered historic

18 Art. 6, 22 y 46 of the Federal Act relating to the Sea (Ley Federal del Mar), 1986.

19 Art. 17, section XIII, 1944 General Law on National Assets (Ley General de Bienes Nacionales) and Article 2, section VI and XVII, 1982 General Law on National Assets (in force in 2021).

20 Art. 2, 1986 Organic Law of the INAH (Ley Orgánica del INAH) (in force in 2015).

21 Art. 28, 1972 Act (as amended).

> monuments, according to the terms of the relevant declaration or by the determination of the Law.[22]

While Article 36 provides a more detailed exposition, as follows:

> The present Law determines that historic monuments shall be:
> 1. Buildings constructed from the sixteenth to the nineteenth century, and intended to be used: as churches or annexes thereto, archbishops' or bishops' palaces, or presbyteries; as seminaries, convents, or buildings for the administration, propagation, teaching or practice of a religious faith; for education or instruction provided for charitable reasons or for social betterment; for public service or embellishment, and for the purposes of the civil and military authorities. Any movable objects that may be found or have already been found in such buildings, and civil works of a private nature produced from the sixteenth to the nineteenth century inclusive, are also included.
> 2. Documents and papers belonging, or that have belonged, to bureaux and archives of the Federation, States or municipalities and presbyteries.
> 3. Original manuscripts relating to the history of Mexico and books, pamphlets and other matter printed in Mexico or abroad between the sixteenth and the nineteenth centuries and which, by virtue of their rare nature and importance to Mexican history deserve to be kept in the country.
> 4. Collections and craft tools and artefacts may be promoted to this category by means of an appropriate declaration.[23]

As can be seen from the material quoted above, throughout these definitions archaeological monuments are fully protected. There is comprehensive coverage, from ceramic fragments to pre-Hispanic cities. However, in the case of 'historic monuments', pursuant to the Act, this application is limited to certain buildings erected between the sixteenth and nineteenth centuries, to the movables inside them or previously found inside them, and to some documents and archives, but leaving open the possibility of including others by way of declaratory action. There was thus no explicit reference to cultural remains (moveable assets) found in a submerged context.

22 Art. 35, 1972 Act (as amended).
23 Art. 36, 1972 Act (as amended).

This shortcoming was addressed by appending to Article 28 TER to the Act, in which it is stipulated that:

> The provisions on conservation and research in the field of monuments and areas of archaeological and historic monuments will be applicable to traces of human existence that have a cultural, historical or archaeological character, located in the marine zone of the United Mexican States, which have been partially or totally underwater, periodically or continuously, such as: the sites, structures, buildings, objects and human remains, together with its archaeological and natural context; vessels, aircraft, other means of transport or any part thereof. Its cargo or other content, together with its archaeological and natural context; and the objects of prehistoric character.
>
> The vessels and aircraft of foreign States, any part of them, their cargo or other content, which enjoy immunity, shall be exempt from the preceding paragraph being sovereign under international law.
>
> The authorisations to carry out research and exploration of the goods referred to in the first subparagraph shall be subject to the provisions of Article 30 of this Regulation.[24]

This text, which draws significantly upon the 2001 Convention (aside from the 100-year time limit), lists "those traces of human existence that have a cultural, historical or archaeological character, located in the marine zone of the United Mexican States". It does not redress the legal vacuum regarding the status of shipwrecks or other cultural property as 'historic monuments' in the Act, which leads to two problems. The first being that this description refers to the definition of historic monuments, which regards them solely as:

> ... the goods linked to the history of the nation, starting from the establishment of Hispanic culture in the country, in the terms of the declaration of the law.[25]

In other words, the only way to ensure the protection of shipwrecks is by proving that they have some kind of connection with the history of Mexico, or by declaring them historic monuments by Presidential Decree.

The second problem lies in the specificity created by delimiting their location to the 'marine zone', thus leaving any remains or historic properties

24 Art. 28 TER 1972 Act, added by Decree on June 13, 2014.

25 Art. 28 1972 Act.

located in inland waters outside of scope and so unprotected.[26] Both issues may prompt a future update of this Act, which could explicitly consider shipwrecks as objects of protection. The provisions regarding archaeological and historic monuments may be extensive and extend to submerged cultural heritage, but in this context a distinction should be made. The provisions apply only to works involving preservation and investigation, without considering the ownership issue.

It is also noteworthy to highlight Articles 30 and 31 of the 1972 Act, in which it is stipulated that all forms of material work to discover or explore archaeological monuments will only be carried out by the INAH or by scientific institutions of 'recognised moral solvency', subject to prior authorisation. These provisions operate to filter motions submitted by treasure hunters masquerading as academic researchers.

Before the 2014 amendment of the 1972 Act, the only law that explicitly took into account shipwrecks, or 'derelicts', was the 2006 Maritime Navigation and Trade Act (Ley de Navegación y Comercio Marítimos), which defines them as follows:

> It shall be considered as derelict, the vessels that are adrift in a state of non-navigability, together with their machines, anchors, remains of vessels and aircraft, goods thrown or falling into the sea and in general terms, all objects, including those of old origin, on which the owner has lost possession, which are found either floating or at the bottom of the sea or in any waterway or waters where the United Mexican States exercise sovereignty or jurisdiction.[27]

Furthermore, it states that any person who discovers a derelict shall be under the obligation to communicate it immediately to the competent port authority. Under Article 174 the derelicts and any objects located inside them, which possess any archaeological, historical, or cultural characteristic of interest, will be considered the property of the Nation. This last point contradicts the provisions of Article 28 TER of the 1972 Act and the 2001 Convention due to the fact that the necessary adjustments and reforms in Mexican legislation are not yet in place.

In addition, compulsory technical regulations fulfil official Mexican standards. For example, since 2002 the INAH's Division of Underwater Archaeology

26 Permanent bodies of water on or below the surface of the Earth.

27 Art. 172 of the 2021 Maritime Navigation and Trade Act (Ley de Navegación y Comercio Marítimos).

has participated in the five-yearly drafting and updating of regulations issued by the Ministry of Tourism (Secretaría de Turismo) regarding SCUBA diving activities. In this regard, guidelines have been drawn up for diving on sites with submerged cultural remains. These guidelines proscribe touching, extracting, removing, and tampering with archaeological contexts. These regulations comprise the NOM-05-TUR-2003, on minimum safety requirements that must be observed by all diving operators; the NOM-09-TUR-2002 setting out guidelines that specialised guides taking part in specific activities must conform to; and NOM-012-TUR-2014 regulating tourist diving services.[28]

2.2.2 International Legislation

With respect to international law, Article 19 of the 1972 Act allows the application of international conventions in the absence of express provision in Mexican law regarding the conservation and protection of movable and immovable archaeological monuments.

One of the normative instruments, which made it possible to establish a firm stance against commercial exploitation (before the signing of the 2001 Convention and the addition of Article 28 TER to the 1972 Act) was the LOSC. This includes two Articles establishing the international legal basis regarding the treatment of archaeological or historical objects found on the sea or seabed and its subsoil, outside the limits of national jurisdiction. Article 149 states that:

> All objects of an archaeological and historical nature found in the Area shall be preserved or disposed of for the benefit of mankind as a whole, particular regard being paid to the preferential rights of the State or country of origin, or the State of cultural origin, or the State of historical and archaeological origin.[29]

Article 303 further provides that:

> 1. States have the duty to protect objects of an archaeological and historical nature found at sea and shall cooperate for this purpose. 2. In order to control traffic in such objects, the coastal State may, in applying article

28 The official Mexican standards are technical and compulsory regulations applied to products, processes or services that could constitute a risk for people, animals, and plants, and also for the environment in general. Secretaría de Economía, Catálogo Mexicano de Normas, 2014.

29 Art. 149 1982 LOSC.

> 33, presume that their removal from the seabed in the zone referred to in that article without its approval would result in an infringement within its territory or territorial sea of the laws and regulations referred to in that article.[30]

Another very useful international instrument was the International Charter on the Protection and Management of Underwater Cultural Heritage,[31] which seeks to promote the protection and management of UCH within inland and near-shore waters, in shallow seas and deep oceans. This Charter, which formed an annex to the 2001 Convention, establishes as one of its fundamental principles the *in situ* conservation of UCH as a first consideration and it emphasises the specific attributes and circumstances of this heritage.

Finally, the 2001 Convention, ratified by Mexico as noted above, deserves a special mention, given Mexico's active participation in its formulation, particularly as a result of the work of Pilar Luna Erreguerena. As with the two previous treaties, this Convention aims at ensuring and strengthening the protection of this heritage, considering *in situ* conservation as the first consideration for long-term conservation. It establishes basic principles for the protection of UCH, which include favouring a system of international cooperation while maintaining an absolute respect for customary and international laws. It also provides practical guidelines for research related to this type of heritage. Furthermore, it stipulates that this heritage shall not be commercially exploited and that responsible non-intrusive public access to these sites should be encouraged, for observation or documentation purposes, as a means of promoting public awareness of this heritage, as well as its recognition and protection.

It lays down a broad definition for UCH, thus covering the full gamut of phenomena, processes, and contexts from across the globe:

> ... all traces of human existence having a cultural, historical or archaeological character which have been partially or totally under water, periodically or continuously, for at least 100 years such as: (i) sites, structures, buildings, artefacts and human remains, together with their archaeological and natural context; (ii) vessels, aircraft, other vehicles or any part

30 Art. 303, Clause 2 of 1982 LOSC.

31 ICOMOS, Charter On The Protection And Management Of UCH (Carta Internacional sobre la Protección y Gestión del Patrimonio Cultural Subacuático, 1996) <https://www.icomos.org/images/DOCUMENTS/Charters/underwater_e.pdf>.

> thereof, their cargo or other contents, together with their archaeological and natural context; and (iii) objects of prehistoric character.[32]

The 2001 Convention also provides that pipelines, cables and other placed on the seabed and still in use shall not be considered as underwater cultural heritage. At the same time, it establishes special considerations for 'State vessels and aircraft', which are defined as meaning warships and other vessels or aircraft that were owned or operated by a State and used, at the time of sinking, only for government non-commercial purposes.

Both the LOSC and the 2001 Convention establish principles that refer to objects of an archaeological or historical nature, rather than to a structured conceptual definition. This normative strategy, through an inclusive approach, contributes towards taking account of the greatest possible amount of archaeological and historical property, which could eventually become an object of attention or dispute between coastal and flag States.

The 2001 Convention prioritises preservation, international cooperation between State Parties, and knowledge at the service of humanity. However, even though it was one of the most critical issues at the time of its formation, it left aside the determination of ownership and jurisdiction applicable in cases of dispute.

3 Consolidation of the Underwater Archaeology Division in Mexico

Mexico has a long history of research in the field of underwater archaeology. The first dives to locate archaeological remains date back to 1892, when Francisco del Paso y Troncoso sent divers in diving suits to prospect the waters in Villa Rica, Veracruz, with the aim of finding conquistador Hernán Cortes' sunken ships. There are photographs of this expedition, depicting the pioneering work of this great scholar of the history of ancient Mexico, and director of the National Museum of Antiquities (Museo Nacional de Antigüedades), which was undertaken concurrently with the Cempoala archaeological excavation.[33]

The beginning of the twentieth century, up to the 1960s, witnessed several interventions by collectors and plunderers in different sites throughout Mexico. Examples of this include the acquisition, for a derisory sum, of the land

32 Art. 1, 2001 Convention.

33 R. Junco, C. Horell, M. Damour and F. Hanselman, 'Tras los barcos de Hernán Cortes Arqueología Subacuática en la Villa Rica de la Veracruz' (2020) in *Arqueología Mexicana* vol. XXVIII Number 164 pp. 40–45.

where the archaeological site of Chichén Itzá is located, by the first American consul to Mexico, Edward Thompson. Between 1904 and 1911, Thompson dredged the site's cenotes (sinkhole) and extracted over 30,000 pieces, which included bone (human and animal), copal (tree resin), golden fabrics and artifacts, jade, wood, obsidian, copper, and rubber. Between 1954 and 1967, sports divers extracted from the lakes inside the Nevado de Toluca, Estado de Mexico, copal spheres and cones, ceramic pots and wood carved in a wavelike fashion, as well as artifacts, bones, and fossils from the Media Luna spring in San Luis Potosí. Furthermore, in 1957 in Quintana Roo, Robert Marx, a known treasure hunter, tracked down and removed, using dynamite, the sunken ship known as the *Matancero* but whose true identity was never determined. From this wreck he removed bottles, plates, crucifixes, silver and brass cutlery, amongst other items, although he was arrested by the police. Years later, the Mexican Exploration and Water Sports Club (Club de Exploraciones y Deportes Acuáticos de Mexico) carried on with the exploitation of this site, extracting anchors and canons that are currently in a deplorable state of conservation.

Academic interest in the rituals of Pre-Columbian peoples settled around bodies of water, dates back to the 1960s. The first attempts at exploring inland water bodies were carried out by archaeologist Víctor Segovia under the direction of archaeologist Román Piña Chan at the Sacred Cenote in Chichén Itzá, and by archaeologist Roberto Gallegos at the Agua Azul Cenote in Chinkultic, Chiapas.[34] Unfortunately, these first interventions were unsuccessful given the complete lack of visibility underwater at the Chichén Itzá Cenote, and the absence of an appropriate methodology to document the *in situ* remains and for their safe removal.

Since 1972, archaeological projects started to contemplate the need to understand the Pre-Columbian peoples' different dynamics, processes and ways of relating to marine and inland bodies of water. Some examples of this are the research carried out at the Media Luna spring in San Luis Potosí; in rivers and dams (Coatlán, Morelos; Arroyo Medio, Veracruz; and Presa de la Angostura, Chiapas); in the marine area (Xel-Ha, Quintana Roo, carried out by archaeologists Jesús Mora, Humberto Besso-Oberto, Rafael Alducín and Carlos Navarrete).[35]

---

34 R. Alducin, 'Antecedentes de la arqueología subacuática oficial en Mexico. Sus perspectivas y futuro' in inah *1er Foro por la Defensa del Patrimonio Arqueológico, Histórico y Subacuático* (INAH, 1988).

35 Both during the 1960s and 1970s, civil associations and diving clubs, as well as some amateurs participated in some of the projects, with the authorisation of the INAH. Alducin *ibid* at p. 71.

These initiatives led to the establishment in 1973 of the archaeological diving unit of the National School of Anthropology and History (*grupo de buceo arqueológico* en la Escuela Nacional de Antropología e Historia) (ENAH) by student Humberto Besso-Oberto and graduates Ernesto Díaz Infante and Alfonso Pérez Munguía, which constituted a first step towards training archaeologists to become divers and to raise their awareness on the importance of the study of the materials remains of culture in aquatic environments. The idea to create the Underwater Archaeology Division was put forward for the first time in 1975, by Besso-Oberto, although the representatives of the Institute did not immediately take it into consideration.

Over the course of six years, archaeologists were trained in diving techniques, and by 1979, the group invited Dr. George Bass to teach a course on underwater and maritime archaeology, and the project to create an underwater archaeology division was once again put forward. That same year, American divers discovered two sunken ships from the sixteenth and eighteenth centuries respectively, on the Cayo Nuevo reef, Gulf of Mexico. They informed the Mexican authorities of these finds in February 1980. The attention given to this report finally led authorities to acknowledge the urgent need to create a special division within the Institute specialising in research, protection, conservation, and management of Mexican UCH and dissemination of such expertise, spearheaded by Pilar Luna M.A. until 2017.

Since then, there have been several projects developed in order to attend to this UCH, both in marine and inland waters, and whose themes include the study of fossil remains and human remains of the first inhabitants of the Yucatan peninsula, rituals surrounding bodies of water, pre-Hispanic cemeteries inside flooded caves and shipwrecks from the sixteenth to the twentieth centuries, to mention but a few.[36]

4 Implementation of the 2001 Convention

Mexico, motivated by concern about the threat to UCH presented by commercial exploitation worldwide and the absence of an international legal instrument to protect it, became one of the main promoters of the drafting and acceptance of the 2001 Convention, as expressed by Pilar Luna:

36 Other than the INAH, some universities, such as the Autónoma de Yucatán and the Autónoma de México, have developed for some years now projects on subaquatic and marine archaeology, respectively. P. Luna, 'Mexico' in C. Ruppé and J. Barstad (eds.) *International Handbook of Underwater Archaeology* (Plenum Publishers, 2002).

> From 1998 to 2001, experts from several countries, including Mexico, met at the headquarters of the United Nations Educational, Scientific and Cultural Organization (UNESCO) in Paris, to discuss the issues that should be included in such an important document. We had to overcome critical moments, make difficult decisions and move beyond extreme positions to reach an agreement for the sake of protecting and researching the heritage that lies beneath our planet's waters.[37]

Mexico ratified this Convention in 2006, as a result of which the country became a member of the Convention's first Scientific and Technical Advisory Body (STAB), which has made it possible to provide scientific and technical advice on research and protection of heritage located under marine and inland waters on an international scale.[38] Furthermore, Mexico was part of the taskforce responsible for formulating the Convention's Operational Guidelines, published in 2015.[39]

Those projects since carried out in Mexico, both in marine and inland waters, have been aligned with the most important principles of the 2001 Convention, such as: non-invasive work in matters relating to the obligation to preserve the cultural heritage; and the *in situ* preservation of UCH as a first consideration. This is considered a fundamental aspect, since the premise is to avoid the extraction of materials whose conservation cannot be guaranteed. Thus, the only objects that shall be recovered are those used for diagnostical purposes or that are at risk of being plundered or destroyed. Other principles underlying projects in Mexico include the non-exploitation of this heritage, the training of experts, and regional and international cooperation.[40]

With regard to the component of international cooperation, Mexico participated in the two introductory workshops on underwater archaeology and management of UCH, with the aim of training a new cadre of specialists (capacity building) in this discipline, who could also contribute to the consolidation of underwater archaeological practice in Latin America and the Caribbean. Instructors from Mexico, Argentina, Great Britain, and Spain participated in these workshops. The first course on 'Research and management

37 P. Luna, 'México y la Convención 2001: un apoyo vital y mutuo' in F.J. López y F. Vidargas, (eds.) *Convenciones UNESCO Una visión articulada desde Iberoamérica*. (INAH, 2013).

38 U. Guérin, 'Diseñar el Camino para la Cooperación Internacional y promover una visión global' in R. M. Roffiel, H. Barba y R. Junco, (coord.) *Pilar Luna Erreguerena Pionera de la Arqueología Subacuática en México*. (INAH, 2022).

39 UNESCO, Operational Guidelines for the Convention on the Protection of the Underwater Cultural Heritage, 2015.

40 Luna *supra* note 37 at p. 98.

in underwater and maritime archaeology', coordinated by UNESCO and INAH, took place in September 2010, and featured the participation of 27 representatives from Cuba, Chile, Colombia, Argentina, Ecuador, Guatemala, Paraguay, Peru, Uruguay, Panama, Nicaragua, the Dominican Republic, El Salvador, and Mexico. The second was organised by the Spanish Government, UNESCO and INAH, and the State and municipal governments of Campeche. It was held in July 2019, for the benefit of 19 archaeologists and experts in related disciplines such as anthropology, history, and marine biology, from Bolivia, Chile, Costa Rica, Cuba, Dominican Republic, Ecuador, Honduras, Nicaragua, Panama, Paraguay, and Uruguay. In this same vein of international cooperation for research and protection of UCH, it is noteworthy that in 2014, Mexico signed a Memorandum of Understanding with Spain.[41]

As for the legal aspect, adjustments still needed to be made regarding certain legal instruments in terms of archaeological and historical property and monuments to ensure consistency between them. To cite one example, Article 174 2006 Navigation and Maritime Trade Act (Ley de Navegación y Comercio Marítimo), as noted above, contradicts the stipulations put forward both during the 2001 Convention and by the 1972 Act in relation to the sovereign immunity of warships under international law.

Ultimately, commercial exploitation remains one of the main problems that Mexico's UCH must face on a daily basis. The sheer size of marine waters that are under Mexican jurisdiction, together with inland waters (rivers, lakes, lagoons, springs, cenotes and flooded caves and estuaries etc.), which may contain traces of UCH, make it virtually impossible to monitor and protect them all. Human, material, and financial resources, and the INAH's available infrastructure are insufficient. Therefore, the best option is to raise awareness in society, that is to say, to educate and to disseminate on the importance of UCH, as the only means of promoting knowledge related to it, explaining its value, and of preserving and protecting it.

5 Conclusion

This chapter has considered some of the legal instruments that provide for, or promote, the protection of cultural heritage, with emphasis on those that are feasible to apply to the particularities of submerged or underwater heritage

41 For information see UNESCO, Culture and Development: Underwater Cultural Heritage in Latin America and Caribbean (2015 Regional Office for Culture in Latin America and the Caribbean, Havana) at page 28.

and that are consistent with what the 2001 Convention provides. Nevertheless, one can pinpoint gaps in Mexican legislation, such as those highlighted by the 2014 addendum, when Section 28 TER was added to the 1972 Act. This addendum incorporates in part the definition of UCH in the 2001 Convention, taking care only to mention the implementation of the provisions on preservation and research with regard to archaeological and historic monuments, while leaving out the subject of protection and ownership. This is so as to avoid disputes with international law, which deals with the ownership of State vessels and aircraft. As noted above, this provision also conflicts with Article 174 of the 2006 Maritime Navigation and Trade Act, which states that derelicts, as well as the objects located inside them and that present archaeological, historical, or cultural characteristics, shall be considered the property of the nation.

Although Mexico ratified the 2001 Convention, the national legal framework regarding UCH has yet to be updated, with a view to strengthening its scope of protection and to avoid the aforementioned contradictions.

Sunken ships are part of a submerged cultural heritage that gives an account of past human activities of cultural significance, and they rest in various aquatic environments. Therefore, all objects are of equal importance, even small and isolated ones, since their study permits a better understanding of different historical processes. To destroy, move or remove them, is to destroy a part of history that gives identity to a human group. Also, sunken ships not only represent a part of the cultural heritage of humanity, but also become habitats for aquatic life, providing refuge and substrate for various species of flora and fauna.

However, although the regulatory framework is the basis for the legal protection of UCH, it should not be forgotten that the informed and responsible participation of public society is paramount for its effective safeguarding. Mexico participated in shaping the text of the 2001 Convention and it ratified it in 2006. Since its entry into force, Mexico has participated as a member of the STAB. Likewise, Mexico has participated in related international summits, such as the Decade of Ocean Science for Sustainable Development.[42]

It should be noted that the INAH's participation via the DUA in the 2001 Convention positioned Mexico as a recognised leader amongst those nations comprising the Latin American and Caribbean region, fostering the creation of similar institutions/initiatives in those countries. This international collaboration has made it possible to strengthen various initiatives, such as the signing of bilateral treaties like the Memorandum of Understanding between Spain

42 United Nations Decade of Ocean Science for Sustainable Development (2021–2030), see <https://unesco.org/en/decades/ocean-decade>.

and Mexico; the development of research projects with the participation of researchers from different countries; and the capacity building of two generations of underwater archaeologists, not only in Mexico, but also in Latin America. We also need to add participation in the Mexican ICOMOS, through the Scientific Committee on CSP and in the International Committee on the UCH.

Mexico's diverse UCH is documented through inventories which have led to research projects, the results of which have been disseminated widely and over an uninterrupted period of time through the publication of scientific books and papers in high impact journals, and through lectures, conferences and documentaries transmitted in mass and electronic media. All this is intended to generate visibility and awareness regarding the safeguarding of UCH while promoting democratic access to such information.

Some of these projects have been awarded international prizes. For example: the Hoyo Negro Underwater Archaeological Project (Proyecto Arqueológico Subacuático Hoyo Negro), which received the Field Discovery Award from the Shanghai Archaeology Forum of the Chinese Academy of Social Sciences; the documentary film presented at the third International Showcase of Audiovisual Works on Intangible Cultural Heritage; as well as recognition awarded by the Advisory Council on Underwater Archaeology in 2021 to the SAS. In addition to this, UNESCO has awarded Mexico with three endorsements for Best Practice: Museo de Arqueología Subacuática; fuerte de San José el Alto, Campeche; and the UCH of the Nevado de Toluca and Banco Chinchorro, all of which are unique to the American continent.[43]

In several regions, the SAS has developed programmes and projects linked to the protection, conservation, research, dissemination, and enhancement of UCH, which includes interdisciplinary work, both intra-agency and with national and foreign research and educational institutions. It has applied new technologies for *in situ* archaeological work, the analysis of materials and their conservation, with the involvement of members of the government, of surrounding communities and underwater explorers.

Nationwide, approximately 600 submerged archaeological sites have been recorded by INAH's Single System of Public Registration of Monuments and Archaeological and Historical Areas. However, the extensive and complex marine and inland water bodies' territory has a high potential for discoveries and ongoing studies on UCH, requiring the recording and monitoring of each piece.

With regard to protecting UCH, the SAS has focused on dealing with reports by carrying out inspections, surveys, recoveries, and salvage, issuing opinions

43 UNESCO, Best Practices of Underwater Cultural Heritage, see <https://unesco.org/en/underwater-heritage/best-practices>.

and, when resources permit, carrying out monitoring. However, on some occasions and despite institutional efforts, the lack of knowledge and application of current legislation on the protection of UCH by authorities and society in general remains a problem. To this, we need to add non-application of the law, mainly due to bureaucratic factors, even when looting and damage to UCH has been reported.

Over the years, it can be said that Mexico has successfully developed an infrastructure to manage the study, conservation, dissemination, and protection of UCH. This has succeeded in pushing forward legislative development on the matter and is cognisant of attempts to deviate from this path. The contemporary reality is that there is both the building of human capacity and an institutional and legal framework to continue this work. In this sense, whilst recognising the need to avoid complacency, it can be said that Mexico has significant potential to become a beacon in relation to the protection of UCH.

All websites last accessed February 2025.

Selected Bibliography

Cottom, B. 2001 'Patrimonio cultural nacional: El marco jurídico y conceptual', *Derecho y Cultura*, 4, Legal Research Institute-UNAM, pp. 79–107, https://revistas-colaboracion.juridicas.unam.mx/index.php/derecho-cultura/article/view/7328/6598.

Cottom, B. *Nación patrimonio cultural y legislación: los debates parlamentarios y la construcción del marco jurídico federal sobre monumentos en Mexico* (Miguel Ángel Porrúa, 2008).

M. G. Espinosa, *Modelo de gestión para la conservación del patrimonio arqueológico en México* Master's thesis in Anthropology, (Universidad Nacional Autónoma de México, 2007).

Online Legal Library of the UNAMs Institute for Legal Research, L. López *El caso particular de la legislación sobre los monumentos arqueológicos* pp. 185–204, https://revistas-colaboracion.juridicas.unam.mx/index.php/rev-facultad-derecho-mx/article/viewFile/28863/26094#:~:text=El%20Congreso%20de%20la%20Uni%C3%B3n,de%20la%20Inspecci%C3%B3n%20de%20Monumentos.

P. Luna, 'Mexico y la Convención 2001: un apoyo vital y mutuo' in F.J. López y F. Vidargas, (eds.) *Convenciones UNESCO Una visión articulada desde Iberoamérica.* (INAH, 2013).

U. Guérin, 'Diseñar el Camino para la Cooperación Internacional y promover una visión global" in R. M. Roffiel, H. Barba and R. Junco, (cord.) *Pilar Luna Erreguerena Pionera de la Arqueología Subacuática en Mexico.* (INAH, 2022).

CHAPTER 13

The Netherlands

*Andrea Klomp**, *Thijs Maarleveld*†, *and Martijn Manders***

1 Introduction

The Netherlands is a maritime country, with maritime commerce shaping its history and its culture. This maritime identity has traditionally resulted in a strong legal stance in international law. The legacy of Hugo Grotius and his 'Mare Liberum' of 1609 is anchored in Dutch thinking: the freedom to trade wherever and with whomever.[1] After 400 years, this still has a strong basis within maritime history, traditions, and common uses. It is thus perhaps idiosyncratic that reasonable legal protection of tangible maritime heritage, comprised in archaeological sites buried under sediment and water, has taken so long to crystallise.

The protective policies and legal instruments for cultural heritage, and particularly underwater sites, have seen major changes during the last few decades. These changes are ongoing, fortunately in the right direction. Large shifts were triggered by the recognition that heritage could be also found underwater (in the 1970s and 1980s), by the implementation of the Council of Europe (CoE) Convention on the Protection of Archaeological Heritage (revised),[2] better known as the Valletta Convention, and more recently the ratification process of the UNESCO Convention for the Protection of the Underwater Cultural Heritage (the 2001 Convention).[3] During the General Assembly of UNESCO in 2001, the Netherlands abstained from voting. In 2016, a governmental decision to ratify was finally taken and the process to implement the necessary changes in legislation started. However, other political priorities and several legislative complications in adjusting the existing juridical system to the demands of the

* Consultant at Rijksdienst voor Cultureel Erfgoed.
† Head of the Maritime Policy Department at the predecessor of the Cultural Heritage Agency of the Netherlands.
** Professor by special appointment in Underwater Archaeology and Maritime Heritage Management at the Faculty of Archaeology, University of Leiden.

1 A. Woudenberg and Th.J. Maarleveld, 'Hugo de Groot en UNESCO op gespannen voet' (2002) 77 *Nederlands Juristenblad* 1025.

2 ETS 143, Valletta 16.1.1992.

3 2562 UNTS 1.

 | DOI:10.1163/9789004510883_015

2001 Convention have caused progress in the ratification process to be disappointing. That said, in the last decades, many steps have been taken to protect underwater cultural heritage (UCH) in the Netherlands in a much-improved way than was the case under the first heritage legislation in 1961. Both capacity and financial means have increased substantially. There is no doubt that the 2001 Convention will be ratified eventually, but the planned date of 2023 has again prooved to be infeasible. Its Annex has been long accepted as a guideline for dealing with UCH, as is the case in many countries. However, whether there is enough support within the Dutch community of professional practitioners in development-led archaeology for their work to reflect it, is another question. For them, another quality system, that of the Dutch Quality Standards for Archaeology, is daily business. As the scope of their work is largely determined by the 'disturber pays' principle, they have expressed apprehension to embrace new aspects, such as involvement of the public, museums, and scientific institutions, for this may increase the cost of archaeological research. As part of the ratification process, planning differences in both systems must be smoothed out. A lot of ground, or water, has been covered to date, but a long and winding road is still ahead.

2 Development of the Regulatory System Applicable to UCH

2.1 *Early Protection and the Role of the National Government*

The Netherlands became involved with the management of UCH in several ways. First, was the management of heritage in inland and territorial waters. Thirty years ago, the latter still had the traditional width of 3 nautical miles (nm). In 1985, after conclusion of the United Nations Convention on the Law of the Sea 1982 (LOSC),[4] this was broadened to 12 nm from the baseline.[5]

Although not explicitly mentioned in heritage legislation until 1988, UCH in inland and territorial waters has arguably been under Dutch jurisdiction all along: heritage is heritage, no matter where it is. However, no consistent regime for its management was deployed before the 1980s, nor was its nature well-understood. Occasional finds had traditionally surfaced through dredging, and during the twentieth century additionally through diving and commercial salvage. Publicly, this was manifested mostly through well-visited antiquities markets and auctions. The frequency of activities producing finds increased when equipment for SCUBA-diving became more widely available and affordable in

4 1833 UNTS 397.

5 Wet grenzen Nederlandse territoriale zee, *Staatsblad* 1985, 129.

the 1960s and 1970s. At the time, most of these activities were unregulated. The excitement of the finds resonated well with museums and historians, for whom the artefacts were merely an illustration of historical facts. This followed a more ancient and orthodox tradition that had largely ceased to exist in terrestrial archaeology: dealing with historical and art collections as commercial objects for limited benefit. Some collections were presented as important historical or art pieces for a wider audience in museums and exhibition spaces, although without much regard for their archaeological context. Unregulated appropriation prompted discussion and disputes arose, although these were generally focussed upon issues associated with ownership, rather than archaeological value, public interests and (governmental) responsibilities.

In the decades after the Second World War (WWII), heritage management was largely centralised and executed by two separate agencies: the National Service for Built Heritage (Rijksdienst voor de Monumentenzorg (RDMZ)) and the National Service for Archaeology (Rijksdienst voor het Oudheidkundig Bodemonderzoek (ROB)). While the management and protection of built heritage focused on preservation and restoration, archaeological heritage was mainly used for the sake of knowledge building, i.e., investigating by excavation. The ROB originally developed as a 'rescue and research' institution, with excavation activities and their regulation as the key issue. The listing and enduring management of sites were of limited importance by comparison and there was a strong bias for visible monuments, such as burial mounds and megalithic monuments.

2.2 *The Early Stages of Underwater Heritage Management*

The management of maritime and underwater heritage developed on two fronts, as not all heritage with a maritime component is necessarily submerged. Throughout the twentieth century more data and information were collated on the potential of archaeological sites deeply buried in the soil and underwater. Large-scale works, such as the reclamation of agricultural land in the former Zuiderzee and the Rotterdam harbour extension, clearly showed the archaeological potential of the sea and waterbeds around the Netherlands, with the discovery of many shipwrecks, remains of extensive inhabited, prehistoric landscapes and Roman and medieval sites.[6] To research those shipwrecks found during reclamation of the Zuiderzee area, a museum with excavation

6 See, for example G.D. van der Heide, *De Zuiderzee. Van land tot water, van water tot land* (Haren, 1974 and L.B.M. Verhart, 'Mesolithic barbed points and other implements from Europoort, The Netherlands' *Oudheidkundige Mededelingen uit het Rijksmuseum van Oudheden* 68, 145–194.

capacity was set up, within the IJsselmeerpolders Development Authority (Rijksdienst voor de IJsselmeerpolders (RIJP)). This happened in parallel to developments at the ROB but within a different ministry. What both the museum and the ROB had in common was a focus on knowledge building.

The first steps toward the management of UCH were taken in 1980, when the Ministry of Culture, Recreation and Social Work appointed a coordinator for underwater archaeology to prepare a policy document on UCH. This resulted in the creation of an underwater archaeology unit under the direct responsibility of the Ministry and separate from the ROB. From 1980 onwards, the management of UCH within Dutch territory was slowly brought into alignment with its terrestrial equivalent. In 1999, the above unit for underwater archaeology and the shipwreck museum of the IJsselmeerpolders Development Authority joined together to form the Nationaal Instituut for Scheeps – en Onderwater Archeologie (NISA), housed in Lelystad, the capital of Flevoland province. NISA comprised both a diving team for underwater research and a unit for shipwreck excavations on land, comprehensive facilities for conservation and restoration, and a large-scale repository for ship finds from all over the country. It became the maritime division of the ROB, but still based at a separate location. This physical separation proved an obstacle for rapprochement between the two organisations, causing maritime archaeology to remain somewhat isolated from mainstream archaeology. Things began to change in 2001, when a unit for maritime heritage policy was embedded within the ROB structure and stationed at its headquarters in Amersfoort.

2.3 *The Cultural Heritage Agency and Its Current Role*

RDMZ and ROB merged in 2006, followed in 2011 by the incorporation of the Instituut Collectie Nederland (ICN), responsible for the care of the national art collection. Together, they formed the Cultural Heritage Agency of the Netherlands (RCE),[7] as it is today, covering the domains of built heritage, (underwater) archaeology, cultural landscapes, and movable heritage. In 2016, both in an attempt to integrate maritime and underwater cultural heritage work more with the activities executed on land and at the same time a cost-cutting measure, the maritime research and repository facilities in Lelystad were divested, the maritime collection was brought under the management of the neighbouring museum, Stichting Erfgoedpark Batavialand, and all maritime

---

7 The English name of the RCE – Cultural Heritage Agency of the Netherlands – is actually incorrect. The RCE is a full governmental body, a department of the Ministry of Education, Culture and Science (OCW) and not an agency.

and underwater archaeological and cultural heritage management activities were placed in Amersfoort.

In the latter part of the twentieth century many public tasks were decentralised and privatised. The management of archaeological heritage was no exception. In implementing the principles of the Valletta Convention, numerous heritage protection responsibilities were transferred to local authorities (municipalities) and development-led archaeology was left to private parties. These developments had far-reaching impact on the role of the RCE as the National Service. From an institute mainly involved with research and executing statutory tasks, it evolved into a centre of expertise for all stakeholders in heritage management, generating and disseminating knowledge, advising on policies and legislation, and implementing them at a national level. Through the National Agency for Public Works and Water Management (Rijkswaterstaat), it obtained a formal advisory role concerning archaeological heritage in large-scale development projects, such as the construction of the high-speed railroad (HSL) and the dredging of a fairway from Amsterdam to the Northern provinces (Vaarweg Amsterdam-Lemmer). In relation to the management of UCH, the RCE retained more of a research role. This was because, firstly, a substantial part of UCH is situated in the Territorial Sea (TS), outside of municipal boundaries, and thus the sole responsibility of the national government. Secondly, where located within municipal borders, stakeholders can be apprehensive about taking full responsibility for UCH, due to the specific knowledge it requires, the long-term management commitments and research, and the high costs involved. Funding from developers, for example, may be absent in situations where UCH is threatened by natural causes or by the ongoing effects of long-past activities. All this caused local and regional authorities to appeal to the national government to step in.

Another reason supporting a more intensive involvement of the RCE in maritime cultural heritage management is the role it can play in international UCH protection. The sovereignty and thus ownership of wrecks entails an, at least moral, obligation to be involved in the management of this heritage. Heritage is also relevant to more general diplomatic relations between the Netherlands and other States: discussion and negotiation on protecting heritage can often 'break the ice' and provide for a sense of unique bonding (see section 7.3 below).

3 Sites and Activities: Legal Protection

The Netherlands' earliest decree regulating the protection of archaeological remains dates from 1734 and concerned protection of megalithic tombs (hunebedden) that were at risk. The indirect cause was the introduction of shipworm (*Teredo navalis*) in Dutch waters, which were eating wooden posts placed as revetments for the dykes around the Zuiderzee. The danger created prompted the use of stone replacements, thus threatening the megalithic tombs, which might have their stones taken. Arguably, this protection ensured the survival of these visible large stone monuments. However, despite such early evidence, even when archaeology and heritage management further developed, legal protection lagged behind, especially where UCH was concerned.

3.1 *Monumentenwet* (*Monuments and Historic Buildings Act*)

In 1961, the Monumentenwet (Monuments and Historic Buildings Act) was enacted.[8] It was the first comprehensive national regulation regarding the protection of built monuments and archaeological sites and created a legal framework for the activities of both National Services (RDMZ and ROB) and of any other institution or private person with an interest in monuments and sites in the Netherlands.

The Act defined a monument as anything 50 years or older and of public interest because of its beauty, its scientific or cultural-historical value, including specific spatial assemblages of buildings, structures and their surroundings based on their visual quality, and provided for the listing of 'protected monuments' in an official Register. Approximately 60,000 historic buildings and 1,600 archaeological sites have since been included on the Register.[9] The Act also offered blanket protection of archaeological heritage, via two complementary means: a general prohibition of archaeological excavations, under Article 22, unless licenced by the Minister of Education, Culture and Science; and under Article 24, an obligation to report any chance discovery to the mayor of the relevant municipality.

The definition of an archaeological excavation entailed disturbing the earth in order to trace or investigate archaeological remains. Disturbing the earth for other purposes or investigating a site by visual or other non-intrusive means was thus not prohibited. A licence to excavate could be provided to both institutions and individuals. However, in practice, excavations remained the prerogative of the ROB, the National Museum of Antiquities, several academic

---

8 Wet van 22 juni 1961, houdende voorzieningen in het belang van het behoud van monumenten van geschiedenis en kunst (Monumentenwet) *Staatsblad* 1961, 200.

9 Currently there are 1,467 archaeological monuments, of which nine are situated underwater. See for the National Monument Register: <https://monumentenregister.cultureelerfgoed.nl/>.

institutions and of historic cities, such as Amsterdam and Rotterdam, that established their own archaeological services.

The obligation to report chance discoveries was the other cornerstone of blanket protection. It applied to any object which the finder 'knows or can reasonably assume' is a monument (Article 24(1)). The obligation to report implied the provision of information and making discovered objects available for scientific research. In such cases of chance discovery, Article 25 also provided that a ministerial order could stop any work, wholly or partially for a definite or indefinite period or/and permit scientific/archaeological research. Projects incurring extra costs caused by any resulting delay were to be compensated by the State.

3.2 *Monumentenwet 1988 (Monuments and Historic Buildings Act 1988)*

In 1988, the 1961 Act was amended, principally to adjust regulation to reflect changing views on the respective roles of central and local government. Thus, the changes gave municipalities a more active role, and responsibility for the care of immovable cultural heritage.

In archaeological terms, the Monumentenwet 1988 addressed some technical deficiencies and lack of clarity associated with the earlier legislation, but the general framework of protection remained unchanged. However, an important step was made regarding UCH. Whilst the definitions in the 1961 Act did not exclude its application to underwater sites, finds and activities, it was quite evident that it had not been written with this form of heritage in mind. The 1988 Act addressed this by including express application to it.

In addition, as underwater activities intensified, more archaeological discoveries were made in waters outside any municipality's competence. The formal trajectory of reporting ran through the offices of the relevant municipality's mayor and, although in practice this was usually followed up by the predecessors of the RCE, some argued that at sea, in the absence of municipal competence, no reporting obligation existed. In 1985, this led the then Minister of Culture to declare that the 1961 legislation would thenceforth be interpreted in such a way that its obligations applied independently of the municipal organisation and that he would establish a Department for Underwater Archaeology to administer reports on underwater sites. This was a milestone, and the protection of UCH would now be explicitly organised through the same system as other heritage.

3.3 *Further Developments of the Monumentenwet 1988*

In 1992, the Netherlands signed the Valletta Convention. Under its implementation, via passing of the Wet op de Archeologische Monumentenzorg

(Archaeological Monuments Protection Act) in 2007,[10] the Monuments and Historic Buildings Act as well as other legislation including the Spatial Planning Act (Wet Ruimtelijke Ordening) and the Earth Removal Act (Ontgrondingenwet) were changed, making *in situ* preservation the leading principle for archaeological heritage management. This principle was given effect by making archaeology an integral part of the spatial planning process and introducing the 'disturber pays' principle.

As the spatial planning process in the Netherlands is predominantly executed at municipal level, the role of local government in archaeological heritage management became pivotal. Municipalities were instructed to weigh archaeological interest in spatial development processes, by means of an archaeological assessment. Based on the outcome, authorised development could be subject to conditions protecting the archaeological heritage or an obligation to excavate it. The new legislation stipulated that archaeological finds would become property of the province in which they were excavated,[11] or State property when found at sea, outside of municipal borders. For this, each province had to appoint and maintain an archaeological repository.[12] The national government remained in charge of maintaining a facility for ship finds, via the maritime repository in Lelystad. In practice, there was gradual transition to these new roles and responsibilities, since the *modus operandi* of the archaeological field adjusted to them long before they became officially stipulated in the 2007 legislation.

Although the Wet op de Archeologische Monumentenzorg codified important changes to the organisation of management of archaeological heritage, the basic principles of the system of blanket protection remained unchanged. The novelty was its extension to the Contiguous Zone (CZ), to 24 nm, which the Netherlands claimed in 2006, and included UCH. However, the incorporation of archaeology into the planning process for activities with incidental

---

10 Wet van 21 december 2006 tot wijziging van de Monumentenwet 1988 en enkele andere wetten ten behoeve van de archeologische monumentenzorg mede in verband met de implementatie van het Verdrag van Valletta (Wet op de archeologische monumentenzorg) *Staatsblad* 2007, 42.

11 Although decision-making regarding archaeological sites was placed at the local level, provinces are responsible for the storage of archaeological finds and documentation, for reasons of both efficiency and to prevent fragmentation of archaeological collections. Municipalities may obtain ownership if they can demonstrate that they are equipped with a suitable repository to house archaeological artefacts.

12 Most provinces already maintained such a repository, but the Wet op de Archeologische Monumentenzorg, explicitly gave provinces the primary responsibility for the artefacts retrieved from excavations.

effects on UCH in the TS and in the Exclusive Economic Zone (EEZ) and Continental Shelf (CS) remained incomplete.[13] In 2007, it was thought sufficient to limit archaeological obligations to activities with the largest impact: aggregate extraction and projects requiring environmental impact assessment (EIA). This perspective was to change in the following decade, as marine planning became established.

The Dutch implementation of the Valletta Convention largely focussed on development control. As a result, those situations where no development was occurring but where protective interventions were nevertheless needed, tended to be overlooked. No legal responsibility for *in situ* management could be established. This acted as a particular disadvantage for UCH, which frequently needs active management measures to prevent destruction by natural causes or illegal salvage and a gap filled by the Cultural Heritage Agency.

In 2012, the Monuments Act 1988 was changed, in particular to accommodate the modernisation of the management of historic buildings.[14] One of the changes made, however, also affected archaeological heritage: the 50-year age limit for monuments was abolished. The main reason being that meaningful buildings were sometimes disappearing before reaching this age.[15] To keep a level of uniformity in the definition of both buildings and archaeological monuments, the age limit was also abolished for the latter.

This abolition has raised an issue for more recent shipwrecks. The 50-year limit had been, rightfully or not, a clear boundary for avocational divers and others, such as salvagers, in terms of those wrecks not to touch. With this boundary no longer in place both younger and older wrecks now need some form of significance assessment to determine whether they fall under the blanket protection of the legislation or not.

3.4 *Omgevingswet* (*Environment and Planning Act*) *and Erfgoedwet* (*Cultural Heritage Act*)

In 2010, the national government started a process of consolidating environmental legislation, merging 26 Acts into one, in order to simplify the regulation

---

13 The EEZ was established in 2000 (Besluit grenzen Nederlandse exclusieve economische zone, Staatsblad 2000-167). Its limits coincide, as was agreed with both Belgium and the United Kingdom, with the borders of the Dutch Continental Shelf.

14 Wet van 6 juni 2011 tot wijziging van de Monumentenwet 1988 en de Wet algemene bepalingen omgevingsrecht in verband met de modernisering van de monumentenzorg *Staatsblad* 2011, 330.

15 *Kamerstukken II*, 2009/10, 32433 nr. 3 (MvT).

of environmental and planning affairs.[16] Heritage legislation was included, ensuring compliance with relevant CoE conventions, such as the aforementioned Valletta Convention, the Convention for the Protection of the Architectural Heritage of Europe (Granada 1985)[17] and the European Landscape Convention (Florence, 2000).[18] For UCH, it offered the opportunity to implement Article 5 of the Valletta Convention more thoroughly than the Wet op de Archeologische Monumentenzorg had.[19] Under the new legislation, called the Omgevingswet, competent authorities can request an archaeological assessment for the main activities at sea subject to licensing that can incidentally affect UCH, both in the TS and on the Dutch CS.[20] An obligation to report chance archaeological finds during these activities was also added.[21] The Omgevingswet was approved by Parliament in 2016,[22] but its entry into force has been postponed several times, for a large extent due to delay in completing the digital infrastructure necessary for its execution. At the time of writing, its entry into force was set as 1 January 2024.

In the slipstream of the reform of environmental legislation, heritage legislation was also transformed. With most heritage regulations concerning the spatial domain being transferred to the Omgevingswet, it was decided that the remainder could best be integrated into one new Act, the Erfgoedwet (Cultural Heritage Act).[23] This new legislation enabled changes in the legal provisions regarding archaeology, prompted by evaluation of the Wet op de Archeologische Monumentenzorg. One of these was substitution of the licensing system for archaeological excavations, overseen by the Minister of Education, Culture and Science, by a third-party certification system, lessening the State's involvement. The new system requires archaeological contractors

16 Regeerakkoord-vvd-cda, Vrijheid en verantwoordelijkheid. Regeerakkoord VVD en CDA, p. 29. <https://www.rijksoverheid.nl>.

17 ETS 121, Granada 01.12.1987.

18 ETS 176, Florence 20.10.2000.

19 Article 5 of the Valletta Convention deals with the integrated conservation of archaeological heritage, by, *inter alia*, the participation of archaeologists "in the various stages of development schemes".

20 Besluit van 3 juli 2018, houdende regels over activiteiten in de fysieke leefomgeving (Besluit activiteiten leefomgeving), hoofdstuk 7: Activiteiten in de Noordzee *Staatsblad* 2018, 293.

21 Idem, art. 13.7.

22 Wet van 23 maart 2016, houdende regels over het beschermen en benutten van de fysieke leefomgeving (Omgevingswet) *Staatsblad* 2016, 156.

23 Wet van 9 december 2015, houdende bundeling en aanpassing van regels op het terrein van cultureel erfgoed (Erfgoedwet) *Staatsblad* 2015, 511.The Erfgoedwet entered into force on 1 July 2016, repealing the Monuments Act 1988.

to demonstrate their ability to meet a professional standard for archaeological work to be certificated by a private body, which monitors quality through regular audits. Public archaeological services, including the Cultural Heritage Agency's archaeological team, are subject to the same rules.

A specific amendment relating to UCH was made, as a reaction to an increasing number of detrimental activities directed at it, in particular the salvage of metal parts from historic shipwrecks dating from both World Wars (WWI and WWII). In 2011, salvage attempts of the British WWI shipwrecks HMS *Aboukir*, *Cressey* and *Hogue* generated controversy in both English and Dutch media and led to Parliamentary questions. A petition was submitted to the Dutch Secretary of State for Culture, requesting better protection of UCH, together with a plea for ratification of the 2001 Convention.[24] Subsequent consultation with the Dutch prosecutor for the North Sea clarified that taking legal steps against unwanted interference with UCH would be difficult under the existing legislation. The main obstacle concerned the legal definition of archaeological excavations. The Monumentenwet 1988 stated that an archaeological excavation must comprise disturbance of the soil (Article 1 (2)(h)). This definition makes perfect sense for archaeological remains on land, especially in the Dutch situation where sedimentation by either marine or riverine processes have almost always caused archaeological remains to be covered by thick layers of clay and sand. For underwater archaeological sites, however, this is not always the case. In more dynamic areas, such as the North Sea and the Wadden Sea, archaeological remains, in particular shipwrecks, can periodically surface and at least become partially uncovered. Although there will be little doubt by those who are well-versed in maritime archaeological practice that removing objects from the seabed will involve at least some disturbance of the seabed, the prosecution of illegal excavation proved to be challenging.[25]

To address this issue, the Erfgoedwet amended the definition for archaeological excavations for underwater archaeological heritage, bringing it more in line with the definition of activities directed at UCH contained in the 2001 Convention. The new definition (Article 5.1 (1)) comprises all activities with the purpose of finding, researching, or acquiring UCH that involve the complete or partial replacement or removal of its parts. These activities are prohibited, except for professional bodies that are in the possession of the required archaeological certificates.

24 See for example, <https://www.waddenacademie.nl/en/news/news-archive-article/zijlstra-vindt-goede-bescherming-van-wrakken-in-de-noordzee-belangrijk/>.

25 *Kamerstukken* II 2014/15 34109, nr. 3, p. 34 (MvT).

3.5 *Regulations for Avocational Divers*

The Erfgoedwet also introduced substantial changes regarding the position of volunteers. The high standards prescribed for archaeological work could only be met by professionals, therefore limiting the role of volunteers in archaeological heritage management considerably. Although volunteers were allowed to participate in professionally-led archaeological research, the economic model of commercial archaeology left little real opportunity.[26] Reflecting changing trends favouring citizen participation in the public domain, triggered by the CoE Convention on the Value of Cultural heritage for Society (Faroe Convention, 2015),[27] the Erfgoedwet created opportunities for volunteers to conduct archaeological excavations without the need to comply with professional standards. Opportunities include the use of a metal detector in the top 30 cm of the subsoil,[28] and permission to excavate in areas where the (local) government has decided that no professional archaeological research is necessary.[29] The latter is usually related to areas where preliminary, professional research has demonstrated that no archaeological remains of high cultural interest are present.

Despite these exemptions, the new legislation was not received well by avocational divers, as it did not accommodate their interests. Their motivation for being involved with UCH is often the excitement of discovering new sites, establishing their identity, and collecting artefacts for identification purposes or recovery from dynamic underwater environments is one of the most appealing components. Under the Erfgoedwet, this was now explicitly ruled out. As a result, the diving community felt their activities had become criminalised, instead of being seen as a contribution to the management of UCH and it objected against the new legislation and the RCE, for being "bureaucratic and arrogant".[30] Significantly, the search for a better and more workable legal framework had in practice resulted in more distance between the government and one if its main stakeholders. After a period of reconciliation and renewed cooperation, an additional exemption for diving volunteers is now being

26 An additional difficulty in the cooperation between professional and avocational archaeologists, especially in underwater archaeology, is the legislation in regard to working conditions. This is not the place to get into this in detail, but the authority relationship in combination with professional rules for a safe working environment, makes this cooperation difficult in practice.

27 ETS 199, Faro 27.10.2005.

28 Besluit Erfgoedwet archeologie, art. 2.2 *Staatsblad* 2015, 155.

29 *Ibid*, Art. 2.3.

30 Bouman, D., 2015, Eindrapportage van het onderzoek: Duiken op Wrakken. Vrijwilligers in de onderwater archeologie, MR & C, p 33.

developed to enable small-scale activities under supervision of the RCE, with the purpose of identification of UCH and the safeguarding of objects under immediate threat by natural erosion. At the time of writing, this exemption has been drafted and is under consultation.[31]

4 A System of Quality Control

As above, the signing of the Valletta Convention triggered an intensive review of the organisation of archaeology in the Netherlands. The result was that archaeological work was no longer the sole domain of government and scientific institutes. In turn, demand for commercial archaeological companies increased and new responsibilities were placed upon developers, who now became part of the decision-making process regarding archaeological site management. This prompted the need for a quality system for archaeological activities. A choice was made to establish a self-regulating system for archaeological contractors, developers, and governmental bodies. Public archaeological services remained players in the field, but other stakeholders now had an equal voice.

Archaeological activities became standardised and subject to the Quality Standards for Dutch Archaeology (KNA). Largely, the KNA protocols and rules are in line with the 'operational rules' of the Annex to the 2001 Convention but are far more elaborate. At the heart of the standards is a programme of requirements necessary for each archaeological intervention, including research questions, based on the relevant (archaeological) research agendas at national and regional level, to demonstrate the scientific relevance of the project.[32] This is broadly consistent with the demands for a project design in Rule 10 of the Annex.

The KNA is process-oriented, generating an archaeological heritage 'care-cycle', from desk-based research to excavation and *in situ* protection. Earlier versions contained different quality standards for both terrestrial and nautical activities. The newest version integrates the two, albeit with separate protocols on how to execute different actions.[33] Responsible persons are subject to high standards and actor-status registration.[34] Their different functions/titles come

---

31 <http://www.internetconsultatie.nl/archeologiebesluit>.

32 Nationale Onderzoeksagenda Archeologie <noaa.cultureelerfgoed.nl>.

33 For the current version of the Dutch Quality Standard for Archaeology (KNA) see: <https://www.sikb.nl/archeologie/richtlijnen/brl-sikb-4000>.

34 For activities directed at UCH an actor can have the status of a prospector, senior underwater archeologist, specialist and/or field technician.

with a set of rules relating to competences, education, qualifications, and experiences. These aspects are monitored and must be updated yearly, thus giving effect to Rules 22 and 23 of the Annex to the 2001 Convention.

4.1 *The Evaluation of UCH*

Developments have delivered a significant amount of new research and archaeological data. However, in the past few years discussions have started on its scientific quality and public benefit. This is partly due to forthcoming ratification of the 2001 Convention and the implementation of archaeological heritage management in the Omgevingswet, discussed above, which has a primary focus on the quality of living in general, but also coincides with a larger debate within the Netherlands and across Europe. Increasingly, greater significance has been given to science and public involvement during archaeological activities, in turn influencing decisions on what is important heritage (or not). Discussions on who should stipulate the value of heritage and who needs to be involved in this decision-making process began in the early 2000s. Originally, with UCH mainly seen as of archaeological interest, assessment of value focussed on gaining knowledge. The changes started during the establishment of a Maritime Programme in 2012, when other values, such as commemorative, experiential and biodiversity values, became part of the assessment. This Maritime Programme was established at the RCE to address backlogs in UCH management, not only in the fields of law and policy, but also in the quality of work and capacity.[35] Maritime and UCH management was first implemented in the standard RCE structure in 2022. It was also the year that the University of Leiden first appointed a professor in maritime archaeology and cultural heritage.[36]

5 Law Enforcement

As noted, legal protection of UCH is relatively new in the Netherlands. The acceptance that there is such a thing, and that it is threatened, needs to become part of a universal value, which can only come through awareness raising, and as such the prevailing start point is a soft approach in heritage management.

---

35 For the results of the Maritime Programmes that were established to resolve the backlogs see: International Programme for Maritime heritage 2017–2021: <https://www.cultureelerfgoed.nl/publicaties/publicaties/2022/01/01/eindrapportage-programma-maritiem-erfgoed-internationaal and Maritime Programme Netherlands (2018–2020): file:///C:/Users/MMand/AppData/Local/Temp/1/MicrosoftEdgeDownloads/257d655b-1c83-4664-ad1d-486613fb6fa4/Resultaten+Maritiem+Erfgoed+Nederland.pdf>.

36 This position was taken by one of the authors, Martijn Manders.

However, should it not, legislation and law enforcement provide the key. International law, or the formulation of international principles, can trigger changes in the accepted body of values to which Dutch society wishes to conform. The fact that regulation follows acceptance, rather than the other way around, may explain why the implementation of multilateral international agreements in domestic legislation takes such a long time. The UNESCO Convention 1970[37] and the Valletta Convention are illustrative of the point[38] and the 2001 Convention is no exception. In the meantime, the 2001 Convention is undoubtedly influencing public values and raising the status of maritime heritage management on the political agenda. The result is a substantial increase in resources for management and law enforcement.

Supervision of compliance with heritage legislation is the responsibility of the Information and Heritage Inspectorate (IOE), part of the Ministry of Education, Culture and Science (OCW), but able to act independently.[39] The IOE ensures that archaeological research and documentation complies with existing standards. Privatisation of the quality control system, as discussed above, shifted the basis of supervision from individual research projects and archaeological contractors towards that of the functioning of the system as a whole. Oversight of the legality of activities directed at cultural heritage also rests with the IOE, including enforcement of law regarding UCH in Dutch territorial waters and the CZ. When the 2001 Convention is ratified, its role will be extended towards activities directed at UCH performed by Dutch flagged ships.

Surveillance at sea is coordinated in the Maritime Information Point (Maritiem Informatie Knooppunt (MIK-NL). Hosted by the Netherlands Coastguard, it is a partnership of public bodies that executes law enforcement and border control tasks for 15 Ministries. Enforcement of the Erfgoedwet is not one of its tasks, but the OCW may join the partnership, which would help to strengthen the protection of UCH, and underpin the forthcoming ratification of the 2001 Convention.

6 Ownership of Archaeological Objects

Private ownership rights are a feature of Dutch law.[40] The management of public interests and responsibilities in public law seems to avoid interference

37 UNTS 11806, Paris 1970.

38 The Netherlands transmitted the instrument of acceptance of the UNESCO Convention 1970 on 17 July 2009 (*Staatsblad* 2009, 256). The Valletta Convention entered into force in the Netherlands on 12 December 2007 (*Tractatenblad* 2007, 126).

39 See <https://english.inspectie-oe.nl/>.

40 W.J. Slagter, *Juridische en economische eigendom* (Deventer, 1968).

with ownership rights as much as possible, although regulating the protection of previously unknown material necessitates determination of ownership. Nevertheless, longstanding principles of private law have strongly influenced practice in subsequent legislative actions.[41]

6.1 *Objects from Excavations and Chance Discoveries*

In line with Rules 33 and 34 of the Annex to the 2001 Convention, collections of objects issuing from archaeological sites are regarded as integral assemblages, which should be kept according to professional standards, together with relevant documentation. There are two approaches adopted under Dutch law, related to the two mainstays of blanket protection, namely the obligation to report and the prohibition upon unauthorised excavation (as explained above).

Whether the finder may become the owner depends on if it was an incidental find made in the course of an activity that was not an excavation. If so, the finder may be entitled to the object under private law.[42] Besides reporting, the finder should keep the object for six months and make it available for study.[43] In so doing, they will remain in consultation with the competent authority, which may request they surrender the object in order that it is preserved in an appropriate repository, together with any material collected previously, or through intended excavation in the future. However, there is no obligation to do so.[44]

Authorisations for excavation are subject to a range of conditions. Authorised parties have responsibility for keeping the material that they excavate, as prescribed by the quality system. They do not, however, become the owner of the material.[45] Movable objects arising from excavations become public property, to be deposited in public repositories.[46]

---

41 The Monumentenwet 1961 respected the ownership arrangements of movable goods in Dutch Civil Law (BW5, Article 4–18). It did so by regarding the authorised excavating party as a finder. The authorised excavating party was allotted ownership, and the property owner could claim financial compensation of half the value. In practice, keeping collections is governed by heritage obligations, rather than rights of ownership. Under the Monumentenwet 1988 and the Wet op de Archeologische Monumentenzorg this private law principle was partly abandoned. Since then, ownership of finds from excavations falls either to the State, the province, or to the municipality. Financial compensation is no longer considered appropriate, except for chance discoveries. For the latter, the above mentioned stipulations in the Dutch Civil Code on property rights (BW5) are still applicable.

42 See above.

43 Erfgoedwet Art. 5.10(2).

44 In this aspect the regulations differ considerably from those in surrounding countries.

45 As used to be the case between 1961 and 1988.

46 Erfgoedwet Art. 5.7–5.9.

An exception to the rules defining ownership of archaeological material is where someone can prove a better title. Although exceptional in the context of present-day archaeological excavations on land, this is relevant regarding ships and cargoes lost in relatively modern times. It should be stressed, however, that title never extends to the archaeological assemblage as a whole and is limited to those objects to which a party can claim original ownership. An assemblage derived from a shipwreck, for instance, is comprised of items that are likely to have had different owners: ship, tackle, equipment, and cargo may have one owner, but is unlikely to include personal belongings of the crew or contraband. That said, there can be multiple reasons influencing ownership in different ways. For example, a ship and/or its cargo could have been insured, which makes the insurer the owner; in wartime, ownership of a ship may be transferred between States; and personal items of a ship's crew could have been bought with a loan, thus making the loan provider the owner. Establishing the ownership of an object is thus not straightforward. Established practice in archaeology, however, is to keep collections together. Their value for science is often – fortunately – above their economic value. The 2001 Convention, understandably, incorporated this principle by restricting the application of salvage law and denouncing the commercial exploitation of UCH.[47] As a prelude, the Netherlands had already in 1997[48] made the relevant exception on accession to the International Convention on Salvage 1989.[49]

6.2 *Antiquities and the Market*

The strength of ownership rights referred to above, is balanced by third-party protection. Possession in good faith is readily assumed. Possession itself is title enough to put up an object for sale and as long as the possession remains undisputed, such possessory rights are respected. This equally applies to antiquities. If there is suspicion that an object put up for sale is stolen or otherwise illegally retrieved, it can be seized. However, this is not undertaken lightly. To suspect that an object has been illegally excavated, there must be evidence beyond the simple fact that such an object has most likely come from an archaeological context. Consequently, prosecutions are rare.

Feeding the antiquities market through illegal excavations on terrestrial sites in the Netherlands seems to be marginal as compared to the total volume of authorised excavations. Basically, it appears limited to small-scale illegal operations, in conjunction with demolition works in historical towns where

47 Art. 4 and Rule 2 of the Annex of the 2001 Convention.

48 *Tractatenblad* 1997, 321.

49 1953 UNTS 165.

the municipality has not taken proper responsibility for archaeological heritage, or where the archaeological infrastructure is still developing. Whenever this comes to light, it may be a reason for concerted action although in the Netherlands it does not seem to be a substantial problem that calls for legislative change. In stark contrast is the situation for underwater sites. Prestigious auction sales of retrieved historical cargoes have been a feature of the Amsterdam antiquities market since the 1970s. Evidently, this was stimulated by the former policies relating to the salvage of Dutch historical shipwrecks in foreign waters, discussed in section 7.1 below.

These sales were also the incentive for many adventurously inclined individuals who acquired a ship, learnt to dive, and set out for adventure and to make discoveries. They fed web-based markets such as 'Marktplaats' and 'Ebay' with archaeological objects. This remains a significant issue that is difficult to control. The reporting of finds has been improved in recent years following development of the online database, Portable Antiquities of the Netherlands (PAN) by Vrije University, Amsterdam, and part of the European Public Finds Recording Network (EPFRN).[50] Private owners of archaeological finds are encouraged to register them in order to make them accessible for scientific research. Objects can be reported anonymously if desired, and critical questions are asked on provenance. Whilst a means of acquiring more information, including for research, one downside is of finds being potentially laundered through the system.

In 2009, the Netherlands ratified the UNESCO Convention on the Means of Prohibiting and Preventing the Illicit Import, Export and Transfer of Ownership of Cultural Property 1970 (1970 Convention).[51] Before that, steps had already been taken towards enhanced control of imports, exports, and transits of antiquities, through the implementation into Dutch legislation of several European directives.[52] The 1970 Convention and the EU directives share the

50 See <www.portable-antiquities.nl>.

51 There are no signs that the Netherlands intends to ratify the UNIDROIT Convention on Stolen or Illegally exported Cultural Objects 1995.

52 Council Regulation (EEC) No. 3911/92 of 9 December on the export of cultural goods OJ 1999 L395/1; Council Directive 93/7/EEC of 15 March 1993 on the return of cultural objects unlawfully removed from the territory of a Member State OJ 1993 L74/74; Directive 2014/60/EU of the European Parliament and of the Council of 15 May 2014 on the return of cultural objects unlawfully removed from the territory of a Member State and amending Regulation (EU) No 1024/2012 (Recast) OJ 2014 L159/1. Also, the Wet Behoud Cultuurbezit of 1984, incorporated into the Erfgoedwet in 2016, has made it illegal to export specific heritage without a permit. An amendment to this Act in 1995 made the Act applicable to all categories of goods listed in the annex of European Regulation 3911/92, including archaeological collections.

common basis that the cultural property in question must have been removed from the territory of a member state to apply. This immediately poses a problem for UCH. This heritage is frequently found outside territorial waters, although even when it has been retrieved from within the territorial waters of a member state, it is difficult to prove when the finder claims otherwise. The 2001 Convention, especially Article 14, was therefore an important addition to the international law on illicit trade.

Whereas illegal salvaging of cultural heritage with the aim to sell the objects is a significant threat to UCH as a whole, compared to widespread issues such as bottom trawling, its impact is limited. Another, apparently increasing threat is the salvaging of shipwrecks purely as a source of valuable materials. In the last decade, many WWII wrecks have been prone to illegal salvage. Although perhaps not immediately seen as objects of high archaeological value, they offer a potential source of iron and lead uncontaminated by Alpha radiation ('low background metals'), which have a high value on the market and are used for medical machines and instruments.[53] However, many of these sites are considered war graves and places of commemoration and the illegal salvage of Dutch WWII wrecks in the Java Sea in Indonesia and the waters of Malaysia, but also closer to home in the North Sea, has prompted concern from both relatives and the public. This has led to intensified government focus on the management of UCH, including law enforcement, and on the cooperation in Dutch shipwreck management with several coastal States.[54]

7 International Policies

It is undeniable that there is, or should be, some coherence between the heritage policies implemented nationally and those deployed in the international arena. Within Europe, prompted by the encouragement of the CoE, national

53 See for example <https://www.good.is/articles/the-search-for-low-background-steel>.

54 *Kamerstukken II* 2017/18, 1755. Antwoord van Minister van Engelshoven (Onderwijs, Cultuur en Wetenschap), mede namens de Minister van Defensie (ontvangen 13 april 2018). See for more information on the case of the three illegally salvaged Dutch wrecks in the Java Sea: M.R. Manders, R.W. de Hoop, S. Adhityatama, D.S. Bismoko, P. Syofiadisna, D. Haryanto (2021) 'Battle of the Java Sea: One event, multiple sites, values and views', *Journal of Maritime Archaeology* 3, 39–56. For more on the submarines in Malaysia, see: M. Manders, R. de Hoop, M.H.W. Verrijth, C.H. Trommel, H. Meinsma, I. Jeffery,T.A. van der Velden, Ruzairy Bin Arbi, Farizah Binti Ideris, Ahmad ZaharuddinBin Abdul Kadir, Khairil Amri, Bin Abdul, Ghani (2019) *Report on the fieldwork at the sites of the Dutch submarines O16 and K-XVII, Cultural Heritage agency of the Netherlands*, Amersfoort.

bodies charged with the management of archaeological heritage throughout Europe have formed the Europae Archaeologiae Consilium (EAC).[55] Its primary mission is to support the management of archaeological heritage throughout Europe and to serve the needs of national archaeological heritage management agencies by providing a forum for organisations to establish closer and more structured co-operation and exchange of information.

7.1 *Alignment of Maritime Policies*

For maritime archaeology, the alignment of policies might even be more urgent than for its land-based counterpart, given the inevitable movement between different territorial/jurisdictional zones. Ships under different flags pass multiple coastal States and in the High Sea it is the legislation of the individual flag State that influences how people interact with UCH. Differences in approach create lack of clarity, so whilst full harmonisation may not be possible, operating under the same/similar principles and approaches should be a starting point. The 2001 Convention should partly fill this gap, but only has direct influence on those countries that have ratified it.

Dutch policy alignment for management of State-owned shipwrecks outside the Netherlands did not happen until recently. A predominantly object-orientated approach, focused on rights rather than responsibilities, continued for a long time. The Netherlands had been issuing salvage contracts for State-owned vessels of the Dutch East India Company (Verenigde Oostindische Compagnie, VOC) since the 1960s and was quite content with this practice. These contracts were not uniform – some had an expiry date, others not. Sometimes objects ended up at auction, sometimes it was a museum that acquired a (large) part of the collection, with major museums having the pick of finds salvaged, rather than the State getting a percentage of the value. This approach, with finds on display in a museum, was considered more beneficial to society.

In general, salvage contracts were concluded with private persons or companies that were motivated by the adventure and/or personal gain. An exception was the transfer of rights of four Dutch VOC shipwrecks found in West-Australian waters in the 1960s: the *Batavia* (1629), *Vergulden Draak* (1656), *Zeewijk* (1727) and *Zuiddorp* (1712).[56] In November 1972, the Agreement between the Netherlands, Western Australia, and the Federal Government of Australia concerning old Dutch shipwrecks was concluded. At its core, this agreement

---

55 <https://www.europae-archaeologiae-consilium.org/>.

56 See, for example, the Western Australian Museum Shipwreck Database, M. van Huystee, Report 77, 1994 <https://museum.wa.gov.au/maritime-archaeology-db/maritime-reports/dutch-references-batavia-vergulde-draak-zuiddorp-zeewijk-and-other-vessels>.

was similar to other salvage contracts, containing stipulations on the division of artefacts between Australia and the Netherlands. However, the Australian Netherlands Committee on Old Dutch Shipwrecks (ANCODS) was appointed to oversee execution of the Agreement, which formed the basis for co-operation in science and heritage management. In 2010, ANCODS was suspended until further notice and all the objects that had been appointed to the Netherlands were transported back to Australia to be reunited with the collections there, and future finds will remain in Australian care. Yet to be discovered finds of other Dutch wrecks off the coast of Western Australia are not included but eventually could be a reason to reactivate ANCODS.[57] Regardless of ownership rights, in all future cases the verifiable links of both Australia and the Netherlands regarding these wreck sites, together with the added value of cooperation, will be the basis of any management decision.

The situation of these four wrecks and the cooperation with Australia will probably remain unique. However, after criticism of the salvage law-based approach of the Dutch Government, a more holistic approach was put into place in 2002 through an interdepartmental framework to guide management decisions on Dutch shipwrecks outside Dutch waters.[58] This policy framework positioned ownership rights as a tool for protection, rather than a goal in itself and referred to the Annex of the 2001 Convention as the guiding principles for activities directed at these wrecks. These days, the transfer of ownership is not taken lightly since the ownership claim by the flag State and the shared commitment from the coastal State form a strong safety net for maritime heritage abroad and an important tool for its management.

7.2 *New Beginnings*

Fortunately, the practice of issuing salvage contracts has now ended.[59] In 2007–2008 an investigation by the Ministry of Finance concluded that the salvage contract for the VOC ship *Rooswijk* (1740), located in the UK's TS and designated a protected site in 2007, was the only one still active. This was resolved in 2017, by the salvor handing it over to the RCE to enable commencement of an archaeological excavation.[60] It remains unclear how many salvage contracts there have been in total. Many contracted wrecks have never been found,

57 The ANCODS Agreement covers all VOC wrecks off the coast of Western Australia.

58 *Kamerstukken II* 2001/02, 28000-V, nr. 62. Brief van de staatssecretarissen van Buitenlandse zaken, van Onderwijs, Cultuur en Wetenschappen en van Financiën.

59 Officially the interdepartmental framework still leaves the option open, but in practice it is impossible to execute.

60 <https://english.cultureelerfgoed.nl/topics/m/maritime-heritage/rooswijk1740>.

others were lying in waters of countries that did not permit UCH to be salvaged or did not accept the Dutch ownership claim.

Although primarily focused on shipwrecks of the VOC, since 2012, when the RCE started its International Maritime Programme, the interdepartmental framework has applied to all State-owned historic vessels. These include wrecks of the West India Company (WIC), Admiralty warships and more modern Navy ships. This practice was formalised in a revised policy document published in 2019.[61] Despite the fact this set out the categories of ships subject to Dutch sovereignty, the actual number of sites involved was still unknown. Therefore, between 2019 and 2021, the RCE, in conjunction with the Netherlands Institute for Military history (NIMH) and the University of Leiden, executed a wreck count. It resulted in a list of more than 1,600 Dutch State-owned ships wrecked worldwide between 1600 and 1960.[62] This figure would be many times higher if non-State owned, commercial, ships were included.

7.3 *Mutual, Shared, and Contested Heritage*

In the name of trade, the Netherlands colonised several areas in the world, starting from the early seventeenth century onwards. The marks of colonialism and decolonisation are still very much visible in our society and that of the colonised countries. With intensified discussions on discrimination, equality, privilege, and distribution of wealth in the world, these subjects are now contentious. Part of such discussions are issues related to ownership of heritage and even heritage itself, researching, protecting, and managing what a society thinks is important, particularly given each can value heritage differently. Questions and issues remain to be resolved, such as to ownership of the remnants of the heritage of a former colonised country, including where that country has split up, and of the role of sovereign immunity in ownership claims. It is clear, however, that most of these issues can best be solved through cooperation and by making mutual, shared, or even contested heritage values the primary consideration. In this way, heritage projects can become a vehicle for cultural diplomacy between countries that have a shared history.

International projects addressing 'mutual, shared or contested heritage' with which the Netherlands has a verifiable link now qualify for a subsidy,

61 *Kamerstukken II* 2018/19 32156, nr. 98. Brief van de ministers van Onderwijs, Cultuur en Wetenschap van Defensie.

62 M. Manders, A. van Dissel, W. Brouwers, M. Fink, J. Spoelstra, R. de Hoop, M. Heijink, A. Lemmers, A. Heitz, O. de Vroomen: Wrakkentelling. Een kwantitatief onderzoek naar historische Nederlandse scheepswrakken in de wereld. Rijksdienst voor het Cultureel Erfgoed (Amersfoort 2021).

and a budget, administered jointly by the Minister of Foreign Affairs and the Minister of Culture, has been set aside for this purpose. For its allocation, criteria were developed in the early 1990s and 2000s, the former colonies being afforded a substantial proportion. Projects were executed under a Shared Heritage Programme in cooperation with ten priority countries, all with a high amount of Dutch tangible (and intangible) heritage. These are, Australia, US, Japan, Indonesia, India, Sri Lanka, South Africa, Brazil, Suriname, and Russia.[63] In 2021, the International Heritage Programme focus was extended to 23 countries, including Belgium, Germany, and the UK. In deploying its international cultural policies,[64] the Netherlands tries to enter into specific Memoranda of Understanding (MoU), Letters of Intent, or Letters of Agreement, setting out means of cooperation and long-term goals. MoUs for UCH extend beyond the above 23 priority countries due to the nature of the heritage, previously extending to Brazil, Suriname, and South Africa and currently in place with Australia, Indonesia, Malaysia, Japan, and Cuba.

Not all partner countries in UCH projects recognise Dutch claims to ownership. However, given the previous potential to gain salvage rights via the Dutch Government this was probably a blessing, resulting in wrecks remaining preserved. Overall, efforts to recognise the value of sites outside of a State's territory as undertaken by the Netherlands are relatively rare and has led to cooperation projects in which exchange of expertise and training align with hands-on archaeological heritage management practice, reflected in UNESCO Foundation Courses and Training Manuals, to which the Cultural Heritage Agency substantially contributed.[65]

8 Developments in Light of the 2001 Convention

The Netherlands was an early adopter in the international arena of protection of UCH, as could be expected of a country with a history closely connected with the sea and seafaring. Despite issues, as discussed below, the goal of the

63 In an early stage, Ghana was also part of this group.

64 International Cultural Policy 2021–24, see <https://dutchculture.nl/sites/default/files/atoms/files/dutch-international-cultural-policy-2021-2024_eng.pdf>.

65 M.R. Manders and C.J. Underwood (Eds.), 2012, Training Manual for the UNESCO Foundation Course on the Protection and Management of Underwater Cultural Heritage in Asia and the Pacific, UNESCO Bangkok. M.R. Manders and C. J. Underwood (Eds.), 2021, The UNESCO Training Manual for the Protection of the Underwater Cultural Heritage in Latin America and the Caribbean, Netherlands. Ministry of Education, Culture and Science. Cultural Heritage Agency, UNESCO Publishing.

2001 Convention of protecting UCH has been supported by the Dutch Government from the beginning, with the rules guiding maritime heritage policies and practice.[66]

Much has been written about potential incompatibility of the 2001 Convention with the LOSC and especially the danger of creeping coastal jurisdiction in the EEZ and on the CS.[67] In the Netherlands, this has been the cause of a considerable ambivalence towards the 2001 Convention, as both its maritime history and the principle of freedom of the seas are valued highly. It formed an impediment to voting in favour of the Convention during the 31st Assembly of the UNESCO General Conference on 6 November 2001 and this attitude continued for most of the decade.[68] However, despite principled objections, a positive attitude towards international legislation to protect UCH[69] was reflected in the Netherlands declaring it would look into the possibilities of signing the 2001 Convention and expressing commitment to its principles and the operational rules of the Annex.

The entry into force of the 2001 Convention on 2 January 2009 created new momentum for the Ministry for Education, Culture and Science and the Ministry of Foreign Affairs to reassess the Dutch position.[70] To inform the discussions, the Netherlands National Commission for UNESCO (NatCom) organised an international debate with both legal experts and maritime archaeologists. Based on this, NatCom drafted a position paper, the conclusions of which stressed that Dutch ratification was important in order to be able to protect UCH outside of its territorial waters and to maintain its "international reputation as a protector of underwater cultural heritage".[71] On the other hand, it also mentioned that ratifying the Convention "could increase the risk of existing

66 The aforementioned interdepartmental decision framework for dealing with Dutch ship finds outside of Dutch waters, for example, stipulates that archaeological investigations must be conducted in conformity with the Annex of the 2001 Convention.

67 For example, Le Gurun, G. 2006, p. 77,78 in S. Dromgoole: The Protection of the Underwater Cultural Heritage. National perspectives in light of the UNESCO Convention 2001 and Aznar, M. 2014, the Contiguous Zone as an Archaeological Maritime Zone, in: International Journal of Marine and Coastal Law, Vol, 29, Issue 1.

68 The Netherlands was one of the 15 states that abstained from voting during the 2001 assembly.

69 In their declaration during the ratification process of the LOSC in 1996, The Netherlands stated that there may be need for further international legislation to protect the UCH.

70 Netherlands National Commission for UNESCO, 2001: International Experts' Debate on the 2001 Convention on the Protection of the Underwater Cultural Heritage, The Hague / The Netherlands 5 and 6 July 2011. Position Paper.

71 See above, p. 6 and 10.

maritime laws losing their effectiveness" and "damage the Dutch position as a strong proponent of this integrity".[72]

Subsequently, Ministers asked the Advisory Committee on Public International Law (CAVV) to advise the government on the relationship between the 2001 Convention and the LOSC.[73] The research questions were predominantly directed at the relationship between Articles 9 and 10 of the 2001 Convention and the competences of the flag and the coastal State provided for in the LOSC.[74] The advice was outspoken in its conclusion that the 2001 Convention was not in contradiction with the LOSC, although a critical note was made about some of its formulation: "the wording of the Convention is unclear in a number of places". The overall conclusion was that the limited increase in competences of the coastal State, contemplated in Articles 9 and 10, could be seen as implementation of Article 303(1) of the LOSC.[75]

The combination of these two, generally positive, advisory reports made way for a letter to parliament announcing that the government had decided to examine steps towards ratification of the 2001 Convention.[76] Finally, on 19 May 2016 an unequivocal announcement was made by the Minister of Education, Culture and Science that the Netherlands would ratify the 2001 Convention, on the condition it would also make a declaration on the importance of the 2001 Convention being interpreted in conformity with the LOSC by all State Parties.[77] This announcement marked the official start of the process to bring Dutch legislation and policies in line with the 2001 Convention. This slow-moving pace towards ratification can be explained by the complexity of legislative issues on the one hand and the fact that other legislative and policy endeavours (such as the previously mentioned Omgevingswet and Erfgoedwet) have received much attention. Regardless, considerable steps have been made. In 2017, the Convention, including the official Dutch translation, was published in the Dutch Treaties Bulletin (Tractatenblad) by the Minister of Foreign

72 See above, p. 9.

73 Brief aan Prof. Dr. M. Kamminga dd. 16 September 2011, registr. nr. DJZ/IR-177/2011. The Advisory Committee on Public International Law (CAVV) is an independent body which advises the government, the House of Representatives, and the Senate of the Netherlands on international law issues.

74 The Advisory Committee on Public International Law, 2001. Advisory report on the UNESCO Convention on the Protection of the Underwater Cultural Heritage (translation), CAVV report 21 <https://www.advisorycommitteeinternationallaw.nl>.

75 See above, p. 4, p. 8. p. 10.

76 *Kamerstukken II* 2013/14 33750 V, nr. 6. Vaststelling van de begrotingsstaten van het Ministerie van Buitenlandse Zaken (V) voor het jaar 2014.

77 *Kamerstukken II* 2015/16 34300 VIII, nr. 146. Vaststelling van de begrotingsstaten van het Ministerie van Onderwijs, Cultuur en Wetenschap (VIII) voor het jaar 2016.

Affairs.[78] Furthermore, an extensive study of the legal measures necessary for implementation of the 2001 Convention has been completed and the process of legislative drafting is now underway. In parallel to these administrative efforts, the operational and financial implications of the 2001 Convention are being examined in order to prepare the executive bodies, in the Netherlands as well as in the six islands of the Kingdom of the Netherlands in the Caribbean, for the additional tasks that stem from its provisions.

Meanwhile, the influence of the 2001 Convention has been noticeable in Dutch maritime heritage management for some time. Maarleveld observed in 2006 that the political commitment of the Netherlands to the Rules of the Annex to the 2001 Convention and the concept of the 'verifiable link' influenced maritime archaeological policy and practice both nationally and in dealing with Dutch UCH abroad.[79] The formal decision to ratify the 2001 Convention increased its influence and created a climate in which interest in issues regarding the protection and management of UCH has grown. With the subject higher on the political agenda, the availability of structural resources for management, research and enforcement has increased, with additional financial support and creation of maritime programmes between 2012 and 2021. These brought UCH management up-to-date and have set the agenda for coming years. The restructuring and replacement of underwater management in the organisation of the RCE as a permanent department with an adequate fixed budget can be seen as a result of these programmes and the level of success that has been achieved.

8.1 *Caribbean Parts of the Kingdom of the Netherlands*

The decision to ratify the 2001 Convention was made exclusively for the European part of the Kingdom of the Netherlands and the Caribbean Isles of Bonaire, St. Eustatius and Saba, which are public entities within the Netherlands' constitutional system.[80] Curacao, Aruba and Sint Maarten, having the status of autonomous countries within the Kingdom of the Netherlands, were formally asked if they wished the application of the Convention to be extended to them, which they all agreed to. At the time of writing, they have started the ratification process and, with the assistance of the Netherlands, are drafting

78 Verdrag inzake de bescherming van het cultureel erfgoed onder water (met Bijlage); Parijs, 2 november 2001 *Tractatenblad* 2017, 3.

79 Maarleveld, T., 2006, p. 187, 188 in Dromgoole, S.: The Protection of the Underwater Cultural Heritage. National Perspectives in Light of the UNESCO Convention 2001.

80 This means the 2001 Convention will apply to these isles as well, unless during ratification a declaration is made, based on Article 239 of the 2001 Convention, to limit the geographical scope. At this point in time the Netherlands is not considering this possibility.

legislation. This positive attitude may not be surprising since diving tourism is an important source of income for many islanders and therefore the protection and conservation of UCH represents a substantial economic interest.

9 Conclusion

Since the first heritage law in 1961, the protection of UCH has come a long way. The threat of treasure hunting on Dutch VOC wrecks in the 1980s first triggered the need for protection in the Netherlands and subsequent policies to protect these wrecks abroad. Initial isolation from mainstream archaeology was followed by the gradual acceptance of UCH as an integral part of archaeological heritage, but in need of a certain degree of customised care.

Major changes in cultural heritage management, such as the implementation of the Valletta Convention and the Omgevingswet, are the legal consolidations of the way the Netherlands perceives and treats cultural heritage in its living environment which is as an integral part of that environment and less for, and more with, others. Cultural heritage protection has become more inclusive and quite rightly so. With implementation of the CoE's Faro Convention this will only increase. Although still evolving, it is good to see UCH now being considered from the start in these changes. This is also paving the way for the ratification of the 2001 Convention, hopefully soon. Ratifying it will offer a major anchoring for the protection of UCH in mainstream heritage management and is a logical step for a country of people with saltwater running through their veins.

All websites last accessed February 2025.

Acknowledgements

In 2006, Thijs Maarleveld, head of the Maritime Policy Department at the predecessor of the Cultural Heritage Agency of the Netherlands, wrote a chapter in the first edition of this book. On 11 March 2021, Thijs sadly died after a long battle against cancer. In memory of the founding father of maritime heritage policy in the Netherlands and his active involvement on the subject all over the world, we have used his previous chapter as a template for this one, which includes changes that have occurred in relation to Dutch maritime and underwater cultural heritage management since 2006. This is also the reason why Thijs Maarleveld remains one of the authors of this chapter, alongside Andrea Klomp, Consultant at Rijksdienst voor Cultureel Erfgoed and Martijn

Manders, Professor by special appointment in Underwater Archaeology and Maritime Heritage Management at the Faculty of Archaeology, University of Leiden.

Selected Bibliography

Bouman, D., 2015, Eindrapportage van het onderzoek: Duiken op Wrakken. Vrijwilligers in de onderwater archeologie, MR & C,

Commissie van Advies inzake Volkenrechtelijke Vraagstukken, December 2011, Advies over het UNESCO – Verdrag inzake cultureel erfgoed onder water, Advies No. 21, The Hague. Available at: https://www.eerstekamer.nl/overig/20120605/cavv_advies_over_het_unesco/document

Manders, M.R., 2017, Preserving the layered history of the Western Wadden Sea. Managing an underwater cultural heritage resource, dissertation Leiden University. <https://hdl.handle.net/1887/58544>.

Manders, M.R. and C. J. Underwood (Eds.), 2021, The UNESCO Training Manual for the Protection of the Underwater Cultural Heritage in Latin America and the Caribbean, Netherlands. Ministry of Education, Culture and Science. Cultural Heritage Agency, UNESCO Publishing.

Manders, M., A. van Dissel, W. Brouwers, M. Fink, J. Spoelstra, R. de Hoop, M. Heijink, A. Lemmers, A. Heitz, and O. de Vroomen, 2021, Wrakkentelling. Een kwantitatief onderzoek naar historische Nederlandse scheepswrakken in de wereld. Rijksdienst voor het Cultureel Erfgoed, Amersfoort.

Woudenberg, A and Th.J. Maarleveld, 2002, Hugo de Groot en UNESCO op gespannen voet, 77 Nederlands Juristenblad 1025.

CHAPTER 14

Aotearoa/New Zealand

Piers Davies and Paul Myburgh***

1 Introduction

Aotearoa/New Zealand (NZ) has a coastline of approximately 15,000 km (the ninth longest in the world), comprising two main islands and smaller islands scattered throughout the southern Pacific Ocean.[1] NZ's maritime boundaries are defined by the Territorial Sea, Contiguous Zone, and Exclusive Economic Zone Act 1977. The Act asserts NZ sovereignty over the Territorial Sea (TS, 12 nautical miles (nm)); establishes a Contiguous Zone (CZ, 12 nm beyond the TS); and an Exclusive Economic Zone (EEZ, 200 nm).[2] The Continental Shelf Act 1964 regulates the economic exploitation of NZ's CS, which includes the seabed and subsoil up to the EEZ limit and extends to the outermost edge of the continental margin where this falls beyond EEZ limits.

NZ's EEZ and CS claims overlap with those of Australia. In 2004, the two governments reached an agreement delimiting common maritime boundaries between the two countries.[3] NZ concluded similar treaties with France and the United States and intends to negotiate common maritime boundaries with Fiji and Tonga. NZ also claims the Ross Dependency, a territory in Antarctica, but the limits of this are yet to be determined.

NZ was settled much later than most of the world as it is surrounded by sea for thousands of kilometres. Although the exact dates of Polynesian exploration and settlement are a matter of debate, it is possible that Polynesians visited NZ during the first millennium C.E., with Polynesian settlement established around 1300 A.D., which evolved into the Māori tribes (iwi) occupying

* Retired maritime lawyer.

** Professor, Auckland University of Technology Law School, New Zealand.

1 Legislation Act 2019 s. 13: statutory references to 'New Zealand' include "the islands and territories within the Realm of New Zealand", but do not include the Cook Islands, Niue, Tokelau, or the Ross Dependency.

2 Territorial Sea, Contiguous Zone, and Exclusive Economic Zone Act 1977 ss. 3, 5–6A, 9.

3 Treaty between the Government of Australia and the Government of New Zealand establishing Certain Exclusive Economic Zone and Continental Shelf Boundaries, done in Adelaide on 25 July 2004, entered into force on 25 January 2006, [2006] *New Zealand Treaty Series* (NZTS) 1, A.51.

 | DOI:10.1163/9789004510883_016

NZ when European explorers arrived.[4] Polynesian explorers were skillful navigators, using large double-hulled canoes (waka) up to 24 metres long with sails, for venturing around the Pacific. No large seafaring waka has been found, but smaller examples have been discovered.[5] In addition, Māori stone fish traps, shell middens, and oven sites have been uncovered in tidal zones and harbour margins. There is also a submerged pā (fort) site in Lake Okataina, near Rotorua, with the remains of a palisade.

The first known European to sight NZ was the Dutch explorer Abel Tasman in 1642, but there was no follow-up until Captain Cook landed in 1769. The earliest underwater artefacts recovered in NZ with an undisputed provenance are anchors of the French explorer de Surville, which were lost in 1769 and recovered nearly 200 years later by Kelly Tarlton. The first known European shipwreck, the *Endeavour*, occurred in 1795 in Dusky Sound. Thereafter, there were numerous shipwrecks, particularly of vessels hunting seals and whales at the beginning of the nineteenth century, and during the gold rushes on the West Coast of the South Island in the 1860s and 1870s. The sites of most are not accurately known. Often, strong tides and stormy seas destroyed any traces of these wrecks. Casualties included several warships, the best known being the HMS *Orpheus* lost on the Manukau Bar in 1863, resulting in the deaths of 189 people.[6]

European settler occupation only became significant from 1840 onwards. NZ's underwater cultural heritage (UCH) includes the submerged remains of old jetties, wharves, and other structures, such as the remains of the settlement of Cromwell, submerged when Lake Dunstan was created for hydro-electricity generation. There are also a small number of significant wrecks of aircraft around the NZ coast, including two aircraft of the Royal New Zealand Air Force. Explorers and excavators of wrecks in NZ tend to be commercial or recreational divers, rather than professional salvors. In the late 1960s and early 1970s, when SCUBA diving equipment became generally available, there was

---

4 Te Ara, 'When was New Zealand first settled?', see <https://teara.govt.nz/en/when-was-new-zealand-first-settled/page-1>; N. Prickett, 'First Settlement Date and Early Rats' (2002) 45 *Archaeology in New Zealand* 288.

5 See Dilys A. Johns, Geoffrey J. Irwin and Yun K. Sung, 'An Early Sophisticated East Polynesian Voyaging Canoe Discovered on New Zealand's Coast' (2014) 111 (41) *Proceedings of the National Academy of Sciences* 14728, see <https://www.pnas.org/doi/10.1073/pnas.1408491111>.

6 Most known NZ shipwreck sites are listed in S. Locker-Lampson and I. Francis, *The Wreck Book* (2nd ed., Halcyon Press, 1994); Eric Heath and Gavin McLean, *Shipwrecks around New Zealand* (Grantham House Publishing, 1994); C.W.N. Ingram, *New Zealand Shipwrecks* (8th ed., Reed, 2007); Lynton Diggle, *Shipwrecks of New Zealand: Companion to the 8th Edition of New Zealand Shipwrecks* (2nd ed., self-published, 2014).

a ‘free-wheeling’ approach to excavating wrecks. The main purpose was to recover treasure or metal objects and the use of explosives was not unknown. In most wreck excavations, divers were looking for propellers, portholes, condensers, and other metallic objects of value for souvenirs or scrap purposes, or even treasure.

NZ has a tradition of skilled and dedicated volunteers working in this area. This is reflected in the way many divers work on excavating wrecks, and concomitantly in the activities of the New Zealand Underwater Heritage Group (NZUHG),[7] and the Maritime Archaeological Association of New Zealand (MAANZ), including the operation of its conservation laboratory.

However, NZ has one of the longest coastlines and largest EEZ s in the world, with only a small proportion surveyed.[8] Balanced against this, the NZ population is only just over five million. Inevitably, this means that the NZ Government is under-resourced to deal with such a substantial area of responsibility and the number of government staff available to administer issues relating to UCH is limited. Heritage New Zealand Pouhere Taonga (HNZPT – formerly the Historic Places Trust) has a limited annual budget (NZ$ 23.89 million in 2022). Its main responsibilities are land-based, with marine archaeology only just starting to become significant.

2 Existing Legal Framework

There is no single NZ statute specifically dealing with UCH,[9] and no uniform or general definition of UCH on the statute books. Instead, several statutes, administered by various government departments or organisations, regulate, or affect, different aspects of UCH. These statutes fall into three broad categories. First, there are general cultural heritage statutes, such as the Heritage New Zealand Pouhere Taonga Act 2014 (HNZPT Act) and the Protected Objects Act 1975 (POA). The primary focus of these statutes is land-based, but they extend to cover UCH to a lesser or greater degree. Secondly, there are maritime law statutes, such as the Admiralty Act 1973 and the Maritime Transport Act 1994 (MTA), which tend to focus on commercial and public safety issues involving

7 See <https://www.underwaterheritage.co.nz>.

8 The OS 20/20 Strategy was launched in March 2005 to survey NZ’s CS and EEZ by 2020. It appears to have stalled in 2014.

9 There is also a dearth of NZ legal writing on UCH – a rare exception is J.S. Blackie, *The UNESCO Convention on the Protection of Underwater Cultural Heritage – Is the Time Right for New Zealand?* (Unpublished LLM dissertation, University of Auckland, 2004).

salvage, ownership, and removal of wrecks, rather than on cultural heritage concerns. Indeed, some of the provisions in these statutes potentially clash with the aim of *in situ* preservation of UCH sites. Thirdly, there is a raft of other statutes not expressly drafted in terms of UCH or wrecks, but which have the potential to impact on UCH. The most important of these are the Resource Management Act 1991 (RMA), the Marine Reserves Act 1971 (MRA), and the Marine and Coastal Area (Takutai Moana) Act 2011 (MACA).

2.1 *Cultural Heritage Statutes*

2.1.1 HNZPT Act

The Historic Places Act 1980 marked the beginnings of a regime placing more emphasis on preservation of wreck sites for their archaeological value. The 1980 Act was replaced by the Historic Places Act 1993, and subsequently by the HNZPT Act. The purpose of the HNZPT Act is to 'promote the identification, protection, preservation, and conservation of the historical and cultural heritage of New Zealand'.[10] HNZPT, a Crown entity, administers and enforces the Act.[11] The Act provides that it is unlawful to destroy, damage or modify the whole or any part of any archaeological site 'if that person knows, or ought reasonably to have suspected, that the site is an archaeological site', or to carry out any archaeological investigation that may destroy, damage, or modify any archaeological site, without prior authorisation from HNZPT.[12] HNZPT may impose designations or heritage orders in respect of historic sites, historic areas, wāhi tūpuna, wāhi tapu, or wāhi tapu areas,[13] and is charged with continuing and maintaining a register of historic places, as well as establishing a list of places of outstanding national heritage value.[14]

In terms of the Act, an 'archaeological site' is:

> ... any place in New Zealand, including any building or structure (or part of a building or structure), that –

10 HNZPT Act s. 3.

11 For more information on HNZPT and its activities, see <https://www.heritage.org.nz/>.

12 HNZPT Act s. 42. Sections 44–55 set out the procedures for applying for an authority to destroy, damage, or modify an archaeological site, and the granting, denying, or imposing of conditions on authorities.

13 *Ibid.*, s. 6 defines wāhi tapu as a place sacred to Māori in the traditional, spiritual, religious, ritual, or mythological sense, wāhi tapu area as land that contains one or more wāhi tapu, and wāhi tūpuna as a place important to Māori for its ancestral significance and associated cultural and traditional values.

14 *Ibid.*, s. 13(1)(i) read with Part 8 of the RMA.

i. was associated with human activity that occurred before 1900 or is the site of the wreck of any vessel where the wreck occurred before 1900; and
ii. provides or may provide, through investigation by archaeological methods, evidence relating to the history of New Zealand.[15]

There are obvious difficulties with this definition, which is both wide-ranging and vague. First, the express limitation of archaeological sites to places 'in New Zealand' indicates that the Act applies only to UCH sites in inland waters and the TS. UCH sites in the NZ CZ, EEZ or CS cannot be said to be 'in New Zealand', however historically significant they may be.[16] Although most known NZ historic shipwrecks occurred relatively close to the coastline, there are some further out to sea, including those of the *Turakina* and the *Rangitane*.[17] The possibility of discovering further significant UCH sites beyond the TS cannot be discounted.[18]

Secondly, the use of a fixed cut-off date of 1900 for protected archaeological sites gives rise to anomalies,[19] such as, for example, not protecting aircraft wreck sites. This is unfortunate, as there are several historically significant aircraft wrecks around the NZ coast.[20]

15 *Ibid.*, s. 6.

16 See too the definitions of 'historic place' and 'historical area' *ibid.*, in s. 6, which are expressly limited to places and areas lying 'within the territorial limits of New Zealand'. The Legislation Act 2019 s. 13 provides that 'territorial limits of New Zealand', 'limits of New Zealand', and similar statutory expressions mean 'the outer limits of the territorial sea of New Zealand'. It therefore seems clear that Parliament did not intend the Act (or its predecessors) to have extra-territorial application.

17 Merchant ships sunk by German raiders in World War II: see <https://nzhistory.govt.nz/turakina-sunk-by-german-raider-in-tasman-sea and https://nzhistory.govt.nz/page/liner-sunk-german-raiders>.

18 See Ministry for the Environment/Manatū Mō Te Taiao *Improving Regulation of Environmental Effects in New Zealand's Exclusive Economic Zone* (Discussion Paper, 2007) 3: 'Management of shipwreck sites in the EEZ might also become of increased importance as technology allows deeper sites to be reached'.

19 A. Dodd, 'Opportunities for Underwater Archaeology in New Zealand' (2003) 46 *Archaeology in New Zealand* 151, 154–155. Blackie, *supra* n. 9, at p. 39, describes the cut-off date as 'illogical and short sighted'. Although s. 43 of the HNZPT Act does allow the NZHPT to protect post-1900 significant archaeological sites by notification, this has not been much utilised in practice so far as shipwrecks are concerned, with the important exception of the wreck site of the SS *Ventnor*, which sank in 1902 and was gazetted as an archaeological site on 8 May 2014.

20 See Locker-Lampson and Francis, *supra* n. 6, at pp. 122–124, for a description of these aircraft wreck sites.

Thirdly, the definition focuses on the *site* of the wreck of the vessel, rather than the physical wreck itself, wreck material, or artefacts. Although this legislative focus on the wreck site is in keeping with the maritime archaeology objective of preserving entire wreck sites *in situ* as 'time capsules', it does not consider the reality that most NZ wrecks have broken apart, scattered, or drifted from the original wreck site. It does not explicitly protect material or artefacts found outside designated wreck sites, which may be treated as 'find spots', rather than as part of the original archaeological site. It also does not deal with the problem of material or artefacts removed from designated wreck sites and sold on to third parties. The protection afforded by the Act to historical wreck material and artefacts is therefore less than comprehensive.

Finally, the Act does not define 'wreck', which potentially results in further uncertainty. It is not clear whether 'wreck' should be construed in the stricter common law sense of the concept, as including only ships, cargo, materials or artefacts washed ashore after shipwreck,[21] or whether coverage also extends to wrecks in the broader sense of any lost vessels, cargo, materials or artefacts remaining *in situ* in the sea or upon the seabed.[22] If NZ courts favoured the stricter common law definition, the HNZPT Act regime would largely be rendered ineffective as far as *in situ* preservation of historic shipwreck sites is concerned.

A key provision of the Act is that any person who wants to destroy, damage, or modify the whole or any part of an archaeological site must apply to the HNZPT for authority to do so via a process set out in the statute. Under the Act, failure to apply for authority, or breaches of any HNZPT authority granted, may be prosecuted, with significant maximum fines.[23] Section 94 of the HNZPT Act provides that in 'a prosecution for an offence against section 87 or 88, it is not necessary to prove that the defendant intended to commit the offence', thereby seemingly creating strict liability offences of modifying or destroying archaeological sites or breaching the conditions of HNZPT authority. However, section 94(2) of the HNZPT Act spells out two specific defences that may be raised, namely the saving or protecting of life or the prevention of serious damage to cultural heritage; or an action or event beyond the control of the defendant, provided certain conditions are met.[24]

---

21 *Robinson v. Western Australian Museum* [1977] HCA 46; (1997) 138 CLR 283; (1977) 16 ALR 623.

22 Another argument is that the broader statutory definition of 'wreck' in the MTA s. 98, discussed in section 1.2.2 *infra*, should be applied.

23 See HNZPT Act ss. 85–90.

24 At the time of writing, there have been only two reported prosecutions under s. 94: *HNZPT v. Dayniel Ltd* [2022] NZDC 25516 and *HNZPT v Chen* [2023] NZDC 2687.

To further muddy the waters, an element of the offence under section 87 is that the offender 'knows, or ought reasonably to have suspected, that the site is an archaeological site', which suggests a *mens rea* offence. This tension between strict and fault-based liability was also present in previous versions of the HNZPT Act. Although unfortunate from a legal point of view, it may be useful from a practical perspective. Since most UCH sites are covered by sand or mud, they will often be difficult to identify without removing this, which immediately creates a risk of damage to, or modification of, the wreck site. Although the whereabouts of many NZ wreck sites are known in principle, most have broken up and been scattered. Since it may be difficult to know if wreck remains constitute an archaeological site, a completely strict liability regime could be unfair. Prosecutions are a very expensive way of preventing damage to archaeological sites: success can turn on relatively fine points. As will be discussed below in sections 3 and 4, it may be more effective to encourage a positive relationship between the HNZPT, the government departments concerned, and the diving community.

2.1.2 Protected Objects Act 1975

The POA was passed to regulate the export of protected NZ objects; prohibit the import of unlawfully exported and stolen protected foreign objects; provide for their return; provide compensation in certain circumstances; give domestic effect to the UNESCO Convention on the Means of Prohibiting and Preventing the Illicit Import, Export and Transfer of Ownership of Cultural Property 1970[25] and the UNIDROIT Convention on Stolen or Illegally Exported Cultural Objects 1995;[26] establish and record the ownership of ngā taonga tūturu;[27] and control the sale of ngā taonga tūturu within NZ. The POA, which was actually promulgated in 2006,[28] replaced the outdated and ineffective Antiquities Act 1975.

In addition to ngā taonga tūturu, the POA regulates 'protected foreign objects'[29] and 'protected New Zealand objects'.[30] The POA prohibits the

25 823 UNTS 231.

26 2421 UNTS 457.

27 Defined in s. 2 as meaning an object that '(a) relates to Māori culture, history, or society; and (b) was, or appears to have been,(i) manufactured or modified in New Zealand by Māori; or (ii) brought into New Zealand by Māori; or (iii) used by Māori; and (c) is more than 50 years old'.

28 See the Protected Objects Amendment Act 2006 (2006 No 37). On the POA generally, see Piers Davies and Paul Myburgh, 'The Protected Objects Act in New Zealand: Too Little, Too Late?' (2008) 15 *International Journal of Cultural Property* 321.

29 See POA s. 2. This is based on the definition of 'cultural property' in Article 1 of the 1970 UNESCO Convention. The POA also regulates the trafficking of protected foreign objects, *ibid.*, in ss. 10A–F.

30 *Ibid.*, s. 2 and Sch. 4, which sets out the categories of protected NZ objects in some detail.

export of protected NZ objects without the permission of the Chief Executive of Manatū Taonga/the Ministry for Culture and Heritage (MCH). Any export without permission 'or without reasonable excuse in the circumstances', amounts to an offence punishable by a fine and/or imprisonment.[31] Protected NZ objects include NZ archaeological objects, which consist 'of any objects, assemblages, scientific samples, and organic remains derived from a New Zealand archaeological site, as defined by the [HNZPT Act]'.[32] The POA therefore regulates the exportation of any objects found on wreck sites within NZ territorial waters, provided they are 'derived from' an archaeological site as defined. Apart from evidentiary complications that may arise in linking the object to an original wreck site, this means that the protection provided by the POA also suffers from the deficiencies in the definition of 'archaeological site' in the HNZPT Act, discussed above.

Ngā taonga tūturu are regulated separately in Part 2 of the POA, which provides that any taonga tūturu found anywhere in NZ or in the territorial waters of NZ are *prima facie* deemed the property of the Crown.[33] If actual or traditional ownership, rightful possession, or custody of any taonga tūturu is subsequently claimed, the Chief Executive or any person having any proprietary interest may apply to the Māori Land Court to determine the issue.[34] Anyone finding taonga tūturu in NZ or in the territorial waters of NZ must notify either the Chief Executive or the nearest public museum. Anyone 'knowing or having reasonable cause to suspect that it is a taonga tūturu' who does not comply with the POA, commits an offence punishable by a fine and/or imprisonment.[35]

The specific treatment of Māori UCH by the Act (e.g., waka, fish traps etc.) is beneficial in some respects, as protection of ngā taonga tūturu extends to Māori objects more than 50-years old, as opposed to the overly stringent pre-1900 requirement imposed by the HNZPT Act. However, it is unclear why the maximum penalties for illegal dealing in ngā taonga tūturu are lower than those

---

31 *Ibid.*, s. 5, representing a significant increase from the maximum penalties under the Antiquities Act 1975, which were risibly low.

32 *Ibid.*, Sch. 4, cl. 6.

33 However, POA s. 11A provides that nga taonga tūturu found within a customary marine title area in the common marine and coastal area of NZ are dealt with separately under the MACA s. 82: see section 2.3.3 *infra*.

34 See e.g., *Chief Executive of the Ministry for Culture and Heritage – Re Taonga Tūturu found at Cook's Cove, Tolaga Bay* (2017) 71 Tairāwhiti MB 267 (71 TRW 267); *Acting Chief Executive of the Ministry for Culture and Heritage – Re Taonga Tūturu found at Kerikeri* [2015] NZMLC 75 (3 July 2015); (2015) 106 Taitokerau MB 210 (106 TTK 210); *Jones v. Wickliffe* [2012] NZHC 1960 (7 August 2012); *Chief Executive, Ministry for Culture and Heritage – Re Taonga Tūturu found at Plimmerton* (2012) 283 Aotea MB 166 (283 AOT 166) [2012] NZMLC 27 (4 May 2012); *Holden - Nga Taonga Tūturu* [2010] NZMLC 2 (3 February 2010).

35 POA s. 11(3).

imposed for illegal dealing in NZ protected objects. This is an oddity given the definition of NZ protected objects includes ngā taonga tūturu,[36] making the demarcation of, and relationship between, these two parallel regulatory and enforcement schemes less than clear.

2.2 *Maritime Law Statutes*

2.2.1 Salvage Regime: Part XVII of the Maritime Transport Act 1994

The MTA enacted statutory provisions anticipating the incorporation of the International Convention on Salvage 1989[37] into NZ domestic law.[38] NZ only acceded to the Salvage Convention in 2002 and it acquired the force of law in 2003.[39] There has been some confusion whether the Salvage Convention applies in NZ to 'maritime cultural property of prehistoric, archaeological or historic interest ... situated on the sea bed', as provided for in the Article 30(1)(d) reservation to the Convention. There was no indication in the Parliamentary proceedings that NZ intended to exercise this reservation, and section 216 of the MTA provides without qualification that the 'provisions of the Convention shall have the force of law'.[40] However, the official International Maritime Organization (IMO) website indicates in respect of NZ's accession to the Salvage Convention that:

> [the] Government of New Zealand, in respect of Article 30(1)(d) of the Convention, reserves the right not to apply the provisions of the Convention when the property involved is maritime cultural property of prehistoric, archaeological or historic interest and is situated on the sea bed; and declares that this accession shall extend to Tokelau.[41]

It is crucial for the correct position to be made plain in domestic legislation. The lack of a clear-cut demarcation between the commercial salvage regime in the MTA and the UCH regimes in the HNZPT Act and POA creates legal uncertainty and tensions in respect of the rights and interests of finders of UCH. This issue will most definitely require clarification if NZ is to ratify the 2001 Convention, especially in the light of its 'salvage clause' in Article 4.

---

36 *Ibid.*, Sch. 4, cl. 4.
37 1953 UNTS 165 (28 April 1989).
38 MTA Part 17 and Sch. 6.
39 Maritime Transport Act Commencement Order 2003 (SR 2003/259).
40 'Convention' is defined in MTA s. 215 as meaning the English text of the Salvage Convention 'as set out in Schedule 6'. Sch. 6 contains no indication of a maritime cultural property reservation.
41 See <https://www.imo.org/en/About/Conventions/Pages/StatusOfConventions.aspx>.

2.2.2 Wreck Regime: Part 9 of the Maritime Transport Act 1994

The traditional NZ wreck regime, based on its UK counterpart, underwent significant updating in 1999.[42] The office of Receiver of Wreck was abolished, with any remaining powers and duties vested in the Director of Maritime New Zealand (MNZ) and the Police. The 1999 amendments also updated the definition of 'wreck'. Section 98 of the MTA now provides that this includes:

a. any ship or aircraft which is abandoned, stranded, or in distress at sea or in any river or lake or other inland water, or any equipment or cargo or other articles belonging to or separated from any such ship or aircraft or belonging to or separated from any ship or aircraft which is lost at sea or in any river or lake or other inland water; and
b. shipping containers and property lost overboard or similarly separated from a ship, other than cargo lost in the course of its unloading or discharge from the ship while the ship is in a port.

Although the primary focus of the MTA regime is on modern wrecks, this definition is broad enough to cover historic shipwrecks and sunken aircraft, as well as their artefacts. The Director of MNZ may give orders 'for the preservation of' wrecks,[43] but from the context these provisions are obviously aimed at the physical preservation of ships and aircraft in current emergencies, rather than archaeological sites.

Section 105 of the MTA requires anyone who:

> ... finds or takes possession of any wreck within the limits of New Zealand or takes possession of and brings within the limits of New Zealand any wreck found outside those limits ...

to notify the Director of MNZ. Failure to comply 'without reasonable excuse' is an offence, resulting in the finder losing any salvage claim and a fine of double the value of the wreck. Finders who are not the owner of the wreck must deliver it to the Police or allow them to take possession of it. This is clearly inappropriate in the case of historical wrecks, which often require immediate, specialised care to preserve them: a task well beyond the expertise and job description of the Police.[44] The MTA provides that the Director of MNZ 'may'

---

42 See specifically Maritime Transport Amendment Act 1999 s. 13(3).

43 MTA ss. 100, 100A, 101.

44 See New Zealand Underwater Heritage Group Inc *Submissions on Heritage New Zealand Pou[h]ere Taonga Bill*, 17 June 2012, p. 2, which describes this as an 'untenable situation': see <https://www.parliament.nz/resource/en-NZ/50SCLGE_EVI_00DBHOH_BILL11133_1_A259154/00be7e2ff33c0c35db8eab9a32a364e9da72e55d>.

share information regarding the wreck with persons or agencies 'as the Director thinks appropriate' but falls short of making information-sharing with HNZPT mandatory for historic shipwrecks (even if the HNZPT Act might apply to them). MNZ did not report any wrecks to HNZPT between 2008–2021.[45] MNZ has had an 'integrated readiness and response strategy in regard to maritime incident response since the *Rena* incident'.[46] HNZPT confirms that it is usually members of the public that alert them to historic wreck finds, rather than MNZ.[47]

Section 110 of the Act gives the Director of MNZ powers to remove and sell wrecked or derelict ships or aircraft considered a hazard to navigation, if the owner fails to arrange to secure and remove the hazard, and the wreck does not lie within the jurisdiction of a regional council. The wreck removal regime is, again, clearly aimed at modern navigation hazards, but its scope is broad enough to cover historic wrecks posing a threat to navigation. However, as with the wreck protection provisions, there is no requirement for the Director of MNZ to consult with HNZPT before exercising removal powers regarding historic wrecks.[48]

2.3 *Statutes Affecting UCH*

2.3.1 Resource Management Act 1991

The RMA is the key statute regulating the use of land, air, and water resources in NZ.[49] It extends to control of the coastal marine area, which includes the seabed and coastal water to the outer limits of the TS. In 2003, the RMA was amended to include explicit protection for historic heritage. Section 12(1)(g) now provides that no-one may:

> … destroy, damage, or disturb any foreshore or seabed (other than for the purpose of lawfully harvesting any plant or animal) in a manner that has or is likely to have an adverse effect on historic heritage …

45 Nigel Clifford, MNZ, email of 3 August 2021.

46 Nigel Clifford, MNZ, email of 26 May 2021.

47 Vanessa Tanner, HNZPT, email of 4 June 2021.

48 The MTA s. 110(1)(d) requires the Director of MNZ to comply with the RMA in removing wrecks but does not require compliance with the HNZPT Act.

49 The RMA was in the process of being reformed and replaced by the Spatial Planning Act 2023 and the Natural and Built Environment Act 2023, both of which came into effect on 24 August 2023. These two reform Acts were intended to be implemented gradually over the next ten years. However, a change of government saw these two Acts repealed in December 2023. The RMA thus remains in force while the current Government formulates its own reforms of the RMA.

unless this is expressly permitted by a rule in a regional coastal plan, or unless a resource consent has been granted by a regional council.

'Historic heritage' is defined in section 2 as meaning 'those natural and physical resources that contribute to an understanding and appreciation of New Zealand's history and cultures', and includes historic sites, structures, places and areas, archaeological sites, and sites of significance to Māori. Although the definition of historic heritage does not expressly refer to UCH or wreck sites, it is sufficiently broadly framed to cover such sites. Indeed, the definition is broader than that contained in the HNZPT Act and is not subject to a specific age requirement. Section 6(1)(f) further requires regional councils to consider matters of national importance when implementing the RMA, including 'the protection of historic heritage from inappropriate subdivision, use, and development'.

The response of regional councils to the inclusion of 'historic heritage' in the RMA since 2003 has been uneven.[50] Some have taken no concrete steps in regional plans to protect UCH sites within their jurisdiction, whilst others have been far more pro-active. Regional coastal plans must conform to the New Zealand Coastal Policy Statement produced by the Department of Conservation, most recently in 2010. Policy 17 on historic heritage identification and protection, requires regional councils to protect historic heritage in the coastal environment.[51] This has been invoked in several Environment Court cases dealing with applications for resource consents under the RMA and disputes over regional coastal plans.[52]

---

50 Resource Management Review Panel *New Directions for Resource Management in New Zealand* [2020] NZAHGovRp 1 (30 June 2020) at [97]: 'Many historic heritage sites – such as jetties, wharves, archaeological sites and sites of significance to Māori – span the land-sea divide and lack of coordination can mean inconsistent management and gaps in protection for such heritage places.'

51 See <https://www.doc.govt.nz/about-us/science-publications/conservation-publications/marine-and-coastal/new-zealand-coastal-policy-statement>. The Department also provides detailed guidance notes on Policy 17. Section 77 of the MACA requires the Minister of Conservation to seek and consider the views of customary marine title groups when proposing to prepare, issue, change, review, or revoke a New Zealand coastal policy statement.

52 See e.g., *Karaka Harbourside Estate Ltd v. Auckland Council* [2012] NZEnvC 236; *Whangaroa Maritime Recreational Park Steering Group v. Northland Regional Council* [2014] NZEnvC 92; *Friends of Nelson Haven and Tasman Bay Inc. v. Tasman District Council* [2018] NZEnvC 46; *Motiti Rohe Moana Trust v. Bay of Plenty Regional Council* [2020] NZEnvC 73. On the relationship between the New Zealand Coastal Policy Statement and lower-order plans, see *Port Otago Ltd v. Environmental Defence Society Inc* [2023] NZSC 112; [2023] NZRMA 422.

2.3.2 Marine Reserves Act 1971

The MRA provides that marine reserves are to be established and maintained in their natural state within the TS, internal waters, or foreshore of the coast of NZ, and that the public is to have a right of entry.[53] Marine reserves have been established in several places off the coast of the main islands of NZ and around the Kermadec and Auckland Islands. There are wrecks in at least two of these marine reserves.

Unlike the HNZPT Act, there is no specific provision in the MRA spelling out that wrecks are not to be damaged, modified or destroyed.[54] However, under section 18I(3)(b) it is an offence to 'wilfully' interfere with or disturb in a marine reserve any marine life, foreshore, or seabed or any of the natural features. If there is significant disturbance of a wreck, it would also probably disturb some marine life or the foreshore and seabed. This is clearly a *mens rea* offence. In contrast, section 18I(3)(d) provides that it is an offence to take or remove from a marine reserve any marine life, mineral, sand, shingle, 'or other natural material or thing of any kind', which seems broad enough to cover unlawful removal of shipwrecks or artefacts, with wording that suggests a strict liability offence. However, the maximum penalty is not particularly substantial. Therefore, if there was any damage, modification, or destruction of a wreck in a marine reserve, the logical approach would be to use the HNZPT Act provisions. However, the MRA could apply to historic wrecks that sank after 1900, whereas the HNZPT Act would not.

2.3.3 Marine and Coastal Area (Takutai Moana) Act 2011

The MACA was enacted to repeal the controversial Foreshore and Seabed Act 2004, which vested ownership of the foreshore and seabed in the Crown, and to restore customary interests extinguished by that Act.[55] The MACA purports,

---

53 MRA ss. 2, 3 and 4.

54 The Marine Reserve (Auckland Islands-Motu Maha) Order 2003 cl. 4 expressly permits salvage or recovery of shipwrecks, including the *General Grant*, in the Auckland Islands marine reserve if approved by the Director-General of Conservation. See also the Marine Reserve (Long Island-Kokomohua) Order 1993 cl. 3(a), which preserves any ownership rights over the wreck *Elsie* situated in the reserve.

55 However, the MACA has proved equally controversial, with the Waitangi Tribunal releasing *The Marine and Coastal Area (Takutai Moana) Act 2011 Inquiry Stage 2 Report: WAI 2660* in pre-publication format in October 2023. The Tribunal found that the MACA does not sufficiently support Māori in their kaitiakitanga (guardianship) duties and rangatiratanga (sovereignty/self-determination) rights, fails to provide a fair and reasonable balance between Māori rights and other public and private rights, and is in breach of the Treaty of Waitangi. The Tribunal recommended that the Crown make several amendments to the MACA.

in accordance with te Tiriti o Waitangi/the Treaty of Waitangi, to recognise and promote customary interests of Māori[56] in the common marine and coastal area of NZ.[57]

Section 8 of the MACA makes it plain, however, that the sovereignty of NZ under international law over the marine and coastal area remains unaffected, as do the rights and obligations of NZ under international law, or provisions in any other enactment relating to international legal rights and obligations. This means that the provisions of the MACA cannot override the operation of the Salvage Convention in the marine and coastal area. It is therefore important that the (non-)application of the Salvage Convention to UCH in which Māori have a customary interest is clarified.

Sections 18 and 19 of the MACA regulate structures within the common marine and coastal area. 'Structure' is defined in accordance with the RMA as any building, equipment, device, or other facility made by people 'and which is fixed to land', so does not cover shipwrecks or artefacts.[58] Section 18 provides that owned structures are deemed separate from the seabed, and section 19 deems abandoned structures to be owned by the Crown. A structure is defined as abandoned if the relevant regional council has, after due inquiry, been unable to ascertain the identity or whereabouts of its owner.

Sections 78 and 79 provide mechanisms for customary marine title groups to protect wāhi tapu and wāhi tapu areas within the common marine and coastal area. Section 82 regulates the finding of nga taonga tūturu found in a customary marine title area. These are *prima facie* deemed to be the property

---

56 The statutory test for customary marine title (CMT) has proven to be fraught: see *Whakatōhea Kotahitanga Waka (Edwards) v. Te Kāhui and Whakatōhea Māori Trust Board* [2024] NZSC 164, where the Supreme Court reversed the Court of Appeal's more liberal interpretation of CMT. The current Government had introduced the Marine and Coastal Area (Takutai Moana) (Customary Marine Title) Amendment Bill into the House in 2024 to overturn the Court of Appeal's interpretation. It remains to be seen if the Supreme Court's narrower approach to CMT will be sufficient to assuage the Government's concerns.

57 Defined in s. 9 as including the area between the line of mean high-water springs and the outer limits of the TS, as well as river beds that are part of the coastal marine area (within the meaning of the RMA), excluding specified freehold land, Crown-owned land, and the bed of Te Whaanga Lagoon in the Chatham Islands.

58 In the Marine and Coastal Area (Takutai Moana) Bill 2010, cl. 20(3) originally provided that 'structure includes a vessel of any description'. This provision was deleted after the Select Committee hearings. For a critique of the Bill from a UCH perspective, see Matthew Carter's and Andrew Dodd's joint *Submissions on the Marine and Coastal Area (Takutai Moana) Bill*, 23 November 2010, available at <https://www.parliament.nz/resource/en-NZ/49SCMA_EVI_00DBHOH_BILL10309_1_A153198/feaa34c0de6e121a388a27b4b71711639c910ea4>.

of the relevant customary marine title group.[59] Section 82 applies the POA process to such taonga tūturu, but with modifications: the relevant customary marine title group is entitled to have interim custody of nga taonga tūturu, at the discretion of the Chief Executive and subject to any conditions that are considered fit; and the public notice given must provide for six months from the notice for any claims of ownership to be lodged. Section 89 of the Act places an obligation on HNZPT to have regard to planning documents lodged by customary marine title groups when considering an application under section 44 of the HNZPT Act to destroy or modify an archaeological site within a customary marine title area.

2.3.4 Other Statutes and Conventions

Several other statutes have a potential impact on UCH in NZ:

- Fisheries Act 1996: section 186 enables the Governor-General to make regulations recognising and providing for customary food gathering by Māori, which may impact on UCH sites.
- Crown Minerals Act 1991: this applies to minerals in land covered by water and includes the foreshore and seabed out to the outer limits of the TS. Licensing of mineral exploration and retrieval may affect UCH sites.
- Continental Shelf Act 1964: this applies, *inter alia*, to minerals in the seabed or subsoil of the CS, exploration, or excavation of which may affect UCH sites.

NZ is also party to the UNESCO Convention for the Protection of World Cultural and Natural Heritage 1972,[60] and has three listed World Heritage sites, one of which is the NZ Sub-Antarctic Islands.[61] Several important wrecks, including the *General Grant*,[62] lie near the Auckland Islands, which are part of this site. However, the Sub-Antarctic Islands have been listed for their natural rather than cultural heritage.[63] Therefore, although additional protection may be afforded to wrecks within World Heritage sites, e.g., oil exploration is prevented, this protection is indirect. In 2006, New Zealand published a tentative list of other proposed World Heritage sites, but this does not seem to

---

59 As opposed to nga taonga tūturu found on land or in territorial waters not part of the common marine and coastal area; see POA ss. 11(1), 11A.

60 UNESCO, Convention for the Protection of the World Cultural and Natural Heritage, No 15511, 1037 UNTS 151 (16 November 1972).

61 See <https://www.doc.govt.nz/about-us/international-agreements/world-heritage/ and https://whc.unesco.org/en/list/>.

62 See <https://nzhistory.govt.nz/page/wreck-general-grant>.

63 See G. Law and K. Greig, 'Protecting Archaeological Heritage through Public Heritage Lists' (2004) 47 *Archaeology in New Zealand* 99.

have progressed any further.[64] The list of proposed sites potentially includes sites with UCH. However, it may be difficult for any of the known shipwreck sites around NZ to come within the Article 1 definition of cultural heritage as 'including archaeological sites which are of outstanding universal value from the historical, aesthetic, ethnological or anthropological point of view'.

2.4 *Ownership of Wrecks*

Under NZ law, the ownership of a wreck remains with the owner of the vessel unless it is abandoned. Often, the owner of the wreck had it insured, and the insurer becomes the successor to the ownership rights after reimbursing the insured. In instances where no ownership can be established, the wreck becomes Crown property in accordance with the *bona vacantia* principle. The Ministry of Transport, through the Receiver of Wreck, traditionally dealt with ownership of wrecks by issuing letters granting salvage rights to abandoned wrecks, including historic shipwrecks. However, after the 1999 amendments to wreck law, the Ministry discontinued this practice, and no substitute regime has been implemented. Thus, no agency or government department currently takes responsibility for determining ownership of shipwrecks, or licensing their salvage if they are *bona vacantia*.[65] Although the Minister of Finance and the Treasury are ultimately charged with exercising the Crown's rights and powers regarding *bona vacantia*,[66] no relevant procedures or guidelines have been developed. Thus, it could be argued that the issue of ownership of abandoned wrecks seems considered a nuisance in NZ, with no government department keen to take responsibility.

2.5 *Crown and Foreign State Immunity*

There is no legislation specifically relating to sunken NZ Crown-owned or foreign State-owned ships or aircraft. Sunken State vessels and aircraft are generally covered by the MTA, HNZPT Act, and other legislation previously referred to, with two exceptions. First, an admiralty action *in rem* cannot be brought against NZ Crown-owned vessels to enforce salvage or property claims; they have to be enforced by bringing an action *in personam* against the Crown.[67] Secondly, the Salvage Convention 1989 does not apply to foreign State-owned

64 See <https://www.doc.govt.nz/globalassets/documents/about-doc/role/international/our-world-heritage.pdf>.

65 Roger Brown, Ministry of Transport (email, 6 May 2021).

66 Public Finance Act 1989 s. 75(1).

67 Crown Proceedings Act 1950 s. 28. The MTA s. 217 provides that, subject to the Crown Proceedings Act, the Salvage Convention 1989 applies to salvage of NZ warships, or any other NZ State-owned ships or other property.

warships or other non-commercial vessels, or their cargo which are entitled, at the time of salvage, to sovereign immunity, unless the foreign State waives immunity.[68] Although NZ does not have State immunity legislation like the UK and USA, NZ courts recognise the restrictive theory of sovereign immunity, based on the distinction between acts of State *iure imperii* and acts *iure gestionis*.[69] The NZ courts apply the restrictive theory of sovereign immunity to both actions *in rem* and actions *in personam*.[70]

There are few known NZ wreck sites of foreign State-owned vessels. Several British warships and vessels, like the HMS *Orpheus*, were wrecked during the nineteenth century, but most have disappeared, or if there are remains, have not yet been discovered. One example is the *l'Alcmene*, a French Government corvette, lost in 1851, which was discovered in 1976 by Kelly Tarlton, and one iron cannon, two anchors, and two bronze swivel guns were recovered. Ownership of the wreck was purchased from the French Government for a nominal sum and the NZ Government granted financial aid for the restoration of these artefacts.

3 Overall Assessment of the Current Position

3.1 *Improvements to the Legislative Framework*

The current legislative regime for UCH in NZ is fragmentary and inefficient.[71] Regulation of different aspects of UCH is administered under several statutes, by a variety of departments and agencies. This has led to unfortunate gaps, and different departments and agencies implementing policy in a narrow fashion without reference to the whole sector. There has long been a pressing need for 'joined-up thinking'[72] and a co-ordinated, holistic legal approach to the preservation of UCH in NZ.

3.2 *Recording of UCH*

There is no comprehensive national register of UCH in NZ. Some items of UCH are recorded, but many are not, and records, which are held by different bodies

68 See arts. 4 and 25.

69 *Buckingham v. Hughes Helicopter* [1982] 2 NZLR 738, 739.

70 See *Marine Steel Ltd v. Government of the Marshall Islands* [1981] 2 NZLR 1, 8–9; *Reef Shipping Co Ltd v. The Ship 'Fua Kavenga'* [1987] 1 NZLR 550, 568–570.

71 Blackie, *supra* n. 9, at p. 38, refers to 'a 'scatter-gun' approach aimed at various particular areas.

72 P. Roberts and S. Trow, *Taking to the Water: English Heritage's Initial Policy for the Management of Maritime Archaeology in England* (English Heritage, 2002) p. 16.

for different purposes, are not necessarily integrated, with some computerised and others out of date. The New Zealand Archaeological Association (NZAA) holds records in a subscription-only database, ArchSite.[73] The Department of Conservation also records information relating to shipwrecks, but only those on the foreshores that the Department administers. Auckland Council's Cultural Heritage Inventory has a comprehensive and detailed schedule of shipwrecks, hulks, and other UCH items but only within its jurisdiction.[74] The Australasian Underwater Cultural Heritage Database (AUCHD) represents a major positive development in this regard.[75] Since 2013, HNZPT has entered its UCH sites into the AUCHD, which at the time of writing contained 2,196 NZ shipwreck records. It is administered by the Australian Department of Climate Change, Energy, the Environment, and Water, serves as the register of protected UCH for the Australian Underwater Cultural Heritage Act 2018 (Cth), and provides a portal for the public to submit notifications and permit applications required under the HNZPT.[76]

3.3 *Education*

Educating the diving fraternity and the general public on UCH is another important issue. NZ has a long history of public access to a large proportion of the coastline. Some members of the public believe that artefacts and wrecks are public property, which they can purloin with no feelings of guilt.[77] Timber and other materials from shipwrecks have also traditionally been recycled and used in the construction of baches (holiday homes).[78] For example, when the 1865 wreck of the *Daring* surfaced on Muriwai Beach in 2018, part of it was damaged by local fossickers, and round-the-clock security was needed to protect it.[79]

---

73 See <https://nzarchaeology.org/>.

74 See <https://www.aucklandcouncil.govt.nz/arts-culture-heritage/heritage/Pages/search-cultural-heritage-inventory.aspx>.

75 See <https://www.dcceew.gov.au/parks-heritage/heritage/underwater-heritage/auchd>.

76 See Andrew Viduka, 'Going for the Win-Win: Including the Public in Underwater Cultural Heritage Management through Citizen Science in Australia and New Zealand' (2020) 49 *International Journal of Nautical Archaeology* 87.

77 New Zealand Archaeological Association Inc., *Submission on Oceans Policy Working Paper 7: Marine Cultural Heritage*, 7 April 2003. (No longer accessible online. Copy with authors.)

78 See Kurt Bennett and Madeline Fowler, '"In my Memory, it says *Rarawa*": Abandoned Vessel Material Salvage and Reuse at Rangitoto Island, Aotearoa/New Zealand' (2017) 21 *International Journal of Historical Archaeology* 27.

79 (Autumn 2019) *Heritage Quarterly* 13.

3.4 *Incentives*

Experienced divers argue for more recognition of those finding and reporting wrecks, like that afforded at the Mangawhai Museum for the exploring and surveying of the RMS *Niagara* wreck.[80] Financial awards would also be attractive. The costs of finding, surveying, and identifying wrecks are high. Although finder's fee regimes have their critics, they have been successfully implemented in other countries and their use should be explored in NZ, even though the current financial climate discourages this. The present regime provides few incentives to disclose wreck discoveries to the authorities, which are seen as unwelcoming of divers. Considerable progress could be made in this area at minimal cost if authorities were prepared to encourage a real dialogue with divers, leading to meaningful participation in the finding and preservation of UCH. The *Daring* provides an example of what can be achieved with the positive combination of locals' enthusiasm, philanthropic trust money, skilled tradespeople, and the authorities' support. This is an area of potentiality that needs developing: paying for the expensive work of surveying and preservation of wrecks requires corporate and philanthropic support, particularly if government funding continues to be limited.[81]

3.5 *Increased Funding for Preservation Facilities*

Preservation of items recovered from the seabed is always a matter of urgency, since often it is only a matter of hours before items deteriorate. MAANZ's laboratory has a limited ability to deal with certain types of items.[82] Additional government or private sector funding needs to be made available to assist in the preservation of recovered items.

3.6 *Increasing Protection of UCH*

Even with enhanced recording of sites, the question of how to best protect them remains. There has been difficulty in protecting land-based sites, where recording and archaeological issues are much further advanced.[83] Most local authorities do not have jurisdiction below the mean high-water line. Regional councils do have jurisdiction within the TS, but only Auckland Council currently has a significant heritage list relating to UCH. Although there is a limited range of protection tools in the marine environment compared to on land, there are RMA tools available, which need to be taken up more resolutely.[84]

80 Keith Gordon and Dave Moran (discussion, 14 May 2021).

81 *Ibid.*

82 New Zealand Archaeological Association, *supra* n. 77.

83 G. Law and K. Greig, *supra* n. 63.

84 Oceans Policy Secretariat *Working Paper 7: Marine Cultural Heritage*, 14 March 2003 pp. 9–10.

4 Prospects for the 2001 Convention in NZ

4.1 *Ratification of the 2001 Convention*

NZ is not a party to the 2001 Convention, and the official government view of the Convention may be characterised as cautious. Although the MCH supports, in principle, the Convention's objectives and general intent, it is unwilling to commit to a specific position on ratification until 'a balanced analysis of potential legislative and regulatory implications, as well as associated benefits and costs'[85] has been carried out. The rub, however, is that the national interest analysis required to decide on ratification does not form part of the MCH's existing working programme, nor are there currently plans to include it. While the MCH has not ruled out ratification, it seems clear that this is unlikely to be actively considered in the immediate future. Whilst Australia has passed the Underwater Cultural Heritage Act 2018 (Cth), which came into effect on 1 July 2019, and is in the process of consultation and consideration of ratifying the Convention, the MCH view is that, while it will follow Australia's progress with interest, such ratification will not have a material bearing on the factors NZ would need to consider in its analysis. For instance, there may be specific implications regarding the Treaty of Waitangi.[86] However, HNZPT does support the principles of the 2001 Convention and the rules in its Annex.[87] There seem to be several reasons for this current situation, which will be discussed in turn.

4.1.1 Priorities

UCH is not a high-profile issue in NZ. The NZ UCH resource is relatively small and commercially inconsequential by international standards and has therefore not been subjected to concerted exploitation by professional salvors. This seems to have influenced the MCH's view that immediate ratification of the 2001 Convention is unnecessary.

Additionally, HNZPT rarely receives reports of maritime archaeological site damage by recreational divers and considers those flouting the law to be a minority.[88] However, problematic incidents at the site of the *Daring*[89] suggest that unlawful disturbance of UCH and the clandestine removal of artefacts is an ongoing issue. Equally, responsible divers are frustrated by the lack of a clear legislative framework and believe that the processes under the HNZPT

---

85 Polly O'Brien, Manager Heritage Policy, MCH (email, 17 May 2021).

86 *Ibid.*

87 Tanner, *supra* n. 47.

88 *Ibid.*

89 See *Heritage Quarterly*, *supra* n. 79.

Act are dilatory and frustrating. A consistent and positive outreach to divers is needed by HNZPT and MCH. The low priority currently accorded to UCH, and the fragmentary nature of the legislative framework, have arguably contributed to a climate where less scrupulous finders are not reporting sites or finds. The UCH they discover is not being scientifically assessed and is thus lost to the NZ public. Ratification of the 2001 Convention would assist in providing a focus for reviewing the legislative framework and processes, and in turn a clearer and more effective regime for UCH protection.

A related argument is that there are other heritage conventions which should enjoy a higher legislative priority than the 2001 Convention. NZ lags behind other States in terms of ratifying heritage conventions and is in a catch-up process. As discussed above, updating the Antiquities Act with the POA in 2006 was seen as a more urgent priority, and has resulted in enhanced protection against removal from and trafficking of UCH in NZ territorial waters. However, since 2012, the focus of the MCH seems to have shifted back to national cultural interests and issues. Indeed, apart from the Te Kāhui o Matariki Public Holiday Act 2022, the MCH has not been responsible for the enactment of any legislation since 2014.[90]

The obvious difficulty with postponing ratification of the 2001 Convention is that the domestic legislative framework regarding *in situ* preservation of UCH sites will remain manifestly inadequate, particularly in respect of sites falling outside NZ's TS, which currently enjoy no legal protection. The enactment of the POA and the MACA has only provided a partial solution to preserving the integrity of NZ's UCH, and in some respects has added further complexity and fragmentation to the existing legal regime. A focused, comprehensive, cross-departmental review of all legislation affecting UCH is highly unlikely to occur unless the NZ Government makes a positive commitment to ratifying the 2001 Convention.

The MCH's statement of strategic intentions for 2018–2022 made no reference to the 2001 Convention (or indeed any other heritage conventions) and contained only the vague and anodyne goal of '[e]nsuring New Zealand's international obligations are being met and opportunities explored on cultural matters, particularly with Australia'.[91] Given Australia's work on the AUCHD and its enactment of the Underwater Cultural Heritage Act 2018 (Cth), collaborating and co-operating with Australia to implement the 2001 Convention effectively, thereby ensuring a comprehensive and uniform approach to protection of

90 See <https://mch.govt.nz/about-ministry/legislation>.

91 Now updated, see *infra.*, n. 93.

UCH across the Australasian, or indeed the Pacific region,[92] would seem to be precisely the sort of opportunity that the MCH ought to be exploring as a priority. MCH's current statement of strategic intentions for 2021–2025 is almost entirely focused on te ao Māori (the Māori world). While this is highly laudable, and long overdue, the statement is remarkably short on specific details and again makes no mention of any international heritage conventions.[93]

4.1.2 Resource Constraints

HNZPT has a limited budget, already strained by conserving terrestrial heritage sites. HNZPT has also been required to undertake an ever-increasing range of heritage functions and obligations at national, regional, and local community level, to the extent that it has been described as 'coming apart at the seams'.[94] There are comparatively few heritage and archaeological consultants specialising in UCH in NZ, and HNZPT does not employ specialist staff to deal solely with UCH issues. If the 2001 Convention is ratified in NZ, its implementation must be accompanied by a meaningful commitment to properly resource underwater archaeology in NZ, either by providing HNZPT with additional resources, or by funding a dedicated maritime archaeology unit.[95]

It has been suggested that, given the scarce resources available to the cultural heritage sector, it would not be wise to stretch these further to accommodate the 2001 Convention's regime. This argument overlooks the fact that the NZ Government made a commitment to preserve and protect UCH under the HNZPT Act and its predecessors. Since 2003, regional councils also have a statutory duty to protect UCH within their jurisdictions. With a few exceptions, however, they are still struggling to achieve their land-based cultural heritage responsibilities, and do not necessarily have the expertise or fiscal resources to protect UCH at the regional level. Funding a specialised marine archaeology unit, either within HNZPT or on an independent basis, would provide a central pool of expertise that can be used to protect UCH at both national and regional levels.

Regardless of whether the 2001 Convention is ratified, increased funding, or a more imaginative and collaborative use of existing resources in other

92 See Andrew Viduka, 'Australia and Pacific Countries: The Need to Collaborate to Protect Underwater Cultural Heritage' (2019) *Historic Environment* 88.

93 See <https://www.mch.govt.nz/sites/default/files/2023-10/Strategic%20Intentions%20web%202021-25%20(D-1124009).pdf>.

94 H. Allen, *Protecting Historic Places in New Zealand* (University of Auckland, 1998) 64, see <https://researchspace.auckland.ac.nz/bitstream/handle/2292/4526/4526.pdf>.

95 Andrew Dodd (email, 9 May 2021).

government departments or agencies,[96] is crucial to meeting existing responsibilities in respect of UCH sites under the HNZPT Act and RMA. The current climate of chronic under-funding does not provide a sound justification for refusing to ratify the 2001 Convention.

4.1.3 Compliance Costs

There have been concerns that ratifying and complying with the 2001 Convention would incur additional costs but, as the MCH itself has pointed out, until an analysis is undertaken, such costs are not quantifiable.[97] It is difficult to pre-assess the level of such compliance costs, but they would not seem to present a hurdle to ratifying the 2001 Convention. Apart from the standard initial costs of undertaking the treaty examination process and drafting legislation implementing the 2001 Convention's provisions in NZ (which might involve a stand-alone statute on UCH,[98] but is more likely to take the form of amendments to the HNZPT Act, the POA, the MTA and the RMA), the ongoing costs of implementing the 2001 Convention are unlikely to be substantial.

One of the main areas in which extra compliance costs will be incurred are reporting and notification requirements under Articles 9, 10 and 11 of the 2001 Convention. However, these requirements will be invoked infrequently, as they relate to wrecks beyond territorial waters and the bulk of NZ's shipwreck sites are along the coastline. Notifications to other States Parties and consultations, if required, can be arranged through diplomatic exchanges. Thus, it seems unlikely that the costs would be high.[99]

Arguably, ratification of the 2001 Convention could give rise to cost savings, result in a clearer definition of UCH, clarify that *in situ* preservation of UCH sites is the primary aim and that commercial salvage law is inapplicable to UCH, and lay down more robust guidelines for reporting discoveries of, and activities dealing with UCH. With previous criminal prosecutions and administrative challenges illustrating the wasted costs of protecting UCH through litigation, the 2001 Convention scheme could ensure a greater degree of legal

---

96 Dr Bridget Buxton (email, 1 May 2021) points out that the costs of assessing and preserving UCH sites can be minimised by utilising the existing capabilities of government departments and agencies, or by encouraging the development of marine archaeology as an academic discipline and the establishment of marine archaeology laboratory facilities in one or more NZ universities. The real strength in NZ is the spirit of volunteerism. What is needed is government leadership and a commitment to a co-ordinated approach to UCH in NZ.

97 O'Brien, *supra* n. 85.

98 Cf. the Underwater Cultural Heritage Act 2018 (Cth).

99 Patrick O'Keefe (email, 9 June 2005).

certainty and provide for more efficient cultural heritage administration: more 'time can now be spent on actual site evaluation and formulating appropriate management schemes, rather than fighting in court'.[100]

4.1.4 Adequacy of the Existing Legal Framework

There is a perception that the existing domestic legislative framework for heritage management already addresses many issues covered in the 2001 Convention.[101] Although it is true that UCH is protected to varying extents by the HNZPT Act, the POA, and, since 2003, by the RMA, the domestic legislative framework nonetheless fails to deal with the issue of protection of UCH in a comprehensive, co-ordinated manner. There are shortcomings in the HNZPT Act, not least the enforcement provisions and the 1900 trigger-date for archaeological sites. None of the existing statutes affords any protection to NZ's UCH on the CS or EEZ, let alone on the High Seas, or on the seabed.

The current legislative framework also neither requires nor assists international co-operation in respect of UCH of significance to NZ. By contrast, Article 6 of the 2001 Convention encourages States Parties to enter into bilateral, regional or multilateral arrangements that further the aims of the 2001 Convention. Several shipwrecks in NZ waters are of foreign origin. The 2001 Convention will allow for, and encourage, international collaborative and co-operative research programmes in respect of such wrecks. Ratifying the 2001 Convention would give NZ enhanced access to maritime archaeological resources and expertise in other countries.

Finally, because of the lack of express reference in the MTA to NZ's UCH reservation to the Salvage Convention 1989, the current domestic legislative framework for heritage management is vulnerable to challenge from salvors attempting to exercise their commercial rights under the Convention. Ratifying the 2001 Convention will ensure that relevant statutes are reviewed, co-ordinated and amended to afford adequate *in situ* protection to the whole of NZ's UCH resource in accordance with international legal norms. The 2001 Convention is likely to strengthen NZ's ability to control what happens out to the edge of its CS, and to seek the return of illegally removed material.

4.1.5 Treaty of Waitangi Obligations

It has been suggested that the 2001 Convention fails to address important maritime cultural heritage issues for NZ, such as protection for structures other than shipwrecks, including sites of significance to Māori. Considerations of the

100 *Ibid.*

101 O'Brien, *supra* n. 85.

Crown's Treaty of Waitangi obligations have been raised as relevant to whether NZ will ratify the 2001 Convention. Full and appropriate consultation with Māori will, of course, be crucial for the success of NZ's ratification.

However, it is difficult to see that this issue is problematic from a legal perspective, given the broad definition of UCH in Article 1(1)(a) of the 2001 Convention as including 'all traces of human existence having a cultural, historical or archaeological character'. The 2001 Convention expressly applies to 'sites, structures, buildings, artefacts and human remains, together with their archaeological and natural context'. As such, its definition of cultural heritage is broader than that of the HNZPT Act. As an international instrument, it is not surprising that the 2001 Convention does not refer to specific peoples' cultural values. Equally, however, there is nothing in the 2001 Convention that prevents its regime from being supplemented with appropriate indigenous heritage management practices if proper practices are observed in accordance with the Rules. Indeed, Article 7(1) of the 2001 Convention expressly recognises that States Parties:

> ... in the exercise of their sovereignty, have the exclusive right to regulate and authorise activities directed at UCH in their internal waters, archipelagic waters and territorial sea.

Questions of consultation, co-operation and co-management of Māori cultural heritage sites are internal political and administrative matters and are, quite rightly, not regulated by the 2001 Convention.

4.1.6 A Divided Constituency

The MCH has noted that there has not been significant pressure from the wider heritage sector in NZ to make any further commitment to the 2001 Convention. Protection of UCH is, of necessity, a highly specialised area. As discussed above, there are comparatively few experts in NZ specialising in marine archaeology. Our informal survey of relevant government departments, academia, the diving community, and the broader heritage community suggests that the provisions and implications of the 2001 Convention are generally not well-known or understood in NZ. More information dissemination and education are required before one can draw any meaningful conclusions from lack of pressure to ratify the 2001 Convention. The marine archaeology experts consulted support the 2001 Convention's objectives and principles.[102] In contrast, experienced divers

102 Dodd, *supra* n. 95.

are sceptical about ratifying the 2001 Convention. They do not see practical benefits encouraging them to research, discover and report wrecks now that MCH and HNZPT apply the 2001 Convention principles and rules, which they consider favour the viewpoints of marine archaeologists. They consider that the current relationship with HNZPT is very fragile and could be hampered by another layer of bureaucracy. However, they do find the information produced by UNESCO on UCH worthwhile.[103]

The 2001 Convention's emphasis on *in situ* preservation and its exclusion of traditional commercial salvage law from the area of UCH is, of course, controversial. There are those who suggest that the balance between competing interests has tipped too far in favour of *in situ* preservation.[104] On the other hand, there is a compelling argument that, because UCH is a non-renewable resource, its exploitation is unsustainable and commercial rights should not apply:

> The archaeological record contains information important to the understanding of New Zealand history and past standards of living that is often not available in any other form. ... [H]istoric shipwrecks in New Zealand waters are the shared property (and heritage) of all New Zealand and not just those that have the resources and desire to exploit them for commercial gain.[105]

5 Conclusion

Regardless of whether the 2001 Convention is ratified in NZ, it is possible and, in the opinion of the authors highly desirable, that it should and will influence the future development and reform of domestic legislation relating to NZ's UCH. The value of the 2001 Convention in setting international standards of best practice in relation to UCH has already been recognised by the Oceans Policy Secretariat.[106] Since the 2001 Convention has entered into force internationally, the hortative effect of its principles and rules has significantly

103 Gordon and Moran, *supra* n. 80.

104 See also Sean A. Kingsley, 'Shipwrecked in Situ: Saving the Sunken Past or Scapegoat Archaeology?' [2019] *Maritime Heritage Foundation*. These concerns were acknowledged and responded to in the 2019 UNESCO *Evaluation of the 2001 Convention on the Protection of Underwater Cultural Heritage* IOS/EVS/PI/174/REV, p. 44 para 238, see <https://unesdoc.unesco.org/ark:/48223/pf0000368560>.

105 Dodd, *supra* n. 95.

106 Oceans Policy Secretariat *supra* n. 84, at p. 2.

increased.[107] As the 2001 Convention's influence grows, its principles and rules are likely to provide a framework of customary public international law that will thus shape the general practice of both Parties and non-Parties to the 2001 Convention in years to come.[108]

All websites last accessed February 2025.

Acknowledgements

We are grateful to those who responded to informal surveys on the UNESCO Convention on Underwater Cultural Heritage 2001.

Selected Bibliography

Andrew Viduka, 'Going for the Win-Win: Including the Public in Underwater Cultural Heritage Management through Citizen Science in Australia and New Zealand' (2020) 49 *International Journal of Nautical Archaeology* 87.

A. Dodd, 'Opportunities for Underwater Archaeology in New Zealand' (2003) 46 *Archaeology in New Zealand* 151.

C.W.N Ingram, *New Zealand Shipwrecks* (8th ed., Reed, 2007).

James A.R. Nafziger, 'The UNESCO Convention on the Protection of the Underwater Cultural Heritage: Its Growing Influence' (2018) 49 *Journal of Maritime Law and Commerce* 371.

J.S. Blackie, *The UNESCO Convention on the Protection of Underwater Cultural Heritage – Is the Time Right for New Zealand?* (Unpublished LLM dissertation, University of Auckland, 2004)

Piers Davies and Paul Myburgh, 'The Protected Objects Act in New Zealand: Too Little, Too Late' (2008) 15 *International Journal of Cultural Property* 321.

---

107 Dodd, *supra* n. 95.

108 James A.R. Nafziger, 'The UNESCO Convention on the Protection of the Underwater Cultural Heritage: Its Growing Influence' (2018) 49 *Journal of Maritime Law and Commerce* 371, 400.

CHAPTER 15

Nigeria

Edwin Egede[*]

Introduction

Nigeria, which was for a long period under the colonial rule of the United Kingdom (UK), came into existence as a legal entity in 1914 with the amalgamation of the then British Southern and Northern Protectorates.[1] It eventually gained independence from British colonial rule in 1960 and thereafter became a Republic in 1963.[2] Nigeria is a federal State, consisting of a Central Government and 36 Unit States.[3] Located in West Africa, and bordering the Atlantic Ocean, it has one of the longest African coastlines, measuring 853 km.[4] At the coast, it shares borders to the west with the Republic of Benin, while it shares its eastern border with the Republic of Cameroon, with the Atlantic Ocean as the southern boundary.[5]

Although the Nigerian coastline is littered with shipwrecks, there has to date been no discovery of high-profile or significant underwater shipwrecks, similar to the *Bredenhof* and *Santissimo Sancremento* off the coasts

* Professor of International Law and International Relations, Cardiff School of Law and Politics, Cardiff University, Wales, UK and Adjunct Professor, Department of Public Law, Nelson Mandela University, Port Elizabeth, South Africa.

1 See the Nigeria Protectorate Order in Council 1913, 22 November 1913, S.P. Vol. 106, 583. The amalgamation took place during the tenure of the British colonial Governor-General, Lord Lugard, whose wife is believed to have coined the name 'Nigeria'. See M Van der Linden, *The Acquisition of Africa (1870–1914): The Nature of International Law* (2016, Brill) chapter 5 especially at 95.

2 See the Nigerian Independence Act 1960, Ch 55, enacted by the British Parliament, available at <https://www.legislation.gov.uk/ukpga/1963/57/enacted>.

3 See sections 2 and 3 of the Nigerian 1999 Constitution, *Official Gazette* vol 86 No 27 of 05.05.1999. This Constitution came into force on 29 May 1999 when the military regime of General Abdulsalam handed over power to the democratically elected government of President Olusegun Obasanjo.

4 See S Orupabo, 'Coastline migration in Nigeria' (2008), available at <https://www.hydrointernational.com/content/article/coastline-migration-in-nigeria>.

5 See O Fadahunsi, S Pe'eri and A Armstrong, 'Characterisation of the Nigerian Shoreline Making Use of Publicly Available Satellite Imagery' (2014) January/February *Hydro International* 22 at 22.

 | DOI:10.1163/9789004510883_017

of Mozambique and South Africa respectively, or the *Mary Rose* in the waters of the UK.[6] In addition, the majority of known shipwrecks in Nigerian waters do not fall within the 100 years or more threshold required by the 2001 UNESCO Convention on the Protection of the Underwater Cultural Heritage (the 2001 Convention).[7] There have also been no obviously maritime, high profile traces of human existence falling under the 2001 Convention's definition of underwater cultural heritage (UCH) found partially or totally within Nigerian maritime zones. However, in relation to internal waters, there has been a significant find, albeit contentious as to its characterisation as UCH. The find, made in 1987, was of the 'Dufuna Canoe'. This was determined to be over 8,500 years old (dating from *circa* 6000 B.C.). It was discovered in Dufuna, a village in Yobe State, north-east Nigeria, which lies mainly in the dry savannah belt, at a depth of 5 metres below the surface. The find has been discussed in relation to UCH and has even been described as a shipwreck in certain literature.[8] This argument is based on the undoubted age of the find as falling within the 100 years or more threshold, along with a hypothesis that Lake Chad, and its tributaries, may have been considerably more extensive, thus explaining the context of the find, which was water-logged and found on a bed of sand with clay layers i.e., that it rested in possibly alluvial deposits such as would be found in a former river system or flood plan/water basin.[9] However, it is debatable as to whether it can be rightly regarded as UCH on the basis that the canoe was discovered in "the seasonally flooded plain of the small, often-dry Komadugu Gana River".[10] There is therefore a potential argument that it may not meet the 2001 Convention's definitional requirements as set out in Article 1(a) of having been 'partially or totally underwater, periodically or continuously for at least 100 years'.[11] The 'Dufuna Canoe' as a find, can be contrasted with that

6 In 1753, the Dutch East India Company's ship *Bredenhof* foundered on a reef 120 miles south of Mozambique and 13 miles off the South African coast, near the Cape of Good Hope. The Portuguese ship *Santissimo Sancremento* was wrecked in 1647 in Sardinia Bay near Port Elizabeth, South Africa. While the English monarch, Henry VIII's flagship, *Mary Rose*, sank during the Battle of the Solent in 1545.

7 2562 UNTS 1.

8 See Afolasade Adewunmi, 'Dufuna Canoe Find: Birthing the Underwater Cultural Heritage in Nigeria', (2014) 4 *University of Ibadan Journal of Public and International Law*, pp. 1–12. See also Stewart Gordon, *A History of the World in Sixteen Shipwrecks*, (2015, ForEdge) at pp. 1–2 where the Dufuna canoe is listed as one of sixteen shipwrecks.

9 Adewunmi, *ibid* pp. 5–6.

10 Gordon, *supra* n.8 at p. 1.

11 See Craig Forrest, 'A New International Regime for the Protection of Underwater Cultural Heritage', (2002) 51(3) *The International and Comparative Law Quarterly*, p. 511 at 523 in footnote 55 explains that "'periodically underwater' will refer to those objects that lie in

of a 4000-year old dugout canoe discovered underwater in Lake Constance in Southern Germany, which could be regarded as UCH.[12] Thus, whilst the 'Dufuna Canoe' is unquestionably an item of important and valuable cultural heritage, one which fortunately is being preserved and exhibited in the museum complex[13] of the Nigerian National Commission for Museums and Monuments (the Commission) in Damaturu, Yobe State capital,[14] it is argued that it is not able to be defined as UCH in the strict sense.

Although no significantly historical UCH has yet been discovered in Nigerian waters, this is not to say it does not exist. At a global level, it has been estimated that there are more than three million shipwrecks on the ocean floor, and that less than one per cent of these shipwrecks have been discovered and/or explored.[15] As Nigeria has a rich seafaring history, as well as having played a significant role in the transatlantic slave trade, there is the potential for future discoveries to be made, including of shipwrecks, that fit within the 2001 Convention's definition of UCH. For instance, there is a Slave History Museum in Calabar, that is located on the site of a fifteenth century slave-trading warehouse in Marina Beach, which was a significant embarkation point during the transatlantic slave trade.[16] The 'Slave Wrecks Project' has estimated that about 1000 ships navigating the Atlantic were wrecked, and in 2015 confirmed the first documented discovery of a sunken slave ship known to have been carrying human cargo.[17] Many of these wrecks remain undiscovered. In addition, UCH has been identified in the Osun River, on the banks of which is the Osun-Osogbo Grove, a UNESCO World Heritage Site since 2005, and other

---

the inter-tidal zone and are only submerged during high tides." See also Craig Forrest, 'Defining 'underwater cultural heritage'', (2002) 31(1) *The International Journal of Nautical Archaeology*, pp. 3–11 where the author identifies some ambiguities in the definition of underwater cultural heritage.

12 See '4,000-year-old boat recovery begins in southern Germany', 31 March 2021, <https://www.dw.com/en/4000-year-old-boat-recovery-begins-in-southern-germany/a-57068160#:~:text=An%20excavation%20began%20this%20week,the%20second%20half%20of%202018>.

13 See generally <https://museum.ng/>.

14 As explained by Adewunmi, *supra* n.8 at p. 6. See Art. 1 of the UNESCO Convention Concerning the Protection of the World Cultural and Natural Heritage 1972, 1037 UNTS 151. Nigeria ratified this Convention on 23 October 1974.

15 Jay Bennett, 'Less than 1 percent of the World's Shipwrecks Have Been Explored', *Popular Mechanics*, January 18, 2016, <https://www.popularmechanics.com/science/a19000/less-than-one-percent-worlds-shipwrecks-explored/#:~:text=But%20most%20wrecks%20don't,surveyed%20or%20visited%20by%20divers>.

16 See <http://slaveryandremembrance.org/partners/partner/?id=P0027>.

17 See <https://global.si.edu/projects/slave-wrecks-project>.

UCH may potentially be found in Nigeria's extensive internal waters.[18] Thus, the possibility of future discoveries, of shipwrecks, human remains, and/or other cultural objects, in Nigerian waters is not ruled out,[19] though to the best of this author's knowledge no such investigation is currently planned. In that connection, this chapter will first examine Nigeria's participation in international treaties regulating UCH. It will then proceed to explore challenges in the domestic implementation of these treaties and examine the status of legislation that regulates UCH in Nigeria, before offering a series of reflections in the conclusion.

1 Treaties Regulating UCH and Nigeria

Nigeria became a Party to the United Nations Convention on the Law of the Sea 1982 (LOSC) on 14 August 1986.[20] The LOSC has rather sparse provisions on UCH, with Articles 149 and 303 specifically referring to objects of an archaeological and historical nature. State Parties, including Nigeria, 'have the duty to protect objects of an archaeological and historical nature found at sea and shall cooperate for this purpose'.[21] It should be noted that Article 303 does not specify the scope of the duty in terms of what must be done, or how it should be carried out, so States can and do take a very narrow interpretation.[22] The LOSC also does not define what is meant by objects of an archaeological and historical nature found at sea. It states that a coastal State Party may establish an archaeological zone in its Contiguous Zone (CZ) to control the traffic of

18 See Evaluation of UNESCO's standard-setting work of the Culture Sector, part VI – 2001 Convention on the Protection of Underwater Cultural Heritage (2019, UNESCO), at p. 8, para.43: <https://unesdoc.unesco.org/ark:/48223/pf0000368446>. On the Grove as a World Heritage Site see <https://whc.unesco.org/en/list/1118/> and <https://museum.ng/whs/osun-osogbo-sacred-grove/>.

19 Phillip J. Turner, Sophie Cannon, Sarah DeLand, James P. Delgado, David Eltis, Patrick N. Halpin, Michael I. Kanu, Charlotte S. Sussman, Ole Varmer and Cindy L. Van Dover, 'Memorializing the Middle Passage on the Atlantic seabed in Areas Beyond National Jurisdiction', (2020) 122 *Marine Policy*, p. 1 at 3–4, (104254). As regards the possibility of slave trade related UCH through the Badagry seaport located in Lagos State, Nigeria see Wale Oyediran, 'Port of Badagry, a Point of No Return: Investigation of Maritime Slave Trade in Nigeria' in Lynn Harris (ed.), *Sea Ports and Sea Power: African Maritime Cultural Landscapes* (2017, Springer) pp. 13 at 13–17.

20 Dec. 10, 1982, 1833 U.N.T.S. 397.

21 Art. 303(1).

22 See Michail Risvas, 'The Duty to Cooperate and the Protection of Underwater Cultural Heritage', (2013) (2)3 *Cambridge Journal of International and Comparative Law*: 562 at 564–572.

such objects.[23] Nevertheless, it is emphasised that the relevant provisions on archaeological and historical objects at sea do not affect the rights of identifiable owners, the law of salvage or other rules of admiralty, or laws and practices with respect to cultural exchanges.[24] It also points out that the provisions of Article 303 are without prejudice to other international agreements and rules of international law in respect of such objects.[25]

The 2001 Convention, which complements LOSC,[26] goes into more detail than the latter on UCH. It came into force on 2 January 2009, and Nigeria was the first African State Party to ratify the Convention on 21 October 2005. There is extensive literature reviewing the 2001 Convention, so this chapter provides only a summary of key aspects.[27] It suffices to state that the 2001 Convention, in seeking to define UCH, adopts an inclusive approach. This makes it clear that the focus goes beyond a shipwreck-centric approach, to extend to:

> all traces of human existence having a cultural, historical, or archaeological character which have been partially or totally under water, periodically or continuously, for at least 100 years.[28]

It includes sites, structures, buildings, artefacts, human remains, vessels, aircraft, other vehicles or any part of these items, their cargo or other contents, 'together with their archaeological and natural context and objects of prehistoric character', as well as objects of prehistoric character.[29] The central aim of the 2001 Convention is to protect and preserve UCH for the benefit of

---

23 Art. 303(2).

24 Art. 303(3).

25 Art. 303(4).

26 Art. 3 of the 2001 Convention.

27 See, for example, Sarah Dromgoole, *Underwater Cultural Heritage and International Law* (Cambridge University Press, 2013); Ariel W Gonzalez, Patrick O'Keefe and Michael Williams, 'The UNESCO Convention on the Protection of the Underwater Cultural Heritage: a Future for our Past?' (2009) 11(1) *Conservation and Management of Archaeological Sites*, pp. 54–69; Roberta Garabello and Tullio Scovazzi (eds.), *Underwater Cultural Heritage: Before and After the 2001 UNESCO Convention* (Martinus Nijhoff, 2003); Sarah Dromgoole, '2001 UNESCO Convention on the Protection of the Underwater Cultural Heritage', (2003) 18(1) *The International Journal of Marine and Coastal Law*, pp. 59–108; G. Carducci, 'New Developments in the Law of the Sea: The UNESCO Convention on the Protection of Underwater Cultural Heritage', (2002) 96 *American Journal of International Law*, pp. 419–434 and Craig Forrest, 'A New International Regime for the Protection of Underwater Cultural Heritage', *supra* n. 11.

28 Art. 1(1)(a).

29 Art. 1(a)(i), (ii) and (iii).

humanity, with the preservation of the UCH *in situ* as the preferred option.[30] The rather technical nature of the 2001 Convention highlights the critical need for capacity-building, especially for developing States, so as to be able to comply with the appropriate international and scientific standards of protecting and preserving such heritage within their waters and to effectively implement the Convention. Related to this, Article 22 of the 2001 Convention obliges Parties to establish a 'competent authority', setting out its responsibilities as:

> the establishment, maintenance and updating of an inventory of underwater cultural heritage, the effective protection, conservation, presentation and management of underwater cultural heritage, as well as research and education.

Inventories are considered a 'key component' of UCH management plans.[31] Facilitating the ability of States to develop these by offering a standard guideline, is a UNESCO Model Sheet for Inventories of UCH.[32]

In November 2013, Nigeria hosted the first African Regional Meeting on the Protection of Underwater Cultural Heritage in Yenagoa, Bayelsa State, which was jointly organised by UNESCO and the Nigerian Federal Ministry of Tourism, Culture and National Orientation (FMTCNO). An outcome of this meeting was an Action Plan, which included a decision by the Nigerian Government to establish an Underwater Cultural Heritage Research and Imaging Centre in Yenagoa, which would provide support to the region in respect of capacity-building and other services to enable African States to better protect their UCH.[33] It secured a premises for the Centre and began the process of seeking to identify individuals who would assist in building up the necessary skills to operationalise the Centre. It also sought to create a maritime archaeology/underwater cultural heritage Chair in either the University of Port Harcourt, Rivers State, one of the Unit States in the country, or at the Maritime Training School in the capital, Abuja. Unfortunately, to date, neither the Centre, nor the process of identifying appropriate personnel as Chair and staff of the proposed

30 Art. 2 of the 2001 Convention and Rule 1 of the Annex concerning activities directed at UCH.

31 UNESCO Practical Tools for Protection, available at <https://en.unesco.org/underwater-heritage/threats-and-protection>.

32 Resolution 4/MSP4 para 8. The form is available at. <https://www.unesco.org/sites/default/files/medias/fichiers/2024/11/UCH_Model-sheet-Inventory_EN.pdf?hub=412>.

33 See Action Plan for First African Regional Meeting on Protection of UCH, <http://www.underwaterarchaeology.net/News/Windhoek/ActionPlan.pdf>.

Centre, has been achieved.[34] Shafman points to a "[l]ack of political will, funding, skilled personnel and academic prospects" in this highly technical field of seeking to protect and preserve UCH as key factors that hinder African States from operationalising the provisions of the 2001 Convention.[35] He points out that Nigeria, as the first African State to ratify the Convention, has struggled to build the capacity required to implement the duties of its designated 'competent authority', as outlined by the Convention. This is despite certain structural changes, such as the merger of the FMTCNO with the Ministry of Information and which is now known as the Ministry of Information and Culture.[36]

Although, there is an indication that attempts have been made to carry out some sort of inventory of UCH within Nigerian waters, with the help of the Nigerian Navy (under the Nigerian Armed Forces Act 1994),[37] it is not clear if such an inventory has in fact been completed by the Federal Ministry. It is crucial for this to be completed as promptly as possible since it is an essential element in ensuring the effective protection and management of UCH. It is also not clear if Nigeria, in seeking to create this inventory, has taken advantage of the Model Sheet for Inventories of Underwater Cultural Heritage.[38] It is pertinent that the Nigerian National Commission for Museums and Monuments, discussed further in section 2 below, as well as Nigerian coastal communities, which are likely to be aware of any UCH within Nigerian waters close to their community,[39] should be involved in the creation of any such inventory.

---

34 See Jonathan Shafman, *Troubled Waters: developing a new approach to maritime and underwater cultural heritage in sub-Saharan Africa* (Leiden University Press, 2017) pp. 50–5.1.

35 *Ibid* at p. 50.

36 In June 1999, the Federal Government of Nigeria created the Federal Ministry of Culture and Tourism. By mid-2006, this was renamed the Federal Ministry of Tourism, Culture and National Orientation. In November 2015, the Ministry of Culture and Tourism was merged with the Ministry of Information and is now known as the Ministry of Information and Culture. See <https://fmic.gov.ng/culture/culture/>.

37 See Evaluation of UNESCO's standard-setting work of the Culture Sector, part VI – 2001 Convention on the Protection of Underwater Cultural Heritage (2019, UNESCO), p. 29, para.166. See s. 1(4)(a)(II) of the Nigerian Armed Forces Act 1994, which states that the Nigerian Navy would amongst other things be responsible for 'enforcing and assisting in co-ordinating the enforcement of national and international maritime laws ascribed or acceded to by Nigeria'. So far there is no such UCH inventory list in Nigerian waters available in the public domain.

38 See *supra* n.32.

39 See Evaluation of UNESCO's standard-setting work of the Culture Sector, part VI – 2001 Convention on the Protection of Underwater Cultural Heritage (2019, UNESCO), p. 29, para. 166, which states 'to contribute to awareness-raising of UCH as well as its safeguarding,

Unquestionably, lack of capacity, including the absence of skilled personnel, as indicated by Shafman,[40] is a key challenge faced by Nigeria in respect of the domestic implementation of the provisions of the 2001 Convention. It is, however, difficult to sustain an argument that the Nigerian Government has not had, or lacked, political will in this respect. As well as Nigeria being, as noted above, the first African State to ratify the Convention, its hosting of the first African Regional meeting, the planned establishment of a research and imaging centre, as well as its designation of a key Federal Ministry as the competent authority, are all demonstrative of the requisite political will. Besides, in the African region, Nigeria has further demonstrated the political will to preserve cultural heritage by its 2010 ratification of the Charter for African Cultural Renaissance (the Charter).[41] The objectives of the Charter are set out in Article 3, and include 'to preserve and promote the African cultural heritage through preservation, restoration and rehabilitation' and:

> ... to promote in each country the popularization of science and technology including traditional knowledge systems as a condition for better understanding and preservation of cultural and natural heritage.[42]

As a party to the Charter, Nigeria thus commits to protect and develop all tangible cultural heritage.[43] Although the Charter does not explicitly define 'African cultural heritage', it does state that it is guided, among other things, by the 1972 UNESCO Convention Concerning the Protection of the World Cultural and Natural Heritage,[44] which defines cultural and natural heritage as including:

> sites: works of man or the combined works of nature and man, and areas including archaeological sites which are of outstanding universal value from the historical, aesthetic, ethnological or anthropological point of view.[45]

---

inventorying should involve the communities that live nearby. Coastal populations already have knowledge of UCH and are able to explain its value'.

40 See *supra* n. 34 above.

41 Adopted by the 6th Ordinary Session of the Assembly of the African Union in Khartoum, Sudan on 24 January 2006, see <https://au.int/en/treaties/charter-african-cultural-renaissance>.

42 Art. 3(d) and (I) of the Charter for African Cultural Renaissance.

43 Art. 10(2).

44 1037 UNTS 151.

45 Art. 1 *ibid.*

This could be interpreted to include UCH.[46]

UNESCO has several active capacity-building programmes.[47] One, launched in July 2019, is the project 'Building Capacity and Raising Awareness for Underwater Cultural Heritage Research in Africa'.[48] This is claimed to be in response to the perception that UCH in Africa "is under serious threat from treasure hunters, uncontrolled industrial development and lack of supervision".[49] The principal aim of the project is targeted towards raising awareness of the importance of safeguarding Africa's UCH, as well as providing the means to "encourage UNESCO Member States to put in place sound policies for researching, managing and promoting underwater cultural heritage in the African region".[50] Additional activities related to capacity-building include various training workshops, such as one in Accra, Ghana in 2023. This focused on supporting the effective implementation of the 2001 Convention in Nigeria and Ghana, as well as capacity-building and the implementation of an inventory of the two countries' UCH, with the UNESCO representative stating "the [UCH] of our region is not just a collection of artefacts or historical remnants but is a story of our shared past".[51]

However, to be fully effective, capacity-building programmes addressing the needs of Africa must be systematic and consistent, ensuring they extend beyond government officials to include other important key stakeholders, so they in turn can play their key role in supporting and taking ownership of UCH protection.[52] In this connection, the Accra workshop placed significant value on the role of civil society organisations, non-governmental organisations and academic institutions in protecting UCH on the basis that these stakeholders "provide input based on their expertise and advocate for legal frameworks that support conservation efforts".[53]

46 The UNESCO World Heritage List includes a number of Ocean sites, see <https://whc.unesco.org/en/list/>.

47 For general info on UNESCO global capacity-building programmes re intangible cultural heritage see <https://ich.unesco.org/en/capacity-building>.

48 See <https://www.unesco.org/en/articles/unesco-prepares-capacity-building-strategy-protection-underwater-cultural-heritage-africa-region>.

49 *Ibid.*

50 *Ibid.*

51 See <https://ghana.un.org/en/243793-preserving-history-unesco-ghana-holds-3-day-workshop-strengthen-national-capacities-protect#:~:text=The%20three-day%20workshop%3A%20from,the%20Convention%20to%20develop%20and >.

52 See Josh Martin, Harnessing Local and Transnational Communities in the Global Protection of Underwater Cultural Heritage, (2021) 10(1) *Transnational Environmental Law*, pp.85–108.

53 *Ibid.*

For instance, in Nigeria this could entail developing, in collaboration with certain Nigerian universities, degree programmes in maritime archaeology, as well as programmes aimed at training members of the civil society and coastal communities in Nigeria on the importance of UCH. Furthermore, Nigeria could be proactive in seeking to cooperate with other State Parties to the 2001 Convention, particularly those that are more advanced in underwater archaeology. In doing so, it could rely on the Convention, which provides that Parties shall:

> ... cooperate in the provision of training in underwater archaeology, in techniques for the conservation of underwater cultural heritage and, on agreed terms, in the transfer of technology relating to underwater cultural heritage.[54]

Moreover, effective Nigerian implementation of the 2001 Convention, requires not only focused capacity-building training in respect of UCH, as indicated above, but also effective communication and outreach to relevant stakeholders in Nigeria to create an awareness of the significance of UCH as an integral part of cultural heritage.[55] Under the 2001 Convention, there is an obligation on the Nigerian Government to:

> ... take all practicable measures to raise public awareness regarding the value and significance of underwater cultural heritage and the importance of protecting it under this Convention.[56]

Related to this, it has been pointed out that:

> [t]he 2001 Convention is written in technical language and is not always easy to decipher by non-experts in archaeology even within UNESCO. It is therefore particularly important to explain its content to a variety of stakeholders and to learn from implementation experiences around the world ....[57]

---

54 Art. 21, 2001 Convention.

55 These stakeholders could include relevant government officials (federal, unit states and local levels), private sector, civil society organisations, academia, and local coastal communities and those living close to the inland waters.

56 Art. 20, 2001 Convention.

57 See Evaluation of UNESCO's standard-setting work of the Culture Sector, part VI – 2001 Convention on the Protection of Underwater Cultural Heritage (2019, UNESCO), p. 22, para.124.

The currently limited knowledge and understanding of UCH in Nigeria could arguably be the reason why maritime heritage is not promoted domestically in the same manner as its terrestrial counterpart, although Nigeria is certainly not alone in this respect. Given the complexities and cost of managing heritage in the marine environment, many nations' terrestrial heritage regimes are more sophisticated and better resourced than those offshore. In Nigeria, both its National Cultural Policy, adopted in 1988 and currently in force,[58] as well as domestic legislation discussed in the section below, deal with cultural heritage generally. However, neither specifically engage with nor expressly refer to maritime heritage. It is unclear why this is the case, given that Nigeria has ratified the 2001 Convention, although this could perhaps be merely an administrative oversight.

2 UCH and Nigerian Domestic Legislation

In Nigeria, a Federal Republic with 36 Unit States and a Federal Capital Territory, the current Constitution of 1999 (the Constitution), which came into force on 29 May 1999, is 'supreme and its provisions [have] binding force on the authorities and persons throughout the Federal Republic of Nigeria'.[59] Under the Constitution, legislative powers are divided between the Central Government and the Unit States.[60] The Central Government has exclusive powers to legislate on all matters explicitly listed in what is titled as the 'Exclusive Legislative List'.[61] It shares legislative powers with the Unit States on matters set out in a separate list, identified as the 'Concurrent Legislative List'.[62] Those matters not listed are deemed to be residual matters that the Unit States exercise exclusive legislative powers over.[63]

In respect of cultural heritage, the Central Government of Nigeria has the power to legislate on:

58 Nigerian National Cultural Policy September 1988, <http://www.wwcd.org/policy/clink/Nigeria.html>. This policy points out "National cultural policy is generally regarded as an instrument of promotion of national identity and Nigerian unity, as well as of communication and cooperation among different Nigerian or African cultures, while the federal states' cultural policies stand for the affirmation and development of particular (ethnic) cultures".

59 Section 1(1) of the Constitution.

60 Section 4(4) and (7) of the Constitution.

61 Section 4(1) and (2) and Part I of the Second Schedule of the Constitution.

62 Section 4(7)(b) and Part II of the Second Schedule of the Constitution.

63 Section 4(a) and (c), *ibid.*

> The establishment and regulation of authorities for the Federation or any part thereof –
> a. …
> b. To identify, collect, preserve or generally look after ancient and historical monuments and records and archaeological sites and remains declared by the National Assembly to be of national significance or national importance;
> c. to administer museums and libraries other than museums and libraries established by the Government of a state.[64]

Under the 'Concurrent Legislative List', the following legislative powers are given to both the Central Government and Unit States:

> The National Assembly may make laws for the Federation or any part thereof with respect to such antiquities and monuments as may, with the consent of the State in which such antiquities and monuments are located, be designated by the National Assembly as National Antiquities or National Monuments but nothing in this paragraph shall preclude a House of Assembly from making Laws for the State or any part thereof with respect to antiquities and monuments not so designated in accordance with the foregoing provisions.[65]

Under section 12(1) of the Constitution:

> [n]o treaty between the Federation and any other country shall have the force of law except to the extent to which any such treaty has been enacted into law by the National Assembly.

This means that Nigeria operates a dualist system, thus even those treaties that have been ratified by Nigeria, including those relating to the sea and UCH, do not have the force of law until they have been domestically incorporated.[66]

---

64 Item 60 of Part I of the Second Schedule.

65 Item 3 of Part II of the Second Schedule.

66 See the Supreme Court of Nigeria decision in *Abacha v Fawehinmi* ([2000] 6 NWLR (Part 660) 228. See also A O Oyebode, *Of Norms, Values and Attitudes: The Cogency of International Law* (2011) 40–46; E Egede 'Bringing human rights home: An examination of the domestication of human rights treaties in Nigeria' (2007) 51(2) *Journal of African Law* 249 at 250–254; A O Enabulele, 'Implementation of treaties in Nigeria and the status question: Whither Nigerian courts?' (2009) 17(2) *AJICL* 326.

Nigeria does not currently have legislation that specifically incorporates the 2001 Convention, but does have legislation dealing generally with cultural heritage, as will be discussed below, that could be applied to UCH. It is not clear why such legislation has not been enacted, but in reference to the implementation of the 1970 Convention on the Means of Prohibiting and Preventing the Illicit Import, Export and Transfer of Ownership of Cultural Property 2011–2015,[67] a Nigerian Government report 2011–2015 indicated that it was in "the process of establishing a National Committee for the domestification (sic) of all UNESCO/UNIDROIT standard setting instruments into our National Legislation/Domestic Laws".[68] To the knowledge of the author, so far there has been no Bill introduced before the National Assembly of Nigeria to enact legislation specifically to incorporate the 2001 Convention into domestic law.

A key Nigerian legislative provision dealing with cultural heritage that could be applicable to UCH is the National Commission for Museums and Monuments Act (NCMMA).[69] This law established the Commission referred to above. The NCMMA confers responsibility upon the Commission, amongst other things, to administer and establish national museums and 'other outlets' in connection with antiquities, as well as to make recommendations to any of the Unit States or to any other persons or authority in respect of the establishment or management of museums.[70] It also has the duty of making recommendations for 'the preservation of antiquities and monuments, not being national museums or antiquities and monuments declared to be national antiquities and monuments'.[71] Moreover, it may also approve the establishment of museums

67 823 UNTS 231. See <https://www.unesco.org/en/legal-affairs/convention-means-prohibiting-and-preventing-illicit-import-export-and-transfer-ownership-cultural>. This UNESCO Convention, which was adopted 14 November 1970 and came in force 24 April 1972, urges States Parties to take measures to prohibit and prevent the illicit trafficking of cultural property, and establishes a common framework for States Parties to follow in order to prohibit and prevent the import, export, and transfer of cultural property.

68 See Para. 2 of the Nigerian National Report on the Implementation of the 1970 Convention on the Means of Prohibiting and Preventing the Illicit Import, Export and Transfer of Ownership of Cultural Property 2011–2015, see <https://web.archive.org/web/20220403230304/http:/www.unesco.org/new/fileadmin/MULTIMEDIA/HQ/CLT/pdf/Rapport_Nigeria_Web_01.pdf>.

69 1979, Cap.19, Laws of the Federation of Nigeria 2004. It repealed previous legislation – the Antiquities Act 1953, the Antiquities (Amendment) Act 1969, and the Antiquities (Prohibited Transfers) Act 1974, See s.31(1) of the NCCM Act. For discussions on this legislation see Folarin Shyllon, 'Cultural Heritage Legislation and Management in Nigeria', (1996) 5(2) *International Journal of Cultural Property*, p. 235 at 239–241.

70 See section 3(1)(a)(b) and (c).

71 See section 3(1) (c).

that are privately owned and maintained.[72] Although the legislation does not explicitly mention 'cultural heritage', the definition of 'antiquity' contained within the legislation could be said to incorporate cultural heritage. Indeed, 'antiquity', which arguably includes 'marine antiquity', although not expressly stated, is defined as:

(a), any object of archaeological interest or land in which any such object was discovered or is believed to exist; or

(b), any relic of early human settlement or colonisation; or

(c), any work of art or craft work, including any statue; model, clay figure, figure cast or rust metal, carving, house post, door, ancestral figure, religious mask, staff, drum, bolt, ornament, utensil, weapon, armour, or craft work of indigenous origin and –

  (i) was made or fashioned before the year 1918; or

  (ii) is of historical, artistic or scientific interest and is or has been used at any time in the performance and for purposes of any traditional ceremony, and in the case of any object or relic mentioned in paragraph (a) or (b) of this section includes for the purposes of this Act any land adjacent thereto which in the opinion of the Commission, a State Government or, as for the purpose of maintaining the same or the amenities thereof or for providing or facilitating access thereto, or for the exercise of proper control or management with respect thereto.[73]

The Act further defines an 'object of archaeological interest' as including 'any fossil remains man or of animals found in association with man' and 'any antique tool or object of metal, wood, stone, clay, leather, textile, basket wear or other material', that are of archaeological interest,[74] which could extend to include some UCH. Although the Act does not expressly refer to the 100-years or more threshold, in contrast with the 2001 Convention, the reference to antiquity as 'such […] made or fashioned before the year 1918', could now, in

72 See section 3(1)(d).

73 Section 32. Compare this with Art. 1(1)(a) of the 2001 Convention which states: 'For the purposes of this Convention:

1. (a) "Underwater cultural heritage" means all traces of human existence having a cultural, historical or archaeological character which have been partially or totally under water, periodically or continuously, for at least 100 years such as:

  (i) sites, structures, buildings, artefacts and human remains, together with their archaeological and natural context;

  (ii) vessels, aircraft, other vehicles or any part thereof, their cargo or other contents, together with their archaeological and natural context; and

  (iii) objects of prehistoric character.'

74 Section 32.

the 2020s, arguably be said to include UCH that has been underwater for 100 years or more.

The Commission has powers under the NCMMA to grant permission to domestic and foreign archaeologists to carry out excavations,[75] and is required to be notified of the discovery of any object of archaeological interest no later than seven days following such discovery.[76] In addition, the Act prohibits the export of items of antiquity from Nigeria without obtaining a permit from the Commission.[77] Although to some extent it is conceivable that this legislation could be interpreted to include/extend to UCH, as it stands it is grossly inadequate as a domestic legislative scheme to regulate UCH. Reasons for this include that fact that it does not directly engage with crucial issues in the 2001 Convention, such as *in situ* preservation of UCH as the first option in protection and management and the significant issue of the UNESCO requirement to impose restrictions as regards the commercial salvage of such heritage.

Commentators have noted that in relation to cultural heritage generally, "Nigeria very much lags behind in terms of recent legislative measures".[78] This author believes that this is a fair observation, because given the number of international cultural heritage treaties Nigeria has ratified, it would be reasonable to expect the enactment of clear and specific domestic legislation covering various aspects of cultural heritage, including UCH. The reason for this lag could possibly be attributed to the inertia of various legislative bodies.

Nigeria needs to enact domestic legislation specifically directed towards fulfilling its obligations under the 2001 Convention, as required by section 12 of the 1999 Constitution, as quickly as possible. Remarkably, although Nigeria has various laws dealing with the Territorial Sea (TS), Continental Shelf (CS) and the Exclusive Economic Zone (EEZ), namely the Territorial Waters Act, as amended,[79] the Petroleum Act, as amended[80] and the EEZ Act,[81] these laws do not in any way deal with UCH. However, in 2020 a Bill for 'an Act to Repeal the Exclusive Economic Zone Act 2004; and the Territorial Waters Act 2004

75 Section 19.

76 Section 20.

77 Sections 25–27.

78 Folarin Shyllon, 'Africa' in Francesco Francioni and Ana Filipa Vrdoljak (eds), *The Oxford Handbook of International Cultural Heritage Law (Oxford Handbooks Online)*, (Oxford University Press, 2020).

79 Territorial Sea Act No. 5 of 1967. The Act was amended by Act No. 38 of 1971 and Act No. 1 of 1998. ((1999) 38 LOSB 53).

80 Petroleum Act, 1969 (Cap 350, Laws of the Federation of Nigeria), as amended by Act No. 22 of 1998.

81 Act No. 28 of 1978.

and Enact the Nigerian Maritime Zone Act to Provide for Maritime Zones in Nigeria'[82] came before the Nigerian National Assembly, which has not yet been enacted as law. The Bill seeks to consolidate the diverse laws on maritime zones into one piece of legislation. In the view of the author, it would appear that the Bill contains some potential flaws. First, it states:

> [s]ubject to any other law, Nigeria shall with [...] regard to objects of an archaeological or historical nature found in the contiguous zone, [have] the same rights and powers as it has in respect of its territorial water.[83]

This somewhat ambivalent provision appears to be incompatible with the relevant LOSC provisions, which are clear on the distinct rights and powers of a coastal State in these different maritime zones.[84] It is thus suggested that this provision of the Bill could be clearer in stating that Nigeria may regulate and authorise activities aimed at UCH within its CZ, and that this would be some sort of 'archaeological zone', in line with Article 303 of the LOSC.[85]

Furthermore, the Bill makes it a criminal offence to remove such objects from the seabed in the CZ without the permission of the appropriate minister or authority.[86] However, it is unclear why this is limited to 'removing' such objects from the 'seabed' and does not extend to other illegal acts, such as damage or other interference with such objects, even if they are located in the water column. At a fundamental level, the Bill does not define 'objects of an archaeological or historical nature', and there is no existing Nigerian legislation that does. Neither does it make any reference to objects of an archaeological or historical nature in other maritime zones within Nigeria's jurisdiction, as required by the 2001 Convention.[87] Finally, by commencing the provision

82 See <https://shipsandports.com.ng/senate-passes-nigerian-maritime-zone-bill/>.

83 Section6(1) of A Bill for an Act to Repeal the Exclusive Economic Zone Act E7 LFN 2010 and the Territorial Waters Act Cap.T5 LFN 2010 and enact the Maritime Zones Act to provide for the Maritime Zones Act to provide for the Maritime Zones of Nigeria and for Matters Connected Therewith. 2020, [SB49] C1591. See also Art. 8 of the 2001 Convention which states: 'Without prejudice to and in addition to Articles 9 and 10, and in accordance with Art. 303, paragraph 2, of the United Nations Convention on the Law of the Sea, States Parties may regulate and authorize activities directed at underwater cultural heritage within their contiguous zone. In so doing, they shall require that the Rules be applied'.

84 See Arts.2 and 33 of LOSC.

85 See Art.8 of the 2001 Convention.

86 Sections 6(2) and 7(2)(3) and (4) of the Bill for an Act to Repeal the Exclusive Economic Zone Act E7 LFN. 2010 and the Territorial Waters Act Cap.T5 LFN 2010 etc.

87 See Art. 7 (Underwater cultural heritage in internal waters, archipelagic waters and territorial sea); Art. 9 (Reporting and notification in the Exclusive Economic Zone and on the

referred to above on objects of an archaeological or historical nature in the CZ with the opening phrase '[s]ubject to any other law …' the Bill seems to assume that other laws dealing with UCH already exist.

There is other legislation in Nigeria that has marginal relevance in its application to discourse around the protection of UCH. The Nigerian Merchant Shipping Act 2007 (MSA 2007) makes provision for the appointment of a Receiver of Wrecks to be responsible for shipwrecks in Nigerian waters.[88] The Nigerian Maritime Administration and Safety Agency (NIMASA), which has amongst its functions the power of receipt and removal of wrecks under its enabling Act, the NIMASA Act 2007, is appointed as the official Receiver of Wrecks in Nigeria.[89] Remarkably, in stark contrast to, for example, the UK position, neither the Nigerian MSA 2007 nor the NIMASA Act 2007 contain provision for the protection and preservation of wrecks of historical or archaeological value.[90] Moreover, the Nigerian MSA 2007 makes provision for the commercial salvage of vessels, but does not have any provision excluding maritime cultural heritage from such salvage.[91] Notably, although Nigeria is a State Party to the IMO International Convention on Salvage 1989,[92] a treaty that applies domestically under the Nigerian MSA,[93] it did not take advantage of the Convention's provision permitting States Parties:

> … at the time of signature, ratification, acceptance, approval or accession, [to]reserve the right not to apply the provisions of this Convention … when the property involved is maritime cultural property of prehistoric, archaeological or historic interest and is situated on the sea-bed.[94]

Continental Shelf) and Art. 10 (Protection of underwater cultural heritage in the exclusive economic zone and on the continental shelf) of the 2001 Convention.

88 Sections 360–385.

89 Section 22(1) of the Nigerian Maritime Administration and Safety Agency 2007. See also section 44(1) (b), which empowers the NIMASA to make Regulations for removal of wrecks.

90 The Protection of Wrecks Act 1973 states: 'If the Secretary of State is satisfied with respect to any site in United Kingdom waters that –
(a) it is, or may prove to be, the site of a vessel lying wrecked on or in the seabed; and
(b) on account of the historical, archaeological or artistic importance of the vessel, or of any objects contained or formerly contained in it which may be lying on the seabed in or near the wreck, the site ought to be protected from unauthorised interference,
he may by order designate an area round the site as a restricted area'.

91 See Part XXVII of MSA 2007.

92 1953 UNTS 165.

93 See section 388 of the Nigerian MSA.

94 Art. 30(1)(d). Nigeria ratified this Convention on 11 October 1990.

The lack of clarity witnessed across the various Nigerian laws set out above, underpins the necessity of calling for distinct legislation that would comprehensively and thus effectively implement the 2001 Convention. Such legislation would need to provide, *inter alia*, clarity and precision on the definition of UCH, giving priority to *in situ* preservation of such UCH as the first option, whilst simultaneously encouraging "non-intrusive and non-destructive public access" to it.[95] In addition, it should contain rules regulating UCH not only found in Nigerian internal waters, TS, CZ, EEZ and Continental Shelf,[96] but also rules for reporting and notification of UCH located in the Area beyond the limits of national jurisdiction, as required by Article 149 of LOSC. Such legislation would also need to address the place of salvage vis-à-vis UCH; adopt appropriate measures that would ensure both Nigerian nationals and vessels flying its flag do not participate in activities directed at UCH that would infringe on the core principles of the 2001 Convention; and impose sanctions and penalties for breaches of it.[97]

The Nigerian Government could choose to enact comprehensive legislation that deals with both terrestrial heritage and UCH, a development that would be in line with UNESCO's 'Model for a National Act on the Protection of Cultural Heritage', available on its website.[98] Conversely, it could chose to uncouple terrestrial heritage and UCH, and have distinct, standalone legislation dealing with UCH. In either case, the Nigerian Government could take advantage of the ability to seek the assistance of UNESCO in drafting such legislation,[99] naturally taking into consideration any relevant local context in Nigeria.

---

95 Jennifer Clare Corrin and Craig J. S. Forrest, (2014). *A model law to implement the Convention on the Protection of the Underwater Cultural Heritage and its possible application in plural legal regimes in Pacific small islands states: a case study of Solomon Islands*. Asia-Pacific Regional Conference on Underwater Cultural Heritage, Hawaii, 12–16 May 2014, p. 1 at.3.

96 Nigeria's CS is extended to 220 nm, see <https://nimasa.gov.ng/fg-welcomes-un-decision-to-extend-nigerias-maritime-border/>.

97 See Art. 16 of the 2001 Convention. For an interesting analysis of this article see Anna Petrig and Maria Stemmler, 'Art. 16 UNESCO Convention and the Protection of Underwater Cultural Heritage', (2020) 69 *International and Comparative Law Quarterly*, pp. 397–429.

98 See for example, <https://www.unidroit.org/instruments/cultural-property/2012-model-provisions/#:~:text=This%20document%20contains%20model%20legislative,protection%2C%20adopt%20effective%20legislation>. For an interesting discourse of the pros and cons of model legislation in relation to UCH in a pluralist society, such as Nigeria see Corrin and Forrest, *supra* n. 95, at pp. 4–9.

99 See Evaluation of UNESCO's standard-setting work of the Culture Sector, part VI – 2001 Convention on the Protection of Underwater Cultural Heritage (2019, UNESCO), p. 44, para. 241, see <https://unesdoc.unesco.org/ark:/48223/pf0000368446>.

3 Conclusion

Although Nigeria may have been the first African State to ratify the 2001 Convention, it still has a long way to go as regards domestic implementation of it. Unfortunately, Nigeria's attempt to establish an Underwater Cultural Heritage Research and Imaging Centre to create awareness and build capacity after the African Regional Meeting on the Protection of Underwater Cultural Heritage in 2013 has so far not materialised. From all indications, considerable work needs to be done to create and build awareness amongst relevant local stakeholders of the importance and value of UCH, as well as building the required capacity to effectively engage with its future preservation and management.

Even though Nigeria has domestic legislation relating to cultural heritage generally that could potentially be interpreted as applying also to UCH, such legislation is not adequate. The Bill before the legislature is also insufficient, containing as it does several flaws. Clearly, the Nigerian Government, perhaps in cooperation with UNESCO, could draft and enact more comprehensive legislation, as well as create domestic awareness of the value of UCH, such as the opportunities it may present for coastal communities. It also needs to develop a clear strategic plan on how to acquire the relevant local capacity on UCH issues, in collaboration with UNESCO and other States Parties to the 2001 Convention with advanced capacity in UCH issues.

All websites last accessed February 2025.

Acknowledgements

The author dedicates this chapter to his very good friend, Prince Emmanuel, for the invaluable contribution to this manuscript.

Select Bibliography

Afolasade Adewunmi, 'Dufuna Canoe Find: Birthing the Underwater Cultural Heritage in Nigeria', (2014)4 *University of Ibadan Journal of Public and International Law*, pp. 1–12.

Wale Oyediran, 'Port of Badagry, a Point of No Return: Investigation of Maritime Slave Trade in Nigeria' in Lynn Harris(ed.), *Sea Ports and Sea Power: African Maritime Cultural Landscapes*(2017, Springer) pp. 13–25. Folarin Shyllon, 'Cultural Heritage

Legislation and Management in Nigeria', (1996)5(2) *International Journal of Cultural Property*, pp. 235–268.

Jonathan Shafman, *Troubled Waters: developing a new approach to maritime and underwater cultural heritage in sub-Saharan Africa* (Leiden University Press, 2017).

Folarin Shyllon, 'Africa' in Francesco Francioni and Ana Filipa Vrdoljak(eds), *The Oxford Handbook of International Cultural Heritage Law (Oxford Handbooks Online)*, (Oxford University Press, 2020).

Phillip J. Turner, Sophie Cannon, Sarah DeLand, James P. Delgado, David Eltis, Patrick N. Halpin, Michael I. Kanu, Charlotte S. Sussman, Ole Varmer and Cindy L. Van Dover, 'Memorializing the Middle Passage on the Atlantic seabed in Areas Beyond National Jurisdiction', (2020)122 *Marine Policy*, pp. 1–5, (104254).

CHAPTER 16

Philippines

Kathleen D. Tantuico and Bobby C. Orillaneda***

1 Introduction

This chapter provides an overview of the shipwrecks excavated in the Philippines and the legislative framework for the protection of underwater cultural heritage (UCH) in the country. While there are no laws specifically providing for the protection of UCH, the National Cultural Heritage Act 2009 governs the exploration, management, protection of and access to cultural heritage in general, including underwater archaeological areas. The National Museum of the Philippines (NMP) is the only agency, private or public, that governs UCH sites and movable cultural property in the Philippines, and the National Commission for Culture and the Arts (NCCA) is the primary regulatory agency that administers the permit system for archaeological excavations of UCH sites within the country's maritime territorial boundaries. The management of UCH in the Philippines is characterised as highly collaborative, but one that faces some challenges in public engagement. While the Philippines is not a party to the UNESCO 2001 Convention on the Protection of UCH,[1] the legislative framework for the protection of cultural heritage, including UCH, contains objectives and provisions generally compatible with it. Issues needing addressing include the current permit system and an historical lack of political will to create a legislative framework specific to the management and protection of UCH.

2 Highlights in Philippine Maritime History

The Philippines is home to numerous world-renowned shipwrecks. Most of these were chance discoveries by self-contained underwater breathing

* Philippine lawyer-archaeologist and LLM, University of Kent.
** Museum Curator Maritime Underwater Cultural Heritage, National Museum of the Philippines.
1 2562 UNTS 1.

 | DOI:10.1163/9789004510883_018

apparatus (SCUBA) divers, occurring as early as 1967, when the NMP was informed of a shipwreck site at Nasagan Point in Santo Domingo, Albay in Southern Luzon Island. In 1970, another shipwreck was found in Arevalo shoal, off the coast of Guimaras Island in Iloilo, Central Visayas Islands.[2] By 1978, the first NMP employee had received training in underwater archaeology by the Southeast Asia Ministry of Education Organization Project for Archaeology and Fine Arts based in Bangkok, Thailand.[3]

2.1 *The San Diego Shipwreck*

One celebrated shipwreck is that of the Spanish flagship, *San Diego*,[4] a 300-ton, 40-metre long, inter-island merchant ship that was docked in Cavite in Southern Luzon Island for reconditioning and repairs when it was converted into a warship to engage a fleet of Dutch naval vessels which entered the Spanish-controlled Philippines in the late sixteenth century. The subsequent naval battle between the *San Diego* and its counterpart, the Dutch vessel *Mauritius*, resulted in the sinking of the former near Fortune Island, Batangas Province in Luzon on 14 December 1600. The sinking of the *San Diego* is a significant event in the Philippines' maritime history, as a material testament of the first naval engagement between Spain and the Netherlands in the Philippines. The vessel evidences the Spanish shipbuilding tradition in the Philippines in the sixteenth century and the cargo is also remarkable as it comprised both merchant cargo and the possessions of the nobles of Manila on-board.

In preparation for the search for the *San Diego*, the investigators analysed the two primary sources describing the battle.[5] Both gave different versions, thus additional archival research was carried out in the libraries and archive institutions in Spain, Holland, Italy, and France. The search commenced in 1991, employing survey-positioning systems for accurate tracking and navigation, as well as magnetometers, taking four weeks for the site to be located.

---

2 See generally <https://www.yodisphere.com/2021/04/Arevalo-Shoal-Shipwreck.html>.

3 M.J. Calderon 'Underwater Archaeology in the Philippines' (1989) 17 *Philippine Quarterly of Culture and Society 322*.

4 Peralta, J.T. and Villegas, R.M (eds), *Saga of the San Diego (A.D.1600), Concerned Citi-zens for the National Museum Inc. Philippines,* (vera-Reyes Inc 1993); Desroches, J., Casal, G. and Goddio, F. (eds.), *Treasures of the San Diego*. (Association Française d'Action Artistique. Elf Foundation, National Museum of the Philippines (1993); B. Orillaneda, 'Maritime Trade in the Philippines during the Early Colonial Period (Sixteenth and Seventeenth Centuries C.E.)' in Berrocal, M.C. and Tsang, C. (eds) *Historical Archaeology of Early Modern Colonialism in Asia-Pacific*, (University of Florida Press, 2017), 29.

5 See generally, Antonio de Morga, Sucesos de las Islas Filipinas 1609, (Cummins, Ed.), 1971, Routledge; and <https://www.atlasofmutualheritage.nl/en/page/10993/the-sea-battle-at-manila-on-14-december-1600>.

The subsequent excavations in 1991 and 1992 by the NMP, in collaboration with World Wide First (WWF),[6] revealed more than 34,000 archaeological objects, including Asian and Mexican ceramics, weaponry, metal, glass, pottery, and ivory.

After the excavation, the story of the *San Diego* and its cargo was the subject of an international exhibition that started in Paris, France in 1994 and then toured Madrid, Spain (1995), New York, USA (1996), and Berlin, Germany (1997), after which, the artefacts were returned to the Philippines. The NMP's National Museum of Anthropology (previously the Museum of the Filipino People) in Manila, houses the *San Diego* collection,[7] along with a '300 Years of Maritime Trade in the Philippines' exhibit,[8] which displays cargoes from seven shipwrecks dated from the thirteenth, fifteenth, and sixteenth centuries.

2.2 *The 'Butuan Boats'*

Another high-profile maritime archaeology project is the excavation of the Butuan Boats in Butuan City, Mindanao Island, Southern Philippines.[9] In the 1970s, a number of ship remains were accidentally discovered by treasure hunters buried under the flood plains of Barangay Libertad, Butuan, Caraga Region in Mindanao. The NMP carried out a series of archaeological investigations from the 1970s to 2015 that exposed the incomplete remains of at least 11 ancient wooden boats. At this time, only five have been archaeologically examined. Butuan Boats 1, 2, 4, 5, and 9 have planks edge-joined with wooden dowels and no metal fastenings. Butuan Boats 1, 2, 4, and 5 were also built using

6 The World Wide First (WWF) is a research organisation headed by Mr. Franck Goddio and has carried out a number of shipwreck investigations in the Philippines from 1986 until 1995. See <https://www.franckgoddio.org/>.

7 See following for more detail <https://www.nationalmuseum.gov.ph/our-collections/maritime-and-underwater-cultural-heritage/treasures-of-san-diego/>.

8 See the following for more detail <https://www.nationalmuseum.gov.ph/exhibitions/anthropology/>.

9 Peralta, J. T. 1980, 'Balanghai: Ancient boat unearthed', National Museum (Philippines); Ronquillo, W.P. 1987, 'The Butuan archaeological Finds: Profound Implications for Philippine and Southeast Asian Prehistory', *Man and Culture in Oceania* (Special issue 3 p71; Ronquillo, W.P. 1989, 'The Butuan archaeological finds: Profound implications for Philippine and Southeast Asian pre-history, in (Brown, Ed.) *Guangdong Ceramics from Butuan and Other Philippine Sites*, p60, Oriental Ceramics Society of the Philippines/Oxford University Press, Manila.; and Lacsina, L., 2016, 'Examining pre-colonial Southeast Asian boatbuilding: An archaeological study of the Butuan Boats and the use of edge-joined planking in local and regional construction techniques' (Doctoral dissertation, Flinders University, School of Humanities and Creative Arts).

the lashed-lug boatbuilding tradition,[10] common in maritime Southeast Asia. Samples from Boats 1, 2 and 5 were radiocarbon dated in the 1970s and 1980s and a wide discrepancy noted: Boat 1 gave a date of fourth century C.E., Boat 5 reportedly dated to the tenth century C.E. while Boat 2 yielded a thirteenth century C.E. date. To clarify the variation in these dates, seven wood samples from the five boats were subjected to accelerator mass spectrometry carbon-14 dating in 2014.[11] The results revealed a consistent date ranging from the eighth to tenth centuries C.E., confirming Boat 5's original radiocarbon date. Sampling also identified that the boats were made from a variety of trees, all available in the Philippine archipelago and neighbouring countries. The Butuan Boats represent the earliest evidence of watercraft vessels in the Philippines.

The Butuan Boats were declared National Cultural Treasures under the Cultural Properties Preservation and Protection Act (CPPPA) 1987.[12] Boats 1 and 5 are currently on exhibit in the Butuan Archaeological Park and National Museum in Butuan, respectively, while Butuan Boat 2 will be part of an exhibit at the National Museum of Anthropology in Manila expected in 2023. Meanwhile, the excavation of Butuan Boats 4 and 9 are still in progress.[13]

2.3 *Documented Shipwreck Sites in the Philippines*

To date, various selected major shipwreck sites have been officially explored, documented, and recognised by the NMP.[14] Shipwreck excavations carried out, include: the *Marinduque* in 1982; the 'Puerto Galera' shipwreck in 1983 and 1989; and the *Royal Captain Junk*, in 1985. Between 1985 and 1988, the British East Indiaman, *Griffin*, and the *Nuestra Señora de la Vida* were recovered, while the Manila galleon, *San Jose*, was excavated between 1986 and 1988. In 1991 and 1992, the 'Breaker Reef' and 'Investigator Shoal' shipwrecks were excavated. This was followed in 1993 by the 'Pandanan' wreck, the 'San Isidro' wreck in 1996, and

10 A lashed-lug boat building tradition entails the use of a series of drilled, projecting blocks, referred to as lugs, that were carved out from the inner side of the planks to which frames were secured by tying rope or strands of rattan, Lacsina *ibid.*

11 Lacsina ibid, Lacsina, L. and Duivenvoorde, W., 2014. 'Report on C-14 AMS analysis of Butuan Boats', National Museum of the Philippines.

12 Proc. No. 86 (1987).

13 Currently there is a State tentative listing, 'Butuan Archaeological Sites', for World Heritage Status, see <https://whc.unesco.org/en/tentativelists/2071/>.

14 The following information is summarised from a paper to the 2011 Asia-Pacific Regional Conference in UCH, B. Orillaneda and W. P. Ronquillo, 'Protecting and Preserving the Underwater Cultural Heritage in the Philippines: A Background Paper', available from <https://www.researchgate.net/publication/343045489_PROTECTING_AND_PRESERVING_THE_UNDERWATER_CULTURAL_HERITAGE_IN_THE_PHILIPPINES_A_BACKGROUND_PAPER>.

the 'Lena Shoal' shipwreck in 1997. By the end of the decade, excavation also included the *Royal Captain*, a British East Indiaman, and the 'Española' site. At the turn of the century, a major project was the 'Santa Cruz' shipwreck, a late fifteenth century trading vessel, followed by the 'Tagbita Bay' shipwreck, a late nineteenth century European vessel that was excavated between 2003 and 2007. In the same period, excavation occurred off Mangsee Islands of a possible European shipwreck. A series of explorations were also carried out in the Scarborough Shoal in the West Philippine Sea in 2006 and 2010, resulting in the discovery of nine potential shipwreck sites. Additional notable UCH projects during this period included investigation of submerged stone ruins beneath Lake Taal at the former towns of Batangas Province in Luzon Island and the investigation, mapping, and excavation of a deep underwater cave site in Mactan Island, Cebu.

3 Philippine Law and Practice for the Protection of Cultural Heritage

3.1 *Background and Context of the Philippine Legal System*

The Philippines is a democratic and republican State. The three branches of government are the Executive Department, headed by the President; the Legislative Department, composed of Congress, with a Senate (Upper House) and a House of Representatives (Lower House); and the Judicial Department, composed of the Supreme Court and lower courts. National laws passed by Congress and approved by the President are identified as Republic Acts, which are binding at a national level.

Each Congress, as a law-making body, has a term of three years within which the legislative process is carried out. The legislative process starts when a member of either House files a Bill in the originating House and undergoes three readings before being transmitted to the other House, where it will again undergo three readings. If a Bill passes the Third Reading, it will be submitted for approval by both Houses. Once approved, the Bill will be passed to the President for signature. If the President approves it, the Bill becomes law. If the President vetoes it, then Congress can override the vetoed Bill by a vote of two-thirds of the members of each House.[15]

International legal agreements to which the Philippines is party are recognised as valid and effective parts of domestic law and as a source of

15 Republic of the Philippines: House of Representatives. The Legislative Process: How a Bill Becomes a Law. See <https://www.congress.gov.ph/legisinfo/?v=process#PREPARE>.

international obligations if approved by two-thirds of the Senate.[16] The Philippines ratified the UNESCO Convention on the Protection of World Cultural and Natural Heritage 1972 (the 1972 Convention) in 1985;[17] and the UNESCO Convention on the Protection of Intangible Cultural Heritage 2003 (the 2003 Convention) in 2006.[18] At the time of writing, it is not a signatory to the 2001 Convention, nor has there been any statement of interest to become so.

3.2 *Efforts to Create National Law for the Protection of UCH*

The Cultural Properties, Preservation and Protection Act 1966 (CPPPA) was the country's first law to mandate the protection and conservation of cultural heritage. It specifically declared the unlawfulness of exploring, excavating, or digging up archaeological or historical sites for obtaining materials of cultural/historical value without prior written authorisation from the Director of the National Museum.[19] Section 3(o) of the CPPPA states '[f]or the purposes of [this Act] government property covers all lands and maritime areas …'. The Act was amended in 1974 via Presidential Decree to offer a more specific definition of 'cultural property', to include:

> … old buildings, monuments, shrines, documents, and objects which may be classified as antiques, relics, or artifacts, landmarks, anthropological and historical sites, and specimens of natural history which are of cultural, historical, anthropological, or scientific value significance to the nation; such physical, anthropological, … , vehicles or ships or boats in part or in whole.[20]

This extension to UCH is also reflected in the definition of 'archaeological sites', which the Decree defines as places which may be:

> … underground or on the surface, underwater or at sea level which contains fossils, artifacts and other cultural, geological, botanical, zoological materials which depict and document evidence of paleontological and pre-historic events.[21]

16 CONST, art VII, s. 21.
17 1037 UNTS 151.
18 2368 UNTS 3.
19 Rep. Act No. 4846 (1966), s. 12.
20 Presidential Decree No. 374 (1974), s. 3(a).
21 *Ibid*, s. 3(j).

Overall, however, the Act can be described as one more focused on the management of government property under the control of the NMP.[22]

The general protection of UCH, more specifically underwater archaeological sites, and shipwrecks, is mandated only under the National Cultural Heritage Act 2009 (NCHA), outlined in 3.3 below, which is a general law for the protection of cultural heritage. Prior to this, two Bills proposing a separate framework for the specific protection of underwater cultural sites were filed in both the Senate and the House of Representatives. During the 13th Congress[23] in 2004, the Protection of Underwater Cultural Heritage (UCH) Bill was filed in both the Senate and the House of Representatives.[24] In 2006, another UCH Bill was filed in the Senate in response to a strong legislative clamour for the protection of underwater archaeological sites.[25] The Bills provided definitions of underwater archaeology[26] and objects of UCH.[27] No further action after First Reading was taken for the Bill filed with the House of Representatives. The Senate Bills were subsequently substituted by a Senate Bill providing for the NCHA.[28] Notably, this did not include any specific definition of underwater archaeology. During the 14th Congress[29] in 2008, the same Bill was re-filed with the Senate as the UCH Bill.[30] Again, no further actions were taken after First Reading. Two years later, in 2010, the NCHA was enacted into law. Although the said law did not adopt any of the UCH Bills, it included 'underwater' archaeological areas as 'areas of interest'.[31]

22 Y. Jing and J. Li, 'Who Owns Underwater Cultural Heritage in the South Chine Sea', (2019) *Coastal Management*, 47:1, 107, pp. 114–115, available at <https://www.tandfonline.com/doi/pdf/10.1080/08920753.2019.1540908>.

23 The term of the 13th Congress was from 2004–2007.

24 H. No. 01466, 13th Cong., 1st Sess. (2004).; S. No. 282, 13th Cong., 1st Sess. (2004).; S. No. 725, 13th Cong., 1st Sess. (2004).

25 Senate Bill No. 2252.

26 Section 3(d) of Senate Bills No. 22252, 725 and 282 defines Underwater archaeology to include not only maritime archaeology but also riverine and submerged site archaeology.

27 Section 3(f) of Senate Bill Nos. 2252, 725 and 282 includes: Objects of underwater cultural heritage, both movable and immovable includes all shipwrecks, sunken vessels at least 100 years old and all things therein, hulls and underwater archaeological artifacts; places of ancient settlement or where there are vestiges of an ancient civilization; docks, ppiers, aqueducts, tanks, wells; monuments, fragment shards or original documents found underwater dating from prehistoric times and any other object of scientific, cultural, religious, archaeological, anthropological or paleontological interest to the Philippines.

28 S. No. 2613, 13th Cong., 3rd Sess. (2007).

29 The 14th Congress of the Philippines ran from 2007–2010.

30 S. No. 2604, 14th Cong., 2nd Sess. (2008). See <https://legacy.senate.gov.ph/lisdata/83657573!.pdf>.

31 Rep. Act No. 10066 (2010), secs. 3(d), 30(a)(1), 30(a)(2), and 30(a)(9).

While the NCHA provided a framework for protecting national cultural heritage in general, it did not provide a separate framework for protection of UCH. After it was enacted, more Bills proposing such were filed with the House of Representatives in the 16th,[32] 17th[33] and 18th[34] Congresses. To date, however, none of these have been enacted into law. At the time of writing, and since the start of the 19th Congress in July 2022, no UCH Bill or any other proposing a legal framework for the protection of UCH, has been filed or re-filed with Congress.

3.3 *Current Law and Practice*

The NCHA is a general law that provides a system for protecting and conserving national cultural heritage. Its salient features include: definition of cultural property; the categorisation of cultural property as National Cultural Treasures (NCT),[35] Important Cultural Property (ICP),[36] World Heritage Sites;[37] Historical Shrines,[38] Historical Monuments,[39] or Historical Landmarks;[40] the designation of Heritage Zones;[41]the registration and conservation of cultural

32 See the Explanatory Note of H. No. 5723, 16th Cong., 2nd Sess. (2015).

33 H. No. 5476, 17th Cong., 1st Sess. (2017); H. No. 7944, 17th Cong., 3rd Sess. (2018).

34 H. No. 1662, 18th Cong., 1st Sess. (2019).

35 Rep. Act No. 10066 (2010), s. 3(bb) states: "National cultural treasure' shall refer to a unique cultural property found locally, possessing outstanding historical, cultural, artistic and/or scientific value which is highly significant and important to the country and nation, and officially declared as such by pertinent cultural agency'.

36 Rep. Act No. 10066 (2010), s. 3(w) states: "Important cultural property' shall refer to a cultural property having exceptional cultural, artistic and historical significance to the Philippines, as shall be determined by the National Museum and/or National Historical Institute'.

37 Rep. Act No. 10066 (2010), s. 6 states: 'World Heritage Sites. The appropriate cultural agency shall closely collaborate with the United Nations Educational Scientific and Cultural Organization (UNESCO) National Commission of the Philippines in ensuring the conservation and management of world heritage sites, of cultural and mixed sites category, in the Philippines'.

38 Rep. Act No. 10066 (2010), s. 3(u) states: "Historical shrines' shall refer to historical sites or structures hallowed and revered for their history or association as declared by the National Historical Institute".

39 Rep. Act No. 10066 (2010), sec. 3(t) states: "Historical monuments' shall refer to structures that honor illustrious persons or commemorate events of historical value as declared by the National Historical Institute'.

40 Rep. Act No. 10066 (2010), s. 3(s) states: "Historical landmarks' shall refer to sites or structures that are associated with events or achievements significant to Philippine history as declared by the National Historical Institute'.

41 Rep. Act No. 10066 (2010), art. iv.

property;[42] and the regulation of the export, transit, import and repatriation of cultural property.[43]

Notably, there is no separate definition for UCH. The protection of underwater cultural sites is derived from the NCHA's general definition of an 'archaeological area' as:

> any place, whether above or underground, underwater or at sea level, containing fossils, artefacts and other cultural, geographical, botanical, zoological materials which depict and document culturally relevant paleontological, prehistoric and/or historic events.[44]

As such, underwater archaeological sites are under the jurisdiction of the NMP.[45]

3.3.1 Declared Cultural Property

Cultural properties[46] may become Declared Cultural Property on being categorised as an NCT, ICP, World Heritage Site, Historical Shrine, Historical Monument, or Historical Landmark, following assessment and declaration by an appropriate cultural agency.[47] NCTs are considered to be of the

---

42 Rep. Act No. 10066 (2010), art. v.

43 Rep. Act No. 10066 (2010), art. vi.

44 Rep. Act No. 10066 (2010), s. 3(d).

45 Rep. Act No. 10066 (2010), Art. III s. 5.

46 Defined under NCHA 2009 s. 3(o) as '… all products of human creativity by which a people and a nation reveal their identity, including churches, mosques and other places of religious worship, schools and natural history, specimens and sites, whether public or privately-owned, movable or immovable, and tangible or intangible'.

47 Rep. Act No. 10066 (2010) states: 'For purposes of this Act, the following shall be the responsibilities of cultural agencies in the categorization of cultural property:
(a) The Cultural Center of the Philippines shall be responsible for significant cultural property pertaining to the performing arts;
(b) The National Archives of the Philippines shall be responsible for significant archival materials;
(c) The National Library shall be responsible for rare and significant contemporary Philippine books, manuscripts such as, but not limited to, presidential papers, periodicals, newspapers, singly or in collection, and libraries and electronic records;
(d) The National Historical Institute shall be responsible for significant movable and immovable cultural property that pertains to Philippine history, heroes and the conservation of historical artifacts;
(e) The National Museum shall be responsible for significant movable and immovable cultural and natural property pertaining to collections of fine arts, archaeology, anthropology, botany, geology, zoology and astronomy, including its conservation aspect; and

highest national, cultural, or historical significance. An Item of Declared Cultural Property is entitled to certain privileges, such as priority government funding for protection, conservation, and restoration, especially during times of armed conflict and national disaster.[48]

Finds of movable UCH obtained from shipwrecks were among the first archaeological artefacts to be declared as NCT by the NMP under the NCHA,[49] and include a fourteenth century Blue-and-White Porcelain Bowl'[50] recovered from the Pandanan wreck in 1993; a 'Blue-and-White Dish with Flying Elephant'[51] recovered from the Lena Shoal shipwreck in 1997; and a 'Bronze Astrolabe'[52] recovered from the *San Diego* in 1991.[53]

3.3.2 Presumption of Archaeological Materials as Important Cultural Property (ICP)

To protect archaeological materials against exportation, modification or demolition, artefacts and other cultural materials obtained from shipwrecks and other underwater archaeological sites are presumed to be ICP by their intrinsic characteristics.[54] This presumption applies to movable cultural and ethnographic materials that are yet to be discovered and documented, including artefacts that are buried, underwater, or found in shipwrecks, even without being declared as ICPs by the appropriate cultural agency.

3.3.3 Ownership and Possession of Cultural Property

All cultural properties recovered from archaeological excavations on land and underwater belong to the State.[55] The National Commission for Culture and the Arts (NCCA) and a proponent of archaeological excavations may agree on where to store archaeological specimens after a project, provided that the NCCA is allowed to access the artefacts at any time and is informed of any transfer of them.[56] Proponents may also loan artefacts for exhibit and further

---

(f) The *Komisyon sa Wikang Filipino* shall be responsible for the dissemination development, and the promotion of the Filipino national language and the conservation of ethnic languages'.

48 Rep. Act No. 10066 (2010), s. 7.
49 Rep. Act No. 10066 (2010) Art. II s. 3(bb).
50 Accession No. IV-93-V-3000.
51 Accession No. IV-97-H-805.
52 Accession No. IV-91-02-934.
53 National Museum Declaration No. 3–2010, June 14, 2010.
54 Rep. Act No. 10066 (2010), s. 5.
55 Rep. Act No. 10066 (2010), s. 30(a)(1).
56 Section 6.3.2, NNCA Resolution No. 2022–308.

study.[57] For underwater excavations, an exception to State ownership is made for human remains, including those associated with the American or Japanese military, which may be transported for identification or repatriation.[58] Sharing of archaeologically retrieved specimens may be negotiated in a Memorandum of Agreement (MoA) between the NCCA and the proponent.[59]

There are currently four privately owned and funded museums that exhibit materials related to maritime history themes: Museo Maritimo, Museo Marino, Magellan's Landing Maritime Museum, and the Museo de Galleon. The Museo Maritimo is owned by the Asian Institute of Maritime Studies and located in Pasay City, Metro Manila. The museum claims to 'promote and safeguard the Philippines' maritime heritage'.[60] The Museo Marino, operated by the Associated Maritime Officers and Seamen's Union of the Philippines, exhibits objects and narratives related to current Philippine maritime industry. The Magellan's Landing Maritime Museum showcases shipwreck objects from excavations during the 1980s. The displays include ceramics, navigational instruments, as well as parts of different shipwrecks from the sixteenth to the twentieth centuries. The privately owned Museo de Galleon was envisioned as a premiere museum to feature the Manila-Acapulco galleon trade route, including a full-scale replica of a galleon. Whilst the museum had a soft opening in 2017, it has since remained closed.

3.4 *The National Museum of the Philippines (NMP)*

The NMP is the sole agency mandated by the government to undertake research, supervision, and management of the country's UCH under the CPPPA and the NCHA.[61] Additionally, under the NCHA, the NMP is responsible for the conservation of significant movable and immovable cultural property, which includes underwater archaeological sites and the movable cultural materials contained therein.[62] The NMP is mandated to carry out permanent research programmes in archaeology, maritime and UCH.[63] Archaeological and historical artefacts are registered with the NMP as part of a general inventory and catalogue.[64]

Any discovery of underwater archaeological sites requires Local Government Units (LGUs), under whose jurisdiction such sites are located, to report

57 Sections 6.3.3, and 7.4.7, NCCA Resolution No. 2022–308.
58 Section 8.4 NCCA Resolution No. 2022–308.
59 Section 7.4.9, NCCA Resolution No. 2022–308.
60 See <https://www.aimsmuseomaritimo.com/about>.
61 Rep. Act No. 4848 (1966).
62 Rep. Act No. 10066 (2010), s. 31(e).
63 Rep. Act No. 11333 (2019), s. 4.
64 Rep. Act No. 11333 (2019), s. 24.

the discovery to the NMP within five days. Conversely, if such discovery is first made by the NMP, then the aforementioned agencies must report the same to the LGU having jurisdiction over the place where the discovery was made. In all instances, the NMP must immediately suspend all activities that may affect the integrity of the site and/ or the archaeological and cultural materials located therein, until a systematic recovery of such archaeological materials considered as ICP is accomplished.[65]

A systematic recovery of underwater archaeological material is not necessarily mandatory in all cases. Nonetheless, what is mandatory in all cases is an investigation and evaluation of the site. Under the NMP's Operations Manual 2018, the guidelines for the verification and inspection of both land and underwater sites is limited to ocular and documentation activities. In case of positive verification, coordination regarding the security of the site with the LGU, the Philippine National Police (PNP) and other private individuals concerned shall be done. The Underwater Archaeology Section (UAS) of the NMP's Archaeology Division will then prepare a report to be submitted to the Director of the NMP for study and further action.[66]

3.4.1 The Maritime and Underwater Cultural Heritage Division of the NMP

In 1980, the NMP's Underwater Archaeology Unit (UAU) was formed under the then NMP's Anthropology Division. At that time, the staff were certified SCUBA divers with no archaeology background. In 1988, the creation of the Archaeology Division upgraded the UAU into the Underwater Archaeology Section (UAS) headed by an archaeologist. The Maritime and Underwater Cultural Heritage Division (MUCH) was created in 2016.[67] The Division's tasks extend beyond underwater archaeology, such as shipwrecks and other submerged cultural resources, to coastal and foreshore archaeological sites related to ancient maritime activities, as well as the assessment, investigation, and protection of World War II shipwrecks.[68]

65 Rep. Act No. 10066 (2010), s. 30(b).

66 National Museum Operations Manual. See <https://www.nationalmuseum.gov.ph/wp-content/uploads/2021/07/NM-Operations-Manual.pdf>.

67 Orillaneda, B. and Jago-on, Recent Updates on Philippine Maritime Archaeology, *Proceedings of the International Symposium Past, Present and Future of ASEAN Maritime Heritage*, Bangkok, Thailand, 2018, p.255; and Labrador, AMT. and Paz-Tauro, M., 'Engaging Museum Audiences through Protection and Promotion of Collections at the National Museum of the Philippines', *Collections Care: Staying Relevant in Changing Times Conference Proceedings*, Singapore, 2019, p. 67.

68 Orillaneda and Jago-on, *Ibid.*

3.4.2 The National Commission for Culture and the Arts (NCCA)

While the NMP is the country's lead agency for exploration and research in the cultural heritage sector, the NCCA was created by law to formulate policies for the development of culture and arts, and to implement these policies in coordination with affiliated cultural agencies, such as the NMP.[69] The NCCA promulgates rules and regulations and undertakes measures to implement its mandate and to regulate activities inimical to the preservation and conservation of national cultural heritage and/or properties.[70] In 2019, the NCCA was granted regulatory powers to issue permit systems for both terrestrial and underwater archaeological exploration and excavation.[71] In August 2022, the NCCA released guidelines (the Guidelines) for the issuance of permits for land and underwater archaeological exploration and excavation in the Philippines.[72]

The Guidelines provide that only qualified archaeologists and registered organisations in the field of science, education and archaeology, with proven ability to do archaeological work, may be granted permits for the exploration or excavation of archaeological sites.[73] For underwater archaeology, a list of certified divers involved in the scientific underwater archaeological work, including a Dive Safety Officer (DSO) or, in the alternative, a document detailing the team's safety plans and emergency procedures, among others, must be included in a formal letter of application for a permit to explore or excavate underwater archaeological sites in the Philippines.[74] All underwater archaeological explorations and excavations shall be supervised and monitored by the NCCA or its representative archaeologists empowered by an authority to supervise the same.[75]

Permits for both land and underwater archaeological activities, are divided into two categories: archaeological exploration and archaeological excavation. 'Archaeological exploration' is also known as a survey, foot survey, or

69 Rep. Act No. 7356 (1992).

70 Rep. Act No. 7356 (1992), s. 12 (k) and (l).

71 Rep. Act No. 11333 (2019), s. 30.

72 National Commission for Culture and the Arts Resolution No. 2022–308, 'Approving and Adopting the NCCA Guidelines Governing the Issuance of Permits for Land and Underwater Archaeological Exploration and Excavation in the Philippines', see <https://ncca.gov.ph/wp-content/uploads/2022/08/Board-Resolution-No.-2022-308-Approving-and-Adopting-the-NCCA-Guidelines-Governing-the-Issuance-of-Permits-for-Land-and-Underwater-Archaeological-Exploration-and-Excavation-in-the-Philippines.pdf?fbclid=IwAR366rLZtOt-YxFr-UQ86oTe8C3cpvp8OnLWsCeaoco4vNzo5-7sS51Es18>.

73 Section 5.1, NCCA Resolution No. 2022–308.

74 Section 5.2, NCCA Resolution No. 2022–308.

75 Section 5.4, NCCA Resolution No. 2022–308.

reconnaissance with the objective of finding or checking a reported site, with the intention to collect materials.[76] 'Archaeological excavation' is defined as the systematic and controlled investigation and digging of an archaeological site, whether on land or underwater, by an archaeological team that aims to scientifically record archaeological context, artefacts and features, and to make recoveries.[77] Both archaeological exploration and excavation necessitate application for a permit.

Underwater archaeological exploration activities must only be carried out under the supervision of a representative from the NCCA.[78] The maximum area for each application should not exceed 50 square kilometres, although a larger area may be permitted upon proof that modern survey techniques can be implemented.[79] No two applications may overlap in terms of area covered by each permit,[80] and an applicant is limited to two exploration permits at any given time,[81] while exploration permits are only valid for six months and can be renewed for another six after evaluation and payment of applicable fees.[82] The recovery of materials from exploration work is limited to archaeological samples retrieved from the surface only, and shall be under the custody of the NCCA.[83] Recovered archaeological samples from exploration activities are not permitted to be subject to destructive analysis without permission from either the NCCA or the NMP.[84]

For underwater archaeological excavations, permits may be limited to sites whose depths can be worked on safely by appropriately trained and certified divers and where archaeological methods and techniques of excavation and recovery may be applied. This limitation may be waived if the applicant can provide adequate equipment for diving to depths without compromising safety, or if the excavation can be safely practised using manned or unmanned submersible vehicles or remotely operated vehicles.[85]

For areas unaffected by seasonal climatic variations, permits are limited to one year and are renewable for another year.[86] Only one excavation

---

76 See Section 4.1, NCCA Resolution No. 2022–308.
77 See Section 4.2, NCCA Resolution No. 2022–308.
78 See Section 7.4.2, NCCA Resolution No. 2002–308.
79 See Section 7.1.1, NCCA Resolution No. 2022–308.
80 See Section 7.1.2, NCCA Resolution No. 2022–308.
81 See Section 7.1.3, NCCA Resolution No. 2022–308.
82 See Section 7.1.4, NCCA Resolution No. 2022–308.
83 See Section 7.1.5, NCCA Resolution No. 2022–308.
84 See Section 7.1.6, NCCA Resolution No. 2022–308.
85 See Section 7.3, NCCA Resolution No. 2022–308.
86 See Section 7.2.1, NCCA Resolution No. 2022–308.

permit may be granted to an applicant at any one time.[87] For areas affected by seasonal climatic variations, permits are limited to six months, renewable for another six months upon submission of a general report and the payment of applicable fees. The applicability of permits shall not exceed a period of eighteen months.[88]

All archaeological materials obtained during either archaeological exploration or excavation activities, all fragmentary materials, such as shards, organic, and inorganic materials recovered during the project, as well as all rare, unique pieces/items retrieved, shall belong to the State.[89] Nonetheless, aside from the NCCA, the applicant is granted the right of first refusal for loan of the artefacts for the purposes of documentation, exhibition, and analysis.[90]

Under the NCHA, and as stipulated in the NCCA Guidelines, the destruction, demolition, mutilation or damaging of archaeological sites, and their exploration, excavation or digging for the purpose of obtaining materials of cultural historical value without prior written authority from the NCCA is prohibited. These acts are punishable by a fine of not less than 200,000 Philippine Pesos (currently around 3,000 Pounds Sterling) or imprisonment of not less than ten years, or both, upon conviction.[91] At the time of writing, there have been no reports of convictions under these provisions.

3.5 *Collaborative Approach to Research on Maritime Archaeology and UCH*

At present, the NMP is the only agency, government or private, that caters to the supervision, management, and research access to the country's UCH, as compared to neighbouring Southeast Asian nations, such as Indonesia, where various cultural agencies manage such sites, and Laos, Myanmar, and Timor Leste that do not have any such agencies.

In the 1980s, driven by a realisation of the importance of UCH and the government's inability to conduct prohibitively expensive underwater surveys and excavations, the NMP facilitated collaboration with private entities to curb shipwreck lootings and to carry out research projects. In the late 1980s, such collaborations included partnerships with archaeologists from the Western Australia Maritime Museum and the State Heritage Branch, Department of Environment and Planning, in Adelaide. One recent collaboration was on the

87 See Section 7.2.2, NCCA Resolution No. 2022–308.
88 See Section 7.2.1, NCCA Resolution No. 2022–308.
89 See Sections 7.4.8 and 7.4.9, NCCA Resolution No. 2022–308.
90 See Section 7.47, NCCA Resolution No. 2022–308.
91 Rep. Act. No. 10066 (2010), s. 48; at Section IX of NCCA Resolution No. 2022–308.

Manila Galleon Project with Dr. Jun Kimura of Tokai University, Japan, which aimed to examine and document the keel of the Manila galleon *Nuestra Señora De La Vida* that sank in 1620, and involved the study of ship construction, particularly of galleons built in the early seventeenth century.

In 1982, UAS created Underwater Archaeology Policy Guidelines[92] that contain rules and regulations for the issuing of permits for parties who wished to engage in underwater archaeological activities within the archipelago's maritime territory. They also provide more established and systemic guidance on the methodology of survey, exploration, excavation, and post-excavation activities, including collaborations for the exploration of shipwrecks, not only in the Philippines but all over the world. Over the years, the guidelines have been modified, with the latest amendment in 2013. To date, a MoU serves as the binding legal instrument between the NMP and its collaborators.

The NMP's collaborative partners have been mostly private concerns, along with a small number of academic institutions. The private partners come from diverse backgrounds, many of whom have a limited knowledge of archaeology and archaeological methods. The most successful partnership has been with French archaeologist Franck Goddio, who has been working with NMP since 1985. This collaboration has resulted in several explorations and excavations that have led to publications and exhibitions. Museum-to-museum partnership happened in the late 1980s with partnership between the archaeologists of the NMP and the Western Australia Maritime Museum and Australia's State Heritage Branch, Department of Environment and Planning that investigated the Butuan boats and other ancient wooden hulls.

3.6 *Engagement with the General Public on Maritime Archaeology and UCH*

Engaging the general public with maritime archaeology in the Philippines remains a challenge. In the past, information was disseminated through a number of publications but did not reach wide public coverage. This situation has changed with the advent of social media platforms. In August 2020, for example, the NMP's Facebook page featured '#MaritimeMonday', which highlighted shipwrecks, shipwreck-related artefacts, and other submerged cultural resources. This has helped immensely in disseminating information on Philippine maritime archaeology and in creating public awareness.

At present, interaction between maritime archaeologists with the public falls into four general categories: grassroots, schools and universities, media,

92 UAS 2013. Rules and Regulations for Underwater Archaeology in Exploration and Excavation in Philippine Waters, National Museum of the Philippines.

and academic venues. At the grassroots level, archaeologists visit local government officials and coastal residents of areas affected by archaeological activities to inform affected stakeholders and conduct information dissemination drives. In some cases, post-fieldwork activities and results are also presented to the local populace. These interactions have been valuable since local authorities and residents' knowledge about archaeology is practically non-existent, resulting in questions about its impact on the local fishing economy and treasure hunting, among other topics. In the Philippines, the latter, most especially in local communities, is a complex topic, given that the treasure hunting of unmarked archaeological sites, including those underwater, is permitted in the country (see section 2.6 below). Furthermore, archaeologists speak at high schools, colleges, and universities about maritime archaeology and UCH. Presentations include standalone lectures and team events related to archaeology, history, and the ocean environment. Virtual Reality (VR) is also being considered as a medium of public engagement for UCH. In the academic setting, archaeologists have presented their research findings in both local and international venues. These academic gatherings are the most frequent way of disseminating and exchanging information and often result in collaborative publications and projects. However, the reach of these publications is quite limited outside academic circles.

3.7 *Treasure Hunting Permit System*

Treasure hunting, or the unsystematic search for hidden treasures, such as gold bars, jewellery, and other objects of financial value, is widely popularised in local films and folklore, which has led to the looting of archaeological sites. In fact, the NMP has attributed the discovery of many of its UCH sites to treasure hunting activities, which leave archaeologists with disturbed and incomplete archaeological sites.[93]

For decades, a permit system has made government agencies a key player in regulating the practice of treasure hunting. The legality of treasure hunting can be traced to 1980, upon the issuance of Presidential Decree (PD) No. 17260-A.[94] This PD was released in the context of the discoveries of "hidden treasures buried for years or centuries underground" that "have, in most cases, been found

93 Peralta, J. (1984) Country Report of the Philippines for SPAFA Consultative Workshop and Research on Maritime Shipping and Trade Networks in Southeast Asia, SPAFA Final Report, West Java, p. 323; Matias and Belmonte (2001), 'Shipwreck looted in Zambales', Philippine Star, 21 May 2001, available at <https://www.philstar.com/headlines/2001/05/21/90743/shipwreck-looted-zambales>; Orillaneda et al. (2006), 'A Field Report on the Underwater Archaeological Survey of Scarborough Shoal', Archaeology Division, National Museum.

94 See <https://www.chanrobles.com/presidentialdecreeno1726-a.htm#.Yq7hmqJBxPY>.

to be possessed of great cultural significance aside from their monetary values".[95] A treasure hunting permit application system was then installed under the Office of the President, who had the sole authority to authorise any such treasure hunting in the country. Under the NCHA, treasure hunting is allowed in the Philippines, provided permits are secured from the appropriate government cultural agency beforehand.[96]

In 2021, the NCCA released guidelines for the issuance of treasure hunting permits (Treasure Hunting Guidelines).[97] Under these, treasure hunting permits cover the disposition of recovered hidden treasures or things of value hoarded in undisclosed places and the transport or sale of hoarded gold bars, gold coins, platinum silver, nickel babbitts, jewellery, gemstones, etc., on both public and private land.[98] Hidden treasures are any unknown deposits of money, jewellery or other precious objects whose ownership is unknown.[99] This definition does not cover cultural or ethnographical materials as contemplated under the NCHA. The items discovered through treasure hunting will be assessed by a relevant government agency deputised by the NMP's Executive Director, either *in situ* or after being transported to the relevant agency. If the items are deemed to be culturally or historically significant, they must be turned over to the NMP or the appropriate government cultural agency.[100]

Any Filipino citizen, of legal age, and partnerships, associations, and corporations with the financial ability to undertake treasure hunting activities may apply for a treasure hunting permit.[101] In contrast to archaeological exploration and excavation (discussed above), a representative of the NCCA is not required to supervise any authorised treasure hunting activities. However, a notable feature of the current Treasure Hunting Guidelines is that permits will not be issued if they cover areas that include archaeological sites and on any shipwrecks, other historical zones, and anthropological reservations.[102] This provision effectively bans treasure hunting in archaeological sites, in contrast to previous guidelines. This development may have its roots in the fact that from 1987 to 2010, prior to the enactment of the NCHA, treasure hunting

95 *Ibid,* (First Paragraph).

96 Rep. Act. No. 10066 (2010), s. 30(a)(8).

97 NCCA Resolution No. 2021–308, available at <https://ncca.gov.ph/wp-content/uploads/2021/08/CTC-NCCA-Board-Resolution-2021-308-Guidelines-Governing-the-Issuance-of-Permits-for-Treasure-Hunting.pdf>.

98 NCCA Resolution No. 2021–308 (2021) Section II.

99 NCCA Resolution No. 2021–308 (2021) Section 4.9.

100 NCCA Resolution No. 2021–308 (2021) Section IX.

101 NCCA Resolution No. 2021–308 (2021) Section V.

102 NCCA Resolution No. 2021–308 (2021) Section VI. C. 5.

permits specifically provided for the salvaging of shipwrecks or sunken vessels. In that period, the function of issuing treasure hunting permits rested with either with the Office of the President or the Department of Environment and Natural Resource (DENR) and its sub-offices.[103] Under the DENR's rules governing the issuance of treasure hunting and shipwreck/sunken vessel recovery, items recovered had to be turned over to the NMP if it determined they had cultural value.[104]

In 2003, Phil Greco, a controversial American treasure hunter, allegedly spirited away 10,000 pieces of Chinese porcelain and pottery from shipwrecks in the Philippines.[105] While some reports claimed that Greco purportedly secured the necessary treasure hunting permit for such activity,[106] the NMP contended that it had not issued him any permit for archaeological exploration or excavation.[107] Nonetheless, he was still able to export items of likely cultural value. This demonstrated that while the treasure hunting permit system aimed to encourage non-archaeological methods to obtain so-called 'hidden treasures', it may have encouraged treasure hunters to get away with smuggling Philippine artefacts at the expense of archaeological research. Whilst the DENR's rules are no longer in effect, they were in force for more than two decades. Actual data on the number of treasure hunting permits issued during this period is unavailable, although some government offices have stated that they did not issue any such permits from 2004 to 2010.[108]

All previous and current rules and guidelines for treasure hunting were issued pursuant to national laws that allows treasure hunting. At the time of writing, no proposals calling for the repeal or amendment to such laws have been filed, indicating that there is no political will to ban treasure hunting in the country.

---

103 Rev. Adm. Code, book IV, title IX, chapter 1, s. 4(8) states: 'The Department shall ... Issue licenses and permits for activities related to the use and development of aquatic resources, treasure hunting, salvaging of sunken vessels and other similar activities'; Exec. Order No. 35 (2001); DENR Adm. O. No. 4 (2002); DENR Adm. O. No. 35 (2004).

104 DENR Adm. O. No. 33 (2004), s. 6.

105 Haithman, D. (2003), 'The Fortune Hunter', Los Angeles Times, available at <https://www.latimes.com/archives/la-xpm-2003-aug-13-et-haithman13-story.html>.

106 Diaz, J. (2003), 'US treasure hunter brings artifacts out of RP, probe sough', Philippine Star, available at <https://www.philstar.com/headlines/2003/06/17/210439/us-treasure-hunter-brings-artifacts-out-rp-probe-sough>.

107 Haithman, *supra* n.105.

108 The authors conducted a personal email inquiry on the number of treasure hunting permits issued under DENR Adm. O. No 33 (2004).

4 Dispute with China over the West Philippine Sea

The geography of both China and the Philippines has led to long-standing territorial disputes over island and maritime territory. One of the contested areas is Scarborough Shoal, off the western coast of northern Luzon Island. In 2006, the NMP received reports of ceramic artefacts being looted by fishermen from the Scarborough Shoal, 221 kilometres from the Municipality of Palauig, Zambales Province. Later, the NMP collaborated with the Far Eastern Foundation for Nautical Archaeology (FEFNA), a NGO based in the Philippines, led by French archaeologist Franck Goddio, to explore and excavate the area (Scarborough Shoal Archaeological Project). Underwater surveys were undertaken in 2006 and 2010, when numerous Chinese ceramics, scattered in the shoal area and embedded in corals, were recovered. While no shipwreck was discovered, underwater archaeological excavations in the area continued in 2011 and 2012. However, in 2012, while the team of archaeologists from the NMP and FEFNA were working on recovering artefacts, a Chinese Marine Surveillance vessel (CMS) with military officers on board arrived. The officers broadcasted on their ship's radio channel a claim to the Scarborough Shoal territory and ordered the archaeologists to stop operations and leave.[109] After a few days' stand-off between the CMS and the Philippine Coast Guard, the archaeologists decided to terminate the project, leaving visible underwater artefacts exposed to the threat of potential looting by fishermen. At the time of writing, a decade after the incident, the Scarborough Shoal Archaeological Project has not been concluded and no other excavations have been undertaken in the area.

In 2016, in proceedings initiated by the Philippines, the Permanent Court of Arbitration (PCA) ruled that there was no basis for China's claims to sovereignty based on the historical 'nine-dash line' theory.[110] The PCA also found China in breach of its obligations under the UN Convention on the Law of the Sea (LOSC)[111] for another incident in 2012, when it had operated law enforcement vessels in the Scarborough Shoal, preventing Filipino fishermen being in the area.[112] At the time of writing, China has yet to recognise the award in favour of the Philippines. Initially, the then Philippine President also did

109 See for further information <https://archive-yaleglobal.yale.edu/content/chinese-territorial-strife-hits-archaeology>.

110 The South China Sea Arbitration (*The Republic of Philippines v. The People's Republic of China*) Case No 2013–19, ICGJ 495 (PCA 2016), 12 July 2016, Permanent Court of Arbitration, p. 67 at 117.

111 1883 UNTS 397.

112 The South China Sea Arbitration *supra* n.110 at 476.

not recognise the award.[113] However, in 2020, he recognised that the award in favour of the Philippines had become part of international law and beyond compromise by governments.[114]

The aborted underwater exploration in Scarborough Shoal is an example of how disputes in maritime territory can affect the protection of underwater archaeological sites. Notably, neither China nor the Philippines are party to the 2001 Convention. While there are international remedies to settle these disputes, the political will of the incumbent administration to enforce any arbitral awards in their respective countries of jurisdiction is also a factor in settling these types of controversies between States. In the case of the Philippines, the President at the time not only initially failed to recognise the PCA's award, but also did not wish to enforce it against China. Thus, the implementation of international law within a specific territorial jurisdiction relies deeply on the political will of the country's officials.

5 Summary and Observations

Analysis of the Philippine legal framework for the protection of cultural heritage reveals that, while the NCHA mandates the protection of cultural heritage in general, at the time of writing, there is no political will to enact a separate law that provides an independent legal framework for the protection of UCH. Nonetheless, some provisions of the NCHA are consistent with the intent of the 2001 Convention (see 4.2 below).

5.1 *Lack of National Laws Providing a Legal Framework for the Specific Protection of UCH*

The NCHA's definition of cultural property[115] does not mention UCH and its categorisation of cultural property[116] does not include a separate category for UCH. The protection of significant underwater sites is only derived from the general

113 See <https://www.theguardian.com/world/2016/jul/12/philippines-wins-south-china-sea-case-against-china>.

114 See <https://thediplomat.com/2020/09/in-un-speech-duterte-stiffens-philippines-stance-on-the-south-china-sea/>.

115 See n.46.

116 Rep. Act No. 10066 (2010), s. 4 states: 'The cultural property of the country shall be categorized as follows: (a) National Cultural Treasures; (b) Important cultural property; (c) World heritage sites; (d) National historical shrine; (e) National historical monument; and (f) National historical landmark'.

definition of archaeological sites, which encompasses underwater areas.[117] The NCHA merely provides specific guidelines for the conduct of archaeological exploration and excavation of underwater archaeological sites.[118] While archaeological materials, including those that have yet to be discovered or retrieved, are presumed to be ICPs that are protected from destruction and illegal exportation from the country, there is no similar provision specifically on UCH.

Factors such as climate change, rising sea levels, environmental degradation, and the exploitation of marine resources called for the formulation of the 2001 Convention. It recognises the need for a separate legal framework for the protection of UCH to be able to address the unique setting in which UCH, such as shipwrecks, can be found.

The legislative campaign for the creation of a separate legal framework for protecting UCH started in 2004, six years before the enactment of the NCHA, but, as discussed above, was not adopted. A review of the NCHA's legislative history and transcript of records during committee deliberations reveals that there were no in-depth discussions on UCH, such as shipwrecks and underwater archaeological areas. Indeed, it appears the NCHA was intended more for built monuments and sites with cultural and historical value. The inaction of Congress on the matter, despite evidence of a legislative ambition to include a separate framework for the protection of UCH, implies that there was, and remains, a lack of political will, not only to enact separate UCH law, but also to recognise UCH as a separate category of cultural property, as the 2001 Convention does.

5.2 *NCHA Provisions Consistent with the 2001 Convention*

Nonetheless, the intent of the NCHA to protect Philippine cultural heritage is consistent with the objectives and general principles under the 2001 Convention, which aims to ensure and strengthen the protection of UCH for the benefit of humanity.[119] It considers the preservation *in situ* of UCH as the first consideration before allowing or engaging in any other activities that may alter its setting.[120] The protection of UCH in specific areas such as internal waters, Territorial Sea, Exclusive Economic Zone, Continental Shelf, and the Contiguous Zone is also provided for. The NCHA contains provisions similar to the

117 Rep. Act No. 10066 (2010), s. 3(d) states: "Archaeological area' shall refer to any place, whether above or under ground, underwater or at sea level, containing fossils, artifacts and other cultural, geological, botanical, zoological materials which depict and document culturally relevant paleontological, prehistoric and/or historic events'.

118 Rep. Act No. 10066 (2010), s. 30.

119 Arts. 2.1 and 2.3 of the 2001 Convention.

120 Art. 2.5 of the 2001 Convention.

2001 Convention's objectives, such as the protection, preservation, conservation, and promotion of the nation's cultural heritage,[121] the supervision of the NMP and the NCCA in all archaeological excavations,[122] and the NMP's internal rules to preserve underwater archaeological sites *in situ* if necessary.

5.3 *The Treasure Hunting System*

As discussed above, the treasure hunting permit system has been operating according to law in the Philippines since the 1980s. At present, after several government reorganisations, the NCCA is the government cultural agency that issues treasure hunting permits. While the NCCA's guidelines for treasure hunting clearly state that no permits will be issued for treasure hunting in archaeological sites and shipwrecks,[123] the absence of supervision from a representative from the NCCA creates difficulty in monitoring actual treasure hunting activities. Treasure hunting in unmarked or undiscovered archaeological areas, including underwater areas, may put the settings of such sites at risk of alteration or destruction.

5.4 *The Enforcement of Arbitral Awards under International Law*

Evidently, the remedies provided for by international law may only be enforced domestically with the political will of the current administration. The tension between the Philippines and China over maritime territory is a classic example of how underwater archaeological sites, such as Scarborough Shoal, are vulnerable to destruction and looting should there be any disputes over maritime territory.

Notably, while both China and the Philippines are not signatories to the 2001 Convention, it provides that in conformity with the LOSC, State Parties are responsible for protecting underwater cultural heritage in marine areas beyond the limits of national jurisdiction. Assuming, for the sake of argument, that the artefact deposit in Scarborough Shoal was not within Philippine territory, adherence to this provision under the 2001 Convention may have avoided such tension.

6 Conclusion and Future Direction

In the Philippines, the protection of UCH is bundled together with the protection of cultural heritage in general, especially built heritage, under the NCHA.

121 Rep. Act No. 10066 (2010), s. 2.
122 Rep. Act No. 10066 (2010), s. 30.
123 NCCA Resolution No. 2021–308 (2021) s. VI.C. 5

The rules and regulations on the specific protection of UCH are the internal rules and regulations of the NMP on underwater archaeology exploration and excavation in Philippine waters. The existence of the treasure hunting permit system for the past decades makes it difficult for the country to accede to the principles of the 2001 Convention. Nonetheless, the NCHA expressly states that the State's policy is to conserve, preserve, and popularise cultural and historical objects, including UCH. Thus, with intensified advocacies and thorough discussions of the benefits of the said Convention within both the executive and legislative branches of government, the Philippines may well accede to the 2001 Convention in the future.

All websites last accessed February 2025.

Acknowledgements

The authors would like to acknowledge Stefanie Klein M. Gatdula, of the University of the Philippines College of Law; and the Philippines' Mines and Geosciences Bureau, for their contribution to this chapter.

Selected Bibliography

Desroches, J., Casal, G. and Goddio, F. (eds.), (1996), Treasures of the San Diego, Association Française d'Action Artistique, Elf Foundation, National Museum of the Philippines.

Goddio, F. et al. (2002), Lost at sea: The strange route of the Lena Shoal junk, London: Periplus Publishing London, Ltd.

Lim, K. A., Orillaneda, B. C. and King, C. P. (2021), People and the sea: A values perspective in the conservation management of maritime heritage in the Philippines, *International Journal of Asia Pacific Studies* 17 (2): 39–73.

Orillaneda, B., Maritime Trade in the Philippines during the Early Colonial Period (Sixteenth and Seventeenth Centuries C.E.) in Berrocal, M.C. and Tsang, C. (eds.) *Historical Archaeology of Early Modern Colonialism in Asia-Pacific*, (University of Florida Press, 2017).

Pearson, N. (2019), Protecting and preserving underwater cultural heritage in Southeast Asia, in Hufnagel, S. and Chappell, D., (eds.) *Palgrave Handbook on Art Crime*, London: Palgrave Macmillan.

Ronquillo, W.P. (1989), The Butuan archaeological finds: profound implications for Philippine and Southeast Asian pre-history, in Brown (ed.) *Guangdong Ceramics from Butuan and other Philippine Sites*, Oriental Ceramics Society of the Philippines/ Oxford University Press, Manila.

CHAPTER 17

Spain

*Mariano J. Aznar**

1 Introduction

Spanish policy towards the protection of underwater cultural heritage (UCH) shows different, and at times contradictory, approaches. Examples of this include, inaction before pillage in the 1970–80s (e.g., *Atocha*, sunk in 1622 in the Florida Keys) or disputable recovery (e.g., in 1992 of the *San Diego*, sunk in 1600 in the Philippines), while in the 1990's sending an archaeological mission to survey the remains of the *San Telmo* at Livingston Island, Antarctica; and successful excavation and protection *in situ* of two eighth century B.C. vessels (*Mazarrón I* and *II*) in southeast Spain in 1993–1995, while neglecting some fundamental sixteenth century coastal sites in Galicia (vessels of the returning 1588 Armada).

Following Spanish ratification of the 1982 UN Law of the Sea Convention (LOSC)[1], new legislation on cultural heritage was enacted: Law 16/1985 on Spanish Historical Heritage (the LPHE),[2] addressing for the very first time the protection of underwater archaeological objects. This was followed by regional legislation, some of which have recent amendments and improvements regarding UCH,[3] including affecting archaeological agencies.[4]

During the 1990s, for the first time, Spain decided to litigate before the United States (US) Admiralty courts against treasure hunters (see the cases of

* Professor of Public International Law, Universitat Jaume I, Spain. Member of the International Committee on Underwater cultural heritage (ICUCH) of the International Council on Monuments and Sites (ICOMOS).

1 1833 UNTS 397. Spain ratified LOSC on 14 February 1997 and the Convention entered into force for Spain on this very date (*Boletín Oficial de Estado* (*BOE*) of 14 February 1997).

2 Law 16/1985, of 25 June 1985, on the Spanish Historical Heritage, see *BOE* No. 155, 29 June 1985. A non-official English version may be found at <https://media.unesco.org/sites/default/files/webform/mhm001/spa_law_16_1985_engtof.pdf>. Amendment (or complete re-drafting) of the LPHE is under discussion (see *infra* n. 88).

3 See below3.1.

4 Initially created in 1980, now the National Museum of Underwater Archaeology (Museo Nacional de Arqueología Subacuática, ARQVA) was established by Royal Decree 1508/2008, of 12 September (*BOE* No. 248, 14 October 2008), with its laboratories in the vicinity. See <https://www.cultura.gob.es/mnarqua/en/home.html>.

 | DOI:10.1163/9789004510883_019

the *Juno* and *La Galga*, discussed in 2.1 below) while, at the same time, adopting a complex negotiating profile during the drafting of the UNESCO Convention on the Protection of the Underwater Cultural Heritage (the 2001 Convention).[5] Another case of looting of Spanish UCH, the *Mercedes* case (see2.3 below), definitely changed the general approach of Spain towards the protection of UCH, both domestically and internationally. Domestically, both administrative and legislative decisions were adopted, most particularly the Law on Maritime Navigation (LMN) in 2014,[6] whilst internationally, Spain decided to play a leading role as a State Party to the 2001 Convention and confirmed a policy of relevant principles through cooperation, new agreements, and judicial claims when necessary.[7]

Giving the relevance of the cases mentioned and how they impacted these administrative and legislative changes, they will be explained first, before discussing how change occurred in their aftermath and Spain's ratification of the 2001 Convention. Following sections will evaluate current domestic legislation (both central and regional), in contrast with international obligations already assumed by Spain.

2 Spanish Litigation on UCH before Courts of the United States

Two landmark cases before US Admiralty courts deserve to be analysed, since they may be considered a turning point in what has been labelled as 'historic salvage',[8] thus influencing other common law jurisdictions. They also had a significant impact on Spanish public opinion.[9]

---

5 2562 UNTS 1. See below section 4.

6 Law 14/2014, 24 May 2014, on Maritime Navigation (*BOE* No. 180, of 25 July 2014).

7 During the *Mercedes* case, Spain faced another case of UCH looting when a US company, Sage Maritime Scientific Research Inc. (SAGE), in collaboration with two well-known local treasure hunters, tried to covertly find and recover cultural objects in coastal waters near Cádiz. See *The M/V Louisa Case (Saint Vincent and the Grenadines v. Kingdom of Spain)*, ITLOS Case No. 18 (available at <www.itlos.org/en/>) and R. Ojinaga, 'The *M/V Louisa* Case: Spain and the International Tribunal for the Law of the Sea' (2013–2014) 18 *Spanish Yearbook of International Law* 199.

8 See T. J. Schoenbaum, 'Pecios históricos y salvamento marítimo: el cambio en la jurisprudencia de los Estados Unidos' (2020) 25 *Revista de Derecho del Transporte* 13. See also O. Varmer and C.M. Blanco, 'The case for using the law of salvage to preserve underwater cultural heritage: The integrated marriage of the law of salvage and historic preservation' (2018) 49 *Journal of Maritime Law & Commerce* 401. See further the US chapter in this book.

9 See I. Rodríguez Temiño, 'The Odyssey Case: press, public opinion and future policy' (2017) 46/1 *The International Journal of Nautical Archaeology* 192.

2.1 *Initial Litigation: the Juno and La Galga Cases*

In 1997, a US private maritime salvage company (Sea Hunt Inc.) claimed to have discovered the wrecks of *La Galga* and the *Juno*, two Spanish frigates wrecked off the coast of Virginia in 1750 and 1802, respectively.[10] Under the US Abandoned Shipwreck Act (ASA) 1987, which gives individual US States title to abandoned shipwrecks embedded in their submerged lands,[11] Sea Hunt was granted permits to conduct salvage operations, including the recovery of artefacts from the wrecks.

From the start, Spain claimed that its title in the vessels had never been abandoned, relinquished, or transferred. However, the US District Court for the Eastern District of Virginia found that Spain had implicitly abandoned its title to *La Galga* when it signed the 1763 Definitive Treaty of Peace Between France, Great Britain, and Spain (and which is still in force between Spain and the US).[12] Spain appealed, and the Fourth Circuit Court of Appeals reversed the District Court decision, upholding Spanish title to both wrecks and denying salvage awards.[13] The Court of Appeals underlined that:

> ... matters as sensitive as these implicate important interests of the executive branch. Courts cannot just turn over the sovereign shipwrecks of other nations to commercial salvors where negotiated treaties show no sign of an abandonment, and where the nations involved all agree that title to the shipwrecks remains with the original owner. Far from abandoning these shipwrecks, Spain has vigorously asserted its ownership rights in this proceeding. Nothing in the law of admiralty suggests that Spain has abandoned its dead by respecting their final resting place at sea.[14]

---

10 See M. White, '*Sea Hunt, Inc. v. Unidentified Shipwrecked Vessel or Vessels*, 221 F.3d 634 (2000), cert. denied, 121 S.Ct. 1079 (2001)' (2001) 95 *American Journal of International Law* 678; M.J. Aznar, 'Treasure hunters, sunken State vessels and the 2001 UNESCO Convention on the Protection of Underwater Cultural Heritage' (2010) 25 *International Journal of Maritime & Coastal Law* 209–236; and T. Scovazzi, 'Sunken Spanish Ships before American Courts' (2018) 34 *International Journal of Maritime & Coastal Law* 245.

11 43 U.S.C. §§ 2101–2106, at 2105 (a) and (c).

12 *Sea Hunt, Inc. v. Unidentified Shipwrecked Vessel or Vessels*, 47 *F. Supp.* 2d 678 (E.D. Va. 1999). The District Court did not hold the same opinion regarding the *Juno* because she sank in 1802, and the preceding 1763 Treaty did not apply. *Ibid* at p. 688, n. 15.

13 *Sea Hunt, Inc. v. Unidentified Shipwrecked Vessel or Vessels*, 221 F.3d 634 (4th Cir. 2000), cert. denied, 148 L. Ed. 2d 956, 121 S.Ct. 1079 (2001). Once Spain won the case, an artifacts' loan agreement for the local display of some remains of the wrecks was signed with the US National Park Service on 17 October 2006.

14 *Ibid.*, at p. 647.

2.2 *Confirmation: the Mercedes Case*

Allegedly trying to find the English warship HMS *Sussex*, wrecked in Spanish waters east of Gibraltar in 1624,[15] the US private company Odyssey Marine Exploration Inc. (Odyssey) suddenly announced in April 2007 the recovery of around 594,000 coins (mainly silver, Spanish *Reales de a Ocho*) and some other historical artefacts.[16] Before the announcement, Odyssey had filed a salvage claim before the US District Court in Tampa (Florida) requesting exclusive salvage rights over the cargo recovered from a publicly undisclosed place.[17] Spain, however, argued that the cargo was recovered from the archaeological site of the *Nuestra Señora de las Mercedes* (the *Mercedes*), a Spanish frigate sunk in combat against a British naval squadron in 1804.[18]

Discussion centred on whether the claimed *res* and Spain were immune from suit under the Foreign Sovereign Immunities Act (FSIA).[19] Odyssey contested this on three grounds: first, FSIA would only apply to foreign government property located in the US, which was not the case with the *Mercedes*; second, that the vessel was incidentally carrying some private cargo and the commercial activity exception to immunity applied; and, third, that if the wreck enjoyed immunity, the private cargo should not. However, while the District Court initially relied on constructive *in rem* jurisdiction for its arrest of the *res*, it concluded it did not have subject matter jurisdiction of the *res* or property under the FSIA, noting that it was a Spanish military ship transporting *specie*

---

15 Operating for the UK Ministry of Defence under a highly controversial contract, Odyssey never disclosed the exact location of the wreck, if any. See S. Dromgoole, 'Murky Waters for Government Policy: The Case of a Seventeenth Century British Warship and Ten Tonnes of Gold Coins' (2004) 28 *Marine Policy* 189.

16 As later confirmed, the cargo was recovered from the Portuguese Continental Shelf, without scientific care of the submerged remains, including human remains, thus irreparably disturbing the archaeological site, as the first Admiralty decision plainly said. *Odyssey Marine Exploration, Inc. v. Unidentified, Shipwrecked Vessel*, 675 F.Supp.2d 1126 (M.D. Fla. 2009). The report of the last Spanish mission to the *Mercedes* archaeological site in 2017 is available at <https://www.libreria.culturaydeporte.gob.es/libro/the-shipwreck-nuestra-senora-de-las-mercedes-third-exploration-and-excavation-campaign_5419/>.

17 The non-disclosure by Odyssey of essential information during the litigation was later sanctioned by the Court as procedural bad faith. See *Odyssey Marine Exploration, Inc. v. Unidentified Shipwrecked Vessel*, 979 F. Supp. 2d 1270 (M.D. Fla. 2013).

18 The case also involved Peru, claiming rights as one of the successor States of Spain in America, and some alleged descendants of those aboard the *Mercedes* at the time of her sinking. However, neither the former nor the later had convincing rights on the case, as the courts finally concluded.

19 28 U.S.C. §§ 1602 *et seq.*

in a time of threatened war and that in treasure shipwreck cases, the cargo is considered an integral part of the shipwreck.[20]

Odyssey, Peru and the alleged descendants of the crew appealed.[21] The Appeal Court ruled that "the evidence in the record fully supports the finding of the District Court that the *res* is the *Mercedes* for the purposes of sovereign immunity",[22] that "[t]he shipwreck of the *Mercedes* is thus unquestionably the property of Spain",[23] and consequently "support[ed] the decision to affirm the District Court's order to release the *res* into Spain's custody".[24] The cargo returned to Spain on 25 February 2012. In December it was handed over to the National Museum of Underwater Archaeology, Cartagena, Murcia, where it is on permanent display.[25]

This case, as well as the earlier *Juno* and *La Galga* and later *La Trinité* cases,[26] confirmed the rule upon which sunken State vessels (including warships), unless expressly abandoned, remain the public property of the flag State. Authoritative international doctrine also supports this rule.[27]

2.3 *Spain's New Policy*

During the *Juno* and *La Galga* case, the US and United Kingdom (UK) Governments supported Spain's legal position.[28] In their aftermath, this position was

20 *Odyssey Marine Exploration, Inc. v. Unidentified, Shipwrecked Vessel*, 675 F.Supp.2d 1126 (M.D. Fla. 2009).

21 *Odyssey Marine Exploration, Inc. v. Unidentified Shipwrecked Vessel*, 657 F.3d 1159 (11th Cir. 2011), cert. denied, 132 S. Ct. 2379 (2012).

22 *Ibid., at* 1171.

23 *Ibid.*, at 1174, see also *supra* n. 8.

24 *Ibid.*, at 1184.

25 See <https://www.cultura.gob.es/mnarqua/en/home.html https://www.culturaydeporte.gob.es/mnarqua/colecciones/piezas-seleccionadas/edad-moderna/nsm.html>.

26 *La Trinité*, the flagship of the French 1565 Fleet of Captain Jean Ribault, sunk in Florida waters. *Global Marine Exploration, Inc. v. Unidentified, Wrecked & (For Finders-Right Purposes) Abandoned Sailing Vessel*, 348 F. Supp. 3d 1221 (M.D. Fla. 2018). See the chapter on the U S.

27 See 'The Legal regime of Wrecks of Warships and Other State-owned Ships in International Law', Resolution adopted by the *Institut de droit international* on 29 August 2015, Tallinn Session, at <https://www.idi-iil.org/app/uploads/2017/06/02-Ronzitti-epave.pdf>.

28 The US in a Statement of Interest of 18 December 1998 (available in the case docket as No. 13) and the UK in a Diplomatic Note of 7 July 1999 (Diplomatic Note no. 41). The US also supported Spain's position during the *Mercedes* case (Statement of Interest and Brief of the United States as Amicus Curiae in Support of the Kingdom of Spain, 27 August 2009).

made explicit by Spain in a public note to the US,[29] claiming sovereign immunity for its State vessels sunk elsewhere, and also for third States' sunken vessels wrecked in Spanish waters. For example, regarding the HMS *Sussex*, Spain recognised British title to the wreck.[30] Several bilateral agreements between other States dealing with title to sunken State vessels,[31] and several domestic measures,[32] also follow this legal position. In the case of Spain, Article 382(1) LMN establishes that:

> ... regardless of the time at which the loss took place and the place where they may be located, shipwrecked or sunken Spanish State ships and vessels, their remains and their equipment or cargo, appertain to the State public domain, may not be disposed of, shall not prescribe and may not be seized, enjoying immunity of jurisdiction.

And paragraph 3 establishes that:

> The remains of foreign warships sunken or shipwrecked in Spanish maritime areas enjoy immunity of jurisdiction pursuant to the terms set forth in Article 50. Notwithstanding this, exploration, tracking, location and extraction operations of these shall be agreed between the competent bodies of the flag State and the Ministry of Defence. In such case, those operations shall be subject to the terms established in the [2001 Convention].[33]

29 Embassy of Spain, Washington, DC, Note No. 128, 19 December 2002, published in *Federal Register*, Vol. 69, No. 24, Thursday, 5 February 2004, Notices, at p. 5647. For a similar position by the US, the UK, France, Germany, Japan and the Russian Federation, see *ibid*, at pp.5647–5648.

30 Note of the Ministry of Foreign Affairs and Cooperation, 23 March 2007 (on file with the author).

31 See different cases cited in Aznar, *supra* note 10, at pp. 221–2.

32 Besides the case of the US, Mexico amended in 2014 its 1972 *Ley Federal de Monumentos y Zonas Arqueológicos, Artísticos e Históricos*, including a new Art. 28 TER preserving flag State's rights upon its sunken State vessels wrecked in Mexican waters. See the chapter on 'Mexico' in this book.

33 Paragraph 2 of the same Article establishes that '[e]xploration, tracking, location and extraction operations of shipwrecked or sunken Spanish State ships and vessels shall require authorisation from the Navy, which holds full powers for their protection, without prejudice to the terms set forth in the laws on historical and cultural heritage, as appropriate'. But see *infra* note 47.

3 Spanish Legislation on UCH

Spain's 1978 Constitution[34] distributes legislative powers between the State and the regions (Comunidades Autónomas). In general terms, matters related to cultural heritage are in the hands of the regions, but in close collaboration with the State. Articles 148(1)(16) and 149(1)(28) make possible the enactment of laws and regulations on cultural heritage by all regions, though retaining relevant powers to the State.[35] Most of this regional legislation applies to UCH,[36] generating a still unresolved legal caveat between the State and regions, since legislation over maritime zones is an exclusive competence of the State. However, so far, both the central and regional administrations seem to have accepted a *de facto* regional competence on UCH, with some variations.

3.1 *General Cultural Legislation*

Under Article 46 of the Constitution, public authorities have the duty to protect cultural heritage. Awaiting amendment, the LPHE remains the basic State law on cultural heritage, including UCH. This Law defines cultural heritage as:

> ... movable and immovable objects of artistic, historical, palaeontological, archaeological, ethnographic, scientific or technical interest. It also comprises documentary and bibliographical heritage, archaeological sites and areas as well as natural sites, gardens and parks having artistic, historical or anthropological value.

In Article 40(1), 'archaeological heritage' is defined as:

> ... movable or immovable property of a historical nature that can be studied using archaeological methodology forms part of the Spanish

34 English translation available at <https://www.lamoncloa.gob.es/documents/constitucion_inglescorregido.pdf>.

35 These powers allocate main responsibility on the State against 'pillaging' (*expolio*), as confirmed by the Spanish Constitutional Court in its Judgment 17/1991, of 21 January 1991 (*BOE* of 25 February 1991).

36 Most regional laws only refer to UCH located in the 'territory' of the region (*i.e.*, not comprising maritime waters which, *per definitionem*, are not comprised within the territory of a region): this applies to the Basque Country, Cantabria, Catalonia, Murcia, and Valencian Community. Some others, like the LPHE, do apply to the Continental Shelf (Andalusia, Asturias, and the Balearic Island). The most recent one (Galicia) only refers to the Territorial Sea; and the case of the Canary Islands refers to the Canary territory, which allegedly includes the 'Canary Waters', traced with straight lines by Law 44/2010, 30 December (*BOE* No. 318, 31 December 2010) but only for domestic purposes.

> Historical Heritage, whether or not it has been extracted and whether it is to be found on the surface or underground, *in territorial seas or on the continental shelf*. Geological and palaeontological elements relating to the history of man and his origins and background also form part of this heritage. (Emphasis added).[37]

When declared, UCH is generally located in what Spanish legislation (both central and regional) labels as an 'archaeological zone', that is, according to Article 15(5) LPHE:

> ... the place or natural landscape where there are movable or immovable properties that can be studied using archaeological methodology, whether or not they have been extracted and whether they are to be found on the surface, underground or below Spanish territorial waters.

There is hence a gap to be resolved, since Spanish UCH may be found up to the outer limit of Spain's Continental Shelf, but archaeological zones cannot be declared beyond the outer limit of the Territorial Sea (TS). In any case, as a by-product of the *de facto* compromise explained above (and a reflection of practical limitations on the material means available to the regions), none of the archaeological zones declared by regions are beyond the outer limit of the TS.[38]

Some regions have further implemented a very useful tool for the preservation of UCH: the 'archaeological preventive zone', which is a delimited space in which it is reasonable to infer the existence of elements of archaeological heritage for which the adoption of precautionary measures is necessary.[39] These preventive zones may include 'archaeological zones', which in turn may

---

37 Contrary to what was decided in the 2001 Convention (see Art. 1(1)), Spain does not include any temporal threshold nor exclude heritage 'still in use' in the definition of archaeological heritage. The legislation enacted by the different regions generally mirrors this definition, with special references to particular local heritage.

38 All zones declared by regions do not stray far from the coastline. Moreover, since 1977 (see *infra* n. 58), straight baselines traced by Spain expand internal waters to cover some of these coastal archaeological zones.

39 See the regional laws of Andalusia (Arts. 48–49, *zonas de servidumbre arqueológica*), Basque Country (Art. 65, *zona de presunción arqueológica*), Catalonia (Art. 49, *espacios de protección arqueológica*), and Valencian Community (Art. 58, *espacios de vigilancia arqueológica*). As a good example, the Andalusian government declared in May 2009 (with another 45 underwater zones) the entire archaeological site of the entrance and surroundings of the Bay of Cádiz, or the 1805 Trafalgar Battle site, with such a level of protection, which included mitigation measures, special permits, and public surveillance.

be protected through the highest preservation regime under Spanish law, that of 'Assets of Cultural Interest' (*Bienes de interés cultural,* BIC), declared either by the State or by a particular region and inscribed in the corresponding 'Register'.[40] Irrespective of being declared BIC, any archaeological element becomes public domain.[41]

BICs are declared by the operation of the Law or by Royal Decree (and analogous instruments at a regional level). By Royal Decree, the asset is protected individually and requires the prior opening and processing of an administrative file.[42] In the case of archaeological underwater sites, the LPHE (as well as regional laws) requires the competent authorities to delimit the affected area by the declaration and, where appropriate, to define and list the component parts, and any belongings and accessories included in the declaration.[43] An immovable property declared BIC is inseparable from its context, and cannot be moved unless this is essential for reasons of *force majeure* or public interest.[44] Local public authorities are bound to draw up an urban special plan for protection of the area.[45] Approval of this plan requires a favourable report from the competent (central or regional) administration.

Any activity directed at UCH must be duly authorised by the competent public authority, either State or regional corresponding authority.[46] Articles 376 and 377 LMN, besides misfortunate drafting,[47] requires the authorisation

---

40 Besides BICs, two other levels of protection are established inthe LPHE: the least is declaration as 'Spanish Historical Heritage', giving the minimum level of protection for an asset (Art. 1). A higher level is the inclusion of an element of cultural heritage in the 'General Inventory of Movable Property', for elements that possess a notable historical, archaeological, scientific, artistic, technical, or cultural value, and not declared BIC (Art. 26). In both cases, such elements, if in private hands, are subject to public inspection and temporary loan for study or exhibition, cannot be freely traded or exported, and the State has a right of pre-emption. Some regional legislation adds another denomination, that of 'Local valuable or relevant Assets' (*Bienes culturales de interés o relevancia local*) which implies (i) a local or regional relevance, (ii) the protection procedure file initiated by the municipalities, and (iii) a lesser, though important, level of protection than that of BICs.

41 Article 44(1) LPHE.

42 A favourable report is also required from any of the State (or respective region) cultural advisory institutions. Once the procedure of declaration begins, the asset receives the highest level of protection as a provisional mitigation measure, which will cease if not finally declared BIC.

43 Article 11(2) LPHE.

44 Article 18 LPHE.

45 Article 20 LPHE.

46 Articles 22 and 42 LPHE.

47 Based on grammatical (use of the term 'extraction'), contextual (included in the section of 'extractions' and without mentioning the particular case of UCH, as in the salvage

of the Navy for the operations of exploration, tracking, location, and recovery (*extracción*) of shipwrecked or sunken vessels or objects in internal maritime waters or in the Spanish TS. Later clarification requires that, if these vessels or objects are defined as UCH, Navy authorisation is to be obtained, although it does not substitute cultural authorities' permits.[48]

Each region establishes the particular prerequisites for issuing a permit, but in general they are all based on the fulfilment of several conditions: qualification standards for applicants,[49] in some cases a 'clean hand' prerequisite,[50] a comprehensive plan of activities,[51] and a continuous feedback process that completes the monitoring system.[52] The surveillance obligations of these cultural agencies are supported by the Navy and the Civil Guard (*Guardia Civil*), which has a specialised group (*Grupo de Patrimonio Histórico*), and naval equipment (*Servicio Marítimo*). Effectiveness has been increased since 2001 via the 'Integrated Off-shore Surveillance System' (*Sistema Integrado de Vigilancia Exterior,* SIVE), which includes a fixed and mobile array of radar, video, infrared and communication system along the coast, facilitating the early location, tracking, and identification of any suspicious vessel navigating in Spain's TS.[53]

---

section), and teleological (giving apparent exclusive competence to the Navy) reasons, these articles have received severe criticism from the archaeological community in Spain.

48 See Royal Decree 371/2020, 18 February 2020, approving the Regulation on Maritime Extractions (*BOE* No. 51, 28 February 2020), Art. 36.

49 Generally speaking, this means that the director of the activity has to be at least a postgraduate in humanities, history, archaeology, or hold a similar university degree. Some regional laws add a requirement for previous experience of underwater archaeology (Andalusia, Balearic Islands, Basque Country, Canary Islands, Cantabria, or Melilla). Curiously, not all legislation explicitly imposes a duty to have diving specialisation (only Andalusia, Cantabria, Catalonia, and Galicia), although it should be implied.

50 Some regional laws impose a prohibition on the authorisation of archaeological activities by those previously engaged in unauthorised or illicit archaeological activities (Asturias, Balearic Islands and Cantabria).

51 Including a detailed plan and chronograph of activities, areas, and objectives. Any change in this plan must be duly notified to the competent authorities. The latter might send aboard, when necessary, staff to survey the appropriate accomplishment of the plan.

52 This includes the notification of charts, results, electronic data, and any other information gathered by the activity, either on an *ad hoc* basis or in periodical reports. A complete inventory and record-book must be created, updated, and available for inspection by the authorities.

53 Initially created to monitor drug traffic in the Strait of Gibraltar, it was adapted to control illicit maritime migrancy and activities directed at any archaeological site, sensitive zones or protected marine installations. So far, it has been deployed on the Andalusian Coast, Balearic and Canary Islands, and some other Mediterranean and Galician areas.

Along Spain's coast, hundreds of 'archaeological zones' have been declared, including UCH (coastal or maritime), with significant numbers in Andalusia and the Balearic Islands. In addition, there are also declared 'archaeological preventive zones', with Andalusia again the leading region. This supposes that many relevant UCH sites are legally protected, with different levels of intensity, although geographical gaps remain, mostly in the north of the country.

3.2 *General Maritime Legislation*

Spain, as a maritime power, has ratified the more relevant law of the sea and maritime international conventions affecting UCH, ratifying LOSC in 1997,[54] and the 1989 Salvage Convention in 2005.[55]

3.2.1 Law of the Sea

Articles 149 and 303 LOSC, provide a minimal protection for UCH beyond the outer limit of the TS.[56] Coastal States' domestic legislation and further agreements on UCH complement and contextualise LOSC in this regard. Spain has enacted and/or declared most LOSC maritime zones:[57]

a. Law 10/1977 declared the Spanish TS up to 12 nm,[58] where Spain enjoys full sovereign rights, including those of exclusive regulation of activities directed to UCH.[59] Article 38 LMN subjects innocent passage through Spain's TS to respect domestic laws and regulations regarding the protection of UCH.

---

54 Spain had previously adhered to the four 1958 Geneva Conventions on 25 February 1971 (*BOE* of 24, 25 and 27 December 1971, in force for Spain on 27 March 1971).

55 International Convention on Salvage, adopted 28 April 1989, entered into force 14 July 1996, 1953 UNTS 165 (*BOE* No. 57, 8 March 2005, in force for Spain on 27 January 2006). Spain has not ratified the IMO Wreck Removal Convention 2008.

56 See T. Scovazzi, 'A Contradictory and Counterproductive Regime' in R. Garabello & T. Scovazzi (eds.) *The Protection of the Underwater Cultural Heritage, Before and After the 2001 UNESCO Convention* (Brill, 2003), pp. 3–17; M. They *La protection internationale du patrimoine culturel de la mer. Les compétences de l'État sur les biens culturels submergés* (Brill/Martinus Nijhoff, 2018), at pp. 101–169.

57 For different reasons (mainly political, but also legal, historical, and geographical), Spain has so far abstained to declare or delimit its maritime zones in the Strait of Gibraltar and northern Africa, including the Gibraltar Rock and the Spanish cities of Ceuta y Melilla, Perejil, Alhucemas and Chafarinas Islets, Vélez de la Gomera Rock. On the case of Gibraltar, see A. del Valle, 'Maritime Zones Around Gibraltar' (2017) 21 *Spanish Yearbook of International Law* 311.

58 Law 10/1977, of 4 January 1977, on the Territorial Sea (*BOE* of 8 January 1977). On the drawing of straight baselines, see Royal Decree 2510/1977, 5 August 1977 (*BOE* No. 234, 30 September 1977). For the Canary Islands, see Law 44/2010 above at note 34.

59 As expressed in Art. 2(1) LOSC, also referring to internal waters as sovereign waters.

b. Law 27/1992 declared a Spanish Contiguous Zone (CZ) up to 24 nm.[60] Its second Additional Provision gives the government competence to adopt the necessary control measures in order to prevent infringement of its customs, fiscal, immigration or sanitary laws and regulations within its territory or TS, as well as to sanction said infractions, without mentioning UCH as foreseen in Article 303(2) LOSC. However, the LMN introduced a novel provision in its Article 23(2), in line with Article 8 of the 2001 Convention:[61]

> Unauthorised extraction of archaeological and historic objects found on the seabed or subsoil of water in the contiguous zone shall be considered a breach of the laws and regulations referred to in the preceding Section, as well as of the provisions on underwater cultural heritage.

And Article 383(2) further establishes that:

> In all cases, administrative authorisation shall be required to extract archaeological or historic objects located on the seabed of the Spanish contiguous zone. Recovery of such goods without the required authorisation shall be penalised as an offence committed in Spanish territory.

c. Under Law 15/1978, Spain declared its Exclusive Economic Zone (EEZ) for the Atlantic coasts,[62] and by Royal Decree 236/2013 it did so for the eastern Mediterranean continental coast (from the limits with France to the Cape of Gata, south-east Spain), thus leaving undeclared the Balearic Islands and the southern coast facing Morocco (from Almeria to

60 Article 8(1) of Royal Legislative Decree 2/2011 of 5 September 2011, approving the consolidated text of the State Ports and Merchant Marine Act (*BOE* No. 253, 20 October 2011).

61 Art. 8 of the 2001 Convention says: 'Without prejudice to and in addition to Articles 9 and 10, and in accordance with Article 303, paragraph 2, of the United Nations Convention on the Law of the Sea, States Parties may regulate and authorize activities directed at underwater cultural heritage within their contiguous zone. In so doing, they shall require that the Rules be applied'. Arguably, this goes beyond LOSC. See M.J. Aznar, 'The Contiguous Zone as an Archaeological Maritime Zone' (2014) 29 *International Journal of Marine and Coastal Law* 1 and 'Article 8: Underwater cultural heritage in the contiguous zone', in T. Scovazzi and P. Vigni (eds), The 2001 UNESCO Convention on the protection of the underwater cultural heritage. A commentary (Oxford University Press, 2025, in print).

62 Law 15/1978, of 20 February 1978, on the Economic Exclusive Zone (*BOE* No. 46, 22 and 23 February 1978).

Càdiz).[63] No mention of UCH is made in these legislative acts regarding the Spanish EEZ. However, Article 383(1) LMN establishes that:

> Regulation and authorisation of activities related to the underwater cultural heritage in the Spanish contiguous zone, as well as authorisation of activities related to underwater cultural heritage in the exclusive economic zone and on the continental platform shall be governed by the terms set forth in the Convention on Protection of the Underwater Cultural Heritage of 2 November 2001 and other treaties to which Spain is a party, as well as the specific legislation.[64]

Combined, this regulation creates a new legal canvas upon which Spain exerts regulatory and enforcement jurisdiction on UCH in its internal waters, TS, and CZ; and subjects authorisation procedure in its EEZ to Articles 9 and 10 of the 2001 Convention.

3.2.2 Law of Salvage and Law of Finds

The law of salvage is not applicable to UCH in Spain. When ratifying the 1989 Salvage Convention in 2005, under Article 30(1)(d) Spain reserved the right not to apply its provisions when the property involved is maritime cultural property of prehistoric, archaeological, or historic interest and is situated on the seabed.[65] The LMN finally clarified this in Article 358(3):

> Any operation whatsoever related to the underwater cultural heritage shall not be considered salvage, as shall be governed by its specific legislation and the international treaties in force to which Spain is a party.[66]

---

63 Royal Decree 236/2013, 5 April 2013, establishing the Spanish Exclusive Economic Zone in the North-West Mediterranean (*BOE* No. 92, 17 April 2013).

64 Existing *ipso jure* by Art. 76(1) LOSC, Spain has not declared its Continental Shelf as such but as already seen, cultural and maritime legislation mentions it regarding UCH protection.

65 That is, Spain *reserved the option* not to apply the Salvage Convention rules, which were not thus definitively precluded in 2005. See the declaration of Spain at *Status of IMO Treaties*, 10 January 2022, available at <https://wwwcdn.imo.org/localresources/en/About/Conventions/StatusOfConventions/Status%20-%202022.pdf>.

66 For the case of recoveries of shipwrecks or other objects located in the bottom of the navigation zones, Art. 369(3) LMN establishes that '[e]xcept for specific provision otherwise in the rules of this Chapter, its rules shall not be applicable to the underwater cultural heritage, which shall be governed by its specific implementing regulations'. For any kind of extractions, a similar limitation exists (Art. 381 LMN).

Regarding the law of finds, it is noteworthy that Article 44(1) LPHE, establishes that:

> All objects and material remains possessing the values of the Spanish Historical Heritage that are discovered as a result of excavations, earth moving or works of any type or by chance are considered public domain. The discoverer shall notify the appropriate Administration of the discovery within a maximum period of thirty days and immediately in the case of casual finds. Under no circumstances shall the provisions of article 351 of the Civil Code be applicable to such finds.[67]

Therefore, as an archaeological element, UCH is thus declared public domain and, as such, *out of the stream of commerce*.[68] This was previously regulated under Law 60/1962[69] (legislation prior to the LMN on finds and salvage) which expressly excluded its application 'to the objects that, by their nature or by legal rules, are exempted from free commerce and which shall be governed by special dispositions on the subject'.[70] However, although the legal concept of 'treasure' is inapplicable to UCH,[71] a reward to finders is still foreseen in Article 44(3) LPHE, under which:

> The discoverer and the owner of the place where the object was found are entitled, as a cash prize, to half of the value attributed to it in the legal appraisal, which will be distributed between them in equal parts. If

67 In accordance with Art. 41(3) of the same Law, '[d]iscoveries of objects and material remains which, having the values of the Spanish Historical Heritage, have taken place by chance or as a result of any type of earth moving, demolition or work of any type are considered chance finds'. See also *infra* n. 71.

68 Under Art. 132 of the Constitution, the land-maritime domain, the beaches, the TS, and the natural resources located in the EEZ and on the CS belong to the public domain. This core principle has been developed by the Law 22/1988, of 28 July 1988, on the Coasts (*BOE* No. 181, 29 July 1998). In its art. 3 this Law qualifies this domain as 'public domain of the State'.

69 Law 60/1962, of 24 December 1962, which regulates aid, salvage, towage, finds and maritime extractions (*BOE* No. 310, 27 December 1962).

70 Article 22(3)) of Law 60/1962.

71 Art. 351 of the Spanish Civil Code, which permits the acquisition of property by find (*tesoro*), states: 'Hidden treasure shall pertain to the owner of the land in which it is found. Notwithstanding the foregoing, if the discovery were to be made by chance in another's property, or in State property, half shall correspond to the discoverer. If the objects discovered were to be of interest to science or art, the State may acquire them for their fair value, which shall be distributed pursuant to the above provisions'.

there are two or more discoverers or owners, the same proportion will be maintained.

Unfortunately, this is applicable to UCH as well. However, some particularities included in Article 44 LPHE deserve to be underlined: first, UCH shall always be found, *per definitionem,* in the public domain (the maritime domain), so the 'owner of the place where the object was found' shall always be the State. Second, finds must be by chance, and normally 'finders' (mostly treasure hunters) do not find by chance. Third, in order to receive the reward, the finder has the duty to 'immediately' notify the chance find and:

> ... until the objects are handed over to the competent authority, the rules on a legal deposit will apply to the finder, unless the objects are given to a public museum.[72]

Fourth, failure to comply with these two conditions, apart from resulting in the forfeiture of the right to a reward,[73] converts the discovery process into an illegal activity, punishable by law.

4 Spain and the 2001 Convention

4.1 *General Attitude and the Negotiation Process*

Initially, Spain joined the so-called 'like-minded' group of States during UNESCO negotiations, due to its status as a maritime power, with UCH located far from its coasts.[74] This led Spain to support a strong regime of protection for UCH, irrespective of its location and the passage of time. However, as negotiations evolved, so did Spain's position. Spain had two objectives: on the one

---

72 Paragraph 2. In accordance with the Civil Code, the depository has stringent duties of custody and conservation.

73 Paragraph 4.

74 The three basic initial assumptions of the 'like-minded' members were the defence of the rights and interests of flag States *vis à vis* the claims of the coastal States, the need to establish a clear link between the new Convention and LOSC, and the defence of consensus instead of voting procedures during the negotiations. See J.A. de Yturriaga Barberán, 'Convención sobre la protección del patrimonio cultural subacuático' in Zlata Drnas de Clément (Coord.) *Estudios de Derecho Internacional en homenaje al Profesor Ernesto J. Rey Caro* (Dirnas-Lernes Ed., 2002) pp. 451–460; C. Espósito and C. Fraile, 'The UNESCO Convention on Underwater Cultural Heritage: A Spanish View' in D.D. Caron and H.N. Scheiber (eds.) *Bringing New Law to Ocean Waters* (Brill, 2004) pp. 201–223; and M.J. Aznar-Gómez *La protección del patrimonio cultural subacuático* (Tirant, 2004).

hand, to favour the adoption of a universal convention, even at the cost of compromising on some of its views; and, on the other, to complement the Convention with subsequent bilateral or regional agreements in order to improve the protection of Spanish UCH.

Concerning jurisdiction, although Spain preferred not to recognise new powers to coastal States beyond those granted by LOSC, it was prepared to afford them a primary co-ordinating function in the zones under their jurisdiction (including the EEZ).[75] At the same time, Spain was in favour of the recognition of certain specific rights to those States that could prove a cultural, historical, or archaeological link with a particular wreck. Last, but not least, Spain firmly supported the inclusion of a provision containing an express recognition of special rights for flag States over sunken State vessels, such as prior consent to begin activities directed at UCH, and a right to be consulted and informed on those activities.

However, negotiations drove Spain to an uncomfortable position (shared by other historical maritime powers) confronting the Latin-American group of the Group of 77 at the UN. Once sunken State vessels were accepted as possible UCH, and given that the majority rejected the inclusion of a sovereign immunity clause, Spain preferred a reasonably privileged regime without prejudice to the flag State's rights of sovereign immunity under international law, even without an express recognition of sovereign immunity.[76] Spain finally opted for an intermediate position resulting in the special regime for State vessels with different requirements depending on the maritime zone involved, on the understanding that the 2001 Convention does not affect title on sunken State vessels.[77] The Spanish position remained thus arguably safeguarded by Articles 1(8), 2(8) and (11), and 3 of the 2001 Convention.

---

75 In the early stage of negotiations, Spain proposed the establishment of a 100-mile zone of protection for UCH (UNESCO General Conference Doc. 28 C/39, 15 October 1995). It has been mentioned that "[a]pparently, this was a proposal originated in the Ministry of Culture, and was not negotiated with other Ministries, such as Foreign Affairs and Fisheries. By the first UNESCO meeting on the UCH, the Spanish position was rectified, and it was clear that Spain rejected the recognition of any maritime zone other than those established by the UNCLOS." Espósito and Fraile, *supra* n. 74, at p. 206.

76 The 2001 Convention eventually included a *réenvoi* clause in its Art. 2(8), upon which, '[c]onsistent with State practice and international law, including the United Nations Convention on the Law of the Sea, nothing in this Convention shall be interpreted as modifying the rules of international law and State practice pertaining to sovereign immunities, nor any State's rights with respect to its State vessels and aircraft'.

77 This included the acceptance of the famous terms '*should* inform' instead of '*shall* inform' (the later preferred by Spain) finally incorporated into Art. 7(3) for sunken State vessels located in internal waters, archipelagic waters and the Territorial Sea, which does not affect title, however. Regarding the EEZ, the CS and the Area, Arts. 10(7) and 12(7) should pre-empt any activity directed at Spanish sunken State vessels located in these areas without its consent.

4.2 *Adoption, Implementation, and Cooperation*

Having voted in favour of its adoption on 2 November 2001, Spain was an early ratifier of the 2001 Convention.[78] The instrument of ratification was deposited with the UNESCO Director-General on 6 June 2005 and the 2001 Convention entered into force for Spain on 2 January 2009.[79] Upon official publication,[80] it formed part of Spanish domestic law.[81] Under the Spanish legal system, international law has primacy over domestic law.

4.2.1 Administrative Questions

Amid the *Mercedes* and *Louisa* cases, on 10 October 2007, the Historical Heritage Council (*Consejo de Patrimonio Histórico*, CPH), the body that coordinates the actions carried out in Spain in the field of cultural heritage, and which includes representatives of the State and all the regions, endorsed the 'National Plan for the Protection of the Spanish Underwater Cultural Heritage' prepared by the Ministry of Culture. On 30 November 2007, the Government approved said Plan. The CPH decided on 12 December 2007 to create a Working Group to draft the Plan's documented programme. The working group, made up of specialists on UCH from the Ministry of Culture, the regions, universities and museums, completed its work on 14 May 2009. The final document was approved by the Historical Heritage Council on 16 July 2009, as was a Green Paper on the National Plan.[82] It proposed a roadmap for Spain's underwater archaeology and the protection of UCH, both domestically and internationally. It foresees activities and decisions regarding:

1. documentation and inventory, such as preparation of UCH charts of the entire coastline, or the design and implementation of a programme for the Integrated Management of Geographical Information of UCH;
2. adoption of physical and legal protective measures, including declaration of new UCH BIC s and other preservation actions;

---

78 In April 2003, the Convention was authorised under Art. 94(1) of the Constitution, which requires a simple majority in the Parliament. This may be seen as a message to current States on former Spanish territories in America and Asia showing Spain's willingness to co-operate in the protection of shared heritage.

79 Articles 26(3) and 27 of the Convention.

80 *BOE* No. 55, 5 March 2009. Spain did not make any reservation under Art. 29 of the Convention (Limitation of geographical scope), nor declared as yet the application of the Annex to inland waters not of maritime character (Art. 28), the procedure of communication of finds under Art. 9(1), or any specific procedure for the peaceful settlement of disputes (Art. 25). The Ministry of Culture is the competent authority in relation to UCH under Art. 22(2).

81 Article 96(1) of the Constitution.

82 Text available in English at <https://www.libreria.culturaydeporte.gob.es/libro/green-paper-national-plan-for-the-protection-of-underwater-cultural-heritage_1040/>.

3. training activities for specialists in research and conservation of UCH, both Spanish and foreign;[83]
4. adoption of coordination measures, including creation of interdepartmental coordination commissions,[84] preparation of an archaeological action protocol for port infrastructures, active use of the Guardia Civil and Armada vessels and other infrastructures,[85] and the negotiation of agreements with other nations;[86]
5. strengthening the role of specialised regional underwater archaeology centres in collaboration with ARQVA (currently those in Andalusia, Catalonia, and Valencian Community), and the planning and performance of prospecting and excavation campaigns in Spain and elsewhere;[87] and
6. design of an outreach and dissemination plan on UCH for the general public.

4.2.2 Legislative Implementation

Pending amendment or re-drafting of the LPHE,[88] the governance of UCH in Spain has been updated and adapted to new circumstances, including the

83 Besides specific workshops and international meetings held in different Spanish cities, Latin-American countries and the Philippines, the University of Cádiz offers a Masters in Nautical and Underwater Archaeology' (for more information see <https://eidemar.uca.es/masters/?lang=en>). This same University, as well as the University of Valencia, the Catalonia's Centre for Underwater Archaeology, and the University Jaume I, are partners of the UNESCO UNITWIN Network for Underwater Archaeology (for more information see <http://www.underwaterarchaeology.net>).

84 The Ministry of Culture has signed interdepartmental agreements regarding UCH with the Ministry of Defence on the collaboration of the Armada (9 July 2009), with the Ministry of the Interior, aimed at applying the SIVE and the response by the Guardia Civil (11 December 2011), and with the Ministry of Foreign Affairs and AECID on the foreign coordination activities (31 August 2011). The central Government has signed different collaboration agreements on the development of the National Plan with the regional governments of Andalusia (*BOE* No. 300, 10 December 2010), the Balearic Islands and Galicia (*BOE* No. 5, 6 January 2011), and Catalonia and the autonomous city of Ceuta (*BOE* No. 27, 1 February 2011).

85 Besides the mention on the uses of SIVE/Guardia Civil (see *ibid* and n. 53), on 5 November 2021, the Armada commissioned the construction of a new 5,000-ton Underwater Intervention Maritime Action Vessel (BAM-IS), operatively expected for May 2025. It will add value to current civil scientific vessel M/V *Sarmiento de Gamboa*, belonging to the Spanish National Research Council (CSIC) (<http://www.utm.csic.es/en/instalaciones/sdg>). For more information on the new navy vessel in English see <https://www.navalia.es/en/news/sectors-news/2434-offshore-patrol-vessel-bam-is-will-be-built-at-navantia-cadiz>.

86 See below section 4.2.3.

87 Mainly in the hands or under supervision of public institutions. Spain still lacks a more developed network of private operators involved in all these activities regarding UCH.

88 While writing this contribution, a first proposal has circulated and received numerous comments, criticisms, and counter-proposals. On UCH protection and management, this

ratification of the 2001 Convention, by new legislation, either central (mainly the 2014 LMN) and regional.

Some other rules were already implemented in international and domestic legislation.[89] This is particularly the case for the *in situ* rule. In addition to the 2001 Convention (Article 2(5) and Rule 1 of the Annex), Articles 4 and 5 of the 1992 Valetta Convention,[90] and the 2008 ICZM Protocol to the 1985 Barcelona Convention (Article 13(2)),[91] mention the *in situ* rule as an already accepted archaeological and legal principle.[92] Domestically, with different wording and diverse extent, almost all coastal regions had included the rule in their legislation: the Basque Country in its Law 7/1990, Catalonia in its Law 9/1993, Valencian Community in its Law 4/1998, Balearic Islands in its Law 12/1998, Canary Islands in its Law 4/1999, and Andalusia in its Law 14/2007; and more explicitly Cantabria in its Law 11/1998, Murcia in its Law 4/2007, and Galicia in its Law 5/2016. Article 1 of Royal Decree 371/2020 on Maritime Extractions also imposes *in situ* preservation, but only for Spanish sunken State vessels and justified by the non-disturbance of human remains rule.[93] To solve this gap, it is expected the rule will be included *expressis verbis* in forthcoming revision of the LPHE.[94]

---

author drafted a report for the Ministry of Culture and ICOMOS Spain proposing a complete re-drafting of the Law, aimed at a better regulation not only of UCH but to intangible heritage, landscapes, *in situ* preservation, and other related questions.

89 The Spanish Supreme Court has accepted the 'self-executing' nature of some treaty provisions, such as the *in situ* rule might be, if their wording is precise enough for its direct application without the need for further legal and regulatory development, and that it represents the will of the contracting States (STS 1613/1998, 10 March 1998, legal ground No. 6) (ROJ 1613/1998).

90 European Convention on the Protection of the Archaeological Heritage (Revised), adopted 16 January 1992, entered into force 25 May 1995, *CETS* No. 143 (*BOE* No. 173, 20 July 2011, into force for Spain on 1 October 2011).

91 Protocol on Integrated Coastal Zone Management, adopted 21 January 2008, entered into force 24 March 2011 [2009] EU OJ L34/19 (*BOE* No. 70, 23 March 2011, into force for Spain on 24 March 2011).

92 See M.J. Aznar, 'In Situ Preservation of Underwater Cultural Heritage as an International Legal Principle' (2018) 13 *Journal of Marine Archaeology* 67.

93 See *supra* n. 48. Article 31 reads as follows: '1. The remains of shipwrecked or sunken Spanish State ships and vessels that constitute permanent burial places for their crews must be respected as such, avoiding unnecessarily disturbing human remains and venerated sites. 2. To make this duty of respect effective, *in situ* conservation will be the priority criterion for the protection of the remains and their extraction may only be carried out when, in addition to the situations in which it is necessary for the safety of the navigation, there are historical, cultural, vulnerability or other reasons that make it necessary or convenient'.

94 Meanwhile, Art. 18 of this law implied the application of the *in situ* rule, but only referring to BICS.

Two main mitigation tools are being used to comply with the duty under Art. 5 of the 2001 Convention to use:

> … the best practicable means at its disposal to prevent or mitigate any adverse effects that might arise from activities under its jurisdiction incidentally affecting underwater cultural heritage.

First, as noted, the creation and development of 'archaeological preservation zones' in different coastal areas; and second, the obligation to perform environmental and archaeological impact assessments. Though environmental assessments have a longstanding tradition in Spanish legislation, reports on archaeological impact evaluation began with Article 20(1) LPHE, with its initial development criticised.[95] In recent decades there has been improvement in its performance, evaluation and feedback.[96] However, these assessments need an adequate adjustment to UCH particularities,[97] avoiding the current practice of treating a lack of objection being raised within a certain period (or administrative silence) as tacit approval.

Other duties imposed by the 2001 Convention, such as the control of illicit traffic,[98] and sanctions for violation of measures taken to implement the Convention,[99] deserve better reflection in Spanish legislation.[100] Regarding illicit traffic, Organic Law 12/1995,[101] correctly typifies smuggling of cultural heritage

---

95 See, for example, M.A. Cerdeño, A. Castillo and T. Sagardoy, 'The Environmental Impact Law and its Effectiveness on the Archaeological Heritage in Spain' (2005) 62/2 *Trabajos de prehistoria* 25 (in Spanish). For subsequent years see R. Ruiz Manteca, 'La evaluación de impacto ambiental y su componente arqueológica subacuática. Aspectos jurídico-prácticos', in X. Nieto and M. Bethencourt (coord.) *Arqueología subacuática española: Actas del I Congreso de Arqueología Náutica y Subacuática Española* (Universidad de Cádiz, 2014), pp. 321–330.

96 For the case of Andalusia, up to 2013, see M. Alzaga and C. García, 'La protección del patrimonio arqueológico subacuático ante actividades legítimas' in X. Nieto, R. Belinchón and P. Prieto (eds.) *Congreso de Arqueología Náutica y Subacuática Española* (Ministerio de Educación Cultura y deporte, 2013), pp. 1040–1053.

97 Sometimes, the lack of qualified personnel and technology make it impracticable to undertake a complete and *ad hoc* assessment of the impact of coastal and marine activities on UCH.

98 Article 14.

99 Article 17.

100 See J.J. Periago Morant and M.J. Aznar Gómez, 'Expolio del patrimonio cultural subacuático: régimen jurídico en España', in *El expolio de bienes culturales* (Universidad de Huelva, 2022), pp. 167-198.

101 Law 12/1995, 12 December 1995, on Repression of Smuggling (*BOE* No. 297, 13 December 1995).

in line with EU Directive 93/7/EEC,[102] and complemented by the 1970 Illicit Traffic Convention,[103] the 1995 UNIDROIT Convention,[104] and Regulation (EU) 2019/880.[105] Regarding general criminal sanctions, the Penal Code includes, in Articles 321–324, a criminal regime for UCH that certainly could be improved (particularly in relation to the identification of various types of damage to archaeological sites constituting a criminal offence).[106] Heritage legislation, both central and regional, on administrative sanctions such as confiscation, damages, reparation and penalty fees, should in this author's view be revised and, perhaps, increased. For example, they could be complemented with a temporary professional disqualification (as Andalusia and Asturias' legislation provides) or a temporary suspension for public servants involved in illicit activities; the revocation of authorisations regarding any activity related to cultural heritage (including UCH); the suspension or revocation of copyrights related to scientific heritage activities (such as those related to the publication of results); and/or the reimbursement of public financial aid received. All these measures have been proposed via revision of the LPHE.

4.2.3 International Cooperation

Article 2(2) and (4) of the 2001 Convention enshrine international cooperation as one of its landmark features, specified in, for example, Articles 9–12 (cooperation system), 19 (information sharing) and 21 (training in underwater archaeology). Article 6(1) of the Convention is instrumental to these types of international cooperation. It foresees and encourages States Parties:

> ... to enter into bilateral, regional or other multilateral agreements or develop existing agreements, for the preservation of underwater cultural heritage. All such agreements shall be in full conformity with the provisions of this Convention and shall not dilute its universal character.

---

102 Council Directive 93/7/EEC, 15 March 1993, on the return of cultural objects unlawfully removed from the territory of a Member State (OJ L074, 27 March 1993).

103 Convention on the Means of Prohibiting and Preventing the Illicit Import, Export and Transfer of Ownership of Cultural Property, adopted on 14 November 1970, 823 UNTS 231, entered into force 24 April 1972 (*BOE* No. 31, 5 February 1986, into force for Spain on 10 April 1986).

104 UNIDROIT Convention on Stolen or Illegally Exported Cultural Objects, adopted 24 June 1995, 2421 UNTS 457, entered into force 1 July 1998 (*BOE* No. 248, 16 October 2002, into force for Spain on 1 November 2002).

105 Regulation (EU) 2019/880 of the European Parliament and of the Council of 17 April 2019 on the introduction and the import of cultural goods [2019] OJ L151, 7 June 2019.

106 See A. Núñez Sánchez, 'La nueva regulación penal del delito de expolio de yacimientos arqueológicos' in C. Guisasola Lerma (dir.) *Expolio de Bienes Culturales. Instrumentos Legales Frente al Mismo* (Tirant, 2018), pp. 166–198.

> States may, in such agreements, adopt rules and regulations which would ensure better protection of underwater cultural heritage than those adopted in this Convention.

Spain has sought various such agreements, not just in 'hard' form (treaties) but also 'soft' ones, such as Memoranda of Understanding (MoU), particularly with States Parties historically linked to Spain (Hispanic-American countries and the Philippines), and maritime powers sharing its concerns on UCH (including title and jurisdictional questions). To this extent, Spain has entered into MoUs with heritage agencies in Mexico (2014) and the US (2010 and 2013) and has proposed a MoU with Colombia regarding the wreck of the *San José* and with Ecuador, Panama, Ireland and Croatia on UCH general cooperation.

In addition, besides permanently financing UCH activities at UNESCO, Spain, mainly through the *Agencia Española de Cooperación Internacional* (AECID), has funded numerous international cultural and outreach activities, workshops, training courses, and other initiatives on the protection of UCH, most particularly in Hispanic-America and the Philippines.

Last but not least, under the cooperative system created by Articles 9 and 10 of the 2001 Convention, Spain decided to declare itself as an 'interested' State in order to be consulted on the Skerki Banks Project, coordinated by Tunisia since 2018 in collaboration with Algeria, Croatia, Egypt, France, Italy, and Morocco.[107]

5 Conclusion

More than 20 years have passed since adoption of the 2001 Convention. In 2021, a revision of its outcomes was published, and an evaluation from the Meeting of States Parties to the Convention is underway.[108] More than a decade after its entry into force, Spain has significantly improved its legal and institutional framework, as well as its infrastructures and programmes regarding the protection and management of UCH. Funds allocated to research, preservation and dissemination activities have also increased, significantly so in particular

107 See <https://www.unesco.org/en/skerki-bank-mission>. Spain proposed (unsuccessfully) to organise this cooperation through the signature of a MoU.

108 See 'Evaluation of UNESCO's standard-setting work of the Culture Sector, part VI – 2001 Convention on the Protection of Underwater Cultural Heritage', UNESCO Doc. IOS /EVS/PI/174 REV, available at: <https://unesdoc.unesco.org/ark:/48223/pf0000368446 .locale=es>.

regions, Andalusia, and Catalonia for example; as has the collaboration, financial and material, of other ministries, including Defence, Interior, and Foreign Affairs. However, all these efforts need to be continued, revisited and enhanced.

Among possible additional mitigation measures, during the process of the amendment of the LPHE, the International Council on Monuments and Sites National Committee in Spain (ICOMOS-Spain) has proposed through its national members of the ICOMOS International Committee on the Underwater Cultural Heritage (ICUCH) the prohibition of metal detectors in the entire coastal public domain, unless otherwise expressly authorised by competent authorities.[109] Closely linked to the use of metal detectors, it was also proposed to eliminate the finder's reward in all cases and irrespective of compliance with a finder's obligations under the law. Having removed salvage law from the UCH equation, the law of finds should also be removed as an attractive excuse for those commercially exploiting or looting cultural heritage. Social recognition could be however encouraged, as has been done, for example, with the *Bou Ferrer* wreck's finders.[110]

On foreign activities, besides the continued effort made by the Ministry of Culture, fully supported by the Main Legal Advisor's Office in the Ministry of Foreign Affairs, several proposals could be (and have been) made regarding the negotiation and signature of MoU with more countries, following the Mexico and US models.[111] Another legal tool, still unexplored and only for Mediterranean waters,[112] might be proposals for sites designated as a 'Specially Protected Area of Mediterranean Importance' (SPAMI) under Section 2 of the Protocol Concerning Specially Protected Areas and Biological Diversity in the

---

109 For example, Art. 101 of Galicia's regional legislation establishes a limited regime for their use, including the negative effect of administrative silence on applications for permits. See A. Yáñez Vega and J.I. Rodríguez Temiño (eds.) *El expoliar se va a acabar: uso de detectores de metales y arqueología: sanciones administrativas y penales* (Tirant, 2018).

110 The *Bou Ferrer*, a Roman merchant ship, wrecked in the mid-first century A.D. off the coast of Villajoyosa, Alicante. was found in 2001 by two local divers, who communicated the find to the competent authorities, thus beginning an on-going project of *in situ* preservation, curation, and dissemination. It was declared as BIC on 18 September 2015. See more information at <https://www.bouferrer.org/en/about>.

111 In addition to those already mentioned other possible MoUs with a more complex situation may be those with Colombia, Uruguay and the Philippines.

112 This could be the case of the Skerki Banks project, as proposed by Spain but still unresolved. See *supra* n. 107.

Mediterranean to the Barcelona Convention.[113] Its Article 3(1)(a) requires State Parties to:

> … protect, preserve and manage in a sustainable and environmentally sound way areas of particular natural or *cultural value*, notably by the establishment of specially protected areas. (Emphasis added).

These areas, if located within the TS of a State, could be unilaterally proposed by a coastal State, and included in the SPAMI list once agreed by a meeting of States Parties to the Protocol.[114] Linked with this model, ICOMOS-Spain has proposed, again through national members of ICUCH, to include in future amending of the LPHE the possibility for the State to create 'archaeological preservation zones'.

These proactive measures need to be accompanied by a vigorous and assertive policy against treasure hunting (domestically and abroad), as well as continuous efforts as part of Spain's foreign cultural policy to respect and promote the 2001 Convention elsewhere. The negotiation and signature of MoUs with other States linked with, or interested in, Spanish UCH is a bold part of this foreign policy. However, much remains to be done, particularly in the internal sphere, where it is expected that reform of the LPHE will allow a critical review and an accurate evaluation of the legal and institutional tools for Spain to better protect and manage UCH.

All websites last accessed February 2025.

Acknowledgements

The views expressed in this chapter are solely those of the author, and do not represent the views of the Kingdom of Spain, nor of the ICUCH/ICOMOS. This contribution revisits, updates, completes, and sometimes corrects the chapter on Spain published in the 2nd edition.

113 Protocol Concerning Specially Protected Areas and Biological Diversity in the Mediterranean, adopted on 10 June 1995, in force since 12 December 1999, OJ L322, 14 December 1999 (into force for Spain on 23 December 1998, *BOE* No. 302, 18 December 1999).

114 Article 9.

Selected Bibliography

Álvarez González, E.M., *La protección jurídica del patrimonio cultural subacuático en España* (Tirant, 2012).

Aznar, M.J. *La protección del patrimonio cultural subacuático* (Tirant, 2004).

Aznar, M.J. 'La aplicación de la Convención UNESCO de 2001 sobre la protección del patrimonio cultural subacuático: algunos problemas nacionales e internacionales', in Castro Ruano, J.L. at al (eds.), *Curso de Derecho Internacional y Relaciones Internacionales de Vitoria Gasteiz 2022* (Tirant, 2023), pp. 122–177.

Crespo Solana, A., Castro, F. and Nayling, N. (eds) *Heritage and the Sea. Maritime History and Archaeology of the Global Iberian World (15th-18th centuries)* (2 vols, Springer, 2022).

Fernández Duro, C. *Armada Española: desde la unión de los Reinos de Castilla y León* (9 vols., Museo Naval de Madrid, 1972–1973).

Ruiz Manteca, R. *Régimen jurídico del patrimonio cultural subacuático* (Ministerio de Defensa, 2013).

CHAPTER 18

Sweden

Thomas Adlercreutz *

1 Background

Statutory measures for the general protection of ancient remains in Sweden were adopted as far back as the seventeenth century. Modern provisions protecting historic wrecks, however, have been existence for merely 57 years. This may seem surprising in light of the spectacular salvage in 1961 of the seventeenth century man-of-war *Vasa*, and its subsequent careful restoration, now to be seen in Stockholm's most visited museum.[1] It is also surprising considering that the brackish waters of the Baltic Sea, in which most of Sweden's Territorial Sea is to be found, provide excellent physical conditions for the natural preservation of the plentiful wooden wreckage deposited over the years by bad weather and naval action. So, for a long time there was a striking discrepancy between a strict cultural heritage regime on land and a total lack of protective rules for remains underwater.

1.1 *Early History*

Records from the sixteenth century show that the Kings of Sweden were interested in ancient remains. In 1599, royal instructions were issued to tour the land to document stones with runic inscriptions.[2] Other missions followed, and in a memorandum of 1630 the scope of the inventory was widened to comprise many elements of what we today think of as cultural heritage. The first instrument for legal protection of ancient remains dates from 1666 – a royal decree of that year, dedicated to the 'immortal glory of the realm', prohibited carelessness with and destruction of ancient 'monuments' and 'antiquities'.[3]

* Former legal counsel to the National Heritage Board of Sweden.

1 <https://sverigesmuseer.se/wp-content/uploads/2023/09/hogsasong-pa-museerna-1.pdf> p. 5. The out-of-doors museum Skansen has more visitors.

2 Torsten Fogelqvist '*Svensk kulturminnesvård. Ett trehundraårsminne*' (2nd edn, 1930), p. 14.

3 The decree seems to have excepted land bestowed of old on the nobility. The decree is sometimes in Sweden hailed as "the oldest antiquities legislation in the world". A deconstruction of that thesis can be found in Thomas Adlercreutz, *The Swedish Royal Placat of 1666. The First Antiquities Legislation in the World?*, Art Antiquity and Law, Volume XXVI Issue 2 2021.

 | DOI:10.1163/9789004510883_020

Furthermore, the decree ordered the repair and conservation of damaged remains. However, there was no mention of remains situated underwater.

Prior to this, there was also a royal interest in valuable finds of precious metals. In Sweden, unlike in Denmark, there was probably never an unconditional royal prerogative right to treasure trove, i.e., finds of gold and silver.[4] The first nationwide Swedish codification, issued in 1350 and 1357, laid down the provision that rare finds on land and shore accrued by two-thirds to the King and one-third the finder.[5] Finds from sea – or lakebed, however, were to be divided equally between King and finder, no doubt as reflection of the greater trouble involved in making finds under difficult conditions.[6] One of the provincial codes,[7] approximately simultaneous with the national code, had the same provisions for finds from sea – and lakebed, but also an interesting exception for wrecks. For unclear reasons, wrecks, unlike other finds from the seabed, would fall by two-thirds to the King, and the remaining third to the finder, i.e., the same partitioning as the national code stipulated for rare finds on land or shore.[8]

Preservation of cultural heritage was not a feature of these early provisions and there is no hint of an intention to glorify the realm, such as the one quoted from the decree of 1666. In that vein, however, in 1684 another royal decree was conceived in which references were made to the old rules for the partitioning of finds in the national code. This decree introduced an element of protection – finders were prohibited from dispersing, melting or in any other way transmuting rare finds. All finds were to be delivered to the Crown, which would then reimburse finders for their share.[9] From the seventeenth century onwards, valuable finds would thus not simply be disposed of for profit but kept in the Royal Treasury and later in museums.

Arguably, the fact that finders received just one-third, or, at best, half the value of the find was likely detrimental to the dutiful reporting of finds. The rules on finder's award were changed in the national codification of 1734. Finds from lake or sea, and other buried hoards, were now to be divided *equally* between *landowner* and finder. Finds of gold and silver (treasure trove) the

4 It should be noted that the Scandinavian countries have had somewhat different concepts of treasure trove than those of the common law of England, Wales and Northern Ireland.

5 Magnus Erikssons allmänna landslag, Tjuvamålsbalken XXXI, and Stadslag, Tjuvamålsbalken XI.

6 Bengt Thordeman 'Skattfyndsregalet i Sverige och Danmark' (1945) 23 *Fornvännen* 190.

7 Östgötalagen, Byggningabalken XXXVII.

8 Thordeman, *Op. cit.* p. 190.

9 *Ibid.* p. 194, I.A. Hedenvind 'Fornfynd och hembudsplikt' in *Ad patriam illustrandam* (1946) p. 37.

finder would have to deliver to the Crown, but then reimbursement was set at the full value plus an increment of one-eighth.[10]

A royal decree of 1827 amalgamated both the older rules for protection of ancient remains and the duty to turn in finds for redemption by the Crown. The latter was expanded in scope: "Anyone, who finds old coins, or older works of gold, silver, copper, metal, stone and wood, or other pieces of art, *either in the soil or in water ...*" had to deliver the find and was – if the Crown decided to keep it – entitled to compensation for the value plus one-eighth. A decree in 1867 retained in different wording the gist of the earlier provisions, but an amendment in 1873 withdrew items of metal (thus also bronze), stone and wood from the duty to report and deliver. There remained no mention of wrecks, to which only general provisions under the law of the sea would be applicable.

1.2 *Development of Present Rules*

Parliament had not been involved in the earlier rules on ancient remains but demands for reform in the 1920s and 1930s led to adoption in 1942 of the Ancient Monuments Act.[11] This Act strengthened the Crown's position with regard to finds. Ownerless objects found on or in connection with a protected ancient monument were proclaimed to become Crown property. Since wrecks were still not considered for inclusion in the categories of protected monuments this provision meant little for objects pertaining to sunken ships. Regarding finds in general, the old rules were retained in essence as concerns finds of gold, silver, and copper, but the provisions were edited differently. An age requirement was introduced: all ownerless objects more than 100 years of age and found in places other than on or near protected ancient monuments, were to accrue to the finder, although this person was under a duty to report the find for redemption by the Crown if the object in question consisted wholly or partly of gold, silver or copper, or was found adjacent to such an object. The mention of a finding place "in the soil or in water" was omitted, although it is doubtful if this omission was intended to lead to any change of the earlier scope of application. An important change was that a finder's reward could be given, in addition to the lawful compensation, which remained at 112.5% (100 + 1/8) for redeemed finds.

10 The introduction of the landowner on the receiving end, replacing the King was probably an influence of Roman law, but a similar order had been practiced in the Middle Ages both on Iceland and on Gotland, where there was no King or the King was weak, Thordeman, *Op. cit.* p. 197.

11 Proposition (Government Bill) 1942:8, Svensk författningssamling 1942:350.

In the 1940s and 1950s, as scuba divers became active in larger numbers, protection against undue exploration of, and the causing of damage to wrecks and other underwater remains, became an increasing concern. The *Vasa* story raised political and public awareness of the value of this hidden heritage. A memorandum published in 1965 by the Ministry of Justice as a result of initiatives from the National Heritage Board and the National Maritime Museum, stated that the existing rules were less than satisfactory in providing protection for shipwrecks and other cultural objects from lake- or seabed.[12] Influenced by rules already adopted in Denmark and Norway, the solution proposed was an extension of the Crown's prerogative right to cover wrecks, finds from wrecks and other finds made in Swedish waters. Provided that the object could be presumed to have been lost more than 150 years ago, and that it seemed apparent that a private owner could not be found, such wrecks and finds should accrue to the Crown.

A solution considered, but not favoured in the memorandum, was one which had been recently adopted in Finland, where the Act on Ancient Monuments 1951 had been amended in 1963 to include shipwrecks among the categories of monuments protected from physical interference directly by law. Such a solution, which does not involve the question of ownership, but which is an expression of State powers under public law, could easily have been implemented in Sweden as well. The Finnish monuments legislation had, in fact, been modelled on the corresponding Swedish legislation, adopting the same public law concepts.

In the end it was the Finnish solution that was adopted in a Government Bill 1967 amending the Act on Ancient Monuments.[13] Under the proposed amendments, shipwrecks became protected in the same way as ancient monuments already were i.e., wrecks, as other categories of remains enumerated in the Act, must not be physically interfered with unless permission had been given by the National Heritage Board (NHB), the government agency responsible for the monitoring of the Act. This would apply regardless of ownership. The State claimed a prerogative right only to *salvaged* ownerless wrecks. The age requirement was that 100 years should be presumed to have elapsed since the vessel was lost. The NHB became authorised to conduct investigations and salvage wrecks, as well as to take other measures for care and protection. With relation to ownerless movable objects pertaining to wrecks, the general provisions of the Act on Ancient Monuments would become applicable, i.e., such items accrued automatically to the Crown, as did finds from protected

---

12 Ju 1965:13.

13 Proposition (Government Bill) 1967:19.

remains. Underwater finds unrelated to a wreck were to be treated as finds on land.[14] The proposed amendments were approved by Parliament and gained legal force as of 1 January 1967.[15]

In 1987, a Ministry for Education report proposed the amalgamation of various statutes and regulations, including the above-mentioned Act on Ancient Monuments, into one comprehensive statute dealing with monuments of an archaeological nature, as well as historic buildings, ecclesiastical buildings and their inventory, and the export of older cultural movables.[16] This proposal resulted in adoption of the Cultural Monuments (etc.) Act 1988, which in 2013 was renamed the Cultural Heritage Act (KML).[17]

2 Current Law

Before detailing the current law there are several points to note. First, the Swedish Constitution has no provisions regarding government obligations to preserve or protect cultural heritage. This does not mean that cultural heritage protection is devoid of constitutional aspects, only that these are not prominent.[18] Of importance, however, is the civil law environment in which the KML is set.[19] Additionally, waters surrounding Sweden are governed by international treaties which Sweden is party to, primarily the UN Convention on the Law of the Sea (LOSC),[20] which have impacted national law in several ways, as detailed below. Since joining the International Maritime Organisation (IMO) in 1959, Sweden is also bound by several of its treaties. However, Sweden abstained from adopting the UNESCO Convention on the Protection of the Underwater Cultural Heritage 2001 (the 2001 Convention),[21] and has declared it will not reassess this position. Finally, protection under the KML in principle is the same for monuments and finds underwater as on land. This is helpful since there are many maritime artefacts now found onshore due to land rise,

14 Ibid p. 24.
15 Svensk författningssamling 1967:77.
16 DsU 1987:9.
17 Svensk författningssamling 1988:950.
18 In the first edition of this chapter a constitutional flaw was described, which has since been remedied.
19 The relationship between the KML and civil law has been treated comprehensively in Thomas Adlercreutz, *Kulturegendomsrätt. Med en kommentar till kulturminneslagen*, Faktainfo 2001.
20 1833 UNTS 397.
21 2562 UNTS 1.

particularly in the northern parts of the Baltic Sea and the adjoining Gulf of Botnia, whilst the opposite phenomenon in the South Baltic and the Strait of Öresund has left Mesolithic settlements underwater.

2.1 *Monument Law*

The KML gained legal force on 1 January 1989.[22] Preparatory works are to be found in the Government Bill and Parliament's committee report, which play a significant role in Swedish statutory construction.[23] The Act is divided into eight chapters, with the second, on ancient remains and finds, of interest here.

2.1.1 Ancient Remains

Under the KML ancient remains are protected directly by law, i.e., no administrative decision will normally be issued to identify what is protected. The scope of protection is defined in Chapter 2, section 1:

> Ancient remains are protected under this Act. Ancient monuments are the following [remains] of human activity in past ages, having resulted from use in previous times and having been permanently abandoned: ... 7. routes and bridges, harbour facilities, beacons, road markings, navigation marks and similar transport arrangements, as well as boundary markings and labyrinths.

The list formerly included a point 8 of 'wrecked ships, if at least 100 years have presumably elapsed since the ship was wrecked'. In 2014, this definition was amended to the much simpler 'remains of craft' with the intention to broaden its scope to include, for instance, aircraft. The translation of the Swedish 'fartygslämningar' to the English 'craft' is inexact so the term wreck will be adopted, covering both shipwrecks and other underwater vehicular remains.

Simultaneously, the general concept of 'ancient remains' was changed to target only remains assumed to have been created (or wrecked) before 1850.[24] This was combined with the addition of a new provision to the effect that remains dated post 1850 could be designated as ancient remains by the County Administration (the State agency responsible at the regional level for managing

22 Svensk författningssamling 1998:950. Translation here used is one unofficially prepared in 1997 by the National Heritage Board. There is no authenticated version in English.

23 Proposition (Government Bill) 1987/88:104, Kulturutskottets betänkande (Report by Committee on Cultural Affairs) 1987/88:21.

24 Proposition 2012/13:96 p – 46 et seq.

the KML), if there are special reasons for doing so due to their historical value (Chapter 2, section 1(a)). Protection of airplane wrecks hinges on how proactive these administrations are, on which the NHB has issued guidance.[25]

Section 2 also provides that:

> An ancient remain includes a large enough area of ground or on the seabed to preserve the remains and to afford them adequate scope with regard to their nature and significance.

This protected area is normally not delimited in advance but may be so by an order of the County Administration.[26]

Protection is defined in section 6 as follows:

> It is prohibited, without permission under this Chapter, to displace, remove, excavate, cover or, by building development, planting or in any other way, to alter or damage an ancient remain.

Section 7 gives State agencies, such as the NHB and the County Administration, access to ancient remains to take measures for their care. For example, they are empowered to 'examine ancient remains, salvage a wreck being an ancient remain and investigate a place where ancient finds have been discovered'. Under section 8 '[i]f a wreck constituting an ancient remain and having no owner is salvaged, it shall accrue to the State'. Section 9 further empowers the County Administration to 'issue regulations for the protection of an ancient remain'. Regulations may also be issued for an area, which under section 2 extends beyond that of the ancient remain if this does not significantly impede current use of the land. The County Administration may issue a protection order for a place where ancient finds have been discovered, if this can be done without causing any significant inconvenience. A protection order may apply until the place has been investigated, as provided in section 8.

All development projects should be preceded by an investigation as to the existence of ancient remains that might be affected, in consultation with the County Administration. If an ancient remain is discovered in the course of works, these are to be immediately suspended (section 10).

Under section 12, any interference with ancient remains is subject to permission by the County Administration, which may not be granted unless the

25 See generally <https://www.raa.se>.

26 Chapter numbers of the KML will in the following be mentioned only if other than 2.

monument causes a disproportionate hindrance or inconvenience. However, it is provided that:

> … [i]n the case of the owner of a wreck or of an ancient find belonging to a wreck, permission may be granted unless there are special reasons to the contrary. – If any person other than the owner of the land or water area or the owner of the wreck applies for permission the application is to be refused if the owner objects to the measure and if there are no particular reasons why the application should be allowed.

In granting permission, under section 13 the County Administration may make reasonable stipulations for special investigations to record the ancient remains, to conserve ancient finds, or for special measures to preserve the remain. According to section 14, the costs are to be borne by the developer, unless certain special criteria are met, one being that the remains were previously unknown. In that connection, section 15 provides for compensation to be paid to the developer '… out of public funds if the ancient monument causes him substantial hindrance or inconvenience …'.

The provisions outlined above relate to all ancient remains, *inter alia* wrecks. In contrast to some other countries' definitions of underwater cultural heritage (UCH), underwater geomorphic or paleontological remains are not protected under the KML. Such remains may be protected under the Environmental Code, but this will not be dealt with here.[27] The focus here will continue with the current provisions for movables considered as UCH.

2.1.2 Ancient Finds

The definition of 'ancient finds' is found in Chapter 2, section 3 of the KML:

> … objects which have no owner when found and which
> 1. are discovered in or near an ancient remain and are connected with it, or
> 2. are found in other circumstances and can be assumed to be from before 1850.

Ancient finds under section 3(1) accrue to the State, whilst other ancient finds accrue to the finder under section 4. The finder is, however, dutybound to invite the State to redeem the find if it:

27 Svensk föfattningssamling 1998:803.

> ... contains objects partly or wholly of gold, silver, copper, bronze or any other copper alloy, or if the find consists of two or more objects which were presumably deposited together.

Anybody who discovers ancient finds, which either accrue to the State or must be offered for redemption, must under section 5 report to the County Administration or certain other authorities. Finds belonging to wrecks may be reported to the Coastguard Service. Upon request the finder must surrender the object in return for a receipt, and report where, when, and how the find was discovered.

Decisions to redeem ancient finds are taken by the NHB. Payment is assessed at an amount which is reasonable with regard to the nature of the find. For objects of precious metals, payment must not be less than the value of the metal by weight, augmented by one-eighth. In addition, a special finder's reward may be paid (section 16).[28] The NHB may also transfer ancient finds to museums (if a non-State museum, ownership is also considered as transferred) – this specifically also applies to shipwrecks.[29]

2.1.3 Common Provisions

The following provisions apply to the protection of both ancient monuments and ancient finds.

1. There is a general ban on the use of metal detectors in Sweden, not just on archaeological sites but everywhere, unless provisions exempting certain usages conducted by authorities apply, or an individual permission has been issued by the County Administration.
2. Sections 21 and 21(a) impose penalties of fines or imprisonment for deliberate and negligent offences contravening the protective rules for ancient remains and ancient finds. In aggravated cases with intent, imprisonment of up to four years may be imposed.
3. To rectify unauthorised infringements, under section 22 enforcement measures can be imposed on offenders acting contrary to protective provisions. This may include forfeiture of ancient finds that do not already accrue to the State, or the value or proceeds of such finds, and metal detectors and other equipment (or their value) used in offences.
4. Under section 23, the County Administration may order its provisions to apply pending final determination of the matter.

---

28 The sum of redemption is for tax purposes considered to be capital gain, but the special reward is tax exempt.

29 Government memorandum DsU 1987:9 p. 135.

5. Sections 24 and 25 contain procedural rules on appeal and the judicial review of decisions. Depending on the matter, the Government, an administrative court, or an environmental court is competent to try appeals or undertake reviews.

2.2 *Related Civil Law*

Under Swedish civil law, finds made on land are in general treated differently from those made in water. In both cases wilfully discarded objects (*res derelicta*) are free for anyone to take possession of. Objects that have been lost inadvertently or by accident remain the property of their owners; ownership is not considered to be time limited. Such objects, if found on land, must be reported by the finder to the police under provisions of the Act on Finds.[30] If no owner appears within certain time limits, the goods accrue to the finder, provided police procedural costs are paid.

The Act concerning Certain Finds from the Waters[31] applies the same principles to those found in lakes, rivers, canals, harbours, bays, and incisions and other water areas between islands, bordering on the Territorial Sea.[32] Finds that must be reported include deserted vessels, shipwrecks, tools, and goods from vessels, regardless of whether taken from the seabed, the shore, or found floating. One difference compared to finds on land is that the police must put on public notice reported finds from the water. Finds claimed are returned to the owner subject to payment of costs for publication, care of the object and a salvor's reward; finds not claimed become the property of the salvor upon payment of police costs.[33] Neither the Act on Finds, nor the Act concerning Certain Finds from the Waters is applicable to ancient finds, which come under the KML. Somewhat paradoxically, this may mean an ancient find becomes the property of the finder more quickly because the temporal requirements of the above two Acts do not apply.

Another aspect of civil law that should be considered with respect to finds are provisions of the Act on Acquisition of Movable Objects in Good Faith.[34] Whereas ownership in principle does not become extinct when an object has been lost, the opposite occurs if an object has been *transferred* to a person

---

30 Svensk författningssamling 1918:121.

31 Svensk författningssamling 1918:163.

32 The definition here given coincides for practical purposes with the definition of internal waters in the Act on Sweden's Territorial Sea, Svensk författningssamling 1966:374.

33 The salvor may acquire exclusive salvage rights under the Act on Exclusive Rights of Salvage, Svensk författningssamling 1984:983.

34 Svensk författningssamling 1986:796, Sections 3 and 4.

who acquires *bona fide*. Title passes regardless of whether the transferor was lawfully in possession of it. Good faith means that the acquirer in all probability ought not to have suspected that the unlawful transferor lacked title, considering the kind of property offered, the circumstances under which it was offered and other circumstances. The former owner, however, has a right to reclaim the object within three months of when they came to know, or ought to have known, from whom to recover, on condition they reimburse the acquirer's costs.

However, as of 1 July 2003 *bona fide* acquisition of stolen or forcibly taken goods is not possible. Ownership remains with the person robbed unless this person fails to reclaim the goods within six months from knowledge or presumed knowledge of who the holder is. No compensation needs to be issued to the holder (who may seek redress from the previous holder). However, after having held the property for ten consecutive years in good faith (without grounds for suspecting lack of title) the holder of stolen or forcibly taken goods does acquire ownership.

Ancient finds are not exempt from this legislation. Therefore, as a breach of the KML provisions prohibiting unlicensed excavation is not legally equated with a theft, it is possible for someone who has acquired such an object in good faith to keep it, or at least receive compensation for surrendering it to the State. This is considered further in 3.2 below.

2.3 *Provisions Relating to International Law*

As of 1979, the breadth of Sweden's Territorial Sea (TS) became twelve nautical miles (nm). Under the Geneva Convention on the Continental Shelf 1958,[35] Sweden has entered into bilateral agreements with other States regarding its extent and has adopted national legislation for the application of the Convention and bilateral agreements.[36] This allows for State control of mineral and other non-living natural resources as well as living resources on the seabed or subsoil thereof. As no attempt has been made to invoke the legislation for protection of UCH, it is safe to assume that such traces of humankind, which are considered part of cultural, rather than natural heritage, are not covered.[37] This does not preclude that knowledge of wrecks and other sunken remains

35 UNTS 499.

36 Continental Shelf Act, Svensk författningssamling 1966:314, and Continental Shelf Regulation, Svensk författningssamling 1966:315.

37 Unlike the situation in, for example, Australia, Ireland, Jamaica, Portugal and Spain, Patrick J. O'Keefe, 'Protection of the underwater cultural heritage: developments at UNESCO', *The International Journal of Nautical Archaeology*, (1996) 25.3 and 4, p. 171.

is collected in the Environmental Impact Assessments needed for permission under this Act.[38]

In 1992, an Act on Sweden's Exclusive Economic Zone (EEZ) was adopted but it does not stretch as far as specifically protecting cultural heritage.[39] However, other legislation regarding pollution from ships and the dumping of environmentally hazardous waste may contribute to better conditions for the preservation of underwater cultural vestiges.[40]

Sweden ratified the LOSC in 1996. Of interest here are those parts of the Convention that apply to 'the Area', particularly Article 149. The concept of the Area dates to a 1970 UN General Assembly Resolution, which declared the seabed and the subsoil thereof beyond national jurisdiction to be 'the common heritage of mankind'.[41] Article 149 obliges State Parties to preserve and dispose of all objects of an archaeological and historical nature found in the Area, with particular regard to preferential rights of States or countries of origin. Although Sweden is far from the deep seabed constituting the Area, certain provisions have been added to the KML to implement its duties under Article 149. Thus, section 4 has been amended to stipulate that ancient finds and wrecks discovered in the Area and *salvaged* by Swedish vessels, or taken to Sweden, accrue to the State, if they can be assumed to be dated prior to 1850.[42] Furthermore, section 17 has been supplemented with a paragraph to the effect that the NHB may assign State rights to salvaged wrecks to museums undertaking their care for the future.

2.3.1 The Contiguous Zone

At the time of its accession to the LOSC Sweden announced it would adopt a Contiguous Zone (CZ), but it took some 20 years before provisions were enacted.[43] The Act is short, with just two provisions. The first proclaims the CZ as a maximum of 24 nm from the baseline, as defined in other provisions on Sweden's naval territory and maritime zones. The second enables measures consistent with the LOSC and international law to control customs, fiscal, immigration and sanitary laws, and protect ancient remains, ancient finds, and other objects of archaeological or historic significance. This latter subsection was made applicable to Chapters 1, 2 and 5–8 of the KML.

---

38 Norman, P. (2022), *Marinarkeologins förvaltningshistoria* Rapport nr 2022:3, Havsmiljöinstitutet.

39 Svensk författningssamling 1992:1140.

40 Svensk författningssamling 1980:424, 1971:1154.

41 Resolution 2749/XXV.

42 The provisions that wrecks and finds should have no owner still apply.

43 Svensk författningssamling 2017:1273.

In the preparatory work for the legislation there was discussion on the extent of Coastal State powers in the CZ.[44] The Swedish Government stated that when applying Article 33 of the LOSC, a Coastal State, pursuant to Article 303.2, was permitted to assume that the removal without its permission of archaeological and historic items from the seabed of the CZ would constitute a contravention on its territory inclusive of its TS of laws and regulations encompassed by Article 33. The government also stated that there was a right, but no obligation, for the Coastal State to monitor its CZ. Responding to an opinion voiced by Stockholm University that this interpretation would need ratification of the 2001 Convention, it further said that it had no intention to undertake such ratification and that its view was consistent with public international law and the rights of other States.

As described above, Chapter 2, section 9 of the KML empowers the County Administration to issue regulations with a scope beyond the location of an ancient remain to protect it, such as prohibitions against diving and/or anchoring. The National Maritime Museums had proposed that this should also be applicable in the CZ. The government, however, found that permanent prohibitions of this nature would not be "possible to the extent they would infringe on existing obligations under public international law".[45] In addition, the CZ was not divided geographically between the 21 counties in Sweden. Therefore, the government declared that responsibilities under the Act would rest with the County Administration in the county closest to the wreck or object in question. The NHB was expected to issue guidelines, for example regarding matters of interpretation of public international law, but to date these have not been forthcoming. Finally, the government announced its intention to issue necessary provisions for monitoring by the Coastguard in the CZ, which can be found in a comprehensive statute on the Coastguard's mission.[46]

A 2019 joint report by the Swedish Agency for Marine and Water Management and the NHB concerning the effects of fisheries on UCH, elaborated further on the issue of heritage protection in the CZ.[47] The report cites the government's position on permanent prohibitions and contains recommendations for the County Administrations when considering the LOSC with regard to free navigation and *force majeure*. It also has interesting observations on fishing in the EEZ and how authorisation procedures under EEZ rules can be

44 Proposition 2016/17:215 p. 545 et seq.

45 *Ibid.*

46 Svensk Författningssamling 2019:32.

47 See for example < https://www.diva-portal.org/smash/get/diva2:1507514/FULLTEXT01.pdf>.

applied to benefit cultural heritage, with recognition of the fact that these rules do not *per se* afford legal protection to wrecks.

2.3.2 MS Estonia Agreement

The passenger ferry MS *Estonia* sank on 28 September 1994 on its way from Tallinn to Stockholm, with the loss of 852 lives, the majority being Swedish nationals. It now rests on the Finnish CS.[48] Cleary, the MS *Estonia* does not qualify as an historic wreck, but its sinking has prompted questions on the application of principles of both international and national law that merit discussion.

The large number of deceased generated turbulent opinions on how to treat the human remains. The government quickly announced its intention to recover as many bodies as possible, but despite opposition it was later decided that the deceased should be left in peace and not recovered. The next intended step, covering the ship in cement to guarantee non-intrusion, was also later rescinded. Instead, in 1995 Sweden, Estonia and Finland entered into an Agreement on MS *Estonia*, declaring a certain area of the High Seas as the final resting place for the victims to be shown due respect.[49]

The Agreement states that the ship will not be raised, with the Parties reserving the right to take measures to cover the wreck and to prevent pollution of the marine environment. Diving that disturbs the peace, and activities with the purpose of recovering victims or property from the wreck and the seabed, are punishable by imprisonment. The Agreement was later followed by another, allowing other States to accede to it and all States around the Baltic Sea, except Germany, have done so.[50] The three original signatories adopted criminal legislation to implement the Agreement (in Sweden in force as of 1 July 1995).[51] Transgressions may lead to a fine or a maximum of two years' imprisonment. Swedish courts were declared competent to adjudicate, even if the regular conditions of the Penal Code were not at hand.

In preparatory work, the Swedish Government declared its view on the international legal position, which was that the site was part of the High Seas and thus the right of free navigation could not be infringed, but any underwater activity should be considered as disturbing the grave.[52] In view of the

48 See for example <https://riksarkivet.se/Media/pdf-filer/NAD/JAIC-haverirapport.pdf>.

49 SÖ 1995:36.

50 <https://svenska.yle.fi/a/7-836120>.

51 Svensk författningssamling 1995:732.

52 Proposition 1994/95:150 p. 8.

danger of pollution from fuel on the vessel, activities preventing this would be excepted if undertaken by any of the three State Parties.

Since 1995, several activities have been considered in breach of the Agreement and related legislation. In 2000, diving operations were conducted from a German vessel by a German journalist and an American financier wanting to investigate the theory that the cause had been an explosion, as opposed to the findings of a 1997 official investigation, which concluded it was a result of the bow door locks failing during a storm. Both operators were arrested *in absentia* by a Swedish prosecutor but were never apprehended.

In 2020, a Swedish documentary was released, which used underwater equipment again operated from a German vessel to film the wreck. This found a four-metre hole in the ship's hull, adding further cause for a suspected explosion or collision. For this filming, two Swedish nationals were charged with disturbing the peace. They were acquitted in the first instance court for lack of jurisdiction under international law – the court found that the equipment used was operated from a vessel registered in Germany and thus not subject to jurisdiction by a Swedish court.[53] This verdict was reversed by the Court of Appeals,[54] which pointed to the declared intention of the Grave Peace Act, as explained in preparatory works,[55] being that Swedish courts are mandated to try cases regardless of culpability under other jurisdictions or the citizenship of the defendant, the limits being set by principles of international law. In this regard, and to cut a long reasoning short, the court found that Article 92 LOSC did not prevent the Parties from exercising jurisdiction over their own nationals, even if the acts in question had been committed on a vessel under another State's flag. The Court of Appeals therefore quashed the lower court's decision and referred the case back to the first instance. This decision could not be appealed, so it gained legal force instantly.

Having been reopened, the case was determined first by the District Court[56] and then by the Court of Appeals.[57] Both courts sentenced the two defendants to a fine (lowered by the Court of Appeals), unanimous in finding that international law did not prevent jurisdiction by Swedish Courts in spite of the fact that the operations had been conducted from a German flag State vessel. Both

53 Göteborgs tingsrätt, Verdict 8 February 2021, case B 18677-19.

54 Göta hovrätt, Decision 15 February 2022, case B 1962-21.

55 Proposition 1994/95 p 11.

56 Göteborgs tingsrätt, Verdict 22 September 2022, case B 2415-22.

57 Göta hovrätt, Verdict 29 March 2023, case B 5637-22.

courts also dismissed other objections from the defendants. The Supreme Court did not grant leave to appeal.[58]

The findings of the film crew prompted the Estonian prime and foreign ministers to meet with their Swedish and Finnish equivalents and to announce that a new technical investigation would take place. To permit this, a change in the Grave Peace Act was enacted whereby investigation of the circumstances causing the loss was added to permitted activities.[59]

The first investigation of the accident had been conducted under an agreement between the prime ministers of Estonia, Finland, and Sweden by the Joint Accident Investigation Commission (JAIC) in the years 1994–1997. Among its conclusions were that the vessel had been seaworthy on departure and the sinking had been caused by a large opening of the bow visor and bow ramp which allowed sea water to ingress into the car deck. The vessel listed very quickly, and water flooded into the cargo deck as well as accommodation decks through broken windows and doors. The flooding progressed and the vessel sank.

These conclusions were already from their publication much criticised, *inter alia*, because most of the survivors had not been interviewed by the Commission. Based on the new evidence brought by the convicted film team from September 2020, the Estonian Safety Investigation Bureau initiated a Preliminary Assessment of the new information along with its counterparts in Finland and Sweden. An Intermediate Report of the Preliminary Assessment of the new investigation was published in January 2023.[60]

The preliminary conclusions were:

- The wreck of MS *Estonia* is in a poor condition with severe structural damage.
- The location of the outcropping bedrock under the hull matches the location of the deformation on the hull.
- Based on the evidence gathered so far, there is no indication of a collision with a vessel or a floating object.
- Based on the evidence gathered so far, there is no indication of an explosion in the bow area.

Based on facts collected by the JAIC – but contrary to its conclusion – the new investigation found that an inspection of the bow parts had not been performed, and thus the related certificate as to seaworthiness should not have been issued. If such an inspection, following regulations, had been carried out, the flaws of the visor construction could have been discovered, and the

---

58 Högsta domstolen, Decision 19 June 2023, case B 3033-23.

59 Svensk författningssamling 2021:557.

60 Accessible via <https://www.shk.se>.

accident would probably not have occurred. Further investigations are ongoing and planned.[61]

3 Sources of Knowledge

3.1 *Register*

As stated, the KML directly protects ancient remains, including wrecks and other maritime artefacts, in that no administrative decision is normally required to identify what is protected. This system places a significant burden on landowners, developers and other users of land and the seabed to understand the law. Recognising the need for practical assistance, since the 1930s there has been systematic archaeological inventorying across the country, with the results entered into a national register (maintained by the NHB), onto maps produced by the National Survey Authority and, to some extent, nautical charts by the Swedish Maritime Administration.[62] The Cultural Heritage Register is now fully digitised and publicly accessible.[63] Before digitisation, the register for UCH was kept by the National Maritime Museum (NMM) in Stockholm. The result of both archival and underwater research, it contained approximately 2,500 known wrecks protected under the KML.

The register has records on almost every known wreck, not just in Sweden's TS, lakes, and rivers, but also in adjacent waters. When the territorial seabed was thoroughly scanned in the 1980s and 1990s in search of suspected foreign submarine activities, knowledge of wrecks grew considerably. However, the knowledge on individual wrecks varies considerably, and some entries can be classified as qualified guesswork. One of the prerequisites for registration is that the remains can be localised. This can pose difficulties as some wrecks are mobile, due to wind, waves, and other oceanic conditions. An additional problem is that many reported losses are without any verifiable confirmation.

As noted above, when a time limit was introduced into the definition of ancient remains, it became obvious that the register contained both entries regarding legally protected remains from before 1850, and entries which were not subject to such protection as they were more recently lost. In addition, lack of sufficient documentation or assessment of real age resulted in a grey area between protected and non-protected remains. Since it was obvious that some more recent remains are of such value to merit legal protection, a new

---

61 <https://www.havkom.se/ovrigt/sok?query=MV+Estonia>.

62 See for example <https://app.raa.se/open/fornsok/>.

63 *Ibid.*

provision in the shape of Chapter 2, section 1(a) was added to the KML to the effect that remains younger than 1850 can be designated as ancient remains by the County Administration through a formal, appealable decision. Since, as discussed above, one of the aims of the change in terminology from 'shipwreck' to 'remains of craft' was to include aircraft, it was obvious that for this intention to have any meaning such a capability was necessary.

The Swedish Agency for Marine and Water Management estimates that some 17,000 wrecks are to be found along the coast of Sweden.[64] A survey, conducted by the NMM before the introduction of the 1850 time limit, revealed that of 784 wrecks registered, only 332 could with certainty be judged as older than 1850, whereas 196 would lose the protection they earlier enjoyed, due to their post 1850 status.[65] At the beginning of 2022, the Cultural Heritage Register contained 2,531 entries for wrecks, with only three of the 196 identified by the NMM as losing status having been subsequently designated as shipwrecks under the revised KML provisions. There is also only one designated aircraft (although 24 others are on the register without any notes on designation). Other designated remains have a maritime connection, such as constructions for timber rafting or harbour facilities.

The KML does not apply just to maritime artefacts currently underwater – it also protects wrecks and related items once underwater but now found on land. This is significant since Sweden provides an ongoing example of tectonic processes resulting in land emerging out of the sea – indeed, since the Mesolithic Age about one fifth of the present surface of the country has risen from underwater. In contrast, in the southernmost part of Sweden and in the Danish Straits the sea has submerged remains of Mesolithic settlements and there are several on-going projects investigating these.[66]

To conclude, the register remains a work in progress: new discoveries are constantly made and excavations provide new knowledge on existing entries.

3.2 *Museums and Research Institutions*

The flagship, in every sense of the word, is the wreck of the *Vasa*, of which the salvaged hull and reconstructed embellishments and riggings are now to be admired in Stockholm's most visited indoor museum. There are, however, other important collections and institutions. The NMM, founded in 1913, has already been

64 See for example <https://www.havochvatten.se/miljopaverkan-och-atgarder/miljopaverkan/fororeningar-och-farliga-amnen/vrak.html>.

65 See for example <https://www.raa.se/in-english/>.

66 Peter Norman, cited in n. 38.

noted. It has a sister museum, the Naval Museum, situated in Karlskrona, where its context is complemented by naval installations, some still in active military service, forming part of a World Heritage Site. In 2021, the Museum of Wrecks was inaugurated next to the *Vasa*, featuring visions of wrecks in their sites, and illustrating marine archaeology at work. There are also collections in Gothenburg, Malmö and Uddevalla (Bohusläns Museum). In the Kalmar regional museum items are displayed from a royal warship, *The Crown*, sunk in an explosion on 1 June 1676 in a battle with the Danish and Dutch navies. Excavation and salvage started in 1980 and continues. Education in maritime archaeology is provided at Södertörn University and archaeology in general can be studied at universities in Stockholm, Uppsala (Uppsala and Visby), Gothenburg, Lund, and Kalmar (Linnéuniversitet). Several of these also conduct doctoral and postdoctoral research, in cooperation with museums.

4 Observations on Scope and Application

4.1 *Two Schools of Thought*

From a comparative perspective, legislation for protection of UCH can be seen to oscillate between two basic conceptions. One is State or public claims to property rights in monuments, fixed or movable. Heritage is seen as a kind of *domain*, to which private possessors may have extensive rights but controlling power rests with an ultimate owner: the monarch, the republic, or nowadays the State through its manifestation in government or a government agency. Legislation dominated by this view may also regulate the transfer of cultural property. The other approach, which seems to be the more modern one, is that the State, in which much authority has been vested under principles of democratic government, has a duty to control the use of property in the interest of the common good.[67] It need not claim property rights to do so: democracy permits restrictions to be imposed in *public law* on owners and those who derive their rights from owners. Either basic view may also be consistent with a delegation of State powers to local levels of government. In a federal society the origin of power may, instead, be considered to rest at regional state level. Of course, in practice there may not be dramatic differences between these two conceptions.

As we can see from the above, in Sweden both concepts are utilised. Restrictions are imposed on ancient monuments *in situ*, among them old shipwrecks,

67 This approach is very evident in § 14 of the German Federal Constitution.

but these apply regardless of ownership.[68] When it comes to ancient finds of a movable nature, then for historic reasons the Crown prerogative rights are still exerted.[69] The State claims ownership to anything that derives from a protected ancient monument, regardless of the fact that the State does not own the monument, and the State also claims a right of redemption, comparable to forced preemption, to many other finds, which under civil law normally would accrue to the finder. (It may be noted that landowners, under Swedish law, have a self-evident right only to fixtures to real property, and very limited rights to ownerless movables found on or in their real property.)

4.2 *The Importance of Age and Ownership*

Swedish law poses two important questions when a new underwater discovery is made or when someone wants to investigate or salvage those already known. If it is a wreck, the first question relates to its age. If the wreck foundered in 1850 or later, the Act concerning Certain Finds from the Waters is applicable. The find must be publicly announced, and further issues of salvage depend on whether an owner appears. So, this would lead to the second question, related to ownership: if there is none, the finder may file for sole rights of salvage under special legislation.[70]

If the wreckage occurred before 1850, the KML alone applies. Regarding the wreck itself, the question of ownership attracts less significance. Under Chapter 2, section 12 there is a presumption that an owner of a wreck, or an ancient find belonging to it, should be given permission to salvage or disturb the remains, unless otherwise prevented. This is a position more favourable to owners of wrecks than to other owners of ancient remains, although the permission to take any measures is not unconditional. It is difficult to predict how strong the owner's position is in practice, as there has, to the author's knowledge, been no determinative litigation on this point.

The reason for this would seem to be that there are seldom any known owners of such wrecks. When commercial interests in salvaging hull and cargo have ceased, ownership is rarely claimed. Even if that should happen, ownership may still be presumed to have been abandoned at an earlier point in time. Although modern techniques of salvage may sometimes revive a commercial interest in wrecks from before 1850, claims to ownership of wrecks of that age

68 Chapter 2, section 7 of the KML *e contrario*.

69 This applies to ancient finds only; other movable heritage items may be under export restrictions without any State claims to ownership. As regards ownerless wrecks, the State becomes owner subject to salvage, Chapter 2, section 8.

70 Act on Sole Rights of Salvage, Svensk författningssamling 1984:983.

so far do not seem to have occurred in Swedish waters. The few claims to ownership of movables that have been made appear to have been settled amicably. In the case of wrecks of Danish men-of-war capsized in Swedish water, where ownership is indisputable, the Kingdom of Denmark has refrained from making any claims and has, informally, pointed to the Swedish authorities as responsible for further investigation. Thus, there is little to report with respect to case law.[71]

However, it would still seem likely that claims could one day convincingly be made by legal successors of a one-time charterer or ship-owner, or by descendants of passengers whose belongings can be traced. If the claim is to the wreck itself, the question of ownership will be relevant for the County Administration in trying an application for salvage or investigation of the wreck, as noted above. The County Administration's primary duty would not be to solve the civil law questions involved, particularly if there are several conflicting claims. However, it may still need to take a position on ownership if it considers it detrimental to heritage interests to grant the application, because if it finds that the application is being made by an owner it would also have to find special reasons for refusing it. If the application is refused, the applicant may appeal to the regionally relevant administrative court of law and from there to the higher echelons of the administrative judicature. If the claims are for ancient finds from a wreck, Chapter 2, section 16 makes it a task for the NHB to determine whether there is evidence to substantiate the claims. If the Board does not accept them, an appeal could be filed with the Administrative Court of Stockholm, and further.

As explained in 2.2 above, ancient finds are not exempt from the Act on Acquisition of Movable Objects in Good Faith. One implication of this is that a find which accrues to the State may still be hard for the State to recover if the finder has turned it over to someone who received it in good faith. Whether the acquirer would pass the good faith test is, of course, a question in itself, but if so, the State would have to negotiate a settlement to secure the object. Many finds from shipwrecks in Swedish waters are pieces of china, of a kind commonly traded, so the prospects of making a successful *bona fide* acquisition are favourable. Regarding the rather recent introduction of an exception for

71 At sea, that is. In 1937, a sumptuous treasure (the socalled Lohe treasure) was found hidden below the floor of a Stockholm Old Town basement. It was claimed by the estates of various descendants of the one-time owners of the property, not necessarily the same as the owner of the treasure, at the probable time of hiding. The Supreme Court upheld the lower court's adjudication that sufficient evidence had not been brought to support the claims, *Nytt juridiskt arkiv*, NJA 1940 110 I.

stolen property to the general *bona fide* acquisition principle, discussed above, it should be pointed out that the taking of ancient finds is not considered as theft under Swedish law for the simple reason that ancient finds by definition are ownerless.

4.2.1 Illustrative Cases

An example of where no good faith could be presumed is demonstrated in a series of events in the 1990s that culminated in legal proceedings in 2002. In 1991, the Norwegian Museum for Defence History received an anonymous offer to purchase two bronze cannons. Accompanying photographs showed the cannons bearing the monogram of Christian II (King of Denmark 1513–1523, of Sweden 1520–1521). At the time these cannons were presumed to have been taken as prize and subsequently mounted on a Swedish man-of-war, lost in the 1520s at an unknown location. Another, later theory is that the cannons had remained on a Danish warship until it foundered in 1566 off the Swedish island of Gotland in the Baltic. The offer to the museum was thought to have been made from Sweden, but the police could find neither cannons nor anyone to whom they could be firmly linked. In 1996, evidence suggested the two cannons were in a port on the Swedish west coast. They were not found there, but two years later the police arrested a suspect who had newspaper articles on the cannons and the earlier investigations. The cannons were subsequently found in a barn belonging to him and were identified as those previously offered for sale. The man was charged and convicted for having kept and concealed ancient finds that should have been reported to the State. The circumstances were considered to be aggravating and he received a suspended sentence and a heavy fine. The cannons were declared forfeited to the State.[72]

The case shows that the legislation, when properly applied, works well. However, somewhat disconcertingly a third cannon belonging to the same series was returned to the person from whom it had been impounded, following a decision not to bring charges against him (other than in the reported case). The suspect claimed that he had found the cannon before 1989 and consequently before the date when ancient finds of bronze had been reinstated as being redeemable by the State.[73]

In another case, a man was charged with having violated the KML by taking a bronze bell from a ship, wrecked in Swedish waters in 1884. This act was considered to have fallen beyond the statutes of limitation under the KML, but it

---

72 Skövde tingsrätt (District Court), Verdict 18 February 2002 in case no. B 1001-00.

73 The earlier provisions for redemption of old objects of *inter alia* bronze had been abolished in 1873, cf. 1.1 above.

nevertheless fell within the bounds of illegitimate disposition under the Penal Code, and as such was judged not to be time-barred. The man was at the same time charged with having taken two ship's bells from another wreck, not old enough to be protected under the KML. He was convicted on both charges (but on the second count for just one of the bells) and received a heavy fine. The first bell was declared forfeited to the State, and the second was awarded to the relevant insurance company.[74]

When cannons are salvaged from an old shipwreck, one can assume that the operation itself must have damaged the ship. This, of course, is also a crime. However, investigation of such crimes is difficult. First, as illustrated in the case of the cannons, the identity and whereabouts of the wreck may not be sufficiently established. If outside of Swedish territorial waters, and not within the Area as defined in the LOSC, it is doubtful whether Swedish jurisdiction applies at all. This issue is discussed further below. If beyond penal action, there may be civil law questions to consider. The first would typically relate to title – even a very old shipwreck may have an owner, who has not relinquished his right to hull and cargo, such as an insurance company. Ownership makes special provisions regarding salvage applicable. If the wreck is a State vessel, questions of sovereign immunity come into play.[75]

4.3 *Complications under International Law*

The first day of June 1676 was a disastrous day in Swedish naval history – not only was *The Crown* lost, but its sister ship *The Sword* was sunk, together with many men-of-war. see 3.2 above. *The Sword's* location remained unknown until 2011, when a private party reported finding it. When requested to reveal the position, the divers refused on two grounds. First, they wanted to prevent the location from becoming publicly known, which would happen if reported to the heritage authorities. Second, they claimed the wreck was a short distance outside of Swedish territorial waters and that they were thus under no obligation under Swedish law to disclose it.[76]

---

74 Tierps tingsrätt (District Court), Verdict 2 December 2004 in case no. B 441-03.

75 This supposition does not appear contradicted by a seemingly rather opposite verdict by the Swedish Supreme Court, in which claims were turned down made by the State of Sweden for restitution to the Federal Republic of Germany of marine research equipment, belonging to the Republic, but held as security by two fishermen for damage caused to their trawl. The Supreme Court did not support the Swedish State's position that it could exercise immunity *ex parte* the Federal Republic. *Nytt Juridiskt Arkiv* 1965 p. 145.

76 <https://www.dykarna.nu/dyknyheter/regalskeppet-svardets-upptackare-kan-polisanmalas-1400.html>.

The NHB reported a suspected crime to the police. Under Chapter 2 section 2(4) of the KML a wreck found on the seabed outside of the bounds of national jurisdiction and which is salvaged by a Swedish ship, or brought to Sweden, accrues to the State. Furthermore, under section 5 anyone who discovers ancient finds that accrue to the State is obliged to report the find to the authorities, stating how and when it was found and to surrender the find. The police investigation established that the wreck was indeed located a few hundred meters outside of the border of the Territorial Sea. In addition, two boards from the hull had been handed over to the authorities, in this case Södertörn University. As there were no formal requirements for how a report should duly be made, and as the wreck itself was situated outside the bounds of national jurisdiction, the public prosecutor decided not to pursue the matter.[77]

This decision was not surprising given the facts. This was well before the Swedish adoption of a CZ and thus the wreck was situated on the Swedish CS and in its EEZ. Few, if any, interpretations of the LOSC consider this as relevant in so far as exercising control of heritage items. Also, it could not be claimed that obligations for treatment of finds of an archaeological or historic nature from the Area under Article 149 of LOSC were relevant. If the public prosecutor's decision was not surprising, the same might be said about the NHB's decision to report to the police. The wording of Chapter 2, section 4 is ambiguous and has been criticised in Swedish juridical doctrine as giving the false impression that Sweden has heritage jurisdiction on the Shelf and the EEZ.[78] The legal situation has changed now that a CZ has been adopted, which is discussed below.

5 Conclusion – Problematic Issues and the Future

5.1 *Newer Remains*

As noted above, many wrecks and other marine remains lost their legal protection when the age limit was moved back to 1850. The remedy, individual designation of remains, in order to fill in the void has so far failed to achieve this end. The direct legal protection that the earlier system created automatically has been replaced by a bureaucratic procedure which the County Administrations have found cumbersome and demanding on already insufficient resources. This calls for increased effort from the NHB and the Ministry of Culture.

77 Decision by Åklagarmyndigheten i Kalmar, 21 June 2012.

78 Hugo Tiberg, *Vem äger vrak och gods*, Svensk Juristtidning, 2000, p. 977, n. 13.

5.2 The MS Estonia

What has happened around the MS *Estonia*, see 2.3.2, illustrates the weakness of international treaties that lack sufficient support. In the first case described above, a German and a US citizen could not be tried in Sweden for the simple reason that they did not set foot on Swedish territory. In the second case, two Swedish nationals were found guilty of disturbing the peace of the grave under the special Act. Balancing the interests of respect for the dead with other interest, the issue of culpability seems more complicated. The purpose of the two defendants was investigating the cause of the average, a question which many had regarded as unresolved by the official JAIC report. As a result of the findings – particularly photos of an unknown crack in the hull – this purpose was added to what is permissible under the special legislation. The three governments were quick in ordering their maritime agencies to conduct further investigations which have brought new light on possible causes and are still ongoing. Freedom of information aspects add to what is troublesome in this case. Punishment does not seem obviously fair.

5.3 The Contiguous Zone

The adoption of a CZ clearly widens the scope of heritage protection. However, the government's Bill to Parliament muddled the applicability of one of the most useful tools in preventing unauthorised activities around wrecks i.e., the issuing of an injunction on anchoring and diving. Chapter 2, section 9 of the KML, which enables such injunctions on ancient remains, has been made applicable in the CZ, but the government added the comment that *permanent* injunctions might be seen as infringements of international law, e.g., the right of free navigation. This leaves open the question of what time span is permissible and what should apply when an injunction is over, but a wreck remains in need of protection, which could be interpreted as a 'free for all' signal. The Swedish Government seems to have taken consolation in the offer from the NHB to issue guidelines on what international law demands. However, the fact these are yet to be produced provides for an unhappy lacuna in the use of the CZ as a heritage protection tool.

5.4 The 2001 Convention

When introducing the CZ the government announced in no uncertain terms that it had no intention of taking steps to ratify the 2001 Convention. Deviating a few years from the internationally accepted 100-year time limit for heritage items and instead drawing a line at the year 1850 had already disqualified Sweden from acceding. In 2001, in a declaration accompanying its vote of abstention, Sweden stated the reason for not ratifying was that the Convention had not gathered enough support.At the time of writing, however, it has 78 State Parties, so this reason is less convincing.

There is much to be said in favour of the 2001 Convention and the spirit of cooperation and mutual reporting it set out to promote, along with the so-called Rules, developed by the International Council on Monuments and Sites (ICOMOS), in order to laydown standards for the conduct of marine archaeology. It is difficult to find any official motivation for the negativity, so one has to surmise. The 2001 Convention in most respects is a soft convention that defers to the LOSC and other Law of the Sea conventions (Article 3). Nevertheless, there are possible complications, which the Law of the Sea experts in Sweden seem to not think worthwhile to solve. In addition, there has so far been no political pressure to join the Convention, so on the few occasions the issue of ratification has been raised, the experts' views have prevailed.

Sweden has a history of being a late-comer in joining the international promotion of cultural heritage by way of legal instruments. For example, the Hague 1954 Convention for the Protection of Cultural Property in the Event of Armed Conflict[79] was not ratified until 1985, along with the 1972 UNESCO Convention Concerning the Protection of the World Cultural and Natural Heritage.[80] The UNESCO 1970 Convention on the Means of Prohibiting and Preventing the Illicit Import, Export and Transfer of Ownership of Cultural Property[81] was for a long time assessed as impossible to implement, but in 2002 the mood changed and it was ratified without parliamentary approval or implementing legislation – a reflection of the fact that by that time Sweden had become a Member State of the European Union and under the obligation to return illegally dispatched property, which also facilitated ratification in 2011 of the UNIDROIT 1995 Convention on Stolen and Illegally Exported Cultural Objects.[82]

The day may not be far away when an external event will highlight the advantages of joining the provisions on cooperation and mutual exchange of reports and information of the 2001 Convention. The political preconditions may then swiftly change, and Law of the Sea experts will assist in finding the necessary modes of operation.

All websites last accessed February 2025.

---

79 UNTS 3511.

80 UNTS 15511.

81 UNTS 11806.

82 UNTS 2421.

Acknowledgements

The author extends thanks to Staffan von Arbin, Peter Norman and Nils Åberg for valuable input.

Selected Bibliography

Adlercreutz, Thomas, *Kulturegendomsrätt. Med en kommentar till kulturminneslagen,* Faktainfo 2001 Norman, P. (2022), *Marinarkeologins förvaltningshistoria* Rapport nr 2022:3, Havsmiljöinstitutet.

Preparatory Works

Proposition (Government Bill) 1942:8.
Proposition (Government Bill) 1967:19.
Proposition 2012/13:96.
Proposition 2016/17:215.

Official Reports

Rapport från Riksantikvarieämbetet Kulturhistorisk värdering av fartygslämningar Ett vägledande underlag om skydd av yngre fartygslämningar.

CHAPTER 19

Türkiye

M. Barış Günay, Haluk Gurulkan*, and Yasin Çakır**

1 Introduction

Anatolia has hosted several civilizations since ancient times due to its geographical location, proximity to other commercial centres in and around its periphery, mild climate, and natural resources.[1] Surrounded by the Black Sea, the Aegean Sea and the Mediterranean Sea, and being itself a large peninsula, Türkiye is at the intersection of Asia and Europe, and has a total coastline of 8,333 km.

The seas surrounding Türkiye, especially the Aegean Sea and the Mediterranean Sea, have played a significant role in maritime trade throughout history. Several civilizations such as Carian, Ionian, Lycian and Lydian were established on the coastal regions of Anatolia, mainly engaging in maritime and trade activities. The Roman and Ottoman Empires continued to engage in maritime activities in the seas surrounding Anatolia. Hence, it is common to see historical artefacts in every region of the country. Numerous artefacts found in excavations carried out for years all around the country are exhibited in museums in Türkiye and various countries of the world. Türkiye also has 21 UNESCO World Heritage sites, 19 of which are cultural.[2]

Research activities and excavations have been carried out not only on the mainland but also underwater. The first scientific underwater excavation started with the discovery of a late Bronze Age shipwreck at Cape Gelidonya, Bodrum, a port city in southwestern Türkiye and an important tourism centre. This discovery in 1954, by sponge fisherman Kemal Aras, initiated the first scientific excavation in 1960 by archaeologist, George Bass. The artefacts from the shipwreck were brought to Bodrum Castle. Bodrum Museum, which exhibits numerous artefacts from the shipwreck within the castle, opened its doors

---

* Partner at Gurulkan Çakır Günay Attorney Partnership, Istanbul, Türkiye.

1 Anatolia is a large peninsular in Western Asia and is the western-most extension of continental Asia. The land mass of Anatolia constitutes most of the territory of contemporary Türkiye. See <https://en.wikipedia.org/wiki/Anatolia>. Note also that since June 2022, Türkiye is the official name of the country, see <https://turkiye.un.org/en/184798-turkeys-name-changed-türkiye>.

2 Further information can be found at <https://whc.unesco.org/en/statesparties/tr/>.

to visitors on 6 November 1964.[3] With most of the artefacts exhibited being underwater finds, its name was changed to the Bodrum Underwater Archaeology Museum on 25 March 1981. It was the first underwater archaeology museum in Türkiye and certainly one of the first of its kind in the world. George Bass, the founder of the Institute of Nautical Archaeology, conducted other excavations, such as of a seventh century wreck at Yassıada between 1961 and 1964, excavation of the so-called 'Glass Wreck' at Serçe Port in 1977, and excavation of a Bronze Age shipwreck in 1984, all in Turkish waters.[4]

Underwater excavations, which started in Türkiye in the 1960s, still continue in different regions of the country. An important project called the 'Turkish Shipwreck Inventory Project: Blue Heritage' (TUBEP) has been led by a team from the Institute of Marine Sciences and Technology, Dokuz Eylül University, since 2005.[5] The main aim of the project is mapping, documenting, and monitoring underwater cultural heritage (UCH) along the coast of Türkiye. Within the scope of this project, many shipwrecks from the Bronze Age to the Ottoman Period have been documented and recorded in the Türkiye Underwater Cultural Heritage Geographical Information System (the System). The System is established by the Institute of Marine Sciences and Technology and is one of the most comprehensive databases in the Mediterranean region. The project is not only related to shipwrecks but is also trying to reveal trade routes, by focusing on the coasts from the southwestern Mediterranean Sea to the northern Aegean Sea. Along with many artefacts and shipwrecks, TUBEP discoveries include a Bronze Age wreck, regarded as one of the oldest shipwrecks in Turkish waters, discovered 40 metres deep in the Marmaris Hisarönü Gulf. According to the data of the Ministry of Culture and Tourism (the Ministry), five excavations were carried out in 2022.[6] These were conducted in Kerpe Bay, Black Sea; in Hersek, Marmara Sea; in İznik Lake, city of Bursa; in Bozukkale, Çamçalık, Kızlan, Southern Aegean Sea and in Kumluca, Mediterrenean Sea.[7]

---

3 Further information can be found at <https://www.ktb.gov.tr/EN-120300/the-bodrum-museum-of-underwater-archaeology.html>.

4 Further information can be found at <https://nauticalarch.org/>.

5 Further information can be found at <https://imst.deu.edu.tr/tr/sualt-arkeolojisi/arast-rma-projeleri/>. The team is led by Associate Professor Harun Özdaş.

6 See <https://kvmgm.ktb.gov.tr/Eklenti/110851,2021-sualtikazilaripdf.pdf?0>.

7 Kerpe excavation is conducted by Kocaeli Museum Directorate; Hersek excavation is led by Assistant Professor Serkan Gündüz from Uludağ University; Iznik Lake excavation is led by Professor Mustafa Şahin from Uludağ University; Bozukkale, Çamçalık and Kızlan excavations are led by Associate Professor Harun Özdaş from Dokuz Eylül University and Kumluca excavation is led by Associate Professor Hakan Öniz from Akdeniz University.

Research activities and excavations are conducted under the supervision of archaeologists and the Ministry, which is the highest national institution in the field of protection of cultural heritage. Along with the Ministry, research and archaeology centres founded in several universities also contribute to the protection of UCH.[8] Furthermore, Turkish universities play an important role in the protection of UCH at an international level. For example, Akdeniz University, Uludağ University and Koç University are members of the UNITWIN Network for Underwater Archaeology, which aims to contribute to the protection of UCH by connecting universities and institutions working in the field.[9]

Within this chapter, Türkiye's legislation on the protection of UCH and its position with regards to the UNESCO International Convention on the Protection of the Underwater Cultural Heritage (the 2001 Convention) will be explained.[10]

2 Turkish UCH Law and Practice

2.1 *Background*

The first regulation on the protection of cultural heritage in Turkish legislative history came into force as early as 1869 and was known as the 'Âsâr-ı Atîka Nizamnamesi' (Regulation of 1869).[11] The main aim of this legislation, which consisted of seven articles, was to prevent unauthorised excavation and smuggling of archaeological finds. However, it did not include definition of either 'artefact' or 'cultural heritage'.[12] The Regulation of 1869 was followed

8 Some of the research centres founded in Turkish universities are: Dokuz Eylül Üniversitesi Sualtı Kültür Mirası ve Denizcilik Tarihi Uygulama ve Araştırma Merkezi, further information can be found at <https://sudemer.deu.edu.tr/tr/anasayfa/>; Akdeniz Üniversitesi Sualtı Arkeolojisi Uygulama ve Araştırma Merkezi, further information can be found at <http://www.suua.org/>; Koç Üniversitesi Mustafa V. Koç Deniz Arkeolojisi Araştırma Merkezi, further information can be found at <https://kudar.ku.edu.tr/>; Muğla Sıtkı Koçman Üniversitesi Sualtı Uygulama ve Araştırma Merkezi, further information can be found at <https://sualti.mu.edu.tr/tr>; Ankara Üniversitesi Deniz Hukuku Ulusal Araştırma Merkezi, further information can be found at <http://www.dehukam.org/>; Sinop Üniversitesi Sualtı Arkeolojisi Uygulama ve Araştırma Merkezi, further information can be found at <https://susam.sinop.edu.tr/>.

9 Further information can be found at <http://www.underwaterarchaeology.net/index.htm>.

10 2562 UNTS 1.

11 Âsâr-ı Atîka Nizamnamesi, 13.11.1869.

12 M. Önge, 'Kültür Mirasını Tanımlamak İçin Türkiye'de Kullanılan İlk Özgün Terim: Âsâr-ı Atîka' (2018) 6 (1) *Avrasya Terim Dergisi*, p. 11.

by others under the same title, which came into force in 1874, 1884 and 1906, respectively.

The first specific provision on the protection of UCH is found in the third Regulation, which entered into force in 1884. Osman Hamdi Bey, a painter and archaeologist, who was the director of the Imperial Museum (Müze-i Hümayûn) at the time, contributed considerably to the drafting of the 1884 Regulation.[13] In it, an 'artefact' was described as 'all kinds of artefacts from ancient inhabitants of the lands of the country' and the Regulation provided a long list of objects that were regarded as such.[14] Article 3 of the 1884 Regulation stated that:

> All kinds of artefacts that have been and will be unearthed by future excavations in the Ottoman land and that will be recovered from the seas, lakes, rivers and streams shall entirely belong to the State.[15]

National excavation efforts are deemed to have been started by Osman Hamdi Bey, who made a considerable contribution to Turkish archaeology after his appointment to the role of director of the Imperial Museum.[16] He conducted the first excavations in many regions of the Ottoman Empire, such as Mount Nemrut, which was included on the World Heritage List in 1987.[17] An official letter written by him to the Ministry of Naval Affairs in 1891, requesting a diver to be hired from Edirne to be sent to Bulamaç Island (Farmakosini) for the exploration of gold coins, illustrates the early underwater research attempts in Türkiye.[18]

2.2 *The Law on the Protection of Cultural and Natural Heritage*

Türkiye, although extremely rich in terms of UCH, does not have a specific regulation devoted to it, and the Law on the Protection of Cultural and Natural

---

13 H. Öniz, O. Sütçüoğlu 'Sualtı Kültür Mirası, Osmanlı İmparatorluğu ve Osman Hamdi Bey' (2016) 153 Arkeoloji ve Sanat Dergisi, p. 244; M. Önge, 'Kültür Mirasını Tanımlamak İçin Türkiye'de Kullanılan İlk Özgün Terim: Âsâr-ı Atîka' (2018) 6 (1) *Avrasya Terim Dergisi*, p. 12.

14 M. Önge *ibid.*

15 H. Öniz, O. Sütçüoğlu *supra* n. 13; See also M. Ü. Eriş 'Asar-ı Atika Nizamnamesinden 2863 Sayılı Kültür ve Tabiat Varlıklarını Koruma Kanununa Mevzuatın Karşılaştırmalı Bir İncelemesi', T.C. Kültür ve Turizm Bakanlığı Kültür Varlıkları ve Müzeler Genel Müdürlüğü (Ankara, 2012).

16 E. Tataroğlu, 'Osman Hamdi Bey: 19. Yüzyılın Türk Müzecisi-Devlet Adamı-Ressamı-Sanat Eğitimcisi-Arkeoloğu" (2019) 221 *Milli Eğitim*, p. 177.

17 Further information can be found at <https://whc.unesco.org/en/list/448>.

18 H. Öniz, O. Sütçüoğlu *supra* n. 13 pp. 244–245.

Heritage (PCNH) is applicable to all cultural and natural heritage. The PCNH came into force in 1983.[19] With its enactment, four laws regulating different aspects of the issues related to heritage were repealed.[20] The PCNH has been amended several times over the years, including two broad amendments made in 2004 and 2011.[21] Furthermore, a number of other regulations in relation to cultural and natural heritage have come into force since the enactment of the PCNH.[22]

The main purposes of the PCNH are to define the movable and immovable cultural and natural heritage to be protected; to regulate the actions and activities to be carried out in relation to them; and to determine the roles and responsibilities of the institutions that will implement the necessary measures. Under Article 3(a)(1) of the PCNH, cultural heritage is defined as:

> ... all movable and immovable assets above ground, underground or underwater, which are related to science, culture, religion and fine arts belonging to prehistoric and historical periods, or which have been the subject of social life in prehistoric or historical periods and have a unique scientific and cultural value.

Under the PCNH, concepts of protection and preservation are regulated slightly differently in terms of immovable and movable cultural assets. According to Article 3(a)(4), the meanings of 'preservation' and 'protection' for immovable cultural and natural heritage are stated as conservation, maintenance, repair, restoration, and function replacement procedures, whereas in movable cultural heritage, they are stated as meaning conservation, maintenance, repair, and restoration works.

According to Article 5 of the PCNH, movable and immovable cultural and natural properties that must be protected and known to exist or to be found in immovable properties belonging to the State and public institutions, as well as belonging to real or legal persons, qualify as State property. Articles 6 and 23 of the PCNH determine the scope of movable and

19 Law No. 2863, Official Gazette, 23.07.1983, No. 18113.

20 Hususi Şahıslara Ait Eski Eserlerle Tarihi Abidelerin İstimlaki Hakkında Kanun (Law No. 7463); Eski Eserler Kanunu (Law No.1710); Gayrimenkul Eski Eserler ve Anıtlar Yüksek Kurulu Teşkiline ve Vazifelerine Dair Kanun (Law No. 5805); Gayrimenkul Eski Eserler ve Anıtlar Yüksek Kurulu Teşkiline ve Vazifelerine Dair 2 Temmuz 1951 tarihli ve 5805 sayılı Kanunda Bazı Değişiklikler Yapılması Hakkında Kanun (Law No. 1741).

21 Law No. 5226 entered into force on 27.07.2004 and Statutory Decree No. 648 entered into force on 17.08.2011.

22 For the list of Regulations see <https://teftis.ktb.gov.tr/TR-267730/yonetmelikler.html>.

immovable cultural properties that must be protected. Accordingly, if the cultural and natural properties fall within the scope of Articles 6 and 23 of the PCNH, they qualify as State property. Article 5 of the PCNH is not applicable to cultural and natural properties which are registered to a foundation, as they have a special status. According to the Law on Turkish Territorial Seas,[23] such waters constitute an integral part of Turkish territory and accordingly, UCH discovered in Turkish territorial waters belong to the State if they fall under the scope of Article 6 or Article 23 of the PCNH.

According to the third paragraph of Article 35, the 'regions' (su altı koruma bölgesi) of cultural and natural heritage to be protected under the water are determined and announced by decision of the President.[24] Furthermore, recreational diving is prohibited in 'conservation regions', although research can be carried out with permission granted by the Ministry, and excavation can be carried out with permission granted by the President. However, a new provision, added to the Tourism Incentive Law in 2019, allows recreational diving in areas designated by the Ministry that fall within the boundaries of designated conservation regions.[25]

There have been various decisions taken by the Council of Ministers, and lately by the President, regarding conservation regions. The first decision of the Council of Ministers[26] after enactment of the PCNH was published in the Official Gazette on 22 October 1988 and provided a list of locations in the Marmara Sea, the Aegean Sea and the Mediterranean Sea declared as conservation regions. According to this decision, a diving ban was declared along the entire Black Sea coast and the coast between Alanya and the Türkiye-Syrian border, since the process for determination of conservation regions was not complete at that time. The list of conservation regions has been amended and updated several times since 1988.[27] One of the most significant amendments was a decision

23 Law No. 2674, Official Gazette Date: 29.05.1982, No. 17708.

24 The phrase 'decision of Council of Ministers' was replaced by 'decision of the President' with Article 78 of the Decree-Law No. 700; Official Gazette Date: 7.07.2018 No.30471-bis.

25 Supplementary Article 6 of Tourism Incentive Law (Law No. 2634, Official Gazette Date: 16.03.1982, No.17635).

26 Council of Ministers Decision No. 88/13259; Official Gazette Date: 22.10.1988, No. 19967.

27 Council of Ministers Decision No. 89/14235, Official Gazette Date: 19.08.1989, No. 20257; Council of Ministers Decision No. 98/11087, Official Gazette Date: 30.05.1998, No. 23357; Council of Ministers Decision No. 2001/2952, Official Gazette Date: 24.09.2001, No. 24533; Council of Ministers Decision No. 2001/3297, Official Gazette Date: 22.12.2001, No. 24618; Council of Ministers Decision No. 2002/3591, Official Gazette Date: 06.02.2002, No. 24663; Council of Ministers Decision No. 2016/8743, Official Gazette Date: 20.05.2016, No. 29717; Council of Ministers Decision No. 88/13259, Official Gazette Date: 22.10.1988, No. 19967; President Decision No. 2339, Official Gazette Date: 02.04.2020, No. 31087; President

of the Council of Ministers, taken in 2016, which repealed all previous ones.[28] The list of conservation regions was again updated and new ones have been added to the list, including four in the Black Sea, eight in the Marmara Sea, 47 in the Aegean Sea and finally 21 in the Mediterranean Sea. Scientific diving is not included in the scope of the diving ban. Scientific diving is distinguished from other types of diving as underwater diving techniques are used merely for the purpose of seeking scientific knowledge.[29] At the time of writing, the most recent update, made by decision of the President, has amended the coordinates of a conservation region in the Aegean Sea.[30]

2.2.1 Compulsory Notification

Under Article 4 of the PCNH, those who find movable and immovable cultural and natural heritage, or who know that there are cultural and natural assets in the private property they own or use, or owners and possessors who become aware of such, should notify, within three days at the latest, the nearest museum directorate or local administrative authority. As soon as such notification is received, the relevant authorities must take necessary measures to preserve and protect the heritage discovered. Once notified, the Ministry must be informed, in writing, within ten days.

According to a decision of the Council of Ministers taken in 2016, if cultural property that needs to be preserved is discovered during diving, the nearest local authority must be notified.[31] Any intervention, such as recovering the UCH, is prohibited during this period.[32] The main idea behind this provision is preserving the UCH until relevant authorities take any necessary action.

2.2.2 Rewards

A reward may be given to finders of movable cultural properties, discovered both underground and underwater, who notify the relevant authorities within the notification period of three days.[33] Details of the relevant procedure are regulated by the Reward Regulation.[34]

Decision No. 2802, Official Gazette Date: 28.07.2020, No. 31199; President Decision No. 5068, Official Gazette Date: 06.01.2022, No. 31711.

28 Council of Ministers Decision No. 2016/8743.

29 Article 1 of the Council of Ministers Decision No. 2016/8743.

30 President Decision No. 5068, Official Gazette Date: 06.01.2022, No. 31711.

31 Article 2 of the Council of Ministers Decision No. 2016/8743.

32 Article 2 of the Council of Ministers Decision No. 2016/8743.

33 Article 64 of the PCNH.

34 Taşınır Kültür ve Tabiat Varlıklarını Bulanlara, Haber Verenlere ve Yakalayan Kamu Görevlilerine Verilecek İkramiye ile İlgili Yönetmelik (Reward Regulation), Official Gazette Date: 11.08.1984, No. 18486.

The amount of the reward depends on the place where the cultural heritage is discovered. Within the scope of Article 64, if the cultural heritage is found on the property of the finder, Articles 24 and 25 of the PCNH will apply. If the cultural heritage is discovered in a private property owned by a person other than the finder, 80 per cent of the assessed value is divided equally between the finder and the owner of the property as a reward by the Ministry. If the cultural property is discovered on land belonging to the State, 40 per cent of the assessed value is given as a reward to those who find it. If the discovery is not notified to the relevant authorities within the period determined by the relevant provision of the PCNH, it is still possible to give a reward to those who inform the relevant authorities.[35] It should be noted that no reward will be given for immovable cultural heritage and movable cultural heritage if the Ministry was already aware of its existence, regardless of its location.[36]

2.2.3 Offences and Penalties

A number of offence types have been created by the PCNH to protect cultural heritage. Article 65 of the PCNH regulates offences and penalties: those who intentionally cause destruction, deterioration, or damage to registered protected sites and immovable cultural and natural assets that are under protection, and those who have undertaken any unauthorised construction and/or physical interventions, may be sentenced to imprisonment for two to five years and a judicial fine payable to the State Treasury for up to 5,000 days. The fine is calculated by multiplying the number of days decided by the court, with the amount ascertained for each day. Updated annually by the government, at the time of writing the lower limit is 20 Turkish Liras and the upper limit is 100 Turkish Liras for each day applicable. The court has discretion on determining the amount for each day within these specified limits.

Those who give demolition or zoning permits in violation of the PCNH may be sentenced to imprisonment for two to five years.[37] A judicial fine up to 5,000 days is also applicable. If these acts are committed with the aim of smuggling cultural and/or natural heritage abroad, the penalties to be imposed are doubled. In addition, a person who deliberately violates the notification obligation (see above) without a valid excuse, may be sentenced to imprisonment for between six months and three years.[38]

---

35 Article 64/1(e) of the PCNH.
36 Article 5 of the Reward Regulation.
37 Article 65/2 of the PCNH.
38 Article 67/1 of the PCNH.

2.3 *Protection of Immovable Cultural Heritage*

Article 6 of the PCNH defines and classifies the immovable cultural and natural heritage that must be protected. Immovables, terrestrial or underwater, built before the end of the nineteenth century, or that were built after this date but classified to be protected by the Ministry due to their importance and characteristics, or immovable cultural assets within protected areas, are considered cultural heritage to be protected. Under the PCNH, the immovables that are not classified by the Conservation Boards for protection by virtue of their characteristics of architectural, historical, and other significance are not considered as immovable cultural property to which protection is applied.

Under Article 7 of the PCNH, the immovable cultural and natural heritage, and natural sites, to be protected are determined by considering the history, art, region, and other characteristics of cultural and natural assets. Identification and registration of immovable cultural heritage to be protected is regulated by the Immovable Registration Regulation.[39] The Ministry determines the immovable cultural and natural heritage to be protected by reference to the detailed criteria specified in Article 4 of this Regulation. The determination process is coordinated by the Ministry; accordingly, the team of experts that makes such a determination is appointed by the Ministry depending on the characteristics and location of the immovable property.[40] Once the determination is made, the details regarding the protected immovable cultural heritage are registered with the decision of the Regional Conservation Board. The decision of the registration, together with cadastral information on the registered immovable, is notified to the relevant Land Registry Directorate, and annotated in the Land Registry.[41]

The Ministry takes the necessary measures to ensure the protection of immovable cultural and natural heritage and undertakes various inspections or may delegate this responsibility to other relevant public institutions, organisations, and municipalities. One of the responsibilities of the municipalities imposed by the Law of Municipalities[42] and the Law of Metropolitan Municipalities[43] is the protection of cultural and natural heritage. Thus, municipalities

---

39 Korunması Gerekli Taşınmaz Kültür Varlıklarının ve Sitlerin Tespit ve Tescili Hakkında Yönetmelik (Immovable Registration Regulation), Official Gazette Date: 13.03.2012, No. 28232.

40 Article 7 of the PCNH; Article 3/1(ö) of the Immovable Registration Regulation.

41 Article 7 of the PCNH; Article 8 of the Immovable Registration Regulation.

42 Article 14 of the Law on Municipalities (Law No. 5393, Official Gazette Date: 13.7.2005, No. 25874).

43 Article 7 of the Law on Metropolitan Municipalities (Law No. 5216, Official Gazette Date: 23.7.2004, No. 25531).

also play a key role in ensuring the preservation of cultural and natural heritage within their boundaries.

2.4 *Protection of Movable Cultural Heritage*

Article 23 of the PCNH defines and classifies the movable cultural and natural assets that have to be protected. Accordingly, all kinds of movable cultural assets belonging to geological, prehistoric, and historical periods, which have a value in terms of geology, anthropology, prehistory, archaeology, or art history, and reflecting the social, cultural, technical, and scientific characteristics of the period they belong to, are regarded as movable cultural heritage that must be protected.

According to Article 25 of the PCNH, movable cultural heritage to be protected is classified and registered by the Ministry according to scientific principles. Those that are chosen to be exhibited are handed over to State museums.[44] There are several examples of recovered movable UCH that are conserved and exhibited in Turkish museums. One of these are those artefacts recovered from the Uluburun shipwreck. This ship, sunk in the Bronze Age, was discovered close to the eastern shore of Uluburun (Grand Cape) in 1982. Recovered artefacts include pottery, gold and silver jewellery, bronze tools, and weapons and these have been exhibited in Bodrum Underwater Archaeology Museum.[45] The procedure for classification, registration and admission to museums is regulated by the Movable Registration Regulation.[46] Movable cultural properties that are not classified, registered, and deemed to have a sufficient cultural value to be taken to State museums are returned to their finders.[47]

In addition, movable cultural heritage that is not classified, registered, and deemed to have sufficient cultural value to be taken to State Museums, can be traded under a licence granted by the Ministry. The procedure for the application and renewal of such a trading licence is regulated by the Trading Regulation.[48] Those who want to obtain a licence must make a written application to the nearest museum directorate. The application must include a certified document stating that the applicant is registered with the Chamber

44 Article 25 of the PCNH.

45 See Bass, G.F. 'A Bronze Age Shipwreck at Ulu Burun (Kas): 1984 Campaign' (1986) 90 *American Journal of Archaeology* 269.

46 Korunması Gerekli Taşınır Kültür ve Tabiat Varlıklarının Tasnifi, Tescili ve Müzelere Alınmaları Hakkında Yönetmelik (Movable Registration Regulation), Official Gazette Date: 20.04.2009, No.27206.

47 Article 25 of the PCNH Law.

48 Taşınır Kültür Varlığı Ticareti ve Bu Ticarete Ait İşyerleri ile Depoların Denetimi Hakkında Yönetmelik (Trading Regulation), Official Gazette Date: 11.01.1984, No.18278.

of Commerce and has a separate business to trade movable cultural property, and a document obtained from the Public Prosecutor's Office, stating that the applicant has not been convicted of crimes such as smuggling or illegal excavation. An assessment is made by the museum directorate and then a trading licence may be granted by the Ministry for a period of three years (renewable on application by the licence holder to the relevant museum directorate one month before the expiry date).[49] Licences of those who violate the relevant provisions of the PCNH and/or Trading Regulation may be cancelled. Workplaces and warehouses of licensed movable cultural property traders may be inspected at any time by the Ministry's inspectors and the director of the relevant museum.[50] As of 31 January 2023, there are 54 trading licence holders throughout Türkiye, with 48 of them located in Istanbul.[51] Taking photos and films, making copies of movable and immovable cultural heritage in ruins, or museums affiliated to the Ministry, for the purposes of education, training, scientific research and promotion are subject to the Ministry's permission.[52]

2.4.1 Prohibition on Taking Movables Abroad

Since the Ottoman era, a significant amount of movable cultural heritage discovered in Türkiye has unfortunately been looted and taken abroad. For instance, some is exhibited in the British Museum (such as the Nereid Monument, unearthed in the ancient city of Xanthos, mosaic discovered in the ancient city of Halicarnassus in Bodrum, and the Idrimi Statue, discovered in the Alalah region in Hatay), and some in the Pergamon Museum in Berlin (such as the Pergamon Altar and the Market Gate of Miletus). It is difficult to prevent illegal diving and thus to protect UCH since the Turkish coastline is very long and close to international waters.[53] The Ministry has made constant efforts to have cultural heritage artefacts returned and in a number of instances has been successful.[54]

---

49 Article 7 of the Trading Regulation.

50 Article 11 of the Trading Regulation.

51 See <https://kvmgm.ktb.gov.tr/TR-44149/tasinir-kultur-varligi-ticareti.html>.

52 Article 34 of the PCNH; Article 6 of the relevant Regulation titled 'Müzelerle Müzelere Bağlı Birimlerde ve Örenyerlerdeki Kültür Varlıklarının Film ve Fotoğraflarının Çekilmesi Mülaj ve Kopyalarının Çıkarılması Hakkında Yönetmelik', Official Gazette Date: 26.01.1984 No. 18293.

53 B. Berkaya, 'Türkiye'de Sualtı Arkeolojisi ve Kaçakçılığın Önlenmesi' (1993) 36 *Ankara Üniversitesi Dil ve Tarih-Coğrafya Fakültesi Dergisi*, pp. 297–299.

54 See the updated list of returned movable cultural heritage at <https://kvmgm.ktb.gov.tr/TR-44470/yurt-disindan-iadesi-saglanan-eserler.html>.

According to Article 32 of the PCNH, movable cultural heritage that 'needs to be preserved in the country' cannot be taken abroad. The provision is silent on the criteria to define such cultural heritage. However, in exceptional cases, when considered to be in the best interests of Türkiye, the President has the authority to allow temporary exhibitions of the country's cultural heritage abroad. The relevant procedure on this is stipulated by the Exhibition Regulation.[55] Accordingly, certain conditions must be met to take cultural heritage abroad for exhibition purposes, such as an insurance and a guarantee has to be provided by the authorities of the destination country against any possible damage or loss.[56] In accordance with Article 6 of the Exhibition Regulation, the duration of the exhibition cannot exceed a period of one year from the date of departure for a single country, or two years if the exhibition will cover more than one country. Further permission is required to extend these periods due to the relocation of any exhibition.[57]

2.5 *Archaeological Excavations and Research*

The conditions and procedures to be followed for research and excavation are stipulated in detail in the Excavation Regulation.[58] The right to research and excavate in order to reveal movable and immovable cultural heritage belongs to the Ministry.[59] However, if certain conditions are met, it is possible to grant research and excavation permits to Turkish and/or foreign institutions.[60] To be able to receive permission, the Ministry must be satisfied as to the scientific and financial competence of these institutions. Only the permission of the Ministry is required for research activities, but the President's permission is also required for excavation activities. Article 3 of the Excavation Regulation states that 'excavation activity' means unearthing all kinds of archaeological structures, documents and other remains that have been under soil or water in an archaeological site; 'research activity' means studies carried out in museums, or above-ground, or underwater, without excavation, to investigate and analyse any issue related to cultural heritage.[61]

---

55 Korunması Gerekli Taşınır Kültür ve Tabiat Varlıklarının Yurt Dışına Çıkarılması ve Yurda Sokulması Hakkında Yönetmelik (Exhibition Regulation), Official Gazette Date: 16.02.1984, No. 18314.

56 Article 6 of the Exhibition Regulation.

57 *Ibid.*

58 Kültür ve Tabiat Varlıklarıyla İlgili Olarak Yapılacak Araştırma, Sondaj ve Kazılar Hakkında Yönetmelik (Excavation Regulation), Official Gazette Date: 10.08.1984, No. 18485.

59 Article 35 of the PCNH; Article 7 of the Excavation Regulation.

60 According to Article 49 of the PCNH, research or excavation permission is not granted to the members of Embassies and Consulates of foreign countries in Türkiye.

61 Article 3 of the Excavation Regulation.

Excavation activities must be carried out based on 'scientific principles'.[62] The Excavation Regulation is silent on the meaning of these. However, it provides criteria regarding the qualifications of the team performing any excavation: those who wish to conduct such activities must be a member of a university or a scientific institution and be officially recommended by their university or institution for the excavation. Furthermore, they must: provide certification proving that they are experts about the culture(s) of the site where the excavation will be carried out; have publications on the subject matter; and provide a written undertaking from their university or institution for financial support for the excavation activities.[63] Excavation teams cannot perform excavation activities outside the permitted areas.[64] If an 'important architectural structure' is discovered during the excavation process, further permission from the Ministry is required to remove the finds. However, the Excavation Regulation is silent on the meaning of 'important architectural structure'.

According to Article 48 of the PCNH, one or more representatives of the Ministry shall be present during research and excavations conducted by foreign delegations and institutions. Furthermore, the head of the excavation is obliged to allow inspection, to be carried out by Ministry officials, of all finds recovered during excavation at the premises where these are collected.[65] At the end of each excavation season, and within three months at the latest, the head of the excavation team must submit a report to the Ministry stating the outcomes of the excavation, including photographs of the inventory of the finds and a plan of any architectural remains.[66]

The Excavation Regulation also determines the principles to be followed in research activities. Research cannot be conducted outside the permitted areas. Movable cultural assets found during research activity must be delivered to the relevant museum, together with an inventory list.[67] Researchers who carry out research at museums, are required to comply with the rules determined by the museum directorate. When determining these, issues such as timing, the right to publish and the safety of the assets must be considered. Two copies of the publication covering the research results must be submitted to the relevant museum, with one copy then sent to the Ministry by the museum directorate.[68]

---

62 Article 9/1(a) of the Excavation Regulation.
63 Article 5 of the Excavation Regulation.
64 Article 9/1(b) of the Excavation Regulation.
65 Article 9/1(g) of the Excavation Regulation.
66 Article 9/1(j) of the Excavation Regulation.
67 Article 10 of the Excavation Regulation.
68 *Ibid.*

Excavation licences and research permits are initially granted for a period of one year, which can be extended provided that the head of the excavation team submits a statement that excavation and research are continuing.[69] Within the scope of Article 41 of the PCNH, all movable cultural assets unearthed during excavations, apart from any important architectural structures, are to be transferred to a State Museum to be specified by the Ministry. In addition, all types of movable cultural heritage related to military history recovered during excavation are transferred by the Ministry to military museums with the approval of the Office of Commander in Chief.[70]

Although it is clearly stated in paragraph 3 of Article 35 of the PCNH that it is prohibited to dive for recreational purposes in conservation regions, the Diving Regulation based on supplementary Article 6 of the Tourism Incentive Law, regulates the procedure and principles for the designation of recreational diving zones within the borders of conservation regions.[71] The Underwater Protection Commission (the Commission), established in accordance with the Diving Regulation, is empowered to decide on the designation of such diving zones for recreational purposes. It should be emphasised that for the Commission to decide on the zones, a certain procedure must be followed: first, a diving team has to be formed by the General Directorate of Cultural Heritage and Museums of the Ministry to examine the relevant underwater zone. After this examination, a report has to be prepared by the diving team, which has to include information such as whether there is visible UCH in the zone, whether there is a protected area in the neighbouring land area, the distance around the UCH that needs to be protected and the possible effects of recreational dives on the UCH.[72] A report is then sent to the General Directorate for assessment by the Commission. After this assessment, the Commission determines any zones for recreational diving. This decision is approved and announced on the website of the Ministry.[73] Furthermore, the rules to be followed during all recreational SCUBA dives, the required standards of diver training, the rules to be followed by diving centres and underwater sports clubs that organise diving activities and all procedures and principles relating to SCUBA diving are

---

69 Article 40 of the PCNH.

70 Article 41 of the PCNH.

71 Su Altında Korunması Gerekli Kültür ve Tabiat Varlığı Bulunan Bölgelerde Turizm ve Sportif Amaçlı Dalış Alanlarının Belirlenmesine İlişkin Usul ve Esaslar Hakkında Yönetmelik (Diving Regulation), Official Gazette Date: 20.03.2020, No. 31074.

72 Article 7 of the Diving Regulation.

73 *Ibid.*

regulated under the Scuba Diving Regulation.[74] Article 19 of this Regulation is in line with the PCNH on protection and preservation of UCH.

The Turkish Underwater Sports Federation (the Federation), founded in 1980, is the leading organisation working for the development of underwater sports in Türkiye.[75] One of its branches is SCUBA diving and it sets principles related to recreational diving, including training standards for divers. The Federation has organised workshops for diving instructors relating to the protection of UCH and worked to raise the awareness of UCH amongst the recreational diving community.

In case of a discovery of UCH that needs to be protected outside of the conservation region, the Commission has the authority to take any necessary measures for its protection, together with the local administrative authorities, such as the governorship or district governorship in the region.[76]

3 Türkiye and International Conventions

3.1 *The 2001 Convention*

The inadequacy of the United Nations Convention on the Law of the Sea 1982 (LOSC)[77] regarding the protection of UCH necessitated a detailed study in this area.[78] In 1979, the Council of Europe's Committee of Ministers set up an 'Ad Hoc Committee of Experts' to draw up a European treaty on the protection of UCH. The Committee held plenary meetings between 1980 and 1985[79] with a Draft European Convention on the Protection of Underwater Cultural Heritage finalised in 1985. However, it could not be completed due to disagreement between Türkiye and Greece, which derived from disputes over maritime boundaries in the Aegean Sea.[80]

After the failure of the Council of Europe's attempt to produce a treaty to protect UCH, the International Law Association's (ILA) Committee on Cultural

74 Türkiye Sualtı Sporları Federasyonu Donanımlı Dalış Yönetmeliği (Scuba Diving Regulation), Official Gazette Date: 10.09.2008, No. 26993.

75 Further information can be found at <https://tssf.gov.tr/>.

76 Article 5 of the Diving Regulation.

77 1883 UNTS 397.

78 S. Dromgoole, '2001 UNESCO Convention on the Protection of the Underwater Cultural Heritage' (2003) 18 *International Journal of Marine and Coastal Law* p. 60.

79 S. Dromgoole, *Underwater Cultural Heritage and International Law* (Cambridge, 2013), p. 40; For further information see <https://assembly.coe.int/nw/xml/XRef/Xref-XML2HTML-EN.asp?fileid=14882&lang=en>.

80 S. Dromgoole *supra* n. 78 pp. 60–61. Note, Türkiye is not a party to the LOSC.

Heritage Law started to prepare a draft convention.[81] This was adopted at the ILA's 66th Conference in 1994 and submitted for consideration to UNESCO in 1995.[82] This draft was used as a starting point for the development of the 2001 Convention.[83] As a result of further efforts between 1998 and 2000 within UNESCO, the 2001 Convention was accepted at UNESCO's General Conference held in 2001. Türkiye is not a party to the 2001 Convention and furthermore, along with Russia, Norway, and Venezuela, was among the countries that voted against it.

A statement made by the Turkish Permanent Representative to UNESCO,[84] explains that the 2001 Convention's references in Articles 2, 3, 10 and 25, which regulate the relationship between the 2001 Convention and the LOSC, constituted an obstacle for Türkiye in being a party to the 2001 Convention.[85] Article 25 of the 2001 Convention stipulates that disputes between the parties are to be resolved within the framework of Article 287 of Part XV of the LOSC. In this regard, Türkiye, together with Venezuela and Thailand, made a proposal referring to the methods listed in the first paragraph of Article 33 of the United Nations Charter, but the proposal was not supported by the majority and rejected.[86] Furthermore, the fact that no reservation can be made, with the only exception specified in Article 30 being Article 29, is also one of the main factors preventing Türkiye from accepting the 2001 Convention.[87]

Türkiye's official position was explained at the 20th plenary meeting held on 2 November 2001 as follows:

> Each country, including Turkey, participated in the preparatory work on the draft Convention and spared no efforts in order to arrive at a satisfactory, comprehensive and consequently global legal instrument. Turkey has a rich underwater cultural heritage, not only in the seas around her coasts but also in various parts of the world. During negotiations much

81 S. Dromgoole, *supra* n. 79, p. 49.

82 D. Bederman, 'The UNESCO Draft Convention on Underwater Cultural Heritage: A Critique and Counter-Proposal' 30 *Journal of Maritime Law and Commerce*, p. 332.

83 P. O'Keefe, *Shipwrecked Heritage: A Commentary on the UNESCO Convention on the Underwater Cultural Heritage* (Leicester, 2002), p. 23; S. Dromgoole, *supra* n. 79, p. 50.

84 U. Görgülü, *Ülkemizin Taraf Olmadığı Sualtı Kültürel Mirasının Korunması Sözleşmesi ve Sualtı Kültür Varlıklarımız*, Yüksek Lisans Tezi, (Konya, 2007), p. 53.

85 Ö Berberoğlu, 'Su Altı Kültürel Mirasının Korunmasına Dair 2001 Tarihli Unesco Sözleşmesi ve Türkiye', 20. Su Altı Bilim ve Teknoloji Toplantısı Bildirileri, (Ankara, 2017), p. 43.

86 *Ibid* p. 43.

87 *Ibid* p. 44.

progress was made, but we observed that no consensus was reached on substantial issues. In other words, the document prepared does not enjoy universal approval. For instance, there is no consensus on the coastal State jurisdiction concerning UCH on the continental shelf and the exclusive economic zone. The balance of rights and obligations between maritime States and coastal States had to be preserved. Some articles of the Convention are still ambiguous and constitute some of the weak points of the Convention. In our view, universal acceptance is the best way to guarantee the application of this Convention. However, universal acceptance is lacking, unfortunately, because some substantive issues have not been resolved.

In summary, the principal objections to the 2001 Convention include the following. As noted above, the text of the Convention includes several references to the LOSC, for example in Articles 2, 3, 10 and 25. In fact, the LOSC is mentioned as one of the instruments constituting the legal framework for the 2001 Convention. Türkiye is not a party to the LOSC, therefore it considered that it could not agree with these references and interpretations. As also noted above, Article 25 of the 2001 Convention, which relates to the peaceful settlement of disputes, was another matter which Türkiye found to be unacceptable. Paragraphs 3 and 4 of Article 25 state that if no agreement is reached on the settlement of disputes between States Parties, Part XV of the LOSC, specifically Article 287, shall apply. Again, as Türkiye is not a party to the LOSC, it could not accept this. Another issue with which Türkiye had difficulty, relates to Article 30 of the 2001 Convention, which states that, with the exception of Article 29, no reservations may be made to the Convention.[88] This 'no-reservation' clause is another reason why Türkiye did not become a party to the 2001 Convention. The Türkiye delegation, during preparatory work, proposed a formula stating that any dispute between States Parties concerning the interpretation or the implementation of the Convention ought to be settled primarily by meaningful negotiations or by any other peaceful means, referred to in Article 33 of the United Nations Charter. As noted above, although some delegations were in favour of this, others did not agree.[89]

88 Article 29 permits a State Party upon ratification to enter a reservation relating to the geographical scope of the 2001 Convention.

89 UNESCO: Records of the General Conference 31st Session Proceeding, Paris 2001, v. II, p. 563, see <https://unesdoc.unesco.org/ark:/48223/pf0000128966/PDF/128966mul.pdf.multi>.

3.2 *International Convention on Salvage 1989 (the Salvage Convention)*

Under Article 30(1)(d) of the Salvage Convention,[90] any State Party may reserve the right not to apply the provisions of the Convention when the property involved is maritime cultural property of prehistoric, archaeological, or historic interest and is situated on the seabed. This stemmed from consideration of maritime cultural property during the International Conference held on 17 April 1989: the French delegation's proposal to exclude maritime cultural property from the scope of the Convention was rejected[91] but its subsequent proposal was approved, becoming subparagraph (d) of Article 30(1).[92]

Türkiye has been a party to the Salvage Convention since 27 June 2015 and reserved the right not to apply the provisions of the Salvage Convention when the property involved is maritime cultural property of prehistoric, archaeological, or historic interest and which is located on the seabed.[93] Furthermore, the Turkish Commercial Code (TCC), which entered into force in 2012, has adopted the provisions of the Salvage Convention, with Article 30(1)(d) of it reflected in Article 1298(3)(b) TCC.[94]

One of the concerns of UNESCO while drafting the 2001 Convention was the increasing commercial exploitation of UCH. Article 2(7) of the 2001 Convention states that 'underwater cultural heritage shall not be commercially exploited'. Therefore, Türkiye, despite not being a party to the 2001 Convention, took an important step to protect UCH from treasure hunters by reserving the right not to apply the provisions of the Salvage Convention to UCH.

4 Conclusion

Anatolia has hosted many civilizations throughout history, with Türkiye's seas being significant trading routes for centuries. Therefore, Türkiye is very rich in terms of UCH and new discoveries are frequently made. Since the 1960s, underwater research and excavations have become common in Türkiye.

90 1953 UNTS 165.

91 The Travaux Préparatoires of the Convention On Salvage, 1989, Comite Maritime International, 2003, p. 547, see <https://comitemaritime.org/wp-content/uploads/2018/05/Travaux-Preparatoires-of-the-Convention-on-Salvage-1989.pdf>.

92 *Ibid*, p. 550–551.

93 Law No. 6480, Official Gazette Date: 29.05.2013, No.28661; Council of Ministers Decision, No. 2014/6336 Official Gazette 24.5.2014, No.29009, Date of Deposit of Instrument: 27.6.2014, Date of Entry into Force: 27.6.2015.

94 Law No. 6102, Official Gazette Date:14.02.2011 No. 27846.

Archaeologists under the supervision of the Ministry have been carrying out excavations, research, and scientific activities for the protection of all cultural heritage, including UCH. Many research centres established by universities and government bodies also contribute to underwater research and the preservation of UCH. Underwater research and excavations are carried out in Türkiye every year, and their outcome is reported to the Ministry with scientific publications on the subject.

Unfortunately, Türkiye's cultural heritage has been looted for centuries. Significant amounts of cultural artefacts discovered in Türkiye have been illegally traded, and some are still exhibited in museums abroad. Awareness began to emerge during the second half of the nineteenth century of the imperative to prevent looting and for the protection of cultural heritage. In the same period, legal regulations started to come into being. With increasing awareness on the need for the protection of cultural heritage, many amendments have been made since.

Although not devoted solely to the protection of UCH, the PCNH applies to UCH as well as terrestrial heritage. After the PCNH entered into force in 1983, many regulations have added detail on the protection of cultural heritage. In order to protect UCH, many conservation regions have been declared in the Black Sea, the Marmara Sea, the Aegean Sea, and the Mediterranean Sea. Diving is prohibited in these regions, except for scientific diving, and recreational diving only within certain zones declared by the Ministry. Since underwater archaeological research continues, it is predicted that this matrix of conservational regions will expand with the discovery of new UCH.

Türkiye is not a party to the 2001 Convention. The fact that the LOSC, to which Türkiye is also not a party, was taken as a legal framework during the preparation of the 2001 Convention, has been decisive with regard to its attitude on not becoming a party to the 2001 Convention. On the other hand, Türkiye while becoming party to the Salvage Convention, reserved the right not to apply the Salvage Convention to UCH. The same approach to protecting UCH was taken when enacting the TCC to prevent the possible commercial exploitation of UCH.

The PCNH aims to protect both the cultural and natural heritage effectively and, by providing strict measures, to prevent them from being subject to trade. Although Türkiye is not a party to the 2001 Convention, the PCNH which was drafted with a holistic approach regarding the protection of all cultural heritage, constitutes a comprehensive legal framework and source for the protection of UCH.

All websites last accessed February 2025.

Selected Bibliography

Ö. Berberoğlu, 'Su Altı Kültürel Mirasının Korunmasına Dair 2001 Tarihli Unesco Sözleşmesi ve Türkiye', 20. Su Altı Bilim ve Teknoloji Toplantısı Bildirileri, (Ankara, 2017).

J. Blake, 'The Protection of Turkey's Underwater Archaeological Heritage – Legislative Measures and Other Approaches', 1994, 3(2) *International Journal of Cultural Property*, 273.

S. Dromgoole, '2001 UNESCO Convention on the Protection of the Underwater Cultural Heritage' (2003) 18 *International Journal of Marine and Coastal Law.*

M.B. Günay 'Kurtarma Hukukunda Sualtı Kültür Varlıkları' (2010) 26(2) *Banka ve Ticaret Hukuku Dergisi*, 57.

H. Karan, A. Odeke, K. Var Türk (eds.) The Legal Regime of Underwater Cultural Heritage and Marine Scientific Research (Ankara, 2020).

P. O'Keefe, *Shipwrecked Heritage: A Commentary on the UNESCO Convention on the Underwater Cultural Heritage* (Leicester, 2002).

CHAPTER 20

The United Kingdom

*Jason Lowther**, *Michael V. Williams***, *Joanne Sellick**** *and Georgia Holly*****

1 Introduction

In 2006, Professor Sarah Dromgoole wrote the United Kingdom (UK) chapter in the second edition of this book. This chapter builds upon that by reviewing the changes that have occurred in the field of UCH policy and law since 2006, and the scholarship of Prof. Dromgoole is hereby acknowledged. However, one thing that remains unchanged is the continued failure of the UK to ratify the UNESCO Convention on the Protection of Underwater Cultural Heritage 2001 (2001 Convention),[1] although it uses the Rules contained in the Annex to it as policy guidance.[2]

The UK is divided into the separate jurisdictions of England, Wales, Scotland and Northern Ireland. Regulation and administration of heritage is a devolved function, meaning that there is variance evident in regulators and emphasis between the separate nations due to the legislative authority that the devolved administrations of Scotland, Wales and Northern Ireland enjoy from the Parliament in England.[3] As such, this chapter necessarily presents a situational analysis of the law and policy within four distinct governance models, which share significant common features, including all of the heritage-relevant measures of international law to which the UK is a signatory,[4]

* Associate Professor in Law, University of Plymouth.

** Visiting Professor in Law, University of Plymouth.

*** Associate Professor in Law, University of Plymouth.

**** Post-Doctoral Research Assistant and Marine Archaeologist, University of Edinburgh.

1 2562 UNTS 1.

2 See here the Parliamentary Questions where the commitment was made. <http://www.publications.parliament.uk/pa/cm200405/cmhansrd/vo050124/text/50124w13.htm>.

3 The protection of military remains under the Protection of Military Remains Act 1986 is the responsibility of the UK's Secretary of Defence.

4 The UK is signatory to various international measures relevant to the protection of UCH. These include the Convention for the Protection of Cultural Property in the Event of Armed Conflict (Hague Convention) 1954 249 UNTS 215; Convention on the Means of Prohibiting and Preventing the Illicit Import, Export and Transfer of Ownership of Cultural Property (Paris Convention) 1970 823 UNTS 231; Convention Concerning the Protection

 | DOI:10.1163/9789004510883_022

although with noticeable differences of approach in law and policy at the margins. The material is presented from an England and Wales' perspective in the first instance, with contrasting measures for Scotland and Northern Ireland dealt with separately as they manifest. We start with a policy imperative shared between all of the UK's devolved governments and which has subsequently infused legislative development. In addition it has facilitated an appreciation of UCH in practice by elevating it to become a consideration in non-sector specific legislation, such as marine development and fisheries management.

1.1 *The Marine Policy Statement 2011*

Increased exploitation and use of the marine environment and its resources present opportunities and threats, with unregulated interventions potentially having a negative impact on UCH in terms of both discovery and/or damage or unlawful recovery. The development and expansion of marine planning, to manage the co-existence of differential claims on marine space, has accelerated during the last two decades, resulting in numerous legislative and policy initiatives across the globe. The UK is no different and has developed a comprehensive regime of marine spatial planning through legislation for England and the devolved administrations which is characterised by reference to a shared policy vision.[5]

The Marine Policy Statement (MPS),[6] published in 2011 pursuant to s.44 of the Marine and Coastal Access Act 2009 (MACAA), promulgated a series of policy imperatives to deliver the objective of sustainable management of decisions affecting the marine environment. The primary objectives within the Statement include: the promotion of sustainable economic development;

---

of the World Cultural and Natural Heritage (World Heritage Convention) 1972 1037 UNTS 151;International Convention on Salvage 1989 1953 UNTS 165; Convention for the Protection of the Architectural Heritage of Europe (Granada Convention) 1985 CETS 121; Valetta Convention for the Protection of the Archaeological Heritage of Europe 1992 ETS 143; the Shipwrecked Vessel RMS Titanic Agreement (2003) TREATIES AND OTHER INTERNATIONAL ACTS SERIES 19-1118; and The European Landscape Convention (Florence) 2000 CETS 176. Although adopting the principles of the 2001 Convention as standard practice, the UK has not yet ratified the Convention. On this point see UK National Commission for UNESCO, "UNESCO convention on the protection of underwater cultural heritage: next steps for the UK Government," 2015.

5 See for example, the Marine and Coastal Access Act 2009; the Marine Scotland Act 2010; and the Marine Act (Northern Ireland) 2013.

6 HM Government, Northern Ireland Executive, Scottish Government, Welsh Assembly Government, 'UK Marine Policy Statement', 2011. Available at <https://assets.publishing.service.gov.uk/media/5a795700ed915d042206795b/pb3654-marine-policy-statement-110316.pdf>.

mitigating the UK's carbon footprint and so reducing the impacts of climate change and ocean acidification; ensuring healthy marine ecosystems by protecting habitats, species and 'our heritage assets'; and contributing to the societal benefits of marine resources for local and social economic issues.[7] In this case, 'ensuring a strong, healthy and just society' is dependent on the 'diversity of the *marine environment, its seascapes, its natural and cultural heritage and its resources*'.[8] Following the UK's withdrawal from the European Union (EU) the MPS was updated in 2020 with guidance in respect of the interpretation of EU law.[9]

Location of UCH protection within the context of 'environment' in UK policy does however have a slightly earlier provenance and is traceable to negotiations on the Draft Marine Bill established in 2005 by the UK Government and devolved administrations, within which 'understanding our marine environment, its natural processes and our *cultural marine heritage*' (emphasis added) was included within a set of strategic goals for the marine environment.[10]

Following this, in 2008 High Level Marine Objectives set out in 'Our Seas – a shared resource' were developed, going on to provide a foundation for the consequent MPS in 2011.[11] Within these objectives, 'marine cultural heritage' was defined as:

> the historic environment of the seas includes individual sites and assets of historic, archaeological, architectural or artistic interest, whether or not they are afforded statutory protection by heritage protection legislation.[12]

The recognition of significance regardless of designation is a particularly important step towards the evolution of heritage as part of the surrounding environment in UK policy, particularly considering heritage legislation has

---

7 *Ibid*, p. 3.

8 *Ibid*, p. 11.

9 *Emphasis added.* See here, <https:// https://www.gov.uk/government/publications/uk-marine-policy-statement/guidance-to-the-uk-marine-policy-statement-from-1-january-2021>.

10 Pater, C and Oxley, I, 'Developing marine historic environment management policy: The English Heritage experience', 2014, Marine Policy, vol. 45, pp. 342–348.

11 HM Government, Northern Ireland Executive, Scottish Government, Welsh Assembly Government, 'Our Seas – a shared resource', 2008. Available at <https://www.gov.uk/government/publications/our-seas-a-shared-resource-high-level-marine-objectives>.

12 *Ibid*, p 9.

previously relied on significance-based designation, such as the Protection of Wrecks Act 1973 (PWA).[13]

The inclusion of cultural heritage as a significant factor to which regard should be had in determining the sustainable development of the ocean represents a similar vision to the goals of the 2001 Convention. However, questions have been raised with regards to the clarity of what 'culture' means in this context. This is noted in the Draft Marine Bill Report and formal minutes by the Joint Committee on the Draft Marine Bill in 2008, in which the lack of definition of sustainable development was questioned, particularly in the context of the objectives of the Marine Management Organisation (MMO),[14] the content of the Marine Policy Statement and the associated marine plans (clauses 2, 40 and 46). In commenting on the Marine Policy Statement's reference to 'development in the UK marine area by setting out a UK vision and objectives for the marine area and its uses, incorporating economic, social, cultural and environmental priorities', the Joint Committee stated:

> it is not clear what 'cultural' might mean in the context of sustainable development: whether it refers to the cultural aspects incorporated in the Government's 'well-being indicators' or the historic cultural heritage encompassing ancient geological landscapes beneath the sea and other artefacts (e.g. shipwrecks) that compromise the accepted marine cultural heritage.[15]

Issues of definitional clarity aside, the breadth of the terminology can sensibly accommodate both meanings. The two interpretations offer scope for complementarity, and subsequent policy and law developments, as examined further in this chapter, reflect this.

1.2 *The Fisheries Act 2020*

The Fisheries Act (FA) purports to give the UK full control of its fishing waters following its exit from the EU. Broadly, the Act aims to work towards the

---

13 Available at <https://www.legislation.gov.uk/ukpga/1973/33>.

14 The MMO is an executive non-departmental English public body, which has the purpose to protect and enhance the marine environment and support UK economic growth by enabling sustainable marine activities and development, see for example <https://www.gov.uk/government/organisations/marine-management-organisation>. Equivalent bodies operate in the devolved administrations, Marine Scotland, Marine and Fisheries Division (Wales) and the Marine and Fisheries Division (Northern Ireland). The MMO retains control over the NI offshore (beyond 12nm) marine area.

15 HL Paper 159-I, HC 552-I, 'House of Lords House of Commons Joint Committee on the Draft Marine Bill - Volume 1 Report and Formal Minutes', 2008, p 22 para. 42.

sustainable protection of fisheries, fishing, aquaculture and marine conservation, and makes provisions on the functions of the MMO and its equivalents in the devolved administrations. Commercial seabed fishing has significant potential to cause harm to UCH,[16] and until recently, the needs of the industry have been prioritised over the natural and cultural environment in UK law. The significance of the FA for UCH relates to the power of a Minster to make regulations for the '... purpose of protecting the marine and aquatic environment from the effects of fishing or aquaculture, or of related activities'.[17] In alignment with contemporary legislation, the scope of the marine and aquatic environment is broadly defined to include 'features of archaeological or historic interest'.[18] Such integration contemplates that financial assistance may be given for the conservation of heritage sites,[19] although the provision is limited in this respect to English waters,[20] and at the time of writing, there is no indication that any grant aid has been forthcoming in respect of UCH. Since its enactment, it has been suggested that this could be taken further by including this definition of the environment in the sustainability clause of the FA and for further amendments to be made for the regulation of fishing activities to conserve heritage, thus plugging gaps in current legislation.[21] The FA is applied to offshore fisheries, that is those fisheries exploited beyond 6nm. Within 0-6nm, in England the exploitation of fisheries resources is regulated by Inshore Fisheries and Conservation Authorities (IFCA) with similar provisions undertaken by regulators in Scotland, Wales and Northern Ireland.

A creation of Part 6 of the MACAA, the IFCA are bodies responsible for the management of English inshore fisheries and fisheries resources out to 6 nautical miles (nm), ascribed on a localised basis around the coast of England. There are 10 IFCA in total, with separate inshore fisheries management bodies

---

16 For a consideration of contrasting opinion see, for example, Parham, D, 'RESPONSE OF DAVID PARHAM TO SEAN KINGSLEY'S COMMENTS ON HIS REVIEW OF SEAN KINGSLEY'S *FISHING AND SHIPWRECK HERITAGE: MARINE ARCHAEOLOGY'S GREATEST THREAT?* 2017, the Antiquaries Journal pp. 301–302.

17 Fisheries Act 2020, s.36(2)(b).

18 Fisheries Act 2020, s.52.

19 Fisheries Act 2020, s.33(1) (a) states that 'The Secretary of State may give financial assistance, or arrange for financial assistance to be given, to any person for ... the conservation, enhancement or restoration of the marine and aquatic environment'; powers are given to the devolved assemblies by virtue of Schedule 6.

20 Fisheries Act 2020, s.33(3). By s.33(6) the devolved administrations are granted equivalent powers by virtue of Schedule 6 to the Fisheries Act.

21 Written Evidence submitted by the Honor Frost Foundation (HFF) Steering Committee on Underwater Cultural Heritage (FB09), vol. Fisheries. 2020. See for example <https://publications.parliament.uk/pa/cm5801/cmpublic/Fisheries/memo/FB09.htm>.

in the devolved nations.[22] The purpose of an IFCA is to broaden a narrow focus that was placed solely on fisheries management to include a more holistic approach, taking account of the environmental impacts of fishing and aquaculture. This broader remit includes impacts upon the historic and cultural environment, such that the definition of 'marine environmental matters' includes under section 151(8)(b) MACAA:

> … the conservation or enhancement of the natural beauty or amenity of marine or coastal areas (including their geological or physiographical features) or of any features of archaeological or historic interest in such areas …[23]

At first glance, this potentially imposes a duty on an IFCA to take affirmative action in respect of UCH, although in fact it is solely related to an IFCA's general duty to manage the exploitation of its sea fisheries resources, whilst balancing that consideration with statutory socio-economic factors.[24] The duty to consider UCH is a significant step forward, although it is inexorably tied to the exploitation of fisheries resources, such that it does not confer a power on IFCA to protect UCH without a fisheries connection.

2 England and Wales

2.1 *Marine Licensing and Assessments of Environmental Impact*

Increased development in the marine environment, whether for mineral or aggregate recovery or the location of fixed or floating offshore renewable energy projects has combined with advances in diving and salvage technologies to present a more consistent threat potential to UCH. In the UK, the regulatory landscape has remained relatively constant, although there have been some key developments in policy and law which affect UCH either directly, or as an ancillary by-product of measures directed principally towards the protection of the natural environment. As noted, the fact of devolution has also contributed to the complex and somewhat fragmented legislative framework.

---

22 Beyond 6 nm the MMO is responsible for such management in offshore English waters and those of the devolved administrations.

23 Echoed in a definition of the 'marine environment' at s.186(1) which includes '… features of archaeological or historic interest …'.

24 MACAA, s.153(2)(b).

2.1.1 Marine Licensing

The introduction of the marine licensing regime under Part 4 of the MACAA rates as the most significant legislative addition to the protection of UCH in England and Wales since the PWA. Broadly, a marine licence is required by any person contemplating the undertaking of a 'licensable marine activity',[25] in the UK Marine Area,[26] reflecting wider environmental purposes to be considered in respect of marine development or other interventions. Upon grant of a licence, any authorised activity must be carried out in accordance with it. There are thirteen licensable marine activities contained in the MACAA,[27] with those most relevant to the protection of UCH being:

- To deposit any substance or object within the UK marine licensing area,[28] either in the sea or on or under the sea bed, from any vehicle, vessel, aircraft or marine structure, or any container floating in the sea;
- To deposit any substance or object anywhere in the sea or on or under the seabed from a British vessel, British aircraft or British marine structure, or a container floating in the sea, if the deposit is controlled from a British vessel, British aircraft or British marine structure;
- To use a vehicle, vessel, aircraft, marine structure or floating container,[29] to remove any substance or object from the seabed within the UK marine licensing area;
- To carry out any form of dredging within the UK marine licensing area (whether or not involving the removal of any material from the sea or sea bed).[30]

When it determines an application for a marine licence, the designated regulator, the MMO or Natural Resources Wales (NRW),[31] must have regard to, *inter alia*, the need to protect the environment. For the purposes of marine licensing

25 MACAA s.65(1).

26 The UK Marine Area is defined in MACAA s.42.

27 MACAA s.66(1).

28 The UK marine licensing area encompasses the UK marine area, i.e., the UK Territorial Sea, Exclusive Economic Zone (EEZ) and Continental Shelf, with the exception of the Scottish Inshore Region; s.42(1), s.66(4). The UK declared an EEZ by virtue of the Exclusive Economic Zone Order 2013 (SI 2013/3161), on the basis of the power granted by s.41 MACAA.

29 A floating container would include any buoyancy device, such as a diver's 'lifting bag', which when inflated provides positive buoyancy to lift objects underwater.

30 Dredging is defined as *including* the use of any device to move any material (whether or not suspended in water) from one part of the sea or sea bed to another part; s.66(2)(a). This would include the use of an 'air lift' by a diver to excavate seabed sediment.

31 The licensing authority for marine licences in English territorial waters is the Secretary of State (s.113((8); in Wales it is a shared function of the Secretary of State and Welsh

the environment includes '... any site (including any site comprising, or comprising the remains of, any vessel, aircraft or marine structure) which is of historic or archaeological interest'.[32] While the expression 'historic or archaeological interest' is not defined in the Act itself, a definition has been provided for the Self-Service Marine Licence process, outlined below. It is also important to note that this definition is wider than that used in the PWA as it encompasses any site of historical or archaeological interest, including monuments and flooded landscapes.

Perhaps most significantly, marine licensing has imposed some meaningful restraints upon the otherwise accepted freedom to remove objects from the seabed. In that respect it extends to limit the freedom to conduct salvage other than by hand without prior authorisation, thus creating a baseline position where in many circumstances UCH can be protected from unauthorised disturbance and recovery without the necessity for designation or scheduling under specific UCH legislative provisions. That said, it should be noted that not *all* disturbance and/or recovery of UCH would satisfy the test of what is a 'marine licensable activity' and thus require authorisation by a marine licence, but any large scale disturbance or recovery is almost certainly likely to fall within its contemplation, resulting in a considerable degree of protection offered to UCH and, tellingly, that which to date is not covered by specialist heritage law.

The licensing criteria are broad, encompassing many routine activities. To avoid excessive regulation or administrative burden, three Statutory Orders provide numerous exemptions, obviating the need to apply for a marine licence provided any conditions imposed by these statutory exemptions are compiled with.[33] To take one example intersecting with UCH, Article 24A of the Marine Licensing (Exempted Activities) Order 2011 provides that removal by a harbour authority of marine litter or debris using a vessel or vehicle is exempt only to the extent that it is not '... likely to cause damage to features of archaeological or historic interest in an area where the activities in question occur'.[34] In an attempt to mitigate this administrative tasking and reduce costs in respect of low risk licensable activities, a system of self-servicing for marine

---

Ministers, s.113(4)) although by agreement that function is discharged by the MMO under s.14((1)).

32 MACAA s.115(2). The MMO will consult Historic England in respect of potential impacts of the proposed activity upon UCH.

33 The Marine Licensing (Exempted Activities) Order 2011 (SI 408/2011); the Marine Licensing (Exempted Activities) Order 2013 (SI 526/2013); and the Marine Licensing (Exempted Activities) (Amendment) Order 2019 (SI 2019/893).

34 Article 24A was inserted by art. 9 of the Marine Licensing (Exempted Activities) (Amendment) Order 2019 (SI 2019/893).

licences has been introduced.[35] In relation to UCH it is particularly noteworthy that the self-service activities includes any removal of 'discreet minor objects of archaeological or historic interest from the seabed', described in the associated application.[36] 'Minor objects' are defined as discrete debris, while 'archaeological or historic interest' is defined as that which:

> ... includes all traces of human existence having a cultural, historical or archaeological character such as sites, structures, buildings, artefacts and human remains, together with their archaeological and natural context vessels, aircraft, other vehicles or any part thereof, their cargo or other contents, together with their archaeological and natural context; and (iii) objects of prehistoric character.[37]

This is an extremely wide definition, which mirrors largely that contained in the 2001 Convention,[38] and encompasses, through the marine licensing system, all UCH, in contrast to the more clearly defined triggers of legislation with a specific heritage focus as elaborated later in this chapter.[39] The removal of such objects under a self-service marine licence is subject to specified criteria and conditions, including a consent from Historic England or an approved methodology.[40]

Lobbying by the avocational archaeological diving sector prompted more detailed guidance from the MMO on practices which could be undertaken without a marine licence in order to clear up practical uncertainties.[41] MMO guidance states that a marine licence is not required to use a floating container,

---

35 Available at <https://www.gov.uk/government/publications/self-service-marine-licensing>. The fee for a self-service marine licence is £50.00, which is a considerable cost reduction.

36 Available at <https://www.gov.uk/government/publications/self-service-marine-licensing/self-service-activities-table>. The meaning of 'discreet' is unclear but presumably relates to what are termed by marine archaeologists disarticulated objects that have become detached from any structure or are free standing, such as items of cargo or personal possessions.

37 *Ibid.*

38 See here <https://www.unesco.org/en/underwater-heritage>.

39 The definition is not without its problems, in that the expression '*cultural, historical or archaeological character*' remains undefined, especially in a chronological sense.

40 A template for such approval is available at <https://www.gov.uk/government/publications/self-service-marine-licensing>.

41 The recreational diving activity table is available at <https://www.gov.uk/government/publications/marine-licensing-guidance-for-recreational-divers/recreational-dive-activity-table>.

such as a lifting bag, to remove an object from the seabed where the object does not require a total lifting capacity greater than 100kg and the object to be removed has not been on the seabed for longer than 12 months.[42]

The utility of this means of regulation for the protection UCH has been confirmed in the courts, with successful enforcement action taken by the MMO in circumstances where removal of materials from wrecks was undertaken without a valid marine licence. The first case involved the SS *Cheerful*,[43] a Liverpool based steamship which sank off the coast of Cornwall in 1855 with a cargo of tin ingots. In 2013 the MMO, backed by the support of a Royal Navy fisheries patrol vessel, HMS *Severn*, intercepted and boarded the salvage vessel, MV *Bela*. The enforcement officers discovered in excess of £50,000 worth of tin ingots which had been removed from the wreck without a licence. The skipper of the *Bela*, a Dutch national, pleaded guilty to the charges and was subject to a fine and costs. His British business-partner, a self-declared 'salvage consultant', was found guilty and sentenced to a community order and a costs order. The ingots were forfeited. While the sanctions were not at a high level, the fact of enforcement and the accrued losses in costs were significant and reverberated through the diving and UCH communities.

A more recent prosecution related to the SS *Harrovian*.[44] The ship, a merchant freighter with a cargo of copper ingots, was sunk in 1916 by a German submarine en route from the USA to France. She lay in deep water some 70 miles south of the Isles of Scilly, a small archipelago to the far southwest of the UK. Upon boarding and inspection of the vessel, it was discovered that £90,000 worth of copper and steel had been removed from the vessel. The skipper did not have a marine licence and had dimmed its AIS system in an attempt to disguise its presence at the site. Further investigations showed that the ship, operated by Dutch company Friendship Offshore BV, had made three unlicensed salvage operations at the site. A guilty plea from the defendants saw fines and costs in excess of £50,000 imposed, as well as a confiscation

42 MMO guidance on this matter is available at < https://marinedevelopments.blog.gov.uk/2017/08/23/why-do-i-need-a-licence-to-remove-lost-abandoned-or-discarded-fishing-gear-from-the-sea-bed/>.

43 For details of the wreck, see <https://www.wrecksite.eu/wreck.aspx?76266>; and for detail of the case, see <https://www.gov.uk/government/news/man-found-guilty-of-marine-licensing-offences-relating-to-salvage-of-shipwreck>.

44 For details of the wreck, see <https://www.wrecksite.eu/wreck.aspx?81179>; and for details of the subsequent prosecution, see <https://www.gov.uk/government/news/master-and-owner-charged-for-illegal-salvage-of-sunken-vessel>.

order under proceeds of crime legislation to deprive the offenders of any benefit from the unlawful activity.[45] In this case the vessel was 'of interest' to the MMO and the Ministry of Defence (MOD) as it was suspected as having been in used in salvage operations on wrecks lost during the battle of Jutland in the North Sea. The case highlights also the targeted nature of the interception, reflecting the UK's greater commitment to inter-agency working, as will be outlined further below.

In both cases, the application of the marine licensing regime beyond the 12nm TS offers a greater reach to the enforcement authorities over most heritage-based designation systems. It is also worthy of note that neither wreck was the subject of a specific scheduling or designation as to their heritage value, although both reflected stories of trade, in and out of wartime. Statements from Historic England were provided to the court and assisted in the sentencing, where the heritage value of the wrecks was explicitly mentioned. The trend towards using legislation targeting benefits accrued to an illegal salvor, as well as the development of specific sentencing guidelines, represent a positive development, offering additional consequences after the fact of disturbance, thereby enhancing deterrence.[46]

The application of more broadly environmental regulatory schemes to encompass heritage matters reflects a more systems-thinking approach to the management of the natural and heritage environments. The two are not exclusive and arguably should not be treated as such in law. Naturally, illicit salvage or damage to UCH through the removal of objects of cultural value is only one of the threats to heritage assets. Offshore development has increased considerably in the last few decades adding new threats to the matrix. Within the UK marine area this has been governed principally by the device of Environmental Impact Assessment (EIA), which, to a degree, dovetails with the marine licensing provisions: the former representing a vehicle for detail to inform licence conditions.[47]

---

45 The enabling legislation is contained in Part 2 of the Proceeds of Crime Act 2002, C.29.

46 For further details on sentencing guidance see, for example < https://historicengland.org.uk/images-books/publications/heritage-crime-guidance-sentencers/heag054a-guidance-for-sentencers/ >.

47 For greater detail on the EIA approach, see for example, Lowther, J., Williams, M., 'Beyond National Legislation: using European regulation to manage the UK's Underwater Cultural Heritage', 2012, Proceedings of 3rd International Congress on Underwater Archaeology (IKUWA 3) Henderson, J. (ed.) pp. 95–104, UNESCO/RGK, Bonn; and <https://www.gov.uk/guidance/marine-licensing-impact-assessments>.

2.1.2 Environmental Impact Assessment and Environmental Outcomes Reports

At the time of writing there remain obligations for EIA placed on developers in the UK marine area. Initially, formal EIA within the UK planning system was conceived within the EU by way of a directive. Directives require a member state to achieve a certain outcome by a set date, although the form of the domestic implementing measures is left to the member state's legal system.[48] The original EIA Directive was agreed in 1985 and was required to be implemented from 1988.[49] It has since been modified to reflect a broader range of environmental imperatives.[50] At its simplest, EIA requires that a systematic evaluation of development projects falling into certain defined categories is undertaken in respect of their potential environmental consequences, as a precursor to any development decision being made.[51] Such impacts may be consequent upon licensable activities and to the extent that their impact is significant they may require an EIA as part of the licensing process. 'Environment' is given a broad meaning to include '... material assets and the cultural heritage', meaning that there is a clear application to UCH.[52] In addition, the geographical scope of the EIA Directive extends to the margins of a State's Continental Shelf (CS).[53]

Transposition of the EIA Directive into UK law was complex and piecemeal, generating a considerable body of secondary legislation. At its heart are the Town and Country Planning (Environmental Impact Assessment) Regulations 2017 (the EIA Regulations)[54] and the Marine Works (Environmental

48 Art 288 of the Treaty on the Functioning of the European Union.

49 Directive 85/337/EEC on the assessment of the effects of certain public and private projects on the environment, OJ L175, 1985, p40-48, Article 12.

50 Directive 85/337/EEC was codified by Directive 2011/92/EU on the assessment of the effects of certain public and private projects on the environment OJ L, 2011, p. 1–21, as amended by Directive 2014/52/EU on the assessment of the effects of certain public and private projects on the environment OJ L 124, 2014, p. 1–18.

51 Also included is a requirement for 'strategic EIA' – so that broader scale plans and programmes are brought within it remit, see, for example, Directive 2001/42/EC on the assessment of the effects of certain plans and programmes on the environment, OJ L 197,2001, pp. 30–37.

52 Art 4 EIA Directive.

53 This was confirmed in case C-6/04 *Commission v UK* [2005] I-09017, in respect of the application of the Habitats Directive and has been subsequently applied to EIA in more recent legislative Acts.

54 The Town and Country Planning (Environmental Impact Assessment) Regulations 2017 (SI 2017/571) as amended.

Impact Assessment) Regulations 2007 (the Marine Works Regulations).[55] Together, the measures provide for the MMO to take either the role of an appropriate authority, under the Marine Works Regulations or consultation authority under the EIA Regulations. The crucial difference between the two schemes is that the latter apply more in respect of municipal planning authority boundaries, meaning that, in the UCH context, it applies to impacts on material situated in the intertidal zone; whilst the Marine Works Regulations apply below the low water mark.

Commentators have observed that the system of EIA has flaws, notably in respect of the developer-led nature of scheme, which in effect permits a developer to determine the basis of the environmental impact.[56] Additionally, a negative EIA does not guarantee development will not proceed. In a marine context this is evident in the unsuccessful Judicial Review of a licensing decision to enable aggregate extraction in a proposed Marine Conservation Zone (MCZ). While MCZ s of themselves are designed to protect specific designated features of the natural environment, the area in question, the Goodwin Sands, is an exceptional repository of historic wreck due to its geomorphology and benthic turbidity which has claimed hundreds of unfortunate vessels over centuries.[57]

How long this system remains in effect in the UK context is currently uncertain. The Levelling-up and Regeneration Act 2023 (LRA) proposes to replace EIA as currently constituted with a new regime requiring an obligation for a developer to generate an 'environmental outcomes report' (EOR).[58] The relevant sections of the LRA are not yet in force and the proposed EOR system has been the subject of consultation, which has now ended.[59]

---

55 The Marine Works (Environmental Impact Assessment) Regulations 2007 (SI 2007/1518), as amended in 2011 and 2017 and the Environment, Food and Rural Affairs (Environmental Impact Assessment) (Amendment) (EU Exit) Regulations 2019 (SI 2019/25), amongst others.

56 On the wider point, see for example Jane Holder, 'Environmental Assessment: The Regulation of Decision Making', 2004 OUP, Oxford.

57 On the case see: Lowther, J and Sellick, J, 'Marine Licensing in Marine Conservation Zones - *Thomson v Marine Management Organisation* [2019] EWHC 2368 (Admin)', (2020), 26(4) Journal of Water Law pp184-189. On the Goodwin Sands and wrecks more generally see, Larn, R, 'Goodwin Sands Shipwrecks', 1977, David & Charles, London; and the Goodwin Sands Conservation Trust's resource at <https://goodwinsands.org.uk/why-so-important/history-heritage/shipwrecks/>. Ultimately, dredging did not proceed for non-environmental reasons unspecified by developer.

58 Levelling-up and Regeneration Act 2023, Ch.55.

59 See here <https://www.gov.uk/government/consultations/environmental-outcomes-reports-a-new-approach-to-environmental-assessment/environmental-outcomes-report-a-new-approach-to-environmental-assessment>.

Reception amongst regulators to the consultation seems lukewarm. It is notable that the UK's overall environmental watchdog, the Office for Environmental Protection (OEP) in its consultation response pointed to the limitations of the current system being attributable to cultural as opposed to structural reasons.[60] Historic England's response, whilst welcoming the inclusion of the historic environment (albeit one that is recognised in current EIA), is also clear that the development of targets for integrating cultural heritage more holistically would be beneficial. Given constraints of space it is not possible to give a full account of the consultation responses here, save to note that support for the perceived benefits of the replacement system in its current form is equivocal.[61] If adopted as it is there is certainly scope for future research into its efficacy as regards UCH.

When the new law becomes effective, Part 3 of the LRA requires that a planning authority must have '... special regard to the desirability of preserving or enhancing the asset or its setting ...'.[62] Preservation in this context contemplates '... preserving or enhancing any feature, quality or characteristic of the asset or setting that contributes to the significance of the asset'.[63] Both the terms 'asset' and 'significance' are given meaning with the former including wrecks designated under section 1 of the PWA and monuments scheduled pursuant to the Ancient Monuments and Archaeological Areas Act 1979 (AMAAA). The 'significance' aspect is determined by the trigger points for designation/scheduling and are related to the intrinsic qualities of the asset.[64]

2.1.3 Marine Conservation Zones

Part 5 of MACAA introduced Marine Conservation Zones (MCZ). Primarily a natural environment designation, conferring a specific Marine Protected Area (MPA) status, they have not been used, to date, to further the protection of UCH in England and Wales. Provision exists, tangentially, to designate an MCZ

60 See, for example, <https://www.theoep.org.uk/sites/default/files/reports-files/OEP%20response%20to%20Environmental%20Outcomes%20Reports%20%28EOR%29%20Consultation.pdf>, p. 3.

61 See for example, Historic England's and the Joint Nautical Archaeology Policy Committee's responses, available at < https://historicengland.org.uk/content/docs/consultations/response-environmental-outcomes-consultation-jun23/> and < https://jnapcorg.files.wordpress.com/2023/06/jnapc-response-on-environmental-outcomes-reports-consultation-07.06.23.pdf> respectively.

62 Levelling-up and Regeneration Act 2023, s.102(1).

63 Levelling-up and Regeneration Act 2023, s.102(2).

64 Levelling-up and Regeneration Act 2023, s.102(3).

for their 'geomorphological interest',[65] which might be stretched to include anthropogenically altered landscape features. There is no basis for the designation of wrecks in this statutory provision however, and to date no designation has been made on grounds related to non-natural heritage. There is provision in the MCZ designation process for the designating authority to have regard to 'any economic or social consequences of doing so', which contemplates impacts upon sites '... in that area (including any sites comprising, or comprising the remains of, any vessel, aircraft or marine installation) which are of historic or archaeological interest.[66] As noted in section 5 below, there is some variation in the legislative approach adopted across the devolved nations.

3 UCH Specific Measures

Aside from ancillary protective benefits ushered in by the extension of laws primarily centred on issues other than UCH, but where the carrying out of those activities may be harmful, UK law has significant bespoke heritage legislation that applies to UCH. This part updates the position in respect of developments in the law and policy regarding such measures, first by considering a recent and novel device using a specific international treaty and then UK specific measures adopted across the respective nations.

3.1 *The Endurance and the Antarctic Treaty*

In an innovative approach to UCH protection, in 2018 the UK's Foreign and Commonwealth Office published a Strategy for The Conservation and Protection of Underwater Cultural Heritage in The British Antarctic Territory.[67] Spurred on by, ultimately successful, attempts to locate the *Endurance*, Shackleton's famous expedition ship which was crushed by sea ice and sunk in 1915, the UK Government sought to make use of the Historic Sites and Monuments provisions under Annex V of the Protocol on Environmental Protection to the Antarctic Treaty.[68] Specifically, it was proposed that *Endurance* be added to the List of Historic Sites and Monuments (the List) in accordance with Annex V,[69] which prior to this had been used solely for terrestrial features. The wreck, all

65 MACAA, s.117(1)(c).

66 MACAA, s117(7) and (8).

67 The Strategy is available at <https://www.gov.uk/government/publications/british-antarctic-territory-underwater-cultural-heritage>.

68 Antarctic Treaty 1959, 402 UNTS 71; Protocol on Environmental Protection to the Antarctic Treaty, Madrid, 1991, UNTS 2941.

69 Article 8(2) Annex V of the Protocol on Environmental Protection to the Antarctic Treaty.

artefacts contained or formerly contained within it, and a defined debris field, was added to the List in 2019 by the Committee for Environmental Protection (CEP).[70] The inclusion occurred despite *Endurance's* precise location at the time being unknown, other than it was beneath the Weddell Sea ice, demonstrating a degree of pragmatic creativity within the designation system.[71] In 2021, Spain successfully secured the listing of the *San Telmo* wreck by the same process.[72] At the time of writing, both vessels are yet to be fully subject to management measures: the *Endurance* will be subject to a management plan in 2024/25 and the *San Telmo* must first be discovered.

3.2 *Military UCH Remains*

The advent of marine licensing within the UK Marine Area represents a very significant contribution to the protection of UCH. However, marine licensing did not entirely replace the utility of the Protection of Military Remains Act 1986 (PMRA), since recoveries by hand by divers or by the hand hauling of ropes remain outside the marine licensing regulatory regime. Consequently, mechanisms such as the PMRA and, within the UK's Territorial Waters, the PWA and the AMAAA remain very relevant. Consequently, it is important to distinguish between protection for military UCH located within UK Territorial Waters and that located beyond this 12 nautical mile limit.

3.2.1 Military UCH Remains within UK Territorial Waters

Within the UK's Territorial Waters, the framework for the protection of military UCH remains fragmented. Since 2006 the PMRA has continued to be applied as the primary tool for protection of military UCH within UK Territorial Waters. resulting by 2019 in thirteen Controlled Sites, where all exploratory diving must be licensed by the MOD, and a further ninety-three wrecks designated as Protected Places where diving is permitted on a 'look but do not touch' basis.[73]

However, as Prof. Dromgoole noted, there is an overlap between the applicability of the PMRA and that of the PWA and the AMAAA, with no clear policy demarcation as to the selection of which Act to use in some instances.[74] This is

70 HSM 93 adopted by Measure 12 (2019) – ATCM XLII – CEP XXII, Prague, available at < https://www.ats.aq/devAS/ToolsAndResources/SearchAtd?lang=e&top=404>.

71 Since its discovery *Endurance's* listing has been amended to reflect its known location, see Measure 18 (2022) – ATCM XLIV – CEP XXIV, Berlin.

72 HSM 95.

73 The Protection of Military Remains Act 1986 (Designation of Vessels and Controlled Sites) Order 2019; <https://www.legislation.gov.uk/uksi/2019/1191/schedule/1/made>.

74 An example of a vessel that could have been protected under the PMRA 1986 but was designated under the PWA 1973 is the minesweeper trawler HMT *Arfon*, lost on 30th April 1917

well illustrated by the scheduling as a monument under the AMAAA of a World War II (WWII) Lockheed Lighting fighter near Harlech in North Wales. Located in the intertidal zone, the substantial remains of the aircraft are automatically a Protected Place under the PMRA but were also scheduled by the Welsh Government as a monument in November 2019.[75] While it may seem somewhat redundant to have military UCH protected by two separate legislative provisions Cadw, the Welsh heritage agency, confirmed that the scheduling was undertaken in order to make possible the future heritage management provisions of the AMAAA, including funding provision. This underlines the lacuna in the PMRA that it was intended primarily to protect the last known resting place of lost service personnel solely by restricting public interference and not as a proactive heritage management tool. Indeed, beyond the prohibition of disturbance and/or public access, the PMRA provides no duties or powers of conservation, nor is the MOD, the parent department for the Act, charged with heritage management. These are significant limitations upon the utility of the Act as a heritage management tool.

The consequence of this is that all the ongoing archaeological investigation of military UCH protected under the Act has been undertaken on a voluntary basis by third party individuals or organisations, licensed by MOD under the Act. This in no way has detracted from the quality of the investigations undertaken, which has resulted in several impressive survey reports.[76] However, it does underline that this management of military UCH under the PMRA is being undertaken on a somewhat arbitrary and *ad hoc* basis, rather than being the product of a predetermined research framework. This is undoubtedly the result of the Act's limited objectives and the fact that it is administered by the MOD, a non-heritage department. Apparently, in 2018 and again in 2024 the MOD was considering reform of the PMRA, but to date nothing has yet materialised.

---

by mining; <https://historicengland.org.uk/listing/the-list/list-entry/1432595?section=official-list-entry>. In the case of vehicles neither the PMPA 1986 nor the PWA 1973 would apply, as instanced by the scheduling of early prototype amphibious tanks in Poole Bay; see further <https://historicengland.org.uk/listing/the-list/list-entry/1459754>.

75 <https://www.gov.wales/harlech-p-38-scheduled-its-historic-importance-and-future-protection>.

76 HMS *Vanguard* Battleship lost by explosion 9th July 1917 and HMS *Royal Oak* Battleship torpedoed September 1939, both in Scapa Flow; <https://www.huskyan.com/diving/hms-vanguard> and <https://discovery.dundee.ac.uk/ws/portalfiles/portal/56863842/Royal_Oak_80_Final_Report_v10_combined_FIN.pdf>; HMS *Hampshire* Cruiser torpedoed off Orkney 5th July 1916; <https://core.ac.uk/download/pdf/286356244.pdf>; in the summer of 2022 the Nautical Archaeology Society surveyed HMS *Natal* lost by explosion Cromarty Firth 30th July 1915 and a survey report is in preparation.

Within England, use of the AMAAA had been far more constrained. Due to resource implications, it seemed that Historic England would not schedule UCH even when its own evaluations concluded that the site meet all the criteria for scheduling. Eventually pressure from the archaeological community led to a revision of this policy, with two UCH sites, those of a sunken Landing Craft and sunken tanks associated with the D-Day landings, being scheduled in UK Territorial Waters.[77]

2.2.2 Military UCH Remains beyond within UK Territorial Waters

Beyond UK Territorial Waters the protection of military UCH is less well provided for. The PWA and the AMAAA do not operate beyond the 12nm limit and, while the PMRA 1986 has extra territorial jurisdiction, beyond this limit the Act applies only to British nationals or UK-flagged vessels. Consequently, apart from the limited applicability of the PMRA, protection for military UCH beyond 12nm is reliant upon the marine licensing system, which will not apply to recoveries by hand, and primarily the concept of Sovereign Immunity.[78] Guidance issued in 2014 by the MOD and the Department of Digital, Culture, Media and Sport (DCMS) states the UK takes the view that customary international law affords Sovereign Immunity to State owned or operated vessels used for non-commercial purposes at the time of their loss.[79] This immunity includes the right not to have salvage services imposed upon them without express authorisation of the vessel's Flag State. This view is not universally shared by States but does reflect the position under the Brussels Convention on Salvage 1910,[80] and the International Salvage Convention 1989.[81] Whether this position is reflected adequately in the 2001 Convention is disputed but the UK continues to take the view it is not.[82] This apparently remains a cornerstone of the UK's refusal to sign the 2001 Convention.

77 Lowther, J., Parham, D., Williams, M., 'All at Sea: When Duty meets Austerity in Scheduling Monuments in English Waters', JPL (3) 2017 pp. 245–334. Since the initial scheduling of the two monuments, a further 26 sites have gained this protected status under the AMAAA.

78 Merchant Shipping Act 1995, s.230 states that the law of civil salvage, with some limited exceptions, shall apply to salvage services rendered to Her Majesty's vessels. The current interpretation by MOD is that it removes the Sovereign Immunity from salvage of such vessels within UK Territorial Waters, but not beyond.

79 The guidance is available at <https://www.gov.uk/government/publications/protection-and-management-of-historic-military-wrecks-outside-uk-territorial-waters>.

80 Convention for the Unification of Certain Rules of Law respecting Assistance and Salvage at Sea, Brussels September 1910, Art. 14.

81 1953 UNTS 165, Art. 4.

82 Pers.comm 28th November 2017.

An additional consequence of the inapplicability of the PWA and the AMAAA beyond the UK's Territorial Waters is that there are no funding mechanisms for marine archaeology apart from developer-led funding through marine licensing. This resource lacuna has had very undesirable results in respect of military UCH as occurred for example with the HMS *Victory* (1744).[83] The predecessor of the current HMS *Victory* preserved in Portsmouth; this was a First-Rate warship launched in 1737. Returning from the Mediterranean, the ship disappeared with all hands in a gale on 5th October 1744.[84] In February 2009, Odyssey Marine Exploration (OME) announced that it had located the wreck site.[85]

The MOD subsequently undertook a public consultation as to how archaeological investigation might be resourced.[86] There was no public funding mechanism identified and the MOD's solution was to gift the wreck in January 2012 to a charity, the Maritime Heritage Foundation (MHF) upon trust for it to undertake future management of the site for the benefit and education of the Nation.[87] This was a newly created charity with no obvious funding stream sufficient to resource a major archaeological investigation and recovery some 45nm offshore.[88] The Deed of Gift provided, *inter alia*, that the charity was not to disturb, remove from the seabed, sell, charge, lease or otherwise dispose of any part of the vessel or anything connected with it in the vicinity of the site.[89] Additionally, 'Key Principles' were agreed between the MOD and MHF, which stipulated, *inter alia*, that the project was "categorically not salvage" and the project would adhere to the Rules of the Annex to the 2001 Convention, Rule 2 of which prohibits commercial exploitation of UCH.[90] An Advisory Group was also established, comprising representatives from MOD, Historic England, the Receiver of Wreck and the National Museum of the Royal Navy. Later, the MOD and the Department of Culture, Media and Sport

---

83 This resource lacuna will also apply to non-military UCH and is discussed below in relation to UK Government policy on UCH within the UK Marine Area.

84 <http://www.victory1744.org/thecannon.html>.

85 <https://rescue-archaeology.org.uk/2015/03/victory/>.

86 The outcomes of the consultation are available at <https://assets.publishing.service.gov.uk/government/uploads/system/uploads/attachment_data/file/72858/HMSVictory1744-options-consultation.pdf>.

87 See here <https://www.gov.uk/government/news/hms-victory-1744-a-rare-gift-to-foundation>.

88 See here <https://register-of-charities.charitycommission.gov.uk/charity-search/-/charity-details/5016772>.

89 The detail of the deed is available at <https://assets.publishing.service.gov.uk/government/uploads/system/uploads/attachment_data/file/27932/victory_1744_deed.pdf>.

90 <http://www.victory1744.org/keyprinciples.html>.

(DCMS) appointed an Expert Panel comprised of persons with expertise in marine archaeology, survey and UCH law.

MHF subsequently appointed OME as an archaeological contractor, under a contract whereby OME would be reimbursed for its work with 80% of the value of artefacts recovered, with the possibility that this recompense could be in artefacts rather than cash. This immediately caused considerable concern within the marine archaeological community, since the contract's terms appeared difficult, if not impossible, to reconcile with adherence to the Annex's Rule 2 and the Key Principles. On 24th October 2014 the Secretary of State for Defence granted consent to MHF to recover at risk surface items, but in March 2015 withdrew this consent in the face of a threatened Judicial Review.[91] The proposed review was based upon the contention that the consent authorised commercial exploitation of UCH in breach of the UK's policy of adherence to the Rules of the Annex; and that neither an adequate Project Design had been submitted nor adequate funding arrangements put in place, both of which the Rules required.[92] The MOD then reconsidered the consent.[93]

On 19th July 2018, MHF was informed that consent would not be given for the project to proceed and that *in situ* preservation would be pursued.[94] Perhaps inevitably, the Secretary of State subsequently faced another Judicial Review brought by MHF in respect of this decision. This action was based upon a legitimate expectation that consent would not be withheld, and that the decision was unreasonable in that there were no material factual changes since consent had first been granted.[95] In any case, the court ruled the claim failed and the wreck remains preserved *in situ*.[96] In February 2024, the MOD issued a tender for a detailed survey of the wreck.

A number of significant conclusions can be drawn from these events, the most obvious of which is that the structure of management of the UK's military UCH beyond 12nm was not sufficiently developed to respond robustly to a discovery of highly significant UCH in the UK Marine Area but outside UK

91 The Judicial Review was brought by Mr. Robert Yorke, Chair of the UK's Joint Nautical Archaeology Policy Committee (JNAPC).

92 <http://www.brickcourt.co.uk/news/detail/secretary-of-state-for-defence-forced-to-retake-decision-concerning-the-raising-of-artefacts-from-the-wreck-of-the-18th-century-hms-victory>.

93 *The Maritime Heritage Foundation v The Secretary of State for Defence v Secretary of State for Digital, Culture, Media and Sport* [2019] EWHC 2513 (Admin) para. 30.

94 *Ibid.* para. 1.

95 *Ibid.* para. 2.

96 *Ibid.* paras. 80–85.

Territorial Waters.[97] This appeared to result in an *ad hoc* response to put a management process in place and insufficient consideration appears to have been given to how outsourced management of such UCH could be achieved within the UK's self-imposed constraints of adherence to the Rules of the Annex. It seems there was a constant tension between a perceived need by MOD officials to resource the management and the reality that no public funding would be made available. This resulted in an attempt to outsource such management to the voluntary sector, without due diligence being undertaken as to whether the chosen charity had the resources to execute this management without exposing the UCH to the risk of commercial exploitation. The fact that MOD was the responsible department but is not a heritage department, and that the chosen charity had no track record of involvement in the discipline of marine archaeology, also appear to have been contributory factors. These, combined with the fact that DCMS was not initially involved in the decision-making process and that external expert advice was not available to MOD officials, led to an insufficient appreciation of the policy complexities. An additional aggravating factor is that gifting the title to the wreck to a charity meant the site probably lost its entitlement to Sovereign Immunity. While it would appear unlikely that management of military UCH beyond UK Territorial Waters will be outsourced to charities in the future, at least not by transfer of ownership, this funding and policy lacuna, both for military and non–military UCH situated in the UK Marine Area will continue to have an adverse impact on the UK's UCH in the absence of the applicability of seabed developer funding.[98]

Beyond the UK Marine Area, the UK has, in terms of military UCH, actively pursued a policy of 'shared heritage' with co-operative Coastal States in whose waters UK military UCH is located. Normally, the UK retains title while ceding heritage management to the Coastal State in question, as for example with both HMS *Fowey* and HMT *Bedfordshire*, discussed below. An exception to this usual policy is agreement concluded with Canada over HMS *Terror* and HMS *Erebus*, lost circa 1848 on Franklin's ill-fated Artic Expedition.[99] In 1997 the UK

97 See also a presentation entitled 'HMS Victory 1744 A Case Study' given by Ms. Elisabeth Bussey-Jones at an ESRC seminar "Enhancing Past Sacrifices" at Plymouth University in November 2021 and available at <https://www.youtube.com/watch?v=ehW1ar_xUqw>.

98 At the time of writing assertions of a similar failure of adequate management of military UCH situated just outside UK Territorial Waters have emerged. These are in respect of the wreck of HMS *Gloucester*, lost in 1682. See <http://thepipeline.info/blog/2023/02/04/exclusive-kentucky-fried-shipwreck-the-real-story-of-the-discovery-of-hms-gloucester-norfolks-mary-rose/>.

99 <https://www.rmg.co.uk/stories/topics/hms-terror-erebus-history-franklin-lost-expedition>.

granted control and custody of the wrecks to Canada and in 2017 ownership of the wrecks was gifted to it.[100]

HMS *Fowey* was sunk on a reef on 26th June 1778 in what is now Biscayne National Park near Miami. The wreck is of national importance to the USA and UK. In August 2013, the U.S. National Park Service (NPS) and the UK entered into a Memorandum of Understanding (MOU). This recognises UK title to and the Sovereign Immunity of the wreck, while endorsing co-operation for further protection, monitoring and research. The MOU apparently commits the NPS to management of the site in accordance with its own policies, the American Sunken Military Craft Act 2004 and the principles of the 2001 Convention.[101]

HMT *Bedfordshire* was sunk on 11th May 1942 with the loss of all hands by the German submarine *U-558* while serving off the east coast of the USA. In January 2016, the U.S. National Oceanic and Atmospheric Administration (NOAA) similarly concluded a MOU with the UK, recognising the UK's title to the wreck and its Sovereign Immunity and committing NOAA to co-operation in respect of protection and monitoring, research into and education about the wreck, as well *in situ* preservation according to NOAA's policies and practices and the principles of the 2001 Convention.[102]

It is also understood that tentative discussions have occurred in relation to a similar agreement being reached with Uruguay in respect of the wreck of HMS *Agamemnon*,[103] which is already the subject of a joint archaeological investigation between Uruguayan and UK institutions.[104] However, it is believed that this instance has thrown up potential difficulties surrounding the concept of Sovereign Immunity. Like many South American Coastal States, Uruguay has expressed reservations concerning the application of Sovereign Immunity to UCH, though its current position in relation to HMS *Agamemnon* is uncertain.[105] In contrast, the UK may well expect acknowledgement of its ownership and the Sovereign Immune status of the wreck before entering into any shared heritage agreement. While the Director of the National Museum of the Royal Navy has characterised this debate as "sterile", in the sense that it does not address the main challenge as to how is cultural benefit to be secured

100 <https://www.gov.uk/government/news/defence-secretary-announces-exceptional-gift-to-canada>.

101 <https://www.nps.gov/bisc/learn/news/fowey-agreement.htm>.

102 <https://monitor.noaa.gov/shipwrecks/bedfordshire.html>.

103 Reputed to be Lord Nelson's favourite ship, this 64-gun Royal Navy vessel was lost at the mouth of the River Plate.

104 <https://www.bucklershard.co.uk/news/new-exhibition-agamemnon/>.

105 See, further the chapter on Uruguay in this book.

for mankind, it is indicative that geo-politics often accompanies the management of UCH.[106]

Underlying this shared heritage approach is the fact that the UK, as a result of former Empire and world conflicts, has military UCH located across the globe and no realistic prospect of funding protection, archaeological investigation and conservation of this heritage. A shared heritage policy is therefore both a pragmatic solution and a political and a fiscal inevitability, provided the Coastal State in question has adequate resources and is committed to adherence to the principles, if not the exact Rules of the Annex to the 2001 Convention. Indeed, it is interesting that neither the USA nor the UK have signed the 2001 Convention, but the principles thereof are clearly influencing these shared heritage agreements, suggesting that the Rules of the Annex are becoming an international yardstick in terms of heritage management, even for those States not party to the 2001 Convention. Reflecting these imperatives, the National Museum of the Royal Navy wishes to work across jurisdictions ensuring public enjoyment of UK military UCH and facilitating this by using technology for greater access. However, to-date the agreements with Canada and the USA have been with countries that adhere to the principle of Sovereign Immunity of sunken military UCH, irrespective of time lapsed and with well-developed heritage management organisations, polices, regulatory frameworks and resources. To what extent this shared heritage approach will function with Coastal States that have less developed resources and/or a different perspective on Coastal State jurisdiction and Sovereign Immunity remains to be seen.

3.3 *UK Heritage Policy and Co-Ordination*

While there has been since 2006 no structural changes to the regulatory framework, with the exception of the introduction of the marine licensing legislation discussed above, much attention has been focused in recent years on the lack of a coherent UCH policy and administration, as well as a lack of funding.[107] These concerns are especially acute in relation to UCH beyond UK Territorial Waters but within the UK Marine Area. This attention has principally been driven by the JNAPC.

---

106 See a presentation entitled 'Shared Underwater Heritage' given by Dominic Tweddle at an ESRC seminar "Enhancing Past Sacrifices" at Plymouth University in November 2021 and available at <https://www.youtube.com/watch?v=ehW1ar_xUqw>.

107 At the time of writing the Historic Environment (Wales) Act 2023, has been passed by the Welsh Assembly (Senedd), although the Act is not yet in force, see < https://cadw.gov.wales/advice-support/historic-environment-wales-act-2023>.

In addition to the case of HMS *Victory* (1744), these concerns had been crystalised by a number of instances involving what the marine archaeological community considers to be inadequate co-ordination between government departments and heritage agencies and a lack of funding to permit mitigation for seabed development. The most significant of these instances is the case of the *Galloper* wreck. This was discovered in July 2016 during a survey for unexploded ordnance (UXO) prior to construction of the Galloper Offshore Wind Farm. Since the purpose of the survey was to detect UXO, no specific archaeological survey was undertaken on behalf of the developer. It is believed that this previously unknown wreck, is most likely to be that of a warship, with at least 13 bronze cannons present. The location of the site was leaked to the commercial and recreational diving communities and the site has become significantly threatened by interference and from illicit recovery.[108] The environmental stability of the site is also undetermined.

In January 2019, JNAPC wrote to DCMS requesting that funding be made available for an archaeological survey of the wreck. In April 2019, a DCMS official responded saying:

> Given that DCMS has no remit in relation to wreck sites located outside of our territorial waters, I regret that unfortunately we cannot contribute public funds for the assessment of this site [Galloper], or other sites in similar locations.[109]

JNAPC responded in August 2019, pointing out that this was an incorrect statement of the legal position. JNAPC's challenge to DCMS's assertion was based upon the duty imposed under Article 303(1) UN Law of the Sea Convention (LOSC) and Section 44 of the MACAA, under which all UK authorities are expected to adopt the MPS. The MPS, while arising in the context of marine planning, is a broad inter-departmental statement of the UK's marine policy, which makes it compulsory for *all public authorities providing any authorisations or enforcement*, relating to the marine environment, to observe the Statement.[110] The MPS has been adopted by the Secretary of State and all Devolved Administrations as 'a key step towards achieving the vision shared by the UK Administrations … of having clean, healthy, safe, productive and biologically

108 'Galloper Wreck: Position Paper' JNAPC 1st July 2019, unpublished.

109 Letter DCMS to JNAPC 23rd April 2019, unpublished.

110 'Marine Policy Statement', (2011) Op cit. p. 13 – *emphasis added.* Available from <https://assets.publishing.service.gov.uk/government/uploads/system/uploads/attachment_data/file/69322/pb3654-marine-policy-statement-110316.pdf)>.

diverse oceans and seas.'[111] The government thereby set its High Level Marine Objectives inside the MPS, which 'recognises the protection and management needs of marine cultural heritage according to its significance',[112] given that 'heritage assets are a finite and often irreplaceable resource and can be vulnerable to a wide range of human activities'.[113] The MPS therefore imposes a duty on public authorities to be sensitive to 'any potential impacts on sites of particular significance including those … designated in relation to cultural heritage [or] of particular social or economic significance'.[114] Throughout the MPS, the importance of protecting the historic environment is an explicit consideration of the UK's wider marine strategy. This is emphasised by the statement that:

> '[o]pportunities should be taken to contribute to our knowledge and understanding of our past by capturing evidence from the historic environment and making this publicly available'.[115]

Thus, given that the DCMS is the primary government department responsible for preserving, promoting, protecting and supporting research into the UK's cultural heritage, JNAPC argued it is clearly incumbent on it to consider these duties towards cultural heritage in the marine environment.

It was only in January 2021, 17 months later, that DCMS responded saying:

> DCMS has lead responsibility for UCH … DCMS will continue to explore opportunities across Government and more widely to enhance the protection and management of UCH, including that located in the UK Marine Area but outside UK territorial waters.[116]

This appeared to confirm that DCMS does indeed have a remit in relation to wreck sites located outside Territorial Waters, but within the UK Marine Area. However, to date no new funding has been provided. A further concern arising from this case is that discovery during pre-seabed development is not seen as an adverse impact upon UCH. Consequently, if a developer can avoid direct physical disturbance of UCH no requirement for archaeological investigation is imposed. However, as the *Galloper* wreck has demonstrated, knowledge of

111 *Ibid*, p. 3.
112 *Ibid*, p. 12.
113 *Ibid*, p. 21.
114 *Ibid*, p. 14.
115 *Ibid*, pp. 21–22.
116 DCMS letter to JNAPC 19th January 2021 unpublished.

such discoveries inevitably enters the public domain and results in a threat to the site. Discovery of UCH in the course of development therefore needs to be recognised as an adverse impact *per se*.

Other instances of inconsistent application of UK policy on UCH beyond 12 nm include the awarding of salvage contracts in respect of WWI and II mercantile war casualties and their cargoes by the Department of Transport (DfT), His Majesty's Treasury (HMT) and the Government Legal Department (GLD). As of 2019, JNAPC has determined that none of these Departments has a formal requirement to consult with DCMS or a heritage agency prior to issuing a salvage contract, nor are these Departments or DCMS or the heritage agencies always consulted by the MMO when considering marine licence applications relating to such wrecks.[117] Moreover, the MMO appears to be inconsistent in its requirements for marine licence applicants to supply heritage information.[118]

JNAPC has proposed several solutions for more consistent management of UCH, especially that beyond UK Territorial Waters but within the UK Marine Area. These include DCMS taking a proactive leadership role in respect of UCH policy, greater adherence to the UK MPS by government departments and public agencies and the formalisation of data sharing and consultation between government departments and agencies.[119]

Since June 2019, JNAPC has repeatedly sought a meeting with DCMS to discuss these proposals. Its Chair ultimately met with the former Minister Lord Parkinson, in early 2024, although any outcome is now subject to the change of government following the UK's 2024 General Election. JNAPC had earlier been supported by the All-Party Parliamentary Archaeological Group in 2021.[120] Until recently, the indication was that there was little or no appetite within DCMS to address the funding lacuna or the inconsistent application of UK UCH policy. Ultimately, like all matters of resource allocation in society, this comes down to a question of political priorities. In a manifestation of what has been termed 'sea blindness', it would appear that within the UK central government the protection and conservation of UCH has little or no political priority. The

117 Following controversy surrounding DfT's granting of a salvage contract for recovery of a cargo of silver from the SS *Gairsoppa*, sunk in the Western Approaches in February 1941, DfT appears to have temporarily stopped awarding salvage contracts. See <https://theconversation.com/sunken-ship-yields-silver-booty-but-should-we-let-sleeping-wrecks-lie-3575>.

118 *'Cross Government Policy for Underwater Cultural Heritage: Proposals for Consistent Management'* JNAPC Paper submitted to DCMS.

119 *Ibid.*

120 *'Request to the All-Party Parliamentary Archaeology Group to consider the responsibilities and actions of DCMS regarding Underwater Cultural Heritage'* JNAPC Paper May 2021 unpublished.

newly elected Labour Government, at the time of writing, has not declared any policy intentions with respect to UCH.

4 Enforcement

A striking feature of the UK experience over the period since the last edition of this volume has been a policy shift that places greater emphasis on the development of enforcement mechanisms by the principal heritage regulators: Historic England and its devolved counterparts.[121] The enforcement matrix has been fortified with use of common criminal offences such as theft or criminal damage, applied alongside heritage specific offences as detailed in the legislation discussed above. In parallel, numerous initiatives in terms of detection, interdiction and investigation, as well as post-conviction measures such as sentencing guidance,[122] the use of impact statements and application of generic sentencing tools, such as proceeds of crime orders,[123] have helped to provide increased visibility in respect of heritage crime. The development has been incremental and systematic and, while having a primarily terrestrial provenance, has been successfully extended to apply to UCH.[124] Strategically, the protection of UCH is identified in the National Strategy for Maritime Security as a task for government. It provides for:

> ... focus on in-situ preservation alongside safety and environmental management. This involves a number of government departments and agencies who focus on protecting military remains, cultural heritage and preventing illegal salvage activity of our historic and sensitive underwater sites.[125]

---

121 In Wales, Cadw; Northern Ireland DEARA; and Scotland, Historic Environment Scotland.

122 See for example, Fisher, J and Harrison, M, 'Guidance for Sentencers: Heritage Crime', 2017, Historic England, available at < https://historicengland.org.uk/images-books/publications/heritage-crime-guidance-sentencers/ >.

123 As discussed above in respect of SS *Cheerful* and SS *Harrovian;* and also see in respect of a salvage prosecution < https://www.theguardian.com/uk-news/2014/jul/02/divers-pay-60000-plunder-artefacts-wrecks-fail-declare-haul>.

124 For a thorough explanation of the English experience, see Lowther, J., Gall, S. Bean, E. and Williams, M. (2019) Enhancing Protection of Underwater Heritage Assets, (Historic England Project Number 7146), available at < https://historicengland.org.uk/images-books/publications/enhancing-protection-underwater-heritage-assets/ >.

125 HM Government, 'National Strategy for Maritime Security', 2022, CP724, London, page 28. Available at < https://assets.publishing.service.gov.uk/media/62fcbf748fa8f504bd84581f/national-strategy-for-maritime-security-print-version.pdf>.

Despite this, none of the UK's heritage agencies has the power to enforce and prosecute for heritage offences *per se*. Instead, reliance has traditionally been placed on the police for the majority of interventions. Given the particular challenges of enforcement offshore, whether in terms of location, knowledge of offences and/or evidence gathering, specialist policing is required, although the MMO/Receiver of Wreck assume an enforcement role for marine licensing/salvage offences. The MACAA empowers certain marine enforcement officers, to include officers of armed-services vessels or aircraft.[126] Contemporary legislation, in the shape of the Policing and Crime Act 2017 (PACA), has offered additional opportunity both to respond and to provide a deterrence to crimes perpetrated against UCH.

Part 4 of PACA provides, so far as relevant for UCH offences, that a 'an enforcement officer'[127] may, exercise any of the 'maritime enforcement powers'[128] set out in it regarding vessels in English (and Welsh) Territorial Waters. These powers, including powers of entry, search, seizure and arrest, exist for the purpose of preventing, detecting, investigating or prosecuting an offence, which include those created under the Merchant Shipping Act 1995 (MSA), the PWA, the AMAAA, the MACAA and the PMRA. In all cases, the trigger for the exercise of the powers is that the officer has reasonable grounds to suspect that an offence in respect of UCH is being or has been committed on the ship; or that the ship is being used in the commission of an offence.[129]

There are certain jurisdictional limits on the use of marine enforcement powers which relate to the flag status of the ships involved and/or their location in English and Welsh, or international waters.[130] Secretary of State authority is required in certain circumstances, and so far as material to UCH, this would apply to non-UK ships either within English and Welsh Territorial Waters, or in international waters.[131] Noting the position consequent upon

126 MACAA 2009, s.235. An offence is created in MACAA s.292 should a person fail to act in accordance with a direction of a marine enforcement officer, to complement the exercise of specific powers of enforcement.

127 PACA 2017, s.84(3) is broadly cast in that it includes the Police, Ministry of Defence Police, special constables, British Transport Police, port constables (appointed under s.7 Marine Navigation Act 2013), designated customs officers, designated National Crime Agency officers or other persons designated by the Secretary of State.

128 PACA 2017, ss.88–90. This includes UK Border Force, which has the most significant marine resources aside from the armed forces.

129 PACA, 2017, s.88(1).

130 PACA 2017, s.84(1).

131 PACA 2017, s.85 – note here that reference to the Secretary of State is to the Secretary of State for the Home Office.

the devolved status of UCH protection, s.86 PACA empowers law enforcement officers to exercise marine enforcement powers in circumstances of 'hot pursuit' into Scottish Territorial Waters.[132] More generically, the Export of Objects of Cultural Interest (Control) Order 2003, could apply as the term cultural goods includes archaeological material over 100 years old recovered from the sea.[133] Attempting to export cultural goods could engage s.68(1) of the Customs and Excise Management Act 1979, which governs the export or shipment of any goods subject to a prohibition or restriction in respect of those goods under any enactment. Additionally, offences related to dealing in 'tainted objects' are set out in the Dealing in Cultural Objects (Offences) Act 2003. In short, exporting cultural goods would be in breach of both the specific Order, as well as the more generic customs offences.

The expansion of the regulatory tool-kit is certainly welcomed. However, the extent to which it will secure beneficial outcomes is uncertain and will rely on a commitment to ensure that resources are made available for training and the means to be able to police challenging offshore environments. In that regard and noting that none of the enforcement agencies has tasking for UCH protection as their principal duty or area of focus, a Common Enforcement Manual (CEM) will be launched by Historic England in the latter part of 2025. The CEM, a recommendation of previous work,[134] will provide a legal resource for agencies with offshore capabilities to ascertain, disrupt and enforce illicit operations affecting UCH.

5 Scotland

5.1 *Introduction*

The following sections build upon a foundational understanding of specific aspects of UK policy and legislation relating to UCH, with a specific focus on Scottish management systems.

Within the wider context of management of the marine environment, the Scottish Marine Protected Areas Project combines the efforts of Historic Environment Scotland (HES) with Marine Scotland, Scottish Natural Heritage, the Scottish Environment Protection Agency and the Joint Nature Conservation Committee to appropriately manage and prioritise marine natural and cultural

132 Although, Secretary of State approval is required in respect of non-UK ships.

133 Export of Objects of Cultural Interest (Control) Order 2003 (SI 2003/2759), as amended, Art 1(3).

134 See *supra* n. 124.

resources through Nature Conservation MPAs, Demonstration and Research MPAs and Historic MPAs. To facilitate designation, Scottish marine legislation and policy provides powers to designate all types of MPAs to conserve the marine environment for the benefit of future generations.

Scotland's TS contains an extensive archaeological record spanning thousands of years of human interactions with the sea and Continental Shelf. In addition, Scotland's UCH is intrinsically linked to the identity and well-being of Scottish people, a factor which has been integrated within its UCH legislation.

As well as playing a significant role in the development of the discipline of maritime archaeology, Scotland houses a number of influential bodies and organisations within the field. As such, the current state of UCH protection in Scotland is particularly interesting; considering the UK's progressive influence in the field of maritime archaeology, the legislation in place to protect UCH has been described as neglectful, and in need of significant reform.[135]

Taken as a whole, the UK's governance of its UCH has not changed dramatically over the last half a century, with incremental and ad hoc policy changes as described above. The PWA, as noted, was initially developed as a reaction to an increase in diver interference with historic wrecks. Despite being developed as a temporary measure,[136] the PWA remains among the primary methods of managing UCH in English, Welsh and Northern Irish Waters.[137]

5.1.1 The Protection of Wrecks Act 1973

Scotland has disregarded s.1 of the 1973 Act and replaced it with Part 5 of the Marine (Scotland) Act 2010. In this case, HES advises Marine Scotland regarding the designation of Historic Marine Protected Areas (HMPAs).[138] These are not to be confused with Highly Protected Marine Areas (HPMAs), exclusively related to natural environment features and species, although the acronyms are very similar. There remains ongoing

135 See for example, Gribble J, Parham D, Scott-Ireton, D 'Historic wrecks: risks or resources?', Conservation and Management of Archaeological Sites, 2009, vol. 11, no. 1, pp. 16–28; and Martin, J.B. and Gane, T, 'Weaknesses in the Law Protecting the United Kingdom's Remarkable Underwater Cultural Heritage: The Need for Modernisation and Reform', Journal of Maritime Archaeology, vol. 15, no. 1, pp. 69–94, 2020.

136 A. Firth, 'Making archaeology: the history of the Protection of Wrecks Act 1973 and the constitution of an archaeological resource', International Journal of Nautical Archaeology, 1999, vol. 28, no. 1, pp. 10–24.

137 See here proceedings of a seminar on the 50th Anniversary of the PWA at the Society of Antiquaries of London, <https://www.youtube.com/watch?v=9jhsb1ky9Zw>.

138 I. Oxley, 'Towards the integrated management of Scotland's cultural heritage: examining historic shipwrecks as marine environmental resources, World Archaeology, 2001, vol. 32, no. 3, pp. 413–426.

discourse in Scotland surrounding HPMAs, with most recent proposals controversially rejected in June 2023.[139] HMPAS protect multiple forms of UCH. Unlike the restrictive powers of the PWA, divers are encouraged to visit HMPAS with the intention to record, appreciate or conserve unless special restrictions are in place. No artefacts may be salvaged and there must be no disturbance to the site, and planning permission or marine licences must be acquired to carry out activities such as development and construction.[140] The concept of a wreck licensee, maintaining general responsibility for and oversight of the wreck, as required in England, is also no longer applicable in Scotland.[141] As a result of these amendments, the management of UCH in Scotland is significantly more integrated with the natural environment. Consequently, Scottish management of UCH and the marine environment is philosophically and theoretically different to the rest of the UK. Otherwise, the AMAAA, PMRA, MSA and parts of the MACAA all continue to have application in Scotland.[142]

Within the system of Scottish HMPAs, the evolution in the conceptualisation of UCH considered in the debates on the Marine and Coastal Access Bill referenced in 1.1 above, may fit more neatly, given it provides a broader base for understanding heritage within the realm of sustainable development, and as part of community identity and well-being. This dimension is expanded upon in the following section.

5.2 *Historic Marine Protected Areas (HMPAs)*

Replacing Section 1 of the UK's PWA the HMPAs, designated under Section 67 of the Marine (Scotland) Act 2010, aim to protect 'marine historic assets', which are defined broadly as to include underwater structures such as vessels and aircraft, as well as scattered remains, groups of artefacts on the seabed and submerged prehistoric landscapes offering a more inclusive set of categories

139 As later confirmed in November 2023. For further details on the scheme and the controversy, see for example, <https://www.gov.scot/policies/marine-environment/highly-protected-marine-areas/>.

140 Historic Environment Scotland, 'Scotland's Historic Marine Protected Areas', 2019, available at < https://www.historicenvironment.scot/archives-and-research/publications/publication/?publicationId=fe248e27-0c19-4e4e-8d65-a62d00a2ce6a>.

141 Section 2 of the PWA, which allows the Maritime and Coastguard Agency through the Receiver of Wreck to designate a 'prohibited area' around a wreck if its contents may be dangerous to life or property, is retained in Scotland.

142 In addition, the Merchant Shipping and Maritime Security Act 1997, s.24, enables the Secretary of State for Transport to take part in international agreements for the protection of wrecks in international waters. The Secretary of State may designate, prohibit access, and provide licences to enter designated sites. The power has only been used twice, in respect of RMS *Titanic* and the ferry *Estonia*.

than the PWA, for example.[143] Section 73(2) includes reference to specific 'preservation objectives' for the asset. Similar to an environmental MPA, planning permission and marine licences are necessary for activities within the HMPA, and it is a criminal offence to disturb or affect the protected asset in any way, including in respect of the preservation objectives, pursuant to section 96. Offences may be committed intentionally or recklessly, with defences available in cases where the operation was carried out lawfully and that reasonable precautions were taken. To determine whether an asset is of national historic importance it must satisfy the criterion of cultural significance manifested in its 'artistic, archaeological, architectural, historic, traditional, aesthetic, scientific, or social interest'.[144] The designation is flexible and considers changing cultural significance over time. In addition, cultural significance is considered under three distinct headings:

- Intrinsic Characteristics: which are those essentially relating to how the physical remains of a site/place contribute to our knowledge of the past.
- Contextual Characteristics: which note the relationships between a site/place and its surrounding environment, and our knowledge of the past.
- Associative Characteristics: those reflecting the relationships between a site/place and society, including the people, practices, traditions, events and historic and social movements.[145]

In addition, these characteristics must exhibit one or more value/s to society, which closely reflect the language used by the United Nations in its Sustainable Development Goals.[146] The implications of the decision to designate are also considered, so that even if a site or place meets the criteria, it may not necessarily be appropriate to designate it.[147] The contemplated values/criterion encompassed in the assessment of cultural significance are stated thus:

- The site/place must have the potential to make a significant contribution to our understanding/appreciation of the past either on its own or through extended research. This can be done as a single site/place, as a specific type of site/place, or as part of a group of related assets.

143 Section 73 Marine (Scotland) Act 2010.

144 Historic Environment Scotland, 'Marine Protected Areas in the Seas around Scotland: Guidelines on the selection, designation and management of Historic Marine Protected Areas', 2019.

145 Historic Environment Scotland, 'Scotland's Historic Marine Protected Areas', 2019, p. 7.

146 Detail in respect of which is available at < https://sdgs.un.org/goals>.

147 Historic Environment Scotland, 'Scotland's Historic Marine Protected Areas, 2019, p. 8. The example given being a decommissioned oil platform which may have historical significance but would be required to be recovered as a result of other legal obligations.

- It must maintain structural, decorative, technical or physical attributes which make a significant contribution to our understanding/appreciation of the past.
- When assessed in the context of the history and archaeology of Scotland, its seas and its place in the wider world, the site/place must be a particularly rare or representative example of a historic marine asset.
- The site/place must make a significant contribution to the historic and wider marine environment. This could include relationships between historic assets or features in the surrounding area'.
- The place/site must have associations with historic, traditional, social or artistic figures, events or movements that are of national importance.[148]

These values themselves represent Key Principles, which, adapted from Scotland's Historic Marine Protected Areas, Historic Environment Scotland (2019), reflect certain characteristics. These include that recognition of the cultural significance of sites/places supports effective decision making, in turn ensuring that site recognition requires an understanding of it and that numerous diverse factors contribute to the concept of significance. Knowledge about and information on the marine historic environment is key to the understanding of our past, present and future and that this is shaped by changed appreciation over time alongside the historic environment. This understanding is created and enhanced through research and knowledge exchange and that a broad spectrum of experience and contribution, recognising public participation, is brought to its interpretation. Decision making should be well informed, transparent, robust, consistent and proportionate. Finally, every person is recognised as a stakeholder and that protecting the marine environment has a universal benefit to current and future generations.

The Scottish MPA network currently covers approximately 22 per cent of Scottish waters. Of the 231 MPAs in Scotland, 8 of these are HMPAS.[149] Alongside rising international pressure for spatially increasing MPA coverage, the UK has increasingly diversified MPA considerations and stakeholders. As noted in 5.1.1 above, Scotland is in a transition period, whereby the policy decision to create HMPAS has received critical pushback from the coastal communities of Scotland. Fundamentally, the lack of community consultation, engagement, and inclusion within Highly Protected MPAs resulted in rejection of the

148 Historic Environment Scotland, 'Scotland's Historic Marine Protected Areas', 2019, pp. 7–8.

149 For detail see <https://marine.gov.scot/information/historic-marine-protected-areas-mpas-hes-wms>.

initial plans to designate at least 10 per cent of Scotland's seas by 2026.[150] In response, The Cabinet Secretary has committed to develop an evolved pathway for marine protection, with a renewed focus on community-led, co-developed marine conservation. Although plans for this course of action are yet to be published, it would be sensible to look to community-centred legislation which is already in place in the marine environment within HMPAS.

As a result of the broad contestation surrounding the management of Scottish MPA s, there is a pool of critical assessment available from various sources which have wide ranging opinions on the process.[151] Yet, when assessing the literature on the diversity of methods and services protected by Scotland and the rest of the UK, the values and uses of HMPAS are usually either disregarded as irrelevant for marine conservation or are not included at all.[152] The context of the available literature primarily focusses on diversifying the socio-cultural relations attached to the seascape in marine conservation policy,[153] and the place of Cultural Ecosystem Services within environmental MPAS.[154] Categorised under 'Other Area Based Measures', HMPAS have to date had little review by academia or heritage practitioners.

Since 2011, HES has conducted two monitoring assessments to determine the condition and vulnerability of marine historic sites in Scotland. According to the 2018 Marine Protected Areas Report to the Scottish Parliament,[155] the

150 See for example <https://www.gov.scot/policies/marine-environment/highly-protected-marine-areas/>.

151 G. J. Pita, C., Theodossiou, I. and Pierce, 'The perceptions of Scottish inshore fishers about marine protected areas,' Mar. Policy, 2013, vol. 37, pp. 254–263; and T. Hopkins, C.R., Bailey, D.M. and Potts, 'Navigating future uncertainty in marine protected area governance: Lessons from the Scottish MPA network,' Estuarine and Coastal Shelf Science, 2018, vol. 207, pp. 303–311.

152 Of the 1,019 papers available at time of writing on Scottish MPA s available on the Web of Science, only one discussed the protection of cultural heritage within these systems, and four discussed heritage values.

153 J. O. Jobstvogt, N., Watson, V. and Kenter, 'Looking below the surface: The cultural ecosystem service values of UK marine protected areas (MPA s),' Ecosystem Services,2014, vol. 10, pp. 97–110; and R. E. Brennan, 'The conservation 'myths' we live by: Reimagining human–nature relationships within the Scottish marine policy context,' Area, 2018, vol. 50, no. 2, pp. 159–168.

154 S. Pike, K; Wright, P; Wink, B; Fletcher, 'The assessment of cultural ecosystem services in the marine environment using Q methodology,' Journal of Coastal Conservation, 2014, vol. 19, no. 5, pp. 1–9; and, to a limited extent, M. J. Ruiz-Frau, A., Edwards-Jones, G. and Kaiser, 'Mapping stakeholder values for coastal zone management,' Mar. Ecol. Prog. Ser., 2011, vol. 434, pp. 239–249.

155 Available at <https://www.gov.scot/publications/marine-protected-area-network-2018-report-scottish-parliament/>.

conservation status of HMPAs has been generally progressing, with four sites considered to be in a stable condition, one in a stable to declining condition, and three in an unknown condition. HES has, however, advised that internal monitoring has shown that 88 per cent of scheduled monuments in Scotland were in a stable condition during the period of 2012–2017.[156]

When assessing HMPAs by the standards of the UK's current heritage management legislation, it appears that several of the concerns associated with the protection of UCH in the UK are overcome. For example, HMPAs have a much broader definition of UCH than that provided by statutory heritage protection in the UK,[157] and potentially a more inclusive provision for public access. Furthermore, in Scotland, following the replacement of section 1 of the PWA, the primary differences lie in the extent of heritage protected,[158] and the active encouragement of research, public access, and engagement within the sites. Part 2 of the HES HMPA Guidelines, states 'HMPAs should not be thought of as no-go areas'.[159] If it is deemed necessary to prohibit, restrict, or regulate activities within the boundaries of an HMPA, a Marine Conservation Order may be put in place in a specified area, as is the same for the natural marine environment.[160] In this manner, it may be argued that HMPAs are closer to National Parks than to conventional designated underwater heritage sites in the UK.

Integration is facilitated within the criteria, which dictate significant and important interaction with the surrounding environment as a factor for designation as noted. Furthermore, section 3.7 of the 2019 Historic MPA Guidelines acknowledges the future for integration between natural and cultural heritage resources:

> There is a recognition that areas designated for cultural heritage reasons may also be of value for nature conservation and in turn, areas recognised for nature conservation value may have the potential to deliver incidental benefits for cultural heritage.[161]

---

156 See, <https://marine.gov.scot/sma/assessment/historic-environment-and-cultural-heritage>.

157 The PWA 1973 provides protection for designated 'vessels lying wrecked on the seabed', The AMAA 1979 may not be applied to 'sites without structures' including scattered objects or landscapes, the Protection of Military Remains Act 1986 may protect military aircraft and vessels lost at sea while in military service.

158 HMPAs can be used to protect a variety of UCH types including wrecks or prehistoric landscapes, as well as the associated artefact scatters, and debris fields.

159 HMPA Guidelines, 2019, section 5.1.

160 *Ibid*, section 8.1.

161 *Ibid*, section 3.7.

It goes on to introduce the capacity to undertake integrated work between Scottish MPA managers regarding biodiversity, geodiversity, and historical surveys and assessments designed to enhance national and regional inventories of archaeological sites. To overcome the issues associated with applying natural environment principles to cultural heritage policy, the preservation objectives of HMPAs state:

> There is an established tradition in formulating conservation objectives for nature conservation, based around the principles of restoring a feature to, or maintaining it in, 'favourable condition'. However, unlike marine natural features, marine historic assets represent a non-renewable resource, without the capacity to 'recover' where their condition deteriorates. With these key differences in mind, the preparation of preservation objectives for HMPAs will focus on objectives that are appropriate and practicable for marine cultural heritage and in line with the Historic Environment Policy for Scotland (HEPS).[162]

The effectiveness of HMPAs is yet to be fully researched, as there is currently no formal method or reporting process for HMPA assessment within the Scottish or UK Governments. It may be the case that this type of UCH management could extend to the rest of the UK, using methods already established within the UK system. In discussion with HE on the extent of UCH integration in English policy in 2021, it was stated:

> heritage is not included in the 'environment' for place-based management tools such as Marine Conservation Zones (MCZs); which otherwise have all the tools available to protect heritage alongside the environment, in compliance with the 2001 Convention.[163]

Integrating the protection of UCH in MCZs may provide an option for place-based protection without the need for altering the PWA; but further analysis would be necessary. Scotland's development of UCH-centred MPAs is a novel step aligning with a more holistic view of marine capital. Despite this, the greater context of Scottish marine resource management, particularly regarding HPMAs, remains contested, with critical parties citing a lack of community inclusion in management strategies. As such, although HMPAs provide a clear example of sustainable development-led, cultural-natural marine resource

162 *Ibid*, section 3.26.
163 Historic England, Pers. Com. 2021.

management, they exist within an oxymoronic system. Yet, it is reasonable to conclude that the legislation protecting UCH in Scotland demonstrates the country's commitment to preserving its rich maritime history and establishes a robust framework for the protection, management, and responsible sharing of its UCH.

6 Northern Ireland

The picture in the Devolved Nations is completed with a consideration of the somewhat hybrid position that Northern Ireland displays.[164] Some of the legislation, applicable to the 12nm TS limit is shared with that generally applicable in England and Wales. The PWA is retained in full, in contrast to the position in Scotland, and the provisions of the PMRA and MSA are also applied to UCH. The licensing regime under the MACAA is also applicable, in conjunction with the Marine Act (Northern Ireland) 2013, to Northern Irish inshore and offshore regions of the Marine Plan area.[165] Taken together, the Marine Plan area borders the Scottish, Welsh, Isle of Man and Republic of Ireland's marine areas, making it somewhat more contained than those comprising the UK offshore plan area. According to the Department of Agriculture, Environment and Rural Affairs' (DEARA) statement of public participation, the Marine Plan for Northern Ireland was to be operational by the end of December 2023.[166] As with its UK counterparts, it reflects the key environmental and heritage imperatives of the MPS.

There are, however, differences in terms of the responsible heritage and regulatory bodies.[167] The Marine and Fisheries Division of DEARA,[168] has specific responsibility for planning, and thus marine licensing decisions. Otherwise, heritage functions are shared with the Historic Environment Division of the

164 The authors are grateful to Mr Colin Dunlop, Marine Historic Environment Advisor, Marine and Fisheries Division, Department of Agriculture, Environment and Rural Affairs for his valuable insights.

165 Part 2 of the Marine Act (Northern Ireland) 2013 permits DEARA to prepare a marine plan for all or part of the NI inshore region.

166 The Statement can be accessed at <https://www.daera-ni.gov.uk/sites/default/files/publications/daera/Annex.pdf>.

167 At the time of writing the picture in NI is made more complex due to the very recent reformulation of the Assembly Government after years of suspension, although the Marine Plan, containing marine heritage protection as a core objective, is anticipated to be in place by the end of 2024.

168 See, for example <https://www.daera-ni.gov.uk/articles/marine-historic-environment#toc-1>.

Department for Communities (DfC).[169] DEARA is the principal regulator in this arrangement with (DfC) acting as specialist advisor in respect of archaeological and historic building situations, which encompasses UCH. Otherwise, where there is a possibility that a scheduled monument is likely to be affected by a development intervention or marine licence application, DfC becomes the lead regulator. The relationship between the bodies is cemented in that DfC provides advice to the UK's DCMS and the MOD for wrecks designated under the PWA and PMRA. Of these, the wreck of *La Girona*, a Spanish Armada vessel lost in 1588, is Northern Ireland's most celebrated wreck. Despite being the subject of unregulated salvage following discovery in the late 1960s *La Girona* was not designated under the PWA until the early 1990s. Anyone seeking to dive the site is required to obtain a PWA licence, via DEARA. Officially recovered finds from the wreck are displayed in the Ulster Museum ensuring their retention for research and access.

Aside from the generally applicable legislation, Northern Ireland has its own specific heritage measure in the Historic Monuments and Archaeological Objects (Northern Ireland) Order 1995 (HMAO), separate to the AMAAA. Article 3 of the HMAO provides for the scheduling by the Department of the Environment of monuments, as defined in Article 2.[170] An additional and separate provision for archaeological licensing is included in Article 41, creating an offence in respect of intervention either without a licence or outside of its scope. There are some constraints in respect of archaeological licensing of UCH under the HMAO as it only applies to land above the mean low water mark, internal waters and the foreshore,[171] and with a specific exception for Crown title, for which no archaeological licences for investigation may be granted. However, monuments on the seabed, those areas permanently covered by the sea, are able to be scheduled, regardless of Crown title.[172] In such circumstances, the regulator may apply conditions in respect of scheduled monument consent, which could include a request to undertake investigation or excavation of a wreck.[173] In 2017, HMS *Drake* was the first wreck scheduled under the HMAO. A WWI heavily armoured cruiser, it was torpedoed and lost

169 See, for example <https://www.communities-ni.gov.uk/landing-pages/historic-environment>.

170 Historic Monuments and Archaeological Objects (Northern Ireland) Order 1995, (NISI 12995/1625 (N.I.9) Article, 3(4)(a).

171 With some exceptions in respect of bays, as per LOSC.

172 Historic Monuments and Archaeological Objects (Northern Ireland) Order 1995, Articles 37–38.

173 Historic Monuments and Archaeological Objects (Northern Ireland) Order 1995, Article 5.

in 1917.[174] Given its rarity, it fell within UK policy set out in the MPS to ensure its protection. Similarly, the *Devereux*, a nineteenth century Barque, and the SS *Lochgarry*, a WWII requisitioned troop transport ship, were scheduled in 2023 due to their high level of preservation and regional heritage significance.

7 Conclusions

The complex of regulatory arrangements spread across the UK's jurisdictions is, to the casual observer, perhaps indicative of an unnecessary patchwork. However, balancing the traditions and expectations of the Devolved Nations has demanded that there is a link to specific as well as shared heritage; and that the very different cultures apparent are equally represented in the legislative matrix. Indeed, maritime boundaries by their nature are somewhat false, the 'wholeness' of ocean systems dictates that action in one jurisdiction may have impacts in another in a way that would not be the case on land.

The placement of heritage, and UCH by association, within the UK's broader marine policy, is possibly the most significant development since the last edition of this work. The law that has grown from that policy is arguably more inclusive, focused and, due to the idiosyncrasies of the UK, diverse. There are some shared aspects. Marine licensing offers significant scope to, at least, offer a point at which to consider systematically the impacts of licenced activities on *all* UCH, not only that known and already protected by some form of legal device, such as the PWA. Marine licensing also offers a greater spatial reach, extending beyond the UK TS. Alongside this, the PMRA continues to be an effective means to ensure the preservation of military wrecks, at least within the UK Marine Area, and to restrict the activities of UK-flagged vessels seeking to interfere with the remains elsewhere. HE's reappraisal of the utility of the AMAAA for UCH has proved a significant additional contemporary means to protect UCH falling outside of the more restrictive categorisations required by the PWA or PMRA, but nonetheless representing a significant heritage value. Since the initial declarations of UCH 'monument' sites in 2019, there are now, at the time of writing, 26. The ability to offer 'look but don't touch' access, without a licence, is something that arguably promotes the value of and interest in the UK's UCH, and HE should be commended for its vision, and its agility in performing a policy *volte-face*.

174 The scheduling documents are available at < https://www.daera-ni.gov.uk/sites/default/files/publications/daera/Drake_Scheduling_Docs_2017.pdf>.

In Scotland, the evolution of new designations to value both the natural and cultural environments is progressive and may evidence innovation in acknowledgement of the complex eco-systems of the benthos,[175] upgrading the predecessor PWA and improving access to UCH, by removing the requirement for a licence to access a wreck in an HMPA. The co-location of natural and cultural heritage offers scope for conservation of both in a way greater than the sum of its parts and is clearly an important consideration going forward, which reflects the concept of marine net gain.

What we have hopefully demonstrated in this chapter is the ongoing evolution of measures across the UK which may enhance the status, and contribute to the protection, of UCH in a sustainable manner. Looking ahead, recognition of the fact that 'discovery' is of itself a potential adverse impact, as seen with the *Galloper* situation, is perhaps something that can be reflected in EIA screening or scoping. Making greater use of shared heritage agreements for specific wrecks and capitalising more effectively on the synergies with natural and cultural environment rhetoric may reap dividends for the protection of UCH more systematically. Given the UK remains a non-ratified party to the 2001 Convention, and it is more than 50 years since the PWA, there certainly remains scope for further means to enhance the protection of UCH assets. There is evidence of innovation, modernisation and reform across the 4 nations of the UK, and it would appear, an appetite to move forward, although ratification of the 2001 Convention may be a chimera for the time being.

Finally, the success of any of these measures depends upon effective enforcement. The tools are in place, and the rolling out of a Common Enforcement Manual in the latter part of 2025 will offer a further layer of protective engagement, implemented by marine-capable regulatory agencies, none of which have UCH as their primary tasking, but which have indicated their willingness to contribute to its conservation.

All websites last accessed February 2025.

Selected Bibliography

Lowther, J., Gall, S., Williams, M., Bean, E., 'Enhancing Protection of Underwater Heritage Assets, 2019, Historic England Project 7146. Available at <https://historicengland.org.uk/images-books/publications/enhancing-protection-underwater-heritage-assets/>.

175 See for example in this connection, Hickman (et al.), 'Shipwrecks act as de facto Marine Protected Areas in areas of heavy fishing pressure', 2023, Marine Ecology 45(1), 12782.

Lowther, J., Parham, D., Williams, M., 'All at Sea: When Duty meets Austerity in Scheduling Monuments in English Waters', Journal of Planning and Environmental Law (3) [2017] pp. 2–21. Sweet and Maxwell, London.

Lowther, J., Williams, M., 'Beyond National Legislation: using European regulation to manage the UK's Underwater Cultural Heritage', 2012, Proceedings of 3rd International Congress on Underwater Archaeology (IKUWA 3) Henderson, J. (ed.) pp. 95–104, UNESCO/RGK, Bonn.

Martin, J.B., Gane T., Weaknesses in the Law Protecting the United Kingdom's Remarkable Underwater Cultural Heritage: The Need for Modernisation and Reform', Journal of Maritime Archaeology <https://doi.org/10.1007/s11457-019-09240-1>.

Parham, D., Williams, M., 'Public Involvement in Maritime Archaeology', 2012, Proceedings of 3rd International Congress on Underwater Archaeology Henderson, J. (ed.) pp. 470–474 UNESCO/RGK, Bonn.

Parham, D., Williams, M., Lowther J., Maritime Archaeology Sea Trust, 'Headline Strategy for the Conservation and Protection of Underwater Cultural Heritage in The British Antarctic Territory, 2018, Foreign and Commonwealth Office, London. Available at <https://www.gov.uk/government/publications/british-antarctic-territory-underwater-cultural-heritage>.

CHAPTER 21

Uruguay

*Gonzalo Rodríguez Prado**

1 Introduction

Uruguay possesses an important concentration of archaeological evidence of the last 500 years of European seafaring. This phenomenon is due to historical and natural factors. For example, the north coast of the River Plate constitutes the only navigable waterway for entering the heart of the continent (towards the foundational cities of Asunción, Charcas, and Potosí) and what is now known as the Paraná-Paraguay-Uruguay waterway, which was used particularly between the sixteenth and seventeenth centuries to gain access for the extraction of metals in America. In addition, in the eighteenth century, Cape Horn replaced the old Paso de Veragua in Panamá as the commercial connection between the Atlantic and the Pacific. The navigation of the Southern Atlantic gained new importance, prompting the Spanish empire to designate the Port of Montevideo as the last Ultra Marine port of destination in the Southern Atlantic and the General Captaincy of the interoceanic pass. Natural factors compounded these historical reasons: at the time, sailors used visual coastline navigation, and faced prevailing SW-SE winds that could push vessels towards the coast.

Uruguay's internal and territorial waters thus preserve unique testimonies from Portuguese, Spanish, British, Dutch, and French seafaring.[1] By way of example, in these maritime zones, we find the underwater archaeological site of Puerto de las Naos de San Salvador (1527 to 1529), where the first contact between indigenous peoples and Europeans in the area took place. It was also here that Lord Nelson's favourite ship, the HMS *Agamemnon*, sank in Maldonado Bay in 1809, and the first naval battle of the Second World War

* Assistant (U.R.), Institute of Public International Law, Law School, Universidad de la República, Uruguay.

1 In accordance with Art. 14 of Law N° 17.033 of 20 November 1998, the baselines for measuring the width of the Territorial Sea and the rest of Uruguay's maritime zones are the normal baselines and the straight baselines established in Annex I, including the straight line that marks the outer limit of the River Plate from the lateral maritime border with Argentina up to Punta del Este, the latter in conformity with what is established in the Treatise of the River Plate and its Maritime Front, of 19 November 1973.

DOI:10.1163/9789004510883_023

took place, with the subsequent sinking of the Battleship *Admiral Graf von Spee* in December 1939.

Despite the historical importance that underwater cultural heritage (UCH) holds for Uruguay, there has been little analysis of the regulations that govern it, and the legal situations that result. For this reason, this chapter analyses the most relevant aspects of the UCH regulatory regime, and the issues involved and shared with other South American States, such as commercial exploitation, the sovereign immunity status of naval wrecks, and legal ownership. Additionally, it considers best practices developed to strengthen the change of paradigm related to these artefacts, to create a new sustainable, blue economy approach, while identifying potential future directions to strengthening the current legal and management regime, such as ratification of the 2001 Convention and its articulation within the legal regime.

2 Uruguayan Legislation and Policy

2.1 *Background: an Inadequate Regime*

> No venderé el rico patrimonio de los orientales al bajo precio de la necesidad.[2]

In Uruguay, historical shipwrecks were subject to rules reflecting different legal values than currently. An example is the Sunken Hulls Law (SHL),[3] passed in 1975, with the objective of prioritising safety in maritime navigation, by 'the elimination of dangerous obstacles to navigation'.[4] The SHL allowed companies to contract with the Uruguayan Coast Guard for finding and recovering national and foreign sunken ships within Uruguayan jurisdictional waters, granting the maritime authority the possibility of selling them or keeping them in their custody.[5]

---

2 J. G. Artigas, A.D. 1764–1850. "I will not sell the rich heritage of the 'orientales', at the low price of necessity". The Oriental Republic of Uruguay is named after its location, to the East or 'orient' of the Uruguay River. These historical and geographical factors, among others, gave the country its name and, as a result, the inhabitants of Uruguay are still called 'orientales', even though it is evident that Uruguay belongs to the Western Hemisphere.

3 Law-Decree 21 March 1975, n. 14.343, "Prefectura Nacional Naval, Se establecen disposiciones referentes a embarcaciones nacionales o extranjeras hundidas, semihundidas o varadas", Published in the 'Diario Oficial' (suppl to No 19492) 9 April 1975.

4 Declaration of reasons for the creation of the Law-Decree 21 March 1975, n. 14.343. Sessions Journal of the State Council, Volume 9, 19/03/1975, item 17.

5 Law-Decree 21 March 1975, n. 14.343, Art. 20.

According to Article 15 of the SHL, shipwrecks belonging to the State, obtained by way of abandonment, are those that were not extracted before 31 December 1973, *de facto* renouncing their flag, if it was foreign.[6] Likewise, Decree No. 692/986 of 28 October 1986, regulating Article 15 of the SHL, established that in the resolution of the National Naval Prefecture, which authorises the search for ancient ships (all of them sunken, semi-sunken or stranded in national jurisdictional waters before 31 December 1973),[7] a ruling should be issued on 'profit-sharing of the interested parties, for the case of the search and extraction of the ship or its cargo'.[8] In this sense, it was agreed in recovery contracts that profit-sharing would amount to a 50/50 split between the State and the permit-holder(s).

2.1.1 Negative Financial Results for the State

The above legal regime encouraged hundreds of applications for the search and removal of wrecks, with the objective of selling archaeological artefacts.[9] In this sense, the most relevant case, one which attracted the attention of treasure hunters,[10] was the case of the Spanish ship *Nuestra Señora de la Luz* (mistakenly called *El Preciado*), supposedly discovered off the coast of Montevideo in 1990, by a private operator. According to the permit-holder's declaration, 70,000 gold and silver coins, ingots, and flasks were sold for about US$ 3,000,000 in a public auction organised by Sotheby's: "The Government received 50% and we received the other 50%, which was barely enough to pay for the expenses and a few other things".[11]

---

6 Art. 15 of the SHL outlines the abandonment regimen of 'ancient ships' in favour of Uruguay. See section 2.1.

7 Arts. 15 of Decree-Law No. 14.343 and 1 of Decree No. 692/986.

8 Art. 4.d of Decree No. 692/986.

9 E. Martínez and J. Silveira, 'Patrimonio Cultural Subacuático en Uruguay. El Río de la Plata atesora fragmentos de historia y secretos de vida' (2001) *Memoirs of the Scientific Congress of Underwater Archaeology* ICOMOS, National Institute of Anthropology and History. México City: National Institute of Anthropology and History, p. 103.

10 Stainforth defines treasure-hunting activities as "the search for intrinsically valuable objects from archaeological sites for personal profit or private gain". M. Stainforth and others, 'International approaches to underwater cultural heritage', in J. Harris (ed) *Maritime Law Issues: Issues, Challenges and Implications* (Nova Science Publishers 2009), see <http://www.academia.edu/385246/International_Approaches_to_Underwater_Cultural_Heritage>.

11 Declaration of the rescuing permit holder before the Commission of Education and Culture of the House of Representatives of the Legislative Power of Uruguay. Tachigraphic version N° 495 de 2006. See <https://parlamento.gub.uy/documentosyleyes/documentos/versiones-taquigraficas?Cpo_Codigo=All&Lgl_Nro=46&Fecha%5Bmin%5D%5

Irrespective of this case, the economic losses for Uruguay have been significant. This is reflected in the institutional expenses required over several decades to analyse the large volume of administrative requests for search and retrieval.[12] Likewise, it is worth considering the financial losses from the legal proceedings started by treasure hunters, due to the lack of a coherent regulatory scheme incorporating both recovery activities and cultural legislation. An example can be seen in the case of the Spanish vessel, *Nuestra Señora de Loreto*, which sunk in 1792 within the Port of Montevideo, and which was supposedly discovered by a treasure hunter in 1985. To preserve the integrity of the archaeological site, the Executive Power (without direct knowledge beyond the private operator's declarations to the press), at the request of the National Heritage Commission, proceeded to extend it legal protection by declaring it a 'Historical Monument'. With recovery works now impossible, the salvor started legal proceedings against the Uruguayan State for damages, finally being granted around US$ 1,000,000.[13] Paradoxically, it was subsequently scientifically proven that there was neither a hull nor a shipwreck at the coordinates marked by the permit holder.

In another case, a permit holder claimed in the Uruguayan courts for a credit right to 50 per cent of the material removed, as the holder of contracts for search and recovery made with the National Coastal Guard and connected with the recovery of a Nazi eagle and rangefinder from the German Battleship, *Admiral Graf von Spee*. A dispute arose concerning the State's alleged breach of contract regarding the sale of the artefacts. The permit holder demanded that the National Ministry of Defense (MOD) comply with its obligations so they could obtain their credit. On this point, the first instance verdict ruled that the

---

Bdate%5D=15-02-2005&Fecha%5Bmax%5D%5Bdate%5D=14-02-2010&Cms_Codigo=All&Dtb_Nro=&tipoBusqueda=T&Texto=ruben+collado&Cuerpo=>.

12 In this sense, the then President of the National Heritage Commission stated that in 2006, although the Uruguayan state received around US$1,500,000, over twenty years, it spent much more than that amount to attend to the requests of people requesting permits: "It means it is a negative business". Participation of Mr. M. Esmoris before the Commission of Education and Culture of the House of Representatives of the Legislative Power of Uruguay, on 23 August 2006. Tachigraphic Version N° 728 de 2006. See <https://parlamento.gub.uy/documentosyleyes/documentos/versiones-taquigraficas?Cpo_Codigo=All&Lgl_Nro=46&Fecha%5Bmin%5D%5Bdate%5D=15-02-2005&Fecha%5Bmax%5D%5Bdate%5D=14-02-2010&Cms_Codigo=All&Dtb_Nro=&tipoBusqueda=T&Texto=manuel+esmoris&Cuerpo=>.

13 *Collado Ruben v. Estado* (*Daños y Perjuicios*) [2004] Sentence of the Supreme Court of Justice of Uruguay of 26 April 2004, n. 117. Said sentence set the stage to determine the amount to pay to the private operator. The final amount of US$1,000,000 was set by the then President of the National Heritage Commission in the declaration, see n.12.

MOD should carry out the onerous transfer and distribution of the profit from the sale of the artefacts and was required to pay the permit holder 50 per cent of the gross earnings, but not necessarily through public auction, as the permit holders had requested.[14] Finally, the Supreme Court of Justice dismissed the lawsuit on the grounds that the claimed credit had expired.[15]

The above are two examples of several lawsuits filed against the State by treasure hunters partnered with it in the search and recovery of historical shipwrecks. Although most of these claims have been dismissed by the Uruguayan courts, the State has had to invest money, time, and human resources (lawyers, archaeologists, and managers of UCH), in order to settle these disputes, at the expense of other work. In addition, excavations conducted by recovery operations have created a financial liability on the State, given its duty to preserve, conserve and curate a considerable part of the cultural property removed.

2.1.2 Substantive Incompatibility of Maritime Archaeology with Commercial Exploitation of UCH

The Uruguayan experience is also useful to prove that the development of maritime archaeology is incompatible with the activities of treasure hunters. When Decree 692/86 was passed, the National Heritage Commission, established via the Ministry of Education and Culture, assumed competence for advice and control of works that might affect historic wrecks, with the Coast Guard responsible for licensing decisions concerning search and recovery. The purpose was to exert a degree of scientific control over such activities. In this way, and as an attempt to limit the activities of treasure hunters, the appropriate national authority started to make the presence of archaeologists mandatory in salvage operations.

The introduction of this requirement left archaeologists to grapple with ethical and professional dilemmas, which divide the national and international archaeological community. Some archaeologists vehemently refused to work for treasure hunters: others claimed that the State would never be able to subsidise necessary excavations and that it would in fact be possible to carry out a scientific project "as long as the investors follow the directions of the

14 *Scariato Fernandez, Maria y otros c/ Prefectura Nacional Naval y otro (Demanda de cumplimiento de contrato más daños y perjuicios)* [2019] Sentence of the Civil Court of 20 June 2019, n. 31. See <https://bjn.poderjudicial.gub.uy/BJNPUBLICA/busquedaSimple.seam>.

15 *Scariato Fernández, María y otros c/ Prefectura Nacional Naval y otro (demanda de cumplimiento de contrato más daños y perjuicios – casación)* [2022], Sentence of the Supreme Court of Justice of 24 November 2022, n. 1083. See <https://bjn.poderjudicial.gub.uy/BJNPUBLICA/busquedaSimple.seam>.

archaeologists".[16] It was also claimed that those recovering the artefacts were better able to preserve and repair them than State institutions.[17] Time proved the first group of archaeologists, who refused from the beginning to take part in the activities of treasure hunters, right. Some of those who did, ended up resigning a lack of trust in the treasure hunters, which affected their work on sites, scientific knowledge and the preservation of the UCH[18] and, in reality, their role was reduced to fulfilling a formal requirement.[19]

Those who claimed that Uruguay was not capable of developing maritime archaeology without the backing of treasure hunters were also wrong. The first maritime archaeology project conducted in Uruguay, which incorporated archaeologists from Uruguay, the UK and Mexico, without any previous connection with treasure hunting companies,[20] was proof of this. This initiative, developed in 2005, helped to change the perception of UCH by the public and politicians, and proved that "it is indeed possible to undertake maritime archaeology in Uruguay".[21]

2.1.3 Affected UCH

With regards to the heritage being affected, lengthy interventions were undertaken at different scales for the removal of cultural objects in dozens of archaeological and historical sites. Thousands of artefacts and tons of cultural material were removed between 1989 and 2005. By way of example, the recovery of *El Salvador* and HMS *Agamemnon* alone included an approximate total of 10,000 artefacts,[22] twice the number of objects found in the tomb of Tutankhamun. In some cases, the operations of salvage companies have involved archaeological sites including human remains, as in the shipwreck of the Spanish frigate *El Salvador*, known as *El Triunfo*, sunk in 1812, and the English slave trade ship, *Sea Horse*, wrecked in 1728 near Gorriti Island, Maldonado Bay. Because of the

---

16 E. Martínez and J. Silveira, *supra* n.9 p. 107.

17 *Ibid.*

18 F. Méndez, 'UN MUNDO INFINITO: arqueólogos subacuáticos, piratas y patrimonio' (2014) 11 *Lento* 42.

19 At the 1996 Meeting of Experts for the Draft Convention on the Protection of Underwater Cultural Heritage, Paris, 22–24 May 1996 (UNESCO doc. CLT-96/CONF.605/6), paras. 45–52, some arguments were in favour of the possibility that archaeologists could monitor the works of salvors.

20 J. Adams and others, 'Maritime Archaeology in Uruguay: Towards a Manifesto' (2010) 1 *Journal of Maritime Archaeology* 5.

21 *Ibid*, p. 66.

22 Resolution of the Ministry of National Defence N° 72383 of 18 April 2018, published in the Bulletin of the Ministry of National Defence, VOLUME CCV AÑO LXXXIX Montevideo, April 25, 2018. Nro. 12.339 Annex.

principle of profit and financial return governing these salvage operations, most of the affected sites and the materials removed are currently in a state of abandonment and decay.

In summary, the Uruguayan experience subjecting UCH to a commercial exploitation and management system was negative, both from a financial and, most of all, a cultural standpoint. For this reason, in 2006, the Executive Power suspended granting new permits, and now only scientific projects that have prior approval of the National Heritage Commission are authorised.[23] In this sense, the cultural authority utilises regulations inspired by the Rules contained in the Annex of the 2001 Convention for any scientific activity directed at UCH.[24]

2.2 *Current Legal Protection and Institutional Framework*

The current system for legal protection of UCH in Uruguay is backed by a complex framework comprising global, regional, and national regulations. At the global level, it is worth noting the Convention for the Protection of the World's Natural and Cultural Heritage (UNESCO World Heritage Convention),[25] which was incorporated into Uruguay's legal system in 1988.[26] Based on this Treaty, in February 2005 the Ministry of Education and Culture included in the tentative list the insular area and bay of Colonia del Sacramento, which has relevant UCH sites.[27] Likewise, Uruguay approved the United Nations Convention on the Law of the Sea 1982 (LOSC) in 1992.[28] Despite the generic, and even counterproductive character of its provisions regarding UCH,[29] it is at least worth remembering Uruguay's duty of cooperation with other nations with an interest in the protection of underwater archaeological artefacts.[30] In this sense, at the regional level it is worth noting the bilateral agreements of Protection and Restitution of Imported, Exported or Illegally Transferred Cultural Goods,

---

23 Art. 4 of Decree 306/06.

24 "Procedimiento de Evaluación y Validación de los Proyectos de Investigación Arqueológica dirigidos hacia Patrimonio Cultural Subacuático", approved by Resolution of the National Heritage Commission in the year 2007 and updated on 9 December 2020.

25 1037 UNTS 151.

26 The UNESCO World Heritage Convention was approved by Law No 15.964 of 28 June 1988.

27 See <https://whc.unesco.org/en/tentativelists/2034/>.

28 1883 UNTS 397. The LOSC was approved by Law No 16.287 of 29 July 1992.

29 In this sense, Scovazzi considers that Art. 303(2) "can be interpreted as a covert invitation to the looting of the underwater cultural heritage" in accordance with a private law approach to historic wreck salvage. See T. Scovazzi, The Law of the Sea Convention and Underwater Cultural Heritage, (2012) 27 *The International Journal of Marine and Coastal Law* 754.

30 See LOSC Art. 303(1).

signed between Uruguay and Perú,[31] Bolivia,[32] Colombia[33], and Ecuador,[34] the scope of which includes UCH, either specifically or generically.

At the national level, UCH legislation is supported by regulations within national (laws), and sub-national jurisdiction (Decrees of the Departmental Boards with power of law in their jurisdiction).[35] Based on Article 34 of the Constitution of the Republic,[36] the heritage protection system was originally developed under Decree-Law No 14.040 of 20 October 1971, as regulated by Decree No 536–72, its modifying and complementary rules. The Ministry of Education and Culture[37] created the National Heritage Commission, entrusting it with the preservation of 'historical monuments'. This is the only *ad hoc* heritage protection mechanism provided by said law, applicable to both buildings and movable property, such as ships. It was applied in the case of the Spanish vessel, *Nuestra Señora de Loreto*, which was declared a 'historical monument' by the Executive in February 1986,[38] thus preventing a private salvor from prospecting.

For its part, the MOD is currently enforcing a protectionist policy regarding UCH, with implementation entrusted to the Coordinating Group for Findings, Shipwrecks and Archaeological Artefacts (GCH-PEMA).[39] Its main goal is to coordinate the execution of works regarding discoveries, shipwrecks, and archaeological artefacts. This spans location, detection, inspection, recovery, and conservation tasks.

---

31 Law No. 18.142 of 15 June 2007 Art. 2 expressly includes the UCH within the scope of cultural, archaeological, artistic and historical properties, but with a definition. Likewise, both States acknowledge that 'the cultural heritage of each country is unique and its own and that it *cannot be the object of commerce*' (emphasis added).

32 Law 18422 of 21/11/2008.

33 Law No. 19.499 of 16/06/2017.

34 Law No. 19.751 of 17/05/2019.

35 Uruguay is divided into 19 administrative jurisdictions called departments.

36 Constitution of the Republic of Uruguay Art. 34 'The entire artistic or historic wealth of the country, no matter who its owner is, constitutes the Nation's cultural treasure; it shall be under the safeguard of the State, and the law shall establish whatever it deems appropriate for its defence'.

37 The National Heritage Commission consists of delegates of the Executive Power, the Ministry of Education and Culture, the Ministry of Transport and Public Works, as well as the University of the Republic (Law 14.040 Art. 1 in the wording provided by Law No 19.355 de 19/12/2015 Art. 427).

38 Executive Resolution 25 February 1986, n. 285, Published in the 'Diario Oficial' (Registro Nacional de Leyes y Decretos: Volume: 1, Semester: 1, Year: 1986, Page: 588) 15 May 1986.

39 Resolution of the Ministry of National Defense No 70.536 of 26 April 2017 published in the Bulletin of the MDN No 12.210.

The heritage protection system is also developed through other rules that, in general terms, primarily concern natural heritage. These laws also have in mind the cultural heritage dimension. For example, Law 17.234 of 22 February 2000, through which the creation and management of a 'National System of Protected Natural Areas' is declared of general interest, is an instrument of application of national environmental protection policies and plans. In this sense, the regulation creating the protected area 'Cabo Polonio' stands out, and which expressly prohibits:

> The collection or extraction of archaeological and historical artefacts, including those corresponding to the underwater heritage, except for research purposes, and as established by the management plan.[40]

As an example, the management plan[41] requires research activities to be authorised by the Area Director, including any corresponding permits or authorisations as defined by current applicable regulations, for example, those required by the National Heritage Commission.[42] The area is managed by a National Commission (created on 27 August 2007 by the Ministry of the Environment, the Ministry of Livestock, Agriculture and Fisheries, and the Ministry of Tourism) among other agencies.

Likewise, the 'General Law for Environmental Protection' declares 'landscape protection' and the formulation, instrumentation, application of the national environmental and sustainable development policy as of general interest, whereas the Environment Law, and its Regulatory Decree,[43] require prior environmental authorisation by the Ministry of the Environment for activities, construction and works that could potentially affect the cultural component of the human environment.[44] In this connection, the National Director of the Environment enacted Resolution No 492/019, under which

40 Executive Decree 20 July 2009, n. 337, Published in the `Diario Oficial' on 29 July 2009, Art. 3.d).

41 Resolution of the Ministry of Housing, Spatial Planning and the Environment passed on 14/02/2019, Approval of the management plan of the Cabo Polonio national park, Art. 7.3. This protection presents the natural area called 'Cerro Verde' created by Executive Decree of 10 August 2011, n. 285, published in the `Diario Oficial' on 22 August 2011.

42 See *supra* note 24.

43 `Environmental Impact Assessment and Environmental Authorizations Regulation' approved by Executive Decree of 21 September 2005, n. 349/005, Published in the `Diario Oficial' on 3 October 2005.

44 Law No 17.283 of 10 January 2001 `General Law for Environmental Protection'. Law N° 16.466 of 19 January 1994 Environment Law'.

'Guidelines for the analysis of the effect on historical and cultural heritage assets of projects subject to Prior Environmental Authorization' was approved. Regarding the protection of UCH, this suggests registration, documentation, recovery and relocation as possible protection measures, and management by the work's licensee.

Also, the Land-use Planning and Sustainable Development Law[45] establishes a complex management system, enshrining legal tools that UCH protection policy could make use of, at both the national and regional (totaling 19) government level. An example is the local land-use plan corresponding to a micro-region of the River Plate,[46] which includes within its guidelines the identification of underwater sites of archaeological value as a protective and revaluation measure. Additionally, the land-use planning and sustainable development of the coastal area of the Atlantic Ocean and the River Plate establishes that the land-use management instruments that refer to the coast[47] must identify and define archaeological sites, among other vulnerable components, for their protection.[48] With regard to non-compliance with any of the land-use planning instruments, the Land-Use Planning and Sustainable Development Law provides for financial and administrative sanctions.[49]

2.3 *Distinctive Aspects of the Legal and Management Framework*

In light of the above discussion, the general legal regime regarding UCH may be considered as a complex legal landscape: sectoral, incomplete, and relatively weak. Is it complex because, within the same spatial scope, several organisations have expertise, although with different degrees of decentralisation and administrative autonomy. Moreover, there is a sectoral element, because there is not just one legal instrument that regulates UCH in a specific and integrated manner. Rather, there are several regulations of varying strength and value,[50]

45 Law No. 18.308 of 18 June 2008 'Land-Use Planning and Sustainable Development Law'.

46 "Plan Local Directrices de Ordenamiento Territorial de la Microrregión de Costa de Oro" approved by Decree of Canelones Departmental Board No 13/017, dated 6 December 2017.

47 Land-use planning and sustainable development of the coastal area of the Atlantic Ocean and the River Plate Law, No. 19.772 of 17/07/2019, Art. 2, states: "The Uruguayan coastal zone constitutes a space of the national territory defined by unique and specific natural, demographic, social, economical and cultural features, with interaction processes between the River Plate and the Atlantic Ocean, and the land".

48 Art. 6 of Law No. 19.772 of 17/07/2019.

49 See Art. 71 Law 18.308.

50 In accordance with Uruguay's legal system, as long as the law is in effect, and has not been repealed, it shall be applied by administrative executive organs and the courts, unless it has been declared as unconstitutional by the Supreme Court of Justice. In which case, it shall not be applicable to the concrete case to which the declaration is referring. By

most generic, undermining the coherence and rationalisation to which every legal system must strive. Although there are inter-institutional coordination mechanisms, especially at the environmental level, it is in fact necessary to strengthen the management of UCH within these measures, so as to avoid regulatory contradictions and the possible incidental impact of activities such as cruise tourism, trawl fishing, fossil fuel exploration and underwater cable-laying.

It may also be considered incomplete, because *lacunae* can be identified, such as the lack of a UCH definition, as well as a specific regimen of criminal and civil sanctions. Finally, the current legal system is relatively weak. For example, administrative regulations create agencies, stipulate institutional competencies, and limit inhabitants' rights, when all of these should be established by law. For this reason, possible sanctions may be declared null and void by the national competent jurisdictional body, thus rendering the current legal framework for sanctions ineffective. Moreover, the current legislation, which suspends non-scientific interventions into UCH, could be easily modified in the future by passing a new Executive Power Decree, allowing once more the sale of archaeological underwater objects. That is why it is necessary to strengthen the current legal protection system, through the creation of a new law or ratification of the 2001 Convention. In this sense, it is interesting to review the position that Uruguay has had regarding the 2001 Convention, given that, as with other countries in the region, there are issues such as the sovereign immunity status of wrecks and their legal ownership regimes.

3 Uruguay and the 2001 Convention

3.1 *Sovereign Immunity of State-Owned or Operated Wrecks*

Despite Uruguay actively participating in the creation process of the 2001 Convention and taking a favourable stance on its ratification, ultimately the

'force' of the rules, we understand the possibility of a legal act to repeal or modify what is provided by another act (H. Cassinelli *Derecho Público* (FCU, 1999), p. 29). For example, if contradiction between a treaty and national law arises, either previously or after the fact, it shall first be necessary to determine their repealing power. In Uruguay, the position of the Supreme Court of Justice has oscillated regarding the hierarchical level that a treaty occupies with respect to a national law. In this sense, although in the past the treaty was assigned a position above national law, recent jurisprudence is inclined to assign it a hierarchy equivalent to a law, so that a subsequent national law contrary to a treaty, in the domestic sphere, would have the strength to repeal it. Until a change occurs in this new jurisprudential criterion, this would be the current hierarchical position that national jurisprudence grants to treaties.

Uruguayan delegates voted to abstain.[51] When consulted as to the reasons that motivated this, the then Ministry of Foreign Affairs expressed to the Parliament in 2004 that the main objection was the conflict between the rights of flag States and the rights of coastal States and/or States with shared watercourses, such as rivers. The Ministry also expressed concerns that the State would be severely compromised should there be contracts with private bodies authorising the extraction of shipwreck remains prior to enforcement of the Convention. This references the responsibility that would fall upon the State under the legal regime prior to 2006, which would require it to give private operators credit equivalent to 50 per cent of the earnings obtained after the sale of any artefacts recovered. In fact, on ratifying the 2001 Convention, the Government would be barred from selling these goods, thereby incurring a contractual liability with such companies for indemnity for economic damages. At present, this argument is based on the existence of only one precedent.

Another objection pointed out by the Ministry, referred to the sovereign immunity regime applied to State-owned or operated ships, as stipulated in the 2001 Convention,[52] which implies that any actions related to historically sovereign immune wrecks must only be undertaken with the express consent of the ship's flag State. In the opinion of Rengifo Lozano, Colombia's main objections referred to the fact that the sovereign immunity regime set out in Article 2(8) of the 2001 Convention exceeds that elaborated in LOSC, making it applicable not only to warships, but also to other vessels or aircraft owned or operated by a State and used, at the time of sinking, for non-commercial government purposes, without time or maritime space constraints.[53] In addition, Lozano understands that the object of immunity of warships itself would be

51 The abstention was taken at the 31st Session of the General Conference of the UNESCO (Commission IV) of 2 November 2001. On that occasion, the delegate from Uruguay expressed in a generic way "… it is clear that the text does not fully take account of Uruguay's interests and we are therefore bound to abstain and to explain our position. First, we believe that this Convention does not adequately safeguard the legitimate rights of coastal countries in internal waters, in the territorial sea, in archipelagic waters, on the continental shelf and in the exclusive economic zone. Secondly, the rights set forth in this Convention are not sufficiently compatible with pre-existing acquired rights". See <https://unesdoc.unesco.org/ark:/48223/pf0000128966> at page 566.

52 Art. 2(8) of the 2001 Convention states: 'Consistent with State practice and international law, including the United Nations Convention on the Law of the Sea, nothing in this Convention shall be interpreted as modifying the rules of international law and State practice pertaining to sovereign immunities, nor any State's rights with regards to its State vessels and aircraft'.

53 A. Rengifo Lozano, 'Las objeciones de Colombia a la Convención Internacional de la UNESCO sobre Protección del Patrimonio Cultural Subacuático' (2009) 25 *Pensamiento Jurídico. Derecho y Política en la era de la Sostenibilidad* 143.

altered, since "what military secret would deserve to be protected in a historical shipwreck that took place 300 years ago?".[54]

For its part, the definition of `State vessels and aircraft´ in Article 1(8) of the 2001 Convention, could affect the abandonment regime of the ships recovered, in favour of the Uruguayan State, as established in Article 15 of the SHL, according to some authors.[55]

The following two considerations counter the arguments presented above. Firstly, and related to the scope of the sovereign immunity notion stated in Article 2(8) of the 2001 Convention, it is worth remembering that the prior International Convention on Salvage 1989[56] (ICS 1989), also afforded sovereign immunity to State-owned vessels or State-operated vessels used for non-commercial purposes at the time of sinking. In this sense, we can consider the 2001 Convention sovereign immunity concept to mirror the ICS 1989. For this reason, it is not surprising that States such as Uruguay have ratified this international instrument.[57]

Secondly, it should be noted that Article 7(3) of the 2001 Convention[58] advises, not obligates, coastal States that they *should* report the discovery of identifiable State vessels and aircraft within their Territorial Sea (TS) to the flag State. This leads to the conclusion that in this area, no consent would be necessary from the flag State prior to an intervention by the coastal State on identifiable State vessels and aircraft. The absence of this requirement would be more evident with regard to historical shipwrecks located within the internal

---

54 *Ibid*, p. 145.

55 In this sense, Prof. Dromgoole states "the employment in Article 1(8) of a definition derived from examples that apply to operational –rather than sunken – craft leads to the result that vessels and aircraft appear to be covered by the definition even in circumstances where the ownership has been lost after sinking, through abandonment or otherwise." S. Dromgoole, *Underwater cultural heritage and international law* (Cambridge University press, 2013), at p. 155. The Uruguayan legal regime with regards to the property of historic shipwrecks is described in section 1.2.

56 1953 UNTS 165.

57 Uruguay approved the ICS 1989 by Law No 19.622 of 17 May 2018. Art 4(1) of ICS states 'State-owned vessels (1) Without prejudice to article 5, this Convention shall not apply to warships or other non-commercial vessels owned or operated by a State and entitled, at the time of salvage operations, to sovereign immunity under generally recognized principles of international law unless that State decides otherwise'.

58 Art. 7(3) of the 2001 Convention states: 'Within their archipelagic waters and territorial sea, in the exercise of their sovereignty and in recognition of general practice among States, States Parties, with a view to cooperating on the best methods of protecting State vessels and aircraft, should inform the flag State Party to this Convention and, if applicable, other States with a verifiable link, especially a cultural, historical or archaeological link, with respect to the discovery of such identifiable State vessels and aircraft'.

waters of coastal States. In this connection, Blumberg, the leader of the USA delegation, observed that, contrary to what is established otherwise in Article 7 of the 2001 Convention, paragraph 3 makes no mention of internal waters. This led him to conclude that the omission "creates a negative implication that flag States have no rights at all over their vessels in these areas".[59]

Uruguay's then Minister of Foreign Affairs shared a similar sentiment, after a request for information from the Parliament in 2005, related to the Nazi bronze eagle extracted from the debris of the Battleship *Graf Spee* by a private operator intending to sell it by public auction. In that case, the German Embassy made verbal representations to the Uruguayan Foreign Affairs Office, making a case for the applicability of sovereign immunity regarding the recovered artefacts. The position of the Uruguayan Foreign Affairs Minister was as follows:

> … the customary law advanced is not applicable, by virtue of the fact that it refers to ships sunk by the enemy, or within the context of actions or displacement, due to collisions with other ships -even of the same flag- or by accident. On the contrary, the *Graf Spee*, was planned and methodically dynamited, blown up and destructed -with the subsequent sinking- by its own crew, who abandoned ship, in an orderly fashion, before it was blown up. To this, it might be added, that said action of destruction and abandonment was carried out in Uruguay's internal waters, without notification or consent from the authorities.[60]

On the basis of this, it may be inferred, *a contrario sensu*, that the position of the Ministry of Foreign Relations was, at least until 2005, in favour of recognising as an international practice the sovereign immunity of State vessels, but not to the specific case of ships that, like the *Graf Spee*, were intentionally sunk or situated within internal waters. For that reason, it also would not be

---

59 R. Blumberg, 'International Protection of Underwater Cultural Heritage' in M. Nordquist, J. Norton Moore and Kuen-chen Fu (eds.) *Recent Developments in the Law of the Sea and China* (Leiden and Boston: Martinus Nijhoff Publishers, 2006), 506, cited by Dromgoole, *supra* n. 55, at p. 157.

60 Words of the then Minister of Foreign Affairs, Mr. Reinaldo Gargano, in a meeting held with the Commission of International Affairs in the Chamber of Representatives of the Legislative Power of Uruguay, on July 11th, 2007. Tachigraphic version N° 1141 of 2007. See <https://parlamento.gub.uy/documentosyleyes/documentos/versiones-taquigraficas?Cpo_Codigo=All&Lgl_Nro=46&Fecha%5Bmin%5D%5Bdate%5D=15-02-2005&Fecha%5Bmax%5D%5Bdate%5D=14-02-2010&Cms_Codigo=All&Dtb_Nro=&tipoBusqueda=T&Texto=graf+spee&Cuerpo= >.

applicable, even though it was not explicitly mentioned, to the case of historical shipwrecks intentionally sunk and located in Uruguay's TS, due to the application of Article 2(1) of LOSC.

Despite these antecedents, on 11 October 2022 the Executive Power presented the text of the 2001 Convention to parliamentary approval, for later ratification, based on the need to solve the problem presented by the absence of relevant legislation, as well as a clear cultural policy that guarantees the protection of archaeological heritage in accordance with best international practices.[61] During the parliamentary discussion, although the scope of the sovereign immunity of State-owned or operated wrecks was not specifically analysed, doubts were raised about the possible impact on Uruguayan sovereignty in matters of UCH. As an example, it was questioned which State would have priority to reunite the dispersed collections that have been seized within the framework of Article 18 of the 2001 Convention.[62] In relation to this and according to Dromgoole:

> [t]he seizing state has the power to determine that disposition and the interest of any linked states are just one of the factors that must be taken into account when it does so.[63]

However, considering the high cost that implementation of the measures provided in the above mentioned Article would imply, the author considers it as probable that the seizing State would accept the offer of the State with the verifiable link to receive, care and ensure the disposition of seized material for

61 El Proyecto fue aprobado por la Cámara de Senadores en marzo de 2023 y actualmente (28/11/2023) se encuentra a studio de la Cámara de Representantes. Message from the Executive Power to the Parliament. Carpeta Nº 798 de 2022 Repartido No 607 March 2023. See <https://parlamento.gub.uy/documentosyleyes/documentos/repartido/senadores/49/607/0/PDF>.

62 Declaration of Member of Parliament, N. Viera Díaz, before the Commission of International Affairs of the House of Representatives of the Legislative Power of Uruguay. Tachigraphic version No 1481 of 2023. See <https://parlamento.gub.uy/documentosyleyes/ficha-asunto/156605/tramite>. Art. 18(4) of the 2001 Convention states: 'A State Party which has seized underwater cultural heritage shall ensure that its disposition be for the public benefit, taking into account the need for conservation and research; the need for reassembly of a dispersed collection; the need for public access, exhibition and education; and the interests of any State with a verifiable link, especially a cultural, historical or archaeological link, in respect of the underwater cultural heritage concerned'.

63 Dromgoole, *supra* n. 55, at p. 130.

the public benefit. Thus, the seizing State would be indirectly in compliance with the obligation in Article 18(4) of the 2001 Convention.

In summary, the recent request for approval of the 2001 Convention to Parliament reflects a change of position on the part of the Uruguayan Executive Power regarding the reasons that motivated the original abstention. Specifically, cultural authorities consider that Article 7 of 2001 Convention is clear in its wording that the flag State could not take part in management of the UCH located within the internal waters and TS of coastal States without prior consent. However, they make no further references to how this could be articulated within the concept of the sovereign immunity of State-owned or operated wrecks.[64]

3.2 *Ownership Rights*

An issue closely related to sovereign immunity is the right to ownership of shipwrecks. The difficulties that arose during the negotiation of the 2001 Convention related to this, inexorably determining that the only way to achieve its adoption was by making "no references to ownership at all".[65] Consequently, the pragmatic approach is to leave ownership as a matter to be determined by domestic law and national courts.[66] Thus, it is pertinent to consider Uruguay's legal framework in respect of UCH ownership.

The ownership of sunken vessels and their cargos has been regulated since 1975 by Article 15 of the SHL, which enshrines an abandonment regime for domestic and foreign sunken ships in favour of the Uruguayan State:

> Vessels, objects and remains of any nature, both national and foreign, as well as the cargo and equipment belonging to them, that might have sunk, half-sunk or aground in jurisdictional national waters (...), prior to 31 December 1973 and whose extraction, removal or demolition did not begin four months before the publication of this law, shall be

---

64 Declaration of cultural authorities before the Commission of International Affairs of the House of Representatives of the Legislative Power of Uruguay. Tachigraphic version No 1462 of 2023. See <https://parlamento.gub.uy/documentosyleyes/documentos/versiones-taquigraficas/representantes/49/1462/0/CAR>.

65 Dromgoole, *supra* n. 55, at p. 117. In the same sense A. González, 'Negotiating the Convention on Underwater Cultural Heritage: Myths and Reality' in R. Garabello, and T. Scovazzi (eds.) *The Protection of the Underwater Cultural Heritage* (Martinus Nijhoff Publishers, 2003), at p. 83; G. Carducci 'The UNESCO Convention versus Existing International Law' in G. Camarda and T. Scovazzi (eds.) *The protection of the Underwater Cultural Heritage. Legal Aspects* (Giuffrè editore, 2002), at p. 164.

66 Dromgoole *supra* n. 55, at p. 117.

> automatically considered as abandoned in favour of the State, ceasing *de facto* its flag, if foreign ....

The legitimacy of such a provision is perhaps questionable. Under the current constitutional order of Uruguay, which, with regards to the most substantial aspects of this topic, stems from the Constitution of 1830, the State can only take away the property rights of private parties by means of expropriation in cases of public necessity or utility, established under law and always if receiving 'prior and fair compensation'.[67]

Likewise, automatic 'abandonment' expressed in the Article referenced above is arguable, since sunken ships or those whose remains are 'thrown to the coast', would continue to belong to their owners.[68] In such cases, the doctrine of *res derelictae* applies because there is a lack of intention by the owner to abandon the property.[69] This interpretation relies on the Roman Law exclusion from said category of things 'thrown or lost at sea', precisely due to the absence of that element of intention.[70] Thus, it may be observed that Articles 6 to 8 of the SHL clearly show that it is not detached from that old theoretical interpretation, as it empowers the National Coast Guard to request agreement with the owners for the extraction of sunken national or foreign vessels situated within national jurisdictional waters, under warning of considering them abandoned in favour of the Uruguayan State. This leads to the conclusion that the use of the automatic 'abandonment' principle by Article 15 of the SHL could be arbitrary.

In contrast to the above considerations, in April 2014, the Supreme Court of Justice[71] upheld the decision of the Court of Appeal confirming the ownership by the Uruguayan State of archaeological property, based on Article 15 of the SHL.[72] In this case, a salvor company filed a judicial claim for the ownership

67 Art. 32 of the Constitution of the Republic of Uruguay states: 'No one shall be deprived of their right to own property, except for cases of public necessity and utility established by a law and always receiving from the National Treasury a fair and prior compensation'.

68 Art. 1452 of the Code of Commerce states 'If a ship is lost due to a grounding or sinking, its owners and those interested in the cargo shall suffer individually the losses and damages that occur in their respective properties, thus belonging to them the remains that can be salvaged ...'.

69 Art. 719 of Civil Code states: 'Things whose property voluntarily leaves its owner, such as coins tossed so that the first passenger can have them in his or her possession, may become an object of finding'.

70 R. Mezzera Alvarez, *Curso de Derecho Marítimo* (Alcali, 1954), at p. 101.

71 Sentence of the Uruguayan Supreme Court of Justice 06 August 2014, n. 732.

72 Decree 692/86 regulated until 2006 the search and recovery of `ancient vessels´, through contracts between the Uruguayan Government and companies, sharing the benefit of the value of the object recovered. For more information about Decree 692/86 see section 1.1.

of three archaeological objects recovered from the German Battleship, *Graf Spee*, a Nazi bronze emblem stern figurehead, a rangefinder, and a cannon. The Court of Appeal, stated:

> In compliance with the regulations in force there is no doubt that the remains of *Admiral Graf Von Spee* must be considered as abandoned in favour of the Uruguayan State and, as a consequence, that is the only owner.[73]

Notwithstanding this decision, it is worth pointing out that the determination of the ownership of these objects took place between the salvor and the State, without intervention of the flag State of the ship involved. In this sense, the passivity of flag States in the face of judicial procedures in Uruguay could be interpreted as an *implicit* abandonment of their shipwrecks. Despite the position of several maritime powers of demanding an express relinquishment to consider their sunken warships abandoned, in the case of Uruguay, such could be inferred from other relevant circumstances. This may permit the execution of contracts entered into between the government and permit holders for the search and rescue of shipwrecks under the legal regime prior to 2006. This would also apply to their successive renewal and of subsequent administrative actions aimed at achieving sale of the rescued assets.

To summarise, it is possible to conclude that both Uruguayan legislation and jurisprudence acknowledge State claims of ownership to historic shipwrecks. Thus, it is premature to say that, at present, the practice and policy of the maritime powers on asserting their rights over sunken State vessels located within the TS and internal waters of coastal States effectively reflects rules of international law. Indeed, the position of the Group of 77 within the preparatory works of the 2001 Convention, and the final adopted provision of Article 7(3), reflect the strength of the contrary position.[74] Hence, more time will be necessary to confirm the international practice of maritime States regarding this issue.

---

73 Sentence of the Uruguayan Civil Court of Appeal n. 1, 17 July 2013, n. sef 0003-000112/2013, "Etchegaray Carvallido, Alfredo y otros c/ Ministerio de Defensa – Cesación de condominio" I.U.E.2-1793/2011. This position was recently followed by decision of a court of first instance. See *supra* n. 14.

74 Chile also expressed its doubts in the Commission regarding matters that may affect the ownership of UCH, see <https://unesdoc.unesco.org/ark:/48223/pf0000128966> at p. 560.

3.3 *Moving from a UCH Commercial-Exploitation Model to a Sustainable Blue-Economy Model*

The work carried out over the last 27 years by government organs, academia and civil society has been fundamental to attaining and deepening the paradigm shift in UCH management toward a sustainable model that benefits the public. Examples of this include the National Heritage Commission, with implementation between 1995 and 1997 of an expert exchange agreement with the National Institute of Anthropology and History of Mexico, which oversees the Project Nueva España Fleet, among which were Drs. Pilar Luna and Jorge Manuel Herrera. In 2000, an agreement was reached with Canada's Park Service to deliver the first Nautical Archaeological Society course for Latin American professionals. It is also important to highlight the scientific work carried out in 2004 by Dr. Herrera, Professor Jon Adams, and the underwater team of the National Heritage Commission, who, thanks to a fellowship from the British Royal Academy, developed a research agreement with Southampton's University Maritime Archaeology Center.[75]

The underwater archaeological site of San Salvador, found in 2011 by local divers, with the initial intervention undertaken on a precautionary basis by the experts of the National Heritage Commission, is one of the most important findings in the history of Uruguay's archaeology. It constitutes a site where there is simultaneous work on land and underwater, which provides archaeological information of a poorly represented historical period, and seldom contemplated by the discipline in the region i.e., the period of the first European contacts in the Northern region of the American continent.[76] In the same year, at the initiative of Uruguay's National Office of Culture, the National Heritage Commission and Spain's National Museum of Underwater Archaeology (ARQUA) undertook the 'Project for strengthening the conservation of the UCH in the Southern Cone', with the support of the Inter-government Committee of the Ibermuseums Program. Also, and with the goal of increasing public awareness of UCH, the experts of the National Heritage Commission took part in carrying out a photo exhibition project, 'Cultural Secrets Under the Waves', organised by the UNESCO Office in Montevideo, among other public national institutions. The same activity was developed later in Perú, with Uruguayan and Peruvian specialists.

As a result of the work of the National Heritage Commission, international cooperation agreements on UCH have been agreed with the governments of

---

75 See *supra* n. 20.

76 V. Buffa, A. Cordero, and Gerardo Sosa, 'Río San Salvador. Resguardo de las primeras naves' (2015), 13 *Cultura y desarrollo* 32.

Peru, Chile, and Brazil, as well as with international universities and multilateral agencies. In 2017, the MOD, through the GCH-PEMA, collaborated in the development of localisation tasks and photogrammetry of the wreck of the HMS *Agamemnon*. This work was developed by specialists of the National Heritage Commission as well as international experts and supported by funding provided by a scientific fund of the National Geographic Society WDC.

At the academic level, it is worth noting the existence of the Coastal Heritage Research Center of the Eastern Region University Center (Universidad de la República), directed at student education and scientific research in Underwater Archaeology. This academic institution is part of the UNESCO UNITWIN Network for Underwater Archaeology and constitutes a centre with an important human and logistical capacity for research and the conservation of underwater materials.[77]

Also important is the role of Non-Government Organisations (NGOs) in the promotion of UCH public awareness. A successful example of this was the traveling audiovisual exhibition related to the HMS *Agamemnon*, with the support of national and world-renowned British institutions.[78] The work underlines not only the importance of maritime archaeology, but also the possible impact of climate change and alien species on the site, as well as on the blue economy, particularly that relating to fishers, who rely on catch near the wreck. The exhibition also highlighted the importance of UCH for the implementation of the Sustainable Development Goals (SDGs) as well as for the implementation of the LOSC and of the principle of co-operation in shared heritage.[79] Moreover, the work carried out in Maldonado Bay by experts of the Fisheries Technology Laboratory of the Uruguayan National Fisheries Office is of interest.[80] As a result of the monitoring and characterisation of existing fleets in the area (cruise, merchant, military, fishing) in the period between 2012 and

---

77 For more information on the work carried out by the Coastal Heritage Research Center see <https://cipac.cure.edu.uy/publicaciones/>.

78 Some of the British institutions involved in the traveling audiovisual exhibition of the HMS *Agamemnon* were the British Embassy Montevideo, the National Museum of the Royal Navy, the Centre for Maritime Archaeology, University of Southampton, the Faculty of Sciences & Technology, University of Bournemouth, Beaulieu Enterprises Limited and the Buckler's Hard Maritime Museum, the Maritime Archaeology Trust, and the Joint Nautical Archaeology Policy Committee. And at national level, the Yacht Club Punta del Este, Museo Ralli, Instituto Cultural Anglo-Uruguayo, the Town hall of Maldonado, and the British Society in Uruguay, among other institutions.

79 Some related to this project are SDGs 4, 8, 11 and 14.

80 J. Chocca and Y. Marín, 'Planificación, patrimonio subacuático y actividades marítimas. El caso de la Bahía de Maldonado' (2020), unpublished report.

2019, the survey was able to identify risks, threats and possible impacts to UCH, as well as areas of different vulnerability. Based on this, the implementation of mitigation measures of different scales (extreme, high, and moderate) is recommended, as well as the need for an integrated management mechanism including the aquatic and coastal space.

Last but not least, it is important to point out, as a good example of public policy for the promotion of cultural projects, the existence of the 'Fondos de Incentivo Cultural' (Cultural Incentive Funds), comprised of donations from companies and private individuals who, in exchange, obtain fiscal benefits of up to 65 per cent in credit certificates.[81] The direct beneficiaries of these funds are private stakeholders interested in promoting cultural projects, including those that have as their object the protection and dissemination of UCH.

In summary, based on the importance of discovered sites such as Puerto de las Naos de San Salvador, experience has been gained both at the public institutional level, as well as the academic, and with NGOs. This covers the specificities required by the management of UCH, such as maritime archaeology, the conservation of materials saturated in water, and their protection.

4 Conclusions and Future Directions

At present, it is paradoxical that the search for, and recovery of, historical wrecks in Uruguay is based, at its core, on a law created in 1975, which has as its purpose solving a `problem´ that was confined to their recovery and subsequent sale. In this sense, the Uruguayan experience has been useful in that it demonstrates that a model of commercial UCH management is unsuccessful. It could be convincingly argued that this failure is apparent in every sense. This is fundamentally a result of the fact that the interests of treasure hunters do not represent the interests of Uruguayan society nor those of humanity, but their own, based on the desire for personal profit.

With the accession of Uruguay to the 2001 Convention, several of the observed weaknesses could be resolved. In fact, through a legal regime it would

81 Arts. 235 to 250 of Law No. 17.930 of 19/12/2005 create the National Board of Evaluation and Promotion of Artistic and Cultural Projects, the Registry of Artistic and Cultural Projects, the Incentive Funds and the managing trust for the funds. In accordance with Article 239, natural persons or legal entities who pay the Income Tax and Equity Tax, who make cash donations for declared cultural artistic development projects, will enjoy, depending on the case, up to 65 per cent of the deposit made in an account authorised for such purposes, imputed as payment on account of the aforementioned taxes. In turn, donors may deduct 25 per cent of the total amount donated from the Income Tax.

be possible to incorporate the concept of UCH into the internal legal system, prohibit its commercial exploitation (with the selling contemplated in Article 20 of SHL tacitly repealed for that objective), as well as enshrine the principle of *in situ* preservation as a priority option before initiating any activity on a heritage site. Likewise, cooperation between Party States would be encouraged for the exchange of information and collaboration in research, excavation and preservation of underwater sites, something that has been poorly developed so far. This is particularly evident in respect of those wrecks where there are non-Uruguayan flag States involved and where this applies to sunken State vessels. In addition, the application of the regime of salvage law to UCH, which is provided by Law No 17.121 of 21 June 1999, by virtue of Article 4 of the 2001 Convention, would be substantially limited.[82]

Whilst the above identifies the benefits to ratification of the 2001 Convention, there are a number of issues remaining that require resolution if Uruguay is to do so. First, it would be recommended to carry out a prior analysis of the viability of its implementation that includes all the elements of governance related to the UCH located in Uruguay. In particular, it is necessary to carefully analyse the current institutional capacities to face the obligations arising from the Convention, in order to avoid incurring possible international liability. In this sense, and as reported by national experts, important challenges would arise *a priori* related to the absence of a national plan to carry out and publish an underwater archaeological inventory, and weaknesses in terms of human and economic resources, especially to use the best practicable means to prevent or mitigate any adverse effects that might arise from activities under its jurisdiction incidentally affecting UCH.[83]

Second, in the case that Uruguay believes itself in a position to move to implementation of the 2001 Convention, it will need to produce effective law to do so, set within a defined national policy clearly based on the

---

82 Law 21 June 1999, No 17121, Competencias de la Armada Nacional a través de la Prefectura Nacional Naval, en aguas de jurisdicción o de soberanía nacional o puertos de la República. Coordinación y control de la actividad de asistencia y salvamento de embarcaciones, artefactos navales o bienes deficientes en peligro o siniestrados, published in the `Diario Oficial' (suppl. to No 25306) July 5th, 1999. In accordance with Art. 2 the notion of salvage refers to 'every act or activity carried out to assist or dispose of a vessel, naval artefact, either in danger or wrecked in waters of national jurisdiction or sovereignty or ports in the Republic'.

83 Declaration of Mr. A. Cordero before the Commission of International Affairs in the Chamber of Representatives of the Legislative Power of Uruguay, on 6 September 2023. Tachigraphic version No 1539 of 2023, see <https://parlamento.gub.uy/documentosyleyes/documentos/versiones-taquigraficas/representantes/49/1539/0/CAR>.

Convention's objectives and considerations. A systemic vision of UCH would aid in strengthening inter-institutional cooperation, and in maximising public resources. To that end, the new law should create coordination and monitoring mechanisms for the application and effective enforcement of the provisions of the 2001 Convention. Likewise, the creation of a national plan for the protection and dissemination of the lessons we can all learn from the study of UCH would greatly assist in defining the applicable measures for its correct implementation through participation of all competent public organs, academia, and, especially, civil society, based on the principle that "[h]eritage protection without community involvement and commitment is an invitation to failure".[84] In particular, it would be advisable to develop a strategy to recruit, select and capitalise on the result of public-private alliances, especially with NGOs, as an additional proposal for public management of cultural heritage.[85]

At the same time, the new law for UCH should align with tourism policies, something that has not been fully developed in Uruguay to date. Underwater sites may broaden the appeal and attractiveness to visitors, evidence of this likelihood being the abovementioned traveling audiovisual exhibition related to the HMS *Agamemnon*. The outcomes of such cultural exchange should also be linked to educational and promotional policies in order to maximise their benefit and ensure the presence of all educational levels in the design of policies for the protection and promotion of the UCH.

A sufficiently effective regime of sanctions for illegal activities is essential, including fines and seizures, for it to dissuade behaviors that undermine the integrity of UCH. Law No 14.040 sets out a relatively mild punitive system, within a challenging enforcement landscape, making the law ineffective. For these reasons, better control should be implemented at first through a range of policies such as those creating awareness of the value of UCH, along with measures designed to dissuade inappropriate interference with UCH. Ultimately, this would need to be underpinned by the creation and

84 World Heritage Committee 31st Session, Christchurch, New Zealand, 23 June–2 July 2007, WHC-07/31.COM/13B, Paris, 23 May 2007, see <https://whc.unesco.org/archive/2007/whc07-31com-13be.pdf>.

85 In this sense, it is worth noting the existence of the 'Gaiola' and 'Baia' underwater parks in Naples, as successful public-private partnership examples for the control, sensitisation, and development of sustainable tourism related to UCH. G. Rodríguez Prado, 'International experiences in the legal protection and management of underwater cultural heritage and their possible implementation in Uruguay' (2014) The United Nations -The Nippon Foundation Fellowship Programme Thesis.

implementation of a sufficiently severe punitive system to act as a deterrent to discourage infractions linked to any damage made to, the deterioration, and illegal traffic of UCH.[86]

In addition, it is necessary to update and reinforce the institutional structure of the Competent Cultural National Authority, with the purpose of adopting the obligations in the 2001 Convention. In this sense, it would be necessary to assign new legal powers to the current National Heritage Commission, as well as to reflect the most efficient institutional legal modality for compliance with the tasks provided for by the 2001 Convention.[87]

If adherence to the 2001 Convention takes place, there would be a degree of doubt as to possible effects upon the abandonment regime of foreign ships established in Article 15 of Law No. 14.343, as per the sovereign immunity regime of State ships, set out in Articles 2(8) and 1(8) of the 2001 Convention, at least within the Contiguous Zone and the remainder of the Exclusive Economic Zone.[88] Anyway, the use of 'should' in Article 7(3) of the 2001 Convention, and the absence of reference to internal waters within this paragraph, could confirm that flag States no longer enjoy the sovereign immunity of State vessels in this zone, as well as in the TS.

Based on the above, it is worth pointing out the need for strengthening international cooperation for the protection and dissemination of UCH. For that it is preferable to leave aside radical positions surrounding ownership issues, to better preserve UCH for the benefit of present and future generations, thus promoting the related sustainable blue economy.

All websites last accessed February 2025.

---

86 See Art. 17(2) of the 2001 Convention.

87 One of the possible institutional management proposals consists of the creation of a Public Cultural Heritage Institute, with its own legal name and assets, with agile operations and the capacity to partner with other public and private organisms, national and international, and of producing additional financial resources through the provision of services and the commercialization of cultural products (A. Quintela, 'Institucionalidad del Patrimonio Cultural en el Uruguay' in A. M. Sosa González, M. L. Mazzucchi Ferreira and W. Rey Ashfield (eds.) *Patrimônio cultural: Brasil e Uruguai: os processos de patrimonialização e suas experiências* (UFPel, 2013).

88 See *supra* n. 60.

Selected Bibliography

J. Adams and others 'Maritime Archaeology in Uruguay: Towards a Manifesto' (2010) 1 *Journal of Maritime Archaeology* 5.

V. Buffa, A. Cordero, and Gerardo Sosa 'Río San Salvador. Resguardo de las primeras naves' (2015), 13 *Cultura y desarrollo* 32.

S. Dromgoole. Underwater cultural heritage and international law (Cambridge University press, 2013).

A. Quintela 'Institucionalidad del Patrimonio Cultural en el Uruguay' in A. M. Sosa González, M. L. Mazzucchi Ferreira and W. Rey Ashfield (eds.) *Patrimônio cultural: Brasil e Uruguai: os processos de patrimonialização e suas experiências* (UFPel, 2013).

A. Rengifo Lozano `Las objeciones de Colombia a la Convención Internacional de la UNESCO sobre Protección del Patrimonio Cultural Subacuático´ (2009) 25 *Pensamiento Jurídico. Derecho y Política en la era de la Sostenibilidad* 145.

G. Rodríguez Prado 'International experiences in the legal protection and management of underwater cultural heritage and their possible implementation in Uruguay' (2014) The United Nations-The Nippon Foundation Fellowship Programme Thesis.

T. Scovazzi `The Law of the Sea Convention and Underwater Cultural Heritage´ (2012) 27 *The International Journal of Marine and Coastal Law* 754.

CHAPTER 22

United States of America

*Ole Varmer**

1 Introduction

The public interest and duty to protect the oceans' heritage is reflected in the UN Law of the Sea Convention (LOSC),[1] the UNESCO Convention on World Heritage (1972 Convention),[2] the Convention on the Protection of Underwater Cultural Heritage (2001 Convention),[3] and domestic laws. Public interest in the United States (US) in protecting its heritage is reflected in the laws and policies discussed in this chapter. The US has shown some leadership in the development of such law, in part because US salvors have been at the forefront of unauthorised commercial salvage of underwater cultural heritage (UCH).

1.1 *History*

The US preservation movement of the early 1800s involved the purchase of buildings associated with its founders. The Antiquities Act 1906 (AA) was the first heritage law and by the 1980s preservation evolved to include RMS *Titanic* and abandoned shipwrecks. However, there is no law that provides comprehensive protection of all UCH.

1.2 *Overview of US Heritage Management System*

At the national level, all federal agencies have a responsibility to identify and preserve historic resources that are subject to their jurisdiction and control, as per the National Historic Preservation Act 1966 (NHPA)[4] and the Archaeological Resource Protection Act 1979 (ARPA).[5] Under these Acts, the Department of Interior (DOI), National Park Service (NPS), plays the leading role in protecting archaeological resources, including UCH, in DOI protected areas.

* Senior Advisor on Ocean Heritage, The Ocean Foundation.

1 1833 UNTS 397.

2 1037 UNTS 151.

3 2562 UNTS 1.

4 The National Historic Preservation Act of 1966, 16 U.S.C. §§ 470a *et seq.* (enacted October 15, 1966).

5 Archaeological Resources Act of 1979, 16 U.S.C. §§ 470aa *et seq.* (enacted October 31, 1979).

 | DOI:10.1163/9789004510883_024

Under the Department of Commerce (DOC), the National Oceanic Atmospheric Administration (NOAA) manages historic sanctuary resources, certain marine national monuments, and sunken NOAA craft. The Navy History and Heritage Command (NHHC)[6] manages the sunken military craft of the Department of Defense, wherever located. The DOI Bureau of Ocean Energy Management (BOEM) manages energy development activities on the Outer Continental Shelf (OCS) and thus controls such activities that may inadvertently affect UCH.[7] The US federal agencies involved in UCH management have indicated that they will adhere to the Annex Rules of the 2001 Convention since they are consistent with the Federal Archaeology Program (FAP).[8]

2 US Statutes Controlling Activities Directed at UCH

2.1 *Antiquities Act 1906* (AA)

Since the second edition of this book, one of the most significant developments regarding UCH is the use of the AA, a terrestrial-based law, to protect natural and cultural heritage within the Exclusive Economic Zone (EEZ)/OCS.[9]

2.1.1 Purpose and Scope

The AA provides authority for the President to set aside lands that are 'owned or controlled' by the US to conserve historic landmarks, historic and prehistoric structures, and other objects of historic or scientific interest.[10] The AA was enacted to protect Native American heritage on terrestrial land from looting. DOI, however, also applied it on federal submerged lands and the OCS for years, until a court ruled in *Treasure Salvors* (*Atocha*) that the AA did not apply on the OCS.[11] However, that case has been distinguished. For example, an AA permit was subsequently required for salvage within the Florida Keys sanctuary for

---

6 Historically the Navy protected its wrecks relying on US Property law. The 2004 Sunken Military Craft Act discussed in section 2.6 is much more comprehensive. See the Naval Heritage and History Command website at< https://www.history.navy.mil/>.

7 The OCS generally extends out the 200 nautical mile (nm) limit of the US Exclusive Economic Zone (EEZ), however, those portions extending beyond that are referred to as the US Extended Continental Shelf. The inner limit of the OCS is the seaward limit of State Submerged Lands generally 3 nm.

8 NPS webpage on FAP available at <https://www.nps.gov/orgs/1187/index.htm>.

9 Antiquities Act of 1906, 16 U.S.C. §§ 431–433 (2011).

10 See the second edition of this book and O. Varmer, *UCH Law Study* for more details and citations.

11 *Treasure Salvors v. The Unidentified Wrecked and Abandoned Sailing Vessel* (the *Atocha*), 569 F.2d 330, 337 (5th Cir. 1978).

UCH on the OCS. The AA has also been applied on the OCS to establish national marine monuments, including Papahānaumokuākea (Hawaiian), which has been inscribed on the World Heritage List for mixed natural and cultural heritage and the boundary for which extended seaward 50 nautical miles (nm), increased to 200 in 2016 so a substantial portion of it is within the EEZ/OCS. Four more marine national monuments have subsequently been established within the EEZ.[12]

2.1.2 Authorisation for Activities Directed at UCH

The AA requires permits for research and recovery of antiquities on lands 'owned or controlled' by the US, including Marine Protected Areas. Admiralty courts have recognised that the AA and the Rivers and Harbors Act 1899 (RHA)[13] have altered substantive maritime law of salvage and ordered compliance with these Acts before conducting salvage activities.[14]

2.1.3 Sanctions

Section 1 of the AA authorised a civil penalty of not more than $500 and imprisonment for not more than ninety days or both.

2.1.4 Gap Analysis

As discussed above, the *Treasure Salvors* case has been distinguished and the AA applies in the EEZ/OCS. It is a good authority for implementing the obligations under the 2001 Convention on the OCS. However, permits on the OCS, which were withdrawn as a result of *Treasure Salvors*, have yet to be reinstated. Notice to the public about the scope of application of the AA, including the EEZ/OCS, is recommended, as well as an amendment to the AA increasing the

---

12 The Marianas Trench, Pacific Remote Islands, Rose Atoll and Northeast Canyons and Seamounts Marine National Monuments. For a list of the monuments see annotations in 16 U.S.C. § 431. See also <https://www.npca.org/advocacy/79-protect-america-s-marine-monuments> for marine monuments.

13 Rivers and Harbors Act of 1899, 33 U.S.C. §§ 401 *et seq.* (enacted as 'An Act Making appropriations for the construction, repair, and preservation of certain public works on rivers and harbors. And for other purposes' March 3, 1899).

14 *Kohala Coast Enterprises, LLC v. Unidentified Shipwrecked Vessel*, Case No. 1:12-cv-00552-SOM-RLP, Warrant Arrest Order, January 4, 2013 (D. Haw, 2012) (Judge Mollway issued an order that would be an excellent model for all admiralty courts to consider in the future: "prior to any physical contact with the Vessel, Plaintiff is responsible for obtaining any necessary permits and authorizations from local, state or federal authorities, including but not limited to authorities whose areas of expertise and enforcement are the ocean, environment, endangered or threatened species, historic preservation, and/or cultural protection or preservation. Plaintiff shall also comply with all applicable local, state or federal statutes or regulations ...").

potential limits of civil and criminal sanctions consistent with the Sunken Military Craft Act 2004 (SMCA)[15] and the National Marine Sanctuaries Act 1972 (NMSA).[16] The current AA sanctions are dated and pale in comparison with those in the NMSA. Finally, an express definition of 'antiquities' that includes UCH is recommended.

2.2 *Archaeological Resources Protection Act 1979 (ARPA)*

2.2.1. Purpose and Scope

The ARPA addressed the vagueness of 'antiquity' with a clear definition of 'archaeological resources' that applies to objects at least 100-years old and of archaeological interest. ARPA also involves updating the criminal and civil enforcement provisions. Unfortunately, its permitting system does not apply on the OCS because the 'public lands' definition expressly excludes it. Fortunately, the trafficking provision (see below 2.2.3) has been applied to objects recovered from private lands in the US and abroad and has been determined to be applicable to UCH, including objects recovered from RMS *Titanic*.

2.2.2 Authorisations of Activities Directed at UCH

ARPA requires a permit for activities directed at archaeological resources (including UCH) located on public lands. Such permits are not granted unless the proposed activities are determined to be consistent with the standards of the Federal Archaeological Program (FAP), which in turn is consistent with the 2001 Convention's Annex Rules.

2.2.3 Sanctions Including Trafficking of UCH from Abroad

The penalties for looting include forfeiture, civil, and criminal sanctions. The prohibition on trafficking of such resources serves as a catch-all to reinforce state and local laws protecting archaeological resources, including foreign laws.[17] It prohibits the sale, purchase, exchange, transport, receipt, or offer to do so, in interstate or foreign commerce, of any unlawfully taken archaeological resource. This enforcement tool has been used for trafficking heritage within the US looted from national parks,[18] private land, Spain and the Vatican

15 Sunken Military Craft Act of 2005, Pub. L. No. 108–375, Stat. 2094–2098 (codified at 10 U.S.C. §§ 13 (2011)).

16 National Marine Sanctuaries Act, 16 U.S.C. §§ 1431 *et seq.* (2000) as amended by Public Law 106–513, November 2000.It is Title III of the Marine Protection Research and Sanctuaries Act of 1972.

17 16 U.S.C. § § 470aa *et seq.* Section 66(c).

18 See *U.S. v. Hampton*, Nos. P169925, P169927, and P169928 (S.D. Fla. 1986): ARPA case ending in plea bargain brought against treasure hunters in Key Biscayne National Park.

City.[19] In sum, the ARPA trafficking provision may be applied within US territory, Territorial Sea (TS), and Contiguous Zone (CZ)[20] for UCH looted from a site on the OCS, the seabed Area under the High Seas, and/or from a foreign nation.

2.2.4 Gap Analysis

To fill the gap in coverage on the OCS, the definition of public lands should be amended to include it. The prohibition on trafficking (section 6(c)) has not yet been tested in a case involving UCH, therefore a notice should be published so the public knows that the trafficking provision applies to the trafficking of UCH looted from the OCS, High Seas/Area and foreign nations.

2.3 *National Marine Sanctuaries Act 1972 (NMSA)*

The Office of National Marine Sanctuaries (ONMS) celebrated the fiftieth anniversary of the NMSA in 2022. This Act is a model of integrated protection and management of natural and cultural heritage and has resulted in the establishment of 15 sanctuaries.

2.3.1 Purpose and Scope

The NMSA is an early marine spatial planning law authorising DOC/NOAA to set aside special marine areas from ocean dumping and other activities inconsistent with the primary purpose of protection. While the initial focus was on natural heritage, the first sanctuary was the historic shipwreck USS *Monitor*.[21] The initial scope included the 3 nm TS and the CS, but it was amended to include the seaward limit of the 12 nm TS and the 200 nm EEZ. The NMS

19 See *US v. Melnikas*, 929 F. Supp. 276 (S.D. Ohio 1996) (professor caught attempting to sell manuscript pages stolen from the Vatican and two cathedrals in Spain) and *US v. An Archaic Etruscan Pottery Ceremonial Vase C. Late 7th Century, B.C. and a Set of Rare Villanovan and Archaic Etruscan Blackware, c. 8th–7th Century B.C., Located at Antiquarium, Ltd., 948 Madison Avenue, New York, New York, 10021*, 96 Civ. 9437 (1996) (company possessed artefacts know to have been looted from site in Italy and purchased in foreign commerce).

20 See M. J. Aznar 'The Contiguous Zone as an Archaeological Maritime Zone' (2014) *Int'l J. Marine and Coastal Law* 29 1–51 for excellent analysis of the evolution of the CZ into LOSC and customary international law because of State practice.

21 The USS *Monitor* was the Union Navy's first ironclad warship used in the Civil War. The vessel sank in 1862 off the coast of North Carolina and rediscovered in 1973. The site was designated as the first marine sanctuary under NMSA in 1975. For more information see: <https://monitor.noaa.gov/shipwrecks/uss_monitor.html> and the second edition of this book.

System includes Papahānaumokuākea and Rose Atoll marine national monuments.[22]

2.3.2 Authorisation of Activities Directed at UCH

A permit or authorisation is required when conducting an activity within a sanctuary that is otherwise prohibited, including moving or removing UCH. Activities that may inadvertently affect UCH, such as excavation or any alteration of the seabed, are also prohibited without a permit. A Special Use Permit is available to control concessions and other activities determined consistent with the primary purpose of protection.

2.3.3 Sanctions

The enforcement provisions collectively provide perhaps the broadest, and most comprehensive, civil enforcement authority of any US preservation law. Offenders are strictly liable for violations; no proof of negligence being required. NOAA must only demonstrate that an offender caused the destruction of, or injury to, sanctuary resources. While the AA and ARPA provide for criminal enforcement mechanisms, the NMSA relies on civil remedies and penalties for violations involving sanctuary resources. Since other federal and state laws may also apply to these activities, the civil penalty enforcement tool provides managers and counsel with supplemental enforcement authority.[23] This dual-track authority for enforcement is relatively unique.

2.3.4 Gap Analysis

While the NMSA is ample authority for implementing the 2001 Convention in sanctuaries, a 2014 study on UCH law offered a proposed amendment to expand its scope to control salvage and other activities directed at UCH located outside of sanctuaries and monuments. The NMSA could also be amended to provide authority for implementing US international agreements protecting UCH in the High Seas, such as the RMS *Titanic*.

2.4 *R.M.S. Titanic Maritime Memorial Act 1986 (1986 Act)*

RMS *Titanic* is perhaps the most famous shipwreck. Its sinking and the loss of life was a catalyst for the first Safety of Life at Sea Convention (SOLAS) and the

22 Mallows Bay-Potomac River and Wisconsin-Shipwreck Coast. See NOAA website on sanctuaries at <https://sanctuaries.noaa.gov/>.

23 See discussion of *Craft* in the second edition of this book and the cooperative enforcement under the NMSA with NPS.

establishment of the International Maritime Organisation (IMO).[24] Its discovery in 1985[25] was quickly followed by enactment of the R.M.S. Titanic Maritime Memorial Act 1986 (1986 Act), thanks to Bob Ballard.[26] This eventually led to the international agreement on *Titanic*, discussed below, and NOAA guidelines for its exploration, research, and if determined appropriate, salvage, encouraged in the 1986 Act.[27]

2.4.1 International Agreement

The Agreement Concerning the Shipwrecked Vessel RMS Titanic (the Agreement) was negotiated by Canada, France, the UK, and the US between 1997 and 2000.[28] The UK ratified it in 2003, implementing it through an order.[29] The US signed the Agreement in 2004, subject to its 'acceptance', meaning that the US would need implementing legislation authorising it to carry out the Agreement's obligations before it could become a party to it. The Agreement entered into force in 2019, after passing of the Consolidated Appropriations Act 2017[30] and an extensive review of other laws available to the US, enabling it

---

24 An explanation of the sinking of *Titanic* and development of SOLAS is available at <https://www.imo.org/en/MediaCentre/PressBriefings/Pages/11-titanic.aspx> and <https://www.cdn.imo.org/localresources/en/OurWork/Safety/Documents/TITANIC.pdf>.

25 It was a US-French expedition involving L'Institut Français de Recherche pour l'Exploitation de la Mer (IFREMER) and US Bob Ballard, Woods Hole Oceanographic Institute (WHOI). IFREMER and WHOI had been cooperating for years on exploration and mapping of the Mid-Atlantic Ridge. The US Navy was a sponsor. It was revealed a couple of years ago that the expedition was a cover for secretly investigating the sunken nuclear submarines, USS *Thresher* and USS *Scorpions*. The National Geographic exhibition was approved by the US Navy. See J. Roach 'Titanic Was Found During Secret Cold War Navy Mission' (December 2018).

26 16 U.S.C. §§ 450rr-450rr-6. *See* NOAA GCIS *Titanic* pages for details on acts, agreement, guidelines, history, authorisations and salvage litigation.

27 The 1986 Act 'directed' DOS and NOAA to negotiate the Agreement and guidelines, However, under the US Constitution the Executive Branch has the lead on international negotiations. So, in President Reagan's signing statement he used the term 'encouraged' and clarified the discretionary authority of the President to negotiate treaties, see <https://www.gc.noaa.gov/documents/102186-titanic_signing.pdf>.

28 This coincided with the negotiation of the 2001 Convention. The Annexes are essentially the same. The express reliance of Flag State and other jurisdictions consistent with the LOSC in the Agreement on RMS *Titanic* was hoped to be a model of clarity so as to avoid 'creeping jurisdiction.'

29 Protection of Wrecks (RMS Titanic) Order 2003 No. 2496 under the Merchant Shipping Act 1995.

30 Public Law 115–31 see NOAA webpage at <https://www.govinfo.gov/content/pkg/PLAW-115publ31/pdf/PLAW-115publ31.pdf>.

to formally accept the legal obligations under the Agreement. On 14 June 2023, the IMO issued Circular Letter No.4731 to its members, other international organisations, and NGOs in consultative status regarding a 25 May 2023 Communication from the Governments of the United Kingdom of Great Britain and Northern Ireland and the United States of America urging other governments to consider becoming a party to the Agreement and offering to provide guidance and assistance to any government with an interest in acceding to it.

The tragic loss of life associated with the 18 June 2023 implosion of the *Titan* submersible at the wreck site of *Titanic* has resulted in investigations into the incident reminiscent of the investigations in the US and UK that resulted in the development of maritime safety standards in SOLAS and other laws. While it is currently unclear whether this will result in new safety requirements for submersibles, cooperation among nations is necessary and appropriate. It is also clear that Canada is the best nation to take the lead in such cooperation to protect RMS *Titanic* under the Agreement and the 2001 Convention.

2.4.2 The Consolidated Appropriations Act 2017

Section 113 of this Act states:

> No person shall conduct any research, exploration, salvage, or other activity that would physically alter or disturb the wreck or wreck site of the RMS *Titanic* unless authorized by the Secretary of Commerce per the provisions of the Agreement Concerning the Shipwrecked Vessel RMS *Titanic*. The Secretary of Commerce shall take appropriate actions to carry out this section consistent with the Agreement.[31]

There are many reasons why it took so long to get implementing legislation and for the Agreement to enter into force, including opposition from RMS Titanic Inc. (RMST) after its hostile takeover by some shareholders in 2000. RMST unsuccessfully sued the US DOS/NOAA to try to prevent the signing of the Agreement and its implementation.[32] Also, Congress did not act on draft legislation proposed by the USG (DOS/NOAA) submitted a few times to

31 *Ibid.* Under Art. 4 each Party is to take 'appropriate actions' to enforce measures taken pursuant to the Agreement against its nationals and vessels flying its flag and to prohibit activities in its territory, including its maritime ports, territorial sea, and offshore terminals, that are inconsistent with the Agreement.

32 RMST argued it would interfere with their right to salvage. Prior to this, the US had consulted RMST during negotiations and addressed concerns about Admiralty jurisdiction, their rights and even incorporated certain orders including the prohibition of recovery of artefacts inside the hull. We were unable to get parties to agree that there would be just

Congress. In 2012, Senator Kerry's Bill on *Titanic* made it out of his Senate Foreign Relations Committee, but it did not become law. Bob Ballard, again, was the voice that convinced Congress to enact legislation to implement the Agreement in 2017.

2.4.3 Gap Analysis

Legislation is recommended for comprehensive enforcement tools, such as those in the NMSA. This could be accomplished with an amendment to the 1986 Act. Alternatively, the NMSA could be amended so its enforcement tools are available to protect RMS *Titanic*. The amendment could also expressly address the relationship of these Acts and the Agreement, with the maritime law of salvage and Admiralty jurisdiction of federal courts required under Article III of the US Constitution. The amendments could, for example, propose a ban on the application of the law of finds and salvage, as Congress did in the SMCA and the Abandoned Shipwreck Act 1987.[33]

2.5 *Abandoned Shipwreck Act 1987* (ASA)

2.5.1 Purpose and Scope

The ASA is a property law enacted to transfer ownership of abandoned shipwrecks on state submerged lands for state management and control to prevent the application of the law of finds and salvage.[34] Unfortunately, the ASA did not require any minimum standards for historic preservation and conservation in the event of intrusive research and recovery. States therefore have wide discretionary authority to implement the ASA. However, NPS did publish guidelines for states and federal agencies for implementing it.

2.5.2 UCH Law of Several US Coastal States

There are dozens of nations with a federal system, including the US. In the US, states have the lead in the protection and management in state lands and waters, generally 3 nm from the coastline or baseline, an exception being that the seaward limit of the state submerged lands and waters is 9 nm in Texas, and the Gulf Coast of Florida. The territory of Puerto Rico also extends out 9 nm.

---

one collection. Regardless, Tulloch supported the Agreement, which was a catalyst for the hostile takeover.

33 Abandoned Shipwreck Act of 1987, 43 U.S.C. §§ 2101 *et seq.*

34 The ASA's transfer of title and ownership of abandoned shipwrecks is consistent with the transfer of the title and ownership of submerged lands under the Submerged Lands Act 1953 (SLA) 1953, 43 U.S.C. §§ 1301 *et seq.* (2006).

US states and territories have programmes for implementing the NHPA and ASA.[35] Some states employ effective legislation to protect UCH and foster a sense of stewardship with members of the public. For example, Florida, California and Vermont both have state-run underwater heritage reserves and SCUBA diving trails. Divers can register with the state and visit certain protected UCH sites, learning about the steps necessary to protect the resources.[36] For example, Alaska helps promote public involvement in UCH by requiring all findings to be made available in order for a permit to be issued[37] and Washington works to involve private landowners, and ensure any excavations are done properly by qualified parties in UCH management, by requiring consent from owners of both private and public lands subject to the permit.[38] Any field investigations on private land must also be conducted by professional archaeologists and disclosure of sites is encouraged, though confidential.[39]

As indicated, states have the discretionary authority to manage UCH as they see fit. Some are more rigorous than others. States and territories have State Historic Preservation Offices (SHPOs). Several states, including Alaska, Florida, Maryland, Texas, Virginia, and South Carolina, employ underwater archaeologists and staff in their SHPO.[40] Most US states and territories have passed legislation that applies to UCH protection.[41] Consistent with the rule of thumb under the NHPA, some states that protect UCH have a lower threshold than

35 NPS website Archaeology Program State Submerged Cultural Resources Laws available at <https://www.npshistory.com/publications/archeology/state-statutes.pdf>.

36 See Vermont's Underwater Historic Preserves and Lake Champlain Maritime Museum available at <https://www.lcmm.org/archaeology/vermont-underwater-historic-preserves/> and California's Maritime Underwater Heritage Trail, available at <https://www.parks.ca.gov/?page_id=1160>.

37 AS §080.

38 For Washington, see RCW §27-53-60.

39 RCW §27-53-60 (1) states: 'On the private and public lands of this state it shall be unlawful for any person, firm, corporation, or any agency or institution of the state or a political subdivision thereof to knowingly remove, alter, dig into, or excavate by use of any mechanical, hydraulic, or other means, or to damage, deface, or destroy any historic or prehistoric archaeological resource or site, or remove any archaeological object from such site, except for Indian graves or cairns, or any glyptic or painted record of any tribe or peoples, or historic graves as defined in chapter 68.05 RCW, disturbances of which shall be a class C felony punishable under chapter 9A.20 RCW, without having obtained a written permit from the director for such activities'.

40 NHPA Section 101(b)(3)(C) as amended (54 U.S.C. §302303) see NPS website on state preservation plans at <https://www.nps.gov/subjects/historicpreservationfund/federal-requirements-for-statewide-historic-preservation-plans.htm>.

41 See NPS website Archaeology Program State Submerged Cultural Resources Laws *supra* n.35.

the 100 years underwater included in the 2001 Convention. For example, Georgia lists a 50-year requirement[42] and Washington declares that archaeological resources abandoned for 30 years or more, specifically any sunken water or aircraft, are also property of the state.[43] In contrast, Texas and Louisiana only protect pre-twentieth century material.[44] This means, for example, World War II wrecks may not be protected under state UCH law, although, as indicated above, they are likely protected under the SMCA, and salvage activities that disturb the seabed likely need a state permit under laws implementing the SLA.[45]

States vary on how they address public access to UCH. Some facilitate public access for divers but strictly regulate intrusive research and recovery, as is the case in most national marine sanctuaries. Florida, for example, is a dive destination, but has law preserving archaeological sites and objects of antiquity for the public benefit, limiting exploration, excavation, and collection of such matters to qualified persons and educational institutions possessing the requisite skills and purpose to add to the general store of knowledge concerning history, archaeology, and anthropology.[46] Other states are more in line with the NPS, which has stricter regulations on public access, such as requiring a permit for metal detectors or use of survey equipment. For example, Alabama allows recreational diving licences but no object recovery.[47] South Carolina has a programme that is distinguishable from NOAA, NPS and most other states in that it issues hobby licences to divers permitting the recovery of up to ten artefacts per diver per wreck.[48]

The ASA has addressed the application of the law of finds on state submerged lands. Consistent with the Supreme Court ruling in the case involving *Brother Jonathan*, when the legal issue of whether the ASA or salvage law arises between a salvor and a state, it must be decided by an Article III federal court sitting in Admiralty jurisdiction.[49] Since the second edition of this book, there

42 GA Code §12-3-80. ARPA has a 100-year-old threshold while the 2001 Convention UCH is defined to be underwater fully or partially for at least 100 years.

43 RCW §27.53.040 and § 27.53.045.

44 Louisiana State Statutes Chapter 13 § 1605 and the Antiquity Code of Texas § 191.002.

45 Submerged Lands Act of 1953 43 U.S.C. §§ 1301 *et seq.*

46 Florida Historic Resources Act §267.14.

47 Underwater Cultural Resources Act <https://ahc.alabama.gov/PDF/Alabama_Underwater_Cultural_Resources_Act.pdf >.

48 South Carolina Underwater Antiquities Act § 54-7-670.

49 *California v. Deep Sea Research, Inc.*, 523 U.S. 491 (1998), *aff'g in part, vacating in part, and remanding sub nom. Deep Sea Research, Inc. v. The Brother Jonathan*, 102 F.3d 379 (9th Cir. 1996) (*Brother Jonathan*).

have been a couple of such decisions including the *Mercedes* case, discussed in section 6 below.[50]

2.5.3 Abandonment under the ASA

In the *Northeast Research* case involving salvage of the so-called *Dunkirk Schooner*,[51] a federal court sitting in Admiralty jurisdiction found that 'abandonment' may be inferred by clear and convincing evidence including that: the vessel had been wrecked for over 150 years; salvage technology existed at the time it sank; and nobody had tried to locate the wreck.[52] The plaintiff-salvor, Northeast Research LLC, filed a claim for salvage rights and title to an early nineteenth century inland schooner embedded in submerged lands of New York's Lake Erie, nicknamed the *Dunkirk Schooner* as it was located near Dunkirk, New York. The state intervened, asserting title to the wreck under the ASA, the SLA, and various provisions of New York State Law. The case was referred to a Magistrate Judge whose recommendation that the state's motion for summary judgment be granted and awarded title to the wreck was adopted by the Admiralty court.

2.5.4 State Control over Submerged Lands Helping Prevent Unauthorised Salvage

In the *Great Lakes* case, a salvage company brought an *in rem* action seeking an arrest warrant for what it believed to be the remains of La Salle's ship, *Le Griffon*.[53] The State of Michigan intervened asserting title under the ASA.[54] The Admiralty court held that a federal court may require a salvor to reveal the precise location of a vessel after a state has intervened to assert a claim under the ASA. The court is also free to issue a conditional arrest warrant limiting salvage operations, or to take other actions designed to protect the interests and concerns of both parties. As the alleged wreck was that of a French explorer, France also intervened. In 2010, an agreement was reached between the salvor, Michigan, and France on research of the site to determine if it was the

---

50 See the second edition and M. Aznar's chapter on Spain in this book for a discussion of the *Juno* and *La Galga* ASA case that provides context here and to the *Mercedes* case discussed in section 6.

51 *Northeast Research v. One Shipwrecked Vessel, her Tackle, Equipment, Appurtenances, and Cargo*, 790 F.Supp.2d 56 (W.D.N.Y. 2011).

52 790 F.Supp.2d 56 (W.D.N.Y. 2011).

53 *Great Lakes Exploration Group, LLC v. Unidentified Wrecked and (For-Salvage Right Purposes), Abandoned Sailing Vessel, etc.*, 522 F.3d 682 (6th Cir. 2008). *Le Griffon* was one of the first sailing vessels to navigate the Great Lakes.

54 *Ibid.*

historic French wreck. A 2013 expedition did not result in a consensus view and Michigan has not authorised any intrusive research or recovery. While claims of the discovery of this 'Holy Grail' of the Great Lakes continue, Michigan is recognised as being in control of the site, in large part because permits are required to disturb state 'bottomlands' under the SLA and implementing legislation.

2.5.5 Gap Analysis

One gap is the lack of a definition of 'abandoned' in the Act, which was because Congress was relying on maritime case law at the time related to the law of finds, e.g., the *Treasure Salvors* case and its progeny. This could be addressed with an amendment that defined 'abandoned' and addressed the relationship with the law of salvage, including the *Brother Jonathan* case. There could also be an amendment to the ASA or perhaps the Coastal Zone Management Act[55] to provide a financial incentive for coastal States to adopt the federal standards and requirements for conservation consistent with the FAP and the Annex Rules of the 2001 Convention, through grants or other financial assistance.

2.6 *Sunken Military Craft Act 2004 (SMCA)*

The threat of salvage of the sunken Spanish warships *Juno* and *La Galga,*[56] and the lack of clarity in the 2001 Convention regarding the treatment of sunken warships within the Territorial Seas of nations, were catalysts for DOS to get Congress to enact the SMCA. It also recognises the need for cooperation among nations regarding UCH.[57]

2.6.1 Purpose and Scope

According to its website, under the SMCA the US Navy protects and manages more than 17,000 US sunken military craft around the world, dating from the American Revolution to the beginnings of the nuclear age. Thus, the scope includes US military craft in all maritime zones around the world, including the Area under the High Seas and the maritime zones off the coast of foreign nations. Consistent with evolving State practice of regulating activities directed at all UCH in the Contiguous Zone, the SMCA provides authority

---

55 This law provides financial assistance to coastal States that get an approved coastal program that meets minimum federal standards, states may include UCH as managed resources under this Act.

56 See M. Aznar chapter on Spain in this book.

57 10 U.S.C. §§ 113 et seq.

to regulate activities directed at foreign sunken military craft within the US 24 nm CZ.[58]

2.6.2 Authorisations of Activities Directed at UCH

The SMCA requires permits or authorisations for activities directed at such craft. This is consistent with the 2001 Convention, but it is clearer in requiring the consent of the US for its sunken military craft located within the territorial waters of foreign nations. Like the ASA and the 2001 Convention, the SMCA expressly prohibits the application of the law of finds and salvage.[59]

2.6.3 Sanctions

The SMCA may be enforced against any person who violates it, or any regulation or permit, including penalties up to $100,000 per day for each violation, as well as costs and damages resulting from the disturbance, removal, or injury to protected craft and cargo. It may not be enforced against foreign nationals and vessels except in a manner consistent with the LOSC. Damages may include the reasonable costs of storage, restoration, care, maintenance, conservation, and curation of the craft, as well as the cost of retrieving any information of an archaeological, historical, or cultural nature from the site. Violators may also be subject to otherwise applicable criminal law sanctions.[60]

2.6.4 Gap Analysis

The SMCA filled many gaps in protecting such craft, but does not cover some non-military public vessels, like those used by NOAA for scientific research. However, such wrecks are protected by US property law. It should, however, be amended to provide the US authority to control US salvors and their activities directed at foreign sunken military craft wherever located. This control may be based on US Flag State jurisdiction and other jurisdiction consistent with the LOSC. It may also rely on Admiralty jurisdiction, as in cases such as RMS *Titanic*.

58 This is an important US recognition of coastal State jurisdiction over UCH creeping beyond the TS and even LOSC Art. 303 which the US is not a party to. See Aznar, *supra* n. 20.

59 See NHHC SMCA webpage on their permit system at <https://www.history.navy.mil/research/underwater-archaeology/policy-and-resource-management/permits.html>.

60 *Ibid.*

3 High-Profile UCH Cases of Salvage Law

3.1 *RMS Titanic Salvage and Litigation*

In 1987, Titanic Ventures' (TV later RMST) George Tulloch, convinced IFREMER to revisit the wreck site and, consistent with the suggestion of Bob Ballard, they carefully recorded and recovered artefacts outside of the two large hull portions of the ship, leaving them undisturbed as a memorial to those who lost their lives that fateful night.[61] Tulloch and his company promised IFREMER to limit the salvage to artefacts outside of the two large hull portions, keep the collection of artefacts together for cultural purposes, and not be involved in operations that dispersed the collection.[62] These promises were also made conditions in the French Administrative Tribunal award of artefacts from the 1987 expedition.[63] RMST made these same promises to the Admiralty court in Virginia as part of its plea to be granted exclusive rights to salvage RMS *Titanic*.[64] The US (DOS/NOAA) subsequently consulted with RMST regarding the agreement it was negotiating in an effort to harmonise the US negotiation position with the 1986 Act, Admiralty court orders and the rights of RMST under those orders.

The issue of salvage archaeology and the *in situ* preservation of RMS *Titanic* has been in dispute since its discovery. RMST's rights to salvage were limited to the field of artefacts between the two large hull portions that should remain undisturbed as a memorial to those who lost their lives in the sinking. This was consistent with RMST's business plan and incorporated conditions of the French award and the US court orders. Unfortunately, the Geller and Harris hostile takeover of RMST was designed to change its business plan so that it could pierce the hull and salvage inside it.[65] Upon learning of RMST plans

61 See Statement by Bob Ballard at the Hearing of the House Merchant Marine and Fisheries Committee on H.R. 3272 bill to Designate the Shipwreck of the Titanic as a Maritime Memorial (October 29, 1985) p. 21.

62 924 F. Supp. 714, 716 (E.D. Va. 1996) (summarising RMST promises to keep the collection together and not salvage hull and contents) fn 10.

63 *Procés-Verbal* (salvage award) from French Administrative Tribunal for the artefacts from the 1987 expedition with IFREMIR on October 20, 1993, the subject 1,800 artefacts were brought back to France for conservation and curation and are now called the French Collection in US court orders.

64 See *RMST Titanic*, 924 F. Supp. 714, 716 fn 10 (E.D. Va. 1996). RMST exclusive salvor in possession acting with due diligence under the circumstances including expensive deep water salvage expeditions.

65 RMST stockholders Arnie Geller and Michael Harris were successful in expelling Tulloch and suing the US DOS and NOAA to prevent the Agreement from coming into effect. They were found guilty of violating securities law, paid fines but retained control.

to do this, the court reiterated a previous order prohibiting disturbance of the hull.[66]

RMST then tried, unsuccessfully, to claim ownership over the wreck and those artefacts it had salvaged under the law of finds. As it eventually learned, US Admiralty courts do not have authority to determine title over wrecks located outside of the court's territorial jurisdiction. Courts do have *in personam* jurisdiction over salvors and their activities and may rely on *in rem* jurisdiction over the *res* or property within the court's territory to determine its disposition. The court ruled that RMST did not own RMS *Titanic* but that it could seek an award for services rendered under salvage law.[67] The ruling was upheld by the Fourth Circuit Court of Appeals with an important clarification – the salvage award may be conditioned to protect the public interest in RMS *Titanic*.[68] This led RMST to voluntarily negotiate the conditions of such award with the US Departments that represent the public interest in RMS *Titanic* under the 1986 Act.[69] At the conclusion of negotiations, RMST then proposed these for consideration by the court for conditioning its salvage award.

3.1.1 Covenant and Conditions of Salvage Award

In an Order by Chief Judge Smith, RMST was awarded title to the artefacts recovered in the 1993, 1994, 1996, 1998, 2000, and 2004 salvage expeditions (American Collection) subject to certain specified covenants and conditions (C&Cs).[70] The artefacts salvaged by IFREMER and TV/RMST in 1987 are subject to a salvage award by the French Administrative Tribunal (French Collection). Nonetheless, RMST voluntarily agreed to include them in certain provisions regarding management of the *Titanic* Collection of artefacts, which comprises both the American and French Collections. Just as the court relies on its *in personam* jurisdiction over RMST and its salvage activities outside of the court's territorial jurisdiction, so it may rely on its *in personam* jurisdiction over

66 Order dated July, 2001.

67 *R.M.S. Titanic, Inc.*, Case no. 2:93cv902 (Sept. 26, 2001 E.D. Va.). The court prohibited RMST from further arguments of title to artefacts under the law of find but will proceed with a hearing on a salvage award.

68 *R.M.S. Titanic, Inc.*, 286 F.3d 194, 203 (4th Cir. 2002) RMST appealed the 4th Circuit's decision to the Supreme Court, but the Supreme Court denied RMST's petition for *certiorari*. RMST subsequently sought a salvage award in the E.D. of Virginia. *See R.M.S. Titanic*, 327 F. Supp. 2d 664 (E.D. Va. 2004); 323 F. Supp. 2d 724, 743 (E.D. Va. 2004), *aff'd in part, vacated in part, remanded sub nom.*, 435 F.3d 521 (4th Cir. 2006).

69 The DOC-NOAA, and Dept. of Justice (DDOJ) negotiated with RMST.

70 Order dated Aug. 15, 2011, is available on the NOAA GC International Section website on *Titanic* at <https://www.gc.noaa.gov/documents/gcil_titanic_order_081511.pdf>.

RMST to enforce the C&Cs including those provisions involving the French Collection.

During negotiations of the C&Cs, RMST spent a lot of time proposing conditions that would address what would happen in the event of bankruptcy. NOAA engaged the expertise of Russel Craig, a DOC expert in bankruptcy, which in turn engaged bankruptcy experts at DOJ, as this whole agreement, process, and conditioning of a salvage award had never been done before. It did not surprise the author that RMST subsequently filed for bankruptcy and tried to use bankruptcy law and process to trump the Admiralty Court's C&Cs, or at least to get authorisation to sell some of the artefacts from the French Collection.

3.1.2 Bankruptcy of RMST/Premier Exhibitions

Premier Exhibitions (PE) experienced what appears to the author to be self-inflicted financial troubles with its 'Saturday Night Live' television show exhibition that led to requests to NOAA and ultimately the court to sell some artefacts from the French Collection.[71] RMST was unsuccessful, as breaking up the collection would be inconsistent with the C&Cs. RMST then voluntarily filed for Chapter 11 Bankruptcy in the Middle District of Florida.[72]

3.1.3 Titanic Collection and the C&Cs Survive Bankruptcy Law and Process

The bankruptcy court authorised the sale of RMST/PE stock, resulting in a reorganisation and new owners. Fortunately, the bankruptcy court recognised the subject matter jurisdiction of the Admiralty court orders and the applicability of the C&Cs.[73] While the bankruptcy judge did question the C&Cs related to the French Collection, it noted that RMST/PE risked litigation in the Admiralty court. While RMST/PE maintained its ability to sell artefacts from the French Collection, it ultimately withdrew its plan to auction some or all of the Collection and got approval for addressing the debt to creditors through the sale of its stock. Since then, the 'new' leaders at RMST have turned their attention back

71 Premier handles exhibitions of collections while RMST handles salvage, and the court orders apply to both.

72 Instead of the ED VA as agreed to under the C&Cs.

73 RMST, et al. Debtors, Case No. 3:16-bk-02230-PMG, US Bankruptcy Ct, M. D. of Florida (Decided Jul 22, 2016) the court noted that the Admiralty court had subject matter jurisdiction over the American Collection but not the French Collection citing *R.M.S. Titanic*, 435 F.3d 521 (4th Cir. 2006). However, it also noted that NOAA has consistently maintained that the C&Cs do not allow a sale of the French Artefacts separately from the American Artefacts and has repeatedly indicated that it would vigorously challenge any effort to break up the Titanic Collection (French or American).

to the Geller/Harris business plan of piercing the hull and salvaging artefacts. This time, however, with a very specific request, what they characterise as careful removal of the Marconi equipment.

3.1.4 Order Authorising the Salvage of the Marconi Equipment Is Vacated

RMST presented 'new' evidence of rapid deterioration of the hull portion that houses the Marconi equipment and its plan for its salvage.[74] RMST was not successful in getting NOAA to agree to a joint proposal to the court. RMST then requested that the court amend its 2000 Order prohibiting RMST from piercing the hull, by authorising the salvage the Marconi equipment from its interior. Despite the objections of the US, the UK and others, the court agreed with RMST and issued an Order authorising it to:

> minimally … cut into the wreck only as necessary to access the Marconi Suite, and to detach from the wreck the Marconi wireless device and associated artefacts.[75]

The court did not address the position that an authorisation from DOC/NOAA was required under the 2017 Act noting that the US is not a party but rather an *amicus*-friend of the court, so the US made a motion to intervene as a party to the case, asking the court to: reconsider its order and opinion authorising salvage; seek a declaratory judgment that the 2017 Act requires that RMST obtain an authorisation from DOC/NOAA before conducting 'any research, exploration, salvage, or other activity that would physically alter or disturb the wreck or wreck site of the RMS Titanic'; and enjoin RMST from conducting such activity unless and until it has obtained the DOC/NOAA authorisation. The US also appealed to the Fourth Circuit.

The Court of Appeals vacated the lower court authorising order because it did not address the US (DOJ/NOAA) motion to intervene and its argument that an authorisation by NOAA/DOC is required under the 2017 Act. It did, however, note that the lower court has the jurisdiction to consider a subsequent request for salvage of the Marconi equipment *after* it considers the US motion to intervene and addresses its argument for the application of the 2017 Act.[76]

---

74 Concerns about deterioration were first raised shortly after its discovery and raised periodically afterwards.

75 *RMS Titanic, Inc.*, 461 F. Supp. 3d 336, 342 (E.D. Va. 2020).

76 March 5, 2021, Order of the 4th Cir. Ct. of Appeals, Case No. 20-1684 (2:93-cv-00902-RBS) RMST, Inc., vs. [*Titanic*], Robert C. Blumberg, … [DOS]; Ole Varmer, [NOAA/DOC], etc. Case

On 21 May 2021, the District Court noted that the previous orders have been vacated and that RMST has no authorisation for its plan to salvage. The US emergency motion to intervene was considered moot and it noted that the US remains an *amicus* as it has been for the past twenty years. The Court also noted that the US is free to resubmit its motion to intervene if, and when, RMST submits a subsequent plan for salvage, or earlier if it wants.

In sum, RMST cannot legally salvage the Marconi equipment. RMST may try to challenge the 2017 Act's application to its activities and may question whether the 2017 Act is constitutional, presumably under Article III of the US Constitution. However, the US Supreme Court in *Brother Jonathan* has already upheld Congress' authority to ban the law of salvage under the ASA. That ban is constitutional, provided an Article III court sitting in Admiralty jurisdiction addresses cases in which there is an issue of whether the law of salvage or the ASA applies to a particular wreck.

In the case of RMS *Titanic*, section 113 of the 2017 Act just integrates and implements the Agreement and requires an authorisation or permit from DOC/NOAA. There is no ban or even an attempt to change the Admiralty jurisdiction of Article III courts. To the contrary, the US (DOJ/NOAA) continues its longstanding practice of respecting the court's Admiralty jurisdiction while also respecting its treaty obligations and relevant Acts of Congress, including the 2017 Act. The public interest in RMS *Titanic* is world-wide, as reflected in US statutes and policy, maritime law, and international law and policy. Thus, all these laws must be considered, and complied with, in future considerations of salvage of RMS *Titanic* by RMST and the courts. Moreover, Admiralty courts have ruled that treaties to which the US is party are to be respected and guide rulings in salvage cases, such as was done in the case of the *Mercedes*.

3.2 *Odyssey's Unauthorised Salvage of Mercedes*

3.2.1 Odyssey's 'Black Swan'

With some facilitation from persons working at the US DOS, Odyssey Marine Exploration (Odyssey) entered an agreement with the UK for "the exploration of the shipwreck believed to be HMS *Sussex* and the conservation and documentation of any artefacts that may be retrieved from the shipwreck".[77]

---

was filed against the author and his colleague as lead negotiators of the Agreement; DOJ subsequently got RMST to correctly file against the Secretaries of State and Commerce and Administrator of NOAA.

77 HMS *Sussex* was a British flagship that sank on 19 February 1694 with ten tons of gold. Working with the UK Ministry of Defence in a controversial contract, Odyssey never disclosed the exact location of the wreck. See S. Dromgoole, 'Murky Waters for Government

The ship sank off the east-coast of Gibraltar, an area of long-standing dispute between Spain and the UK. Spain was concerned about salvage of its shipwrecks and asserted rights to oversee the activities, entering into an agreement with the UK and Odyssey whereby a Spanish archaeologist would be an on-board observer. Odyssey was also exploring another area associated with what Odyssey called the 'Amsterdam Project', west of the Strait of Gibraltar, discovering what it called the 'Black Swan' site.

3.2.2 Salvage

In March 2007, while operating 100 miles from Gibraltar on the Portuguese CS, Odyssey recovered a cargo of around 594,000 coins (mainly silver Spanish Reales) and some other historical artefacts. Odyssey claimed that the site of salvage was in 'international waters' beyond the TS or CZ of any nation.[78] Odyssey quickly air freighted the 17 tons of coins from its base camp in Gibraltar to its home base in Tampa.[79]

On 9 April 2007, Odyssey filed an *in rem* court claim in Florida asserting ownership of the coins under the law of finds and alternatively rights to them as an *in specie* award under the law of salvage.[80] On 22 May 2007, Spain contacted the US to notify it about the salvage of coins from what it believed to be a Spanish archaeological site and to preserve its interests.[81] After research and analyses by expert Dr. James P. Delgado, Spain determined that the site of unauthorised salvage was around the site in which the *Mercedes* was sunk by the British during the 1804 Battle of Cape Saint Mary.

On 31 May 2007, Spain intervened claiming that the property in this salvage case was from a wreck still owned by Spain and subject to its sovereign

---

Policy: The Case of a Seventeenth Century British Warship and Ten Tonnes of Gold Coins' (2004) 28 *Marine Policy* 189.

78 OME initially stated that there was no evidence of a shipwreck at the site and subsequently argued it may be associated with more than one shipwreck. The court noted that "[b]y 2006, Odyssey listed the *Mercedes* with thirty other shipwrecks of interest (the 'Amsterdam Project')" at 1129.

79 *Odyssey Marine Exploration, Inc. v. Unidentified Shipwrecked Vessel*, 675 F. Supp. 2d 1126 (M.D. Fla. 2009) (*Odyssey*) (artefacts indicating the site was a Spanish warship were left in Gibraltar).

80 *Ibid.*

81 Diplomatic cable from Spain to the US dated 24 May 2007, obtained from WikiLeaks website and the website on the 'Story of Nuestra Señora de las Mercedes shipwreck' on VictoryShipModels.com available at <http://victoryshipmodels.com/mercedes-ship-treasure-story.html>.

immunity. Spain requested the specific location of the salvage site from Odyssey for it to properly determine its interest and rights regarding it.

3.2.3 Order to Disclose Site of Salvage and Related Information

From the outset, Odyssey maintained its need to keep the salvage site secret. Spain's counsel, successfully argued that Odyssey must, as a matter of law, provide the precise location and related information about the site, citing cases relying on the certain rules for Admiralty cases.[82]

Odyssey continued to maintain that it had not discovered evidence of a shipwreck but based upon its research said it believed the coins were associated with a nineteenth century ship. After many pleadings from Spain, the court ordered and compelled Odyssey to share its information. After a review of Odyssey's information about the site, including survey videos, Spain was convinced that it was the wreck site of the *Mercedes* and moved to dismiss the case 'for lack of subject matter jurisdiction' as *Mercedes* and its contents and cargo were subject to sovereign immunity from all claims or arrest in the US under the Foreign Sovereign Immunities Act 1976 (FSIA).[83] Peru and individual claimants joined Odyssey in asserting rights to the coins. The US subsequently filed a Statement of Interest and an *amicus* brief in support of Spain.

3.2.4 Courts Rule in Favour of Spain

In 2009, the court held that it was the wreck site of *Mercedes.* As such it was still owned by Spain, subject to sovereign immunity and therefore immune from judicial arrest in US courts under the FSIA.[84] These rulings were upheld on appeal and the US Supreme Court denied *certiorari* thus ending Odyssey's legal options in the US.[85] Spain then successfully moved to get reimbursed for its legal fees and associated costs. Judge Merryday said:

> In sum, Odyssey's persistent denial and feigned uncertainty about the existence and identity of the wrecked vessel was a demonstrably purposeful and *bad faith* litigation posture effected from the beginning of this action to deflect, delay, and if possible, defeat (or, at least, compromise) Spain's rightful claim. (Emphasis added)[86]

---

82 *Great Lakes*, 522 F.3d 682 (6th Cir. 2008) and *Fathom Exploration v. Unidentified wreck*, 352 F. Supp. 2d 1218 (S.D. Ala. 2005).

83 Foreign Sovereign Immunities Act (FSIA), 28 U.S.C. §§ 1602–1611.

84 *Odyssey*, 675 F. Supp. 2d 1126 (M.D. Fla. 2009).

85 *Odyssey*, 657 F.3d 1159 (11th Cir. 2011) *cert. denied*, 132 S. Ct. 2379 (2012).

86 *Odyssey*, 979 F. Supp. 2d 1270 (2013) at 1272.

Odyssey was ordered to pay over a million dollars for Spain's legal fees.[87] This case should discourage unauthorised salvage of UCH and is likely to guide the courts and others on some important issues.

3.2.5 The Sovereign Immunity of Mercedes Extends to Private Cargo and Effects

An issue of first impression in the US was whether the scope of sovereign immunity of a sunken warship extended to privately owned cargo. Spain and the US argued that it was important that the scope of immunity include all private cargo and personal effects. The US noted that should the court rule otherwise, wrecks such as the USS *Arizona* Memorial and USS *Monitor* could be salvaged to try to recover private property and personal effects. The court agreed and ruled accordingly. Additionally, the comity principles, and the need to protect Spain's sovereign interests, favoured returning the salvaged property to Spain.[88]

3.2.6 Peru's Claims

On behalf of Peru, Professor John Norton Moore[89] argued that the preferential rights of the State of origin under LOSC Article 149 regarding such resources in the Area should be applied in this proceeding to a wreck site on the CS of Portugal, was curious and questioned.[90] There was also a claim that Peru had rights and ownership under the international law of the succession of States, in sum that the Spanish coins were part of Peru's sovereign patrimony. Judge

---

87 *Ibid.*

88 *Odyssey*, 657 F.3d 1159 (11th Cir. 2011), *cert. denied*, 132 S. Ct. 2379 (2012).

89 Moore was the U.S. Ambassador for the negotiation of the Law of the Sea Convention under Presidents Richard Nixon and Gerald Ford. He is law professor at the University of Virginia Law School and oversaw the development of the UVa Commentary on the LOSC that has been called 'the Bible' on the LOSC by colleagues at the US DOS and Navy.

90 Peru and the US are not parties to the LOSC. Most of the LOSC was a codification of existing customary international law. Article 149 was developed at UNCLOS III and was not customary international law in 1982. However, the author has argued that the duty to protect and cooperate for that purpose in LOSC Arts. 149 and 393 are now customary international law. See O.Varmer, 'Duty to Protect Underwater Cultural Heritage and to Cooperate for that Purpose,' 77–117 in H. Karan, Ed. *The Legal Regime of Underwater Cultural Heritage and Marine Scientific Research* (Ankara U. Research Center of the Sea and Maritime law, 2020) (Duty to Protect and Cooperate now customary international law). Moore's argument that it applied in this case and the court's dicta recognising how the Art. 149 principles may be appropriate in another forum are further recognition that this duty to protect and cooperate are customary international law now.

Merryday respectfully ruled that the US court was not the appropriate forum for a dispute between the governments of Spain and Peru over the cargo.[91]

3.2.7 Duty to Comply with LOSC Article 149

Moore noted that while the US is not a party to the LOSC "it nevertheless carries the weight of law from the date of its submission by the President to the Senate."[92] In addition, Moore noted that the provisions of the LOSC, including Article 149, are legally binding because they reflect customary international law.[93] While the author would agree that Article 149 provides the framework of preferential rights and interests for UCH in the Area, it is about interests; it is not a rule addressing issues of ownership and the disposition of property.[94] Moreover, the site was not in the Area but on the CS of Portugal, which apparently recognised and respected the Flag State jurisdiction of Spain over its sunken warship. In sum, the court correctly ruled that the US court sitting in Admiralty jurisdiction is not the appropriate forum for determining the issues raised by Peru against Spain regarding a Spanish wreck, 4000 miles from Florida.

3.2.8 Treaty of Friendship 1902 and Relations between the US and Spain

This treaty guided the court on the reciprocal treatment required in this case. It requires the US to treat Spanish sovereign wrecks in the same manner as US law and policy treats US sovereign wrecks, which would include the SMCA and the ASA. Under these laws, the cargo associated with a ship is treated as part of the shipwreck. Since the private cargo is not severable from the shipwreck under SMCA and ASA, it concluded that "the protections awarded to a sunken sovereign vessel also extend to the cargo aboard that vessel" in this case.[95]

Under LOSC Articles 149 and 303, the US has a duty to protect UCH and to cooperate with other nations for that purpose. Thus, US Friendship Treaties may be instrumental in future UCH cases in Admiralty court and otherwise.

---

91 *Odyssey* at 1127.

92 Quoting from *US v. Royal Caribbean Cruises*, 11 F. Supp. 2d 1358, 1372 (S.D. Fla. 1998).

93 See *Sarei v. Rio Tinto, PLC.*, 456 F.3d 1069, 1078 (2006), *US v. McPhee*, 336 F.3d 1269, 1273 (11th Cir. 2003) and the Restatement of Foreign Relations Law at Introductory Note to Part V (Law of the Sea).

94 M. Aznar, 'The Notions of Preferential Right and Interest of States in the Protection of the Underwater Cultural Heritage' (2019) *Revista Electrónica de Estudios Internacionales* 1 (DOI: 10.17103/reei.38.07).

95 *Odyssey*, 657 F.2d at 1181.

4 US Cooperation with Other Nations

The *Titanic* Agreement is the best example of expressly implementing the LOSC duty to protect UCH and cooperate for that purpose. Other examples of cooperation with the UK include the NPS agreement on HMS *Fowey* in Biscayne Park[96] and the NOAA agreement on protecting the World War II (WWII) wreck HMT *Bedfordshire*.[97]

In terms of other nations, in 2016 NOAA entered a Memorandum of Understanding (MoU) with Spain, renewing an agreed framework to jointly identify, protect, manage and preserve UCH of mutual interest within their respective areas of responsibility. NOAA also consulted and cooperated with Germany regarding protecting U-boats in its Battle of the Atlantic Program. Upon discovery of the *U-576* off the coast of North Carolina, Germany was notified, briefed, and consulted on how to protect and cooperatively manage it. As the wreck was intact it was of particular interest. The *U-576*, and other U-boats, have been placed on the National Register for Historic Places and are subject to the NHPA.

NOAA also entered into an agreement to cooperate with Australia in its efforts to protect US sunken military craft off the coast of Australia to commemorate the seventieth anniversary of the WWII Naval Battle of the Coral Sea.[98] Australia declared that the three US warships sunk during the Battle (the USS *Lexington*, the USS *Sims*, and the USS *Neosho*) were protected under the historic preservation law of Australia. It recognises that these shipwrecks are a tangible link to one of the most dramatic events in Australian and US military history and to one of the most defining moments of WWII. It was made possible in part through collaboration between Australia and the NOAA ONMS Maritime Heritage Program. This collaboration was also consistent with the MoU and the US-Australia Science and Technology Agreement.[99]

---

96 See NOS Press Release <https://www.nps.gov/bisc/learn/news/fowey-agreement.htm>.

97 Agreement between the UK and NOAA Regarding the Protection of HMT *Bedfordshire* (Historic WWII Wreck Off North Carolina) (January 2016) available on the NOAA GC International Section website at https://www.gc.noaa.gov/documents/hmt-bedfordshire.pdf. For more information about the wreck see NOAA ONMS website Battle of the Atlantic *Exploring WWII in the Graveyard of the Atlantic* HMT *Bedfordshire* available at <https://sanctuaries.noaa.gov/missions/battleoftheatlantic2/bedfordshire.html>.

98 NOAA and Australia's Department of the Environment, Water, Heritage, and the Arts Australia' Memorandum of Understanding (May 7, 2012).

99 For more information, see Friends across the Pacific: Shared WWII maritime heritage of Australia and the US at <https://www.gc.noaa.gov/documents/2012/shipwrecks-friends-across-the-pacific.pdf>.

Cooperation with other nations to protect their WWII UCH has also extended to wrecks of Japan. Following Terry Kerby of the Hawaii Undersea Research Lab's (HURL) discovery of a Japanese Midget submarine in Pearl Harbor,[100] controversy ensued when the Institute of Aeronautical Archaeological Research, Inc., which was aboard in search of a different wreck, used the HURL video in support of its *in rem* claim in Admiralty against the wreck, seeking a $5,000,000 award. Terry Kerby objected to them and the court and asked NOAA and NPS for advice. This resulted in a two-pronged approach to prevent any salvage, and protect the wreck, led by DOS and DOJ. The DOS notified Japan and the cooperation resulted in an agreement under which the US would protect and manage the wreck.[101] As the owner of the property, it enabled the application of US property law to protect it. DOJ's Phil Berns intervened in the salvage case.[102] As the US was now the owner of the wreck, salvage could be denied, but more importantly he obtained a permanent injunction from the Admiralty court prohibiting any person from:

> ... directly or indirectly, taking any action of any nature in relation to defendant sunken vessel, including salvaging, attempting to salvage, moving, disturbing, removing, touching, making contact with the sunken vessel, its components, appurtenances, engines, boilers, appliances, furnishings, parts, etc., within the rectangular area encompassed by [certain] Latitudes ... and Longitudes ... without a permit from the US.[103]

While the SMCA has filled a gap in the law for foreign sunken military craft within the CZ, this case is nonetheless an excellent example of how to use maritime and property law to prevent looting and unwanted salvage elsewhere.

US cooperation with France on UCH goes back at least to the 1980s, with the discovery of RMS *Titanic* and subsequent negotiations and agreements on

---

100 J. P. Delgado, T. Kerby, H.K. Van Tilburg, S. Price, O. Varmer, M. D. Cremer, and R. Matthews *The Lost Submarines of Pearl Harbor* Ch. 7: Archaeology, Memory, Management, and Protection, Legal and Policy Issues (Ed Rachal Foundation Nautical Archaeology Series) (Texas A&M University Press & the Texas Book Consortium, 2016) 169–173 (Kerby used targets provided by NPS Larry Murphy and Dan Lenihan).

101 In an exchange of diplomatic notes, Japan and the US agreed the US owns these submarines located deep off the entrance of Pearl Harbor. Agreement between the US and Japan (Feb. 12, 2004): *See* NOAA GCIS Japanese Midget Sub webpage at <https://sanctuaries.noaa.gov/maritime/japanese-mini-subs/>.

102 *Institute of Aeronautical Archaeological Research, Inc. v. Wreck of Type A "Midget" Japanese Submarine*, Civ. No. 92-0052-BMK (D. Hawai'I, July 1, 1993) reported in Digest of US Practice in Int'l Law (2004), 1991– 99: 1619–20.

103 *Ibid.* See also J. P. Delgado *et al. supra* n. 100 at p. 171.

it, on the CSS *Alabama* off the coast of France, and *La Belle* off the coast of Texas.[104] James A. Goold, who was so successful in protecting Spanish heritage against unwanted salvage by US companies, was also successful in getting a US court sitting in Admiralty jurisdiction to dismiss the claim of salvage rights to an unidentified wreck that France argued was *La Trinité*, the flagship of the Royal Navy of France, 1565 Fleet of Captain Jean Ribault.[105] With the support of the State of Florida and the US, the court agreed with France's expert, Dr. James P. Delgado, that the wreck was indeed *La Trinité*, still owned by France, subject to sovereign immunity and thus immune from arrest under the law of salvage.[106] France and Florida have entered into an agreement on how to protect and manage the wreck.[107] The US has also cooperated with France in regard to activities involving *Le Griffon*, and the *Bonhomme Richard*.

The US cooperated with the self-described 'Major Maritime Powers' (MMP) at the UNESCO negotiation meetings.[108] They all expressed concerns with the text, which resulted in them not signing the 2001 Convention at the completion of negotiations. Serge Segura, France's Ocean Ambassador, subsequently very diplomatically explained to the US that France no longer shared those concerns, and it became a party.[109]

5 Why the US is Not a Party to the 2001 Convention

The US delegation stated its support of the general principles, the Annex Rules and most of the 2001 Convention's provisions protecting UCH. However, the US also noted its concern about the new requirements for notification, reporting, and regulation within the EEZ/CS as upsetting the balance of Flag and coastal State jurisdiction under the LOSC: DOS and the Navy remain concerned with creeping coastal State jurisdiction over UCH within the EEZ/

104 CSS *Alabama* Agreement between France and US (March 8, 1995) and *La Belle* Agreement between France and US (March 31, 2003). See second edition of this book for discussion.

105 *Global Marine Exploration, Inc. v. Unidentified, Wrecked & (For Finders-Right Purposes) Abandoned Sailing Vessel*, 348 F. Supp. 3d 1221 (M.D. Fla. 2018).

106 *Ibid.*

107 Florida Dept. of State Press Release Republic of France and State of Florida Sign Declaration of Intention to Embark on a Historic Partnership to Research and Preserve the Trinité Shipwreck available at <https://dos.myflorida.com/communications/press-releases/2018/republic-of-france-and-state-of-florida-sign-declaration-of-intention-to-embark-on-a-historic-partnership-to-research-and-preserve-the-trinit%C3%A9-shipwreck/>.

108 S. Dromgoole, 'Reflections on the position of the major maritime powers with respect to the UNESCO Convention on the Protection of the Underwater Cultural Heritage 2001', *Marine Policy* vol. 38(C) (2013)116–123.

109 The author was at the meeting with France.

OCS and the treatment of sunken warships within the TS. After 24 years, it is clear those party to the 2001 Convention have acted consistently with the LOSC and respect Flag State jurisdiction, with no examples of creeping jurisdiction. Since 2001, France has become a party and others are realising that the 2001 Convention is being interpreted consistently with the LOSC and their views of jurisdiction and the treatment of sunken vessels. The author hopes that the US DOS and Navy will therefore revisit their views to enable the US to become a party.

6 Conclusion – Future Direction and Reforms

Our ocean heritage includes the natural and cultural resources and property that we wish to pass along to present and future generations. The US and other nations need to be more holistic in their views and integrate the research and conservation of both natural and cultural heritage in the UN Decade of Ocean Science for Sustainable Development and in the context of Climate Change.

The World Heritage Convention 1972[110] is perhaps the best example of integrating the protection and management of national and cultural heritage. It needs to be extended to our ocean heritage in the High Seas and the Area. Moreover, the guidelines for inscription need to be revisited so as to include wreck sites being preserved *in situ* as first option.

In regard to addressing the gaps in law controlling looting and unauthorised salvage on the OCS, the AA, ARPA and/or the NMSA could be amended to apply to activities directed at UCH outside of monuments, and sanctuaries.[111] In the interim, DOI should reassert application of the permit requirements on the OCS. The AA could also be amended to make its civil penalties consistent with NMSA or SMCA sanctions. Regarding RMS *Titanic*, the NMSA, or the 1986 Act, should be amended to provide more comprehensive enforcement tools such as those in the NMSA and SMCA.

WWII wrecks are not yet covered by the 2001 Convention and are subject to unauthorised salvage, particularly in the Pacific. The salvage threatens our ocean heritage, the environment and livelihoods that are so dependent upon a clean marine environment.[112] A resolution or amendment to the IMO Salvage

---

110 1037 UNTS 151.

111 See O. Varmer *UCH Law Study*, Section 7, Recommendations draft bill to amend the NMSA.

112 See generally, Threats to Our Ocean Heritage: Potentially Polluting Wrecks (Springer, 2024) (available for free download at <https://link.springer.com/book/10.1007/978-3-031-57960-8>).

Convention 1989 should clarify that the law of salvage does not apply to sunken warships without the express consent of the Flag State. A resolution or amendment to the IMO Salvage Convention should similarly be done to harmonise it with the 2001 Convention in relation to the salvage of UCH.

In the dreams of this author, the US remains in UNESCO and becomes a party to the 2001 Convention. The US has made progress over the last couple of decades in developing laws and policies to implement its duty to protect UCH and cooperate with other nations for that purpose. There is still much to do, including building upon on an integrated approach to conserving ocean heritage and using the best available science as a beacon.

All websites last accessed February 2025.

Acknowledgments

The author would like to thank the Ocean Foundation for its support including the assistance from Charlotte Jarvis, who helped with editing as well as writing the section on the UCH law of US states. This update of the second edition focuses on significant developments since 2006 and draws from O. Varmer, *Underwater Cultural Heritage Law Study,* (BOEM 2014-005, 2014) available at <https://espis.boem.gov/final%20reports/5341.pdf>.

Selected Bibliography

M. Aznar, 'The Notions of Preferential Right and Interest of States in the Protection of the Underwater Cultural Heritage' (2019) *Revista Electrónica de Estudios Internacionales* 1 (DOI: 10.17103/reei.38.07).

M. J. Aznar, 'The Contiguous Zone as an Archaeological Maritime Zone', (2014) *Int'l J. Marine and Coastal Law,* 29 1–51.

S. Dromgoole, 'Murky Waters for Government Policy: The Case of a Seventeenth Century British Warship and Ten Tonnes of Gold Coins', (2004) 28 *Marine Policy,* 189.

O. Varmer, 'Duty to Protect Underwater Cultural Heritage and to Cooperate for that Purpose,' 77–117 in H. Karan, Ed. *The Legal Regime of Underwater Cultural Heritage and Marine Scientific Research* (Ankara U. Research Center of the Sea and Maritime law, 2020).

O. Varmer, *Underwater Cultural Heritage Law Study*, (BOEM 2014-005, 2014) available at https://espis.boem.gov/final%20reports/5341.pdf.

Index

If you have any questions regarding this title, please contact:

Koninklijke Brill BV
Plantijnstraat 2
2321 JC Leiden
Email: info@brill.com

Batch number: 08533313